Board + CUET

CL MASTER SERIES

CBSE STUDY GUIDE

12th CLASS

with special focus on CUET examination

ACCOUNTANCY

Includes

**CUET Solved Paper 2022 &
CBSE Solved Papers 2022 (Term I and II)**

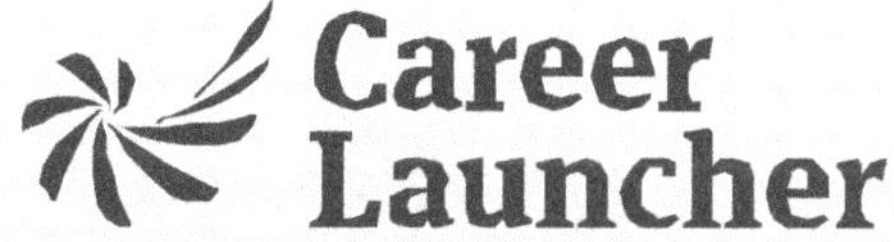

Title   : **CL Master Series** : CBSE Class XII - Accountancy (Study Guide)

Language   : English

Editor's Name : Akshika Gupta

Copyright ©   : 2022 CLIP

No part of this book may be reproduced in a retrieval system or transmitted, in any form or by any means, electronics, mechanical, photocopying, recording, scanning and or without the written permission of the Author/Publisher.

Typeset & Published by :

Career Launcher Infrastructure (P) Ltd.

A-45, Mohan Cooperative Industrial Area, Near Mohan Estate Metro Station, New Delhi - 110044

Marketed by :

G.K. Publications (P) Ltd.

Plot No. 9A, Sector-27A, Mathura Road, Faridabad, Haryana-121003

ISBN   : **978-93-95101-41-7**

Printer's Details

For product information :

Visit *www.gkpublications.com* or email to *gkp@gkpublications.com*

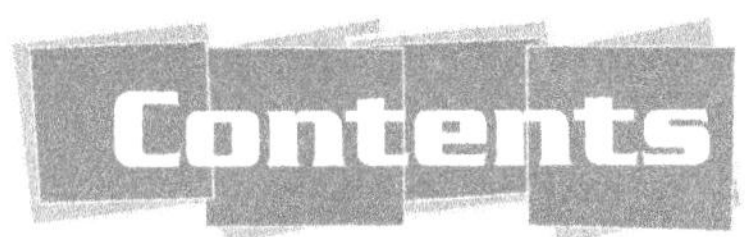

PART I

PART I

Accounting for Partnership Firms – Fundamentals

 Concepts of Partnership, Partnership Deed, Maintenace of Capital A/C, Distribution of Profit Among Partners, Interest on Capital, Intrest on Drawings

Summary

Partnership is a separate business entity from the accounting viewpoint.

Partnership is a relationship between person who has agreed to share the profits of a business carried on by all or any of them acting for all.

Nature of Partnership:

1. **Two or more persons:** There must be at least two persons to form a valid partnership. The maximum number of partners cannot exceed the number of partners prescribed by Companies Act, 2013 which is 50 in any business whether banking or non-banking.

2. **Agreement:** Partnership comes into existence by an agreement (either written or oral among the partners. The written agreement among the partners is called Partnership Deed.

3. **Existence of business and profit motive:** A partnership can be formed for the purpose of carrying on legal business with the intention of earning profits. A joint ownership of some property by itself cannot be called a partnership.

4. Sharing of Profits: An agreement between the partners must be aimed at sharing the profits. If some persons join hands to run some charitable activity, it will not be called partnership. Futher, if a partner is deprived of his right to share the profits of the business, he cannot be called as partner.

5. **Business carried on by all or any of them acting for all:** It means that each partner can participate in the conduct of business and each partner is bound by the acts of other partners in respect to the business of the firm.

6. **Relationship of Principal and Agent:** Each partner is an agent ad well as a partner of the firm. An agent, because he can bind the other partners by his acts and principal, because he himself can be bound by the acts of the other partners.

Partnership Deed: The relationship between the partners may be expressed formally (oral or written) or implied by their conduct. A partnership agreement which is written and signed by all the partners and is duly stamped according to the stamp act.

Contents of the Partnership Deed

The Partnership Deed usually contains the following details:

- Names and Addresses of the firm and its main business;
- Names and Addresses of all partners;
- Amount of capital to be contributed by each partner;
- The accounting period of the firm;
- The date of commencement of partnership;
- Rules regarding operation of Bank Accounts;
- Profit and loss sharing ratio;
- Rate of interest on capital, loan, drawings, etc;
- Mode of auditor's appointment, if any;
- Salaries, commission, etc, if payable to any partner;
- The rights, duties and liabilities of each partner;
- Treatment of loss arising out of insolvency of one or more partners;
- Settlement of accounts on dissolution of the firm;
- Method of settlement of disputes among the partners;
- Rules to be followed in case of admission, retirement, death of a partner, and
- Any other matter relating to the conduct of business. Normally, the partnership deed covers all matters affecting relationship of partners amongst themselves. However, if there is no express agreement on certain matters, the provisions of the Indian Partnership Act, 1932 shall apply.

Benefits of Partnership Deed

(1) It regulates the rights, duties and liabilities of each partner.

(2) It helps to avoid any misunderstanding amongst the partners because all the terms and conditions of partnership have been laid down beforehand in the deed.

(3) Any dispute amongst the partners may be settled easily as the partnership deed may be readily referred to.

Hence, it is always best course to have a written partnership deed duly signed by all the partners and registered under the Act.

Types of partners:

(a) **Active partner:** A partner who contributes capital and takes an active part in the management of the partnership

(b) **Sleeping partner:** A partner who merely contributes capital for the business but does not take part in the management of the partnership business.

Provisions of Partnership Act Relevant for Accounting :

The important provisions affecting partnership accounts are as follows:

(a) **Profit Sharing Ratio:** If the partnership deed is silent about the profit sharing ratio, the profits and losses of the firm are to be shared equally by partners, irrespective of their capital contribution in the firm.

(b) Interest on Capital: No partner is entitled to claim any interest on the amount of capital contributed by him in the firm as a matter of right. However, interest can be allowed when it is expressly agreed to by the partners. Thus, no interest on capital is payable if the partnership deed is silent on the issue.

(c) Interest on Drawings: No interest is to be charged on the drawings made by the partners, if there is no mention in the Deed.

(d) Interest on Loan: If any partner has advanced loan to the firm for the purpose of business, he/she shall be entitled to get an interest on the loan amount at the rate of 6 per cent per annum. (e) Remuneration for Firm's Work: No partner is entitled to get salary or other remuneration for taking part in the conduct of the business of the firm unless there is a provision for the same in the Partnership Deed.

Maintenance of Capital Accounts of Partners:

There are two methods by which the capital accounts of partners are maintained. They are the following:

(a) Fixed Capital Method

(b) Fluctuating Capital Method

(a) Fixed Capital Method: Under the fixed capital method, the capitals of the partner shall remain fixed or unaltered unless some additional capital is introduced or some amount of capital is withdrawn with the consent of all the partners.

In this method, two accounts for each partner are to be maintained:

1. Capital Account

2. Current Account.

1. Capital Account: This account is credited with the amount of capital introduced by the partner. This account will continue to show the same balance from year to year unless some amount of capital is introduced or withdrawn. This account always appears on the liabilities side in the balance sheet.

2. Current Account: All entries relating to drawings, interest on capital, interest on drawings, salary or commission, the share of profit or loss, etc. are made in this account. This account is debited with drawings, interest on drawings, the share of loss, etc. and credited with the interest on capital, salary, commission, the share of profit, etc. The balance of this account will fluctuate from year to year. If it has a credit balance then it will appear on the liabilities side of the Balance Sheet and if it has a debit balance then it will appear on the assets side of the Balance Sheet.

PARTNER'S CAPITAL ACCOUNT

Dr.   **Cr.**

Date	Particulars	J.F.	Amount (Rs.)	Date	Particulars	J.F.	Amount (Rs.)
	Bank (permanent withdrawal of capital)		xxx		Balance b/d (opening balance)		xxx
	Balance c/d (closing balance)		xxx		Bank (fresh capital introduced)		xxx
			xxx				**xxx**

PARTNER'S CURRENT ACCOUNT

Dr.   Cr.

Date	Particulars	J.F.	Amount (Rs.)	Date	Particulars	J.F.	Amount (Rs.)
	Balance b/d (in case of debit opening balance) Drawings		xxx		Balance b/d (in case of credit opening balance) Salary		xxx
	Interest on drawings		xxx				xxx
	Profit & Loss a/c		xxx		Commission Interest on capital Profit &		xxx
			xxx		Loss Appropriation		xxx
	Balance c/d (in case of credit closing balance)		xxx		(share of profit) Balance c/d		
					(in case of debit closing balance)		xxx
			XXXX				**XXXX**

Fig. 2.1: Proforma of Partner's Capital and Current Account under Fixed Capital Method.

(b) **Fluctuating Capital Method:** Under this method, only one account i.e. Capital Account is maintained for each partner. All the entries relating to the interest on capital, salary, commission to partners, the share of profit and loss, drawings, interest on drawings, etc. are directly recorded in the capital accounts of the partners. The balance of this account fluctuates from year to year. The format of Fluctuating Capital Account is as follows:

PARTNER'S CURRENT ACCOUNT

Dr.   Cr.

Date	Particulars	J.F.	Amount (Rs.)	Date	Particulars	J.F.	Amount (Rs.)
	Balance b/d (in case of debit opening balance) Drawings		xxx		Balance b/d (in case of credit opening balance) Salary		xxx
	Interest on drawings		xxx				xxx
	Profit & Loss a/c		xxx		Commission Interest on capital Profit &		xxx
			xxx		Loss Appropriation		xxx
	Balance c/d (in case of credit closing balance)		xxx		(share of profit) Balance c/d		
					(in case of debit closing balance)		xxx
			XXXX				**XXXX**

Fig. 2.2: Proforma of Partner's Capital Account under Fluctuating capital Method.

Profit and Loss Appropriation Account

In partnership, net profit after adjustment of partner's interest on capital, salary, and commission to partner's, interest on drawings, etc. is distributed among the partners in the agreed profit sharing ratio. For this purpose, a separate account is prepared called Profit and Loss Appropriation Account.

Journal Entries relating to Profit and Loss Appropriation Account:

1. **Transfer of the balance of Profit and Loss Account to Profit and Loss Appropriation Account:**

    (a) If Profit and Loss Account shows a credit balance (net profit):

    Profit and Loss A/c Dr.

    To Profit and Loss Appropriation A/c

    (b) If Profit and Loss Account shows a debit balance (net loss)

    Profit and Loss Appropriation A/c Dr.

    To Profit and Loss A/c

2. **Interest on Capital:**

    (a) For Allowing interest on capital:

    Interest on Capital A/c Dr.

    To Partner's Capital/Current A/cs (individually)

    (b) For transferring interest on capital to Profit and Loss Appropriation Account:

    Profit and Loss Appropriation A/c Dr.

    To Interest on Capital A/c

3. **Interest on Drawings:**

    (a) For charging interest on drawings to partners' capital accounts:

    Partners Capital/Current A/c's (individually) Dr.

    To Interest on Drawings A/c

    (b) For transferring interest on drawings to Profit and Loss Appropriation Account

    Interest on Drawings A/c Dr.

    To Profit and Loss Appropriation A/c

4. **Salary to Partner(s):**

    (a) For crediting partner's salary' to partner's Capital/Current A/c:

    Salary to Partner A/c Dr.

    To Partner's Capital /Current A/c (Individually)

    (b) For transferring partner's salary to Profit and Loss Appropriation A/c:

    Profit and Loss Appropriation A/c Dr.

    To Salary to Partner A/c

5. **Commission to Partner(s):**

    (a) For crediting partner's commission to partner's Capital/ Current A/c:

    Commission to Partner A/c Dr.

    To Partner's Capital/Current A/c (Individually)

    (b) For transferring partner's commission to Profit and Loss Appropriation A/c:

    Profit and Loss Appropriation A/c Dr.

    To Commission to Partner A/c

6. **Share of Profit/Loss after adjustments:**

    (a) If Profit

    Profit and Loss Appropriation A/c Dr.

    To partner's Capital/Current A/c (Individually)

    OR

    (b) If Loss:

    Partner's Capital/Current A/c (Individually) Dr.

    To Profit and Loss Appropriation A/c

PROFIT AND LOSS APPROPRIATION ACCOUNT

Dr.   **Cr.**

Particulars	Amount (Rs.)	Particulars	Amount (Rs.)
Profit and Loss (if there is loss)	xxx	Profit and Loss (if there is profit)	xxx
Interest on Capital	xxx	Interest on Drawings	xxx
Salary to Partner	xxx	Partner's Capital/Current Accounts (distribution of Loss)	xxx
Commission to Partner	xxx		
Partner's Capital/Current Accounts (distribution of profit)	xxx		
	XXXX		**XXXX**

Interest on Capital:

Interest on Capital is generally provided for in two situations:

1. When the partners contribute unequal amounts of capital but share profits equally.

2. When the capital contribution is the same but profit sharing is unequal.

    Interest on Capital = Amount of Capital × Rate / 100 × Time

Interest on Drawings:

Drawings is the amount withdrawn, in cash or in-kind, for personal use by the partner(s). Interest on drawings is calculated with reference to the date of withdrawal.

The calculation of interest on drawings under different situations is shown as under:

When drawings are made:

1. At the beginning of each month of the financial year:

    $$\text{Interest on Drawings} = \text{Interest on Drawings} = \text{Total Drawings} \times \frac{\text{Rate}}{100} \times \frac{6^{1/2}}{12}$$

    Here, time period is $6\frac{1}{2}$ months.

2. At the middle of each month of the financial year

    $$\text{Interest on Drawings} = \text{Total Drawings} \times \frac{\text{Rate}}{100} \times \frac{6}{12}$$

    Here, time period is 6 months.

3. At the and of each month of the financial year:

$$\text{Interest on Drawings} = \text{Total Drawings} \times \frac{\text{Rate}}{100} \times \frac{5^{1/2}}{12}$$

Here, time period is $5\frac{1}{2}$ months.

4. At the beginning of the eaclr quarter of the financial year:

$$\text{Interest on Drawings} = \text{Total Drawings} \times \frac{\text{Rate}}{100} \times \frac{7^{1/2}}{12}$$

Here, time period is $7\frac{1}{2}$ months.

5. At the end of each quarter of the financial year:

$$\text{Interest on Drawings} = \text{Total Drawings} \times \frac{\text{Rate}}{100} \times \frac{4^{1/2}}{12}$$

Here, time period is $4\frac{1}{2}$ months.

(b) **When Varying Amounts are withdrawn at Different Intervals:** When the partners withdraw different amounts of money at different time intervals, the interest is calculated using the production method. In this method, each amount of drawing is multiplied by the number of days/months (from the date of drawings to the last date of the financial year) to find out the product and then all the products are totaled. Here, the total product and interest for 1 month at the given rate are calculated.

$$\text{Interest on Drawings} = \text{Total Drawings} \times \frac{\text{Rate}}{100} \times \frac{1}{12} \ \text{ or } \ \frac{1}{365}$$

(c) When dates of Withdrawal are Not Specified: When the total amount withdrawn is given but the dates of withdrawals are not specified, then it is assumed that the amount was withdrawn evenly throughout the year. Here, the time period is taken 6 months.

$$\text{Interest on Drawings} = \text{Total Drawings} \times \frac{\text{Rate}}{100} \times \frac{6}{12}$$

Multiple Choice Questions   [1 Mark]

Q.1. Devika and Tanmay are partners in a firm. They are entitled to interest on their capital but net profit was not sufficient for paying his interest, then the profit will be disturbed among partner in

(a) 1 : 2   (b) Profit sharing Ratio   (c) Capital ratio   (d) Equally

Ans. (c)

Q.2. Closing entry for interest on loan allowed to partners   [CBSE 2020]

(a) Interest on partner's loan   ...Dr.

  To profit and loss A/c

(b) Interest on loan   ...Dr.

  To profit and loss appropriation A/c

(c) Profit and loss appropriation/c   ...Dr.

  To interest on partner's loan A/c

(d) Profit and loss appropriation A/c   ...Dr.

  To interest on loan A/C

Ans. (c)

Q.3. Salary to a partner under fixed capital account is credited to

    (a) Partner's capital A/c   (b) Partner's current A/c

    (c) Profit & loss A/c   (d) Partner's loan A/c

Ans. (b)

Q.4. In the absence of partnership deed partner share profit and loss in

    (a) Ratio of capital employed   (b) Equal ratio

    (c) 2 : 1   (d) 1 : 2

Ans. (b)

Q.5. As per section a minor may be admitted for the benefit of the partnership if:-

    (a) One partner agree   (b) More than one agree

    (c) All partner agree   (d) Both (a) or (b)

Ans. (c)

Q.6. If the partner carries on the business that is similar to firm competition with the firm and profit earned from it, the profit

    (a) Shall be retained by the partner   (b) Shall be paid to firm

    (c) Can be retained or gained to the firm   (d) Both (a) or (b)

Ans. (b)

Q.7. The relation of the partner with the firm is that of

    (a) An owner   (b) An agent and A principal   (c) An agent   (d) Manager

Ans. (b)

Q.8. Which one of the following item cannot be recorded in profit and loss appropriation account?

    (a) Interest on capital   (b) Manager's commission

    (c) Interest on drawings   (d) Partner's salary

Ans. (b)

Q.9. Which of the following accounts would be opened when capitals of partners are fixed?

    (a) Only currents accounts.   (b) Only capital accounts

    (c) Capital accounts and current accounts.   (d) Either capital accounts or current accounts.

Ans. (c)

Q.10. It is necessary to have a partnership deed in writing because______________.

    (a) Partnership deed sets out the -duties, rights and obligations of the partners and , thus, avoids any dispute among them

    (b) Liability of partners is limited

    (c) Interest on loan is at the expense of the firm

    (d) All of the above.

Ans. (a)

Q.11. Even if all the partner agree a minor cannot be admitted as a partner because _________.

    (a) It should be in the agreement

    (b) A minor is not competent according to contract act

    (c) Consent of all partners is required

    (d) All of the above

Ans. (b)

Q.12. In the absence of an agreement, partners are entitled to:

    (a) Salary   (b) Profit share in capital ratio

    (c) Interest on loan and advances   (d) Commission

Ans. (c)

Q.13. Salman and Shahrukh are partners in a firm. Which of their claims is valid?

    (a) Salman is an active partner and wants a salary of Rs. 10,00,000 per year.

    (b) Sharukh had advanced a loan to the firm and claims interest 10% P.A

    (c) Shahrukh wants interest on capital to be credited @6% per annum.

    (d) The capitals contributed by Salman and Sahrukh are Rs. 20,00,000 and Rs. 50,00,000 respectively. Salman wants that profit be shared equally.

Ans. (d)

Q.14. Which of the following statements is false in the context of partnership:

    (a) If the partnership deed is silent, interest @6% would be charged on the drawings made by partnership.

    (b) Maximum number of partners can be 50.

    (c) Partnership is the result of an agreement. But written agreement is not necessary for a valid partnership.

    (d) If the partnership deed is silent, interest @6% will be given on partner's loan.

Ans. (a)

Q.15. How are mutual relation i.e, rights and obligation of partner are government if there is no partnership deed?

    (a) Companies Act   (b) Partnership Act

    (c) Cooperative societies Act   (d) Contract Act

Ans. (b)

Very Short Answer Type   [1 Mark]

Q.16. A and B are partner sharing profit equally. A draw regularly Rs. 4.000 at the end of every month for 6 month. Years ended on 30th September 2018, calculate interest on drawings @ rate 5% p.a

Ans. Rs. 250

Q.17. Which section of the indian partnership act 1932 define partnership as the relation between person who have agreed to share the profit to the business carried on by all or any of them acting for all?

Ans. Section 4

Q.18. Amit and Nitin are partners without any agreement. Amit has given a loan of Rs. 5,00,000 to the firm at the end of year firm incurred a loss. How much interest be paid on Amit's loan?

Ans. @6%p.a.

Q.19. If fixed amount is withdrawn on the last day of every month and interest on drawing charged is 10% p.a. Interest on drawing amounted to Rs 2,750 what will we drawing amount.

Ans. Rs. 5,000 per month

Q.20. If date of drawings of a partner is not given, interest on drawings will be charged for

Ans. 6 months

Q.21. If a partner withdraws fixed amount in the beginning of every month, how much interest is charged on the whole amount?

Ans. 6.5 months

Q.22. Ram and Sohan are partners in a firm, having no partnership deed. Sohan has given a loan of Rs. 5,00,000 to the firm. At the end of the year, loss was incurred in the business. How much interest will be paid to Sohan by the firm?   [CBSE 2014]

Ans. @6% p.a.

Q.23. A and B are partners in a firm having no partnership deed. How much amount of interest on capital will be allowed to them, if they have invested Rs. 5,00,000 and Rs. 4,00,000 respectively into the business?

Ans. No interest on capital

Q.24. Salary to partners will be shown in __________.

Ans. Profit and loss appropriation account

Q.25. Harshita and Soham are partners. They do not have a partnership deed. How will they divide profit and loss the business?

Ans. Equally

Q.26. The partnership deed is silent on payment of salary to partners. Anita, a partner, claimed that, since she managed the business, she should get a monthly salary of Rs 10,000. Is she entitled for the salary? Give reason.   [CBSE 2014]

Ans. No, Anita is not entitled for the salary. Since, the partnership deed is silent on the payment of salary to partners, in that case provisions of Partnership Act will be followed, which prohibit payment of remuneration of any kind to the partners.

Q.27. State the provisions of Indian Partnership Act, 1932 regarding the payment of remuneration to a partner for the services rendered.   [CBSE 2012]

Ans. In the absence of partnership deed, a partner is not entitled to get any remuneration from the firm.

Q.28. What share of profit would a 'sleeping partner', who has contributed 75% of the total capital, get in the absence of a deed?   [Delhi 2011]

Ans. In the absence of partnership deed, sleeping partner will get equal share of profit, no matter how much share of total capital he has contributed.

Q.29. Is a sleeping partner liable for the acts of other partners?   [Delhi 2011 C]

Ans. Yes, a sleeping partner is also liable for the acts of other partners.

Q.30. What is meant by a partnership deed?   [Delhi 2011,2010; All India 2010]

Ans. Partnership deed is a document which contains the terms and conditions of partnership agreement.

Q.31. What is meant by 'unlimited liability of a partner'?   [CBSE 2013]

Ans. Unlimited liability of a partner means that each partner is liable jointly and also severally with all the other partners to the third party for all the acts of the firm done, while he is a partner. His private assets can also be used for paying off the firm's debts.

Q.32. A, B and C decided that interest on capitals will be provided to each partner @ 5% per annum, but after one year C wants that no interest on capital is to be provided to any partner. State how 'C' can do this?

[CBSE 2012]

Ans. C can do this only when all partners agree to it or if there is no partnership deed.

Q.33. A and B are partners in a firm without a partnership deed. A is an active partner and claims a salary of Rs 18,000 per month. State with reasons whether the claim is valid or not.   [Delhi 2008]

Ans. According to Indian Partnership Act, 1932, no salary is allowed to partners in the absence of partnership deed. So, the claim of A for salary of 7 18,000 per month is not valid.

Short Answer Type - I   [2 Marks]

Q.1. Partnership deed is not compulsory to make but it is always advisable to prepare it, write benefits of having a deed .   [CBSE 2011]

Ans. Benefits of Partnership Deed

   (1) It regulates the rights, duties and liabilities of each partner.

   (2) It helps to avoid any misunderstanding amongst the partners because all the terms and conditions of partnership have been laid down beforehand in the deed.

   (3) Any dispute amongst the partners may be settled easily as the partnership deed may be readiy referred to.

   Hence, it is always best course to have a written partnership deed duly signed by all the partners and registered under the Act.

Q.2. Define partnership according to Indian partnership act 1932 section 4.

Ans. Partnership is a relationship between person who has agreed to share the profits of a business carried on by all or any of them acting for all.

Q.3. Explain relationship of agent and principal of partners.   [CBSE 2015]

Ans. Relationship of Principal and Agent: Each partner is an agent as well as a partner of the firm. An agent, because he can bind the other partners by his acts and principal, because he himself can be bound by the acts of the other partners

Q.4. A and B are partner's sharing profit in the ratio 2:1 on 31st march 2019 firm's net profit is Rs. 72,000 the partnership deed provided interest on capital to A and B Rs. 5,000 to Rs.7,000. What is the net amount transferred to partner's capital A/c as share of profit?

Ans. 72,000 – (5,000 + 7,000)

$\qquad$ = 60,000 (in 2 : 1)

$\qquad$ = 40,000 and 20,000.

Q.5. X is a manager in a firm, who is entitled to get a commission of 10% of the net profit after charging such commission. The net profit of the firm before charging any commission was Rs. 5,50,000. Calculate the amount of commission payable to X. $\hfill$ **[CBSE 214]**

Ans. $5,50,000 \times \dfrac{10}{110} = Rs.50,000$

Q.6. On 1st April, 2020, X's capital was Rs. 300000. On 1st Jan 2021, he introduces additional capital of Rs. 200000. Interest on capital at the rate of 5% p.a. on 31st March 2021 will be -

Ans. $\qquad$ $3,00,000 \times 5/100 = 15,000$

$\qquad$ $2,00,000 \times 5/100 \times 3/12 = 2,500$

$\qquad\qquad$ = 15,000 + 2500

$\qquad\qquad$ = Rs. 17,500

Q.7. Hardik is a partner in a firm. He withdrew Rs. 5,000 per month on the last day of every month during the year ended 31st March 2021.If interest on drawings is charged at the rate of 8% p.a., the interest charged (in Rs) will be

Ans. $\qquad$ Total drawings = 5000 × 12 = 60,000

$\qquad\qquad$ = 60,000 × 8/100 × 5.5/12

$\qquad\qquad$ = Rs. 2200

Q.8. Sunny is a partner in a firm. She withdrew Rs. 10,000 in the beginning of each quarter during the year ended 31st March 2021. Interest on her drawings (in Rs.) at the rate of 9% p.a. will be -

Ans. $\qquad$ Total drawings = 10,000 × 4 = 40,000

$\qquad\qquad$ = 40,000 × 9/100 × 7.5/12

$\qquad\qquad$ = Rs.2250

Q.9. X and Y are partners in a firm sharing profits and losses in the ratio of 2:1. Their capitals are Rs. 500000 and Rs. 300000 respectively. Interest on capital is allowed at the rate of 7% p.a. Firm earned a profit of Rs. 80,000 for the year ended 31st March 2021. Interest on capital will be -

Ans. X – Rs.35,000

$\qquad$ Y – Rs. 21,000

Q.10.

I	Maximum number of partners	A	6% p.a.
II	Partnership Deed	B	50
III	Interest on partner's loan	C	Written agreement

(a) I-A; II-B; III-C $\quad$ (b) I-B; II-A; III-C $\qquad\qquad$ (c) I-C; II-B; III-A $\qquad$ (d) I-B; II-C; III-A

Ans. Maximum number of partners = 50

Partnership Deed = Written agreement

Interest on partner's loan = 6% p.a.

Q.11. Chhavi and Neha were partners in a firm sharing profits and losses equally. Chhavi withdrew a fixed amount at the beginning of each quarter. Interest on drawings is charged @ 6% p.a. At the end of the year, interest' on Chhavi's drawings amounted to ₹900. Pass necessary journal entry for charging interest on drawings.

[CBSE 2013]

Ans.

Date	Particulars		L.F.	Dr. (₹)	Cr. (₹)
	Chhavi Capital A/c	Dr.		900	900
	To Interest on Drawing A/c				
	(Being Interest on Drawings is charged)				

Short Answer Type - II

[3 Marks]

Q.1. Aman ,Bhuvan and charan are partners sharing profits in the ratio of 2:2;1.Aman drew Rs 5,000 at the Beginning of each month, Bhuvan drew Rs 6,000 at the end of each month and Charan drew Rs 4,500 at the middle of each month. Interest on drawings is charged at 9% p.a. Determine the amount of interest if this process is continued for a period of 6 months ending 30th September ,2021.

Ans. Total drawings of Aman = 5000 × 6 = Rs.30,000

Total drawings of Bhuvan = 6000 × 6 = Rs.36,000

Total drawings of Charan = 4500 × 6 = Rs.27,000

Particulars	Aman (Beginning)	Bhuvan (End)	Charan (Middle)
Average Period	$\dfrac{6+1}{2} = 3.5$ months	$\dfrac{5+0}{2} = 2.5$ months	$\dfrac{5.5+0.5}{2} = 3$ months
Interest on Drawings	$\dfrac{30000 \times 9 \times 3.5}{100 \times 12}$ = Rs.787.50 or Rs.788	$\dfrac{36000 \times 2.5 \times 9}{100 \times 12}$ = Rs.675	$\dfrac{27000 \times 9 \times 3}{100 \times 12}$ = Rs.607.50 or Rs.608

Q.2. Compute interest on drawings @ 12 % p.a. for the year ending 31st March 2022. If Aarav withdrew followings amount during the year

Date	Amount (RS.)
May 01	3,000
July 31	4,000
September 01	3,000
December 31	5,000
February 01	7,000
March 31	2,000

Ans. Calculation of Interest on Drawings

as at 31st March 2022 (Product Method)

Date of Drawings	Amount Rs.	Months up to March 31	Product
May 01	3,000	11	33,000
July 31	4,000	8	32,000
September 01	3,000	7	21,000
December 31	5,000	3	15,000
February 01	7,000	2	14,000
March 31	2,000	0	0
		Total	**1,15,000**

$$\text{Interest on Drawings} = \frac{\text{Total of Product} \times \text{Rate of Interest}}{100 \times 12}$$

$$= \frac{1,15,000 \times 12}{100 \times 12} = \text{Rs.}1,150$$

Q.3. In the following questions identify correct options given below.

[A]   **Statement I:** Interest on capital to a partners is payable only out of profits.

Statement II: Interest on capital is an appropriation of profit which is required to be provided irrespective of profits or loss.

(a) Only statement I is correct.

(b) Only statement II is correct.

(c) Both statements are correct

(d) Both statements are Wrong.

Ans. (c)

[B] **Statement I:** It is considered desirable to have a partnership agreement in writing.

Statement II: It helps in setting any disputes with regard to the terms of partnership and acts as an evidence in the court of law.

(a) Only statement I is correct.

(b) Only statement II is correct.

(c) Both statements are correct.

(d) Both statements are Wrong.

Ans. (c)

[C] **Statement I:** Salary paid to a partner is debited to profit and loss account.

Statement II: Salary paid to a partner is an appropriation of profit.

(a) Only statement I is correct.

(b) Only statement II is correct.

(c) Both statements are correct.

(d) Both statements are Wrong.

Ans. (b)

Q.4. A and B are partners in a firm sharing profits and losses in the ratio of 7 : 3. Their fixed capitals were : A ₹ 9,00,000 and B ₹ 4,00,000. The partnership deed provided the following:

[CBSE Compt. 2019]

(i) Interest on capital @ 10% p.a.

(ii) A's salary ₹ 50,000 per year and B's salary ₹ 3,000 per month.

Profit for the year ended 31st March 2019 ₹ 2,78,000 was distributed without providing for interest on capital and partner's salary.

Showing your working clearly, pass the necessary adjustment entry for the above omissions.

Ans.

JOURNAL

Date	Particulars		Dr. (₹)	Cr. (₹)
2019 Mar 31	A's Current A/c To B's Capital A/c (Being omission of interest on Capital and salary, now rectified)	Dr.	11,200	11,200

Table showing Past Adjustments:

Partners	Interest on Capital (Cr.) (₹)	Salary (Cr.) (₹)	Profit Dr. (₹)	Net effect	
				Dr. (₹)	Cr. (₹)
A	90,000	50,000	1,51,200	11,200	-
B	40,000	36,000	64,800	-	11,200
	1,30,000	86,600	2,16,000	11,200	11,200

Q.5. A and B were partners in a firm sharing profits in the ratio of 5 : 3. Their fixed capitals on 31st March, 2017 were: A ₹ 60,000 and B ₹ 80,000. They agreed to allow interest on capital @ 12% p.a. The profit of the firm for the year ended 31st March, 2018 before allowing interest on capitals was ₹ 12,600.

Pass necessary journal entries for the above transactions in the books of A and B. Also show your working notes clearly.   **[CBSE : 2018]**

Ans.

JOURNAL

Date	Particulars		LF	Dr. (₹)	Cr. (₹)
	Interest on Capital A/c To A's Current A/c To B's Current A/c (Being interest on capital credited to Partner's Current A/c)	Dr.		12,600	5,400 7,200
	P & L Appropriation A/c To Interest on Capital A/c (Being interest on capital transferred to P&L Appropriation A/c)	Dr.		12,600	12,600

Working Notes:

Interest on Capital:

A = 12% of 60,000 = 7,200

B = 12% of 80,000 = 9,600

Total interest = 16,800

Since profits are insufficient interest on capital will be distributed in the ratio of 7,200:9,600 i.e. 3:4

A = 3/7 of 12,600 = 5,400

B = 4/7 of 12,600 = 7,200

Q.6. Krishna, Sandeep and Karim are partners sharing profits in the ratio of 3 : 2 : 1. Their fixed capitals are: Krishan ₹ 1,20,000, Sandeep ₹ 90,000 and Karim ₹ 60,000. For the year 2013-14, interest was credited to them @ 6% p.a. instead of 5% p.a. Record adjustment entry.   **[CBSE 2014]**

Ans.

ADJUSTMENT TABLE

	Particulars	Krishna	Sandeep	Karim	Total
Add:	Interest as capital provided in excess @ 1% to be debited	(1200)	(900)	(600)	(2700)
Less:	Correct distribution of ₹ 2,700 in 3 : 2 : 1 to be debited]	1350	900	450	2700
	Net effect	150 Cr.	Nil	(150) Dr.	Nil

ADJUSTING JOURNAL ENTRY

Date	Particulars		L.F	Dr. (₹)	Cr. (₹)
	Karim's current A/c	Dr.		150	
	To Krishna's current A/c				
	(Being error is rectified)				150

Q.7. Anubha and Kajal are partners of a firm sharing profits and losses in the ratio of 2 : 1. Their capital were ₹ 90,000 and ₹ 60,000. The divisible profit during the year were ₹ 45,000. According to partnership deed, both partners are allowed salary @ ₹ 700 per month to Anubha and ₹ 500 per month to Kajal. Interest allowed on capital @ 5% p.a. The drawings at the end of the period were ₹ 8,500 for Anubha and ₹ 6,500 for Kajal. Interest is to be charged @ 5% p.a. on drawings. Prepare partners capital accounts, assuming that the capital accounts are fluctuating.   **[CBSE 2015]**

Ans.

Dr.   **PARTNER'S CURRENT A/C**   **Cr.**

	Particulars	Anubha (₹)	Kajal (₹)	Particulars	Anubha (₹)	Kajal (₹)
To	Drawings A/c	8,500	6,500	By Balanced b/d	90,000	60,000
To	Interest on Drawings A/c	212.50	162.50	By Salary A/c	8,400	6,000
				By Interest on Capital A/c	4,500	3,000
To	Balance c/d	1,24,187.50	77,337.50	By P & L App. A/c (Profit)	30,000	15,000
		1,32,900	84,000		1,32,900	84,000

Note:

(1) It has been assumed that profit given is divisible profit.

(2) It has been assumed drawings have been made in the middle of the year. Normally, in the absence of date, drawings are assumed to have been made in the middle of the year.

Q.8. Following is the extract of the Balance Sheet of Neelkant and Mahadev as on March 31,2013:   **[CBSE 2013]**

BALANCE SHEET AS AT MARCH 31, 2013

Liabilities	(₹)	Assets	(₹)
Neelkant's Capital	10,00,000	Sundry Assets	30,00,000
Mahadev's Capital	10,00,000		
Neelkant's Current Account	1,00,000		
Mahadev's Current Account	1,00,000		
P&L Appropriation (March 2013)	8,00,000		
	30,00,000		30,00,000

During the year Mahadev's drawings were 7 30,000. Profits dining 2013 is 7 10,00,000. Calculate interest on capital @ 5% p.a. for the year ending March 31,2013.

Ans. Interest on Neelkant's Capital $= ₹10,00,000 \times \dfrac{5}{100} = ₹\,50,000$

Interest on Mahadev's Capital $= ₹\,10,00,000 \times \dfrac{5}{100} = ₹\,50,000$

Note:

Since the capitals are fixed, profit and drawings must have been transferred to Current Accounts. Therefore, capitals must be fixed in beginning as well as at the end.

Q.9. Raj and Neeraj are partners in a firm. Their capitals as on April 01, 2013 were 72,50,000 and 71,50,000, respectively. They share profits equally. On July 01, 2013, they decided that their capitals should be 71,00,000 each. The necessary adjustment in the capitals were made by introducing or withdrawing cash by the partners Interest on capital is allowed @ 8% p.a. Compute interest on capital for both the partners for the year ending on March 31,2014.   **[CBSE - 2014]**

Ans. Interest on Ram's Capital @ 8% p.a.

From 1 April 2013 to 1 July 2013 $= 2,50,000 \times \dfrac{8}{100} \times \dfrac{3}{12} = ₹5,000$

From 1 July 2013 to 31 March 2014 $= 1,00,000 \times \dfrac{8}{100} \times \dfrac{9}{12} = ₹\,6,000$

Total Interest on Ram's Capita l$= ₹\,11,000$

Interest on Neeraj's Capital @ 8% p.a

From 1 April 2013 to 1 July 2013 $= 1,50,000 \times \dfrac{8}{100} \times \dfrac{3}{12} = ₹3,000$

From 1 July 2013 to 31 March 2014 $= 1,00,000 \times \dfrac{8}{100} \times \dfrac{9}{12} = ₹\,6,000$

Total Interest on Neeraj's Capital $= ₹\,9,000$

Case Study Based Questions

Read the following information carefully and answer the questions that follow:

X and Y are partners in 3 : 2. Their capital balances as on 1st April 2020 amounting to ₹ 2,00,000 each. On 1st February, 2021, X contributed an additional capital of ₹1,00,000. Following are the terms of deed:

(a)   Interest on capital @ 6% per annum

(b)   Interest on drawings @ 8% per annum

(c)   Salary to X ₹1500 per month

(d)   Commission to Y @10% on net profit after charging interest on capital, salary and his commission.

Drawings of the partners were ₹20,000 and ₹30,000 respectively during the year. Net profit earned by the firm was ₹2,08,000.

Choose the correct option based on the above information:

Q.10. What is the amount of Interest on capitals of X and Y:

(a) ₹ 12,000 each   (b) ₹ 12,000 to X and ₹ 13,000 to Y

(c) ₹ 13,000 to X and ₹ 12,000 to Y   (d) None of the above.

Q.11. What is the amount of interest on drawings of X and Y:

    (a) ₹ 1200 and ₹ 1800 respectively   (b) ₹ 800 and ₹ 1200 respectively

    (c) ₹ 1200 and ₹ 800 respectively   (d) ₹ 1600 ₹ 2400 respectively

Q.12. What is the amount of commission payable to Y?

    (a) ₹ 15000   (b) ₹ 16500   (c) ₹ 20800   (d) None of these

Ans.

1	C	IOC to X = $(2,00,000 \times 6/100) + (1,00,000 \times 6/100 \times 2/12)= 13,000$ IOC to Y = $2,00,000 \times 6/100 = 12,000$
2	B	IOD will be calculated for an average period of six months since time of drawings is not given.
3	A	$2,08,000 - 13,000 - 12,000$(IOC) $- 18,000$(salary) $= 1,65,000 \times 10/110 = 15,000$.

Q.13. Michal and Jackson were partners in a firm with capitals of Rs.80,000 and Rs.40,000 respectively. The firm earned a profit of Rs.30,000 during the year.Calculate Michal's share in the profit.

Ans. Rs. 15000

    In the absence of partnership Deed, profits are shared equally among the partners.

Q.14. R and S are partners sharing profits in the ratio of 2 : 1. S has advanced a loan of Rs.1,00,000 to the firm on 1st October, 2020. The net profit earned by the firm for the year ending 31st March, 2021 is Rs.90,000. What amount will be credited to S's capital account?

Ans. Rs.29,000

    Net profit of the firm = 90,000 – 3,000(interest on loan) = 87,000. S's share in profit = 87,000 × 1/3 = 29,000. Only share of profit is credited to Partner's Capital a/c, interest on loan is credited to Partner's Loan A/c.

Q.15. Akhil and Ravi are partners sharing profits and losses in the ratio of 7:3 with capitals of Rs. 8,00,000 and Rs. 6,00,000 respectively. According to partnership deed interest on capital is to be provided @ 8% p.a. and is to be treated as a charge. Profit for the year is Rs.80,000. Journalise.

Ans. A will be credited by Rs. 41,600 and B will be credited by Rs. 38,400.

    IOC to Akhil = Rs. 64,000 less share of loss = Rs. 22,400 (32,000 × 7/10).

    Net amount paid to Akhil = Rs. 41,600.

    IOC to Ravi = Rs. 48,000 less share of loss = Rs. 9,600 (32000 × 3/10).

    Net amount paid to Ravi = Rs. 38,400.

Q.16. Write Essential Features of Partnership.   **[CBSE 2010]**

Ans. Essential Features of Partnership 1. Two or More Persons 2. Agreement 3. Lawful Business 4. Mutual Agency 5. Sharing of Profit 6. Relationship of Mutual agency among the partners

    Note: By virtue of Section 464 of the Companies Act 2013, the Central Government is empowered to prescribe maximum number of partners in a firm but the number of partners cannot be more than 100 · The Central government has prescribed the maximum number of partners in a firm to be 50 under Rule 10 of the Companies (Micellanous) Rules, 2014, So, a partnership firm cannot have more than 50 partners.

Q.17. Write the relevant provisions of Indian partner-ship act In the absence of partnership deed/if partnership deed is silent.

Ans. In the absence of partnership deed/if partnership deed is silent (the relevant provisions of the

1. Profits/losses are shared equally by all the partners

2. Interest on capital is not allowed to partners.

3. Interest on drawing is not charged from partners

4. Interest on advances/loan by a partner is paid @ 6% p. a.

5. Remuneration (Salary and Commission etc.) to Partners not allowed.

Q.18. Difference between Charge against profit and Appropriation of Profit.   **[CBSE 2012]**

Ans. Charge against profit

1. It is always debited to profit and loss account (whether profit or loss) before appropriation.

2. Examples are rent paid to a partner, interest on partners loan.

Appropriation of profit

1. It is debited to profit and loss appropriation account (If profit available) after charging.

2. Examples are salary/ commission to partners, interest on capital, transfer of profits to general reserve.

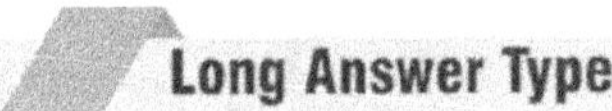 **Long Answer Type**   **[5 Marks]**

Q.1. Explain partnership deed.   **[CBSE 2012]**

Ans. Partnership Deed: The relationship between the partners may be expressed formally (oral or written) or implied by their conduct. A partnership agreement which is written and signed by all the partners and is duly stamped according to the stamp act. Contents of the partnership Deed.

The Partnership Deed usually contains the following details:

- Names and Addresses of the firm and its main business;
- Names and Addresses of all partners; " Amount of capital to be contributed by each partner;
- The accounting period of the firm;
- The date of commencement of partnership
- Rules regarding operation of Bank Accounts;
- Profit and loss sharing ratio;
- Rate of interest on capital, loan, drawings, etc;
- Mode of auditor's appointment, if any;
- Salaries, commission, etc, if payable to any partner;
- The rights, duties and liabilities of each partner;
- Treatment of loss arising out of insolvency of one or more partners;
- Settlement of accounts on dissolution of the firm;
- Method of settlement of disputes among the partners;
- Rules to be followed in case of admission, retirement, death of a partner; and

- Any other matter relating to the conduct of business. Normally, the partnership deed covers all matters affecting relationship of partners amongst themselves. However, if there is no express agreement on certain matters, the provisions of the Indian Partnership Act, 1932 shall apply.

Q.2. Aalu and Bhalu are partners in a firm sharing profits in the ratio of 60% and 40%. The following trial balance was extracted from their books as at 31st March, 2022.   **[CBSE guide line]**

TRIAL BALANCE as at 31st March 2022

Dr. Balances	Rs.	Cr. Balances	Rs.
Opening Stock	36,000	Sales	9,40,000
Purchases	6,20,000	Returns Outwards	4,000
Returns Inwards	12,000	Sundry Creditors	43,000
Sundry Debtors	1,25,000	Interest	1,000
Computer	50,000	Aalu's Capital	3,00,000
Rent(for11 months)	22,000	Bhalu's Capital	1,50,000
Salary to Staff	1,20,000		
Land & Building	3,52,000		
Wages	16,000		
General Charges	30,000		
Cash at Bank	25,000		
Aalu's Drawings	20,000		
Bhalu's Drawings	10,000		
	14,38,000		**14,38,000**

You are required to prepare the Trading, Profit and Loss Account and Profit and Loss Appropriation Account for the year ended 31st March 2022 and a Balance Sheet as on that date, considering the following adjustments:

(i) Stock on 31st March 2022 was valued at Rs.60,000.

(ii) Rent for the month of March 2022 was valued at Rs.60,000.

(iii) Depreciate Computer by 20%.

(iv) Bhalu is to be allowed a Salary of Rs.5,000 per month and partners are entitled to interest on Capital @6% p.a.

Ans.

TRADING AND PROFIT & LOSS ACCOUNT OF THE FIRM

Dr.   **for the year ended 31st March 2022**   **Cr.**

Particulars	Rs.		Particulars	Rs.	
To Opening Stock		36,000	By Sales	9,40,000	
To Purchases	6,20,000		Less: Returns Inwards	12,000	9,28,000
Less: Returns Outwards	4,000	6,16,000	By Closing Stock		60,000
To Wages		16,000			
To Gross Profit c/d		**3,20,000**			
		9,88,000			9,88,000
To Rent	22,000		By Gross Profit b/d		3,20,000
Add: Outstanding			By Interest		1,000
(22,000 / 11)	2,000	24,000			
To Salary to Staff		1,20,000			

To General Charges	30,000		
To Depreciation on Computer	10,000		
To Net Profit transferred to			
Profit & Loss			
Appropriation A/c	**1,37,000**		
	3,21,000		3,21,000

PROFIT AND LOSS APPROPRIATION ACCOUNT

Dr.   **for the year ended 31ˢᵗ March, 2022**   **Cr.**

Particulars		Rs.	Particulars	Rs.
To Bhalu's Salary		60,000	By Profit & Loss A/c	
To Interest on Capital:			(Net Profit)	1,37,000
Aalu	18,000			
Bhalu	9,000	27,000		
To Profit transferred to:				
Aalu's Capital A/c	30,000			
Bhalu's Capital A/c	20,000	50,000		
		1,37,000		**1,37,000**

BALANCE SHEET OF THE FIRM

as at 31ˢᵗ March 2022

Liabilities		Amount	Assets		Amount
		Rs.			Rs.
Sundry Creditors		43,000	Cash at Bank		25,000
Outstanding Rent		2,000	Sundry Debtors		1,25,000
Aalu's Capital	3,00,000		Closing Stock		60,000
Less: Drawings	20,000		Computers	50,000	40,000
	2,80,000		Les:Depreciation	10,000	
Add: Interest on Capital	18,000	3,28,000	Land & Building		3,52,000
Add .Net Profit	30,000				
Bhalu's Capital	1,50,000				
Less: Drawings	10,000				
	1,40,000	2,29,000			
Add: Salary	60,000	**6,02,000**			**6,02,000**
Add: Interest on Capital	9,000				
Add. Net Profit	20,000				

Q.3. A and B are partner sharing profits and losses in the ratio of 2:1 with capitals of Rs.10,00,000 and Rs.5,00,000 respectively on 1st April 2019. Each partner is entitled to 8% p.a. interest on his capital. B is entitled to a salary of Rs.3,500 p.m. together with a commission of 10% of Net Profit remaining after deducting interest on capitals and salary and after charging his commission. The profits for the year ended 31st March 2020 prior to calculation of interest on capital but after charging salary of B amounted to Rs.4,50,000. Show the division of profit, pass journal entries and prepare Partner's Capital Accounts: (i) When capitals are fixed, and (ii) When capitals are fluctuating.

Ans.

PROFIT AND LOSS APPROPRIATION ACCOUNT

Dr.		for the year ended 31st March 2020		Cr.
Particulars	**Rs.**	**Particulars**		**Rs.**
To B's Salary	42,000	By Profit and Loss A/c ---		
To Interest on Capitals:		(being profit before B's salary)		
A 80,000				
B 40,000	1,20,000	(Rs.4,50,000 + Rs.42,000)		4,92,000
To Commission to B (See Note 1)	30,000			
(To Profits transferred to:				
A's Capital/				
Current × A/c 2,00,000				
B's Capital/				
Current × A/c 1,00,000	3,00,000			
	4,92,000			**4,92,000**

*Current A/c will be written in case of fixed capitals.

Note: (1)

Calculation of Partner's Commission:

Profit = Rs.4,50,000 – Interest on Capital Rs.1,20,000 = Rs.3,30,000

B's Commission (after charging such commission) $= 3,30,000 \times \dfrac{10}{110} =$ Rs.30,000

(i) When Capitals are fixed:

In the Books of A and B

JOURNAL

Date	Particulars		L.F.	Dr. (Rs.)	Cr. (Rs.)
2020					
31-Mar	Profit & Loss A/c	Dr.		4,92,000	
	To Profit and Loss Appropriation A/c				4,92,000
	(Transfer of net profit in Profit and Loss Appropriation Account)				
31-Mar	B's Salary A/c	Dr.		42,000	
	To B's Current A/c				42,000
	(B's salary credited to his Current Account)				

31-Mar	Profit and Loss Appropriation A/c	Dr.		42,000	
	To B's Salary A/c				42,000
	(B's Salary transferred to Profit and Loss Appropriation Account)				
31-Mar	Interest on Capital A/c	Dr.		1,20,000	
	To A's Current A/c				80,000
	To B's Current A/c				40,000
	(Interest on capital allowed to partners)				
31-Mar	Profit and Loss Appropriation A/c	Dr.		1,20,000	
	To Interest on Capital A/c				1,20,000
	(Interest on capital transferred to Profit and Loss Appropriation Account)				
31-Mar	Commission to B	Dr.		30,000	
	To B's Current A/c				30,000
	(B's Commission credited to his Current A/c)				
31-Mar	Profit and Loss Appropriation A/c	Dr.		30,000	
	To Commission to B				30,000
	(B's Commission transferred to Profit & Loss Appropriation Account)				
31-Mar	Profit and Loss Appropriation A/c	Dr.		3,00,000	
	To A's Current A/c				2,00,000
	To B's Current A/c				1,00,000
	(Divisible profit of Rs.3,00,000 credited to partner's Current Accounts in 2:1)				

Dr.   **CAPITAL ACCOUNTS**   **Cr.**

Date	Particulars	A	B	Date	Particulars	A	B
2020		Rs.	Rs.	2019		Rs.	Rs.
March 31	To Balance c/d	10,00,000	5,00,000	April 1	By Balance b/d	10,00,000	5,00,000

Dr.   **CAPITAL ACCOUNTS**   **Cr.**

Date	Particulars	A	B	Date	Particulars	A	B
2020		Rs.	Rs.	2020		Rs.	Rs.
March 31	To Balance c/d			March 31	By Salary		42,000
		2,80,000	2,12,000	March 31	By Interest on Capitals	80,000	40,000
				March 31	By Commission		30,000
				March 31	By Profit & Loss Appropriation A/c (Share of Profit)	2,00,000	1,00,000
		2,80,000	**2,12,000**			**2,80,000**	**2,12,000**

(ii) When Capitals are fluctuating:

In the Books of A and B

JOURNAL

Date	Particulars		L.F.	Dr. (Rs.)	Cr. (Rs.)
2020 March 31	Profit and Loss A/c	Dr.		4,92,000	
	To Profit and loss Appropriation A/c				4,92,000
	(Transfer of net profit to Profit and Loss Appropriation A/c)				
	B's Salary A/c	Dr.		42,000	
	To B's Capital A/c				42,000
	(B's salary credited to B's Capital Account)				
	Profit and Loss Appropriation A/c	Dr.		42,000	
	To B's Salary A/c				42,000
	(B's salary transferred to Profit and Loss Appropriation A/c)				
	Interest on Capital A/c	Dr.		1,20,000	
	To A's Capital A/c				80,000
	To B's Capital A/c				40,000
	(Interest on Capital allowed to partners)				
	Profit and Loss Appropriation A/c	Dr.		1,20,000	
	To Interest on Capital A/c				1,20,000
	(Interest on capital transferred to Profit and Loss Appropriation A/c)				
	Commission to B	Dr.		30,000	
	To B's Capital A/c				30,000
	(B's Commission credited to his Capital A/c)				
	Profit and Loss Appropriation A/c	Dr.		30,000	
	To Commission to B				30,000
	(B's Commission transferred to Profit & Loss Appropriation A/c)				
	Profit and Loss Appropriation A/c	Dr.		3,00,000	
	To A's Capital A/c				2,00,000
	To B's Capital A/c				1,00,000
	(divisible profit of Rs.3,00,000 credited to partner's				
	Capital Accounts in 2 : 1)				

Dr.   **CAPITAL ACCOUNTS**   **Cr.**

Date	Particulars	A	B	Date	Particulars	A	B
2020		Rs.	Rs.	2019		Rs.	Rs.
March 31	To Balance c/d	12,80,000	7,12,000	April 1	By Balance b/d	10,00,000	5,00,000
					By Salary		42,000
					By Interest on Capitals	80,000	40,000

				By Commission		30,000
				By Profit and Loss Appropriation A/c (Share of Profit)	2,00,000	1,00,000
	12,80,000	7,12,000			12,80,000	7,12,000

Note:Commission of manager is written in Profit and Loss A/c as it is a charge, whereas commission of partner is written in Profit and Loss Appropriation A/c as it is an appropriation.

Q.4. Mudit and Sudhir are partners with capitals of Rs.60,000 and Rs.20,000 respectively on 1st April 2021. Net profit (before giving effect to the Partnership Deed) for the year ended 31st March 2022 was Rs.24,000. The Partnership Deed provides salary to Sudhir of Rs.6,000 p.a.

Drawings of partners Mudit and Sudhir are Rs.6,000 and Rs.4,000 respectively.

Interest allowed on capitals of Mudit and Sudhir were Rs.3,600 and Rs.1,200 respectively. Drawings of the partners of Mudit and Sudhir were Rs.6,000 and Rs.4,000 respectively and interest charged on drawings were Rs.200 and Rs.100 respectively.

Show how profit will be distributed between Mudit and Sudhir and also prepare the Capital Accounts of the partners along with their Drawings Accounts:

(i) if they are fixed, and

(ii) if they are fluctuating.

Ans.   **PROFIT & LOSS APPROPRIATION ACCOUNT**

Dr.   **for the year ended 31st March 2022**   **Cr.**

Particulars		Rs.	Particulars		Rs.
To Interest on Capital A/cs:			By Profit & Loss A/c (Net Profit)		24,000
Mudit	3,600				
Sudhir	1,200	4,800	By Interest on Drawings A/cs:		
To Sudhir's Salary A/c		6,000			
To Profit transferred to:			Mudit	200	
(Equal share of profit)*			Sudhir	100	300
Mudit's Capital/Current**A/c	6,750				
Sudhir's Capital/Current**A/c	6,750	13,500			
		24,300			24,300

*Profit is to be shared equally because profit-sharing ratio is not given.

**In case of fixed capitals.

(i) Fixed Capitals

<table>
<tr><td>Dr.</td><td colspan="5" align="center">MUDIT'S CAPITAL ACCOUNT</td><td>Cr.</td></tr>
<tr><td>Date</td><td>Particulars</td><td>Rs.</td><td>Date</td><td>Particulars</td><td>Rs.</td></tr>
<tr><td>2022
March 31</td><td>To Balance c/d</td><td>60,000</td><td>2021
April 1</td><td>By Balance b/d</td><td>60,000</td></tr>
</table>

<table>
<tr><td>Dr.</td><td colspan="5" align="center">SUDHIR'S CAPITAL ACCOUNT</td><td>Cr.</td></tr>
<tr><td>Date</td><td>Particulars</td><td>Rs.</td><td>Date</td><td>Particulars</td><td>Rs.</td></tr>
<tr><td>2022
March 31</td><td>To Balance c/d</td><td>20,000</td><td>2021
April 1</td><td>By Balance b/d</td><td>20,000</td></tr>
</table>

Dr. MUDIT'S CURRENT ACCOUNT **Cr.**

Date	Particulars	Rs.	Date	Particulars	Rs.
2022			2022		
March 31	To Mudit's Drawings A/c	6,000	March 31	By Interest on Capital A/c	3,600
March 31	To Interest on Drawings A/c	200	March 31	By Profit & Loss App. A/c Profit (1/2)	6,750
March 31	To Balance c/d	4,150			
		10,350			**10,350**

Dr. SUDHIR'S CURRENT ACCOUNT **Cr.**

Date	Particulars	Rs.	Date	Particulars	Rs.
2022			2022		
March 31	To Sudhir's Drawings A/c	4,000	March 31	By Interest on Capital A/c	1,200
March 31	To Interest on Drawings A/c	100	March 31	By Sudhir's Salary A/c	6,000
March 31	To Balance c/d	9,850		By Profit & Loss App. A/c Profit (1/2)	6,750
		13,950			**13,950**

Dr. MUDIT'S DRAWINGS ACCOUNT **Cr.**

Date	Particulars	Rs.	Date	Particulars	Rs.
2022			2022		
March 31	To Cash/Bank A/c	6,000	March 31	By Mudit's Current A/c	6,000

Dr.				SUDHIR'S DRAWINGS ACCOUNT	Cr.
Date	Particulars	Rs.	Date	Particulars	Rs.
2022			2022		
March 31	To Cash/Bank A/c	4,000	March 31	By Sudhir's Current A/c	4,000

(ii) Fluctuating Capitals

Dr.				MUDIT'S CAPITAL ACCOUNT	Cr.
Date	Particulars	Rs.	Date	Particulars	Rs.
2022			2021		
March 31	To Mudit's Drawings A/c	6,000	April 1	By Balance b/d	60,000
			2022		
March 31	To Interest on		March 31	By Interest on	
March 31	Drawings A/c	200	March 31	Capital A/c	3,600
				By Profit & Loss App. A/c Profit (1/2)	
	To Balance c/d	64,150			6,750
		70,350			70,350

Dr.				SUDHIR'S CAPITAL ACCOUNT	Cr.
Date	Particulars	Rs.	Date	Particulars	Rs.
2022			2021		
March 31	To Sudhir's Drawings A/c	4,000	April 1	By Balance b/d	20,000
			2022		
March 31	To Interest on		March 31	By Interest on	
March 31	Drawings A/c	100		Capital A/c	1,200
	To Balance c/d	29,850	March 31	By Sudhir's Salary A/c	6,000
			March 31	By Profit & Loss App. A/c Profit (1/2)	6,750
		33,950			33,950

Dr.				MUDIT'S DRAWINGS ACCOUNT	Cr.
Date	Particulars	Rs.	Date	Particulars	Rs.
2022			2022		
March 31	To Cash/Bank A/c	6,000	March 31	By Mudit's Capital A/c	6,000

Dr.				SUDHIR'S DRAWINGS ACCOUNT	Cr.
Date	Particulars	Rs.	Date	Particulars	Rs.
2022			2022		
March 31	To Cash/Bank A/c	4,000	March 31	By Sudhir's Capital A/c	4,000

Q.5. X and Y are partners sharing profits and losses in the ratio of 2 : 3 with capitals of Rs.2,00,000 and Rs.1,00,000 respectively. Pass the necessary Journal entry or entries for distribution of profit/loss for the year ended 31st March, 2018 in each of the alternative cases: **[CBSE 2018]**

Case 1: If Partnership Deed does not provide for interest on capital and the profit for the year if Rs.20,000.

Case 2: If Partnership Deed provides for interest on capital @6% p.a. and loss for the year is Rs.15,000.

Case 3: If Partnership Deed provides for interest on capital @6% p.a. and the profit for the year is Rs.21,000.

Case 4: If Partnership Deed provides for interest on capital @6% p.a. as a charge on profit and the profit for the year is Rs.20,000.

Case 5: If Partnership Deed provides for interest on capital @ 6% p.a. as a charge on profit and the profit for the year is Rs.2,000.

Case 6: If Partnership Deed provides for interest on capital @ 6% p.a. as a charge on profit and the profit for the year is Rs.18,000.

Ans.   **JOURNAL**

Date	Particulars		L.F.	Dr. (Rs.)	Cr. (Rs.)
2018 March 31	Case 1 Profit & Loss A/c To Profit & Loss Appropriation A/c (Net profit transferred to Profit & Loss Appropriation Account)	Dr.		20,000	20,000

	Profit & Loss Appropriation A/c
	  To X's Capital A/c
	  To Y's Capital A/c
	(Profit distributed between X and Y in the ratio of 2 : 3)
		Dr.		20,000	8,000
					12,000

	Case 2 Profit & Loss Appropriation A/c To Profit & Loss A/c (Loss transferred to Profit & Loss Appropriation A/c)	Dr.		15,000	15,000
	X's Capital A/c Y's Capital A/c To Profit & Loss Appropriation A/c (Loss distributed between X and Y in the ratio of 2 : 3) Note: Due to loss, interest on capital is not allowed.	Dr. Dr.		6,000 9,000	15,000

	Case 3			
	Profit & Loss A/c	Dr.	21,000	
	To Profit & Loss Appropriation A/c			21,000
	(Net profit transferred to Profit & Loss Appropriation Account)			
	Interest on Capital A/c	Dr.	18,000	
	To X's Capital A/c			12,000
	To Y's Capital A/c			6,000
	(Interest on capital allowed to Partners @ 6% p.a.)			
	Profit & Loss Appropriation A/c	Dr.	18,000	
	To Interest on Capital A/c			18,000
	(Interest on capital transferred)			
	Profit & Loss Appropriation A/c	Dr.	3,000	
	To X's Capital A/c			1,200
	To Y's Capital A/c			1,800
	(Profit distributed between X and Y in the ratio of 2 : 3)			
	Case 4			
	Interest on Capital A/c	Dr.	18,000	
	To X's Capital A/c			12,000
	To Y's Capital A/c			6,000
	(Interest on capital allowed @6% p.a.)			

Date	Particulars		L.F.	Dr. (Rs.)	Cr. (Rs.)
	Profit & Loss A/c	Dr.		18,000	
	To Interest on Capital A/c				18,000
	(Interest on capital transferred to Profit & Loss Account)				
	Profit & Loss A/c	Dr.		2,000	
	To Profit & Loss Appropriation A/c				2,000
	(Net profit transferred to Profit & Loss Appropriation Account)				
	Profit & Loss Appropriation A/c	Dr.		2,000	
	To X's Capital A/c				800
	To Y's Capital A/c				1,200
	(Profit distributed between X and Y in the ratio of 2 : 3)				

Case 5				
Interest on Capital A/c	Dr.		18,000	
To X's Capital A/c				12,000
To Y's Capital A/c				6,000
(Interest on capital allowed @ 6% p.a.)				
Profit & Loss A/c	Dr.		18,000	
To Interest on Capital A/c				18,000
(Interest on capital transferred to Profit & Loss Account being a charge)				
Profit & Loss Appropriation A/c	Dr.		16,000	
To Profit & Loss A/c				16,000
(Loss transferred to Profit & Loss Appropriation A/c)				
X's Capital A/c	Dr.		6,400	
Y's Capital A/c	Dr.		9,600	
To Profit & Loss Appropriation A/c				16,000
(Rs.18,000-Rs.2,000)				
(Net loss transferred to Capital Accounts of X and Y in their profit sharing ratio)				
Case 6				
Interest on Capital A/c	Dr.		18,000	
To X's Capital A/c				12,000
To Y's Capital A/c				6,000
(Interest on capital allowed as a charge on profit@6% p.a.) (Note)				
Profit & Loss A/c	Dr.		18,000	
To Interest on Capital A/c				18,000
(Interest on capital transferred to Profit & Loss Account)				

Note: Case 6:Profit & Loss Appropriation Account will not be prepared because interest on capital is a charge against profit and hence is debited to Profit & Loss Account. After allowing interest on capital, it results in neither profit nor loss.

Q.6. A and B entered into partnership on 1st April, 2009 without any partnership deed. They introduced capital of Rs. 5,00,000 and Rs. 3,00,000 respectively. On 31st October, 2009, A advanced Rs. 2,00,000 by way of loan to the firm without any agreement as to interest.

The profit and loss accounts for the year ended 31st March, 2010 showed a profit of Rs. 4,30,000, but the partners could not agree upon the amount of interest on loan to be charged and the basis of division of profits.

Pass a journal entry for the distribution of the profit between the partners and prepare the capital accounts of both the partners and loan account of 'A'. **[All India 2011]**

Ans.

JOURNAL

Date	Particulars		L.F	Amt (Dr)	Amt (Cr)
2010		Dr			
March 31	Profit and Loss Appropriation A/c			4,25,000	
	To A's Capital A/c				2,12,500
	To B's Capital A/c				2,12,500
	(Being profit distributed among the partners in equal ratio)				

Dr   **Partner's Capital Account**   **Cr**

Date	Particulars	A	B	Date	Particulars	A	B
2010				2009			
March 31	To Balance c/d	7,12,500	5,12,500	Apr 1	By Bank A/c	5,00,000	3,00,000
				2010			
				Mar 31	By Profit and Loss Appropriation A/c	2,12,500	2,12,500
		7,12,500	5,12,500			7,12,500	5,12,500

Dr   **A's Loan Account**   **Cr**

Date	Particulars	LF	Amt (₹)	Date	Particulars	LF	Amt (₹)
2010				2009			
March 31	To Balance c/d		2,05,000	Oct 31	By Cash A/c		2,00,000
				2010			
				Mar 31	By Interest on Loan A/c		5,000
			2,05,000				2,05,000

Working note

(i)

Dr   **PROFIT AND LOSS APPROPRIATION ACCOUNT**   **Cr**

for the year ending 31st March, 2010

Particulars		Amt (₹)	Particulars	Amt (₹)
		4,25,000	By Net Profit as per Profit and Loss A/c	
To Profit Transferred to			(4,30,000 – 5,000)	4,25,000
A's Capital A/c	2,12,500			
B's Capital A/c	2,12,500			
		4,25,000		4,25,000

(ii) In the absence of partnership deed, interest on partners loan will be provided @ 6% per annum

i.e. Interest on A's loan $= 2,00,000 \times \dfrac{6}{100} \times \dfrac{5}{12} = ₹5,000$

(iii) In the absence of partnership deed, profits among the partners will be divided equally.

TOPIC 2 Guarantee of Minimum Profit, Past Adjustment

Summary

Guarantee of Profit to a Partner

Sometimes a partner may be guaranteed a minimum amount of profit by one or some or by all the partners in the existing profit sharing ratio or some other agreed ratio. The minimum guaranteed amount shall be paid to a partner when his share of profit as per the profit-sharing ratio is less than the guaranteed amount.

Past Adjustments

Sometimes, after making of final accounts and the distribution of profits among the partners, a few omissions or errors in the recording of transactions or the preparation of summary statements are found. These errors or omissions need adjustments for correction of their impact.

This error or omissions may relate to:

1.   Interest on capital may have omitted or have been wrongly treated.

2.   Interest in drawings may have been omitted.

3.   Salary or commission payable has been omitted in the capital account of the partner.

4.   The profit-sharing ratio has been changed from the past.

5.   Interest in the partner's loan has been omitted.

Instead of altering old accounts, necessary adjustments can be made either by:

(a)   through 'Profit and Loss Adjustment Account'

OR

(b)   directly in the capital account of the concerned partners.

(a)   Profit and Loss Adjustment Account:

1.   For omission of Interest on Capital, Salaries to partner(s), Commission to partner, etc.

Profit and Loss Adjustment Account Dr.

To Partner's Capital/Current A/c (Individually)

2.   For omission of Interest on drawings etc

Partner's Capital/Current A/c Dr.

To Profit and Loss Adjustment Account

3.   Calculate the difference or balance of the Profit and Loss Adjustment Account and transfer it to the Capital/Current Accounts of partners in the profit-sharing ratio.

(a) If Profit (Credit balance):

Profit and Loss Adjustment A/c Dr.

To Partner's Capital/Current A/c (Individually)

OR

(b) If Loss (Debit balance):

Partner's Capital/Current A/c (Individually) Dr.

To Profit and Loss Adjustment A/c (b) Adjustment through a single entry or directly in the capital account of the concerned partner(s):

In this case, the following steps should be taken

1. Calculate amount which should have been credited to each partner's Capital/Current Account by way of (Interest on Capital + Salaries to Partner(s) + Commission to Partner(s) - Interest on Drawings etc.)

2. Distribute the amount calculated in step (1) in the current profit sharing ratio.

3. Calculate the difference between the above two steps for each partner (1) - (2) (-) Excess or (+) Short

Multiple Choice Questions   [1 Mark]

Q.1. A,B, and C are partner's sharing profits in the ratio of 5:3:2 according to the partnership agreement C is to get a minimum amount of Rs. 10,000 as his share of profits every year. The net profit for the year ended 31st march, 2019 amounted to Rs. 40,000. How much amount contributed by A?

(a) Rs. 1,350   (b) Rs.1,250   (c) Rs. 750   (d) Rs. 1,225

Ans. (b)

Q.2. When a partner is given guarantee by other partners any deficiency on such guarantee will be borne by:

(a) Firm.   (b) All other partners.

(c) Partner with highest profit ratio.   (d) Partner who has given the guarantee.

Ans. (d)

Q.3. V, G and N are partners sharing profits in the ratio of 5:3:2. According to the partnership deed, N is to get a minimum amount of Rs.1,00,000 as his share of profits every year. The net profit for the year ended 31st march 2019 amounted to Rs. 4,00,000. How much amount would be contributed by V and G to meet the deficiency of profit of N?

(a) Rs. 10,000 each   (b) Rs. 12,500 V and Rs. 7,500 G

(c) Rs. 7,500 V and 12,500 G   (d) Rs. 20,000 V

Ans. (b)

Q.4. A, V and M are partners sharing profit in the ratio of 3: 2: 1. According to partnership deed, M is to get a minimum amount of Rs. 1,00,000 as her share of profits every year. The net profit for the year ended 31st march 2019 amount to Rs.9,00,000. How much profit would be credited to M's capital account as her share of profit?

(a) Rs. 9,00,000   (b) Rs. 1,50,000   (c) Rs. 1,00,000   (d) Rs. 5,80,000

Ans. (b)

Q.5. P, Q and R are partners in a firm in 3:2:1. R is guaranteed that he will get minimum of Rs. 20,000 as his share of profit every year. Firm's profit was Rs. 90,000. Partners will get:

(a) P Rs. 40,000; Q Rs. 30,000; R Rs. 20,000   (b) P Rs. 42,500; Q Rs. 27,500; R Rs. 20,000

(c) P Rs. 45,000; Q Rs. 30,000; R Rs. 15000   (d) P Rs. 42,000; Q Rs. 28,000; R Rs. 20,000

Ans. (d)

Q.6. Mohit, Sohit and Rohit are partners sharing profits and losses in the ratio 2:1:1. Rohit is guaranteed a profit of Rs. 14,000. The firm incurred a profit of Rs. 20,000 during the year. Calculate the amount of deficiency borne by Mohit and Sohit.

(a) Mohit Rs. 4,500 and Sohit Rs. 4,500   (b) Mohit Rs. 3,000 and Sohit Rs. 6,000

(c) Mohit Rs. 3,000 and Sohit Rs. 3,000   (d) Mohit Rs. 6,000 and Sohit Rs. 3,000

Ans. (d)

Q.7. X,Y,and Z are partners in the ratio of 6:4:1.In the firm, X has guaranteed Z for his minimum profit of Rs.15,000. Firm's profit was ? 99,000.In the firm profit X's share will be:

(a) Rs.30,000   (b) Rs.15,000   (c) Rs.60,000   (d) Rs.45,000

Ans. (c)

Q.8. When a partner is given guarantee by other partners, loss on such guarantee will be borne by:

(a) Partnership firm

(b) All the other partners

(c) Partners who give the guarantee

(d) Partner with highest profit sharing ratio.

Ans. (c)

Q.9. Anu and Tanu are equal partners with fixed capitals of ₹2,00,000 and ₹1,00,000 respectively. After closing the accounts for the year ending 31st-March,2019 it was discovered that interest on capitals @ 8%p.a.was omitted to be provided In the adjusting entry:

(a) Anu will be credited by ₹16,000 and Tanu will be credited by ₹8,000

(b) Anu will be debited by ₹16,000 and Tanu will be debited by ₹8,000

(c) Anu will be credited by ₹4,000 and Tanu will be debited by ₹4,000

(d) Anu will be debited by ₹4,000 and Tanu will be credited by ₹4,000

Ans. (c)

Q.10. Assertion Reason Questions

Assertion (A): Guarantee of minimum profit may be given to a partner.

Reason(R): It is compulsory as per Indian Partnership Act, 1932.

In the context of the given codes, which one of the following is correct?

(a) Both Assertion and Reason are true and reason is correct explanation of Assertion.

(b) Assertion and reason both are true but Reason is not the correct explanation of Assertion.

(c) Assertion is false, Reason is true.

(d) Assertion is true, Reason is false.

Ans. (d)

Very Short Answer Type   [1 Mark]

Q.1. True or false

When new partner share of profit is more than the guaranteed profit then he is given only the guaranteed amount of profit.

Ans. False

Q.2. In case of guarantee of minimum profit to a partner deficiency of guaranteed partner is from shared by remaining partner in ____________.

Ans. Agreed Ratio

Q.3. Sony and Romy are equal partners with fixed capitals of ₹4,00,000 and ₹3,00,000 respectively. After closing the accounts for the year ending31stMarch,2019 it was discovered that interest on capitals was provided @ 8% instead of 10%p.a. In the adjusting entry:

Ans. Sony will be credited by ₹1,000 and Romy will be debited by ₹1,000.

Q.4. P and Q are partners sharing profits and losses in the ratio of 2:1 with capitals ₹1,00,000 and ₹80,000 respectively. The interest on capital has been provided to them @ 8% instead of 10%. In the rectifying adjustment entry, Q will be:

Ans. Q will be credited by ₹1,600 (interest@2% to be given to Q) and Q will be debited by ₹1,200(share of Q in loss to the firm). So, finally Q will be credited by ₹400.

Q.5. A and B are partners sharing profits and losses equally. They admitted C as a partner with an equal share giving him a guarantee of minimum ₹50,000 profit p.a. The profit for the year after C's admission was ₹1,20,000. What will be the net amount that will be credited to A's Capital A/c?

Ans. Share of A in profit = 40,000 less Deficiency paid to C = 5,000. So net amount received by A = 35,000.

Q.6. X and Y are partners in the ratio of 3 : 2. Their fixed capitals are ₹2,00,000 and ₹1,00,000 respectively. After closing the accounts for the year ending 31st March 2019, it was discovered that interest on capital was allowed @12% instead of 10% per annum. By how much amount X will be debited/credited in the adjustment entry:

Ans. ₹400(Debit)

Q.7. P, Q and R are equal partners with fixed capitals of ₹5,00,000, ₹4,00,000 and ₹3,00,000 respectively. After closing the accounts for the year ending 31st March 2019 it was discovered that interest on capitals was provided @7% instead of 9%p.a.In the adjusting entry:

Ans. P will be credited by ₹2,000 and R will be debited by ₹2,000.

Q.8. X, Y, and Z are partners in the ratio of 4 : 3 : 2. Salary to X ₹15,000 and to Z ₹3,000 omitted and profits distributed. For rectification, now X will be credited by:

Ans. ₹7,000

Q.9. When a partner Mr. Amitabh is given guarantee by other partners Mr. Abhishek and Mrs.Aishwarya,in the ratio of 3:2, deficiency of Rs.10,000 on such guarantee will be borne by:

Ans. 6,000 Rs. by Mr. Abhishek, 4,000 Rs.by Mrs.Aishwarya.

Q.10. Guarantee given to partner 'A' by the other partners 'B & C'means:

Ans. In case of loss or insufficient profits,'A' will withdraw the minimum guarantee amount.

Short Answer Type - I   [2 Marks]

Q.1. Explain Gurantee of Profit to a Partner.

Ans. Sometimes a partner is admitted into the firm with a guarantee of certain minimum amount by way of his share of profits of the firm. Such assurance may be given by all the old partners in a certain ratio or by any of the old partners, individually to the new partner. The minimum guaranteed amount shall be paid to such new partner when his share of profit as per the profit sharing ratio is less than the guaranteed amount.

Q.2. Write a short note on Past Adjustments.

Ans. Sometimes a few omissions or errors in the recording of transactions or the preparation of summary statements are found after the final accounts have been prepared and the profits distributed among the partners. The omission may be in respect of interest on capitals, interest on drawings, interest on partner's loan, partner's salary, partner's commissions, or outstanding expenses. There may also be some changes in the provisions of partnership deed or system of accounting having impact with retrospective effect. All these acts of omission and commissions need adjustments for correction of their impact. Instead of altering old accounts, necessary adjustment can be made either;

(a) through 'Profit and Loss Adjustments', or

(b) directly in the capital accounts of the concerned partner

Q.3. A and R were partners in a firm sharing profits in the ratio of 2 : 3. Their fixed capitals were Rs. 2,50,000 and Rs. 4,50,000 respectively. After the final accounts of the year had been closed, it was found that interest on capital at 10% per annum as provided in the partnership agreement has not been credited to the capital accounts of the partners. Give necessary adjustment entry.

Ans. Ankita's Current A/c …Dr. 3000

    To Rinkita's Current A/c 3000

Q.4. Akshya, Harsh and Prince are partners in a firm sharing profits in the ratio of 5:3:2. Their capitals were Rs. 3,00,000; Rs. 2,00,000 and Rs. 1,00,000 respectively. For the year 2018-19, interest on capital accounts @ 8% p.a. instead of 10% p.a. pass the necessary adjusting entry.

Ans. Prince's Capital A/c …… Dr. 400

    To Harsh's Capital A/c 400

Q.5. X, Y and Z were partners, sharing profits in the ratio of 2 : 2 : 1. Z was guaranteed a minimum profit of Rs. 20,000. The profits of the firm for the year ended 31.03.2019 were Rs. 80000. Calculate share of Profit.

Ans. X's share Rs. 30000 ;

Y's share Rs. 30000

Z's share Rs. 20000

Q.6. N, A and S are partners in a firm sharing profits in the ratio of 2 : 3 : 5. On 1st April 2018, their capitals were Rs. 50,000 , Rs. 80,000 and Rs. 60,000 respectively on which they were entitled to get interest @ 10% p.a. The accountant omitted to allow interest on capital while distributing profits of Rs. 49000 at the end of the year. Pass necessary journal entry to rectify the error.

Ans. S's Capital A/c …. Dr. 3500

    To N's Capital A/c   1200

    To A's Capital A/c   2300

Q.7. Dinesh and Manish share profits and losses in the ratio of 3:2. They admit Nipun into their firm to 1/6 share in profits. Dinesh personally guaranteed that Nipun's share of profit, after charging interest on capital @ 10 percent per annum would not be less than Rs. 3,00,000 in any year. The capital provided was as follows: Dinesh Rs. 25,00,000, Manish Rs. 20,00,000 and Nipun Rs. 15,00,000. The profit for the year ending March Rs. 20,00,000 The Profit for the year ending March 31, 2019 amounted to Rs. 15,00,000 before providing interest on capital. Calculate the share of the Profit if new profit sharing ratio is 3:2:1.

Ans. Interest on capital:

Dinesh	2,50,000
Manish	2,00,000
Nipun	1,50,000
Total	6,00,000

Now remaining Net Profit 15,00,000 – 6,00,000 = 9,00,000

Profit transferred to capital A/c:

Dinesh 4,50,000 Less : share of deficiency 1,50,000 = 3,00,000

Manish = 3,00,000

Nipun 1,50,000 Add: deficiency recieved from Dinesh 1,50,000 = 3,00,000

Ans. Rs.3,00,000 to each

Q.8. P, D and K are partner's sharing profits in the ration of 5:4:1 K is given a guarantee that her share of profits in any given year would not be less than Rs. 50,000. Deficiency, if any would be borne by P and D equally. Profits for the year amounted to Rs. 4,00,000. Calculate the share of profit.

Ans. Net Profit 4,00,000 transferred to capital A/c:

P 2,00,000 Less: share of deficiency 5000 = 1,95,000

D 1,60,000 Less: share of deficiency 5000 = 1,55,000

K 40,000 Add: deficiency received from P 5,000, from D 5000 = 50,000

Q.9. Partners of a firm distributed the profits for the year ended 31-3-2003 Rs. 75,000 in the ratio 3 : 2 : 1 without providing for the following adjustments:

(a) A and B were entitled to a salary of Rs. 3,000 each p.a.

(b) B was entitled to a commission of Rs. 5,000

(c) B and C have guaranteed a minimum profit of Rs. 35,000 p.a. to A. and any deficiency in profits will be borne by A and B equally

Profits were to be shared in the ratio of 3 :3: 2. Pass necessary journal entry for the above adjustments in the books of the firm.

Ans.

C'S CAPITAL A/c	Dr. 2000	
TO B'S CAPITAL A/C		500
TO A'S CAPITAL A/C		1500

Q.10. M and D share profits and losses in the ratio of 2:1. From January 01, 2019 they admitted R into their firm who is to be given a share of 1/10 of the profits with a guaranteed minimum of Rs. 25,000. M and D continue to share profits as before but agree to bear any deficiency on account of guarantee to R in the ratio of 3:2 respectively. The profits of the firm for the year ending December 31, 2019 amounted to Rs. 1,20,000. Calculate share of Profit .

Ans. Share in profit

M 64200

D 30800

R 25000

Q.11. A, B and C were partner in a firm. On 1st April, 2018, their capitals stood at ₹ 4,00,000, ₹ 3,00,000 and ₹2,00,000 respectively. As per the provisions of the partnership deed. **[Sample paper 2019]**

(i) A was entitled to a salary of ₹5,000 per month.

(ii) Partner were entitled to interest on capital @ 10% p.a.

The net profit for the year ended 31st March 2019, ₹ 3,00,000 was divided among the partners without providing for the above items.

Showing your working clearly, pass an adjustment entry to rectify the above error.

Ans.

JOURNAL

Date	Particulars		Dr. (₹)	Cr. (₹)
2019	B's Capital A/c	Dr.	20,000	–
Mar 31	C's Capital A/c	Dr.	30,000	–
	To A's Capital A/c		–	50,000
	(Being ommission of interest on Capital and salary, now rectified)			

Table showing Past Adjustments:

Partners	Interest on Capital (Cr.) (₹)	Salary (Cr.) (₹)	Profit Dr. (₹)	Net effect	
				Dr. (₹)	Cr. (₹)
A	40,000	60,000	50,000	–	50,000
B	30,000	–	50,000	20,000	–
C	20,000	–	50,000	30,000	–
	90,000	60,600	1,50,000	50,000	50,000

Q.1. A, B and C are partners in a firm sharing profits and losses in the ratio of 2:3:5. Their fixed capitals were 15,000, Rs.30,000 and Rs.60,000 respectively. For the year 2019 interest on capital was credited to them @ 10% instead of 8%. Pass the necessary adjustment entry.

Ans. C's current A/c Dr.   150

    To A's Current A/c   120

      To B's Current A/c   30

(For interest less charged on capital, now rectified)

Q.2. Amit, Sumit and Vinit are partners in a firm. Their Capital A/c on 01st April 2021,was Rs. 2,00,000, Rs.1,20,000 and Rs. 1,60,000 respectively. Each partner withdrew Rs. 15,000 during the year 2021-22 As per the provisions of their partnership deed :

(1) Interest on capital was to be allowed @ 5% p.a.

(2) Interest on drawings was to be charged @ 4% p.a.

(3) Profits and Losses were to be shared in the ratio 5: 4: 1.

The net profit of Rs 72,000 for the year ended 31st March ,2022 , was divided equally amongst the Partners without providing for the terms of deed.

You are required to pass a single adjustment entry to rectify the error (Show working clearly)

Ans.   STATEMENT SHOWING ADJUSTMENT

Particulars		Amit	Sumit	Vinit	Firm
Interest on Capital	(Cr.)	1,000	6,000	8,000	24,000
Less: Interest on Drawings	(Dr.)	(300)	(300)	(300)	(900)
Add: Profit Ratio 5:4:1		9,700	5,700	7,700	23,100
(72000 – 23100 = 48900)		24,450	19,560	4,890	48,900
(a) This should have been done 50	(Cr.)	34,150	25,260	12,590	72,000
(b) Due to mistake profit Rs.72,000					
was divided equally so. It reversed	(Dr.)	24,000	24,000	24,000	72,000
(c) Difference (a-b)		10,150	1,260	11,410	…
		Cr.	Cr.	Dr.	

JOURNAL

Date	Particulars		L.P.	Dr. (Rs.)	Cr. (Rs.)
2022					
April 01	Vinit's Capital A/c	Dr.		11,410	
	To Amit's Capital A/c				10,150
	To Sumit's Capital A/c				1,260
	(Being adjustment entry passed)				

Q.3. Aarti, Archana and Aradhna are partners in a firm having fixed capital of Rs 1,60,000 ,80,000 ,and Rs 1,00,000 respectively sharing profits as 7:6:4. The rate of interest on capital was agreed at 10% p.a., But was wrongly credited to them as 12% p.a.. Give the necessary adjustment entry.

Ans. Statement Showing Adjustment

Particulars	Aarti	Archana	Aradhna	Amount
(a) Interest on Capital credited@12%	19,200	9,600	12,000	40,800
Interest should be credited @10%	16,000	8,000	10,000	34,000
Excess Interest credited (Dr.)	3,200	1,600	2,000	6,800
(b) Profit due to error increased by				
Rs.6,800 credited in 7:6:4 (Cr.)	2,800	2,400	1,600	6,800
Difference (a x b)	400 (Dr.)	800 (Cr.)	400 (Dr.)	…

ADJUSTMENT ENTRY

Date	Particulars		L.F.	Dr. (Rs.)	Cr. (Rs.)
	Aarti's Current A/c	Dr.		800	
	Aradhna's Current A/c				400
	To Archna's Current A/c				400
	(Being excess interest on capital credited now rectified)				

Q.4. Amol, Ajeet and Akhil were partners in a firm sharing profits in 2:1:1. Ratio. Akhil was guaranteed a profit of Rs. 50,000. Amol agreed to meet the liability arising out of guaranteed amount of Akhil . The firm earned a profit of Rs 1,60,000 for the year ended 31.03.2022.

Prepare the Profit and Loss Appropriation Account.

Ans.   **PROFIT AND LOSS APPROPRIATION A/C**

for the year ending 31st March 2022

Dr.   Cr.

Particulars	Amount	Particulars	Amount
To Partners Capital A/c		By Profit and Loss A/c (Profit)	1,60,000
Amol 80,000 – 10,000 = 70,000			
Ajeet 40,000 – = 40,000			
Akhil 40,000 + 10,000 = 50,000	1,60,000		
	1,60,000		**1,60,000**

Q.5. Ashok ,Manoj And Ravi entered into partnership on 01st April 2021 to share profits in the ratio of 2:1:1. It was provided in the deed that Ravi's share of profit will not less than Rs 70,000 p.a. The losses for the year ended 31st March ,2022 were Rs 2,00,000 before allowing interest Rs. 9,000 on Ashok's loan which due for current year.Prepare the Profit and Loss Appropriation Account .

Ans.   **PROFIT & LOSS APPROPRIATION A/C**

for the year ended 31st March 2022

Dr.   Cr.

Particulars	Amount	Particulars	Amount
To Loss (Before Int. on Loan) 2,00,000Add: Int. on loan to Ashok 9,000	2,09,000	By Partners Capital A/c	
		Ashok (2/3) 1,86,000	
To Ram's Capital A/c	70,000	Manoj (1/3) 93,000	2,79,000
(Minimum share of Profit)			
	2,79,000		**2,79,000**

Note: Interest on Partners Loan is a charge against profit

Q.6. Paresh and Parul were partners in a firm sharing profits equally. Their fixed capitals were Rs.1,00,000 and Rs.50,000 respectively. The partnership deed provided for interest on capital at the rate of 10% per annum. For the year ended 31st March, 2016, the profits of the firm were distributed without providing interest on Capital.

Pass necessary adjustment entry to rectify the error.   [C.B.S.E., 2017]

Ans.   **Books of the Firm**

JOURNAL

Date	Particulars		L.F.	Dr. (Rs.)	Cr. (Rs.)
2016	Parul's Current A/c	Dr.		2,500	
April 1	To Paresh's Current A/c				2,500
	(Being the adjustment of interest on capital omitted in previous year)				

Working Notes: Statement Showing Adjustment

Particulars	Paresh (Rs.)	Parul (Rs.)	Total (Rs.)
(a) Interest on Capital be Credited	10,000	5,000	15,000
(b) Profit wrongly distributed be debited	7,500	7,500	15,000
(c) Difference (a – b)	**2,500 Cr.**	**2,500 Dr.**	

Q.7. Rahim, Karim and Ajim were partners in a firm sharing profits and losses in the ratio of 2:1:2. Their capitals were fixed at Rs.3,00,000, Rs.1,00,000 and Rs.2,00,000. For the year 2000, interest on capital was credited to them @ 9% p.a. instead of 10% p.a. The profit for the year before charging interest was Rs.2,50,000.

Show your working and pass the necessary adjustment entry.   [C.B.S.E., 2001]

Ans.   STATEMENT SHOWING ADJUSTMENT

Particulars	Rahim (Rs.)	Karim (Rs.)	Ajim (Rs.)	Total (Rs.)
(a) Interest on capital should be @ 10% p.a. Less: Interest on capital has been charged @ 9% p.a.	30,000	10,000	20,000	60,000
	27,000	9,000	18,000	54,000
Excess interest on capital should be credited to partners	3,000	1,000	2,000	6,000
(b) Thus, excess interest will result in decrease in profit in ratio of 2:1:2				
(c) Difference (a – b)	2,400	1,200	2,400	6,000
	Cr. 600	**Dr. 200**	**Dr. 400**	

JOURNAL ENTRY

Date	Particulars	L.F.	Dr. (Rs.)	Cr. (Rs.)
	Karim's Current A/c Dr.		200	
	Ajim's Current A/c Dr.		400	
	To Rahim's Current A/c			600
	(For less interest on capital provided, now rectified)			

Q.8. Manohar and Udit are partners in a firm sharing profits in the ratio 2:3. Their capital accounts as on April 1, 2015 showed balances of Rs.70,000 and Rs.60,000 respectively. The drawings of Manohar and Udit during the year 2015-16 were Rs.16,000 and Rs.12,000 respectively. Both the amounts were withdrawn on 1st January 2016. It was subsequently found that the following items had been omitted while preparing the final accounts for the year ended 31st March, 2016.

(a) Interest on capitals @ 6% p.a.

(b) Interest on drawings @ 6% p.a.

(c) Manohar was entitled to a commission of Rs.4,000 for the whole year.

Showing your working clearly, pass a rectifying entry in the books of the firm.   [C.B.S.E., 2017-AI-C]

Ans.   **Books of the Manohar and Udit**
                                      JOURNAL

Date	Particulars		L.F.	Dr. (Rs.)	Cr. (Rs.)
2016	Udit's Capital A/c	Dr.		3,408	
April 1	To Manohar's Capital A/c				3,408
	(Rectifying entry for omission of IOC, IOD and Manohar's Commission)				

Working Note: Statement Showing Adjustment

Particulars	Manohar (Rs.)	Udit (Rs.)	Total (Rs.)
(a) Items omitted:			
Interest on Capital	4,200	3,600	7,800
Commission	4,000	....	4,000
	8,200	3,600	11,800
Less: Interest on Drawing	240	180	420
Amount should be Credited	7,960	3,420	11,380
(b) Due to omission, profit was divided in ratio 2:3	4,552	6,828	11,380
(c) Difference (a – b)	**3,408 Cr.**	**3,408 Cr.**	....

Q.9. Karun, Laxman and Manoj were partner in a firm sharing profits in 2:1:1 ratio. Manoj was guaranteed a profit of Rs.25,000. Karun agreed to meet the liability arising out of guaranteed amount of Manoj. The firm earned a profit of Rs.80,000 for the year ended 31.03,2016. Prepare Profit & Loss Appropriation Account.   **[C.B.S.E.,2007-AI modified]**

Ans.   **PROFIT & LOSS APPROPRIATION A/C**
Dr.   **for the year ending 31.03.2016**   **Cr.**

Particulars	(Rs.)	Particulars	(Rs.)
To Profit trans. To Capital A/cs		By Profit & Loss A/c	
Karun 40,000 – 5,000 (to Manoj)	35,000	(Net Profit)	80,000
Laxman 20,000	20,000		
Manoj 20,000 + 5,000 (from Karun)	25,000		
	80,000		**80,000**

Notes:

(i) Profit of Karun, Laxman and Manoj in ratio of 2:1:1 come to Rs.40,000 Rs.20,000 and Rs.20,000 respectively.

(ii) Since Karun guaranteed the profit of Rs. 25,000 to Manoj, so Karun will give Rs.5,000 from his share of profit and Manoj will get Rs.5,000 from Karun.

Q.10. Sarfaraz, Arbaz and Riyaz are partners sharing profits in the ratio 5:3:2. As per agreement, Riyaz is to get a minimum share of profit of Rs.10,000 every year. The profit for the year 2017 amounts to Rs.35,000.

Prepare Profit & Loss Appropriation Account to allocate the share of profit of each partner during 2017.

[C.B.S.E., 2017-AI Set III, modified]

Ans. Profit of 2007 = Rs.35,000

Safaraz's share = $Rs.35,000 \times \dfrac{5}{10}$ = Rs.17,500

Arbaz's share = $Rs.35,000 \times \dfrac{3}{10}$ = Rs.10,500

Riyaz's share = $Rs.35,000 \times \dfrac{2}{10}$ = Rs.7,000

Since the minimum guaranteed profit share of Riyaz is Rs.10,000 so he will get Rs.3,000 (Rs.10,000 – 7,000) more from the remaining partners in the ratio of Sarfaraz and Arbaz i.e. 5:3. Thus,

Sarfaraz will pay = $Rs.3,000 \times \dfrac{5}{8}$ = Rs.1,875

Arbaz will pay = $Rs.3,000 \times \dfrac{3}{10}$ Rs.1,125

Thus, profit share of each partner will be:

Sarfaraz – Rs.17,500 – 1,875 (to Riyaz) = Rs.15,625

Arbaz – Rs.10,500 – 1,125 (to Riyaz) = Rs.9,375

Riyaz – Rs.7,000 + Rs.1,875 (Sarfaraz) + Rs.1,125 (Arbaz) = Rs.10,000

PROFIT & LOSS APPROPRIATION A/C

Dr.   **for the year ended 31st December, 2017**   Cr.

Particulars	(Rs.)	Particulars	(Rs.)
To Profit trans. To Capital A/cs		By Profit & Loss A/c (Net Profit)	35,000
Sarfaraz 17,500 – 1,875	15625		
Arbaz 10,500 – 1,125	9,375		
Riyaz 7,000 – 1,875 + 1,125	10,000		
	35,000		**35,000**

Alternatively, another way is:

Profit of 2017 = Rs.35,000

Profit share of Sarfaraz, Arbaz and Riyaz is 5:3:2 with minimum guaranteed share of Riyaz Rs.10,000

Riyaz's share of profit = $Rs.35,000 \times \dfrac{2}{10}$ = Rs.7,000

Since Riyaz's share of profit comes to Rs.7,000 while his minimum share is Rs.10,000.

So, Total Profit of 2007 = Rs.35,000

Less: Riyaz's Share (Minimum guaranteed share) = Rs.10,000

Remaining profit **= Rs.25,000**

Rs.25,000 will be shared by Sarfaraz and Arbaz in ratio 5:3.

Sarfaraz's share = $Rs.25,000 \times \dfrac{5}{8}$ = Rs.15,625

Arbaz's share = $Rs.25,000 \times \dfrac{3}{8}$ = Rs.9,375

Q.11. A, B and C were partner in a firm. On 1st April, 2018, their capitals stood at ₹4,00,000, ₹3,00,000 and ₹2,00,000 respectively. As per the provisions of the partnership deed. **[CBSE 2019]**

(i) A was entitled to a salary of ₹5,000 per month.

(ii) Partner were entitled to interest on capital @ 10% p.a.

The net profit for the year ended 31st March 2019, ₹3,00,000 was divided among the partners without providing for the above items.

Showing your working clearly, pass an adjustment entry to rectify the above error.

Ans.

JOURNAL

Date	Particulars		Dr. (₹)	Cr. (₹)
2019	B's Capital A/c	Dr.	20,000	–
Mar 31	C's Capital A/c	Dr.	30,000	–
	To A's Capital A/c		–	50,000
	(Being omission of interest on Capital and salary, now rectified)			

Table showing Past Adjustments:

Partners	Interest on Capital (Cr.) (₹)	Salary (Cr.)(₹)	Profit Dr. (₹)	Net effect	
				Dr. (₹)	Cr. (₹)
A	40,000	60,000	50,000	–	50,000
B	30,000	–	50,000	20,000	–
C	20,000	–	50,000	30,000	–
	90,000	60,600	1,50,000	50,000	50,000

Q.12. Radha, Mary and Fatima are partners sharing profits in the ratio of 5 : 4 : 1 Fatima is given a guarantee that her share of profit, in any year will not be less than ₹5,000. The profits for the year ending March 31,2013 amounts to ₹ 35,000. Shortfall if any, in the profits guaranteed to Fatima is to be borne by Radha and Mary in the ratio of 3 : 2. Record necessary journal entry to show distribution of profit among partner. **[CBSE 2013]**

Ans.

Dr.		JOURNAL BOOK				Cr.
Date/S.No.	Particulars			L/F	Dr.(₹)	Dr. (₹)
	Profit and Loss A/c		Dr.		35,000	
	To Profit and Loss App. A/c					35,000
	(Being net profit transferred to Profit and Loss App. A/c)					
					35,000	16,600
						13,400
						5,000

	Profit and loss App. A/c	Dr.			
	To Radha's Capital A/c	[₹ 17,500 – ₹ 900]			
	To Mary's Capital A/c	[₹ 14,000 – ₹ 600]			
	To Fatima's Capital A/c	[₹ 3,500 + ₹ 900 + ₹ 600]			
	(Being share of profit transferred to Capital A/c)				

Working Notes:

Radha's share in profit = ₹ 35,000 × $\dfrac{5}{10}$ = ₹ 17,500

Mary's shar in profit = ₹ 35,000 × $\dfrac{4}{10}$ = ₹ 14,000

Fatima's share in profit = ₹ 35, 000 × $\dfrac{1}{10}$ = ₹ 3,500

Deficiency in Fatima's share in profit = ₹ 5000 – ₹ 3500 = ₹ 1500

Deficiency borne by Radha = ₹ 1500 × $\dfrac{3}{5}$ = ₹ 900

Deficiency borned by Mary = ₹ 1500 × $\dfrac{2}{5}$ = ₹ 600

Q.13. Ram, Mohan and Sohan are partners with capitals of ₹ 5,00,000, ₹ 2,50,000 and 2,00,000 respectively. After providing interest on capital @ 10% p.a. the profits are divisible as follows:

Ram 1/2, Mohan 1/3 and Sohan 1/6. But Ram and Mohan have guaranteed that Sohan's share in the profit shall not be less than ₹ 25,000, in any year. The net profit for the year ended March 31, 2013 is ₹ 2,00,000, before charging interest on capital.

You are required to show distribution of profit.   [CBSE - 2016]

Ans.

Dr.   **PROFIT AND LOSS APPROPRIATION A/C**   **Cr.**

	Particulars		(₹)	Particulars	(₹)
To	Interest on Capital A/c			By Profit and Loss A/c (Net profit)	2,00,000
	Ram	50,000			
	Mohan	25,000			
	Sohan	20,000	95,000		
To	Capitals A/c (Net Profit)				
	Ram	52,500			
(–)	Deficiency borne	4,500	48,000		
		35,000			
	Mohan				
(–)	Deficiency borne	3,000	32,000		
		17,500			
	Sohan				

(+) Deficiency from Ram	45,000			
(+) Deficiency from Mohan	3,000	25,000		
		2,00,000		2,00,000

Note: Profit sharing ratio $= \dfrac{1}{2} \times \dfrac{3}{3} : \dfrac{1}{3} \times \dfrac{2}{2} : \dfrac{1}{6} = \dfrac{3}{6} : \dfrac{2}{6} : \dfrac{1}{6} = 3 : 2 : 1$

Q.14. Ankur and Bobby were into the business of providing software solutions in India. They were sharing profits and losses in the ratio 3 : 2. They admitted Rohit for a 1/5 share in the firm. Rohit, an alumni of IIT, Chennai would help them to expand their business to various South African countries where he had been working earlier. Rohit is guaranteed a minimum profit of ₹ 2,00,000 for the year. Any deficiency in Rohit's share is to be borne by Ankur and Bobby in the ratio 4:1. Losses for the year ₹ 10,00,000. Pass the necessary journal entries. **[CBSE Sample Paper 2015]**

Ans.

JOURNAL

Date	Particulars		L/F	Dr. (₹)	Cr. (₹)
	Ankur's Capital A/c	Dr.		4,80,000	
	Bobby's Capital A/c	Dr.		3,20,000	
	Rohit's Capital A/c	Dr.		2,00,000	
	To Profit and Loss A/c				10,00,000
	(Being loss debited to partner's capital accounts)				
	Ankur's Capital A/c	Dr.		3,20,000	
	Bobby's Capital A/c	Dr.		80,000	
	To Rohit's Capital A/c				4,00,000
	(Being the deficiency borne by Ankur and Bobby in the ratio 4 : 1)				

Q.15. Rehman, Suleman and Hanuman were partners in a firm sharing profits in the ratio of 3 : 2 : 1 respectively. Their fixed capitals were as follows: Rehman ₹ 3,00,000, Suleman ₹ 2,00,000 and Hanuman ₹ 1,00,000. The partnership deed provided for the following for the division of profit:

(i) 10% of trading profit will be transferred to Reserve Account.

(ii) Hanuman was guaranteed a profit of ₹ 50,000. Any loss because of guarantee to Hanuman will be shared by Rehman and Suleman equally.

The trading profit of the firm for the year ended 31. 12. 2012 was ₹ 2,00,000.

Prepare the Profit and Loss Appropriation Account of Rehman, Suleman and Hanuman for the year ended 31. 12. 2012. **[CBSE 2013 Compartment OD]**

Ans.

Dr.   **PROFIT AND LOSS APPROPRIATION ACCOUNT**   **Cr.**

for the year ending 31 st March, 2013

Particulars		(₹)	Particulars	(₹)
To	Reserve A/c	20,000	By Profit and Loss A/c	2,00,000
To	Capital A/c (Profit)			
	Rehman	90,000		
	Less: Transfer to Hanuman	(10,000)　80,000		
	Suleman	60,000		
	Less: Transfer to Hanuman	(10,000)　50,000		
	Hanuman	30,000		
	Add: Transfer from			
	Rehman	10,000		
	Suleman	10,000　50,000		
		2,00,000		2,00,000

Long Answer Type   [5 Marks]

Q.1. Avinash and Vishal share profits and losses in the ratio of 2:1. They admit Narendra as a partner with ¼ share in profits with a guarantee that his share of profit shall be at least Rs.50,000. The net profit of the firm for the year ending March 31, 2014 was Rs.1,60,000. Prepare Profit and Loss Appropriation A/c, Pass necessary journal entry/entries for distribution of profits.   **[CBSE 2014]**

Ans.   New profit sharing ratio of Avinash, Vishal and Narendra = 2:1:1.

Particulars	Amount (Rs.)		Particulars	Amount (Rs.)
To Avinash's Capital A/c			By Profit and	1,60,000
(Share of profit)	80,000		Loss A/c (Net profit)	
Less: Share in deficiency)	(6,667)	73,333		
To Vishal's Capital A/c				
(Share of profit)	40,000	36,667		
Less: Share in deficiency)	(3,333)			
To Narendra's Capital A/c				
(Share of profit)	40,000			
Add: Deficiency received from:				
Avinash	6,667			
Vishal	3,333	50,000		
		1,60,000		1,60,000

Q.2. Abhay and Sanjay were partners in a firm sharing profits in the ratio of 3:2. On 01.04.2020 they admitted Varsha as a new partner for 1/8th share in the profits with a guaranteed profit of Rs.1,50,000. The new profit sharing ratio between Sanjay and Abhay will remain the same but they decided to bear any deficiency on account of guarantee to Varsha in the ratio 2:3. The profit of the firm for the year ended 31.03.2021 was Rs.9,00,000.

Prepare Profit and Loss Appropriation Account of Abhay, Sanjay and Varsha for the year ended 31.03.2021.

Ans. Dr.   **PROFIT AND LOSS APPROPRIATION A/C**   **Cr.**

Particulars		Amount (Rs.)	Particulars	Amount (Rs.)
To Profit tr. To Partners Capital A/c:			By Profit and	
Abhay	4,72,500		Loss A/c (net profit)	
Less: Deficiency	(15,000)	4,57,500		9,00,000
Sanjay	3,15,000			
Less: Deficiency	(22,500)	2,92,500		
Varsha	1,12,500			
Add: Deficiency received:				
From Abhay	15,000			
From Sanjay	22,500	1,50,000		
		9,00,000		**9,00,000**

Q.3. Shiv, Sundar and Sameer are partners sharing profits in the ratio of 3:2:1. Their fixed capitals are: Shiv Rs.1,20,000, Sundar Rs.90,000, and Sameer Rs.60,000. For the year 2020-21, interest on capitals were credited to them @ 6% p.a. instead of 5% p.a. Record adjustment entry. Show your workings clearly.

Ans. Adjustment Entry

Date	Particulars		L.F.	Dr. (Rs.)	Cr. (Rs.)
2021	Sameer's Current A/c	Dr.		150	
31 March	To Shiv's Current A/c				150
	(Adjustment for interest on capital credited @ 6% p.a. instead of 5% p.a.				

Working Notes: **Adjustment Table**

Particulars		Shiv (Rs.)	Sundar (Rs.)	Sameer (Rs.)	Total (Rs.)
Interest on Capital excess credited by 1%, now debited Share in Profit Rs.2,700 less credited, now credited	Dr.	1,200	900	600	2,700
in 3:2:1	Cr.	1,350	900	450	2,700
Adjustment/Net Effect		**Cr. 150**	---	**Dr. 150**	---

Q.4. The firm of Amar, Akbar and Anthony who have been sharing profits in the ratio of 2:2:1, have existed for same years. Anthony wants that he should get equal share in the profits with Amar and Akbar and he further wishes that the change in the profit sharing ratio should come into effect retrospectively were for the last three year. Amar and Akbar have agreement on this account. The profits for the last three years were: 2018-19 Rs.22,000; 2019-20 Rs.24,000 and 2020-21 Rs.29,000.

Show adjustment of profits by means of a single adjustment journal entry. Show your workings clearly.

Ans.

ADJUSTMENT ENTRY

Date	Particulars		L.F.	Dr. (Rs.)	Cr. (Rs.)
31 March	Amar's Capital A/c	Dr.		5,000	
2021	Akbar's Capital A/c	Dr.		5,000	
	To Anthony's Capital A/c				10,000
	(Adjustment redistribution of profits of last 3 years)				

Working Notes:

ADJUSTMENT TABLE

Particulars		Amar (Rs.)	Akbar (Rs.)	Anthony (Rs.)	Total (Rs.)
Cancellation of total profits of last 3 years Rs.75,000	Dr.	30,000	30,000	15,000	75,000
Share of profit credited equally	Cr.	25,000	25,000	25,000	75,000
Adjustment/Net Effect		**Dr. 5,000**	**Dr. 5,000**	**Cr. 10,000**	---

Q.5. Abhinav and Shalini are partners in a firm sharing profit in the ratio of 3:2.

Balance Sheet of Abhinav and Shalini as on 31 March, 2021

Liabilities		Amount (Rs.)	Assets		Amount (Rs.)
Abhinav's Capital	30,000		Drawings: Abhinav	4,000	
Shalini's Capital	10,000	40,000	Shalini	2,000	6,000
			Other Assets		34,000
		40,000			**40,000**

Profit for the year ended March 31, 2021 was Rs.5,000 which was divided in the agreed ratio, but interest @ 5% p.a. on capital and @ 6% p.a. on drawings was inadvertently enquired. Give the adjustment entry. Show your workings clearly.

Ans.

ADJUSTMENT TABLE

Date	Particulars		L.F.	Dr. (Rs.)	Cr. (Rs.)
2021	Shalini's Capital A/c	Dr.		288	
31 March	To Abhinav's Capital A/c				288
	(Adjustment for omission of interest on capitals and drawings)				

Working Notes: (i) Calculation of Opening Capitals and Interest on Capitals:

Details	Abhinav (Rs.)	Shalini (Rs.)
Closing Capital	30,000	10,000
Less: Profit distributed	(3,000)	(2,000)
Opening Capital	**27,000**	**8,000**
Interest on capital @ 5% p.a.	1,350	400

Note: For calculating opening capitals, drawings have not been added as it was not debited to Partner's Capital Accounts.

(ii)

Details		Abhinav (Rs.)	Shalini (Rs.)	Total (Rs.)
Profit already distributed, now cancelled	Dr.	3,000	2,000	5,000
Interest on Drawings @ 6% p.a. for 6 months	Dr.	120	60	180
Total	Dr.	3,120	2,060	5,180
Interest on Capitals	Cr.	1,350	400	1,750
Share of Profits	Cr.	2,058	1,372	3,430
Total	Cr.	3,408	1,772	5,180
Adjustment/ Net Effect		**Cr. 288**	**Dr. 288**	---

Q.6. Mohan, Neeraj and Peeyush are partners in a firm. They contributed Rs. 75,000 each as capital three years ago. At that time, Peeyush agreed to look after the business as Mohan and Neeraj were busy. The profits for the past three years were Rs. 45,000, Rs. 30,000 and Rs. 60,000 respectively. While going through the books of accounts, Mohan noticed that profit had been distributed in 1 : 1 : 2 ratio. When he enquired from Peeyush about this, Peeyush answered that since he looked after the business he should get more profit. Mohan disagreed and it was decided to distributed profits equally with respectively effect for the last three years.

(i) You are required to make necessary corrections in the books of accounts of Mohan, Neeraj and Peeyush by passing an adjustment entry.

(ii) Identify the value which is being ignored by Peeyush.

[All India 2013; VBQ]

Ans. *(i)*

JOURNAL

Date	Particulars		LF	Amt (Dr)	Amt (Cr)
	Peeyush's Capital A/c	Dr		22,500	
	To Mohan's Capital A/c				11,250
	To Neeraj's Capital A/c				11,250
	(Being profits of last three years distributed wrongly, now rectified)				

Working Note

STATEMENT SHOWING ADJUSTMENTS

Particulars	Mohan (₹)	Neeraj (₹)	Peeyush (₹)
Profits wrongly distributed now to be debited (45,000 + 30,000 + 60,000) in the ratio 1 : 1 : 2	33,750 (Dr)	33,750 (Dr)	67,500 (Dr)
Profits to be distributed equally, to be credited	45,000 (Cr)	45,000 (Cr)	45,000 (Cr)
Net Effect	11,250 (Cr)	11,250 (Cr)	22,500 (Dr)

(ii) Value not followed by Peeyush while distributing profits is (Any one)

    (a) **Honesty** Peeyush has not shown honesty towards co-partners by not distributing profits as per Partnership Act.

    (b) **Transparency** Peeyush has not shown transparency while distributing profits as per his wish and not communicating the same to other partners.

    (c) **Equity** Peeyush has not shown equity in profits distribution.

    (d) **Team work** Peeyush has not shown team work by hiding profit sharing ratio from other partners.

Q.7. P, Q and R are partners sharing profits in the ratio of 3 : 2 : 1. However, R is guaranteed Rs. 20,000 as his share of profits every year. Deficiency if any would be borne by the other partners. The profits for the two years ending 31st March, 2008 and 31st March, 2009 had been Rs. 75,000 and Rs. 80,000 respectively. Show the profit and loss appropriation account for the two years. **[CBSE 2010]**

Ans.

Dr $\qquad$ **PROFIT AND LOSS APPROPRIATION ACCOUNT** $\qquad$ **Cr**

for the year ended 31 st March, 2008

Particulars		Amt (₹)	Particulars	Amt (₹)
To Profit Transferred to (WN(i))			By Net Profit as per Profit and Loss A/c	75,000
P's Capital A/c	33,000			
Q's Capital A/c	22,000			
R's Capital A/c	20,000	75,000		
		75,000		75,000

Dr $\qquad$ **PROFIT AND LOSS APPROPRIATION ACCOUNT** $\qquad$ **Cr**

for the year ended 31 st March, 2009

Particulars		Amt (₹)	Particulars	Amt (₹)
To Profit Transferred to (WN(ii))			By Net Profit as per Profit and Loss A/c	80,000
P's Capital A/c	36,000			
Q's Capital A/c	24,000			
R's Capital A/c	20,000	80,000		
		80,000		80,000

Working Note

(i) Distribution of profit of ₹75,000 in the ratio 3 : 2 : 1.

P ₹37,500, Q ₹ 25,000, R ₹ 12,5000

But R is guaranteed ₹ 20,000 as his share of profit every year.

Therefore, the deficiency of ₹ 7,500 (i.e. ₹ 20,000 – ₹ 12,500) will be borne by P and Q in their profit sharing ratio of 3 : 2.

P will pay $7,500 \times \dfrac{3}{5} = ₹ \, 4,500;$ Q will pay $7,500 \times \dfrac{2}{5} = ₹ \, 3,000$

Finally,

P will get 37,500 – 4,500 = ₹ 33,000;   Q will get 25,000 – 3,000 = ₹ 22,000

R will get 12,500 + 4,500 + 3,000 = ₹ 20,000

(ii) Distribution of profit of ₹ 80,000 in the ratio 3 : 2 : 1.

P ₹ 40,000, Q ₹ 26,667, R ₹ 13,333

But R is guaranteed ₹ 20,000 as his share of profit every year. Therefore, the deficiency of ₹ 6,667 (i.e. ₹ 20,000 – ₹ 13,333) will be borne by P and Q in their profit sharing ratio of 3 : 2.

P will pay $6,667 \times \dfrac{3}{5} = ₹ \, 4,000;$ Q will pay $6,667 \times \dfrac{2}{5} = ₹ \, 2,667$

Finally, P will get 40,000 – 4,000 = ₹ 36,000

Q will get 26,667 – 2,667 = ₹ 24,000

R will get 13,333 + 4,000 + 2,667 = ₹20,000

TOPIC 3 Goodwill Theory, Methods of Valuation

Summary

Meaning of Goodwill: Goodwill means the good name or reputation of a business earned by a businessman through his hard work and honesty. This helps the business to earn more profit.

Features of Goodwill

1. It is an intangible asset: Goodwill cannot be seen or touched. It does not have any physical existence. Thus, it belongs to the category of intangible assets such as patents, trademarks, copy rights, etc.

2. It does not have an existence separate from that of an enterprise: Goodwill of an enterprise entirely depends on the enterprise and the situation of its profits. Thus, normally it has realisable value when business is sold.

3. It is helpful in earning higher profits.

4. It is an attractive force: It is an attractive force as it brings in customers regularly to the place of business.

5. It comes into existence due to various factors: The factors affecting the value of a firm's goodwill may be locational advantages, favourable contracts, brands, trademarks, copyrights, market reputation, etc.

6. It is difficult to place an exact value on goodwill: This is because its value may fluctuate from time to time due to changing circumstances which are internet and external to business. Moreover, the value of goodwill is subjective as it depends on the assessment of the valuer.

7. Its value is liable to constant fluctuations: While goodwill does not depreciate, its value is liable to constant fluctuation, its value is liable to constant fluctuations. It is always present as a silent asset in a business where there are super profits (i.e. More than the normal) but declines in value with the decline in earnings

Methods of Valuation of Goodwill

i. **Average profit method** Under this method, goodwill is valued on the basis of simple average or weighted average of profits of the firm multiplied by the number of years' of purchase.

   Value of Goodwill = Average Profit x Number of Years' Purchase

   NOTE Any abnormal gain or abnormal loss should not be taken into consideration while calculating the average profit.

   Number of years' of purchase means for how many years the firm will earn the same amount of profits in future. Average Profits = Total Profits/Number of years A buyer always wants to estimate the future profits of a business. Future profits depend upon the average performance of the business in the past. Past profits indicate as to what profits are likely to accrue in the future. Therefore, the past profits are averaged. But before calculating the average profits, the profits earned in the past must be adjusted in the light of future expectations and the following factors should be taken into account while calculating the average profits: (i) Abnormal income of a year should be deducted out of the net profit of that year. (ii) Abnormal loss of a year should be added back to the net profit of that year. (iii) Income from investments should be deducted out of the net profits of that year, because this income is received from outside the business

ii. **Capitalisation Method: Under this method, goodwill can be calculated in two ways:**

   (i) Capitalisation of Average Profit Method: Under this method first of all we calculate the average profits and then we assess the capital needed for earning such average profits on the basis of normal rate of return. Such capital is also called capitalised value of average profits. It is calculated as under.

   Capitalised value of the firm = Average Profits × 100

   Normal Rate of Return Goodwill is calculated by deducting the actual capital employed in business from the capitalised value of average profits. There will be no goodwill if the actual capital employed in the business exceeds or equals the capitalised value of the average profits.

   Net Assets or Capital Employed = Total assets - Outside liabilities Goodwill = Capitalized value of Average Profits - Capital Employed

   (ii) Capitalisation of Super Profit Method: Under this method first of all we calculate the super profits and then we assess the capital needed for earning such super profits on the basis of normal rate of return. Such capital is actually the amount of goodwill. Super profits are calculated in the same manner as calculated in super profits method.

   Goodwill of the firm = Super Profits x 100 Normal rate of return.

iii. **Weighted Average Profit Method:** Weighted average is multiplied by agreed Number of years of Purchase.

   Weighted Average Profit: = Total Product of Profits / Total Weights

   Goodwill = Weighted Average Profit x No. of years' of purchase.

   Weighted average profit method is considered better than the simple average profit method because it assigns more weightage to the profits of the latest year which is more likely to be earned in future. This method is preferred when profits over the past years have been continuously rising or falling.

iv **Super profit method:** In this method goodwill is calculated on the basis of surplus (excess) profits earned by a firm in comparison to average profits earned by other firms. If a business has no anticipated excess earnings, it will have no goodwill.

   Super Profit are the excess of actual profit over normal profits. Normal profits are profits earned by similar business. If a firm earns higher profit in comparison to normal profit (generally earned by other firms of same industry) then the difference is called Super Profit.

Goodwill is calculated on the basis of Super profit due to future expectations of earning capacity of the firm. Goodwill is calculated by the following formula:

Goodwill = Super Profit x Number of years' of purchase

where, Super Profit = Average profit - Normal profits and

Normal Profit = Investment (Capital Employed) x Normal Rate of Return / 100

Capital Employed = Total Capital of all partners + Free Reserves - fictitious Assets (if any), or

All Assets - (Goodwill, fictitious assets and non-trade Investment) - Outsider's Liabilities

Multiple Choice Questions   [1 Mark]

Q.1. Goodwill is _____

    (a) tangible asset   (b) intangible asset   (c) fictitious asset   (d) both (b) & (c)

Ans. (b)

Q.2. Goodwill of the firm on the basis of 2 years' purchase of average profit of the last 3 years is Rs.25,000. Find average profit.

    (a) Rs.50,000   (b) Rs.25,000   (c) Rs.10,000   (d) Rs.12500

Ans. (d)

Q.3. Calculate the value of goodwill at 3 years' purchase when: Capital employed Rs.2,50,000; Average profit Rs.30,000 and normal rate of return is 10%.

    (a) Rs.3000   (b) Rs.25,000   (c) Rs.30,000   (d) Rs.15,000

Ans. (d)

Q.4. What are super profits

    (a) Actual profit - Normal Profit   (b) Normal Profit - Actual profit

    (c) Actual profit + Normal Profit   (d) None of the above

Ans. (a)

Q.5. The net assets of the firm including fictitious assets of 5,000 are 85,000. The net liabilities of the firm are 30,000. The normal rate of return is 10% and the average profits of the firm are 8,000. Calculate the goodwill as per capitalization of super profits.

    (a) Rs.20,000   (b) Rs.30,000   (c) Rs.25,000   (d) None of the above

Ans. (b)

Q.6. Which of the following items are added to previous year's profits for finding normal profits for valuation of goodwill?

    (a) Loss on sale of fixed assets   (b) Loss due to fire, earthquake etc.

    (c) Undervaluation of closing stock   (d) All of the above

Ans. (d)

Q.7. Under which method of valuation of goodwill, normal rate of return is not considered?

   (a) Loss on sale of fixed assets

   (b) Loss due to fire, earthquake etc.

   (c) Undervaluation of closing stock

   (d) All of the above

Ans. (c)

Q.8. Following are the methods of calculating goodwill except:

   (a) Super profit method   (b) Average profit method

   (c) Weighted Average profit method   (d) Capital profit method

Ans. (d)

Q.9. The excess amount which the firm can get on selling its assets over and above the saleable value of its assets is called:

   (a) Surplus   (b) Super profits   (c) Reserve   (d) Goodwill

Ans. (d)

Q.10. When Goodwill is not purchased goodwill account can:

   (a) Never be raised in the books   (b) Be raised in the books

   (c) Be partially raised in the books   (d) Be raised as per the agreement of the partners

Ans. (a)

Q.11. The goodwill of the firm is not affected by:

   (a) Location of the firm   (b) Reputation of the firm

   (c) Better customer services   (d) None of the above

Ans. (b)

Q.12. Weighted average profit method of calculating goodwill is used when:

   (a) Profits are not equal   (b) Profits show a trend

   (c) Profits are fluctuating   (d) None of the above

Ans. (b)

Q.13. Assertion (A): goodwill is considered as an intangible asset but not a fictitious asset.

   Reason (R): goodwill can neither be seen and touched nor it can be purchased or sold with any other asset.

   In the context of the given codes, which one of the following is correct?

   (a) Both Assertion and Reason are true and reason is correct explanation of Assertion.

   (b) Assertion and reason both are true but Reason is not the correct explanation of Assertion.

   (c) Assertion is false, Reason is true.

   (d) Assertion is true, Reason is false.

Ans. (d)

Q.14. Assertion (A): The factors which affect profits, also affect goodwill

Reason(R): Profits are directly related to goodwill.

In the context of the given codes, which one of the following is correct?

(a) Both Assertion and Reason are true and reason is correct explanation of Assertion.

(a) Assertion and reason both are true but Reason is not the correct explanation of Assertion.

(b) Assertion is false, Reason is true.

(c) Assertion is true, Reason is false.

Ans. (a)

Q.15. Assertion (A): Self - generated goodwill is the internally generated or hard earned goodwill.

Reason (R): It arises due to continued hard work of the organization, its better quality products, etc

In the context of the given codes, which one of the following is correct?

(a) Both Assertion and Reason are true and reason is correct explanation of Assertion.

(b) Assertion and reason both are true but Reason is not the correct explanation of Assertion.

(c) Assertion is false, Reason is true.

(d) Assertion is true, Reason is false.

Ans. (a)

Very Short Answer Type   [1 Mark]

Q.1. Under ---------- method, goodwill is the excess of capitalized value of business over actual capital employed.

Ans. Capitalisation of average profit

Q.2. The value of goodwill is based on ----------- judgment of the value.

Ans. Subjective

Q.3. When the value of goodwill of the firm is not given but has to be inferred on the basis of the net worth of the firm, it is called……………..

Ans. Hidden Goodwill

Q.4. Goodwill is not valued during …………..

Ans. Dissolution of the firm

Q.5. If Super profit of a firm is 10,000, its value of goodwill will be ………….if rate of return is 8%

Ans. 1,25,000

Q.6. Location of business does not affect the goodwill of business.

Ans. False

Q.7. "Average profit method" takes into consideration the future maintainable profits.

Ans. True

Q.8. Goodwill can be sold in part.

Ans. False

Q.9. Purchased goodwill may arise on acquisition of an existing business concern.

Ans. True

Q.10. Self-Generated goodwill is recorded in the books of accounts as some consideration is paid for it

Ans. False

Q.11. How does the nature of business affect the value of goodwill of a firm?　　　　　　**[All India 2011]**

Ans. The firm that produces high value products and has stabilised demand, will be able to earn more profit and more goodwill.

Q.12. What are super profits?　　　　　　**[CBSE 2011c]**

Ans. Super profit is the excess of actual average profit over the normal profit. i.e. Super Profit = Actual Profit - Normal Profit

Q.13. How does the factor 'efficiency of management' affect the goodwill of a firm?　　　　　　**[All India 2010]**

Ans. When the management of a firm is capable and competent, the firm will earn higher profits therefore the 'efficiency of management' surely will affect or increase the goodwill.

Short Answer Type - I　　　　　　**[2 Marks]**

Q.1. Capital invested in a firm is 5,00,000. Normal rate of return is 10%. Average profit of the firm are 64,000(after an abnormal loss of 4,000).Value of goodwill at four times the super profits will be:

Ans. Super profit = av profit – nor profit

$$= 68,0000 – 50,000 = 18000$$

Goodwill = s.p × pur year

$$= 18,0000 × 4 = Rs.72,000$$

Q.2. Harsh and Dev formed a partner ship, for the calculation of goodwill they required super profit.What is the amount of super profit in the given situation?

If Average profit = Rs. 1,60,000

Actual Capital Employed = Rs. 5,00,000

If rate of normal profit = 20%

Ans. Super profit = av profit – nor profit

$$=1,60,000 – 1,00,000$$

$$= Rs. 60,000$$

Q.3. If goodwill is Rs.1,20,000, Average profit is Rs.60,000 Normal. Rate of return of is 10%on capital Employed Rs.4,80,000. Calculate capitalized value of the firm:-　　　　　　**[CBSE 2015]**

Ans. C.V. = Av profit/nor rate × 100

$$= 60,000/10 × 100$$

$$= Rs. 6,00,000$$

Q.4. Tangible assets of the firm are Rs. 14,00,000 and outside liabilities are Rs. 4,00,000, profit of the is Rs. 1,50,000 and normal rate of return is 10% Calculate capital employed

Ans. C.E. = T.A – Outside liabilities

$$= 14,00,0000 – 4,00,000$$

$$= Rs. 10,00,000$$

Q.5. A business has earned super profit of Rs. 1,00,000 during the last few years and normal rate of return in 10% calculate goodwill

Ans. Goodwill = S.P. × 100/ Nor rate

$$= 1,00,000 × 100/10$$

$$= Rs. 10,00,000$$

Q.6. The profits earned by a business over the last 5 years are as follows 12,000; 13,000; 14,000:18,000 and 2,000 (loss). Based on 2 years purchase of the last 5 years profits, value of Goodwill will be :

Ans. Total profit = 55,000

Average profit = 55000/5 = 11,000

Goodwill = 11,000 × 2 = 22,000

Q.7. Explain any two methods for valuation of goodwill. **[Delhi 2008C]**

Ans. The two methods for valuation of goodwill are as follows

(i) Average Profit Method of Valuation of Goodwill Under average profit method, goodwill is valued on the basis of simple average or weighted average profits of the firm, multiplied by the number of years' of purchase.

Average Profit =Total Profit (after adjustments) / Number of Years

Goodwill = Average Profit x Number of Years' of Purchase.

(ii) Valuation of Goodwill by Capitalisation of Super Profit Method Under this method, goodwill is the capitalised value of super profits. For calculating goodwill, the following steps are followed

(a) Ascertain the average profits based on the past few years' performance.

(b) Calculate normal profit on capital employed by applying normal rate of return.

(c) Calculate super profits by deducting normal profit from average profits.

(d) Goodwill = Super Profit x 100 / Normal Rate of Return

Q.8. Akansha, Chetna and Dipanshu are partners in a firm shring profits and losses in the ratio of 3:2:1. They decide to lake jatin into partnership form January 1, 2015 for1/5 share in the future profits. For this purpose, goodwill is to be valued at 2 times the average annual profits of the previous four years. The average profits for the past four years were. **[CBSE 2016]**

Year	(Rs.)
2012	96,000
2013	60,600
2014	62,400
2015	84,400

Calculate the value of goodwill.

Ans. Formula

Average Profit = Total Profits/No. of Years.

Goodwill = Average Profit × Number of years of purchase

Year	(Rs.)
2012	96,000
2013	60,600
2014	62,400
2015	84,400
Total Profits	**Rs. 3,03,400**

Average profit = 3,03,400/4 = Rs. 75,850

Goodwill = 75,850 × 2 = Rs. 151,700

Q.9. A earns Rs. 1,20,000 as its annual profits, the rates of normal profit being 10%. The assets of the firm amounted to Rs. 14,40,000 and liabilities to Rs. 4,80,000. Find out the value of goodwill by capitalization method.

[CBSE 2015]

Ans. Capitalised value of the firm Average Profit $\times \dfrac{100}{\text{Normal Rate of Return}}$

$$= \text{Rs. } \frac{1,20,000 \times 10}{100} = \text{Rs. } 12,00,000$$

Capital employed = Total assets – liabilities

$$= \text{Rs. } 14,40,000 - 4,80,000 = \text{Rs. } 9,60,000$$

Goodwill = Capitalised value – Capital Employed

$$= \text{Rs. } 12,00,000 - 9,60,000 = \text{Rs. } 2,40,000$$

Short Answer Type - II

[3 Marks]

Q.1. The average net profits Expected of the firm in future are Rs. 68,000 per year and capital invested in the business by the firm is Rs. 3,50,000. The rate of interest expected from capital invested in this class of business is 12%. The remuneration of the partners is estimated to be Rs. 8,000 for the year. You are required to find out the value of goodwill on the basis of 2 years purchase of super profits.

Ans. Average profit = 68,000 – 8000 = 60,000

Normal profit = 3,50,000 × 12/100 = 42,000

Super profit= 60,000 – 42,000 = 18,000

Goodwill = 18,000 × 2 = 36,000

Q.2. Define Goodwill and write two main characteristics of goodwill. [CBSE 2012]

Ans. A Goodwill is the value of Reputation, Good name and wide business connections of a firm which enables it to earn higher profits in compare to the normal profit earned by the other firms in the same trade.

main characteristics

(i) it is an intangible asset having a definite value.

(ii) It helps in earning more profit.

Q.3. Name the factors affecting goodwill of a partnership firm. [CBSE 2013]

Ans. The main factors affecting the value of goodwill are as follows: 1. Nature of business 2. Location 3. Efficiency of Management 4. Market Situations 5. Special advantages like low rate and assured supply of electricity, long term contracts for supply of materials, well known collaborators, patents, trademarks, import, licences, etc,. enjoy higher value of goodwill.

Q.4. Explain Categories of Goodwill.

Ans. Categories of Goodwill 1. Purchased Goodwill 2. Self Generated Goodwill

Purchased Goodwill

Goodwill for which a consideration in money or money's worth has been paid in cash is called Purchased Goodwill. Features - 1 It arises on purchase of business or brand. 2. Shown in Balance Sheet as asset. 3. It is amortised (depreciated)?

Self-Generated Goodwill

It is an internally generated Goodwill which arises from a number of factors that a running business possess. 1. It is generated over the years. 2. According to AS-26, it is not recorded in books of accounts. 3. It is also known as "INHERENT GOODWILL"

Q.5. Write the circumstances when Goodwill needs to be valued.

Ans. Goodwill needs to be valued in the following circumstances. 1. Change in Profit Sharing ratio among the existing partners 2. Admission of a New Partner 3. Retirement of a Partner 4. Death of a Partner 5. Dissolution of a firm involving Sale of business as a going Concern. 6. Amalgamation of a Partnership Firm

Q.6. Explain simple average profit method for calculation of goodwill.

Ans. Under this method, the goodwill is valued at the agreed numbers of years of purchase of the average profits of the past years.

STEPS OF CALCULATE GOODWILL

1. Calculate Adjusted Profits/Normal Business Profit: Profit or Loss of the past year ADD : Abnormal losses Loss on Sale of Fixed Assets Overvaluation of opening stock Undervaluation of closing stock Non-recurring Expenses Capital Expenditure charged as Revenue Expenditure LESS : Abnormal gains Profit on sale of Fixed Assets Overvaluation of closing stock Undervaluation of opening stock Non-recurring incomes Partner's remuneration, if it is not deducted Income from Non-trade Investments Any future Expense.

2. AVERAGE PROFIT = TOTAL OF ADJUSTED PROFIT No. of YEARS

3. GOODWILL = AVERAGE PROFIT X NO. OF YEAR'S OF PURCHASE ??

Q.7. M/s Aradhya having the assets of Rs 10,00,000 and Liabilities of Rs 4,20,000. The firm earns the annual profit of Rs. 90,000. The rate of interest expected from the capital having regard to the risk involved is 15%. Calculate the amount of Goodwill by Capitalisation of Super Profit method. [CBSE 2016]

Ans. Super Profit = Average/Actual Profits – Normal Profits

Actual Profits = Rs. 90,000

$$\text{Normal Profit} = \text{Capital Employed} \times \frac{\text{Normal Rate of Return}}{100}$$

Capital Employed = Total Assets – Outside's Liabilities

$$= Rs.\ 10,00,000 - Rs.\ 4,20,000$$

$$= Rs.\ 5,80,000$$

Normal Profit = Rs. $5,80,000 \times \dfrac{15}{100}$ = Rs. 87,000

Super Profits = Rs. 90,000 – Rs. 87,000 = Rs. 3,000

Goodwill

$$= Super\ Profits \times \dfrac{100}{Normal\ Rate\ of\ Return}$$

$$= 3,000 \times \dfrac{100}{15}$$

Ans. Goodwill = Rs. 20,000

Q.8. The profits of a firm for the last five years were:

Year →	2011	2012	2013	2014	2015
Profits (Rs.)	45,000	50,000	52,000	65,000	85,000

Calculate the value of goodwill on the basis of two years of purchase of weighted average profits, the weights to be used are 2011-1, 2012-2, 2013-3, 2014-4 and 2015   **[CBSE 2015]**

Ans.

Year	Profit (Rs.)	Weights	Weights Profit × Weight
2011	43,000	1	43,000
2012	50,000	2	1,00,000
2013	52,000	3	1,56,000
2014	65,000	4	2,60,000
2015	85,000	5	4,25,400
Total		15	9,84,400

Weighted Average Profit: $= \dfrac{Total\ product\ of\ profits}{Total\ of\ weights} = \dfrac{9,84,000}{15} = 65,600$

Goodwill = Weighted Average Profit ✕ No. of years of purchase.

Rs. 65600 × 2 = Rs. 1,31,200

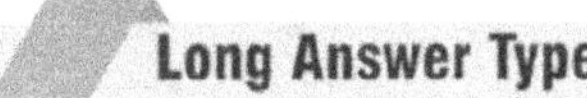

Long Answer Type   [5 Marks]

Q.1. A firm's profits and loss from last five years were as follows :

Year	Profit (Rs.)	
2018	1,60,000	
2019	1,56,000	
2020	(Loss)	(63,000)
2021	1,06,000	
2022	1,80,000	

Calculate the value of goodwill on the basis of 3 years purchase of 5 years average profits.

Ans. Calculation of Goodwill

Year	Amount
2018	1,60,000
2019	1,56,000
2020	(63,000)
2021	1,06,000
2022	1,80,000
Total	5,39,000

Average Profit   = Total Profit / No. of years

   = 5,39,000 / 5 = Rs.1,07,800

Goodwill = Average Profit × No. of years of purchase

   = 1,07,800 × 3 = Rs.3,23,400

Q.2. Abhita purchased business of Dipika from 01st April 2022. The profit of Dipika's business for last three years were as follows :

Year	Profits
2019-20	RS.1,60,000 (Which includes an abnormal gain of Rs. 20,000)
2020-21	Rs.2,00,000 (Which was after charging an abnormal loss of Rs.40,000)
2021-22	Rs.1,80,000 (Which excludes Rs. 20,000 as insurance premium of firm's assets)

Calculate the value of goodwill on basis of 2 years purchase of 3 years average profits.

Ans.   Calculation of Net / Normal Profit

Year	Profit	Adjustment	Normal Profit (Rs.)
2019-20	1,60,000	– Gain 20,000	1,40,000
2020-21	2,00,000	+ Abnormal Loss 40,000	2,40,000
2021-22	1,80,000	– Insurance 20,000	1,60,000
		Total Normal Profit Rs.	5,40,000

Average Profit = Total Profit / No. of years

   = 5,40,000 / 3 = Rs.1,80,000

Goodwill = Average Profit × No. of years of purchase

   = 1,80,000 × 2 = Rs.3,60,000

Ans. Goodwill Rs.3,60,000

Q.3. From the following information, calculate goodwill according of capitalisation of Super Profit Method.

[CBSE 2017]

(i) Total Assets Rs.10,00,000

(ii) External Liabilities Rs. 1,80,000

(iii)Normal Rate of Return 10%

(iv) Average Net Profit Rs. 1,00,000

Ans. Capital employed = Total Assets – External Liabilites

$$= 10,00,000 - 1,80,000 = Rs.8,20,000$$

$$\text{Normal Profit} = \frac{Capital\ Employed \times Rate\ of\ Normal\ Profit}{100}$$

$$= 8,20,000 \times 10/100 = Rs.82,000$$

Super Profit = Average Profit × Normal Profit

$$= 1,00,000 - 82,000 = 18,000$$

$$\text{Goodwill} = \frac{Super\ Profit \times 100}{Rate\ of\ Normal\ Profit}$$

$$= \frac{18,000 \times 100}{10} = Rs.1,80,000$$

Ans. Goodwill = Rs.1,80,000

Q.4. Explain calculation of goodwill by super profit method.

Ans. Under this method, the goodwill is valued at the agreed number of years of purchase of the super profits of the firm .

STEPS TO CALCULATE GOODWILL

(1) Average Capital = Opening capital employed + closing capital employed /2

(2) Calculate average maintainable profit (same as above in average profit method)

(3) Normal of profit = Average Capital Employed × Normal rate of return / 100

(4) Super Profit = Average maintainable profits – Normal Profits

(5) GOODWILL = SUPER PROFIT × NO. OF YEAR'S OF PURCHASE

Calculation of capital employed

- Assets side Approach

- Capital Employed = All Assets (except goodwill, non-trade investments and ficitious assets) – Outside liabilities

- Liabilities side Approach Capital Employed = Capital + Reserves - Goodwill (if exists in books)- Ficitious Asset - Non- trade investments.

Q.5. Explain Capitalisation method of calculation of Goodwill.   **[CBSE 2014]**

Ans. There are two methods ;

Capitalisation of average profits

Capitalisation of super profits .

[1] CAPITALISATION OF AVERAGE PROFITS

Under this method, the value of goodwill is calculated by deducting the actual capital employed from the capitalization value of the average profits on the basis of the normal rate of return

Steps to calculate goodwill

1.   Calculate Average Normal Profit

2.   Capitalised value of the Business = Average profit Normal rate of return × 100

3.   Capital Emloyed = All Assets (except goodwill, non-trade investment and ficitious assets) – Outside liabilities

4.   GOODWILL = Capitalised value of the Business – Net Assets

[2] CAPITALISATION OF SUPER PROFITS

Under this method, Goodwill is calculated by capitalizing the super profits

Steps to calculate goodwill

1. Capital Employed = All Assets (except goodwill, non-trade investments and ficitious assets) – Outside Liabilities

2. Normal Profit = Capital Employed × Normal rate of return 100

3. Calculate average maintainable profit (as above)

4. Super Profit = Average maintainable profits – Normal Profits

5. GOODWILL = Super Profit Normal rate of return × 100

Chapter Practice

Multiple Choice Questions   [1 Mark]

Q.1. The basic elements of partnership are :

(a) Association of two or more person based on agreement

(b) Business is carried on by all or any of them acting for all

(c) Sharing of profits and loss

(d) All above elements

Q.2. In the absence of partnership deed , interest on partner's capital is allowed :

(a) 5%   (b) 6%   (c) at market   (d) No interest is allowed

Q.3. The balance of partner's current account are :

(a) Debit   (b) Credit   (c) Can never be debit   (d) Either debit or credit

Q.4. Partner Ravi drew fixed amount at the end of each month during 2021-22. If interest on drawings at 8% p.a. amounts to Rs. 2200, his monthly drawings was :

(a) Rs. 5500   (b) Rs. 5000   (c) Rs. 6000   (d) None of these

Q.5. Rohan withdraw Rs. 10,000 at the end of each month for 6 months. Interest on his drawings @ 10% p.a. Will be :

(a) Rs.1750   (b) Rs.1250   (c) Rs.1500   (d) None of these

Q.6. Interest on partner's capital is computed on :

(a) Opening Capital (b) Average Capital   (c) Closing Capital   (d) Capital in mid year

Q.7. A dormant partner is also known as .... partner.

(a) Active   (b) Sleeping   (c) Nominal   (d) Minor

Very Short Answer Type   [1 Mark]

Q.8. Six friends started a partnership business.

They decided to share profit equally. Name the terms which they will be called individually and collectively?

Q.9. Why is it necessary to have partnership deed ?

Q.10. Give two circumstances under which fixed capital of partner may change ?

Q.11. Why interest on capital allowed ?

Q.12. Why is Profit And Loss Appropriation A/C prepared by a Partnership Firm ?

Q.13. Is there any limit on maximum number of partners in a firm ?

Q.14. Why should partnership deed be in writing ?

Q.15. Ravi and Manoj were partners in a firm sharing profits in the ratio of 3:2.During the year ended 31 st March 2022 , Ravi withdrew Rs 20.000. Interest on his drawings amounted to Rs. 500. Pass necessary Journal entry for charging interest on drawings assuming that the capitals of the partners were fixed.

Q.16. One of the partner in a firm has withdrawn Rs. 18,000 at the end of each quarter ,throughout the year Calculate interest on drawings at the rate of 6% p.a.

Q.17. A,B,and C were partners in a firm sharing profits in the ratio of 3:2:1. B was guaranteed a profit of Rs. 2,00,000. During the year ,the firm earned a profit of Rs.84,000. Calculate the net amount of Profit/Loss Transferred to Capital account of A and C.

Short Answer Type - I　　　　　　　　　　　　　　　　[2 Marks]

Q.18. Jay and Vijay are partners having capitals Rs.1,00,000 and 80,000 respectively .Interest on Capital is allowed @ 6% p.a. Their profit sharing ratio is 2:3. The profit for the year of the firm before providing. Interest on capital for the year ended 31st March 2022 is Rs. 9,000. Prepare Profit & Loss Appropriation Account.

Q.19. Veena,Vasudha and Vandana are partners in a firm having fixed capital of Rs.80,000,Rs.40,000 and And Rs.50,000 respectively sharing profits as 7:6:4. The rate of interest on capital was agreed at 10%p.a. but was wrongly credited to them as 12% p.a. Give necessary adjustment journal entry.

Q.20. Anita and Babita started business on July, 1,2021, each partner contributed Rs.1,50,000 as her share of Capital. Three months later, on October 1,2021, Babita makes additional contribution of Rs.1,00,000.

Which is treated as loan. The profit for the period ending March ,2022 was Rs.85,000 before charging. Any interest.The partners had drawen Rs.24,000 each on 01st January 2022. Prepare Profit and Loss Appropriation Account for the period ended March 31,2022

Short Answer Type - II　　　　　　　　　　　　　　　　[3 Marks]

Q.21. Veena and Vasudha are partners in a firm. Their capital account as on April.01.2021 showed a balance of Rs. 2,00,000 and Rs. 3,00,000 respectively . On July,01.2021 ,Veena introduced additional capital of Rs.50,000 and Vasudha Rs.60,000. On October 01.2021 Veena withdrew Rs.30,000 and on January 01.2022,Vasudha withdrew Rs.15,000 from their capital. Interest is allowed @8% p.a. Calculate interest on capital for the financial year 2021-22.

Q.22. Priyank withdrew the following amount from the firm during the year ending March 31, 2022. Calculate interest on drawings ,if the rate of interest is 9% p.a.:

Date	Amount(Rs.)
01.04.2021	16,000
30.06.2021	15,000
15.10.2021	10,000
31.12.2021	14,000
01.03.2022	11,000

Q.23. Abhiuank and Dipika are partners in a firm. Abhiyank withdrew Rs.20,000 at the end of each month.

Dipika withdrew Rs.40,000 on quarterly basis at the beginning of each quarter Compute interest on drawings @ 9% p .a. on 31.03.2022

Q.24. Anil, Sunil and Kamal are partners in a firm in the ratio of 2:1:1. It was provided in the deed that Kamal's share of profit will not be less than Rs. 70,000 p.a. The losses for the year ended 31st' March 2022 wereRs.2,00,000 before allowing interest Rs 9,000 on Anil's loan which is due for the current year Prepare Profit and Loss Appropriation A/c for the year ending 31st March, 2022

Long Answer Type   [5 Marks]

Q.25. Ravi, Ashok And Manoj are partners in a firm sharing profits in ratio of 3:1:1. Their Fixed Capital balance are Rs.4,00,000 ,Rs.1,60,000 and Rs.1,20,000 respectvely.Net Profit for the year 31.03.2022 distributed amongst the partners was Rs 1,00,000 without taking into account the following adjustment:

(i) Interest on capital @2.5% p.a.

(ii) Salary to Ravi Rs.18,000 p.a. and commission to Manoj Rs.12,000

(iii)Ravi was allowed a commission of 6% of the divisible profit after charging such commission Pass an adjustment entry in the books of firm. Show your workings clearly.

Q.26. Shailesh and Shobhik are partners in a firm sharing profits in the ratio of 3:1.contributing Rs.1,10,000 each as their capital on 01st April, 2021. The partnership deed provides the following :

(i) Partners are allowed interest on capital @5%

p.a. and are charged interest on drawings @6%p.a.

(ii) Shailesh is entitled to remuneration of 10% of net profit

(iii)Shobhik is also entitled to a commission of 10 % of the net profit after clause(ll) of deed

(iv) Shailesh is entitled to rent of Rs 1,000 per month for the use of his premises by the firm.

(v) During the year, Shailesh withdrew Rs.350 at the beginning of every month and Shobhik withdrew Rs.550 at the end of every month

The profit of the firm during the year 2021-22 before making above adjustment was 1,11,000.

Prepare Profit And Loss Appropriation Account.

Q.27. Dharma, Sharma and Verma started a partnership business. Dharma contributed Rs. 60,000 for the whole year.Sharma contributed Rs.50,000 and after 6 months further introduced Rs.20,000 as capital. Verma Invested Rs.80,000 but withdrew Rs. 20,000 at the end of 8th month. Profit of the firm for the year Rs.29,000. You are required to apportion the profit of the firm in their capital ratio.

CHAPTER 2

Change In Profit Sharing Ratio

 Introduction, Sacrificing Ratio, Gaining Ratio, Treatment Of Goodwill At The Time Of Change In P.S.R.

Summary

Reconstitution of firm: Partnership agreement defines the relationship among the partners and whenever there is change in relationship, it results in reconstitution of the firm. Such reconstitution of the firm always leads to change in profit-sharing ratio among the partners. A firm is reconstituted, whenever there is a :

i. Change in the profit-sharing ratio among the existing partners.

Admission of a new partner.

Retirement of an existing partner.

Death of a partner.

Amalgamation of two or more partnership firms

Change in profit sharing ratio among the existing partners

Meaning: When all the partners of a firm agree to change their profit sharing ratio, the ratio may be changed. In this case one profit is purchasing a share of partner from another one. In other words, share of one partner may increase and share of another partner may decrease.

Meaning and the Computation of Sacrificing and Gaining Ratio:

The prime purpose of computing the sacrificing and gaining ratio is to determine the amount of compensation (goodwill) that the gaining partner shall pay to the sacrificing partner. Following points help us in understanding their meaning:

i. **Sacrificing Ratio:**
   - **Meaning:** It is that ratio in which one or more partners forego their share of profits in favour of one or more partners of the firm. In simple terms, it the ratio of sacrifice made by one or more partners.
   - Computation: Sacrificed Share = Old Share – New Share

ii. **Gaining Ratio:**
   - **Meaning:** It is that ratio in which one or more partners gain share of profit as a result of sacrifice made by other partners of the firm. In simple terms, it the ratio of gained share in profits of two or more partners in terms of the ratio.
   - Computation: Gaining Share = New Share – Old Share

Example : A and B are partners in a firm sharing profits in the ratio of 2:1 . It was decided by them to share profits equally w.e.f. 1 st April 2021. Calculate the sacrificing and gaining ratio.

Solution:

New profit sharing ratio = 1:1

Calculation :

Sacrificed/ gain of each partner.

Sacrificed share = old share – new share

A = 2/3 – 1/2 = 4 – 3 / 6 = 1/6 (i.e , sacrifice)

B = 1/3 – 1/2 = 2 – 3 / 6 = – 1/ 6 (i.e , gain)

Adjustment for Change in Profit Sharing Ratio: Issues that need to be considered at the time of change in Profit Sharing Ratio:

    i. Determining Sacrificing and Gaining ratio,

    ii. Treatment for Goodwill,

    iii. Accounting treatment for Reserves and Accumulated Profit or losses,

    iv. Revaluation of Assets and Reassessment of Liabilities.

    v. Adjusting the capital accounts of the partners for the same.

Accounting treatment of goodwill:

Example : In case of change in profit sharing ratio, the gaining partner must compensate the sacrificing partner by paying the proportionate amount of goodwill.

Illustration 1 A and K were partners in a firm sharing profits in the ratio of 3:2. With effect from January 1,2012 they agreed to share profits equally. For this purpose the goodwill of the firm was valued at ₹60,000. Pass the necessary journal entry.

Solution:

Old ratio of A and K = 3:2 New ratio of A and K = 1:1

Sacrifice or Gain: A = 3/5 – 1/2 = 65/10 = 1/10 Sacrifice

K = 2/5 – 1/2 = 45/10 = 1/10 Gain

JOURNAL

DATE	PARTICULARS	L.F	DEBIT	CREDIT
1ˢᵗ Jan	K's capital A/c Dr.		6,000	
	To A's Capital A/c			6,000
	(Adjustment for goodwill on change in profit sharing ratio)			

Multiple Choice Questions   [1 Mark]

Q.1. Any change in the relationship of existing partners which results in an end of the existing agreement and enforces making of new· agreement is called:

(a) Revaluation of partnership

(b) Reconstitution of partnership

(c) Realisation of partnership

(d) None of the above

Ans. (b)

Q.2. The ratio in which a partner surrenders his share in favour of a partner is known as:

(a) New profit-sharing ratio   (b) Sacrificing Ratio

(c) Gaining Ratio   (d) Capital Ratio

Ans. (b)

Q.3. The ratio in which a partner receives a rise in his share of profits is known as:

(a) New Ratio   (b) Sacrificing Ratio   (c) Capital Ratio   (d) Gaining Ratio

Ans. (d)

Q.4. Sacrificing ratio is the difference between:

(a) New ratio and old ratio   (b) Old ratio and new ratio

(c) New ratio and gaining ratio   (d) Old ratio and gaining ratio

Ans. (b)

Q.5. A and B are partners in a firm sharing profits in the ratio of 3 : 2. They decided to share future profits equally. Calculate A's gain or sacrifice

(a) 2/10 (sacrifice)   (b) 5/10 (gain)   (c) 1/10 (Gain)   (d) 1/10 (sacrifice)

Ans. (d)

Q.6. In case of change in profit-sharing ratio, the gaining partner must compensate the sacrificing partners by paying the proportional amount of

(a) Capital   (b) Cash   (c) Goodwill   (d) None of the above

Ans. (c)

Q.7. The nature of profit and loss adjustment account is

(a) real   (b) personal   (c) Both (a) and (b)   (d) nominal

Ans. (d)

Q.8. At the time of change in profit sharing ratio, accumulated ...... are ...... in partners' capital account.

(a) profits: debited   (b) losses: credited   (c) Both (a) and (b)   (d) None of these

Ans. (d)

Q.9. The steps of treatment of goodwill at the time of change in profit sharing ratio are

(i) Calculate compensation payable by gaining partner(s) to sacrificing partner(s).

(ii) Pass the adjustment entry.

(iii) Calculate the share gained and share sacrificed.

The correct order is

(a) (i) (iii) (ii)   (b) (i) (ii) (iii)   (c) (iii) (i) (ii)   (d) (iii) (ii) (i)

Ans. (c)

Very Short Answer Type   [1 Mark]

Q.1. …….. should compensate …………..in the case of reconstitution of the firm.

Ans. Gaining Partner, Sacrificing Partner

Q.2. A partnership is reconstituted due to change in profit sharing ratio.

Ans. True

Q.3. A,B and C are sharing profits in the ratio of 3:2:1. They decided to share equally in future .B's has neither sacrificed nor gained.

Ans. False

Q.4. Assertion (A) A changes in profit sharing ratio amounts to dissolution of partnership firm.

Reason (R) Exiting agreement comes to an end and a new agreement comes into existence.

(a) Both Assertion and reason are true and reason is correct explanation of assertion.

(b) Assertion and reason both are true but reason is not the correct explanation of assertion.

(c) Assertion is false, reason is true.

(d) Assertion is true, reason is false.

Ans. (c)

Q.5. Assertion (A) It is important to compute sacrificing and gaining ratio at the time of change in profit sharing ratio.

Reason (R) Sacrificing partner compensates the gaining partner by paying him proportion amount of goodwill.

(a) Both Assertion and reason are true and reason is correct explanation of assertion.

(b) Assertion and reason both are true but reason is not the correct explanation of assertion.

(c) Assertion is false, reason is true.

(d) Assertion is true, reason is false.

Ans. (d)

Q.6. Sahil and Vinay are sharing profits and losses equally. With effect from 1st April 2019, they agree to share profits in the ratio of 3:2. What is Vinay's gain or sacrifice.   **(CBSE 2010)**

Ans. $\dfrac{1}{10}$

Q.7. Ekta and Rekha are partners in a firm, sharing profits in the ratio of 2:1. They now decide to share profits equally in future. What is Rekha's sacrifice or gain?

Ans. $\dfrac{1}{6}$

Q.8. Gaurav and Saurabh are sharing profits and losses equally. They agree to share profits in the ratio of 3:2 ____________ is a gaining partner.

Ans. Gaining ratio = New ratio - Old ratio Gaurav

Q.9. Give the meaning of 'reconstitution of a partnership firm'.　　　　　　　　**[CBSE : Delhi2014]**

Ans. Change in the existing agreement of partnership is considered as reconstitution of a partnership firm. Due to this, existing agreement comes to an end and the new agreement comes into existence and the firm continues.

Q.10. State any two occasions on which a firm can be reconstituted.　　　　**[Delhi 2012,2008; All India 2011]**

Ans. A firm can be reconstituted on the following occasions (Any two)

    (i)　When there is a change in the profit sharing ratio of existing partners.

    (ii)　When a new partner is admitted.

    (iii)When an existing partner retires.

    (iv)When an existing partner dies.

Short Answer Type - I　　　　　　　　　　　　　　　　　　　　　　　**[2 Marks]**

Q.1. Define Sacrifice Ratio.

Ans. The ratio in which the old partners have agreed to sacrifice their shares in profit in favour of a new partner is called the sacrificing ratio. This ratio is calculated by taking out the difference between the old profit sharing ratio and the new profit sharing ratio. Sacrificing Ratio = Old Ratio - New Ratio

Q.2. Define Gaining Ratio.　　　　　　　　　　　　　　　　　　　　　**[CBSE 2011]**

Ans. The ratio in which the continuing partners acquire the share of the retiring/deceased partner is called the gaining ratio. The gaining ratio is calculated by deducting the old ratio from the new ratio. Gaining ratio = New ratio - Old ratio

Q.3. Define New Profit Sharing Ratio.

Ans. The new profit sharing ratio of each remaining partner will be the sum total of his old share of profits in the firm and the portion of the retiring partner's share of the profit acquired. New Share of Partner = Old share + Acquired share.

Q.4. Ajit, Gaurav and Vikrant are partners sharing profits in the ratio of $\dfrac{1}{2}, \dfrac{1}{3}$ and $\dfrac{1}{6}$. From April 1, 2014 they decide to change their profit sharing ratio as $\dfrac{1}{3}, \dfrac{1}{3}$ and $\dfrac{1}{3}$. Calculate sacrificing ratio of Ajit and Gaurav.

Ans. Sac Ratio=Old ratio -New ratio

$\dfrac{1}{6}$ Nil

Q.5. X and Y are partners in a firm sharing profits in the ratio of 3:2. With effect from 1st April 2019, they agreed to share profits equally. For this purpose, goodwill of the firm is valued at Rs.75,000. You are required to give journal entry.

Ans. Sac Ratio=Old ratio -New ratio

Y's capital A/C   Dr.   7,500

To X's Capital A/C   7,500

Q.6. A and B are sharing profits and losses equally. With effect from 1st April, 2013, they agree to share profits in the ratio of 4 : 3. Calculate individual partner's gain or sacrifice due to the change in ratio.   **[CBSE 2014]**

Ans. Old Ratio (A and B) = 1 : 1

New Ratio (A and B) = 4 : 3

Sacrificing (or Gaining) Ratio = Old Ratio ? New Ratio

$$\text{A's Share} = \frac{1}{2} - \frac{4}{7} = \frac{7-8}{14} = \frac{-1}{14}\,(\text{Gain})$$

$$\text{B's Share} = \frac{1}{2} - \frac{3}{7} = \frac{7-6}{14} = \frac{1}{14}\,(\text{Sacrifice})$$

$\therefore$ A's Gain = 1/14

B's Sacrifice = 1/14

Q.7. X, Y and Z are sharing profits and losses in the ratio of 5 : 3 : 2. With effect from 1st April, 2018, they decide to share profits and losses equally. Calculate each partner's gain or sacrifice due to the change in ratio.

[CBSE 2017]

Ans. Old Ratio (X, Y and Z) = 5 : 3 : 2

New Ratio (X, Y and Z) = 1 : 1 : 1

Sacrificing (or Gaining) Ratio = Old Ratio – New Ratio

$$\text{X's Share} = \frac{5}{10} - \frac{1}{3} = \frac{15-10}{30} = \frac{5}{30}\,(\text{Sacrifice})$$

$$\text{Y's Share} = \frac{3}{10} - \frac{1}{3} = \frac{9-10}{30} = \frac{-1}{30}\,(\text{Gain})$$

$$\text{Z's Share} = \frac{2}{10} - \frac{1}{3} = \frac{6-10}{30} = \frac{-4}{30}\,(\text{Gain})$$

$\therefore$ Y's Gain = 1/30

Z's Gain = 4/30

X's Sacrifice = 5/30

Short Answer Type - II   [3 Marks]

Q.1. Write the conditions of Reconstitutions of Partnership.

Ans. Partnership is an agreement between two or more persons (called partners) for sharing the profits of a business carried on by all or any of them acting for all.

(i) **Admission of a New Partner:** A new partner may be admitted when the firm needs additional capital or managerial help. According to the provisions of Partnership Act 1932 unless it is otherwise provided in the partnership deed a new partner can be admitted only when the existing partners unanimously agree for it.

(ii) Change in the profit sharing ratio among the existing partners: Sometimes the partners of a firm may decide to change their existing profit sharing ratio. This may happen an account of a change in the existing partners' role in the firm.

(iii) Retirement of an existing partner: It means withdrawal by a partner from the business of the firm which may be due to his bad health, old age or change in business interests.

(iv) Death of a partner: Partnership may also stand reconstituted on death of a partner, if the remaining partners decide to continue the business of the firm as usual.

Q.2. Write the important points which require attention at the time of change in profit sharing ratio.[CBSE 2012]

Ans. Important points which require attention at the time of change in profit sharing ratio:

(i) New profit sharing ratio;

(ii) Sacrificing ratio;

(iii) Valuation and adjustment of goodwill;

(iv) Revaluation of assets and Reassessment of liabilities;

(v) Distribution of accumulated profits (reserves);

(vi) Adjustment of partners' capitals

Q.3. A, B and C shared profits and losses in the ratio of 3 : 2 : 1 respectively. With effect from 1st April, 2018, they agreed to share profits equally. The goodwill of the firm was valued at Rs. 18,000. Pass necessary Journal entries when: (a) Goodwill Account is not opened; and (b) Goodwill Account is opened.   [CBSE 2018]

Ans. Cas (i) When Goodwill Account is not opened

JOURNAL

Date 2018	Particulars		L.F.	Debit Amount Rs	Credit Amount Rs
April 1	C's Capital A/c	Dr.		3,000	
	To A's Capital A/c				3,000
	(Adjustment of goodwill made on change in profit sharing ratio)				

Working Notes:

Old Ratio (A, B and C) = 3 : 2 : 1

New Ratio (A, B and C) = 1 : 1 : 1

Sacrificing (or Gaining) Ratio = Old Ratio – New Ratio

$$\text{A's Share} = \frac{3}{6} - \frac{1}{3} = \frac{3-2}{6} = \frac{1}{6} \text{ (Sacrifice)}$$

$$\text{B's Share} = \frac{2}{6} - \frac{1}{3} = \frac{2-2}{6} = \text{Nil}$$

$$\text{C's Share} = \frac{1}{6} - \frac{1}{3} = \frac{1-2}{6} = \frac{-1}{6} \text{ (Gain)}$$

Goodwill of the firm = Rs 18,000

A will receive for goodwill $= 18,000 \times \dfrac{1}{6} = $ Rs. 3,00

C will give for goodwill $= 18,000 \times \dfrac{1}{6} = $ Rs.3,000

Cas (ii) When Goodwill Account is opened

JOURNAL

Date 2018	Particulars	L.F.	Debit Amount Rs	Credit Amount Rs
April 1	Goodwill A/c Dr. To A's Capital A/c To B's Capital A/c To C's Capital A/c (Being goodwill account opened)		18,000	9,000 6,000 3,000
April 1	A's Capital A/c Dr. B's Capital A/c Dr. C's Capital A/c Dr. To Goodwill A/c (Being goodwill written off in 3:2:1)		9,000 6,000 3,000	18,000

Long Answer Type   [5 Marks]

Q.1. Saqib and Aaqib were partners in a firm sharing profit in the ratio 3 : 2. With effect from 1st April, 2016 they agreed to share profits equally. For this purpose, the goodwill of the firm was valued at Rs.30,000. Pass the necessary journal entry for the treatment of goodwill.

Ans.
JOURNAL

Date	Particulars	L.F.	Dr. (Rs.)	Cr. (Rs.)
2016 April 1	Aaqib's Capital A/c Dr. To Saqib's Capital A/c (For goodwill adjustment on change in profit sharing ratio)		3,000	3000

Working Note.

Calculation of Profit Share Sacrificed/Gained

	Saqib	Aaqib
Old Profit Ratio	$\dfrac{3}{5}$	$\dfrac{2}{5}$
New Profit Ratio	$\dfrac{1}{2}$	$\dfrac{1}{2}$
Difference	(Sacrifice) $\dfrac{1}{10}$	$-\dfrac{1}{10}$ (Gain)

Gaining Partner's Share of Goodwill $= $ Rs.30,000 $\times \dfrac{1}{10} = $ Rs.3,000

Q.2. Mohan, Sohan and Rohan are partners in a firm sharing profits in the ratio of 2:2:1. They decided that N will get 1/4th share in future profit. Goodwill of the firm was valued Rs.80,000. Goodwill already appeared in the books Rs.20,000. **[CBSE 2013]**

Pass necessary journal entries.

Ans. (i) New Profit Sharing Ratio

Let profit of firm $= 1$

Rohan's Share $= \dfrac{1}{4}$

Balance $= 1 - \dfrac{1}{4} = \dfrac{3}{4}$

Old ratio of Mohan and Sohan is

$= 2 : 2 \text{ or } 1 : 1$

Mohan's Share $= \dfrac{1}{2} \text{ of } \dfrac{3}{4} = \dfrac{3}{8}$

Sohan's Share $= \dfrac{1}{2} \text{ of } \dfrac{3}{4} = \dfrac{3}{8}$

New ratio of Mohan : Sohan : Rohan is

$= \dfrac{3}{8} : \dfrac{3}{8} : \dfrac{1}{4} \text{ or } 3 : 3 : 2$

(ii) Calculation of Sacrifice/Gain of Partners

	Mohan	Sohan	Rohan
Old Share	$\dfrac{2}{5}$	$\dfrac{2}{5}$	$\dfrac{1}{5}$
New Share	$\dfrac{3}{8}$	$\dfrac{3}{8}$	$\dfrac{2}{8}$
Difference	$\dfrac{1}{40}$	$\dfrac{1}{40}$	$-\dfrac{2}{40}$
	(Sacrifice)	(Sacrifice)	(Gain)

(iii) Gaining Partner's Share in Goodwill

Rohan's share = Rs.80,000 $\times \dfrac{2}{40}$ = Rs.4,000

(iv) Sacrificing Partner's Share in Goodwill

Mohan's Sacrifice = Rs.80,000 $\times \dfrac{1}{40}$ = Rs.2,000

Sohan's Sacrifice = Rs.80,000 x $\dfrac{1}{40}$

= Rs.2,000

JOURNAL

Date	Particulars	L.F.	Dr. (Rs.)	Cr. (Rs.)
	Mohan's Capital A/c		8,000	
	Sohan's Capital A/c		8,000	
	Rohan's Capital A/c		4,000	
	To Goodwill A/c			20,000
	(For cancellation of goodwill among partners in old ratio)			
			Dr.	
			Dr.	
			Dr.	
	Rohan's Capital A/c . Dr		4,000	
	To Mohan's Capital A/c			2,000
	To Sohan's Capital A/c			2,000
	(For goodwill adjustment due to change in profit sharing ratio)			

Q.3. Sahil and Aahil are partners in the firm sharing profits and losses in the ratio 3 : 2. From 1st April, 2016, they decided to share profits in the ratio of 2 : 3. For this purpose, goodwill of the firm was valued at Rs.50,000. General Reserve appeared in the books at Rs.30,000.

They decided that neither goodwill be shown nor General Reserve be distributed. Pass journal entry to record the change.

Ans. (i)   Calculation of Sacrifice/Gain

	Sahil	Aahil
Old Share	$\dfrac{3}{5}$	$\dfrac{2}{5}$
New Share	$\dfrac{2}{5}$	$\dfrac{3}{5}$
Difference	$\dfrac{1}{5}$	$-\dfrac{1}{5}$
	(Sacrifice)	(Gain)

(ii)

	(Rs.)
Value of Goodwill	50,000
General Reserve	30,000
	80,000

Aahil will compensate Sahil to the extent of

$$= \frac{1}{5} \text{ of Rs.80,000} = \text{Rs.16,000}$$

JOURNAL

Date	Particulars		L.F.	Dr. (Rs.)	Cr. (Rs.)
2016 April 1	Aahil's Capital A/c To Sahil's Capital A/c (For adjustment made for goodwill and General Reserve on change in profit sharing ratio)	Dr.		16,000	 16,000

Q.4. X, Y and Z were partners in a firm sharing profits in the ratio 3 : 3 : 2. On 31st March, 2017, their balance sheet stood as follows:

Liabilities	Rs.	Assets	Rs.
Creditors	20,000	Sundry Assets	1,15,000
Profit & Loss A/c	25,000	Advertisement Suspense A/c	10,000
Capital A/c:			
X 30,000			
Y 30,000			
Z 20,000	80,000		
	1,25,000		**1,25,000**

Partners decided to change their profit sharing ratio to 2 : 3 : 3. For this purpose, goodwill was valued at Rs.45,000.

They decided neither to record goodwill in the books nor want to change any item of the balance sheet. Pass a single journal entry to give the effect of the change.

Ans. (i)   Calculation of Sacrifice/Gain

	X	Y	Z
Old Share	$\dfrac{3}{8}$	$\dfrac{3}{8}$	$\dfrac{2}{8}$
New Share	$\dfrac{2}{8}$	$\dfrac{3}{8}$	$\dfrac{3}{8}$
Difference	$\dfrac{1}{8}$	$\dfrac{0}{8}$	$-\dfrac{0}{8}$
	(Sacrifice)		(Gain)

(ii) Net Amount of Adjustment to be made

	(Rs.)
Profit & Loss A/c	25,000
Value of Goodwill	45,000
	70,000
Less: Advertisement Suspense A/c	10,000
	60,000

(iii) Z must compensate X to the extent of $\dfrac{1}{8}$ of Rs.60,000 = Rs.7,500

JOURNAL

Date	Particulars		L.F.	Dr. (Rs.)	Cr. (Rs.)
2017 March 31	Z's Capital A/c To X's Capital A/c (For adjustment of goodwill, P & L A/c and advertisement suspense A/c due to change in profit sharing ratio)	Dr.		7,500	7,500

TOPIC 2   Adjustmentof Accumulated Profit and Losses, Reserves, Revluation of Assets and Reassesment of Liabilities

Summary

Accounting treatment of Reserves and Accumulated Profits:

At the time of change in profit sharing ratio reserves, accumulated profits and losses exist in the books of the firm , they are transferred to the Partner's capital account (if capitals are fluctuating) or the current accounts (if capital are fixed) in their old profit sharing ratio.

The journal entries passed are :

JOURNAL ENTRIES

Date	Particulars		L.F	Debit	Credit
	General Reserve	Dr.			
	Profit and Loss	Dr.			
	Workmen's Compensation Reserve	Dr.			
	To Old Partners Capital A/c's				
	(Being Reserves and Accumulated profits				
	credited to old partners in their old Ratio)				
	Old partner's Capital A/c's	Dr.			
	To Preliminary Expense				
	To Advertisement Suspense				
	To Profit and Loss A/c				
	To Goodwill				
	(Being Accumulated losses and fictitious assets debited to old partners in their old ratio)				

Workmen compensation reserve :

It is a reserve set aside out of firm' s profit to meet liability on account of compensation to employees , if it arises. It means a claim may or may not arise .

Accounting treatment :

1. When claim against workmen's compensation reserve does not exist

    The amount of workmen compensation reserve is transferred to the partner's capital account in their old profit sharing ratio.

    Workmen Compensation Reserve A/c   ------   Dr.

    To partner's capital (or current) A/c

2. When claim against workmen's compensation reserve exists

    In such situation, treatment shall depend on the amount of liabilities:

    i.   Claim is equal to reserves: Amount of reserves is transferred to Provision for Workmen Compensation Claim Account.

         Entry to be passed:

         Workmen Compensation Reserves A/c ...Dr.

         To Provision for Workmen Compensation Claim A/c

         (Being the provision made for estimated compensation claim)

    ii. Claim amount is lower than the reserve: Excess of Workmen Compensation Reserve over the Workmen Compensation Claim is credited to all partners in their old profit sharing ratio. Entry is:

         Workmen Compensation Reserve A/c ...Dr.

         To Provision for Workmen Compensation Claim A/c

         To Partners' Capital or Current A/c

         (Being the surplus of Workmen Compensation Reserve transferred to Partners' Capital or Current Account in their old profit sharing ratio)

    iii. Claim amount is higher than the reserve: Amount in excess of reserve is debited to Revaluation Account as the loss is to be borne by the partners in old profit sharing ratio.

Entry is:

*   Workmen Compensation Reserve A/c ...Dr.

            Revaluation A/c ...Dr.

    To Provision for Workmen Compensation Claim A/c

    (Being amount of estimated claim debited to Workmen Compensation Reserve and Revaluation Account)

*   Partners' Capital or Current A/cs ...Dr. (In Old Ratio)

    To Revaluation A/c

    (Being the loss on revaluation transferred to Capital or Current Account of partners in their old profit sharing ratio)

Investments Fluctuation Reserve:

i.   It is a reserve which is set aside out of the profits to meet fall in the market value of investments.

ii. In order to decide the treatment of this reserve, it is necessary to first determine whether the book value and the market value are same or different and if different, which value is higher and which is lower.

Accounting Treatment of Investment Fluctuation Reserve:

i.   When Book Value and Market Value are same: Entry has to be passed to transfer the amount of Investment Fluctuation Reserve to Partners' Capital or Current Accounts in their old profit sharing ratio as below:

Investment Fluctuation Reserve A/c ...Dr.

To Partners' Capital (or Current) A/cs [In Old Ratio]

ii. When Market Value if less than the Book Value: In this case, treatment of Investments Fluctuation Reserve shall depend on the quantum of decrease, which has 3 possibilities as follows:

   a. Fall in Value is Less than Investments Fluctuation Reserve: The amount of Investment Fluctuation Reserve to the extent of fall in value, is transferred to Investment Account and balance is distributed among the partners in their old profit sharing ratio for which following entry is to be passed:

   Investment Fluctuation Reserve A/c ...Dr.

   To Investment A/c [Book Value - Market Value]

   To Partners' Capital (or Current) A/cs [In Old Ratio]

   b. Fall in Value is Equal to Investments Fluctuation Reserve: In this case, amount of Investment Fluctuation Reserve is transferred to Investment Account and no amount is distributed among the partners. Entry for the same is as follows:

   Investment Fluctuation Reserve A/c ...Dr.

   To Investment A/c

   c. Fall in Value is More than Investments Fluctuation Reserve: In this case, amount of Investments Fluctuation Reserve along with balance amount of fall in value is transferred to Investment Account and the amount in excess of reserve is debited to the Revaluation Account for which following entries are passed:

- Investment Fluctuation Reserve A/c ...Dr.

   Revaluation A/c ...Dr.

   To Investment A/c

- Partners' Capital (or Current) A/cs ...Dr. [In Old Ratio]

   To Revaluation A/c

iii. When there is an Increase in Market Value of Investment: In this case, total amount of Investment Fluctuation Reserve is distributed among partners and increase in value of investment is credited to Revaluation Account for which following entry is to be passed:

- Investment Fluctuation Reserve A/c ...Dr.

   To Partners' Capital (or Current) A/cs [In Old Ratio]

- Investment A/c ...Dr.

   To Revaluation A/c [Investment Brought up to Market Value]

- Revaluation A/c …Dr.

  To Partners' Capital (or Current) A/cs [In Old Ratio]

  Adjustment of Accumulated Profits, Losses and Reserve through Partners' Capital Accounts, i.e. When Accumulated Profits, Losses and Reserves are to be retained in the Books:

  I.   If the partners of the firm decide that the existing balances of Profit and Loss Account or Reserve should continue to appear at the same amount in the Balance Sheet of the reconstituted firm, then an adjustment entry for the net effect of accumulated profits, losses and reserves is passed since they were earned in past.

  II.   Such entry is passed through the Partners' Capital Accounts using the following steps:

  Step 1: Net effect of Reserves, Accumulated Profits and Losses is to be calculated.

  Step 2: Gain/Loss of Share is to be calculated.

  Step 3: Share of Gaining and Sacrificing Partners in the Net Accumulated Profits, Losses and Reserves is to be calculated as below:

- For Gaining Partner = Net Effect   Share Gained
- For Sacrificing Partner = Net Effect   Share Sacrificed

  Step 4: Adjustment entries are to be passed as follows:

- In case if Positive Effect (Net Profit):

  Gaining Partners' Capital/Current A/cs …Dr.

  To Sacrificing Partners' Capital/Current A/cs

- In case of Negative Effect (Net Loss):

  Sacrificing Partners' Capital/Current A/cs …Dr.

  To Gaining Partners' Capital/Current A/cs

Treatment of reserves, accumulated profits and losses when nothing is mentioned in the question:

Journal Entries to be passed for the mentioned transactions are as follows:

  a.   For distributing reserves and accumulated profits:

  General Reserves A/c …Dr.

  Profit and Loss A/c …Dr.

  Workmen Compensation Reserves A/c* …Dr.

  Investment Fluctuation Reserve A/c** …Dr.

  To All Partners' Capital A/c (In old profit sharing ratio)

  *Amount of workmen compensation reserve distributed shall be excess of reserves over liability. **Amount of investment fluctuation reserve distributed shall be excess of reserve over difference between Book Value and Market Value.

  b.   For writing off accumulated losses:

  All Partners' Capital A/c …Dr.

  (In old profit sharing ratio) To Profit and Loss A/c

Accounting Treatment for revaluation of assets and reassessment of liabilities:

In the event of change in profit sharing ratio of the partners, assets are revalued and liabilities are to be reassessed. Such revaluation will result in gain or loss which is to be distributed to the partners in their old profit sharing ratio. The partners are not necessarily required to record the revised values in the books of the firm. The partners may decide to:

  i.   Record revised values of assets and liabilities; or
  ii.   Not to record the revised values of assets and liabilities.

Accounting treatment under each of the option is different and hence, partners need to be careful of the treatment for the option chosen.

I. Accounting Treatment when revised values of assets and liabilities are to be recorded:

In such situation, revaluation of assets and reassessment of liabilities are to be recorded in an account known as 'Revaluation Account' or 'Profit and Loss Adjustment Account'.

- Understanding Revaluation Account: In the event of change in profit sharing ratio of the partners, assets are revalued and liabilities are to be reassessed. Such revaluation will result in gain or loss which is to be distributed to the partners in their old profit sharing ratio.

  For the purpose recording such increase or decrease on revaluation, revaluation account is maintained.

- Features of Revaluation Account are as follows:

  i.   Increase in assets value and decrease in liabilities are to be credited to the Revaluation Account.

  ii.   Decrease in assets and increase in liabilities are to be debited to the Revaluation Account.

  iii. Unrecorded assets are credited and unrecorded liabilities are to be debited to the revaluation account.

  iv.   If the credit side is bigger than the debit side of the account, it is referred as gain or profit on revaluation.

  v.   If the debit side is bigger than the credit side of the account, it is referred as loss on revaluation.

  vi.   Finally, such profit or loss is credited or debited to the Partners' Capital or Current Accounts in their old profit-sharing ratio.

Accounting entries to record the Revaluation of Assets and Reassessment of Liabilities:

  i.   Increase in the value of an asset:

        Asset A/c (Individually) ...Dr.

          To Revaluation A/c

  ii.   Decrease in the value of an asset:

        Revaluation A/c ...Dr.

          To Asset A/c (Individually)

  iii. Increase in the amount of a liability:

        Revaluation A/c ...Dr.

          To Liability A/c (Individually)

  iv.   Decrease in the amount of a liability:

        Liability A/c (Individually) ...Dr.

          To Revaluation A/c v.

  v.   Recording an unrecorded asset:

        Unrecorded Asset A/c ...Dr.

          To Revaluation A/c

  vi.   Recording an unrecorded liability:

        Revaluation A/c ...Dr.

          To Unrecorded Liability A/c

  vii. Transfer of Balance in Revaluation Account:

        a.   In case of gain in Revaluation Account:

             Revaluation A/c ...Dr. (Individually in old profit sharing ratio)

               To Partners' Capital (or Current) A/cs

    b.   In case of loss in Revaluation Account:

        Partners' Capital (or Current) A/cs …Dr.

        To Revaluation A/c (Individually in old profit sharing ratio)

Treatment for profit or loss arising from the revaluation of assets and reassessment of liabilities:

i.   In the event of change in the profit sharing ratio, assets are revalued and liabilities are reassessed. This is basically done to increase or decrease the value of assets and liabilities up to the date of change in profit sharing ratio.

ii.   The net gain or loss arising on account of such revaluation and reassessment is for the period before the change in profit sharing ratio. Such gain or loss is therefore, credited or debited to the Partner's Capital Accounts in their old profit sharing ratio.

II.   Accounting Treatment when revised values of assets and liabilities are not to be recorded: When revised values of assets and liabilities are not to be recorded in the books, gain or loss on revaluation is adjusted through Partners' Capital Accounts by passing adjustment entry to the Capital or Current Accounts. For the treatment mentioned above, following steps should be followed:

i.   Calculate net effect of Revaluation (i.e. net effect of increase or decrease in assets and liabilities).

ii.   Calculate the share of sacrifice or gain by the partners using formula as follows: Sacrifice/(Gain) = Old Share – New Share

iii.   Calculate proportionate amount of net effect of revaluation.

For Gaining Partner = Share Gained * Net Effect of Revaluation

For Sacrificing Partner = Share Sacrificed * Net Effect of Revaluation

Journal entries :

- In case of gain or profit on revaluation:

    Gaining Partners' Capital A/cs …Dr.

    To Sacrificing Partners' Capital A/cs

- In case of loss on revaluation:

    Sacrificing Partners' Capital A/cs …Dr.

    To Gaining Partners' Capital A/cs

Adjustment of Capital:

- Need to Adjust Capital:

i.   In the event of change in profit sharing ratio, adjustments are made for change in values of assets and liabilities, goodwill and distribution of reserves, accumulated profits and losses, change in partners' capitals.

ii.   Also, if the partners decide total capital of the firm and also that the capital shall be in profit sharing ratio of the partners, then also capital of the partners has to be adjusted.

iii.   In case the partners' capital(s) fall(s) short or has shortage of the required capital, then such partner(s) will have to bring more capital.

iv.   In case the partners' capital(s) is (are) surplus (excess) of the required capital, then such partner(s) may withdraw surplus or excess capital.

v.   Any shortage or surplus of Capital can be adjusted through Current Accounts.

vi.   Accounting Treatment:

- For Adjusting Shortage of Capital:

  Bank A/c or Concerned Partners' Current A/c ...Dr.

   To Concerned Partners' Capital A/c

- For Adjusting Surplus of Capital:

  Concerned Partners' Capital A/c ...Dr.

   To Bank A/c or Concerned Partners' Current A/c

  Adjustment of Partners' Capital, if total Capital of the new firm is already given:

  i.   When total Capital of the new firm (reconstituted firm) is already given, then it is divided among the partners in their new profit-sharing ratio. This respective share of capital will be their new capital.

  ii. Once this is done, the surplus (excess) or deficit (shortage) capital is calculated by comparing the new capital and present adjusted capital.

Multiple Choice Questions [1 Mark]

Q.1. Reserves and accumulated profits are transferred to partners' capital accounts at the time of reconstitution in:

 (a) Old profit-sharing ratio   (b) Sacrificing Ratio

 (c) Gaining ratio   (d) New profit-sharing ratio

Ans. (a)

Q.2. Increase and decrease in the value of assets and liabilities are recorded through:

 (a) Partners' Capital Account   (b) Revaluation Account

 (c) Profit and Loss Appropriation   (d) Balance Sheet

Ans. (b)

Q.3. In which of the following case, revaluation account is debited?

 (a) Increase in value of asset   (b) Decrease in value of asset

 (c) Decrease in value of liability   (d) No change in value of assets

Ans. (b)

Q.4. In which of the following cases, revaluation account is credited?

 (a) Decrease in value of liability   (b) Increase in value of liability

 (c) Decrease in value of asset   (d) No change in value of liability

Ans. (a)

Q.5. Partner's capital account is credited when there is

 (a) Profit on revaluation   (b) Transfer of general reserve

 (c) Transfer of accumulated profits   (d) All of the above

Ans. (d)

Q.6. In case of change in profit-sharing ratio, the accumulated profits are distributed to the partners in

 (a) New ratio   (b) Old ratio   (c) Sacrificing ratio   (d) Equal ratio

Ans. (b)

Q.7. Which Account is to be prepared at the time of change in Profit Sharing Ratio assess the correct value of assets and liabilities.

    (a) Revaluation A/c (b) Realisation A/c   (c) Both a & b   (d) None of the above

Ans. (a)

Q.8. U V and W are partners sharing profits in the ration of 2:3:5.They decide to share the future profits equally. They also decide to record the effect of the following revaluations and reassessments without affecting the book values of assets and liabilities by passing a single adjustment entry:

	Book Value (Rs.)	Revised Value (Rs.)
Land and Building	3,00,000	3,50,000
Furniture	1,50,000	1,00,000
Sundry Creditors	60,000	20,000
Outstanding Salaries	10,000	15,000

The single adjustment entry will

    (a) Dr. W and Cr. U by Rs.10,500   (b) Dr. U and Cr. W by Rs.10,500

    (c) Dr. V and Cr. U by Rs.10,500   (d) None of the above

Ans. (d)

Q.9. X, Y and Z are partners sharing profits and losses in the ratio of 5:3:2.They decide to share the future profits in the ratio of 3:2:1. Workmen compensation reserve appearing in the balance sheet on the date if no information is available for the same will be:

    (a) Distributed among the partners in old profit sharing ratio

    (b) Distributed among the partners in new profit sharing ratio

    (c) Distributed among the partners in capital ratio

    (d) Carried forward to new balance sheet without any adjustment

Ans. (a)

Q.10. A, B and C were are partners in a firm sharing profits in the ratio of 3:4:1 .They decided to share profits equally w.e.f from 1 .4.2019. On that date the profit and loss account showed the credit balance of 96,000.instead of closing the profit and loss account, it was decided to record an adjustment entry reflecting the change in profit sharing ratio .In the journal entry:

    (a) Dr. A by 4,000; Dr. B by 16,000; Cr C by 20,000

    (b) Cr. A by 4,000; Cr. B by 16,000; Dr C by 20,000

    (c) Cr. A by 16,000; Cr. B by 4,000; Dr C by 20,000

    (d) Dr. A by 16,000; Dr. B by 4,000; Cr C by 20,000

Ans. (b)

Q.11. In case of change in profit-sharing ratio, the accumulated profits are distributed to the partners in

    (a) New ratio   (b) Old ratio   (c) Sacrificing ratio   (d) Equal ratio

Ans. (b)

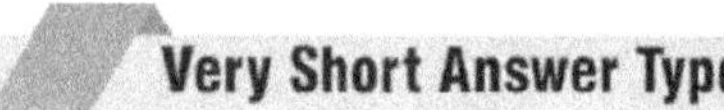 **Very Short Answer Type**   **[1 Mark]**

Q.1. Increase in the value of assets and decrease in the value of liabilities result in ……..for the existing partners and should be ……….to P/L Adjustment a/c

Ans. gain, credited

Q.2. Assertion (A) At the time of reconstitution of firm, assets are revalued and liabilities are reassessed.

Reason (R) the changed in the value of assets and liabilities belongs to the period prior to reconstitution And any gain or loss on revaluation is shared in the old ratio by the partners.

(a) Both Assertion and reason are true and reason is correct explanation of assertion.

(b) Assertion and reason both are true but reason is not the correct explanation of assertion.

(c) Assertion is false, reason is true.

(d) Assertion is true, reason is false.

Ans. (a)

Q.3. Assertion (A) when reserve and accumulated profits / losses are adjusted through capital accounts, they appear in the balance sheet of new firm at the old figures.

Reason (R) If partner decided to record net effects of reserves, etc, a single adjusting entry involving the capital accounts of sacrificing and gaining partners is passed.

(a) Both Assertion and reason are true and reason is correct explanation of assertion.

(b) Assertion and reason both are true but reason is not the correct explanation of assertion.

(c) Assertion is false, reason is true.

(d) Assertion is true, reason is false.

Ans. (a)

Q.4. State the ratio in which the partners share the accumulated profits when there is a change in the profit sharing ratio amongst existing partners.   **[All India 2013]**

Ans. Accumulated profits are distributed in old profit sharing ratio, at the time of change in profit sharing ratio amongst the existing partners.

Q.5. State the ratio in which the partners share profits or losses on revaluation of assets and liabilities, when there is a change in profit sharing ratio amongst existing partners.   **[CBSE - Delhi 2013]**

Ans. Revaluation profits or losses are distributed in old profit sharing ratio, at the time of change in profit sharing ratio amongst the existing partners.

Q.6. Why are 'reserves and surplus' distributed at the time of reconstitution of the firm?   **[Delhi, All India 2010]**

Ans. At the time of reconstitution of the firm, reserves and surplus should be transferred to old partners' capital/ current accounts in their old profit sharing ratio because the new partner is not entitled to any share in such undistributed profits or losses as these are earned/accrued by the old partners.

Short Answer Type - I   [2 Marks]

Q.1. Define Investment Fluctuation Reserve.

Ans. Investments are recorded in the book of a company at cost. However, in the market, it might change. It may be higher or lower than the book value. Investment fluctuation reserve is a reserve set aside out of profit to meet fall in the market value of the investment.

Short Answer Type - II   [3 Marks]

Q.2. Explain treatment of reserves, accumulated profits & losses.

Ans. Accumulate Profits include credit balance of P& LA/c, General Reserves, Reserve Fund, Workmen Compensation Reserve, Investment Fluctuation Reserve etc. Accumulated Losses include debit balance of P& LA/c, Deferred Revenue Expenditure i.e. Advertisement Suspense A/c.

(a) When question is silent or when accumulated profits or losses are to be distributed or when accumulated profits or losses are not to be shown in new balance sheet Contingency Reserve A/c Dr. Reserve Ac/ Dr. P & LA/c (Cr. Balance) Dr. Workmen Compensation Reserve A/c Dr. Investment Fluctuation Reserve A/c Dr. To all Partner's Capital A/cs (Being reserves & accumulate profits transferred to all partners in old ratio) All Partners Capital A/c Dr. To P& LA/c (Dr Balance) To Deferred Revenue exp. A/c

(b) When accumulated profits or losses are not to be distributed or when accumulated profits or losses are to be shown in new balance sheetat same book value. Calculate the net effect of Reserves, Accumulate Profits & Losses- RESERVES + ACCUMULATED PROFITS Less ACCUMULATED LOSSES = Net Effect +/-i)

    (i) In case the Net Effect is Positive

        Gaining Partner's Capital/Current Accounts Dr.

        To Sacrificing Partner's Capital/Current Accounts .

    (ii) In case the Net Effect is Negative

        Sacrificing Partner's Capital/Current/Accounts Dr.

        To Gaining Partner's Capital/Current Accounts.

Q.3. Explain treatment of workmen compensation reserve.

    CASE 1   When there is no Claim

            Workmen Compensation Reserve A/c Dr.

            To Partner's Capital/Current A/cs

    CASE 2   WCC = WCR (equal)

            Workmen Compensation Reserve A/c Dr.

            To Provision's for workmen Compensation Claim A/c

    CASE 3   WCC < WCR (less)

            Workmen Compensation Reserve A/c Dr.

            To Provision for workmen Compensation Claim A/c

            To Partner's Capital/Current A/cs

    CASE 4   WCC > WCR (more)

    (i) Workmen Compensation Reserve A/c Dr.

        Revaluation A/c Dr.

        To Provision for Workmen Compensation Claim A/c

(ii) Partner's Capital/Current A/cs Dr.

　　To Revaluation A/c

　　WCC stands for WORKMEN COMPENSATION CLAIM

　　WCR stands for WORKMEN COMPENSATION RESERVE

Q.4. Explain treatment of investment fluctuation reserve.

CASE 1　BV = MV
　　　　Investment Fluctuation Reserve A/c Dr.
　　　　To partner's Capital/Current A/cs

CASE 2　BV < MV
　　　　Investment Fluctuation Reserve A/c Dr.
　　　　　To Partner's Capital/Current A/cs
　　　　(Entire reserve distributed in partner's old ratio)
　　　　Investments A/c Dr.
　　　　　To Revaluation A/c
　　　　(For increase in value of Investments)
　　　　Revaluation A/c Dr
　　　　　To Partner's Capital/Current A/cs.

CASE 3　BV > MV

(i)　When Fall in value is less than investment Fluctuation Reserve

　　Investment Fluctuation Reserve A/c Dr.

　　　To Investment A/c (BV-MV)

　　　To Partner's Capital/Current A/cs (In old ratio)

(ii)　When Fall in value is equal to Investment Fluctuation Reserve

　　Investment Fluctuation Reserve A/c Dr.

　　　To investment A/c

(iii)　When Fall in value is more than Investment Fluctuation Reserve

　　Investment Fluctuation Reserve A/c Dr.

　　Revaluation A/c Dr.

　　　To Investment A/c

　　Partner's Capital/Current A/cs Dr.

　　　To Revaluation A/c

　　BV stands for Book value of Investments

　　Mv Stands for Market value of Investments

Q.5. Explain revaluation of assets & reassessment of liabilities.

Ans. Revaluation account is a nominal account & prepared to revalue assets & reassess liabilities. When question is silent or when revised values of assets & liabilities are to be recorded. Revaluation A/c is prepared & Profit/ Loss of revaluation is distributed among old partner's in old ratio.

When revised values of assets & Liabilities are not to be recorded.

(Assets & Liabilities will appear in Balance Sheet at old Value) Calculate the net effect of revaluation ------- -

Increase in the value of Assets, Add Decrease in the value of liabilities ,

Less Decrease in the value of Assets ,Less Increase in the value of liabilities , =Net Effect on Revaluation Gain/Loss

For Gaining Partner =Share Gained x Net Effect on Revaluation

For Sacrificing Partner = Share Sacrificed x net Effect on Revaluation

Gaining Partner's Capital/Current Accounts Dr

To Sacrificing Partner's Capital/Current Accounts

Q.6. X, Y and Z were partners sharing profits and losses in the ratio of 5 : 3 : 2. They decided to share future profits and losses in the ratio of 2 : 3 : 5 with effect from 01.04.2017. They decide to record the effect of the following, without affecting their book values:

(i) Profit and Loss A/c

(ii) Advertisement Suspense A/c

    Pass the necessary adjustment entry.

Ans. (i) Calculation of Gain/Loss

	X	Y	Z
Old Share	$\dfrac{5}{10}$	$\dfrac{3}{10}$	$\dfrac{2}{10}$
New Share	$\dfrac{2}{10}$	$\dfrac{3}{10}$	$\dfrac{5}{10}$
Difference	$\dfrac{3}{10}$	$\dfrac{0}{10}$	$-\dfrac{3}{10}$
	(Sacrifice)		(Gain)

(ii) Total amount of adjustment to be made

	Rs.
Profit & Loss A/c (Credit Balance)	24,000
Less: Advertisement Suspence & (Debit Balance)	12,000
Net Amount of Profit	12,000

X's share of sacrifice = $\dfrac{3}{10}$ of Rs.12,000 = Rs.3,600

Z's share of gain = $\dfrac{3}{10}$ of Rs.12,000 = Rs.3,600

JOURNAL

Date	Particulars		L.F.	Dr. (Rs.)	Cr. (Rs.)
2017	Z's Capital A/c	Dr.		3,600	
April 1	To X's Capital A/c				3,600
	(For adjustment made on account of change in profit sharing ratio)				

Q.7. Keshav, Meenakshi and Mohit sharing profit and losses in the ratio of 1:2:2, decide to share future profit equally with effect from April 1, 2015. On that date general reserve showed a balance of Rs. 40,000. Partners do not want to distribute the reserves. You are required to give the adjusting entry.   **[CBSE 2012]**

Ans. Keshav; Meenakshi; Mohit

Old ratio 1/5 : 2/5 : 2/5

New ratio 1/3 : 1/3 : 1/3

Sacrifice or Gain

$$\text{Keshav} = 1/5 - 1/3 = \frac{3}{15} - \frac{5}{15} = -\frac{2}{15} \text{ (gain)}$$

Meenakshi = 2/5 – 1/3

$$= \frac{6}{15} - \frac{5}{15} = \frac{1}{15} \text{ (Sacrifice)}$$

$$\text{Mohit} = 2/5 - 1/3 = \frac{6}{15} - \frac{5}{15} = \frac{1}{15} \text{ (Sacrifice)}$$

JOURNAL

Date	Particulars	L.F	Debit (Rs.)	Credit (Rs.)
2015 Apr.1	Keshav's capital A / c $\left(2,40,000 \times \dfrac{2}{15}\right)$ Dr. To Meenakshi capital A / c $\left(2,40,000 \times \dfrac{1}{15}\right)$ To Mohit's capital A / c $\left(2,40,000 \times \dfrac{1}{15}\right)$ (Adjustment for General reserve on change in profit sharing ratio)		32,000	 16,000 16,000

Long Answer Type   **[5 Marks]**

Q.1. P, Q and R sharing profits and losses in the ratio of 3 : 2 : 1, decide to share profits and losses equally with effect from 1st April, 2021. Following is an extract of their Balance Sheet as at 31st March, 2021:

Liabilities	Rs.	Assets	Rs.
Investment Fluctuation Reserve	30,000	Investment (At Cost)	5,00,000

Show the accounting treatment under the following alternative cases:

Case (i) If there is no other information.

Case (ii) If the market value of Investments is Rs.5,00,000.

Case (iii) If the market value of Investments is Rs.4,88,000.

Case (iv) If the market value of Investments is Rs.4,46,000.

Case (v) If the market value of Investments is Rs.5,06,000.

Ans.

JOURNAL

Date	Particulars		L.F.	Dr. (Rs.)	Cr. (Rs.)
2021 April 1	Case (i)				
	Investment Fluctuation Reserve A/c	Dr.		30,000	
	To P's Capital A/c				15,000
	To Q's Capital A/c				10,000
	To R's Capital A/c				5,000
	(Transfer of excess Investment Fluctuation Reserve to partner's capital accounts in their old profit sharing ratio)				
	Case (ii)				
	Same Solution as given in case (i)				
	Case (iii)				
	Investment Fluctuation Reserve A/c	Dr.		30,000	
	To Investments A/c (5,00,000 4,88,000)				12,000
	To P's Capital A/c				9,000
	To Q's Capital A/c				6,000
	To R's Capital A/c				3,000
	(Transfer of excess Investment Fluctuation Reserve to partner's capital accounts in their old profit sharing ratio)				
	Case (iv)				
	Investment Fluctuation Reserve A/c	Dr.		30,000	
	Revaluation A/c	Dr.		24,000	
	To Investments A/c				54,000
	(Fall in the value of investments adjusted through investment fluctuation reserve and shortfall charged to Revaluation Account)				
	P's Capital A/c	Dr.		12,000	
	Q's Capital A/c	Dr.		8,000	
	R's Capital A/c	Dr.		4,000	
	To Revaluation A/c				24,000
	(Transfer of loss on revaluation to partner's capital accounts in their old profit sharing ratio)				

Date	Particulars		L.F.	Dr. (Rs.)	Cr. (Rs.)
	Case (v)				
	Investment Fluctuation Reserve A/c	Dr.		30,000	
	To P's Capital A/c				15,000
	To Q's Capital A/c				10,000
	To R's Capital A/c				5,000
	(Transfer of excess investments fluctuation reserve to Partners' Capital Accounts in their old profit sharing ratio)				
	Investments A/c	Dr.		6,000	
	To Revaluation A/c				6,000
	(Value of investments brought up to market value)				
	Revaluation A/c	Dr.		6,000	
	To P's Capital A/c				3,000
	To Q's Capital A/c				2,000
	To R's Capital A/c				1,000
	(Transfer of profit on revaluation in old profit sharing ratio)				

Q.2. A, B and C are partners sharing profits and losses in the ratio of 5 : 3 : 2. From 1st April 2021, they decide to share future profits and losses equally. Their Balance Sheet as at 31st March 2021 stood as follows:

Liabilities	Rs.	Assets	Rs.
Sundry Creditors	50,000	Land and Buildings	4,00,000
Salaries Payable	25,000	Computers	60,000
Outstanding Expenses	20,000	Stock	2,00,000
General Reserve	50,000	Sundry Debtors 3,00,000	
Workmen Compensation Reserve	70,000	Less: Provision for	
Capital Accounts:		Doubtful Debts 25,000	2,75,000
A 4,00,000		Cash at Bank	30,000
B 2,50,000		Cash in Hand	10,000
C 1,50,000	8,00,000	Advertisement Suspense	40,000
	10,15,000		**10,15,000**

Partners agreed that:

(i) Value of Land and Building be increased to Rs.5,00,000 and stock be decreased by Rs.20,000.

(ii) Provision for doubtful debts to be written back, since all debtors are good.

(iii) Out of salaries payable, Rs.15,000 was not payable.

(iv) Outstanding expenses are to be written back, being not payable.

(v) A provision for Workmen Compensation Claim be made for Rs.30,000.

(vi) Goodwill is valued at Rs.60,000.

(vii) B was to carry out the work for reconstitution of the firm at a remuneration (including expenses) of Rs.10,000. Expenses paid by b amounted to Rs.4,000.

Pass journal entries and prepare Revaluation Account.

Ans.

Date	Particulars		L.F.	Dr. (Rs.)	Cr. (Rs.)
2021 April 1	General Reserve A/c	Dr.		50,000	
	To A's Capital A/c				25,000
	To B's Capital A/c				15,000
	To C's Capital A/c				10,000
	(Transfer of general reserve in old profit sharing ratio)				
April 1	Workmen Compensation Reserve A/c	Dr.		70,000	
	To Provision for Workmen compensation Claim A/c				30,000
	To A's Capital A/c				20,000
	To B's Capital A/c				12,000
	To C's Capital A/c				8,000
	(Excess of Workmen Compensation Reserve transferred in old profit sharing ratio)				
April 1	A's Capital A/c	Dr.		20,000	
	B's Capital A/c	Dr.		12,000	
	C's Capital A/c	Dr.		8,000	
	To Advertisement Suspense A/c				40,000
	(Transfer of accumulated loss in old profit sharing ratio)				
April 1	Land & Buildings A/c	Dr.		1,00,000	
	Provision for Doubtful Debts A/c	Dr.		25,000	
	Salaries Payable A/c	Dr.		15,000	
	Outstanding Expenses A/c	Dr.		20,000	
	To Revaluation A/c				1,60,000
	(Increase in the value of assets and decrease in liabilities)				
April 1	Revaluation A/c	Dr.		20,000	
	To Stock A/c				20,000
	(Decrease in the value of stock)				
April 1	Revaluation A/c	Dr.		10,000	
	To B's Capital A/c				10,000
	(Remuneration payable to B)				

Date	Particulars		L.F.	Dr. (Rs.)	Cr. (Rs.)
April 1	Revaluation A/c	Dr.		1,30,000	
	To A's Capital A/c				65,000
	To B's Capital A/c				39,000
	To C's Capital A/c				26,000
	(Transfer of gain on revaluation in old profit sharing ratio)				
April 1	B's Capital A/c $\left(\dfrac{1}{30}\text{ of Rs.60,000}\right)$ [1]	Dr.		2,000	
	C's Capital A/c $\left(\dfrac{4}{30}\text{ of Rs.60,000}\right)$	Dr.		8,000	
	To A's Capital A/c $\left(\dfrac{5}{30}\text{ of Rs.60,000}\right)$				10,000
	(Adjustment for goodwill on change in profit sharing ratio)				

Dr.   **REVALUATION ACCOUNT**   **Cr.**

Particulars	Rs.	Particulars	Rs.
To Stock A/c	20,000	By Land & Building A/c	1,00,000
To B's Capital A/c	10,000	By Provision for Doubtful	
To Gain on Revaluation		Debts A/c	25,000
transferred to:		By Salaries Payable A/c	15,000
A's Capital A/c 65,000		By Outstanding Expenses A/c	20,000
B's Capital A/c 39,000			
C's Capital A/c 26,000	1,30,000		
	1,60,000		**1,60,000**

Working Note (1):

Calculation of Sacrifice or Gain:

Old Ratio - 5 : 3 : 2   New Ratio - 1 : 1 : 1

$$A = \frac{5}{10} - \frac{1}{3} = \frac{15-10}{30} = \frac{5}{30}\text{ Sacrifice}$$

$$B = \frac{3}{10} - \frac{1}{3} = \frac{9-10}{30} = \frac{1}{30}\text{ Gain}$$

$$C = \frac{2}{10} - \frac{1}{3} = \frac{6-10}{30} = \frac{4}{30}\text{ Gain}$$

Q.3. A, B and C are partners sharing profits and losses in the ratio of 3 : 3 : 2. Their balance sheet as at 31st March 2019 was as follows:

Liabilities	Rs.	Assets	Rs.
Sundry Creditors	24,000	Cash at Bank	37,000
General Reserve	36,000	Sundry Debtors	44,000
Capital Accounts:		Stock	1,20,000
A 2,00,000		Machinery	1,59,000
B 1,50,000		Building	2,00,000
C 1,50,000	5,00,000		
	5,60,000		**5,60,000**

Partners decided that with effect from 1st April 2019, they would share profits and losses in the ratio of 4 : 3 : 2. It was agreed that:

(i)   Stock be valued at Rs.1,10,000.

(ii) Machinery is to be depreciated by 10%.

(iii) A provision for doubtful debts is to be made on debtors @ 5%.

(iv) Building to be appreciated by 20%.

(v) A liability for Rs.2,500 included in sundry creditors is not likely to arise.

Partners agreed that the revised values are to be recorded in the books. They do not, however want to distribute the general reserve. You are required to prepare journal entries, capital accounts of the partners and the revised balance sheet.

Ans.   **JOURNAL**

Date	Particulars		L.F.	Dr. (Rs.)	Cr. (Rs.)
2019					
April 1	Revaluation A/c	Dr.		28,100	
	To Stock A/c				10,000
	To Machinery A/c				15,900
	To Provision for Doubtful Debts A/c				2,200
	(Decrease in the value of assets and provision made for doubtful debts)				
	Building A/c	Dr.		40,000	
	Sundry Creditors A/c	Dr.		2,500	
	To Revaluation A/c				42,500
	(Increase in the value of building and decrease in creditor)				

Revaluation A/c Dr.[1]		14,400	
To A's Capital A/c			5,400
To B's Capital A/c			5,400
To C's Capital A/c			3,600
(The transfer of profit on revaluation to the capital accounts of partners in old ratio)			
A's Capital A/c Dr.[1]		2,500	
To B's Capital A/c			1,500
To C's Capital A/c			1,000
(The adjustment for general reserve on change in profit sharing ratio)			

Working: (1)

Dr.   **REVALUATION ACCOUNT**   **Cr.**

Particulars	Rs.	Particulars	Rs.
To Stock A/c	10,000	By Building A/c	40,000
To Machinery A/c	15,900	By Sundry Creditors A/c	2,500
To Provision for Doubtful			
Debts A/c	2,200		
To Profit on Revaluation			
transferred to:			
A's Capital A/c (3/8)	5,400		
B's Capital A/c (3/8)	5,400		
C's Capital A/c (2/8)	3,600		
	42,500		**42,500**

(2) Adjustment for General Reserve:

    Old Ratio of A, B and C   3 : 3 : 2

    New Ratio of A, B and C   4 : 3 : 2

    Sacrifice or Gain:

$$A = \frac{3}{8} - \frac{4}{9} = \frac{5}{72} \text{(Gain)}$$

$$B = \frac{3}{8} - \frac{3}{9} = \frac{3}{72} \text{(Sacrifice)}$$

$$C = \frac{2}{8} - \frac{2}{9} = \frac{2}{72} \text{(Sacrifice)}$$

Since A has gained, he will be debited from $\dfrac{5}{72}$ General Reserves of Rs.36,000 = Rs.2,500

Since B has sacrificed, he will be credited from $\dfrac{3}{72}$ of General Reserves of Rs.36,000 = Rs.1,500

Since C has sacrificed, he will be credited from $\dfrac{2}{72}$ of General Reserves of Rs.36,000 = Rs.1,000

Dr.   CAPITAL ACCOUNTS   **Cr.**

Particulars	A	B	C	Particulars	A	B	C
	Rs.	Rs.	Rs.		Rs.	Rs.	Rs.
To B's Capital A/c	1,500			By Balance b/d	2,00,000	1,50,000	1,50,000
To C's Capital A/c	1,000			By Revaluation A/c	5,400	5,400	3,600
To Balance c/d	2,02,900	1,56,900	1,54,600	By A's Capital A/c		1,500	1,000
	2,05,400	**1,56,900**	**1,54,600**		**2,05,400**	**1,56,900**	**1,54,600**

BALANCE SHEET

as at 1st April 2019

Liabilities		Rs.	Assets		Rs.
Sundry Creditors		21,500	Cash at Bank		37,000
General Reserve		36,000	Sundry Debtors	44,000	
Capital Accounts:			Less: Provision for		
A	2,02,900		Doubtful Debts	2,200	41,800
B	1,56,900		Stock		1,10,000
C	1,54,600	5,14,400	Machinery		1,43,100
			Building		2,40,000
		5,71,900			**5,71,900**

Q.4. Shadab, Ishak and Aamir are partners sharing profits and losses in the ratio of 5:3:2. Their Balance Sheet as at 31st March, 2022 stood as follows:

Liabilities		Rs.	Assets	Rs.
Capital A/cs:			Land and Building	2,60,000
Shadab	3,50,000		Machinery	3,50,000
Ishak	2,50,000		Stock	90,000
Aamir	3,00,000	9,00,000	Bills Receivable	70,000
General Reserve		20,000	Sundry Debtors	1,00,000
Workmen Compensation Reserve		30,000	Cash in Hand	25,000
Sundry Creditors		50,000	Cash at Bank	1,05,000
		10,00,000		**10,00,000**

They agreed to share profits and losses in the ratio of 2:2:1 w.e.f. 1st April 2022 on the following terms:

(i) Land and Building be appreciated by 10%.

(ii) Machinery be reduced by 15%.

(iii) Stock be increased to Rs.1,00,000.

(iv) Provision for Doubtful Debts be created @ 5% on Sundry Debtors.

(v) A Creditor of Rs.5,000 is not to claim the dues. Hence, it is to be written back.

(vi) A claim on account of Workmen Compensation is Rs.10,000.

(vii) An expense of Rs.2,000 was paid by the firm for getting the value of Land and Building certified from a Chartered Engineer.

Pass the Journal entries and prepare Revaluation Account.

Ans. **JOURNAL**

Date	Particulars		L.F.	Dr. (Rs.)	Cr. (Rs.)
2022 April 1	General Reserve A/c	Dr.		20,000	
	To Shadab's Capital A/c				10,000
	To Ishak's Capital A/c				6,000
	To Aamir's Capital A/c				4,000
	(General Reserve credited to Partners' Capital Accounts in their old profit sharing ratio)				
	Workmen compensation Reserve A/c	Dr.		30,000	
	To Workmen Compensation Claim A/c				10,000
	To Shadab's Capital A/c				10,000
	To Ishak's Capital A/c				6,000
	To Aamir's Capital A/c				4,000
	(Workmen Compensation Reserve, after adjusting claim, credited to Partners' Capital Accounts in their old profit sharing ratio)				
	Land and Building A/c	Dr.		26,000	
	Stock A/c	Dr.		10,000	
	To Revaluation A/c				36,000
	(Increase in value of land and building and stock recorded)				
	Revaluation A/c	Dr.		57,500	
	To Machinery A/c				52,500
	To Provision for Doubtful Debts A/c				5,000
	(Decrease in value of Machinery recorded and provision for doubtful debts made)				
	Sundry Creditors A/c	Dr.		5,000	
	To Revaluation A/c				5,000
	(Amount not payable written back)				
	Revaluation A/c	Dr.		2,000	
	To Cash/Bank A/c				2,000
	(Expense for valuation of Land and Building)				

Shadab's Capital A/c	Dr.		9,250	
Ishak's Capital A/c	Dr.		5,550	
Aamir's Capital A/c	Dr.		3,700	
To Revaluation A/c				18,500
(Loss on revaluation debited to Partners' Capital Accounts in their old profit sharing ratio)				

Dr.   **REVALUATION ACCOUNT**   **Cr.**

Particulars	Rs.	Particulars	Rs.
To Machinery A/c	52,500	By Land and Building A/c	26,000
To Provision for Doubtful Debts A/c	5,000	By Stock A/c	10,000
To Cash/Bank A/c (Expenses)	2,000	By Sundry Creditors A/c	5,000
		By Loss transferred to:	
		Shadab's Capital A/c 9,250	
		Ishak's Capital A/c 5,550	
		Aamir's Capital A/c 3,700	18,500
	59,500		59,500

Q.5. Kaju, Raju, Aaju and Baju were partners in a firm sharing profits in the ratio of 4 : 3 : 2 : 1. On 1st April 2016 their Balance Sheet was as follows:

BALANCE SHEET
as on 1st April, 2016

Liabilities		Rs.	Assets	Rs.
Capital A/cs:			Fixed Assets	4,40,000
Kaju	2,00,000		Current Assets	2,00,000
Raju	1,50,000			
Aaju	1,00,000			
Baju	50,000	5,00,000		
Sundry Creditors		80,000		
Workmen Compensation Reserve		60,000		
		6,40,000		**6,40,000**

From the above date partners decided to share the future profits in 3 : 1 : 2 : 4 ratio. For this purpose the goodwill of the firm was valued at Rs.90,000. The partners also agreed for the following:

(i) The claim for workmen compensation has been estimated at Rs.70,000.

(ii) To adjust the capitals of the partners according to new profit sharing ratio by opening Partners' Current Accounts.

Prepare Revaluation Account, Partners' Capital Accounts and the Balance Sheet of the reconstituted firm.

Ans. Dr.   **REVALUATIOON ACCOUNT**   **Cr.**

Particulars	Rs.	Particulars	Rs.
To Workmen Compensation Claim A/c	10,000	By Loss on Revaluation transferred to:	
		Kaju's Capital A/c 4,000	
		Raju's Capital A/c 3,000	
		Aaju's Capital A/c 2,000	
		Baju's Capital A/c 1,000	10,000
	10,000		**10,000**

Dr.   **PARTNER'S CAPITAL ACCOUNTS**   **Cr.**

Particulars	Kaju	Raju	Aaju	Baju	Particulars	Kaju	Raju	Aaju	Baju
To Revaluation A/c (Loss)	4,000	3,000	2,000	1,000	By Bal. b/d	2,00,000	1,50,000	1,00,000	50,000
To Kaju' Capital A/c	...	...	...	9,000	By Baju's Capital A/c (WN1)	9,000	18,000	...	...
To Raju's Capital A/c	...	...	...	18,000	By Baju's Current A/c (Bal. Fig.)	...	...	...	1,74,000
To Kaju's Current A/c (Bal. Fig.)	58,000	...	...	...					
To Raju's Current A/c (Bal. Fig.)	...	1,16,000	...	...					
To Balance c/d (WN 2)	1,47,000	49,000	98,000	1,96,000					
	2,09,000	**1,68,000**	**1,00,000**	**2,24,000**		**2,09,000**	**1,68,000**	**1,00,000**	**2,24,000**

BALANCE SHEET OF THE RECONSTITUTED FIRM
as at 1st April 2016

Liabilities		Rs.	Assets	Rs.
Capital A/cs:			Fixed Assets	4,40,000
Kaju	1,47,000		Current Assets	2,00,000
Raju	49,000		Baju's Current A/c	1,74,000
Aaju	98,000			
Baju	1,96,000	4,90,000		
Sundry Creditors		80,000		
Kaju's Current A/c		58,000		
Raju's Current A/c		1,16,000		
Provision for WCR		70,000		
		8,14,000		**8,14,000**

Working Notes:

1. Adjustment of Goodwill:

   Value of Firm's Goodwill = Rs.90,000

   Calculation of Sacrificed/(Gained) Profit Share of each Partner:

Particulars	Kaju	Raju	Aaju	Baju
i. Old Profit Share	4/10	3/10	2/10	1/10
ii. New Profit Share	3/10	1/10	2/10	4/10
iii. Sacrificed/(Gained) Profit Share (I-II)	4/10 – 3/10 = 1/10 (Sacrifice)	3/10 – 1/10 = 2/10 (Sacrifice)	2/10 – 2/10 = 0	1/10 – 4/10 = 3/10 (Gain)

   Journal Entry for Adjustment of Goodwill:

   Baju's Capital A/c (Rs.90,000 x 3/10)

   To Kaju's Capital A/c (Rs.90,000 x 1/10)

   To Raju's Capital A/c (Rs.90,000 x 2/10)

2. Total Capital of the New firm after Adjustment: Rs.

   Kaju (Rs.2,00,000 + Rs.9,000 - Rs.4,000)   2,05,000

   Raju (Rs.1,50,000 + Rs.18,000 - Rs.3,000)   1,65,000

   Aaju (Rs.1,00,000 - Rs.2,000)   98,000

   Baju (Rs.50,000 - Rs.1,000 - Rs.9,000 - Rs.18,000)   22,000

   Total Capital of the New Firm   4,90,000

   Capital of the partners in the new firm as per New Profit sharing Ratio:

   Kaju = Rs.4,90,000 x 3/10 = Rs.1,47,000;

   Raju = Rs.4,90,000 x 1/10 = Rs.49,000;

   Aaju = Rs.4,90,000 x 2/10 = Rs.98,000; and

   Baju = Rs.4,90,000 x 4/10 = Rs.1,96,000.

Q.6. Ravi and Rakhi are partners in a firm sharing profits in the ratio of 2 : 3. The balance sheet of the firm as on 31st March, 2020 is given below

Balance Sheet as at 31st March, 2020

Liabilities		Amount (Rs.)	Assets	Amount (Rs.)
Creditors		6,20,000	Bills Receivable	3,60,000
Bills Payable		1,80,000	Stock	16,00,000
Capital A/c			Machinery	18,40,000
Ravi	16,00,000		Land and Building	10,00,000
Rakhi	24,00,000	40,00,000		
		48,00,000		**48,00,000**

The partners decided to share profits in equal ratio with effect from 1st April, 2020. The following adjustments were agreed upon

(a) Land and building was valued at Rs.16,00,000 and machinery at Rs.16,40,000 and were to appear at revalued amounts in the balance sheet.

(b) The goodwill of the firm was valued at Rs.80,000 but it was not to appear in books.

(i) What was the entry passed in revaluation account with respect to machinery?

   (a) Debit Machinery A/c Rs.2,00,000; Credit Revaluation A/c Rs.2,00,000

   (b) Debit Revaluation A/c Rs.2,00,000; Credit Machinery A/c Rs.2,00,000

   (c) Debit Machinery A/c Rs.16,40,000; Credit Revaluation A/c Rs.16,40,000

   (d) Debit Revaluation A/c Rs.16,40,000; Credit Machinery A/c Rs.16,40,000

Ans. (b)

(ii) What was the final profit/loss of revaluation account?

   (a) Loss Rs.8,00,000 (b) Profit Rs.8,00,000   (c) Profit Rs.4,00,000   (d) Loss Rs.4,00,000

Ans. (c)

(iii) What was the gain/sacrifice of share for Ravi?

   (a) Gain-1/10   (b) Sacrifice-1/10   (c) Sacrifice-1/5   (d) Gain-1/5

Ans. (a)

(iv) What was the Ravi's capital account balance?

   (a) Rs.17,52,000   (b) Rs.17,60,000   (c) Rs.26,40,000   (d) Rs.26,48,000

Ans. (a)

(v) What was the Rakhi's capital account balance?

   (a) Rs.17,52,000   (b) Rs.17,60,000   (c) Rs.26,40,000   (d) Rs.26,48,000

Ans. (d)

Chapter Practice

Multiple Choice Questions   [1 Mark]

Q.1. A Partnership is reconstituted due to:

(a) Change in profit sharing ratio among existing partners

(b) Admission of a partner

(c) Retirement/death of a partner

(d) All above.

Q.2. Any change in the relationship of existing partners which results in an end of the existing agreement and enforces making of a new agreement is called

(a) Revaluation of partnership

(b) Reconstitution of partnership

(c) Realisation of partnership

(d) None of the above

Q.3. Sacrificing ratio of a partner is computed as:

(a) Old Ratio-New Ratio

(b) New Ratio-Old Ratio

(c) Old Ratio-Gaining Ratio

(d) None of these

Q.4. A, B and C are partner in a firm sharing profits in the ratio 3:2:1. They decided to share profits equally in future. B's sacrifice/gain will be:

(a) Sacrifice 1/6   (b) Gain 1/6   (c) No change   (d) None of these

Q.5. The average capital employed of a firm is Rs.4,00000 and the normal rate of return is 15%. The average profit of the firm is Rs.80,000 pcr annum. If the remuneration of the partners is estimated to be Rs.10,000 per annum, then on the basis of two years purchase of super-profit, the value of the Goodwill will be

(a) 10,000   (b) 20,000   (c) 60,000   (d) 80,000

Q.6. Under the capitalisation method, the formula for calculating the goodwill is:

(a) Super profits multiplied by the rate of return

(b) Average profits multiplied by the rate of return

(c) Super profits divided by the rate of return

(d) Average profits divided by the rate of return

Q.7. Gaining ratio of a partner is computed as:

(a) Old Ratio-New Ratio

(b) New Ratio-Old Ratio

(c) New Ratio-Sacrificing Ratio

(d) None of these.

Q.8. A and B are partners in a firm sharing profits and losses equally. They decided to share profits in the ratio of 3:2 in future. A's sacrifice/gain will be

(a) Sacrifice 1/10   (b) Gain 1/10   (c) Sacrifice 3/5   (d) Gain 3/5

Q.9. X Y and Z Are partners sharing profits in the ratio of 3:2:1. They decided to share future profits in the ratio 2:1:1. Thus, Z's sacrifice/gain will be

(a) 4/12 gain   (b) 3/12 gain   (c) sacrifice 1/12   (d) 1/12 gain

Q.10. P and were partners sharing profits and losses in the ratio of 3:2. They decided that with effect from 1st January, 2019 they would share profits and losses in the ratio of 5:3. Goodwill is valued at Rs. 1,28,000. In adjustment entry:

(a) Cr. P by 3,200; Dr. Q by 3,200

(b) Cr. P by 37,000; Dr. Q by 37,000

(c) Dr. P by 37,000; Cr. Q by 37,000

(d) Dr. P by 3,200 Cr. Q by 3,200

Very Short Answer Type   [1 Mark]

Q.11. At the time of change in profit sharing ratio among the existing partners, where will you record an unrecorded liability ?

Q.12. Give two circumstances in which gaining ratio can be applied.

Q.13. Define gaining ratio.

Q.14. X, Y and Z are partners sharing profits and losses in the ratio of 5:3:2.They decide to share the future profits in the ratio of 3:2:1. What will be the treatment of Workmen compensation reserve appearing in the balance sheet on the date if no information is available for the same?

Q.15. Should compensate …………...in the case of reconstitution of the firm.

Short Answer Type - II   [3 Marks]

Q.16. Anu and Bala distributed profits and losses in the ratio 3:2 starting 1st April 2019, they accepted to distribute profits evenly. Goodwill of the business was accounted for at Rs.50,000. Prepare the journal for the accounting of goodwill: When the goodwill is adjusted through Partners' Capital Account.

Q.17. A, B, and C are partners sharing profits in the ratio of 5:3:2. They decided to share the profits in the ratio of 2:3:5. Starting 1st April, they decided to adjust the following accumulated profits, losses and reserves without affecting their book values, by passing an adjustment entry. Journalise

Q.18. Mention the points when a firm reconstitute.

Q.19. Define Investment Fluctuation Reserve. And explain the two types of the accounting treatment of Investment Fluctuation Reserve.

Q.20. Hardeep and Sandeep are partners sharing profits in the ratio of 4:1. They decided to distributed profits equally starting 1st April 2019. Their balance sheet as on 31st March 2019 shows a balance of advertisement suspense of Rs. 20,000. Pass the journal entry at the time of change in profit sharing ratio.

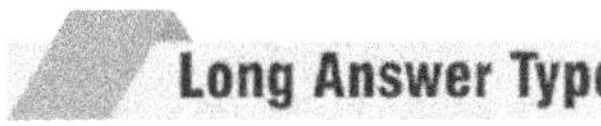

Long Answer Type   [5 Marks]

Q.21. A, B and C were partners producing electronic goods and sharing profits and losses in the ratio of 2 : 3 : 4. They decided to share future profits and losses in the ratio of 4:3:2. They also decided to record the effect of the following without affecting their book value:

General Reserve	Rs. 1,60,000
Profit and Losses account (Cr)	Rs. 80,000
Advertisement suspense account	Rs. 60,000

You are required to give the necessary adjustment journal entry.

Direction: On the basis of the following case, answer the question number (22 to 26):

Ravi and Rakhi are partners in a firm sharing profits in the ratio of 2 : 3. The balance sheet of the firm as on 31st March, 2020 is given below

BALANCE SHEET

as at 31st March, 2020

Liabilities		Amount (Rs.)	Assets	Amount (Rs.)
Creditors		6,20,000	Bills	3,60,000
Bills Pay-able		1,80,000	Receivable	
			Stock	16,00,000
CapitalA/c			Machinery	18,40,000
Ravi	16,00,000		Land and Building	10,00,000
Rakhi	24,00,000	40,00,000		
		48,00,000		**48,00,000**

The partners decided to share profits in equal ratio with effect from 1st April, 2020. The following adjustments were agreed upon

(i) Land and building was valued at Rs.16,00,000 and machinery at Rs.16,40,000 and were to appear at revalued amounts in the balance sheet.

(ii) The goodwill of the firm was valued at Rs.80,000 but it was not to appear in books.

Q.22. What was the entry passed in revaluation account with respect to machinery?

(a) Debit Machinery A/c Rs.2,00,000; Credit Revaluation A/c Rs.2,00,000

(b) Debit Revaluation A/c Rs.2,00,000; Credit Machinery A/c Rs.2,00,000

(c) Debit Machinery A/c Rs.16,40,000; Credit Revaluation A/c Rs.16,40,000

(d) Debit Revaluation A/c Rs.16,40,000; Credit Machinery A/c Rs.16,40,000

Q.23. What was the final profit/loss of revaluation account?

(a) Loss Rs.8,00,000 (b) Profit Rs.8,00,000   (c) Profit Rs.4,00,000   (d) Loss Rs.4,00,000

Q.24. What was the gain/sacrifice of share for Ravi?

(a) Gain-1/10   (b) Sacrifice-1/10   (c) Sacrifice-1/5   (d) Gain-1/5

Q.25. What was the Ravi's capital account balance?

(a) Rs.17,52,000   (b) Rs.17,60,000   (c) Rs.26,40,000   (d) Rs.26,48,000

Q.26. What was the Rakhi's capital account balance?

(a) Rs.17,52,000   (b) Rs.17,60,000   (c) Rs.26,40,000   (d) Rs.26,48,000

Q.27. A, B and C are partners sharing profits and losses in the ratio of 5 : 3 : 2. From 1st April 2021, they decide to share future profits and losses equally. Their Balance Sheet as at 31st March 2021 stood as follows:

Liabilities		Rs.	Assets		Rs.
Sundry Creditors		50,000	Land and Buildings		4,00,000
Salaries Payable		25,000	Computers		60,000
Outstanding Expenses		20,000	Stock		2,00,000
General Reserve		50,000	Sundry Debtors	3,00,000	
Workmen Compensation Reserve		70,000	Less: Provision for		
Capital Accounts:			Doubtful Debts	25,000	2,75,000
A	4,00,000		Cash at Bank		30,000
B	2,50,000		Cash in Hand		10,000
C	1,50,000	8,00,000	Advertisement Suspense		40,000
		10,15,000			**10,15,000**

Partners agreed that:

(i) Value of Land and Building be increased Rs.5,00,000 and stock be decreased by Rs.20,000.

(ii) Provision for doubtful debts to be written back, since all debtors are good.

(iii) Out of salaries payable, Rs.15,000 was not payable.

(iv) Outstanding expenses are to be written back, being not payable.

(v) A provision for Workmen Compensation Claim be made for Rs.30,000.

(vi) Goodwill is valued at Rs.60,000.

(vii) B was to carry out the work for reconstitution of the firm at a remuneration (including expenses) of Rs.10,000. Expenses paid by b amounted to Rs.4,000. prepare Revaluation Account.

Q.28. A, B and C are partners sharing profits and losses in the ratio of 3 : 3 : 2. Their balance sheet as at 31st March 2019 was as follows:

Liabilities		Rs.	Assets	Rs.
Sundry Creditors		24,000	Cash at Bank	37,000
General Reserve		36,000	Sundry Debtors	44,000
Capital Accounts:			Stock	1,20,000
A	2,00,000		Machinery	1,59,000
B	1,50,000		Building	2,00,000
C	1,50,000	5,00,000		
		5,60,000		**5,60,000**

Partners decided that with effect from 1st April 2019, they would share profits and losses in the ratio of 4 : 3 : 2. It was agreed that:

(i) Stock be valued at Rs.1,10,000.

(ii) Machinery is to be depreciated by 10%.

(iii)A provision for doubtful debts is to be made on debtors @ 5%.

(iv) Building to be appreciated by 20%.

(v) A liability for Rs.2,500 included in sundry creditors is not likely to arise.

Partners agreed that the revised values are to be recorded in the books. They do not, however want to distribute the general reserve. You are required to prepare Revaluation account.

CHAPTER 3

Reconstitution of a Partnership Firm – Admission of a Partner

 Introduction, Effect of Admission of Partner on Profit Sharing Ratio, Sacrificing Ratio, Gaining Ratio

Summary

Partnership is an agreement between two or more persons (called partners) for sharing the profits of a business carried on by all or any of them acting for all.

1. **Admission of a New Partner:** A new partner may be admitted when the firm needs additional capital or managerial help. According to the provisions of Partnership Act 1932 unless it is otherwise provided in the partnership deed a new partner can be admitted only when the existing partners unanimously agree for it.

2. **Change in the profit sharing ratio among the existing partners:** Sometimes the partners of a firm may decide to change their existing profit sharing ratio. This may happen an account of a change in the existing partners' role in the firm.

3. **Retirement of an existing partner:** It means withdrawal by a partner from the business of the firm which may be due to his bad health, old age or change in business interests.

4. **Death of a partner:** Partnership may also stand reconstituted on death of a partner, if the remaining partners decide to continue the business of the firm as usual.

Admission of a New Partner: When firm requires additional capital or managerial help or both for the expansion of its business a new partner may be admitted to supplement its existing resources. According to the Partnership Act 1932, a new partner can be admitted into the firm only with the consent of all the existing partners unless otherwise agreed upon. With the admission of a new partner, the partnership firm is reconstituted and a new agreement is entered into to carry on the business of the firm. A newly admitted partner acquires two main rights in the firm-

1. Right to share the assets of the partnership firm; and

2. Right to share the profits of the partnership firm.

Following are the other important points which require attention at the time of admission of a new partner:

1. New profit sharing ratio;

2. Sacrificing ratio;

3. Valuation and adjustment of goodwill;

4. Revaluation of assets and Reassessment of liabilities;

5. Distribution of accumulated profits (reserves); and

6. Adjustment of partners' capitals.

New Profit Sharing Ratio:

The ratio in which all partners including new partner share the future profits is called the new profit sharing ratio. In other words, on the admission of a new partner, the old partners sacrifice a share of their profits in favour of the new partner. On admission of a new partner, the profit-sharing ratio among the old partners will change keeping in view their respective contribution to the profit-sharing ratio of the incoming partner. Hence, there is a need to ascertain the new profit sharing ratio among all the partners.

The new partner may acquire his share from the old partners in any of the following situations:

1. If only the ratio of the new partner is given, then in the absence of any other agreement or information, it is assumed that the old partners will continue to share the remaining profits in the old ratio.

2. If the new partner acquires his share of profit from the old partners equally. In that case, the new profit sharing ratio of the old partner will be calculated by deducting the sacrifice made by them from their existing share of profit.

3. In the new partner acquire his share of profit from the old partners in a particular ratio. In that case, the new profit sharing ratio of the old partners will be calculated by deducting the sacrifice made by them from their existing share of profit.

4. If the old partners surrender a particular fraction of their share in favour of the new partner. In that case, the new partner's share is calculated by adding the surrendered portion of the share by the old partners. Old partners' share is calculated by deducting the surrendered portion from their old ratio.

5. If the new partner acquires his share of profit from only one partner. In that case, the new profit sharing ratio of the old partner will be calculated by deducting the sacrifice made by one partner from his existing ratio.

Sacrificing Ratio

The ratio in which the old partners have agreed to sacrifice their shares in profit in favour of a new partner is called the sacrificing ratio. This ratio is calculated by taking out the difference between the old profit sharing ratio and the new profit sharing ratio.

Sacrificing Ratio = Old Ratio – New Ratio

Multiple Choice Questions [1 Mark]

Q.1. Which of the following is not the reconstitution of partnership?

(a) Admission of a partner

(b) Dissolution of Partnership

(c) Change in Profit Sharing Ratio

(d) Retirement of a partner

Ans. (b)

Q.2. On the admission of a new partner:

(a) Old partnership is dissolved

(b) Both old partnership and firm are dissolved

(c) Old firm is dissolved

(d) None of the above

Ans. (a)

Q.3. Sacrificing ratio is used to distribute ------------------ in case of admission of a partner.

(a) Goodwill

(b) Revaluation Profit or Loss

(c) Profit and Loss Account (Credit Balance)

(d) Both (b) and (c)

Ans. (a)

Q.4. Yash and Manan are partners sharing profits in the ratio of $2:1$. They admit Kushagra into partnership for 25% share of profit. Kushagra acquired the share from old partners in the ratio of $3:2$. The new profit sharing ratio will be:

(a) $14:31:15$ (b) $3:2:1$ (c) $31:14:15$ (d) $2:3:1$

Ans. (c)

Q.5. Which of the following is not true with respect to Admission of a partner?

(a) A new partner can be admitted if it is agreed in the partnership deed.

(b) If all the partners agree, a new partner can be admitted.

(c) A new partner has to bring relatively higher capital as compared to the existing partners

(d) A new partner gets right in the assets of the firm

Ans. (c)

Q.6. Sacrificing ratio is calculated because:

(a) Profit shown by Revaluation Account can be credited to sacrificing partners

(b) Goodwill brought in by the incoming partner can be credited to the new partner

(c) Goodwill brought in by the incoming partner can be credited to the sacrificing partners

(d) Both (a) and (c)

Ans. (c)

Q.7. Match the following:

i.	Sacrificing Ratio	A	Nominal Account
ii.	Gaining Ratio	B	Reconstitution of Partnership
iii.	Revaluation Account	C	New Ratio – Old Ratio
iv.	Admission of a Partner	D	Old Ratio – New Ratio

(a) i- B, ii-C, iii-A, iv-D (b) i- D, ii-B, iii-A, iv-C

(c) i- D, ii-C, iii-A, iv-B (d) i- D, ii-C, iii-B, iv-A

Ans. (c)

Very Short Answer Type   [1 Mark]

Q.1. "At the time of admission, old partnership comes to an end". Is the statement true or false?

Ans. True

Q.2. "As per Section 26 of the Indian Partnership Act, 1932, a person can be admitted as a new partner if it is agreed in the Partnership Deed". Is the statement True or False?

Ans. False

Q.3. "Unless agreed otherwise, Sacrificing Ratio of the old partners will be the same as their Old Profit Sharing Ratio". Is the statement True or False?

Ans. True

Q.4. Assertion (A): It is necessary to ascertain new profit sharing ratio for old partners when a new partner is admitted

Reason (R): New partner acquires his share from old partners which reduce old partners share in profits.

(a) Both Assertion and reason are true and reason is correct explanation of assertion.

(b) Assertion and reason both are true but reason is not the correct explanation of assertion.

(c) Assertion is false, reason is true.

(d) Assertion is true, reason is false.

Ans. (a)

Q.5. State the right acquired by a newly admitted partner. **(All India 2014,2009; Delhi 2008)**

Ans. The right acquired by a newly admitted partner is (Any one):

(i) Share in the future profits of the firm.

(ii) Share in the assets of the firm.

Q.6. State the meaning of sacrificing ratio. **(All India 2011)**

Ans. It is the ratio in which the old partners have agreed to sacrifice their share of profits in favour of new or incoming partner.

Sacrificing Ratio = Old Ratio – New Ratio

Q.7. List any two items that need adjustments in the books of accounts of a firm at the time of admission of a partner. **(CBSE- 2014)**

Ans. Two items that need adjustment at the time of admission are:

(i) Goodwill of the firm.

(ii) Reserves and accumulated profits/losses.

Q.8. State any one purpose for admitting a new partner in a firm. **(All India 2012)**

Ans. A new partner may be admitted for the following purpose (Any one)

(i) For procuring additional capital.

(ii) For acquiring additional managerial skills.

Short Answer Type - I [2 Marks]

Q.1. On 1-4-2016, A and B entered into partnership for sharing profits in the ratio of 4 : 3. They admitted C as a new partner on 1-4-2018 for 1/5th share which he acquired equally from A and B. A , B and C earned profit at a higher rate than the Normal Rate of Return for 31-3-2019. Therefore, they decided to expand their business. To meet the requirements of addition at Capital they admitted D as a new partner on 1-4-2019 for 1/7th share in profits which he acquired from A and B in 7 : 3 ratio.

Calculate:

(a) New Profit Sharing Ratio of A : B : C for 2018-19.

(b) New Profit Sharing Ratio of A : B : C : D on D's admission.

Ans. (a) 33 : 23 : 14   (b) 13 : 10 : 7 : 5

Q.2. Vikram and Abhishek are partners sharing profits and Losses in the ratio of 8 : 5. They admit 'Avishi' and decide that the profit sharing ratio between Abhishek and Avishi shall be the same as existing between 'Vikram' and 'Abhishek'.Calculate New Profit Sharing Ratio and Sacrificing Ratio. **(CBSE 2015)**

Ans. NPSR 64 : 40 : 25

SR 8 : 5

Q.3. A, B and C are partners in a firm for the profit sharing ratio 4 : 3 : 1. They admitted 'D' as a new partner. 'A', sacrifice 1/3rd of his share in favour of 'D' and 'B', Sacrifice 1/4th from his share in favour of new partner C in neutral. Calculate New Profit Sharing Ratio.

Ans. NPSR 8 : 3 : 3 : 10

Q.4. A and B are partners sharing profits in the ratio of 5 : 4. They admit C for 1/1 th share of profit which he acquires in equal proportion from both. Find the new profit sharing ratio. **(Delhi 2011c, 2009)**

Old ratio $= 5 : 4$

C's share $= \dfrac{1}{10}$ th

Which he acquires in equal proportion from both,

$$\therefore \text{A's sacrifice} = \frac{1}{10} \times \frac{1}{2} = \frac{1}{20}; \quad \text{B's Sacrifice} = \frac{1}{10} \times \frac{1}{2} = \frac{1}{20}$$

$$\text{A's new share} = \frac{5}{9} - \frac{1}{20} = \frac{100-9}{180} = \frac{91}{180}$$

$$\text{B's new share} = \frac{4}{9} - \frac{1}{20} = \frac{80-9}{180} = \frac{71}{180}$$

$$\text{C's new share} = \frac{1}{10} = \frac{1}{10} \times \frac{18}{18} = \frac{18}{180}$$

$\therefore$ New ratio among A, B and C $= 91 : 71 : 18$

Q.5. L and M are partners in a firm sharing profits and losses in the ratio of 7 : 3. They admitted N for 3/7th share which he takes 2/7th from L and 1/7 from M. Calculate the new profit sharing ratio. **[CBSE 2014]**

Ans. Calculation of New profit sharing ratio:

$$\text{New share} = \frac{7}{10} - \frac{2}{7} = \frac{49-20}{70} = \frac{29}{70}$$

$$\text{L's new share} = \frac{3}{10} - \frac{1}{7} = \frac{21-10}{70} = \frac{11}{70}$$

$$\text{N's new share} = \frac{2}{7} + \frac{1}{7} = \frac{3}{7} \text{ (given)}$$

$$\text{New ratio among L, M and N} = \frac{29}{70} : \frac{11}{70} : \frac{3}{7} = 29 : 11 : 30/70 \quad 29 : 11 : 30$$

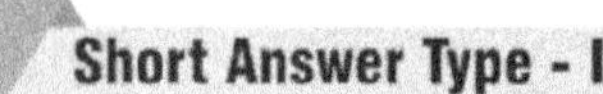 **Short Answer Type - II** [3 Marks]

Q.1. Why a new partner is admitted?

Ans. A new partner may be admitted when the firm needs

(a) Additional Capital

(b) Managerial Help

(c) Both.

Q.2. How can a new partner be admitted?

Ans. Unless it is otherwise provided in the partnership deed a new partner can be admitted only when the existing partners unanimously agree for it.

Q.3. Write main Rights acquired by a newly admitted partner.

Ans. 1. Right to share the assets of the partnership firm.

2. Right to share the profits of the partnership firm

3. Right to participate in the business activity

Q.4. What does a new partner bring to acquire the rights?

Ans. To acquire share in the assets and profits of the firm, the partner brings

(i) An agreed amount of Capital either in Cash or kind and / or some technical skill

(ii) Additional amount known as premium of Goodwill.

Q.5. Define New profit sharing ratio and sacrificing ratio. [CBSE 2015]

Ans. The ratio in which all partners, including new partner will share future profits losses of the firm is known as new profit-sharing ratio.

Sacrificing ratio is the ratio in which old or existing partners forego their share of profit in favour of the new partner.

Q.6. X and Y are partners sharing profits in the ratio of $3:2$. They admit P and Q as new partners. X surrendered 1/3 of his share in favour of P and Y surrendered ¼ of his share in favour of Q. Calculate the new profit sharing ratio of X, Y, P and Q. [CBSE 2016]

Ans. (i) Calculation of Sacrifice share :

$$\text{X surrenders } \frac{1}{3} \text{ of his share in favour of P} = \frac{1}{3} \times \frac{3}{5} = \frac{3}{15}$$

$$\text{Y surrenders } \frac{1}{4} \text{ of his share in favour of Q} = \frac{1}{4} \times \frac{2}{5} = \frac{2}{20}$$

$$\text{X's new share} = \frac{3}{5} - \frac{3}{15} = \frac{9-3}{15} = \frac{6}{15}$$

$$\text{Y's new share} = \frac{2}{5} - \frac{2}{20} = \frac{8-2}{20} = \frac{6}{20}$$

$$\text{New profit sharing ratio} = X:Y:P:Q = \frac{6}{15} : \frac{6}{20} : \frac{3}{15} : \frac{2}{20} = 4:3:2:1$$

Q.7. A, B and C are partners sharing profits in the ratio of $3:2:1$. They admit D for $\dfrac{1}{6}$ share. C would retain his old share. Calculate new ratio of all partners. **[CBSE 2013]**

Ans. (i) Calculation of sacrifice share : (Only A and B sacrifice in ratio of $3:2$)

(ii) A's sacrifices $= \dfrac{3}{5}$ of $\dfrac{1}{6} = \dfrac{3}{30}$ or $\dfrac{1}{10}$

B's sacrifices $= \dfrac{2}{5}$ of $\dfrac{1}{6} = \dfrac{2}{30}$ or $\dfrac{1}{15}$

C's sacrifices $=$ Nil

(iii) Calculation of New profit sharing Ratio :

New share = Old share – Sacrifice share

A's new share $= \dfrac{3}{6} - \dfrac{1}{10} = \dfrac{30-6}{60} = \dfrac{24}{60}$

B's new share $= \dfrac{2}{6} - \dfrac{1}{15} = \dfrac{30-6}{90} = \dfrac{24}{90}$

C's new share $= \dfrac{1}{6} - 0 = \dfrac{1}{6}$

D's new share $= \dfrac{1}{10} + \dfrac{1}{15} = \dfrac{3+2}{30} = \dfrac{5}{30} = \dfrac{1}{6}$

New ratio among A, B, C and D

$\dfrac{24}{60} : \dfrac{24}{90} : \dfrac{1}{6} : \dfrac{1}{6} : \dfrac{1}{6}$

$= \dfrac{72:48:30:12:8:5:5}{180} = 12:8:5:5$

Long Answer Type [5 Marks]

Q.1. X and Y are partners sharing profit in the ratio 3 : 2. They admit P and Q as new partners. X surrendered 1/3rd of his share in favour of P and Y surrendered 1/4th of his share in favour of Q. **[CBSE 2014]**

Calculate (a) Sacrificing ratio (b) New profit sharing ratio X, Y, P and Q.

Ans. (a) Calculation of Sacrificing Ratio

X surrenders $\dfrac{1}{3}$ of his share in factor of P $= \dfrac{1}{3} \times \dfrac{3}{5} = \dfrac{3}{15}$

Y surrenders $\dfrac{1}{4}$ of his share in favour of Q $= \dfrac{1}{4} \times \dfrac{2}{5} = \dfrac{2}{20}$

$= X : Y$

$\dfrac{3}{15} : \dfrac{2}{20}$

$\dfrac{12}{60} : \dfrac{6}{60}$

$12 : 6$ or $2 : 1$

(b) Calculation of New Profit-sharing ratio

$$\text{X's New share} = \frac{3}{5} - \frac{3}{15} = \frac{6}{15}$$

$$\text{Y's New share} = \frac{2}{5} - \frac{2}{20} = \frac{6}{20}$$

$$\text{P's} = \frac{3}{15}$$

$$\text{Q's} = \frac{2}{20}$$

$$X : Y : P : Q$$

$$= 24 : 18 : 12 : 6$$

$$= 4 : 3 : 2 : 1$$

Q.2. X and Y are partners sharing profit and losses in the ratio 3 : 2. They admit Z into the partnership, who acquires 1/4th of his share from X and 3/16th share from Y. Calculate New Profit Sharing Ratio and Sacrificing Ratio.

Ans. Since Z acquires $\frac{1}{4}$ th of his share from X

It means he acquires $\frac{3}{4}$ th of his share from Y.

If 3/4th share of Z = $\frac{3}{16}$ (Received from Y)

$$\text{Z's share} = \frac{3}{16} \times \frac{4}{3} = \frac{1}{4}$$

$$\text{Share acquired by Z from X} = \frac{1}{4} \times \frac{1}{4} = \frac{1}{16}$$

$$\text{Share acquired by Z from Y} = \frac{3}{16}$$

$$\text{Hence, X's new share} = \frac{3}{5} - \frac{1}{16} = \frac{43}{80}$$

$$\text{Y's new share} = \frac{2}{5} - \frac{1}{16} = \frac{17}{80}$$

$$\text{Z's share} = \frac{1}{4}$$

New profit sharing ratio

$$= X : Y : Z$$

$$= 43 : 17 : 20$$

Sacrificing Ratio

$$X : Y = \frac{1}{16} : \frac{3}{16}$$
$$= 1 : 3$$

Q.3. Rekha, Sunita and Teena are partners in a firm sharing profits in the ratio of 3 : 2 : 1. Samiksha joins the firm. Rekha surrenders 1/4th of her share; Sunita surrenders 1/3rd of her share and Teena surrenders 1/5th of her share in favour of Samiksha. Find the new Profit-sharing ratio. **[CBSE 2011]**

Ans. Rekha surrenders for Samiksha $= \dfrac{1}{4} \times \dfrac{3}{6} = \dfrac{3}{24}$

Sunita surrenders for Samiksha $= \dfrac{1}{3} \times \dfrac{2}{6} = \dfrac{2}{18}$

Teena surrenders for Samiksha $= \dfrac{1}{5} \times \dfrac{1}{6} = \dfrac{1}{30}$

New share of Rekha $= \dfrac{3}{6} - \dfrac{3}{24} = \dfrac{9}{24}$

New share of Sunita $= \dfrac{2}{6} - \dfrac{2}{18} = \dfrac{4}{18}$

New share of Teena $= \dfrac{1}{6} - \dfrac{1}{30} = \dfrac{4}{30}$

Share of Samiksha $= \dfrac{3}{24} + \dfrac{2}{18} + \dfrac{1}{30} = \dfrac{97}{360}$

New ratio : $\dfrac{9}{24} : \dfrac{4}{18} : \dfrac{4}{30} : \dfrac{97}{360}$

$= 135 : 80 : 48 : 97$

TOPIC 2 Treatment of Goodwill, Accumulated Profits and Losses, Reserves at the Time of Admission

Summary

Goodwill

Goodwill is the value of the reputation of a firm in respect of the profits expected in future over and above the normal profits earned by other similar firms belonging to the same industry. In other words, a well-established business develops an advantage of good name, reputation and wide business connections. This helps the business to earn more profits as compared to newly set-up business. This advantage in monetary terms called 'Goodwill'. It arises only if a firm is able to earn higher profits than normal.

Factors Affecting the Value of Goodwill: The main factors affecting the value of goodwill are as follows:

1. **Nature of business:** A firm that produces high value added products or having a stable demand is able to earn more profits and therefore has more goodwill.

2. **Location:** If the business is centrally located or is at a place having heavy customer traffic, the goodwill tends to be high.

3. **Efficiency of management:** A well-managed concern usually enjoys the advantage of high productivity and cost efficiency. This leads to higher profits and so the value of goodwill will also be high.

4. **Market situation:** The monopoly condition or limited competition enables the concern to earn high profits which leads to higher value of goodwill.

5. **Special advantages:** The firm that enjoys special advantages like import licences, low rate and assured supply of electricity, long-term contracts for supply of materials, well-known collaborators, patents, trademarks, etc. enjoy higher value of goodwill.

Need for Valuation of Goodwill

1. At the time of sale of a business;
2. Change in the profit-sharing ratio amongst the existing partners;
3. Admission of a new partner.
4. Retirement of a partner;
5. Death of a partner;
6. Dissolution of a firm;
7. The amalgamation of the partnership firm.

Treatment of Goodwill

1. Goodwill (Premium) brought in cash through the firm

    1. Cash A/c or Bank A/c Dr.

        To Goodwill A/c

        (For the amount of Goodwill brought by new partner)

        Goodwill A/c Dr.

        To Old Partner's Capital A/c

        (For the amount of Goodwill distributed among the old partners in their sacrificing ratio)

    2. **When goodwill already exists in books:** If the goodwill already exists in the books of firms and the incoming partner brings his share of goodwill in cash, then the goodwill appearing in the books will have to be written off.

        Old Partner's Capital A/c's Dr.

        To Goodwill A/c

        (For Goodwill written-off in old ratio)

        After the admission of the partner, all partners may decide to maintain the Goodwill Account in the books of accounts.

        Goodwill A/c Dr.

        To All Partner's Capital A/c's

        (For Goodwill raised in the new firm after admission of a new partner in new profit sharing ratio)

    3. **Goodwill does not exist in the books :** When goodwill does not exist in the books, sacrificing partners are credited with their share of goodwill and new partner is debited by the amount of goodwill not brought by him.

        The journal entry in this case is :

        Incoming (New) Partners Current A/c Dr.

        To Sacrificing Partners Capital A/c (individually)

        (Account of goodwill not brought in by new partner)

4.   No goodwill appears in the books:

   Goodwill A/c Dr.

   To Old Partner's Capital A/c's

   (For Goodwill raised at full value in the old ratio)

5.   When goodwill already exists in the books

   1.   When the value of goodwill appearing in books is equal to the agreed value:

   [No Entry is Required]

   2.   If the value of goodwill appearing in the books is less than the agreed value:

   Goodwill A/c Dr.

   To Old Partner's Capital A/c's

   (For Goodwill is raised to its agreed value)

   3.   If the value of goodwill appearing in the books is more than the agreed value:

   Old Partner's Capital A/c's Dr.

   To Goodwill A/c

   (For Goodwill brought down to its agreed value)

Hidden or Inferred Goodwill:

1.   To find out the total capital of the firm by new partner's capital and his share of profit.

2.   To ascertain the existing total capital of the firm: We will have to ascertain the existing total capital of the new firm by adding the capital (of all partners, including new partner's capital after adjustments, if any excluding goodwill)

3.   Goodwill = Capital from (1) - Capital from (2)

Adjustment for Accumulated Profits and Losses:

Sometimes a firm may have accumulated profits not yet transferred to capital accounts of the partners. These are usually in the form of general reserve, reserve and/or Profit and Loss Account. The new partner is not entitled to have any share in such accumulated profits. These are distributed among the partners by transferring it to their capital current accounts in old profit sharing ratio. Similarly, if there are some accumulated losses in the form of a debit balance of profit and loss account and/or deferred revenue expenditure appearing in the balance sheet of the firm. It should be transferred to the old partners' capital accounts.

Accumulated profits and reserves are distributed to partners in their old profit sharing ratio. If old partners are not interested to distribute, these accumulated profits are adjusted in the same manner as goodwill and the following adjusting entry will be passed.

New Partner's capital A/c Dr. (New share)

To old partner's capital A/c (Sacrificing ratio)

Accounting treatment for revaluation of assets and re-assessment of liabilities

The assets and liabilities are generally revalued at the time of admission of a new partner. Revaluation Account is prepared for this purpose in the same way was in case of change in profit sharing ratio. This account is debited with all losses and credited with all gains. Balance of Revaluation Account is transferred to old partner in their old ratio.

The journal entries recorded for revaluation of assets and reassessment of liabilities are following:

1.   For increase in the value of an Assets

   Assets A/c Dr.

   To Revaluation A/c (Gain)

2. For decrease in the value of an Assets
    Revaluation A/c Dr.
        To Assets A/c (Loss)
3. For appreciation in the amount of Liability
    Revaluation A/c Dr.
        To Liability A/c (Loss)
4. For reduction in the amount of a Liability
    Liability A/c Dr.
        To Revaluation A/c (Gain)
5. For recording an unrecorded Assets
    Unrecorded Assets A/c Dr.
        To Revaluation A/c (Gain)
6. For recording an unrecorded Liability
    Revaluation A/c Dr.
        To Unrecorded Liability A/c (Loss)
7. For the sale of unrecorded Assets
    Cash A/c or Bank A/c Dr.
        To Revaluation A/c (Gain)
8. For payment of unrecorded Liability
    Revaluation A/c Dr.
        To Cash A/c or Bank A/c (Loss)
9. For transfer of gain on Revaluation if the credit balance
    Revaluation A/c Dr.
        To Old Partner's Capital A/c's (Old Ratio)
10. For transfer of loss on Revaluation if debit balance
    Old Partner's Capital A/c's Dr.
        To Revaluation A/c (Old Ratio)

Multiple Choice Questions   [1 Mark]

Q.1. Himanshu and Naman share profits & losses equally. Their capitals were Rs.1,20,000 and Rs.80,000 respectively. There was also a balance of Rs.60,000 in General reserve and revaluation gain amounted to Rs.15,000. They admit friend Ashish with 1/5 share. Ashish brings Rs.90,000 as capital. Calculate the amount of goodwill of the firm.

(a) Rs.1,00,000   (b) Rs.85,000   (c) Rs.20,000   (d) None of the above

Ans. (b)

Q.2. Heena and Sudha share Profit & Loss equally. Their capitals were Rs.1,20,000 and Rs.80,000 respectively. There was also a balance of Rs.60,000 in General reserve and revaluation gain amounted to Rs.15,000. They admit friend Teena with 1/5 share. Teena brings Rs.90,000 as capital. Calculate the amount of goodwill of the firm.

(a) Rs.85,000   (b) Rs.1,00,000   (c) Rs.20,000   (d) None of the above

Ans. (a)

Q.3. As per ---------, only purchased goodwill can be shown in the Balance Sheet.

(a) AS 37   (b) AS 26   (c) Section 37   (d) AS 37

Ans. (b)

Q.4. At the time of admission of a partner, Employees Provident Fund is:

    (a) Distributed to partners in the old profit sharing ratio

    (b) Distributed to partners in the new profit sharing ratio

    (c) Adjusted through gaining ratio

    (d) None of the above

Ans. (d)

Q.5. At the time of admission of a new partner, the balance of Workmen Compensation Reserve will be transferred to:

    (a) Old partners in the old profit sharing ratio   (b) Sacrificing partners in the sacrificing ratio

    (c) Revaluation Account   (d) All partners in the new profit sharing ratio

Ans. (a)

Q.6. The firm of P, Q and R with profit sharing ratio of 6 : 3 : 1, had the balance in General Reserve Account amounting Rs.1,80,000. S joined as a new partner and the new profit sharing ratio was decided to be 3 : 3 : 3 : 1. Partners decide to keep the General Reserve unchanged in the books of accounts. The effect will be:

    (a) P will be credited by Rs.54,000   (b) P will be debited by Rs.54,000

    (c) P will be credited by Rs.36.000   (d) P will be credited by Rs.36,000

Ans. (a)

Q.7. Which statement is true with respect to AS-26?

    (a) Purchased goodwill can be shown in the Balance Sheet

    (b) Revalued goodwill can be shown in the Balance Sheet

    (c) Both purchased goodwill and revalued can be shown in the Balance Sheet

    (d) None of the above

Ans. (a)

Q.8. Premium brought by newly admitted partner should be:

    (a) Credited to sacrificing partners

    (b) Credited to all partners in the new profit sharing ratio

    (c) Credited to old partners in the old profit sharing ratio

    (d) Credited to only gaining partners

Ans. (a)

Q.9. Match the following with respect to journal entries for treatment of goodwill.

i.	Incoming partner brings his share of goodwill	A	No Entry
ii.	Incoming partner does not bring his share of goodwill	B	Premium for Goodwill A/c Dr.
			Incoming Partner's Capital A/c Dr.
			To Sacrificing Partners Capital A/c

iii.	Incoming partner pays his share of goodwill privately	C	Premium for Goodwill A/c Dr.
			To Sacrificing Partners Capital A/c
iv.	Incoming partner brings only a part of his share of goodwill	D	Incoming Partner's Capital A/c Dr.
			To Sacrificing Partners Capital A/c

(a) i- B, ii-C, iii-A, iv-D

(b) i- C, ii-D, iii-A, iv-B

(c) i- D, ii-C, iii-A, iv-B

(d) i- D, ii-C, iii-B, iv-A

Ans. (b)

Q.10. Gain / loss on revaluation at the time of change in profit sharing ratio of existing partners is shared by ___ (i)_______ whereas in case of admission of a partner it is shared by____(ii)_____.

(a) (i) Remaining Partners, (ii) All Partners.   (CBSE 2021)

(b) (i) All Partners, (ii) Old partners.

(c) (i) New Partner, (ii) All partner.

(d) (i) Sacrificing Partner, (ii) Incoming partner.

Ans. (b)

Q.11. At the time of admission of a partner, what will be the effect of the following information? Balance in Workmen compensation reserve ₹40,000. Claim for workmen compensation ₹45,000.   (CBSE 2021)

(a) ₹45,000 Debited to the Partner's capital Accounts.

(b) ₹40,000 Debited to Revaluation Account.

(c) ₹5,000 Debited to Revaluation Account.

(d) ₹5,000 Credited to Revaluation Account.

Ans. (c)

Q.12. Kalki and Kumud were partners sharing profits and losses in the ratio of 5 : 3. On 1st April,2021 they admitted Kaushtubh as a new partner and new ratio was decided as 3 : 2 : 1. Goodwill of the firm was valued as ₹3,60,000. Kaushtubh couldn't bring any amount for goodwill. Amount of goodwill share to be credited to Kalki and Kumud Account's will be: (CBSE 2021)

(a) ₹ 37,500 and ₹22,500 respectively

(b) ₹ 30,000 and ₹30,000 respectively

(c) ₹ 36,000 and ₹24,000 respectively

(d) ₹ 45,000 and ₹15,000 respectively

Ans. (d)

Q.13. Angle and Circle ware partners in a firm. Their Balance Sheet showed Furniture at ₹2,00,000; Stock at ₹1,40,000; Debtors at ₹1,62,000 and Creditors at ₹60,000. Square was admitted and new profit-sharing ratio was agreed at 2 : 3 : 5. Stock was revalued at ₹1,00,000, Creditors of ₹15,000 are not likely to be claimed, Debtors for ₹2,000 have become irrecoverable and Provision for doubtful debts to be provided @ 10%. Angle's share in loss on revaluation amounted to ₹30,000. Revalued value of Furniture will be: (CBSE 2021)

(a) ₹2,17,000   (b) ₹1,03,000   (c) ₹3,03,000   (d) ₹1,83,000

Ans. (d)

Q.14. Asha and Nisha are partner's sharing profits in the ratio of 2 : 1. Kashish was admitted for 1/4 share of which 1/8 was gifted by Asha. The remaining was contributed by Nisha. Goodwill of the firm is valued at ₹40,000. How much amount for goodwill will be credited to Nisha's Capital account?   **(CBSE 2021)**

(a) ₹2,500.   (b) ₹5,000.   (c) ₹20,000.   (d) ₹ 40,000.

Ans. (b)

Very Short Answer Type   [1 Mark]

Q.1. "A newly admitted partner cannot pay his share of the goodwill to the sacrificing partners privately". Is the statement True or False?

Ans. False

Q.2. Assertion (A): when reserve and accumulated profits / losses are adjusted through capital accounts, they appear in the balance sheet of new firm at the old figures.

Reason (R): If partner decided to record net effects of reserves, etc, a single adjusting entry involving the capital accounts of sacrificing and gaining partners is passed.

(a) Both Assertion and reason are true and reason is correct explanation of assertion.

(b) Assertion and reason both are true but reason is not the correct explanation of assertion.

(c) Assertion is false, reason is true.

(d) Assertion is true, reason is false.

Ans. (a)

Q.3. Assertion (A): In certain cases, the premium for goodwill paid by the incoming partner is not recorded in the books of accounts.

Reason (R): Sometime, the incoming partner pays his share of goodwill privately to the sacrificing partners, outside the business.

(a) Both Assertion and reason are true and reason is correct explanation of assertion.

(b) Assertion and reason both are true but reason is not the correct explanation of assertion.

(c) Assertion is false, reason is true.

(d) Assertion is true, reason is false.

Ans. (a)

Q.4. Under what circumstances will the premium for goodwill paid by the incoming partner not be recorded in the books of accounts.   **(CBSE 2014)**

Ans. When the incoming partner pays his share of goodwill privately to the sacrificing partners, outside the business, then no entry is passed in the books of the firm.

Q.5. State the need for treatment of goodwill on admission of a partner.   **(Delhi 2010)**

Ans. When a new partner is admitted, his share in future profits of the firm is equal to the sacrifice of profit by an existing partner or partners of the firm. The amount he pays to compensate this sacrifice, is in the form of goodwill. Therefore, it is important to treat goodwill at the time of admission of a partner.

Q.6. Why are assets and liabilities revalued at the time of admission of a partner?   **(CBSE2014)**

Ans. Assets and liabilities are revalued at the time of admission of a partner, so that profit or loss arising on account of revaluation, may be adjusted among old partners in their old profit sharing ratio, since it belongs to them.

Q.7. Profit available in the Balance sheet at the time of admission of a partner is to be credited to all partners' capitals in new profit sharing ratio." - Justify this argument.   **(CBSE-2010)**

Ans. The statement is wrong, because profit available in the balance sheet at the time of admission of a partner is credited only to old partners capital account in old ratio.

Q.8. At the time of reconstitution of the firm, the value of machinery is found less by 10%. What journal entry will be passed for giving effect to the above?   **(CBSE 2012)**

Ans. Revaluation a/c Dr.

To Machinery A/c

Q.9. Share of Goodwill brought in cash by the new partner is called   **(CBSE 2011)**

Ans. Premium / Goodwill / Premium for goodwill

Q.10. Biju and Lijo are partners in a firm sharing profits and losess in the ratio of 5 : 3. They admit Rajan for 1/6 share. The total goodwill of the firm is Rs. 50,000. Existing goodwill is Rs. 25,000. Find the share of goodwill to be brought in by Rajan.   **(CBSE 2013)**

Ans.   Goodwill to be brought in by Rajan $= \dfrac{50,000 \times 1}{6} = 8,333$

Short Answer Type - I   **[2 Marks]**

Q.1. P and Q share profits in the ratio of 7 : 3. R is admitted for 2/7th share in profits. Goodwill already appears in the balance sheet at Rs.1,00,000. Pass necessary journal entries if: **(CBSE 2014)**

     (a)   R cannot bring cash for his share of goodwill Rs.80,000.

     (b)   R brings in cash Rs.40,000 out of his share of goodwill Rs.80,000.

Ans. (a)   R's current A/c Dr. by Rs.80,000; P(Cr.) Rs.56,000 and Q(Cr.) Rs.24000

     (b)   (i)Bank A/c Dr. Rs.40,000; Premium for Goodwill A/c (Cr.) Rs.40,000

         (ii)Premium for Goodwill Dr. Rs.40,000; R's current A/c Dr. Rs.40,000; P(Cr.) Rs.56,000 and Q (Cr.) Rs.24,000.

Q.2. Hari, Ravi and Shri were partners in a firm sharing profits in the ratio of 3 : 2 : 1. They admitted Mihir as a new partner for 1/7th share in the profit. The new profit sharing ratio will be 2 : 2 : 2 : 1 respectively. Mihir brought Rs.3,00,000 for his Capital and Rs.45000 for his 1/7th share of goodwill. Pass necessary Journal entries in the books of the firm.

Ans. Premium for Goodwill Dr. 45000; Shri Dr. 37500; Hari Cr. 67500 and Ravi Cr. 15,000.

Q.3. A firm runs by Akhil, Nikhii and Mukil earns a net profit of Rs. 12,000/- per year. Normally the firms in same type of business earns at a rate of 10%. If the firm's total assets are of Rs. 1,50,000/- and external liabilities are for Rs. 50,000, what will be its value of Goodwill?   **(CBSE 20013)**

Ans. Value of goodwill = Total value of business – Net assets

Total value of business

Net Assets = Assets – Liabilities

$\qquad$ = 1,50,000 – 50,000 = 1,00,000

Goodwill = 1,20,000 -1,00,000 = 20,000

Q.4. Merin and Mallu are partners sharing profits in the ratio 3:2. They admit Dillan as a partner for 1/6th share and he brings Rs.40000 as his capital and could not bring any amount as goodwill. Even then the share of goodwill of Dillan is valued at Rs.10,000/-. **(CBSE 2010)**

Pass necessary entries regarding the above.

Ans. JOURNAL

Date	Particulars		LF	Debit	Credit
	Cash A/c	Dr.		40000	
	To Dillan's capital a/c	Dr.		10000	40000
	(Capital brought by Dillan)				
	Dillan's capital a/c				
	To Merin's capital				6000
	To Mallu's capital				4000
	(The share of goodwill which				
	cannot be brought in by new				
	partner				

Note: Since the ratio of the old partner's does not change, the sacrificing ratio is similar to old ratio ie. 3:2.

Dillan's share of goodwill = 10000

Merin's share of goodwill $= \dfrac{10000 \times 3}{5} = 6000$

Mallu's share of goodwill $= \dfrac{10000 \times 2}{5} = 4000$

Q.5. At the time of admission of a partner revaluation of assets and liabilities will always benefit old partners". Is this statement correct? Why? **(CBSE 2013)**

Ans. Yes, when a partner admitted, he acquires the ownership rights of the assets and also makes himself responsible for the firms liabilities. He should not get any benefit from any appreciation in the value of assets or reduction of liabilities nor should he suffer because of any fall or depreciation in the value of assets or -increase of liabilities as on the date of admission. The result of revaluation (May be either profit or loss. It should be credited or debited to Old Partners Capital Account in their old ratio. It must be clearly understood that result of revaluation does not concern the new partner, it always goes to old partners.

Q.6. A and B are partners with capitals of Rs. 26,000 and Rs. 22,000 respectively. They admit C as partner with 1/4th share in the profits of the firm. C's brings Rs 26, 000 as his share of capital. Give journal entry to record goodwill on C's admission. **(CBSE 2015)**

JOURNAL

Date	Particulars	L.F.	Debit (Rs.)	Credit (Rs.)
	Bank A/c Dr. To C's capital A/c (Being the amount of goodwill brought in by new partner)		26,000	26,000
	C's Capital A/c Dr. To A's Capital A/c To B's Capital A/c (Being the goodwill credited to sacrificing partners' capital a/cs in their sacrificing ratio i.e., equal)		7,500	3,750 3,750

Note :

(1) Calculation of C's share of goodwill :

Total capital of new firm no basis of C's capital i.e., $26{,}000 \times \dfrac{4}{1} = 1{,}04{,}000$

Total capital of A and B and C i.e., Rs. 26,000 + Rs. 22,000 + Rs. 26,000 = 74,000

Goodwill of the firm = total capital of new firm – combined capital = 1,04,000 – 74,000 = 30,000

Thus C's share of goodwill $= 30{,}000 \times \dfrac{1}{4} = 7{,}500$

(2) In the absence of information, profits will be shared equally.

Q.7. A and B are partners in a firm. They admit C as a partner with 1/5th share in the profits of the firm. C brings ₹ 4,00,000 as his share of capital. Calculate the value of C's share of Goodwill on the basis of his capital, given that the combined capital of A and B after all adjustments is ₹ 10,00,000.   **(CBSE Sample Paper 2019-20)**

Ans.

Total Capital as per C's Share (4,00,000 × (5/1))	20,00,000
Less Actual capital of A, B, C (10,00,000 + 4,00,000)	14,00,000
Value of firm's Goodwill	6,00,000

C's share of Goodwill = 6,00,000 × (1/5) = ₹1,20,000

Q.8. Atul and Neera were partners in a firm sharing profits in the ratio of 3 : 2. They admitted Mitali as a new partner. Goodwill of the firm was valued at ₹ 2,00,000. Mitali brings her share of goodwill premium of ₹20,000 in cash, which is entirely credited to Atul's Capital Accoum. Calculate the new profit sharing ratio.

(CBSE 2016)

Ans. Neera

3 : 2

Goodwill = ₹2,00,000

Mitali's share = 2,00,000 × x = 20,000

$$x = \frac{1}{10}$$

$$\text{Autal} = \frac{3}{5} - \frac{1}{10} = \frac{6-1}{10} = \frac{5}{10}$$

$$\text{Neera} = \frac{2}{5} = \frac{4}{10}$$

$$\text{Mitali} = \frac{1}{10}$$

Q.9. A and B were partners in a firm. They admitted C as anewpartnerf or 20% share in theprofits. Afterall adjustments regarding general reserve, goodwill, gain or loss on revaluation, the balances in capital accounts of A and B were ₹ 3,85,000 and ₹ 4,15,000 respectively. C brought proportionate capital so as to give him 20% share in the profits. Calculate the amount of capital to be brought by C.

(CBSE Sample paper 2016)

Ans. Combined capital of A and B = ₹3,85,000 + ₹4,15,000 = ₹8,00,000

$$\text{C's Share} = \frac{1}{5} \text{ th of total capital}$$

$$\text{Remaining share} = 1 - \frac{1}{5} = \frac{4}{5} = ₹8,00,000$$

$$\text{C's capital} = ₹8,00,000 \times \frac{5}{4} \times \frac{1}{5} = ₹2,00,000$$

Q.10. Tvisha and Divya were partners in a firm carrying on a tiffin service in Hyderabad. Divya noticed that a lot of food is left at the end of the day. To avoid wastage, she suggested that the same may be distributed among the needy. Tvisha wanted it to be mixed with the food to be served the next day.

Tvisha then gave a proposal that if her share in the profit is increased, she will not mind free distribution of left over food. Divya happily agreed. So, they decided to change their profit sharing ratio to 3 : 2 with immediate effect. On the date of change in the profit-sharing ratio, the goodwill of the firm was valued at Rs. 50,000. Pass the necessary adjustment entry for the treatment of goodwill. **(Compt. Delhi 2017)**

Ans.

<table>
<tr><td colspan="6" align="center">Books of the Tvisha and Divya
JOURNAL</td></tr>
<tr><td>Date</td><td>Particulars</td><td></td><td>L.F.</td><td>Dr. (₹)</td><td>Cr. (₹)</td></tr>
<tr><td>2016</td><td>Divya's Capital A/c</td><td>Dr.</td><td></td><td>5,000</td><td></td></tr>
<tr><td>Apr 1</td><td>   To Tvisha's Capital A/c</td><td></td><td></td><td></td><td>5,000</td></tr>
<tr><td></td><td>(Treatment of goodwill on changes in Profit sharing ratio)</td><td></td><td></td><td></td><td></td></tr>
</table>

Short Answer Type - II
[3 Marks]

Q.1. Why is new partner required to bring premium?

Ans. This is due to compensate the existing partners for loss of their Share in the Super Profits of the firm. When a person pays for Goodwill, he pays for sacrifice of the profits by old partners.

Q.2. Explain Treatment of Goodwill in case of Admission of a Partner.

(i) When Goodwill is Paid Privately No Entry

(ii) When goodwill is brought in cash or cheque by new partner and retained in the firm

    (a) Cash / Bank A/c Dr.

        To new partner' capital A/c

        To premium for goodwill A/c

      (Being capital and premium for goodwill brought in)

    (b) Premium for Goodwill A/c Dr.

        To Sacrificing Partners' Capital/ Current A/cs

      (Being premium for goodwill is distributed among sacrificing partners' in sacrificing ratio) Current A/c in case of Fixed capitals.

(iii) When Goodwill is brought in cash or cheque by new partner and Withdrawn by sacrificing partners

    Premium for Goodwill A/c Dr.

      To sacrificing Partners Capital / Current A/cs

    (Being premium for goodwill is distributed among sacrificing partners' in sacrificing ratio)

    Sacrificing Partners' Capital / Current A/Cs Dr.

      To Cash / Bank A/c

    (Being withdrawal of premium by the partners)

    Current A/C in case of Fixed capitals

Q.3. A and B share profits and losses in the ratio of 5 : 3. They admit C as a partner who pays Rs.54,000 as premium for goodwill for 1/5th share in the future profits of the firm. Pass journal entries for goodwill and calculate new profit sharing ratio in each of the following case-   **(CBSE 2014)**

(a) If he acquires his share of profits in the Original ratio of existing partner

(b) If he acquires his share of profits in equal proportions from the existing partners.

(c) If he acquires his share in the ratio of 3 : 1 from the existing partners.

(d) If he acquires his share of profits as 1/6th from A and 1/30th from B.

Ans. (a) Cr. A's Capital A/c by Rs.33750 and B's Capital A/c by Rs.20250

      NPSR = 5 : 3 : 2

(b) Cr. A's Capital A/c by Rs.27000 and B's Capital A/c by Rs.27000

      NPSR = 21 : 11 : 8

(c) Cr. A's Capital A/c by Rs.40500 and B's Capital A/c by Rs.13500

      NPSR = 19 : 13 : 8

(d) Cr. A's Capital A/c by Rs.45000 and B's Capital A/c by Rs.9000

      NPSR = 55 : 41 : 24

Q.4. Rahul and Anurag are partners sharing profits in the ratio of 3 : 2. They decided to admit Bajaj as a new partner and to share future profits and losses equally. Bajaj brings in Rs.50,000 as his capital. Goodwill of the firm is valued at Rs.60,000. Pass necessary Journal entries-

(a) When no goodwill appears in books.

(b) When goodwill appears at Rs.50,000.

(c) When goodwill appears at Rs.1,00,000 and goodwill is raised and written off.

Ans. (a) Bajaj (Dr.) Rs.20,000; Rahul (Cr.) Rs.16,000; Anurag (Cr.) Rs.4000

    (b) (i)   Bajaj (Dr.) Rs.20,000; Rahul (Cr.) Rs.16,000; Anurag (Cr.) Rs.4000

       (ii) Rahul (Dr.) Rs.30,000; Anurag (Dr.) Rs.20,000; Goodwill (Cr.) Rs.50,000

    (c) (i)   Rahul (Dr.) Rs.60,000; Anurag (Dr.) Rs.40,000; Goodwill (Cr.) Rs.1,00,000

       (ii) Goodwill (Dr.) Rs.60,000; Rahul (Cr.) Rs.36,000; Anurag (Cr.) Rs.24,000

       (iii) Rahul (Dr.) Rs.20,000; Anurag (Dr.) Rs.20,000; Bajaj (Dr.) Rs.20,000; Goodwill (Cr.) Rs.60,000

Q.5. P, Q and R were partners in a firm sharing profits in the ratio of 1 : 1 : 2. On 31st March, 2018, their balance sheet showed a credit balance of ₹9,000 in the profit and loss account and a Workmen Compensation Fund of ₹64,000. From 1st April, 2018 they decided to share profits in the ratio of 2 : 2 : 1. For this purpose it was agreed that:

(a) Goodwill of the firm was valued at ₹4,00,000.

(b) A claim on account of workmen compensation of ₹30,000 was admitted.

Pass necessary journal entries on reconstitution of the firm.   **(CBSE Delhi 2019)**

Ans.

JOURNAL

Date	Particular		L.F.	Dr. (₹)	Cr. (₹)
	Profit and Loss A/c	Dr.		9,000	
	To P's Capital A/c				2,250
	To Q's Capital A/c				2,250
	To R's Capital A/c				4,500
	(Being Profit and Loss Account credited to Partner's Capital Accounts)				
	Workmen's Compensation Reserve A/c	Dr.		64,000	
	To Workmen's Compensation Claim A/c				30,000
	To P's Capital A/c				8,500
	To Q's Capital A/c				8,500
	To R's Capital A/c				17,000
	(Being Workmen's Compensation Reserve adjusted for claim and the balance distributed among the partners)				
	P's Capital A/c	Dr.		60,000	
	Q's Capital A/c	Dr.		60,000	
	To R's Capital A/c				1,20,000
	(Being adjustment entry made for goodwill)				

Q.6. A man, Bobby and Chandani were partners in a firm sharing profits and losses in the ratio of 5 : 4 : 1. From 1st April, 2018 they decided to share profits equally. The revaluation of assets and re-assessment of liabilities resulted in a loss of ₹5,000. The goodwill of the firm on its reconstitution was valued at ₹ 1,20,000. The firm had a balance of ₹ 20,000 in General Reserve.   **(CBSE Delhi 2019)**

Ans. Showing your workings clearly pass necessary journal entries on the reconstitution of the firm

JOURNAL

Date	Particular		L.F.	Dr. (₹)	Cr. (₹)
	Aman's Capital A/c	Dr.		2,500	
	Bobby's Capital A/c	Dr.		2,000	
	Chandani's Capital A/c	Dr.		500	
	To Revaluation A/c				5,000
	(Being loss on revaluation debited to Partner's Capital Accounts)				
	Chandani's Capital A/c	Dr.		28,000	
	To Aman's Capital A/c				20,000
	To Bobby's Capital A/c				8,000
	(Being adjustment entry made for goodwill)				
	General Reserve A/c	Dr.		20,000	
	To Aman's Capital A/c				10,000
	To Bobby's Capital A/c				8,000
	To Chandani' Capital A/c				2,000
	(Being General Reserve distributed among the partners)				

Q.7. Amar and Akbar are equal partners in a firm. They admitted Anthony as a new partner and the new profit sharing ratio is 4 : 3 : 2. Anthony could not bring his share of goodwill ₹ 45,000 in cash. It is decided to do adjustment for goodwill without opening goodwill account. Pass the necessary journal entry for the treatment of goodwill.   **(CBSE 2015)**

Ans. Old ratio of old partners: Amar and Akbar =1 : 1

New ratio of all partners: Amar, Akbar and Anthony = 4 : 3 : 2

Old ratio of old partners: Amar and Akbar = 1 : 1

New ratio of all partners: Amar, Akbar and Anthony = 4 : 3 : 2

Sacrificing shares = Old shares – New shares

$$\text{Amar's sacrifice} = \frac{1}{2} - \frac{4}{9} = \frac{9-8}{18} = \frac{1}{18}$$

$$\text{Akbar's sacrifice} = \frac{1}{2} - \frac{3}{9} = \frac{9-6}{18} = \frac{3}{18}$$

$$\text{Sacrificing ratio} = \frac{1}{18} : \frac{3}{18} = 1 : 3$$

JOURNAL

Date	Particular		L.F.	Dr. (₹)	Cr. (₹)
	Anthony's Capital / Current A/c	Dr.		45,000	
	To Amar's Capital A/c				11,250
	To Akbar's Capital A/c				33,750
	(Being amount of goodwill adjusted from Anthony to Amar and Akbar in the sacrificing ratio 1 : 3				

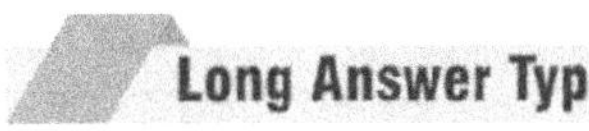 **Long Answer Type** [5 Marks]

Q.1. Aakash, Amber are partners. Their Profit ratio is 3:2. Gagan joins the partnership for ¼ th share in Profit (of which he acquires 2/3 from Aakash and 1/3 from Amber). Gagan brings in Rs.6,00,000 for Capital and Rs.2,40,000 for goodwill. ½ of the goodwill is withdrawn by old partners. Pass necessary Journal entries.

(CBSE 2013)

Ans.

JOURNAL

Date	Particulars		L.F.	DR. (Rs.)	Cr. (Rs.)
(i)	Bank A/c	Dr.		8,40,000	
	To Gagan's Capital A/c				6,40,000
	To Premium for Goodwill A/c				2,40,000
	(Being amount of capital and goodwill brought by Gagan in cash)				
(ii)	Premium for Goodwill A/c	Dr.		2,40,000	
	To Aakash's Capital A/c				1,60,000
	To Amber's Capital A/c				80,000
	(Being goodwill credited to old partners in sacrificing ratio 2:1)				
(iii)	Aakash's Capital A/c	Dr.		80,000	
	Amber's Capital A/c	Dr.		40,000	
	To Bank A/c				1,20,000
	(Being 1/2 of goodwill withdraw by cash)				

Q.2. Akhil and Nikhil are partners in a firm sharing profits in the ratio of 5 : 3. On April 01,2022 they admitted. Sahil as a new partner. The new profit sharing ratio will be 4 :3 : 2. Sahil brought in Rs.1,00,000 in cash as his share of capital. The Firm's goodwill on Sahil's admission was valued At Rs.1,80,000. At the time of Sahil's admission goodwill existed in books of the firm at Rs.2,40,000 Pass necessary journal entries in the books of the firm on Sahil's admission.

Ans.

JOURNAL

Date	Particulars		L.F.	DR. (Rs.)	Cr. (Rs.)
(i)	Akhil's Capital A/c	Dr.		1,50,000	
	Nikhil's Capital A/c	Dr.		90,000	
	To Goodwill A/c				2,40,000
	(Being existing goodwill written off in old profit ratio 5:3)				
(ii)	Bank A/c	Dr.		1,00,000	
	To Sahil's Capital A/c				1,00,000
	(Being amount of goodwill brought in by Sahil for his share)				

(iii)	Sahil's Current A/c (1,80,000 x 2/9)	Dr.		40,000	
	To Akhil's Capital A/c (13)				32,500
	To Nikhil's Capital A/c (13)				7,500
	(Being share of Sahil's goodwill adjusted in sacrificing ratio)				

Working Note: Calculation of Sacrificing Ratio

Sacrificing Ratio = Old Ratio – New Ratio

$$\text{Akhil} = \frac{5}{8} - \frac{4}{9} = \frac{45-30}{72} = \frac{13}{72}$$

$$\text{Nikhil} = \frac{3}{8} - \frac{3}{9} = \frac{27-24}{72} = \frac{3}{72}$$

Sacrificing Ratio = 13 : 3

Q.3. Aditya and Bhaskar were partners in the ratio of $7:5$ .Chanradra was admitted for 1/6 the share. New ratio was decided as 13 : 7: 4 respectively. Chandra brings Rs.2,00,000 as his share of capital but was not able any cash for his share of goodwill. The firm's goodwill was valued Rs.1,92,000. At the time of Chandra's admission. Pass necessary Journal Entries   **(CBSE 2016)**

Ans.   **JOURNAL**

Date	Particulars		L.F.	Dr. (Rs.)	Cr. (Rs.)
(i)	Bank A/c	Dr.		2,00,000	
	To Chandra's Capital A/c				2,00,000
	(Being amount of capital brought in by Chandra for his share)				
(ii)	Chandra's Current A/c	Dr.		32,000	
	To Aditya's Capital A/c (1)				8,000
	To Bhaskar's Capital A/c (3)				24,000
	(Being share of goodwill of Chandra adjusted in sacrificing ratio) (1,92,000/6 = 32,000)				

Working Note: Calculation of Sacrificing Ratio

Sacrificing Ratio = Old Ratio – New Ratio

$$\text{Aditya:} \qquad \frac{7}{12} - \frac{13}{24} = \frac{14-13}{24} = \frac{1}{24} \text{ Sacrifice}$$

$$\text{Bhaskar:} \qquad \frac{5}{12} - \frac{7}{24} = \frac{10-7}{24} = \frac{3}{24} \text{ Sacrifice}$$

Q.4. A, B and C were partners in a firm sharing profits in the ratio of 3 : 2 : 1. D was admitted into the firm with 1/4th share in profit, which he got 3/16th from A and 1/16th from B. The total capital of the firm as agreed upon was ₹ 1,20,000 and D brought in cash equivalent to 1/4th of this amount as his capital. The capital of other partners also had to be adjusted in the ratio of their respective share in profits by bringing in or paying cash. The capitals of A, B and C after all adjustments related to revaluation of assets and reassessment of liabilities were ₹ 40,000; ₹ 35,000 and ₹ 30,000 respectively.

Calculate the new capitals of A, B and C and record the necessary journal entries for the above transactions.

(CBSE 2015)

Ans.

JOURNAL

Date	Particulars		Dr. (₹)	Cr. (₹)
	Cash/Bank A/c	Dr.	30,000	–
	To D's Capital A/c			30,000
	(Being Cash brought in by D as his capital)			
	A's Capital A/c	Dr.	2,500	–
	B's Capital A/c	Dr.	2,500	–
	C's Capital A/c	Dr.	10,000	–
	To Cash/Bank A/c		–	15,000
	(Being cash withdrawn by partners to adjust the capital in the new ratio)			

Calculation of new profit sharing ratio

$$A = \frac{3}{6} - \frac{3}{6} = \frac{3}{16}$$

$$B = \frac{2}{6} - \frac{1}{6} = \frac{13}{48}$$

$$C = \frac{1}{6}$$

$$D = \frac{1}{4}$$

New ratio = 15 : 13 : 8 : 12

So , new capitals of A, B, C are:

$$A = ₹1,20,000 \times \frac{15}{48} = ₹37,500$$

$$B = ₹1,20,000 \times \frac{13}{48} = ₹32,500$$

$$C = ₹1,20,000 \times \frac{1}{6} = ₹20,000$$

$$D = ₹1,20,000 \times \frac{1}{4} = ₹30,000$$

Calculation of cash brought in or paid off

	A (₹)	B (₹)	C (₹)
Existing capitals	40,000	35,000	30,000
Adjusted capitals	37,500	32,500	20,000
Cash withdrawn	2,500	2,500	10,000

TOPIC 3 Revaluation Account, Partner's Capital Accounts, Balance Sheet on Admission of A Partner

Summary

Understanding Revaluation Account

It is an account which is used to record change in value of assets and liabilities. Following are the items which are to be recorded in the Revaluation Account:

    i.   Credited to Revaluation Account:

- Increase in assets,
- Unrecorded assets,
- Decrease in liabilities,
- Writing back excess provision.

    ii.   Debited to Revaluation Account:

- Decrease in assets,
- Increase in liabilities,
- Unrecorded liabilities,
- Liabilities provided.

    iii.   Any gain or loss from the revaluation of assets and liabilities is to be distributed among the partners in their old profit sharing ratio and is adjusted in their Capital or Current Accounts.

    iv.   Assets and liabilities revalued are to be shown in the books of firm at the revalued figures only.

Accounting Treatment when revised values of assets and liabilities are not to be recorded: In such case, the partners may decide that the value of assets and liabilities will continue to appear in the books at their existing values and therefore, any increase or decrease in the value of assets and liabilities is recorded in the Memorandum Revaluation Account.

Dr.		REVALUATION ACCOUNT	Cr.
Particulars	**Amt. (Rs.)**	**Particulars**	**Amt. (Rs.)**
Decrease in value of Assets	xx	Increase in value of Assets	xx
Increase in value of Liabilities	xx	Decrease in value of Liabilities	xx
Unrecorded Liability	xx	Unrecorded Assets	xx
Payment of Liability [Cash A/c]	xx	Sale of Unrecorded Assets [Bank A/c]	xx

Profit tr. Of Capital A/c of old partners		Loss tr. To Capital A/c of old partners	
[Old Ratio]	xx	[Old Ratio]	xx
	xxx		xxx

Adjustment of Capitals

1. When the new partner brings in proportionate capital OR On the basis of the old partner's capital.

    (a) Calculate the adjusted capital of old partners (after all adjustments)

    (b) Total capital of the firm

    = Combined Adjusted Capital × Reciprocal proportion of the share of old partners

    (c) New Partner's Capital

    = Total Capital × Proportion of share of a new partner.

2. On the basis of the new partner's capital:

    (a) Total Capital of the firm = New Partner's Capital × Reciprocal proportion of his share.

    (b) Distribute Total Capital in New Profit Sharing Ratio.

    (c) Calculate adjusted capital of old partners.

    (d) Calculate the difference between New Capital and Adjusted Capital.

1. If the debit side of the Capital Account is bigger then it means he has excess capital

    Partner's (capital Accounts Dr.

    To Cash A /c or Bank A/c or Current A/c

2. If the credit side is bigger then it means that he has short capital

    Cash A/c or Bank A/c or Current A/c Dr.

    To Partner's Capital A/cs

Multiple Choice Questions
[1 Mark]

Q.1. A and B are partners sharing profit and losses in ratio of 5 : 3. C is admitted for 1/4th share. On the date of reconstitution, the debtors stood at Rs.40,000, bill receivable stood at Rs.10,000 and the provision for doubtful debts appeared at Rs.4000. A bill receivable, of Rs.10,000 which was discounted from the bank, earlier has been reported to be dishonored. The firm has sold, the debtor so arising to a debt collection agency at a loss of 40%. If bad debts now have arisen for Rs, 6,000 and firm decides to maintain provisions at same rate as before then amount of Provision to be debited to Revaluation Account would be:

(a) Rs.4,400   (b) Rs.4,000   (c) Rs.3,400   (d) None of the above

Ans. (c)

Q.2. A, and B are partners sharing profits in the ratio of 2 : 3. Their balance sheet shows machinery at Rs.2,00,000; stock Rs.80,000, and debtors at Rs.1,60,000. C is admitted and the new profit sharing ratio is 6 : 9 : 5. Machinery is revalued at Rs.1,40,000 and a provision is made for doubtful debts @5%. A's share in loss on revaluation amount to Rs.20,000. Revalued value of stock will be:

(a) Rs.62,000   (b) Rs.1,00,000   (c) Rs.60,000   (d) Rs.98,000

Ans. (c)

Q.3. If at the time of admission if there is some unrecorded liability, it will be -------------to ------------- Account.

    (a) Debited, Revaluation   (b) Credited, Revaluation

    (c) Debited, Goodwill   (d) Credited, Partners' Capital

Ans. (a)

Q.4. Aryaman and Bholu are partners sharing profit and losses in ratio of 5 : 3. Chirag is admitted for 1/4th share. On the date of reconstitution, the debtors stood at Rs 40,000, bill receivable stood at Rs. 10,000 and the provision for doubtful debts appeared at Rs. 4000. A bill receivable, of Rs 10,000 which was discounted from the bank, earlier has been reported to be dishonored. The firm has sold, the debtor so arising to a debt collection agency at a loss of 40%. If bad debts now have arisen for Rs 6,000 and firm decides to maintain provisions at same rate as before then amount of Provision to be debited to Revaluation Account would be:

    (a) Rs.4,400   (b) Rs.4,000

    (c) Rs.3,400   (d) None of the above

Ans. (c)

Q.5. Revaluation Account is a ------------ Account.

    (a) Real   (b) Nominal

    (c) Personal   (d) Liability

Ans. (b)

Very Short Answer Type   **[1 Mark]**

Q.1. Assertion (A): At the time of reconstitution of firm, assets are revalued and liabilities are reassessed.

Reason (R): the changed in the value of assets and liabilities belongs to the period prior to reconstitution And any gain or loss on revaluation is shared in the old ratio by the partners.

    (a) Both Assertion and reason are true and reason is correct explanation of assertion.

    (b) Assertion and reason both are true but reason is not the correct explanation of assertion.

    (c) Assertion is false, reason is true.

    (d) Assertion is true, reason is false.

Ans. (a)

Q.2. Assertion (A): If the amount of any liability is understated, then revaluation account will be debited to restore the liabilities' s amount to its actual value.

Reason (R): Increase in the amount of liabilities is a profit for the firm.   (CBSE 2021)

    (a) Both Assertion and reason are true and reason is correct explanation of assertion.

    (b) Assertion and reason both are true but reason is not the correct explanation of assertion.

    (c) Assertion is false, reason is true.

    (d) Assertion is true, reason is false.

Ans. (d)

Q.3. Assertion (A): The balance of memorandum revaluation account (second part) is transferred to partners capital account in told profit sharing ratio.

Reason (R): Sometimes, partner decide to show the assets and liabilities in the books of the new firm at their existing values.

(a) Both Assertion and reason are true and reason is correct explanation of assertion.

(b) Assertion and reason both are true but reason is not the correct explanation of assertion.

(c) Assertion is false, reason is true.

(d) Assertion is true, reason is false.

Ans. (c)

Q.4. State a reason for the preparation of 'Revaluation Account' at time of admission of a partner.   **(CBSE 2015)**

Ans. To record the effect of revaluation of assets and liabilities.

Short Answer Type - I   [2 Marks]

Q.1. In the event of admission whether the incoming partner is entitled to the profit on revaluation of assets effected as on the data of admission. Offer your comments.   **(CBSE 2011)**

Ans. No. The profit or loss on revaluation should be . transformed to old partners capital account in old profit sharing ratio.

Q.2. A and B are partners in a firm. They admit C as a partner with l/5th share in the profits of the firm. C brings ₹ 4,00,000 as his share of capital. Calculate the value of C's share of Goodwill on the basis of his capital, given that the combined capital of A and B after all adjustments is ₹ 10,00,000.   **(CBSE Sample Paper 2019-20)**

Ans.

Total Capital as per C's Share (4,00,000 × (5/1))	20,00,000
Less Actual capital of A, B, C (10,00,000 + 4,00,000)	14,00,000
Value of firm's Goodwill	6,00,000

C's share of Goodwill = 6,00,000 × (1/5) = ₹ 1,20,000

Q.3. A and B are partners in a firm sharing profits and losses in the ratio of 3 : 2. On 1st April, 2019 they decided to admit C their new ratio is decided to be equal. Pass the necessary journal entry to distribute Investment Fluctuation Reserve of ₹ 60,000 at the time of C's admission, when Investment appear in the books at ₹ 2,10,000 and its market value is ₹1,90,000.   **(CBSE 2017)**

Ans.

JOURNAL

Date	Particulars		L.F.	Dr. (₹)	Cr. (₹)
2019 April, 1	Investment Fluctuation Reserve A/c	Dr.		60,000	
	To Investment A/c				20,000
	To A's capital A/c				24,000
	To B's Capital A/c				16,000
	(Being the transfer of excess Investment)				
	Fluctuation reserve to partner's capital account in old profit sharing ratio				

Q.4. X, Y and Z are partners in a firm sharing profits and losses in 2 : 2 : 1 ratio. On April 1, 2013, they admitted A as a partner for 1/5th share in profits. On that date, the firm has general reserve of ₹ 35,000, Workmen Compensation Fund of ₹ 20,000, Investments Fluctuation Fund of ₹ 15,000 and accumulated losses of ₹ 10,000. The partners decided to transfer reserves and accumulated losses in their Current Accounts. Pass necessary adjustment entry. (CBSE 2013)

Ans.

JOURNAL

Date	Particulars		L.F.	Dr. (₹)	Cr. (₹)
2013 April, 1	General Reserve A/c	Dr.		35,000	
	Workmen Compensation Fund A/c	Dr.		20,000	
	Investment Fluctuation Fund A/c	Dr.		15,000	
	To X's Current A/c				28,000
	To Y's Current A/c				28,000
	To Z's Current A/c				14,000
	(Being undistributed profit transferred to partners capital in ratio 2 : 2 : 1)				
April, 1	X's Current A/c	Dr.		4,000	
	Y's Current A/c	Dr.		4,000	
	Z's Current A/c	Dr.		2,000	
	To Accumulated Losses A/c				10,000
	(Being accumulated loss transferred to partners capital in ratio 2 : 2 : 1)				

Q.5. John, Brown and Smith are partners in a firm sharing profit and losses in 3 : 2 : 1 ratio. On April 1, 2012, they changed their profit sharing ratio as 4 : 3 : 2. On that date, the firm has general reserve of ₹ 50,000 and accumulated profits of ₹ 40,000. The partners decided to show reserves and accumulated profits in the existing manner. Pass necessary adjustment entry and show your working. (CBSE 2012)

Ans. Sacrificing Ratio = Old Ratio – New Ratio

$$\text{John} = \frac{3}{6} - \frac{4}{9} = \frac{9-8}{18} = \frac{1}{18} \text{ Sacrificer}$$

$$\text{Brown} = \frac{2}{6} - \frac{3}{9} = \frac{6-6}{18} = \frac{0}{18} \text{ No effect}$$

$$\text{Smith} = \frac{1}{6} - \frac{2}{9} = \frac{3-4}{18} = \frac{-1}{18} \text{ Gainer}$$

The Total Transferable Amount to Partner's Capital = (₹ 50,000 + ₹ 40,000) × $\dfrac{1}{18}$

$$= ₹\ 90,000 \times \frac{1}{18} = ₹\ 5,000$$

JOURNAL ENTRY

S.No.	Particulars		L.F.	Dr. (₹)	Cr. (₹)
1	Smith's Capital A/c	Dr.		5,000	
	To John's Capital A/c				5,000
	(Being adjustment made in sacrificing-gaining manner, so no interfare in existing value)				

Q.6. General Reserve of ₹ 24,000 and Profit and Loss Account (Debit Balance) of ₹ 6,000 appearing in the balance sheet of partner's P and Q on the admission of R is to be adjusted. Give the journal entries assuming that P and Q are equal partners. **(CBSE 2014)**

Ans. (i) General reserve a/c Dr 24,000

   P's capital a/c Q's capital a/

(ii) P's capital a/c Dr 3000

   Q's capital a/c Dr 3000

   To P/L A/C

Short Answer Type - II   [3 Marks]

Q.1. Prepare a revaluation account from the following: **(CBSE 2010)**

Assets:

Plant and Machinery – 10000

Furniture – 3000

Patents – 7000

Stock – 3000

Liabilities: Creditors – 15000

The above items were revalued as follows:

(a) Fixed assets revalued at 10% less.

(b) Stock damaged wholly by a fire occurred and become valueless.

(c) Claims received against the loss of value of stock Rs.2000.

(d) Repair bill of Rs.1000 is not in the books of accounts remain unpaid.

Ans. Revaluation a/c

Dr.   **Cr.**

Particulars	Amount	Particulars	Amount
To Plant & Machinery	1000	By Loss transferred to capital a/c	
To Furniture	300		
To Patents	700		4000
To Stock (3000–2000)	1000		
To Repair bill	1000		
	4000		**4000**

Q.2. A, B and C were partners in a firm sharing profits in the ratio of 3 : 2 : 1. D was admitted into the firm with 1/4th share in profit, which he got 3/16th from A and 1/16th from B. The total capital of the firm as agreed upon was ₹ 1,20,000 and D brought in cash equivalent to 1/4th of this amount as his capital. The capital of other partners also had to be adjusted in the ratio of their respective share in profits by bringing in or paying cash. The capitals of A, B and C after all adjustments related to revaluation of assets and reassessment of liabilities were ₹ 40,000; ₹ 35,000 and ₹ 30,000 respectively.

Calculate the new capitals of A, B and C and record the necessary journal entries for the above transactions.

(CBSE 2016)

Ans.

JOURNAL

Date	Particulars		Dr. (₹)	Cr. (₹)
	Cash/Bank A/c	Dr.	30,000	–
	To D's Capital A/c		–	30,000
	(Being Cash brought in by D as his capital)			
	A's Capital A/c	Dr.	2,500	–
	B's Capital A/c	Dr.	2,500	–
	C's Capital A/c	Dr.	10,000	–
	To Cash/Bank A/c		–	15,000
	(Being cash withdrawn by partners to adjust the capitals in the new ratio)			

Calculation of new profit shareing ratio

$$A = \frac{3}{6} - \frac{3}{16} = \frac{15}{48}$$

$$B = \frac{2}{6} - \frac{1}{6} = \frac{13}{48}$$

$$C = \frac{1}{6}$$

$$D = \frac{1}{4}$$

New ratio = 15 : 13 : 8 : 12

So, new capitals of A, B, C are:

$$A = ₹1,20,000 \times \frac{15}{48} = ₹ \, 37,500$$

$$B = ₹1,20,000 \times \frac{13}{48} = ₹ \, 32,500$$

$$C = ₹1,20,000 \times \frac{1}{6} = ₹ \, 20,000$$

$$D = ₹1,20,000 \times \frac{1}{4} = ₹ \, 30,000$$

Calculation of cash brought in or paid off

	A (₹)	B(₹)	C(₹)
Existing capitals	40,000	35,000	30,000
Adjusted capitals	37,500	32,500	20,000
Cash withdrawn	2,500	2,500	10,000

Q.3. Anita, Geeta, Sunita and Lata were partners in a firm. They admitted Kavita as a new partner for 1/5th share in the profits. Kavita acquired her share equally from Anita, Geeta, Sunita and Lata. The total capital of the new firm was agreed at ₹ 4,00,000. Kavita brought cash equal to 1/5th of the total capital as her capital and the capital of Anita, Geeta, Sunita and Lata were to be adjusted according to the new profit sharing ratio. For this necessary cash was to be brought by or paid to Anita, Geeta, Sunita and Lata as the case may be. After doing necessary adjustments related to revaluation of assets and reassessment of liabilities the balances in the capital accounts of Anita, Geeta, Sunita and Lata were Anita ₹ 80,000; Geeta ₹ 85,000; Sunita ₹ 75,000 and Lata ₹ 80,000.

Calculate the new capitals of Anita, Geeta, Sunita and Lata and pass necessary journal entries for the above transactions in the books of the firm.

Ans.

JOURNAL

Date	Particulars		Dr. (₹)	Cr. (₹)
	Cash Bank A/c	Dr.	80,000	
	To Kavita's capital A/c			80,000
	(Being cash brought in by Kavita)			
	Cash Bank A/c	Dr.	5,000	
	To Sunita's capital A/c			5,000
	(Being cash brought in by Sunita)			
	Geeta's Capital A/c	Dr.	5,000	5,000
	To Cash/Bank A/c			
	(Being cash withdrawn by Geeta)			

Calculation of cash brought in or paid off

	Anita (₹)	Geeta (₹)	Sunita (₹)	Lata (₹)
Existing capitals	80,000	85,000	75,000	80,000
Adjusted capitals	80,000	85,000	80,000	80,000
Cash withdrawn/brought in	–	-5,000	5,000	–

Q.4. Ashoo and Rahul are partners sharing profits in the ratio of 5 : 3. Gaurav was admitted for 1/5 share and was asked to contribute proportionate capital and ₹ 4,000 for premium (goodwill). The capitals of Ashoo and Rahul, after all adjustments relating to revaluation, goodwill etc., worked out to be ₹ 45,000 and ₹ 35,000 respectively.

Calculate new profit sharing ratio, capital to be brought in by Gaurav and record necessary journal entries for the same.

Ans.

JOURNAL

Date	Particulars		L.F.	Dr. (₹)	Cr. (₹)
	Cash A/c	Dr.		24,000	
	To Gaurav's Capital A/c				20,000
	To Premium A/c				4,000
	(Being capital and goodwill brought in by Gaurav in Cash				
	Premium A/c	Dr.		4,000	
	To Ashoo's Capital A/c				2,400
	To Rahul's Capital A/c				1,600
	(Being amount of goodwill distributed among old partners in sacrificing ratio 3 : 2)				

(1) Working Note: Capital to be brought in by Gaurav:

New Capital of the Firm = Combined Adjusted Capital of Old Partners × Reciprocal Proportion of Share of Old partners

$$= (45,000 + 35,000) \times \frac{5}{4}$$

$$= 80,000 \times \frac{5}{4} = ₹1,00,000$$

Gaurav's Capital = Capital of the Firm × Proportion of Share of Gaurav

$$= 1,00,000 \times \frac{1}{5} = ₹20,000$$

Q.5. Bhavya and Sakshi are partners in a firm, sharing profits and losses in the ratio of 3 : 2. On 31 st March, 2018 their Balance Sheet was as under:

BALANCE SHEET OF BHAVYA AND SAKSHI

As at 31st March, 2018

Liabilities	Amount (₹)	Assets	Amount (₹)
Sundry Creditors	13,800	Furniture	16,000
General Reserve	23,400	Land and Building	56,000
Investment Fluctuation Fund	20,000	Investments	30,000
Bhavya's Capital	50,000	Trade Receivables	18,500
Sakshi's Capital	40,000	Cash in Hand	26,700
	1,47,200		1,47,200

The partners have decided to change their profit sharing ratio to 1 : 1 with immediate effect. For the purpose, they decided that:

- Investments to be valued at 20.000

- Goodwill of the firm valued at 24,000

- General Reserve not to be distributed between the partners.

You are required to pass necessary journal entries in the books of the firm. Show workings.

(CBSE Sample Paper 2018-19)

Ans.

JOURNAL

Date	Particulars		L.F	Amount (₹)	Amount (₹)
31.3.18	Invest Fluctuation Fund A/c	Dr.		20,000	
	To Investment A/c				10,000
	To Bhavya's Capital A/c				6,000
	To Sakshi's Capital A/c				4,000
	(Being Investment Fluctuation Fund adjusted against the Fluctuations in market Value and balance was distributed amongst partners)				
31.3.18	Sakshi's Capital A/c			2,400	
	To Bhavya's Capital A/c				2,400
	(Being adjustment of goodwill made between partners due to change in profit sharing ratio between partners)				
31.3.18	Sakshi's Capital A/c			2,340	
	To Bhavya's Capital A/c				2,340
	(Being General Reserve adjusted among the partners without writing it off)				

Q.6. A and B are partners in a firm having 2 : 1 profit sharing ratio. On April 1, 2013, they agreed to share profits and losses equally. On this date, they decided to revalue assets as follows:

	Book Value (₹)	Revised Value (₹)
Land and Building	4,00,000	5,50,000
Machinery	2,00,000	2,20,000
Furniture	50,000	40,000
Debtors	60,000	55,000

Partners also decided to record net effect of the revaluation of assets and reassessment of liabilities without affecting their book value by passing a single adjustment entry. Pass the adjustment entry.   **(CBSE 2014)**

Ans.

S.No.	Particulars		L.F.	Dr. (₹)	Cr. (₹)
1	B's Capital A/c	Dr.		25,833	
	To A's Capital A/c				25,833
	(Adjustment made for revaluation without effecting the Market Value)				

Working Note:

$$₹1,55,000 \times \frac{1}{6} = ₹\ 25,833$$

Sacrificing Ratio = Old Ratio – New Ratio

$$A = \frac{2}{3} - \frac{1}{2} = \frac{4-3}{6} = \frac{1}{6} \text{ Sacrificer}$$

$$B = \frac{1}{3} - \frac{1}{2} = \frac{2-3}{6} = \frac{-1}{6} \text{ Gainer}$$

	₹
Increase in value of Land and Building	+ 1,50,000
Increase in value of Machinery	+ 20,000
Decrease in value of Furniture	−10,000
Decrease in value of Debtors	−5,000
Net Effect:	1,55,000 (Profit)

Long Answer Type [5 Marks]

Q.1. A and B share the profits of a business in the ratio of 5 : 3. They admit C, into the firm for 1/4th share in the profits to be contributed equally by A and B. On the date of admission of C, the Balance Sheet of the firm was as follows:

Ans.

Liabilities	Rs.	Assets	Rs.
A's Capital	40,000	Machinery	30,000
B's Capital	30,000	Furniture	20,000
Workmen's Compensation Reserve	4,000	Stock	15,000
Creditors	2,000	Debtors	15,000
Provident Fund	10,000	Bank	6,000
	86,000		**86,000**

Term of C's admission were as follows:

(i) C will bring Rs.30,000 for his share of capital and goodwill.

(ii) Goodwill of the firm has been valued at 3 year's purchase of the average super profits of last four years. Average profits of the last four years are Rs.20,000 while the normal profits that can be earned with the capital employed are Rs.12,000.

(iii) Furniture is undervalued by Rs.12,000 and the value of stock is reduced to Rs.13,000. Provident Fund be raised by Rs.1,000.

(iv) Creditors are unrecorded to the extent of Rs.6,000.

Prepare Revaluation Account, Partner's Capital Accounts and the new Balance Sheet of A, B and C.

Ans.

Dr.   **REVALUATION A/C**   Cr.

Particulars		Rs.	Particulars	Rs.
To Stock A/c		2,000	By Furniture A/c	12,000
To Provident Fund A/c		1,000		
To Creditors		6,000		
To Profit transferred to				
A's Capital A/c	1,875			
B's Capital A/c	1,125	3,000		
		12,000		**12,000**

Calculation of Goodwill:

$$\text{Super Profits} = \text{Average Profits} - \text{Normal Profits}$$

$$= \text{Rs.20,000} - \text{Rs.12,000} = \text{Rs.8,000}$$

$$\text{Goodwill} = \text{Super Profit x No. of years purchased}$$

$$= \text{Rs.8,000} \times 3 = \text{Rs.24,000}$$

C brings in his share of goodwill in cash. Therefore, he brings in Rs.24,000 × ¼ = Rs.6,000 for goodwill which is included in the total amount of Rs.30,000 brought by him. This amount of Rs.6,000 will be divided between A and B equally, because they have sacrificed in equal proportions.

Dr.   **CAPITAL ACCOUNTS**   **Cr.**

Particulars	A	B	C	Particulars	A	B	C
	Rs.	Rs.	Rs.		Rs.	Rs.	Rs.
To Balance				By Balance b/d	40,000	30,000	
c/d	47,375	35,625	24,000	By workmen's			
				compensation			
				reserve	2,500	1,500[1]	
				By Revaluation			
				A/c	1,875	1,125	
				By Bank A/c			24,000
				By Premium for			
				Goodwill A/c	3,000	3,000	
	47,375	35,625	24,000		47,375	35,625	24,000

Note 1.Since there is no specific liability related to Workmen's Compensation Reserve it is divided in old partners in their old profit sharing ratios.

OPENING BALANCE SHEET

Liabilities	Rs.	Assets	Rs.
Creditors	8,000	Machinery	30,000
Provident Fund	11,000	Furniture	32,000
Capital Accounts:		Stock	13,000
A	47,375	Debtors	15,000
B	35,625	Bank	36,000
C	24,000		
	1,26,000		1,26,000

Q.2. Sunaina and Tamanna are partners in a firm sharing profits and losses in the ratio of 3 : 2. Their Balance Sheet as at 31st March, 2020 stood as follows:

BALANCE SHEET

Liabilities		Rs.	Assets		Rs.
Capital Accounts:			Plant & Machinery		1,20,000
Sunaina	60,000		Land and Building		1,40,000
Tamanna	80,000	1,40,000	Debtors	1,90,000	
Current Accounts:			Less: Provision for		
Sunaina	10,000		Doubtful Debts	40,000	1,50,000
Tamanna	30,000	40,000	Stock		40,000
General Reserve		1,20,000	Cash		30,000
Workmen's			Goodwill		20,000
Compensation Reserve		50,000			
Creditors		1,50,000			
		5,00,000			5,00,000

They agreed to admit Pranav into partnership for 1/5th share of profits on 1st April, 2020, on the following terms:

(i) All Debtors are good.

(ii) Value of land and building to be increased to Rs.1,80,000.

(iii) Value of plant and machinery to be reduced by Rs.20,000.

(iv) the liability against Workmen's Compensation Reserve is determined at Rs.20,000 which is to be paid later in the year.

(v) Mr. Anil, to whom Rs.40,000 were payable (already included in above creditors), drew a bill of exchange for 3 months which was duly accepted.

(vi) Pranav to bring in capital of Rs.1,00,000 and Rs.10,000 as premium for goodwill in cash.

Ans.

JOURNAL

Date	Particulars		L.F.	Dr. (Rs.)	Cr. (Rs.)
2020					
April	Land and Building A/c	Dr.		40,000	
1	Provision for Doubtful Debts A/c	Dr.		40,000	
	To Revaluation A/c				80,000
	(Land and Building revalued and provision for doubtful debts written back)				
April	Revaluation A/c	Dr.		20,000	
1	To Plant and Machinery A/c				20,000
	(Plant and Machinery revalued)				
April	Revaluation A/c	Dr.		60,000	
1	To Sunaina's Current A/c				36,000
	To Tamanna's Current A/c				24,000
	(Profit on revaluation credited to partners current accounts)				

April	Creditors A/c		Dr.	40,000	
1	To Bills Payable A/c				40,000
	(Bills accepted in favour of Mr. Anil)				
April	Sunaina's Current A/c		Dr.	12,000	
1	Tamanna's Current A/c		Dr.	8,000	
	To Goodwill A/c				20,000
	(Goodwill written off)				
April	General Reserve A/c		Dr.	1,20,000	
1	To Sunaina's Current A/c				72,000
	To Tamanna's Current A/c				48,000
	(Reserve distributed among old partners)				
April	Workmen Compensation Reserve A/c		Dr.	50,000	
1	To Claim for Workmen Compensation A/c				20,000
	To Sunaina's Current A/c				18,000
	To Tamanna's Current A/c				12,000
	(Provision for Workmen Compensation provided and balance distributed among old partners)				
April	Bank A/c		Dr.	1,10,000	
1	To Pranav's Capital A/c				1,00,000
	To Premium for Goodwill A/c				10,000
	(Capital and premium brought in by new partner)				
April	Premium for Goodwill A/c		Dr.	10,000	
1	To Sunaina's Current A/c				6,000
	To Tamanna's Current A/c				4,000
	(Premium distributed among sacrificing partners)				

Q.3. X and Y are in partnership sharing profits and losses in the ratio of 2 : 1. As from 1st April, 2021 they admit Z into partnership and the new ratio of X, Y and Z is agreed as $\frac{1}{4}:\frac{3}{8}:\frac{3}{8}$. Z is to contribute a sum of Rs.1,50,000 as his capital and Rs.36,000 as his share of goodwill. The Balance Sheet of X and Y as at 31st March, 2021 stood as follows:

Liabilities	Rs.	Assets	Rs.
Creditors	70,000	Land & Buildings	3,40,000
Capital Accounts:		Plant	2,00,000
X	4,00,000	Stock	80,000
Y	2,50,000	Debtors	75,000
		Cash and Bank	25,000
	7,20,000		**7,20,000**

Land & Buildings are to be valued at Rs.3,00,000. Plant is to be depreciated by 10% and stock by Rs.6,000. Give journal entries to record the above transactions and prepare the opening balance sheet of the new firm. Revaluation is to be made through Profit & Loss Adjustment A/c.

Ans. Old Ratio of X and Y = 2 : 1

New Ratio of X, Y and Z = $\dfrac{1}{4} : \dfrac{3}{8} : \dfrac{3}{8}$

Sacrifice or Gain:

$$X = \dfrac{2}{3} - \dfrac{1}{4} = \dfrac{16-6}{24} = \dfrac{10}{24} \text{ (Sacrifice)}$$

$$Y = \dfrac{1}{3} - \dfrac{3}{8} = \dfrac{8-9}{24} = \dfrac{1}{24} \text{ (Gain)}$$

$$Z = \dfrac{3}{8} \text{ or } \dfrac{9}{24} \text{ (Gain)}$$

Only X is sacrificing his share to the benefit of Y and Z. Hence, the whole amount of premium brought in by Z will be credited to X. In addition, Y must also compensate X for acquiring $\dfrac{1}{24}$ share. The value of whole of firm's goodwill on the basis of premium paid by Z is Rs.36,000 $\times \dfrac{8}{3}$ = Rs.96,000. On this basis the amount of compensation to be paid by Y will be Rs.96,000 $\times \dfrac{1}{24}$ = Rs.4,000.

Date	Particulars		L.F.	Dr. (Rs.)	Cr. (Rs.)
2021	Profit & Loss Adjustment A/c	Dr.		66,000	
April	To Land and Building A/c				40,000
1	To Plant A/c				20,000
	To Stock A/c				6,000
	(Decrease in the value of assets)				
	X's Capital A/c	Dr.		44,000	
	Y's Capital A/c	Dr.		22,000	
	To Profit & Loss Adjustment A/c				66,000
	(Transfer of loss on revaluation in the ratio of 2 : 1)				
	Bank A/c	Dr.		1,86,000	
	To Z's Capital A/c				1,50,000
	To Premium for Goodwill A/c				36,000
	(Amount introduced by Z for capital and premium for goodwill)				
	Premium for Goodwill A/c	Dr.		36,000	
	To X's Capital A/c				36,000
	(Premium for goodwill brought in by Z credited to sacrificing partner X)				
	Y's Capital A/c	Dr.		4,000	
	To X's Capital A/c				4,000
	(Adjustment for goodwill on acquiring 1/24 share by Y from X)				

Dr. CAPITAL ACCOUNTS **Cr.**

Particulars	X	Y	Z	Particulars	X	Y	Z
	Rs.	Rs.	Rs.		Rs,	Rs.	Rs.
To Profit & Loss Adj. A/c	44,000	22,000		By Balance b/d	4,00,000	2,50,000	
				By Bank			1,50,000
To X's Capital A/c		4,000		By Premium For Goodwill A/c	36,000		
To Balance c/d	3,96,000	2,24,000	1,50,000	By Y's Capital A/c	4,000		
	4,40,000	2,50,000	1,50,000		4,40,000	2,50,000	1,50,000

BALANCE SHEET
as at 1st April, 2021

Liabilities	Rs.	Assets	Rs.
Creditors	70,000	Land and Buildings	3,00,000
Capital Accounts:		Plant	1,80,000
X	3,96,000	Stock	74,000
Y	2,24,000	Debtors	75,000
Z	1,50,000	Cash and Bank	2,11,000
	8,40,000		8,40,000

Q.4. A and B are partners in a firm. Their balance sheet as at 31st March, 2022 was as follows:

Liabilities	Rs.	Assets	Rs.
Provision for Doubtful Debts	4,000	Cash	10,000
Workmen Compensation Reserve	5,600	Sundry Debtors	80,000
Outstanding Expenses	3,000	Stock	20,000
Creditors	30,000	Fixed Assets	38,600
Capitals: A	50,000	Profit & Loss A/c	4,000
B	60,000		
	1,52,600		1,52,600

C was taken into partnership as from 1st April, 2022. C brought Rs.40,000 as his capital but he is unable to bring any amount for goodwill. New profit sharing ration is 3 : 2 : 1. Following terms were agreed upon:

(i) Claim on account of Workmen's Compensation is Rs.3,000.

(ii) To write off Bad Debts amounting to Rs.6,000.

(iii) Creditors are to be paid Rs.2,000 more.

(iv) Rs.2,000 be provided for an unforeseen liability.

(v) Outstanding expenses be brought down to Rs.1,200.

(vi) Goodwill is valued at $1\frac{1}{2}$ year's purchase of the average profits of last three years. Profits of 3 years amounted to Rs.8,000; Rs.10,000 and Rs.18,000.

Prepare Journal entries, capital accounts and opening Balance Sheet.

Ans. **JOURNAL**

Date	Particulars		L.F.	Dr. (Rs.)	Cr. (Rs.)
2022					
April	A's Capital A/c	Dr.		2,000	
1	B's Capital A/c	Dr.		2,000	
	To Profit and Loss A/c				4,000
	(Loss appearing in the Balance Sheet debited to old partner's accounts)				
	Workmen Compensation Reserve A/c [1]	Dr.		5,600	
	To Liability for Workmen Compensation Claim A/c				3,000
	To A's Capital A/c				1,300
	To B's Capital A/c				1,300
	(Excess reserve (Rs.5,600 – 3,000) shared by old partners)				
	Bad Debts A/c	Dr.		6,000	
	To Sundry Debtors A/c				6,000
	(Bad debts written off)				
	Provision for Doubtful Debts A/c [2]	Dr.		4,000	
	Revaluation A/c	Dr.		2,000	
	To Bad Debts A/c				6,000
	(Bad Debts adjusted)				
	Revaluation A/c	Dr.		4,000	
	To Creditors A/c				2,000
	To Unforeseen Liability A/c				2,000
	(Provision for Liabilities)				

Outstanding Expenses A/c	Dr.		1,800	
To Revaluation A/c				1,800
(Outstanding expenses reduced)				
A's Capital A/c	Dr.		2,100	
B's Capital A/c			2,100	
To Revaluation A/c				4,200
(Loss on revaluation transferred)				
C's Current A/c[4]	Dr.		3,000[3]	
To B's Capital A/c				3,000
(C's share of goodwill credited to B's Capital A/c, as he alone has sacrificed)				
Cash A/c	Dr.		40,000	40,000
To C's Capital A/c				
(Cash brought in by C as capital)				

Dr.   **CAPITAL ACCOUNTS**   **Cr.**

Particulars	A	B	C	Particulars	A	B	C
	Rs.	Rs.	Rs.		Rs.	Rs.	Rs.
To P & L A/c	2,000	2,000		By Bal. b/d	50,000	60,000	
To				By workmen's			
Revaluation	2,100	2,100		Compensation			
To Bal. c/d	47,200	60,200	40,000	fund	1,300	1,300	
				By C's Current			
				A/c		3,000	
				By Cash			40,000
	51,300	**64,300**	**40,000**		**51,300**	**64,300**	**40,000**

OPENING BALANCE SHEET as at 1st April 2022

Liabilities	Rs.	Assets	Rs.
Liability for Workmen		Cash	50,000
Compensation Claim	3,000	Sundry Debtors	74,000
Outstanding Expenses	1,200	Stock	20,000
Unforeseen Liability	2,000	Fixed Assets	38,600
Creditors	32,000	C's Current A/c	3,000
Capitals: A	47,200		
B	60,200		
C	40,000		
	1,85,600		**1,85,600**

Note:

(i) Workmen Compensation Reserve is appearing at Rs.5,600, whereas, the actual liability for workmen's Compensation is Rs.3,000. Therefore, Rs.2,600 will be transferred to the capital accounts of old partners in their old ratio.

(ii) Provision for Doubtful debts appearing in the balance sheet is Rs.4,000, whereas actual bad debts amounted to Rs.6,000. Therefore, Rs.2,000 will be debited to revaluation account as loss.

(iii) Valuation of Goodwill

$$\text{Average Profit} = \frac{8,000 + 10,000 + 18,000}{3} = \text{Rs.12,000}$$

$$12,000 \times 1\frac{1}{2} = \text{Rs.18,000}$$

$$\text{C's share of Goodwill} = 18,000 \times \frac{1}{6} = \text{Rs.3,000}$$

Sacrifice Ratio = (Old Ratio – New Ratio)

$$A = \frac{1}{2} - \frac{3}{6} = 0$$

$$B = \frac{1}{2} - \frac{2}{6} = \frac{1}{6}$$

Hence, B alone has sacrificed.

(iv) From C's share of goodwill, his current A/c has been debited instead of his Capital A/c so that his Capital is not reduced and remains intact at Rs.40,000.

Q.5. Aditi and Parul are partners in a firm with capitals of Rs.35,000 each. They shared profits and losses in the ratio of 3 : 1.

On 1st April, 2017, they admit Chanda into their partnership with 1/5th share in the profits.

Chanda brings in Rs.40,000 as her capital and also brings her share of goodwill in cash

Her share of goodwill is calculated on the basis of her capital contribution and her share of profits in the firm.

At the time of Chanda's admission:

(a) The firm had a Workmen Compensation Reserve of Rs.60,000 against which there was a claim of Rs.20,000.

(b) Creditors of Rs.8,000 were paid by Aditi privately for which she is not to be reimbursed.

(c) There was no change in the value of other assets and liabilities.

You are required to, on the date of Chanda's admission:

(i) Calculate the goodwill of the firm. (Show the workings clearly).

(ii) Pass the necessary journal entries to record the above transactions.

Ans. Calculation of hidden goodwill of the firm: Rs.

Total Capital of the firm based on Chanda's Capital = 5 × 40,000   2,00,000

Less: Net worth of the business:

Adjusted Capitals of all the partners

(Capital + Workmen Compensation Reserve + Creditors)

Aditi   35,000 + 30,000 + 6,000 = 71,000

Parul   35,000 + 10,000 + 2,000 = 47,000

Chanda   40,000   1,58,000

Hidden Goodwill 42,000

Chanda's share of Goodwill = $42,000 \times \dfrac{1}{5}$ = Rs. 8,400

JOURNAL

Date	Particulars		L.F.	Dr. (Rs.)	Cr. (Rs,)
2017					
April	Workmen Compensation Reserve A/c	Dr.		60,000	
1	To Workmen Compensation Claim A/c				20,000
	To Aditi's Capital A/c				30,000
	To Parul's Capitla A/c				10,000
	(Excess of Workmen Compensation Reserve credited in old ratio)				
	Creditors A/c	Dr.		8,000	
	To Revaluation A/c				8,000
	(Gain on creditors being paid by a partner and not to be reimbursed)				
	Revaluation A/c	Dr.		8,000	
	To Aditi's Capital A/c				6,000
	To Parul's Capital A/c				2,000
	(Gain on revaluation transferred in old ratio)				
	Bank A/c	Dr.		48,400	
	To Chanda's Capital A/c				40,000
	To Premium for Goodwill A/c				8,000
	(Capital and premium for goodwill contributed by Chanda)				
	Premium for Goodwill A/c	Dr.		8,400	
	To Aditi's Capital A/c				6,300
	To Parul's Capital A/c				2,100
	(Premium for goodwill credited to old partners in sacrificing ratio of 3 : 1)				

Q.6. Jain and Gupta were partners sharing profits in the ratio of 3 : 2. Their Balance Sheet as at 31st March 2022 was as follows:

Liabilities	Rs.	Assets		Rs.
Creditors	49,000	Cash		14,800
Bills Payable	3,000	Debtors	20,500	
Bank Overdraft	17,000	*Less:* Provision for Bad Debts	300	20,200
Reserve	15,000	Stock		44,000
Jain's Capital	70,000	Plant		40,000
Gupta's Capital	60,000	Building		75,000
		Motor Vehicles		20,000
	2,14,000			**2,14,000**

They agreed to admit Mishra for 1/4th share from 01.04.2022 subject to the following terms:

(a) Mishra to bring in capital to 1/4th of the total capital of Jain and Gupta after all adjustments including premium for goodwill.

(b) Building is undervalued by 25% and Stock is overvalued by 10%.

(c) Provision for bad debts on Debtors to be raised to Rs.1,000.

(d) A Provision be made for Rs.14,800 for outstanding legal charges.

(e) Mishra's share of goodwill/premium was calculate at Rs.10,000 which is brought by him in cash.

Prepare Revaluation Account, Partner's Capital Accounts and the Balance Sheet of the new firm on Mishra's admission.

Ans.

Dr.   **REVALUATION ACCOUNT**   **Cr.**

Particulars		Rs.	Particulars	Rs.
To Stock (Rs.44,000-Rs.40,000)		4,000	By Building	
To Provision for Bad Debts		700	(Rs.1,00,000 –	
To Provision for Legal Charges		14,800	Rs.75,000)	25,000
To Profit transferred to				
Jain's Capital A/c	3,300			
Gupta's Capital A/c	2,200	5,500		
		25,000		**25,000**

Dr. PARTNER'S CAPITAL ACCOUNTS **Cr.**

Particulars	Jain	Gupta	Mishra	Particulars	Jain	Gupta	Mishra
	Rs.	Rs.	Rs.			Rs.	Rs.	Rs.
To Balance c/d	88,300	72,200	....	By Balance b/d	70,000	60,000	.....
				By Reserve	9,000	6,000	
				By Revaluation	3,300	2,200	
				By Premium for Goodwill	6,000	4,000	
	88,300	72,200			88,300	72,200	
By Balance c/d	88,300	72,200	40,125	By Balance b/d	88,300	72,200	
				By Bank A/c[4]			40,125
	88,300	**72,200**	**40,125**		**88,300**	**72,200**	**40,125**

BALANCE SHEET
As at 1st April, 2022

Liabilities		Rs.	Assets		Rs.
Creditors		49,000	Cash		14,800
Bills Payable		3,000	Bank[5]		33,125
Provision for Legal Charges		14,800	Debtors	20,500	
Capital Accounts:			Less: Provision for		
Jain	88,300		Bad Debts	1,000	19,500
Gupta	72,200		Stock		40,000
Mishra	40,125	2,00,625	Plant		40,000
			Building		1,00,000
			Motor Vehicles		20,000
		2,67,425			**2,67,425**

Q.7. Swadesh and Swaraj were partners sharing profits equally. Their Balance Sheet as at 31st March, 2022 was:

Liabilities		Rs.	Assets		Rs.
Creditors		50,000	Cash		12,000
Bills Payable		15,000	Cash at Bank		15,000
Outstanding Expenses		3,000	Debtors	20,000	
			Less: Provision for		
Capital A/cs	60,000		Doubtful Debts	500	19,500
Swadesh	40,000	1,00,000	Stock		20,000
Swaraj			Furniture		10,000
			Machinery		18,000
			Land and Building		73,500
		1,68,000			**1,68,000**

Sambhav is admitted as partner from 1st April, 2022 on the following terms:

(i)   Sambhav will get 1/5th share in profits and he will bring Rs.20,000 as his capital and Rs.5,000 as his share of goodwill.

(ii) Goodwill brought by Sambhav will be withdrawn by Swadesh and Swaraj.

(iii) Provision for Doubtful Debts should be brought up to 5% on Debtors.

(iv) Machinery be reduced by Rs.2,000 and Furniture by 12.5%.

(v)   Stock be valued at Rs.23,000.

(vi) Land and Building be appreciated by 20%.

(vii) Investments of Rs.2,000 which did not appear in books is to be recorded.

(viii) Out of the amount of insurance premium which was debited to Profit & Loss Account, Rs.5,000 be carried forward as prepaid insurance.

(ix) A bill for Rs.5,000 for Electricity was not accounted.

Pass necessary Journal entries and prepare Revaluation Account and Balance Sheet of the new firm.

Ans.   **JOURNAL**

Date	Particulars		L.F.	Dr. (Rs.)	Cr. (Rs.)
2022					
April	Cash A/c	Dr.		25,000	
1	To Sambhav's Capital A/c				20,000
	To Premium for Goodwill A/c				5,000
	(Capital and goodwill brought by Sambhav)				
	Premium for Goodwill A/c	Dr.		5,000	
	To Swadesh's Capital A/c				2,500
	To Swaraj's Capital A/c				2,500
	(Goodwill credited to Swadesh and Swaraj in their sacrificing ratio)				
	Swadesh's Capital A/c	Dr.		2,500	
	Swaraj's Capital A/c	Dr.		2,500	
	To Cash A/c				5,000
	(Goodwill withdrawn by old partners)				
	Revaluation A/c	Dr.		8,750	
	To Provision for Doubtful Debts A/c [(5% of Rs.20,000) – Rs.500]				500
	To Machinery A/c				2,000
	To Furniture A/c				1,250
	To Outstanding Electricity Expenses A/c				5,000
	(Decrease in value of machinery and furniture and increase in Provision for Doubtful Debts and Outstanding Electricity Expenses recorded)				

Stock A/c		Dr.	3,000	
Land and Building A/c		Dr.	14,700	
Investments A/c		Dr.	2,000	
Prepaid Insurance Premium A/c		Dr.	5,000	
To Revaluation A/c				24,700
(Increase in value of assets recorded)				
Revaluation A/c		Dr.	15,950	
To Swadesh's Capital A/c				7,975
To Swaraj's Capital A/c				7,975
(Distribution of revaluation gain (profit) between old partners (WN 1)				

Dr.   **REVALUATION ACCOUNT**   **Cr.**

Particulars	Rs.	Particulars	Rs.
To Provision for Doubtful Debts A/c	500	By Stock A/c	3,000
To Machinery A/c	2,000	By Land and Building A/c	14,700
To Furniture A/c	1,250	By Investments A/c	2,000
To Outstanding Electricity		By Prepaid Insurance	
Expenses A/c	5,000	Premium A/c	5,000
To Gain (Profit) transferred to:			
Swadesh's Capital A/c 7,975			
Swaraj's Capital A/c 7,975	15,950		
	24,700		**24,700**

BALANCE SHEET as at 1st April 2022

Liabilities	Rs.	Assets		Rs.
Bills Payable	15,000	Cash in Hand (WN 2)		32,000
Creditors	50,000	Cash at Bank		15,000
Outstanding Expenses		Stock		23,000
(Rs.3,000 + Rs.5,000)	8,000	Debtors	20,000	
Capital A/cs (WN1):		Less: Provision for		
Swadesh 67,975		Doubtful Debts	1,000	19,000
Swaraj 47,975		Investments		2,000
Sambhav 20,000	1,35,950	Prepaid Insurance		
		Premium		5,000
		Furniture		8,750
		Machinery		16,000
		Land and Building		88,200
	2,08,950			**2,08,950**

Working Notes:

1. Dr.   PARTNER'S CAPITAL ACCOUNTS   Cr.

Particulars	Swadesh Rs.	Swaraj Rs.	Sambhav Rs.	Particulars	Swadesh Rs.	Swaraj Rs.	Sambhav Rs.
To Cash A/c	2,500	2,500	---	By Balance b/d	60,000	40,000	---
To Balance c/d	67,975	47,975	20,000	By Cash A/c	---	---	20,000
				By Premium for Goodwill A/c	2,500	2,500	---
				By Revaluation A/c	7,975	7,975	---
	70,475	**50,475**	**20,000**		**70,475**	**50,475**	**20,000**

2. Dr.   CASH ACCOUNT   Cr.

Particulars	Rs.	Particulars	Rs.
To Balance b/d	12,000	By Swadesh's Capital A/c	2,500
To Sambhav's Capital A/c	20,000	By Swaraj's Capital A/c	2,500
To Premium for Goodwill A/c	5,000	By Balance c/d	32,000
	37,000		**37,000**

Q.8. Karam and Param are partners in a firm. They share profits in the ratio of 3 : 2. Their Balance Sheet as at 31st March, 2022 was:

Liabilities	Rs.		Assets	Rs.	
Creditors		1,50,000	Cash at Bank		1,20,000
Bills Payable		80,000	Debtors	2,00,000	
Outstanding Rent		20,000	Less: Provision for	20,000	
Capital A/cs			Doubtful Debts		1,80,000
Karam	3,00,000		Stock		50,000
Param	1,50,000	4,50,000	Prepaid Expenses		10,000
			Plant and Machinery		3,40,000
		7,00,000			**7,00,000**

They admitted Suresh as partner on 1st April 2022 on the following terms:

(i) Suresh will bring Rs.2,00,000 as capital and the necessary amount for goodwill.

(ii) New profit-sharing ratio among Karam, Param and Suresh will be 5 : 3 : 2.

(iii)Amount of goodwill is to be based on Suresh's share in profits and capital contributed by him.

(iv)Stock is to be reduced by 10%.

(v) Provision for Doubtful Debts is to be Rs.5,000.

(vi)Plant and Machinery is to be reduced by 5%.

(vii)Expenses on revaluation were Rs.1,400 and were paid by the firm.

(viii)An unaccounted Commission Receivable of Rs.1,400 be accounted.

Prepare Revaluation Account, Partners' Capital Accounts, Bank Account and the Balance Sheet of the New Firm.

Ans.

Dr.		REVALUATION ACCOUNT		Cr.
Particulars	Rs.	Particulars		Rs.
To Stock A/c	5,000	By Provision for Doubtful Debts A/c		15,000
To Plant and		(Rs.20,000 – Rs.5,000)		
Machinery A/c	17,000	By commission Receivable A/c		1,400
To Bank A/c		By Loss transferred to:		
(Revaluation		Karam's Capital A/c	4,200	
Expenses)	1,400	Param's Capital A/c	2.800	7,000
	23,400			**23,400**

Dr.				PARTNERS CAPITAL ACCOUNTS			Cr.
Particulars	Karam Rs.	Param Rs.	Suresh Rs.	Particulars	Karam Rs.	Param Rs.	Suresh Rs.
To Revaluation A/c (Loss)	4,200	2,800	---	By Balance b/d	3,00,000	1,50,000	---
				By Bank A/c	---	---	2,00,000
To Balance c/d	3,31,500	1,82,900	2,00,000	By Premium for Goodwill A/c (in Sacrificing Ratio) (WN 1 and 2)	35,700	35,700	---
	3,35,700	**1,85,700**	**2,00,000**		**3,35,700**	**1,85,700**	**2,00,000**

Dr		BANK ACCOUNT		Cr.
Particulars	Rs.	Particulars		Rs.
To Balance b/d	1,20,000	By Revaluation A/c		1,400
To Suresh's Capital A/c	2,00,000	By Balance c/d		2,50,000
To Premium for Goodwill A/c	71,400			
	3,91,400			**3,91,400**

BALANCE SHEET OF THE NEW FIRM

as at 1st April 2022

Liabilities		Rs.	Assets		Rs.
Bills Payable		80,000	Cash at Bank		3,90,000
Creditors		1,50,000	Stock (Rs.50,000 –		
Outstanding Rent		20,000	Rs.5,000)		45,000
Capital A/cs:			Debtors	2,00,000	
Karam	3,31,500		Less: Provision for		
Param	1,82,900		Doubtful Debts	5,000	1,95,000
Suresh	2,00,000	7,14,400	Prepaid Expenses		10,000
			Commission Receivable		1,400
			Plant and Machinery		3,23,000
		9,64,400			**9,64,400**

Q.9. Shailesh , Shoubhik are partners in a firm sharing profits in the ratio of 2 : 3. Their Balance Sheet as at 31 st March, 2022 was as follows:

Liabilities		Amount	Assets		Amount
Salary outstanding		5,000	Cash and Bank		22,000
Creditors		13,000	Debtors	48,000	
General Reserve		5,000	Less: Provision	(2,000)	46,000
Capital Account :			Stock		35,000
Shailesh	80,000		Prepaid Expenses		21,000
Shoubhik	1,20,000		Investment		60,000
			Furniture		38,000
		2,00,000	Advertisement Suspense A/c		1,000
		2,23,000			**2,23,000**

On the above date they admitted Soniya as a partner for ¼ th share in the firm which she acquires equally from Shailesh and Shoubhik. Following are required adjustments:

(a) Soniya will contribute Rs.60,000 as her capital and Rs.3,000 towards goodwill.

(b) Stock is overvalued by Rs.5,000.

(c) Market value of Investment is Rs.54,000.

(d) Provision for doubtful debts to be maintained at 5 % on debtors.

Pass necessary journal entries on Soniya's admission.

Ans.

JOURNAL

Date	Particulars		L.F.	Dr. (Rs.)	Cr. (Rs.)
2022 April 01	General Reserve A/c	Dr.		5,000	
	To Shailesh's Capital A/c				2,000
	To Shoubhik's Capital A/c				3,000
	(Being balance of reserve transferred to old partners capital A/c)				
	Shailesh's Capital A/c	Dr.		400	
	Shoubhik's Capital A/c	Dr.		600	
	To Advertisement Suspense A/c				1,000
	(Being Advertisement suspense A/c written off)				

Date	Particulars		L.F.	Dr. (Rs.)	Cr. (Rs.)
2022 April 01	Bank A/c	Dr.		63,000	
	To Soniya's Capital A/c				60,000
	To Premium for Goodwill A/c				3,000
	(Being capital and premium for goodwill brought by Soniya)				
	Premium for Goodwill A/c	Dr.		3,000	
	To Shailesh's Capital A/c				1,500
	To Shoubhik's Capital A/c				1,500
	(Being goodwill credited to old partner's capital A/c in sacrificing ratio)				
	Revaluation A/c	Dr.		11,400	
	To Stock A/c				5,000
	To Investment A/c				6,000
	To Provision for Bad debts A/c				400
	(Being assets revalued)				
	Shailesh's Capital A/c	Dr.		4,560	
	Shoubhik's Capital A/c	Dr.		6,840	
	To Revaluation A/c				11,400
	(Being loss on revaluation transferred to old partners capital A/c in old profit ratio)				

Q.10. Abhiyank and Priyank are partners sharing profits and losses in the ratio of 3 : 2. Their Balance Sheet as at 31.03.2022 was as follows:

Liabilities	Amount	Assets		Amount
Outstanding Expenses	12,000	Cash and Bank		71,000
Bills Payable	60,000	Debtors	1,50,000	
Creditors	96,000	Less : Provision	(2,000)	1,25,000
Employee Provident Fund	18,000	Stock		50,000
Investment Fluctuation Fund	20,000	Investment		1,20,000
General Reserve	40,000	(Market Value Rs.90,000)		
Capital Account		Machinery		60,000
Abhiyank	2,50,000	Building		2,00,000
Priyank	1,50,000	4,00,000	Profit and Loss A/c	20,000
	6,46,000			**6,46,000**

On 01st April ,2022 they admitted Mayank as a partners for 1/5th share in profits on the following terms :

(1) Mayank will contribute proportionate capital and his share of goodwill in cash.

(2) The goodwill of the firm is valued at RS. 50,000.

(3) Provision on debtors was found to be in excess by Rs. 5,000.

(4) Outstanding Expenses will be increased by Rs 1,000.

(5) A liability of Rs 6,000 included in Creditors is not likely to arise.

Prepare Revaluation A/c, Partner's Capital Account and New Balance Sheet.

Ans.

Dr.   **REVALUATION A/C**   **Cr.**

Particulars	Amount	Particulars	Amount
To Outstanding Exp.	1,000	By Provision for Bad debts	5,000
To Investment	10,000	By Creditors	6,000
	11,000		**11,000**

Dr.   **Partner's Capital A/c**   **Cr.**

Particulars	Abhiyank	Priyank	Mayank	Particulars	Abhiyank	Priyank	Mayank
To P. & L. A/c	12,000	8,000		By Balance b/f	2,50,000	1,50,000	…
To Balance c/d	2,68,000	1,62,000	1,07,500	By G/Reserve	24,000	16,000	…
				By Pre. For Goodwill	6,000	4,000	1,07,500
				By Bank			
	2,80,000	**1,70,000**	**1,07,500**		**2,80,000**	**1,70,000**	**1,07,500**

BALANCE SHEET OF NEW FIRM

Liabilities	Amount	Liabilities	Amount
Outstanding Expenses	13,000	Cash at Bank	1,88,500
Bills Payable	60,000	Debtors 1,50,000	
Creditors	90,000	Less: P.B.D. 20,000	1,30,000
Employee Provident Fund	18,000	Stock	50,000
Capital A/c		Investments	90,000
Abhiyank 2,68,000		Machinery	60,000
Priyank 1,62,000		Building	2,00,000
Mayank 1,07,500	5,37,500		
	7,18,500		**7,18,500**

Working Note: Calculation of Capital brought by Mayank

Total Share 1 – 1/5 : 4/5 Remaining share

Capital of Abhiyank after all adjustment	2,68,000
Capital of Priyank after all adjustment	1,62,000
Capital for 4/5 share	4,30,000

So capital of firm will be 4,30,000 × 5/4 = 5,37,000

Less: Capital for 4/6th share	4,30,000
Capital for 1/5th share	1,07,000

Q.11. Abhita and Dipika were partners sharing profits and losses in the ratio of 5 : 3 Their Balance Sheet as at 31st March, 2022 was as under:

Liabilities	Amount	Assets	Amount
Bills Payable	22,000	Cash at Bank	97,000
Sundry Creditors	45,000	Debtors	80,000
Workmen Compensation Fund	40,000	Stock	66,000
General reserve	70,000	Investment	60,000
Profit and Loss A/c	20,000	Furniture	75,000
Capital Account		Machinery	2,25,000
Abhita 3,20,000		Goodwill	1,04,000
Dipika 1,90,000	5,10,000		
	7,07,000		**7,07,000**

On 01st April 2022 they admitted Vasudha in to partnership firm for 1 /4th share which she Acquired from Abhita and Dipika in the ratio of 2 : 1. Other adjustment were as follows:

(a) The goodwill of the firm valued at Rs.96,000.

(b) Vasudha brings in capital Rs.1,20,000 in Cash but was unable to her share of goodwill in cash.

(c) Create a Provision of 5% for Doubtful Debts.

(d) 50 % of the Investment were taken over by old Partners in their profit sharing ratio. Remaining Investment were valued at Rs.35,000

(e) Claim on Workmen Compensation was established at Rs.16,000

(f) One month salary of Rs.16,000 was outstanding.

Ans.

Dr. **REVALUATION A/C** **Cr.**

Particulars	Amount	Particulars	Amount
To Provision for Bad debts	4,000	By Investment	5,000
To Outstanding Salonies	16,000	By Partners Capital A/c	
		Abhita (5) 9,375	
		Dipika (3) 5,625	15,000
	20,000		**20,000**

Dr. **Partner's Capital A/c** **Cr.**

Particulars	Abhita	Dipika	Vasudha	Particulars	Abhita	Dipika	Vasudha
To Goodwill (w/o)	65,000	39,000	...	By Balance b/d	3,20,000	1,90,000	...
To Investment	18,750	11,250		By we Fund	15,000	9,000	...
To Rev. (Loss)	9,375	5,625	...	By Gen. Reserve	43,750	26,250	...
To Balance c/d	3,14,125	1,84,875	1,20,000	By P. & L. A/c	12,500	7,500	...
				By Vasudha	16,000	8,000	
				Current A/c			
				(Goodwill)			
				By Bank			1,20,000
	4,07,250	**2,40,750**	**1,20,000**		**4,07,250**	**2,40,750**	**1,20,000**

Balance Sheet of New Firm

Liabilities		Amount	Assets		Amount
Bills Payable		22,000	Cash at Bank		2,17,000
Sundry Creditors		45,000	Debtors	80,000	
Provision for Compensation		16,000	Less: Provision	4,000	76,000
Outstanding Salonies		16,000	Stock		66,000
Partners Capital A/c			Investment		35,000
Abhita	3,14,125		Furniture		75,000
Dipika	1,84,875		Machinery		2,25,000
Vasudha	1,20,000	6,19,000	Vasudha's Current A/c		24,000
		7,18,000			**7,18,000**

Q.12. Prepare Revaluation A/c, Partner's Capital Account and Firm's New Balance Sheet 13. On 31St March 2022 the Balance Sheet of Manan and Mansha ,who are partners in a firm sharing Profits in the ratio of 3:2 was as follows :

Liabilities	Amount	Assets		Amount
Capital Accounts		Plant & Machinery		10,000
Manan 10,000		Land & Buildings		8,000
Mansha 8,000	18,000	Debtors	12,000	
General Reserve	15,000	Less: Provision	(1,000)	11,000
Workmen Compensation Fund	5,000	Stock		12,000
Creditors	12,000	Cash at Bank		9,000
	50,000			**50,000**

They admit Shivansh for 1/5th share of profits on the followings terms:

(1) Provision for doubtful debts would be increased by Rs.2,000

(2) The value of Land & Building would be increased to Rs18,000.

(3) The value of stock would be increased by Rs.4,000

(4) The liability against workmen's Compensation fund is determined at Rs.2,000.

(5) Shivansh brought as his share of goodwill Rs.10,000 in Cash .

(6) Shivansh bring further cash as would make his capital equal to 20 % of the total capital of the new firm, after the above all adjustments.

Prepare Revaluation A/c, Partners Capita l Account, Balance Sheet after Shivansh's admission.

Ans.

Dr.   **REVALUATION A/C**   **Cr.**

Particulars	Amount	Particulars	Amount
To Provision for Bad debts	2,000	By Land & Building	10,000
To Partners Capital A/c		By Stock	4,000
Manan 7,200			
Mansha 4,800	12,000		
	14,000		**14,000**

Dr.   **PARTNERS CAPITAL A/C**   **Cr.**

Particulars	Manan	Mansha	Shivansh	Particulars	Manan	Mansha	Shivansh
To Balance c/d	34,000	24,000	…	By Balance b/d	10,000	8,000	…
				By G/Reserve	9,000	6,000	…
				By W.C. Fund	1,800	1,200	
				By Rev. (Profit)	7,200	4,800	
				By Pre. for			
				Goodwill	6,000	4,000	
	34,000	24,000	…		34,000	24,000	…
By Balance c/d	34,000	24,000	14,500	By Balance b/d	34,000	24,000	…
				By Bank	…	…	14,500
	34,000	**24,000**	**14,500**		**34,000**	**24,000**	**14,500**

NEW BALANCE SHEET

(After Admissing of Shivansh)

Liabilities		Amount	Assets	Amount
Creditors		12,000	Plant & Machinery	10,000
Claim for compensation		2,000	Land & Building	18,000
Partners Capital A/c			Debtors	
Manan	34,000		Less: P.B.D.	9,000
Mansha	24,000		Stock	16,000
Shivansh	14,500	72,500	Cash at Bank	33,500
			(9000 + 10000 + 14500)	
		86,500		**86,500**

Working Note: Calculation of Proportionate Capital of Shivansh

Total Capital of Manan and Mansha = 34000 + 24000 = 58000

This capital will be for (1-1/5) = 4/5 share

So total capital of firm will be 58000 × 5/4 = 72500

Now Shivansh capital will be $\dfrac{72500 \times 20}{100} = 14500$

Q.13. On the basis of the following case, answer the question number. (i to v)

Vihaan and Vivaan are partners in a firm with equal ratio.

BALANCE SHEET

as at 31st March, 2019

Liabilities		Amount (Rs.)	Assets	Amount (Rs.)
Creditors		2,00,000	Bank	80,000
Bills Payable		1,20,000	Debtors	1,20,000
General Reserve		80,000	Building	4,00,000
Capital A/cs			Machinery	2,00,000
Vihaan	4,00,000		Investment	80,000
Vivaan	2,00,000	6,00,000	Patents	40,000
			Furniture	40,000
			Goodwill	40,000
		10,00,000		**10,00,000**

Adjustments

(i) Veer comes for 1/5th share and brings capital Rs.2,00,000 and premium Rs.40,000 out of Rs.60,000.

(ii) New ratio 2 : 2 : 1.

(iii)Rs.20,000 included in creditors are not likely to be paid.

(iv) Patents are valueless.

(v) 10% provision for doubtful debts on debtors out of general reserve.

(i)   What is the profit/loss of revaluation account?

(a) Profit Rs.60,000   (b) Loss Rs.60,000   (c) Profit Rs.20,000   (d) Loss Rs.20,000

Ans.(d)

(ii) If the old ratio is equal and new ratio (Between old partners) is also equal, then what would be the sacrificing ratio?

(a) 1 : 2   (b) 2 : 1   (c) 1 : 1   (d) Can't be determined

Ans. (c)

(iii) What was the total of bank account at the end of transactions?

(a) Rs.3,40,000   (b) Rs.3,20,000   (c) Rs.2,80,000   (d) Can't be determined

Ans. (b)

(iv) Vihaan capital account was ……….. by ……… for adjusting the part of goodwill not brought in by Bharat.

(a) debited; Rs.30,000(b) credited; Rs.30,000   (c) debited; Rs.10,000   (d) credited; Rs.10,000

Ans. (d)

(v) By how much amount was Vivaan's capital credited on account of General Reserve?

(a) Rs.80,000   (b) Rs.68,000   (c) Rs.40,000   (d) Rs.34,000

Ans. (d)

Q.14. On the basis of the following case, answer the question number. (i to v)

Surya and Shreyas are partners sharing profits and losses in the proportion of 2 : 3. The following is the balance sheet of Surya and Shreyas on 31st March, 2018.

BALANCE SHEET

as at 31st March, 2018

Liabilities	Amount (Rs.)	Assets	Amount (Rs.)
Bills Payable	10,000	Cash	10,000
Workmen's Compensation Reserve	15,000	Debtors	15,000
General Reserve	30,000	Bills Receivable	15,000
Capital A/c		Stock	10,000
Surya 20,000		Fixtures	20,000
Shreyas 25,000	45,000	Premises	30,000
	1,00,000		**1,00,000**

They admit Shami for 1/5th share into partnership on 1st April 2018, on the following terms.

(i) Z brings Rs.30,000 as capital.

(ii) Goodwill of the firm is valued on the basis of Z's share in profits and capital contributed by him.

(iii)The provision on debtors is to be created @ 5%.

(iv) Fixtures and stock are to be decreased by 10%.

(v) The value of premises be appreciated by 10%.

(i) From which item did partners benefitted at the time of reassessment of assets and liabilities?

(a) Fixtures   (b) Stock   (c) Premises   (d) Debtors

Ans. (c)

(ii) What was loss/profit on revaluation and by how much amount?

    (a) Loss Rs.1,500   (b) Loss Rs.750   (c) Profit Rs.1,500   (d) Profit Rs.750

Ans. (b)

(iii) What was the amount of total capital of firm according to Shami's share?

    (a) Rs.30,000   (b) Rs.90,750   (c) Rs.1,50,000   (d) Rs.75,000

Ans. (c)

(iv) What was the amount of goodwill of the firm?

    (a) Rs.6,150   (b) Rs.30,750   (c) Rs.60,750   (d) Can't be determined

Ans. (b)

(v) General reserve given in the balance sheet will be distributed among …….. partners in …………. ratio.

    (a) new, new   (b) old, old   (c) old, sacrificing   (d) old, new

Ans. (b)

Q.15. On the basis of the following case, answer the question number. (i to v)

Shardul and Siraj were partners in a firm sharing profits and losses in the ratio of 4 : 3. The following is the balance sheet of the firm as on 31st December, 2019.

BALANCE SHEET
as at 31st December 2019

Liabilities		Amount (Rs.)	Assets		Amount (Rs.)
Sundry Creditors		20,000	Cash		14,800
Bills Payable		3,000	Debtors	20,500	
Bank Overdraft		17,000	(-) Provision for Doubtful Debts (300)		20,200
Capital A/cs			Stock		20,000
Shardul	70,000		Plant		40,000
Siraj	60,000	1,30,000	Building		75,000
		1,70,000			**1,70,000**

They agreed to admit Sourabh as a partner with effect from 1st January, 2020 for 1/4th share in profits on the following terms

(i) Sourabh will bring in Rs.47,183 as his capital.

(ii) Building is to be appreciated by Rs.14,000 and plant to be depreciated by Rs.7,000.

(iii) The provision on debtors is to be raised to Rs.1,000.

(iv) The goodwill of the firm has been valued at Rs.21,000.

(i) What will be the net amount of debtors in new balance sheet?

    (a) Rs.20,500   (b) Rs.20,200   (c) Rs.19,500   (d) Rs.19,200

Ans. (c)

(ii) What is the profit/loss on revaluation and by what amount?

    (a) Profit Rs.7,000   (b) Profit Rs.6,300   (c) Loss Rs.7,000   (d) Loss Rs.6,300

Ans. (b)

(iii) What is the sacrificing ratio of Shardul and Siraj?

(a) 1 : 1 (b) 3 : 4 (c) 4 : 3 (d) Can't be determined

Ans. (c)

(iv) What is the total of cash account after this event of admission?

(a) Rs.14,800 (b) Rs.61,983 (c) Rs.67,233 (d) Can't be determined

Ans. (b)

(v) In general, goodwill adjustment is done in accounts of old partners in ……….. ratio.

(a) Old profit sharing (b) Sacrificing ratio (c) Both (a) and (b) (d) New profit sharing

Chapter Practice

Multiple Choice Questions   [1 Mark]

Q.1. X and Y share profits in the ratio of 3 : 2. Z was admitted as a partner who sets 1/5 share Calculate new profit sharing ratio, if Z acquires 3/20 from X and 1/20 from Y :

   (a) 9 : 7 : 4   (b) 8 : 8 : 4   (c) 6 : 10 : 4   (d) 10 : 6 : 4

Q.2. A, B and C are partners in a firm. If D is admitted as a new partner :

   (a) Old firm is dissolved   (b) Old Firm & Partnership is dissolved

   (c) Old Partnership is reconstituted   (d) None of the Above

Q.3. Revaluation Account is a:

   (a) Personal A/c   (b) Real A/c   (c) Nominal A/c   (d) Assets A/c

Q.4. When the balance Sheet is prepared after the new agreement,the assets & liabilities are recorded at

   (a) Historical cost   (b) Current Cost   (c) Realizable Value   (d) Revalued Value

Q.5. Which goodwill is recorded in books of accounts ?

   (a) Self-generated goodwill   (b) Purchased goodwill

   (c) Both can be recorded   (d) None of the above

Very Short Answer Type   [1 Mark]

Q.6. How will you calculate the hidden goodwill ?

Q.7. Give journal entry for unrecorded liability at the time of admission of a partner.

Q.8. What is the Recommendation of accounting standard 10 in case of goodwill?

Q.9. State any two rights acquired by the new partner in a partnership firm.

Q.10. What is the need for treatment of goodwill on admission of a partner ?

Short Answer Type - I   [2 Marks]

Q.11. On April, 2022 an existing firm had assets of Rs. 75,000 including cash of Rs 5,000. The partners capital A/c showed a balance of 60,000 and reserve constituted the rest. If the normal rate of return is 10% and the Goodwill of the firm is valued 24,000 at 4 year's purchase of super profits, find the average profits of the firm.

Q.12. Abhi, Bhavya, Bhavik were in a partners in the ratio of 4 : 3 : 2. Divya was admitted for 2/9 th share. Divyabrings Rs. 4,50,000 as capital and Rs. 2,00,000 as his share of goodwill. The new profit share ratio was 3 : 2 : 2 : 2 respectively. Pass necessary journal entries.

Q.13. Rajinder and Surinder are partners in a firm sharing profits in the ratio of 4 : 1. On April 01, 2022, they Admit Narender as a new partner for1/6 share. On that date there was a balance of Rs.20,000 in General Reserve and a debit balance of 10,000 in the Profit and Loss Account of the firm.

Pass necessary Journal entries.

Short Answer Type - II [3 Marks]

Q.14 . Taru and Tanmay were partners in the ratio of 3 : 2. They admitted Toshi for 1/5th share. New profit ratio after admission will be 2 : 2 : 1. Toshi brought some assets and liabilities in the form of her capital andand for share of her goodwill:

Plant and Machinery	Rs.1,40,000
Stock	Rs.1,80,000
Building	Rs.4,40,000

At the time of admission of Toshi, goodwill of the firm was valued Rs.12,50,000. Passnecessary journalentries for capital and goodwill.

Q.15. Ajay and Akshay partnerswith capital of Rs.1,95,000 and 1,35,000 respectively. They admitted Ankit for 1/5th share. Rs.1,20,000 was brought by Ankit as his share of capital.

Pass necessary journal entries for goodwill and capital.

Q.16. Kanu and Manu are partners sharing profits and losses as 2 : 1. On 01st April 2021, they admit Tanu as

As partner for 1/4 share, who pays Rs. 45,000 as premium for goodwill privately.

On 01st April, 2022 they take Hanu as a partner for 1/5 th share, who brings in Rs. 40,000 as premium

For goodwill, out of which half is withdrawn by the existing partners,

Journalise the above transactions in the books of the firm.

Long Answer Type [5 Marks]

Q.17. Aditya, Gourav, Madhur are partners sharing profit and losses in the ratio 2 : 2 : 1. They admitted Kamlesh for 1/4th share with effect from 1st April 2022. An extract of their Balance Sheet as at 31st March 2022 is as follows:

Liabilities	Amount	Assets	Amount
Workmen Compensation Reserve	80,000	Investments (At cost)	5,00,000
Investment Fluctuation Reserve	30,000		

Other information:

1. Claim for Workmen compensation is estimated at Rs. 1,00,000

2. If market value of Investment is Rs 4,82,000

Pass Necessary journal entries in the books of the firm.

Q.18. Mukul and Nakul were partners in a firm sharing profits in the ratio of 3 : 2. Bakul was admitted for 1/5th share. He paid Rs.80,000 for his capital. Opening capitals of Mukul and Nakul were Rs.1,60,000 Rs.80,000 respectively. Revaluation profit was Rs.30,000 and Reserve stood Rs.40,000 at the time of Admission of Bakul. It was decided that the capital of partners will be in their profit sharing ratio.

Any surplus or deficiency is to be transferred to current Account of the concerned partners..

Find out Capital of the partners,the amount to be transferred to the Current Account, pass necessary Journal entries for such transferred.

Q.19. Himani, Harshita and Shivani are partnership a firm sharing Profit and Losses in the ratio 3 : 2 : 1. Shruti is admitted as a new partner for 1/4th share in a profits of the firm, which she gets 1/8 from Himani And 1/16 each from Harshita and Shivani. The Total capital of the new firm after Shruti's admission will be Rs. 2,40,000. Shruti is required to bring in cash equal to 1/4 of the total capital of new firm. The capital of the old Partners also have to be adjusted in proportion of their profit sharing ratio. The capital of Himani, Harshita and Shivani adjustments in respect of goodwill and revaluation of assets and liabilities have been made are Himani Rs.80,000 , Harshita Rs.30,000 and Shivani Rs.28,000. Calculate the capitals of all partners, record the necessary journal entries for doing adjustment in respect of capitals according to the agreement between Pass Necessary journal entries in the books of the firm.

Q.20. Pareek and Sharma are partners in a firm sharing profits and losses in the ratio of 3 : 2. On 31st March 2022, their Balance Sheet was as under :

Liabilities	Amount	Assets	Amount
Creditors	70,000	Bank	40,000
Capital A/c	1,50,000	Debtors	1,20,000
Pareek	80,000	Stock	60,000
Sharma	2,30,000	Furniture	50,000
Goodwill	30,000		
	3,00,000		**3,00,000**

On the above date Vyas is admitted as a partner . Pareek surrendered 1/6th of his share and Sharma 1/3rd of his share infavour of Vyas. Goodwill is valued Rs.1,20,000. Vyas brings in only 1/2 of his share of goodwill in Cash and Rs.1,00,000 as his capital. Following adjustments are agreed upon :

(a) Stock is to be revalued to Rs. 56,000 and Furniture depreciated by Rs.5,000

(b) There is an unrecorded assets worth Rs. 20,000

(c) One month's Rent Rs. 15,000 is outstanding. Prepaid Insurance is Rs. 2,000

(d) A creditor for goods purchased for Rs. 10,000 had been omitted to be recorded although the Goods had been correctly included in stock.

You are Required to prepare Revaluation A/c, Partners Capital A/c And new Balance Sheet.

Q.21. On 31st March, 2022 the Balance Sheet of Agrawal and Gupta, who are partners in the firm sharing profits in the Ratio3 : 2 wasas follows :

Liabilities		Amount	Assets		Amount
General Reserve		15,000	Plant and Machinery		10,000
Workmen Compensation Fund		5,000	Land & Building		8,000
Creditors		12,000	Stock		12,000
Capital Accounts Cash		9,000			
Agrawal		10,000	Debtors		12,000
Gupta	8,000	18,000	Less: Provision	1000	11,000
		50,000			**50,000**

Theyadmit Jain partnership for 1/5th share of profit on the following terms:

1.   Provision for doubtful debts would be increased by Rs.2,000

2.   The value of Land & Building would be increased to Rs.18,000

3.   The Value of stock would be increased by Rs.4,000

4.   The liability against workmen Compensation Fund is Determined at Rs.2,000

5.   Jain brought his share of goodwill Rs. 10,000 in cash

6.   Jain would bring further cash as would make his capital equal to 20% of the total capital of the new firm, after the above Revaluation A/c and adjustment are carried out.

Prepare RevaluationAccount, Partners Capital Account And Balance Sheet After Jain's admission.

CHAPTER 4

Retirement /Death of a Partner

Summary

Retirement of a Partner

A partner may retire from the partnership firm:

1. with the consent of all other partners;

   or

2. in case of retirement at will i.e. (partnership at will);

   or

3. by giving notice in writing to all other partners by the retiring partner

Ascertaining the Amount Due to Retiring/ Deceased Partner

The sum due to the retiring partner (in case of retirement) and to the legal representatives/ executors (in case of death) includes:

 (i) credit balance of his capital account;

 (ii) (credit balance of his current account (if any);

 (iii) his share of goodwill;

 (iv) his share of accumulated profits (reserves);

 (v) his share in the gain of revaluation of assets and liabilities;

 (vi) his share of profits up to the date of retirement/death;

 (vii) interest on his capital, if involved, up to the date of retirement/death;

 (viii) salary/commission, if any, due to him up to the date of retirement/death.

The following deductions, if any, may have to be made from his share:

 (i) debit balance of his current account (if any);

 (ii) his share of goodwill to be written off, if necessary;

 (iii) his share of accumulated losses;

 (iv) his share of loss on revaluation of assets and liabilities;

(v)   his share of loss up to the date of retirement/death;

(vi) his drawings up to the date of retirement/death;

(vii) interest on drawings, if involved, up to the date of retirement/death.

New Profit Sharing Ratio

The new profit sharing ratio is the ratio in which the remaining partners will share future profits after the retirement or death of any partners. In other words, the new profit sharing ratio of each remaining partner will be the sum total of his old share of profits in the firm and the portion of the retiring partner's share of the profit acquired.

New Share of Partner = Old share + Acquired share from retiring/deceased partner.

(a)   Nothing is mention about the new profit sharing ratio at the time of retirement:

If nothing is stated about the future ratio of the remaining partner, then their old ratio is considered as their new ratio. In other words, in the absence of any information regarding the profit-sharing ratio in which the remaining partner acquire the share of the retiring/deceased partner, then it is assumed that they will acquire it in the old profit sharing ratio and so the share the future profits in their old ratio.

(b)   Remaining partners acquire the share of retiring/deceased partner in the specified ratio:

If the remaining partners acquire the share of retiring/deceased partner in a specified ratio, other than their old ratio, then there is a need to compute a new profit sharing ratio among them. The new profit sharing ratio is equal to the sum total of their old ratio and the share acquired from the retiring/deceased partner.

(c)   Remaining partners may agree on a particular new profit sharing ratio:

If the remaining partners decide a particular profit sharing ratio to share the future profits of the firm, in such a case the ratio so specified will be the new profit sharing ratio.

Gaining Ratio

The ratio in which the continuing partners acquire the share of the retiring/deceased partner is called the gaining ratio.

(a) If nothing is mention in agreement:

If nothing is mention in the agreement about the gaining ratio, then it is assumed that the remaining partners acquire the share of the retiring/deceased partner in their old profit sharing ratio. In that case, the gaining ratio of the remaining partners will be the same as their old profit sharing ratio and there is no need to compute the gaining ratio.

(b) If a new profit sharing ratio is given:

If the new profit sharing ratio is given of the remaining partners then we have to compute the gaining ratio. In this case, the gaining ratio is calculated by deducting the old ratio from the new ratio.

Gaining ratio = New ratio – Old ratio

Multiple Choice Questions   [1 Mark]

Q.1. P, Q and R are partners sharing profits in the ratio of 8 : 5 : 3. P retires. Q takes $3/16^{th}$ share from P and R takes $5/16^{th}$ share from P. What will be the new profit sharing ratio?

   (a) 1 : 1   (b) 10 : 6   (c) 9 : 7   (d) 5 : 3

Ans. (a)

Q.2. X, Y and Z are partners sharing profits and losses in the ratio of 4 : 3 : 2. Y retires and surrenders $1/9^{th}$ of his share in favour of X and the remaining in favour of Z. The new profit sharing ratio will be:

    (a) 1 : 8   (b) 13 : 14   (c) 8 : 1   (d) 14 : 13

Ans. (b)

Q.3. Retiring partner is compensated for parting with the firm's future profits in favour of remaining partners. The remaining partners contribute to such compensation amount in:

    (a) Gaining Ratio   (b) Sacrificing Ratio   (c) Capital Ratio   (d) Profit Sharing Ratio

Ans. (a)

Q.4. As per section _______ of the Indian Partnership Act, a retiring partner becomes entitled to profits after retirement if his dues remain unpaid

    (a) Section 73   (b) Section 26   (c) Section 4   (d) Section 37

Ans. (d)

Q.5. P, Q and R were partners in a firm in the ratio of 5 : 4 : 3. They admit S for 1/7 share. It is agreed that Q would retain his original share. _______ will be the sacrificing ratio between P and R.

    (a) 5 : 4   (b) 1 : 1   (c) 5 : 3   (d) 4 : 3

Ans. (c)

Very Short Answer Type   [1 Mark]

Q.6. "Retiring partner is not liable for firm's acts after his retirement". Is the statement True or False?

Ans. False

Q.7. Assertion (A): If new profit sharing ratio of remaining partner is not given

    Reason (R): It will assume that the remaining partner continue to share profit and losses in the new ratio

    (a) Both Assertion and reason are true and reason is correct explanation of assertion.

    (b) Assertion and reason both are true but reason is not the correct explanation of assertion.

    (c) Assertion is true, reason is false.

    (d) Assertion is false, reason is true.

Ans. (a)

Q.8. Assertion (A): gaining Ratio is calculated when a partner Retires or Dies

    Reason (R): Gaining ratio is calculated only by one method

    (a) Both Assertion and reason are true and reason is correct explanation of assertion.

    (b) Assertion and reason both are true but reason is not the correct explanation of assertion.

    (c) Assertion is true, reason is false.

    (d) Assertion is false, reason is true.

Ans. (c)

Q.9. Assertion (A): On retirement, the old partnership agreement comes to an end and a new partnership agreement comes into existence between the remaining partners.

Reason (R): Retirement of the partnership leads to the reconstitution of the firm.

(a) Both Assertion and reason are true and reason is correct explanation of assertion.

(b) Assertion and reason both are true but reason is not the correct explanation of assertion.

(c) Assertion is true, reason is false.

(d) Assertion is false, reason is true.

Ans. (a)

Q.10. Assertion (A): Ram, Rahim and Ron share profits in the ratio 2 : 3 : 5. Ram decides to retire. The new profit-sharing ratio is 3 : 5. If the profit earned was Rs.1,50,000 before retirement. Rahim's share is Rs.45,000.

Reason (R): The profits are shared in the new profit-sharing ratio.

(a) Both Assertion and reason are true and reason is correct explanation of assertion.

(b) Assertion and reason both are true but reason is not the correct explanation of assertion.

(c) Assertion is true, reason is false.

(d) Assertion is false, reason is true.

Ans. (c)

Q.11. P, Q and R were partners in a firm. On 31st March, 2018 R retired. The amount payable to R Rs. 2,17,000 was transferred to his loan account. R agreed to receive interest on this amount as per the provisions of Partnership Act, 1932. State the rate at which interest will be paid to R.   **(CBSE Delhi 2019)**

Ans.   Rate of interest will be 6% p.a.

Q.12. At the time of retirement how is the new profit sharing ratio among the remaining partners calculated Rs.

(CBSE Compt. 2019)

Ans. The new share of each of the remaining partner is calculated as his/her own share in the firm plus the share acquired from the retiring partner.

Q.13. In which ratio do the remaining partners acquire the share of profit of the retiring partner?

(CBSE Compt. 2017)

Ans. Gaining ratio.

Q.14. At the time of retirement of a partner, state the condition when there is no need to compute gaining ratio.

(CBSE 2013 Compartment OD)

Ans. When the remaining partners share profits in old ratio.

Q.15. State the ratio in which share of goodwill of the retiring partner is debited to Capital Accounts of the remaining partners.   **(CBSE 2011)**

Ans. In their gaining ratio.

Short Answer Type - I   [2 Marks]

Q.1. A, B and C are partners sharing profits in the ratio of 5 : 2 : 1. If the new ratio on the retirement of A is 3 : 2, what be the gaining ratio?   (CBSE 2012)

Ans. 14 : 11

Q.2. P, Q and R are partners sharing profits in the ratio of 5 : 4 : 3. Q retires and P and R decide to share future profits equally. Gaining ratio will be:

Ans. 1 : 3

Q.3. A, B and C are partners sharing profits in the ratio of 1/2 : 1/4 : 1/4. New ratio on the retirement of B will be:

(CBSE 2010)

Ans. 2 : 1

Q.4. A, B and C are partners sharing profits in the ratio of 1/4 : 3/10 : 9/20. The new ratio on the retirement of C will be:

Ans. 5 : 6

Q.5. X, Y and Z have been sharing profits in the ratio of 4; 2 : 1 Z retires X and Y take Z's share equally. New profits sharing ratio will be:

Ans. 9 : 5

Q.6. L, P and G are three partners sharing profits in the ratio 15 : 9 : 8. G retires. L and P decided to share profits in equal ratio. Gaining ratio will be:

Ans. 1 : 7

Q.7. On 1st April, 2022 A, B and C were partners sharing profits and losses in the ratio of 5 : 3 : 2 respectively. On this date B retires. The new profits sharing ratio of A and C will be 3 : 2. Gaining ratio will be:

Ans. 2 : 1

Q.8. B, P and L sharing profits in the ratio 4 : 3 : 2. B retires, P and L decided to share profits inn future in the of 5 : 3 gaining ratio will be:

Ans. 11 : 13

Q.9. P, Q and R were partners sharing profits in the ratio 2 : 2 1. Q retires and the new profits sharing ratio of P and R will be 3 : 1. Gaining ratio will be:

Ans. 7 : 1

Q.10. A, B and C are equal partners in a firm. B retires and the remaining partners decided to share the new firm in the ratio of 5 : 4 gaining ratio will be:

Ans. 2 : 1

Q.11. A, B and C are partners sharing profits or loss in the ratio of 3 : 2 : 1. B retires and after B's retirement A and C agreed to share profit or loss in the ratio of 3 : 2 in future. Their gaining ratio will be:

Ans. 3 : 7

Q.12. A, B and C are partners sharing profit or loss in the ratio of 4 : 3 : 2. C retires and after C" s retirement A and B agreed to share profit or loss in the ratio of 4 : 3 in future. Their gaining ratio will be: **(CBSE 2013)**

Ans. 4 : 3

Short Answer Type - II   [3 Marks]

Q.1. How can a partner retire from a firm?   **(CBSE 2011)**

Ans. Retirement of a Partner Retirement of a partner means ceasing to be partner of the firm. A partner may retire

   (i) If there is Agreement to this effect

   (ii) All Partners' give consent

   (iii) At Will by giving written notice.

Q.2. Explain how to calculate amount paid to retired or deceased partner?

Ans. (i) Amount due to Retiring/Deceased Partner

     (a) Credit Balance of his capital.

     (b) Credit Balance of his current account (if any).

     (c) Share of Goodwill. (To be given by gaining partners)

     (d) Share of Reserves or Undistributed Profits.

     (e) His share in the profit on revaluation of assets and reassessment of liabilities.

     (f) If retirement is during the year, the retiring partner will be given. Share in profits up to the date of retirement.

     (g) Interest on capital if involved. 8. Salary if any up to the date of Retirement/Death

   (ii) Deductions from the above Sum (To be Debited to the Capital Account)

     (a) Debit balance of his current account (if any)

     (b) Share of existing Goodwill to be written off.

     (c) Share of Accumulated loss.

     (d) Drawings and interest on drawings (if any).

     (e) Share of loss on account of Revaluation of assets and liabilities.

     (f) His share of business loss up to the date of Retirement/Death (To P & L suspense A/c)

Q.3. A, B and C are partners sharing profit and loss in the ratio of 3 : 2 : 1 then on retirement of a partner; the gaining ratio/new ratio will be?

Ans. On A's Retirement ratio between B and C will be 2 : 1

   On B's Retirement ratio between A and C will be 3 : 1

   On C's Retirement ratio between A and B will be 3 : 2

Q.4. A, B & C share profit and losses in the ratio 3 : 2 : 1. On C's death his share is taken by A and B in the ratio of 2 : 1 Calculate new ratio.

Ans. In this case gaining ratio = 2 : 1 (given)

A's old share = 3/6,

B's old share = 2/6

C's share = 1/6

A's gain = 2/3 of C's share 2/3 × 1/6 = 2/18

B's gain = 1/3 of C's share = 1/3 × 1/6 = 1/18

A's new share = A's old + A's gain = 3/6 + 2/18 = 11/18

B's new share = B's old share + B's gain = 2/6 + 1/18 = 7/18

Ans. New ratio = 11 : 7

Q.5. A, B, & C share profit in the ratio 3 : 2 : 1 on C's death his taken by A & B in the rate of 2 : 1 Calculate new ratio.

(CBSE 2014)

Ans. In this case gaining ratio = 2 : 1 (given)

A's old share = 3/6 B's old share = 2/6   & C's share = 1/6

A's gain =2/3 of c's share 2/3 × 1/6 =2/18

B's gain = 1/3 of C's share =1/3 × 1/6 =1/18

A's new share = A's old + gain

=2/6 +1/18 = 11/18

B, s new share = B's old share + B's gain

=2/6 + 1/18 = 7/18

New ratio =11 : 7

Q.6. W, X, Y and Z are partners sharing profit and losses in the ratio of 1/3, 1/6, 1/3 and 1/6 respectively. Y retires and W, X and Z decided to share the profit and losses equally. Calculate the gaining ratio.   **(CBSE 2013)**

Ans. Gaining ratio – New ratio – old ratio

Old ratio = 1/2 : 1/6 : 1/3 : 1/6

ie. 2/6 : 1/6 : 26 : 1/6

New ratio = 1 : 1 : 1

W's gain = 1/3 – 2/6 = 0/6

Z's gain = 1/3 – 1/6 = 1/6

Z's gain = 1/3 – 1/6 = 1/6

Gaining ratio = 0 : 1 : 1

TOPIC 2 Treatment of Goodwill, Accumulated Profits and Losses, Reserves and Provisions at the time of Retirement of A Partner

Summary

Treatment of Goodwill

The retiring or deceased partner is entitled to his share of goodwill at the time of retirement/death because the goodwill has been earned by the firm with the efforts of all the existing partners. Hence, at the time of retirement/death of a partner, goodwill is valued as per agreement among the partners the retiring/ deceased partner compensated for his share of goodwill by the continuing partners (who have gained due to acquisition of share of profit from the retiring/ deceased partner) in their gaining ratio.

1. When goodwill does not appear in the books:-

    (a) **Goodwill is raised at its full value and retained in the books:**

         Goodwill A/c Dr.

         To All Partner's Capital A/c's

         (including retiring/deceased partner)

         (For the goodwill raised at its full value and credited to capital A/c's of a'1 partners in their old profit sharing ratio)

         The full value of goodwill will appear in the new balance sheet.

    (b) **Goodwill is raised at its full value and written off immediately:**

         If it is decided that the goodwill will not appear in the balance sheet of the reconstituted firm, then the following journal entries are required:

         1. Goodwill A/c Dr.

             To All Partner's Capital A/c's (For raising of Goodwill and credited to all partners capital A/c's in their old profit sharing ratio)

         2. Continuing Partner's Capital A/c's Dr.

             To Goodwill A/c

             (For written off goodwill between continuing partners in their new profit sharing ratio)

    (c) **Goodwill is raised to the extent of retired/deceased partner's share and written off immediately:**

         1. Goodwill A/c Dr.

             To Retiring/Deceased Partner's Capital A/c (For the goodwill raised by share of outgoing partner)

         2. Continuing Partner's Capital A/c's Dr.

             To Goodwill A/c

             (For the goodwill written off between the continuing partners in their gaining ratio)

    (d) No Goodwill account is raised at all in the firm's books:

         If the outgoing partner's share of goodwill is adjusted in the capital accounts of the continuing partners without opening a goodwill account, the following entry will be required:

         Continuing Partner's Capital A/c's Dr.

         To Outgoing Partner's Capital A/c (For the share of outgoing partner in the goodwill adjusted through capital accounts in the gaining ratio)

Hidden Goodwill: If the firm has agreed to settle the retiring or deceased partner's account by paying him a lump sum amount, then the amount paid to him in excess of what is due to him, based on the balance in his capital account after making necessary adjustments in respect of accumulated profits and losses and revaluation of assets and liabilities, etc., shall be treated as his share of goodwill (known as hidden goodwill)

Revaluation of Assets and Liabilities

The retiring /deceased partner must be given a share of all profits that have arisen till his retirement/death and is made to bear his share of losses that have occurred till that period. This necessitates the revaluation of assets and liabilities. At the time of retirement/death of a partner, there may be some assets and liabilities which may not have been shown at their present values.

Journal Entries:

1. For increase in the value of assets:

   Asset(s) A/c (individually) Dr.

   To Revaluation A/c (For increase in the value of assets)

2. For decrease in the value of assets:

   Revaluation A/c Dr.

   To Assets A/c's (individually)

   (For decrease in the value of assets)

3. For increase in the number of liabilities:

   Revaluation A/c Dr.

   To Liabilities A/c's (individually)

   (for an increase in liabilities)

4. For decrease in the number of liabilities:

   Liabilities A/c's (individually) Dr.

   To Revaluation A/c (For decrease in the liabilities)

5. For an unrecorded asset:

   Assets A/c Dr.

   To Revaluation A/c

   (For unrecorded assets brought into books)

6. For an unrecorded liability:

   Revaluation A/c Dr.

   To Liability A/c

   (For an unrecorded liability brought into books)

7. For the sale of an unrecorded asset:

   Cash A/c Dr.

   To Revaluation A/c (For the sale of unrecorded assets)

8. For payment of an unrecorded liability:

   Revaluation A/c Dr.

   To Cash A/c

   (For the payment of an unrecorded*liability)

9.　For-profit on revaluation:

　　Revaluation A/c Dr.

　　To All Partner's Capital A/c's (individually)

　　(For the distribution of profit on revaluation to all partners in their old profit sharing ratio)

　　Or

10.　For Loss on revaluation:

　　All Partner's Capital A/c's (individually) Dr.

　　To Revaluation A/c

　　(For the distribution of losses on revaluation to all partners in their old profit sharing ratio)

Reserves and Accumulated Profits and Losses

The retiring/deceased partner is also entitled to his/her share in the accumulated profits, general reserve, workmen compensation fund 1 etc. and is also liable to share the accumulated losses.

For this purpose the following journal entries are required:

1.　For Transferring accumulated profits, General Reserves etc.

　　To All Partner's Capital A/c's (individually)

　　(For accumulated profits are transferred to all partner's Capital A/c's in their old profit sharing ratio)

2.　For transfer of accumulated losses:

　　All Partner's Capital A/c's (individually) Dr.

　　To Profit and Loss A/c To Any Accumulated Loss A/c (For accumulated losses transferred to all partner's Capital A/c's in their old profit sharing ratio)

Multiple Choice Questions　　　　　　　　　　　　　　　　　　　　　　　　[1 Mark]

Q.1. Gaining ratio is used to distribute______in case of retirement of a partner.

　　(a) Goodwill　　　　　　　　　　　　　　　(b) Revaluation Profit or Loss

　　(c) Profit and Loss Account (Credit Balance)　　　(d) Both b and c

Ans. (a)

Q.2. X, Y and Z are partners in a firm. Y retires and his claim including his capital and his share of goodwill is R. 1,20,000. He is paid partly in cash and partly in kind. A vehicle at Rs.60,000 unrecorded in the books of the firm and the balance in cash is given to him to settle his account. The amount of cash to be paid to Y will be:

　　(a) Rs.80,000　　　　(b) Rs.60,000　　　　(c) Rs.40,000　　　　(d) Rs.30,000

Ans. (a)

Q.3. At the time of retirement of a partner, share of retiring partner's goodwill will be credited to_____Capital Account(s).

　　(a) Remaining Partner(s)　　　　　　　　　(b) Retiring Partner's

　　(c) Both Sacrificing and Gaining Partner(s)　　　(d) Gaining Partner(s)

Ans. (b)

Q.4. A and B were partners. They shared profits as A- 1/2; B- 1/3 and carried to reserve 1/6. B retired. The balance of reserve on the date of death was Rs.30,000. B's share of reserve will be:

(a) Rs.10,000   (b) Rs.8,000   (c) Rs.12,000   (d) Rs.9,000

Ans. (c)

Q.5. If goodwill is already appearing in the books of accounts at the time of retirement, then it should be written off in —————.

(a) New Ratio   (b) Gaining Ratio   (c) Sacrificing Ratio   (d) Old Ratio

Ans. (d)

Q.6. A, B and C were partners. Their partnership deed provided that they were to share profits as; A 26 per cent; B 34 per cent; C 40 per cent; and that if a partner retires, his capital should remain in the business for a stated period at a fixed rate of interest, but that the retiring partner's share should be credited with an amount for Goodwill, based upon one and a half year's average profits, for the five years prior to his death, but be subject to deduction of 5 per cent from the book debts. C retired, and the profits of the firm for five years were agreed at Rs.20,000; Rs.30,000; Rs.15,000 (loss); Rs.5,000 (loss); and Rs.45,000 respectively. Book Debts stood at Rs.90,000. The share of Goodwill to be credited to C's Account will be:

(a) Rs.2,700   (b) Rs.6,300   (c) Rs.7,200   (d) Rs.3,600

Ans. (c)

Q.7. X,Y and Z were partners in a firm sharing profits in ratio of 3 : 4 : 1 X retired and new profit sharing ratio between Y and Z will be 5 : 4. On X's retirement the goodwill of the firm was valued at Rs. 54,000 journal entry will be:

(a) Y's capital   Dr.   24,000
    Z's capital   Dr.   30,000
    To X's capital   54,000
(b) Y's capital   Dr.   15,000
    Z's capital   Dr.   12,,000
    To X's capital   27000
(c) Y's capital   Dr.   12,000
    Z's capital   Dr.   15,000
    To X's capital   27,000
(d) X's capitals a/c   Dr.   27,000
    To Y's capitals   12,000
    To Z's capitals   15,000

Ans. (c)

Q.8. At the time of retirement, amount remaining in Investment Fluctuation Reserve after meeting the fall in value of Investment is:

(a) Credited in Sacrificing Ratio   (b) Credited in New Profit Sharing Ratio

(c) Credited in Old Profit Sharing Ratio   (d) Credited in Gaining Ratio

Ans. (c)

Q.9. Match the following with respect to the treatment of goodwill:

i.	Change in Profit Sharing Ratio	A.	Gaining Partners Capital A/c To Retiring Partners Capital A/c	Dr.
ii.	Admission of a Partner	B.	Gaining Partners Capital A/c To Sacrificing Partners Capital A/c	Dr.
iii.	Retirement of a Partner	C.	Premium for Goodwill A/c To Sacrificing Partners Capital A/c	Dr.

(a) i-C, ii-A, iii-B   (b) i-A, ii-B, iii-C   (c) i-B, ii-A, iii-C   (d) i-B, ii-C, iii-A

Ans. (d)

Very Short Answer Type   [1 Mark]

Q.10. Assertion (A): retiring partner is entitled to his share of goodwill at the time of retirement.

Reason (R): goodwill earned by the firm is result of efforts of all existing partners in the past

(a) Both Assertion and reason are true and reason is correct explanation of assertion.

(b) Assertion and reason both are true but reason is not the correct explanation of assertion.

(c) Assertion is true, reason is false.

(d) Assertion is false, reason is true.

Ans. (a)

Q.11. Assertion (A): When goodwill is not appearing in the books, retiring or deceased partner's capital account is to be credited with his share of goodwill and gaining partners' capital accounts are to be debited in gaining ratio.

Reason (R): Goodwill needs to be compensated by the gaining partners in the gaining ratio.

(a) Both Assertion and reason are true and reason is correct explanation of assertion.

(b) Assertion and reason both are true but reason is not the correct explanation of assertion.

(c) Assertion is true, reason is false.

(d) Assertion is false, reason is true.

Ans. (a)

Q.12. X, Y and Z were partners sharing profits and losses in the ratio of 3 : 2 : 2. Z retired and the amount due to him was Rs. 85,000. He was paid Rs. 5,000 immediately. The balance was payable in three equal annual instalments carrying interest @ 6% p.a. Pass necessary journal entry for recording the same on the date of Z's retirement.

(Compt. Delhi 2017)

Ans.

Books of the X, Y, Z

JOURNAL

Date	Particulars		L.F.	Dr. (Rs.)	Cr. (Rs.)
	Z's Capital A/c	Dr.		85,000	
	To Cash/Bank A/c				5,000
	To Z's Loan A/c				80,000
	(Amount due to Z on his retirement transferred to his loan A/c after payment of Rs.5000)				

▰ Short Answer Type - I　　　　　　　　　　　　　　　　　　　　　　**[2 Marks]**

Q.13. A, B and C were partners in a firm sharing profits and losses in the ratio of 2 : 2 : 1. The capital balance are Rs.50,000 for A. Rs.70,000 for B, Rs.35,000 for C. B decided to retire the firm and balance in reserve on the date was Rs.25,000. If goodwill of the firm was valued at Rs.30,000 and profit on revaluation was Rs.7,500 then what amount will be payable to B? **(CBSE 2013)**

Ans. Rs.95,000 [70,000 + 10,000 + 12,000 + 3,000]

Q.14. P, O and R are sharing profits and losses equally. R retires and the goodwill is appearing in the books at Rs.30,000. Goodwill of the firm is valued at Rs.1,50,000. Calculate the Net amount to be credited to R's capital A/c

Ans. Rs.40,000 [50,000 – 10,000]

Q.15. Ram, Krishna and Ganesh were sharing profits and losses in the ratio of 5 : 3 : 2. Ram retires and Krishna and Ganesh share the future profits and losses equally. Goodwill of the firm is valued at Rs.1,00,000. Calculate the amount of goodwill to be debited to Krishna's and Ganesh capital A/C.

Ans. Rs.20,000 & Rs.30,000

Q.16. A, B and C were partners sharing profits in the ratio of 6 : 4 : 5. On 1st April, 2016, B retired from the firm and the new profit sharing ratio between A and C was decided as 11 : 4. On B's retirement, the goodwill of the firm valued at Rs.1,80,000. Pass journal entry for treatment of goodwill on B's retirement. **(CBSE Delhi)**

Ans. A's Capital A/c Dr. 60,000

　　To B's Capital A/c　　　　48,000

　　To C's Capital A/c　　　　12,000

　　(Being adjustment of goodwill made on B's retirement)

Q.17. P, O and R are sharing profits and losses equally. R retires and the Goodwill of the firm is valued at Rs.1,50,000. Journalise. **(CBSE Delhi)**

Ans. P's Capital A/c Dr.　　　　25,000

　　O's Capital A/c Dr.　　　　25,000

　　To R's Capital A/c　　　　50,000

　　(Being adjustment of goodwill made on R's retirement)

Q.18. Naresh, Raj Kumar and Bishwajeet are equal partners. Raj Kumar decides to retire. On the date of his retirement, the Balance Sheet of the firm showed the following : General Reserves Rs.36,000 and Profit and Loss Account (Dr.) Rs.15,000.

Pass the necessary journal entries to the above effect. **(CBSE 2015)**

Ans.

JOURNAL

Date	Particulars	L.F.	Dr. (Rs.)	Cr. (Rs.)
	General Reserve A/c　　　　　　　　　　　　　　Dr.		36,000	
	To Naresh's Capital A/c			12,000
	To Raj Kumar's Capital A/c			12,000

To Bishwajeet's Capital A/c				12,000
(Being transferring the general reserve to old partners in old profit sharing ratio 1 : 1 : 1)				
To Naresh's Capital A/c	Dr.		5,000	
To Raj Kumar's Capital A/c	Dr.		5,000	
To Bishwajeet's Capital A/c	Dr.		5,000	
To Profit and Loss A/c				15,000
(Being transferring the balance of profit and Loss A/c to old partners in old profit sharing ratio 1 : 1 : 1)				

Q.19. A, B and C were partners sharing profits in the ratio of 6 : 4 : 5. Their capitals were A Rs.1,00,000, B Rs.80,000 and C Rs.60,000. On 1 st April 2009, B retired from the firm and the new profit sharing ratio between A and C was decided as 11 : 4. On B's retirement the goodwill of the firm was valued at Rs.1,80,000. Showing your calculations clearly, pass necessary journal entry for the treatment of goodwill on B's retirement.

(CBSE 2016)

Ans.

JOURNAL

Date	Particulars		L.F.	Dr. (Rs.)	Cr. (Rs.)
2009	A's Capital A/c	Dr.		60,000	
April 1	To B's Capital A/c				48,000
	To C's Capital A.c				12,000
	(Amount of goodwill adjusted)				

Gaining Ratio = New Ratio – Old Ratio

$$A = \frac{11}{15} - \frac{6}{15} = \frac{5}{15}$$

$$C = \frac{4}{15} - \frac{5}{15} = \frac{1}{15} \text{ (Sacrifice)}$$

B's share of goodwill = Rs.1,80,000 × $\frac{4}{15}$ = Rs.48,000

C's share of goodwill to the extent of sacrifice = Rs.1,80,000 × $\frac{1}{15}$ = Rs.12,000

As A is only gainer, he will compensate both B and C.

Short Answer Type - II   [3 Marks]

Q.1. Why the Retiring or Deceased Partner is entitled to his share of Goodwill at the time of Retirement/ Death?

Ans. Because the Goodwill has been earned by the firm with the efforts of the existing partners, hence at the time of retirement/death of a partner it is valued as per agreement.

Q.2. What is Hidden Goodwill?

Ans. If the firm has agreed to settle the retiring or deceased partner by paying a lump sum amount, then the amount paid to him in access of what is due shall be treated as his share of goodwill and known as hidden goodwill

Q.3. Describe Treatment of Goodwill at the time of retirement or death of a partner.

Ans. Steps to be followed

(i) When old goodwill appears in the books then first of all this is written off in the old ratio. Remember Old Goodwill in Old Ratio.

All Partner's capital A/c Dr.

To Goodwill A/c

(ii) After written off old goodwill, adjustment of retiring partner's share of goodwill will be made through the following journal entry

Gaining Partner's Capital A/c Dr. (in gaining ratio)

To Retiring / Deceased Partner's Current A/c (if any)

To Retiring/Deceased Partners' Capital A/c

Q.4. Ram, Shyam and Mohan are partners sharing profits in the ratio of 5 : 3 : 2. Shyam retired, and goodwill is valued at Rs.1,20,000. Ram and Mohan decided to share future profits in the ratio of 2 : 3. Pass necessary journal entries for treatment of goodwill, if goodwill appears in the books atRs.40,000.   **(CBSE 2015)**

Ans.

JOURNAL

Date	Particulars		L.F.	Dr. (Rs.)	Cr. (Rs.)
	Ram's Capital A/c	Dr.		20,000	
	Shyam's Capital A/c	Dr.		12,000	
	Mohan's Capital A/c	Dr.		8,000	
	To Goodwill A/c				40,000
	(Goodwill appearing in books written off among partners' in old ratio				
	Mohan's Capital A/c	Dr.		48,000	
	To Shyam's Capital A/c				36,000
	To Ram's Capital A/c				12,000
	(Adjustment for goodwill)				

Sacrificing Ratio = New Ratio – Old Ratio

$$\text{Ram} = \frac{2}{5} - \frac{5}{10} = \frac{4-5}{10} = \frac{1}{10}\,(\text{Sacrifice})$$

$$\text{Monan} = \frac{3}{5} - \frac{2}{10} = \frac{6-2}{10} = \frac{4}{10}\,(\text{Gain})$$

As only Mohan has gain, he will compensate Shyam (Rs.36,000) and Ram (Rs.12,000)

$$\text{Shyam's share of Goodwill} = \text{Rs.1,20,000} \times \frac{3}{10} = \text{Rs.36,000}$$

$$\text{Ram's share of goodwill} = \text{Rs.1,20,000} \times \frac{1}{10} = \text{Rs.12,000}$$

Q.5. A firm of A, B and C has Workmen Compensation Fund of Rs.30,000. On retirement of a partner, how Rs. 20,000 will be treated in the following cases:

(a) There is no claim against Workmen Compensation fund.

(b) There is a claim of Rs. 12,000 against Workmen Compensation Fund.

Journalise.

(CBSE 2014)

Ans.

JOURNAL ENTRIES

Date	Particulars		L.F.	Dr. (Rs.)	Cr. (Rs.)
Case (a)	Workmen Compensation Fund A/c	Dr.		30,000	
	To A's Capital A/c				10,000
	To B's Capital A/c				10,000
	To C's Capital A./c				10,000
	(Being entire workmen compensation fund distributed in old profit sharing ratio)				
Case (b)	Workmen Compensation Fund A/c	Dr.		18,000	
	To A's Capital A/c				6,000
	To B's Capital A/c				6,000
	To C's Capital A./c				6,000
	(Being workmen compensation fund distributed in old ratio after setting off claim of Rs.12,000)				

Long Answer Type   [5 Marks]

Analyse the case given below and answer the questions that follow:

Q.6. P and Q and R are partners in a firm sharing Profit in the Ratio of 2 : 2 : 1. Their capitals were 1,50,000; 100,000 and 50,000 respectively. Plant 140,000; Stock 90,000; Patents 18250; Cash 30750; Debtors 80,000 And provision for doubtful debt 4000; Creditors 55000. R retires on the this date and P, Q decided to share future profit and losses in the Ratio of 3 : 2 On the basis of above case. Give the answer of following questions.

[1] Stock to be reduced by Rs.82000 the new amount will shown in

    (a) Debit side of revaluation A/c 8000   (b) Credit side of revaluation A/c 90000

    (c) Credit side of partners capital A/c 8000   (d) None of the above

Ans. (a)

[2] If Patents are valueless then what will be the new amount of patent

    (a) 18,250   (b) zero

    (c) Both amount to be consider   (d) None of the above

Ans. (a)

[3] Profit or loss on Revaluation A/c Transferred to

    (a) Rs.60,000 Profit   (b) Rs.60,000 loss

    (c) Rs.90,000 Profit   (d) Rs.90,000 loss

Ans. (b)

[4] How will you treat an amount of Rs.20,000 had to be paid to an employee injured in accident?

    (a) Bank a/c Credit side of revaluation a/c   (b) Bank a/c Debit side of revaluation a/c

    (c) Bank a/c Credit side of realization a/c   (d) Bank a/c Debit side of Realization a/c

Ans. (a)

Analyse the case given below and answer the questions that follow:

Q.7. P, Q and R are partners sharing profit in the ratio of 5 : 3 : 2 Q retires and new Profit-sharing ratio Between P and R agreed at 2 : 3. They also decided to record the effect of the following without affect their book values: General Reserve 120,000 Contingency reserve 70,000 Profit and Loss (Dr) 30,000 Advertisement suspense a/c 10,000 On the basis of above data give the answer of following questions

    [1] Calculate Sacrificing Ratio of P

        (a) 1/20   (b) 1/10

        (c) 2/10   (d) 2/15

Ans. (a)

    [2] Contingency reserve will be

        (a) Added to General reserve   (b) Subtracted to General Reserve

        (c) Added to Advertisement Expenses   (d) No effect

Ans. (a)

    [3] What will be single Adjusting Entry?

        (a) R's capital A/c Dr. 60,000 To Q's capital a/c 45,000 To P's capital A/c 15,000

        (b) Q's capital A/c Dr. 80,000 To R's capital a/c 45,000 To A's capital A/c 35,000

        (c) R's capital A/c Dr. 60,000 To P's capital a/c 45,000 To Q's capital A/c 15,000

        (d) P's capital A/c Dr. 80,000 To Q's capital a/c 45,000 To R's capital A/c 35,000

Ans. (a)

    [4] What will be the net effect?

        (a) 1,40,000   (b) 1,30,000

        (c) 1,50,000   (d) 2,00,000

Ans. (a)

Analyse the case given below and answer the questions that follow:

Q.8. A, K and S were partners in a firm sharing profits in the ratio of 5: 3: 2. Goodwill appeared in their books at the value of Rs.60,000. 'K' decided to retire from the firm. On the date of his retirement, goodwill of the firm was valued at Rs.2,40,000. The new profit sharing ratio decided among A and S was 2 : 3.

    [1] How much will be transferred to K's Capital Account of the existing goodwill?

        (a) Rs.18,000   (b) Rs.30,000

        (c) Rs.12,000   (d) Rs.72,000

Ans. (a)

    [2] What is A's gaining or sacrificing ratio:

        (a) 1/10 Gain   (b) 1/10 Sacrifice

        (c) 4/10 Gain   (d) 4/10 Sacrifice

Ans. (b)

    [3] What amount of goodwill will be transferred to K's capital account as compensated by A and S?

      (a) Rs.96,000　　　　　　　　　　　　　　　　(b) Rs.72,000

      (c) Rs.24,000　　　　　　　　　　　　　　　　(d) Rs.18,000

Ans. (b)

Analyse the case given below and answer the questions that follow:

Q.9. Rohit, Karan and Karim are partners sharing profits and losses in the ratio of 14 : 5 : 6 respectively. Karan retires and surrenders his entire 5/25th share in favour of Rohit. The goodwill of the firm is valued at 2 years' purchase of Super Profit based on average profits of last three years. The profits for the last three years are Rs50,000, Rs.55,000 and Rs.60,000, respectively. The normal profits for the similar firm are 30,000. Goodwill already appears in the books of the firm at 75,000.

    [1] Who is the gaining partner on retirement of Karan?

      (a) Rohit　　　　　　　　　　　　　　　　　(b) Karim

      (c) Both (a) and (b)　　　　　　　　　　　　(d) Neither (a) nor (b)

Ans. (a)

    [2] What is the value of goodwill determined by using super- profit method?

      (a) Rs.50,000　　　　　　　　　　　　　　　　(b) Rs.10,000

      (c) Rs.30,000　　　　　　　　　　　　　　　　(d) Rs.75,000

Ans. (a)

    [3] In which ratio, existing goodwill of Rs.75000 be written off:

      (a) 14 : 5 : 6　　　　　　　　　　　　　　　　(b) New ratio, after Karan retirement

      (c) In gaining ratio　　　　　　　　　　　　　(d) None of these

Ans. (a)

TOPIC 3　Revaluation Account, Partner's Capital Accounts and Balance Sheet at the Time of Retirement

Summary

Disposal of Amount Due to Retiring Partner

The necessary journal entries recorded are as follows.

1. When retiring partner is paid cash in full.

    Retiring Partners' Capital A/c Dr.

    To Cash/Bank A/c

2. When retiring partners' whole amount is treated as loan.

    Retiring Partners' Capital A/c Dr.

    To Retiring Partners' Loan A/c

3.   When retiring partner is partly paid in cash and the remaining amount treated as loan.

Retiring Partners' Capital A/c Dr. (Total Amount due)

To Cash/Bank A/c (Amount Paid)

To Retiring Partners' Loan A/c (Amount of Loan)

4 .   When Loan account is settled by paying in instalment includes principal and interest.

(a)   For interest on loan Interest A/c Dr.

To Retiring Partner's Loan A/c

(b)   For payment of instalment Retiring Partner's Loan A/c Dr.

To Cash/Bank A/c

Adjustment of Partner's Capital

At the time of retirement or death of a partner, the remaining partners may decide to adjust their capital contribution in their new profit sharing ratio. The adjustment of the remaining partner's capitals may involve any one of the following cases:

1.   When the total capital of a new firm is specified.

Steps:

(a)   Compute the new capitals of the remaining partners by dividing total capital in their new profit sharing ratio.

(b)   Calculate the amount of adjusted old capital of the remaining partners after all adjustments regarding goodwill, accumulated profit and losses, profit or loss on revaluation etc.

(c)   Find out the surplus or deficiency, as the case may be, in each of the remaining partner's capital account by comparing the new capital and the adjusted capital.

(d)   Adjust the surplus by paying cash to the concerned partner or by crediting his Current Account as agreed. Adjust the deficiency by asking the concerned partner to pay cash or by debiting his current account.

Adjustment of Partners' Capitals

At the time of retirement or death of a partner, the remaining partners may decide to adjust their capital contributions in their profit sharing ratio. In such a situation, the sum of balances in the capitals of continuing partners may be treated as the total capital of the new firm, unless specified otherwise. Then, to ascertain the new capital of the continuing partners, the total capital of the firm is divided amongst the remaining partners as per the new profit sharing ratio, and the excess or deficiency of capital in the individual capital account's may be worked out. Such excess or shortage shall be adjusted by withdrawal of contribution in cash, as the case may be, for which the following journal entries will be recorded.

(i)   For excess capital withdrawn by the partner :

Partners' Capital A/c Dr.

To Cash / Bank A/c

(ii)   For amount of capital to be brought in by the partner:

Cash / Bank A/c Dr.

To Partners' Capital A/c

Multiple Choice Questions   [1 Mark]

Q.1. As per Section 37 of the Indian Partnership Act, 1932, interest @_____ is payable to the retiring partner if full or part of his dues remain unpaid.

(a) 9% p.m.   (b) 12% p.m.   (c) 6% p.m.   (d) None of the above

Ans. (d)

Q.2. When the balance sheet is prepared after retirement (subsequent to preparation of Revaluation Account), _____ values are shown in it.

(a) Historical   (b) Realisable   (c) Market   (d) Revalued

Ans. (d)

Q.3. On retirement of a partner, debtors of Rs.34,000 were shown in the Balance sheet. Out of this Rs.4,000 became bad. One debtor became insolvent. 70% were recovered from him out of Rs.10,000. Full amount is expected from the balance debtors. On account of this item loss in revaluation account will be:

(a) Rs.10,200   (b) Rs.3,000   (c) Rs.7,000   (d) Rs.4,000

Ans. (c)

Q.4. If at the time of retirement, there is some unrecorded asset, it will be_____ to_____ Account.

(a) Debited, Revaluation   (b) Credited, Revaluation

(c) Debited, Goodwill   (d) Credited, Partners' Capital

Ans. (b)

Q.5. Anil, Bimal and Chetan are partners sharing their profits and losses in the ratio of 4 : 3 : 2. On 1.7.2013, Chetan retired and on that date the capitals of Anil, Bimal and Chetan after all necessary adjustments stood at Rs.75,000, Rs.65,000 and Rs.45,000 respectively. Anil and Bimal continued to carry the business for 6 months without settling Chetan's account. During the period of six months ending 31st December, 2013, a profit of Rs.50,000 is earned by the firm. Keeping Chetan's interest in mind, the amount payable to Chetan will be:

(a) Rs.1,350   (b) Rs.13,362   (c) Rs.12,162   (d) Rs.1,362

Ans. (c)

Very Short Answer Type   [1 Mark]

Q.6. Assertion (A): At the time of retirement Revaluation account is prepared

Reason (R): revaluation and Reessement is made by the method other than Admission of partner

(a) Both Assertion and reason are true and reason is correct explanation of assertion.

(b) Assertion and reason both are true but reason is not the correct explanation of assertion.

(c) Assertion is true, reason is false.

(d) Assertion is false, reason is true.

Ans. (c)

Q.7. Assertion (A): retiring partner is entitled to Interest @10 %p.a. till the loan is paid off

Reason (R): Instead of Interest he may take that share of profit which has been earned by the firm by the amount due to him

(a) Both Assertion and reason are true and reason is correct explanation of assertion.

(b) Assertion and reason both are true but reason is not the correct explanation of assertion.

(c) Assertion is true, reason is false.

(d) Assertion is false, reason is true.

Ans. (d)

Short Answer Type - I　　　　[2 Marks]

Q.8. Explain Disposal Amount due to Retiring partner.

Ans. The outgoing partners' account is settled as per the terms of partnership deed i.e.

(i)　In lump sum immediately

(ii)　In various instalments with or without interest as agreed

(iii)Partly in cash immediately and partly in instalments at the agreed intervals.

Q.9. What are the provisions if the Retiring Partner is not paid fully at the time of Retirement?　**[CBSE 2015]**

Ans. In the absence of any agreement, Section 37 of the Indian Partnership Act, 1932 is applicable, which states that the outgoing partner has an option to receive

(i)　Either Interest @ 6% till the date of payment

(ii)　Such share of Profits which has been earned with his/her money.

Short Answer Type - II　　　　[3 Marks]

Q.10. Write Accounting Treatments which are required at the time of retirement.

Ans. Following Accounting Treatments are required at the time of retirement.

(i)　Calculation of new profit-sharing ratio and gaining ratio

(ii)　Treatment of goodwill.

(iii)Revaluation account preparation with the adjustment in respect of unrecorded assets/liabilities.

(iv)Distribution of reserves and accumulated profits/loss.

(v)　Ascertainment of share of profit/loss till the date of retirement/death.

(vi)Adjustment of capital if required.

(vii)Settlement of the Accounts due to Retired/Deceased partner

Q.11. Explain Adjustment of Capitals At the time of retirement /death.

Ans. The remaining partners may decide to adjust their capitals in their new profit sharing Ratio. Then following situation may arise

Case 1: When the total capital of the new firm is not given in the question

- Then the sum of their adjusted capitals of remaining partners' will be treated as the total capital of the new firm which will be divided in their New Profit Sharing Ratio.

- Excess or Deficiency of capital in the individual capital A/c is calculated.
- Such excess or shortage is adjusted by withdrawal or contribution in cash or transferring to Partner's current A/cs.

Journal Entries

(a) For excess Capital withdrawn by the partners

    Partner's Capital A/c Dr.

    To Cash/Bank A/c / Partner's Current A/c

(b) For deficiency, cash will be brought in by the partner

    Cash/Bank A/c /Partner's Current A/c Dr.

    To Partner's Capital A/c

Case 2: When the capital of the new firm as decided by the partners is specified, divide the capital in new profit sharing ratio and make adjustments accordingly.

Case 3: When the amount payable to retiring partner will be contributed by continuing partners in such a way that their capitals are adjusted proportionate to their new profit sharing ratio then calculations will be as under > Total capital of the new firm = balance in capital accounts of remaining partners + amount payable to retiring/deceased partner.

Long Answer Type [5 Marks]

Q.12. A, B and C were partners sharing profits and losses in the ratio of 5 : 3 : 2. Their Balance Sheet as at 1st April, 2022 was as follows:

Liabilities		Rs.	Assets	Rs.
Sundry Creditors		10,000	Cash	2,000
Employee's Provident Fund		5,000	Sundry Debtors	8,000
Reserve Fund		6,000	Stock	40,000
Workmen's Compensation			Furniture	13,000
Reserve		2,000	Patents	4,000
Capitals:			Buildings	60,000
A	50,000		Goodwill	6,000
B	35,000			
C	25,000	1,10,000		
		1,33,000		**1,33,000**

Cretires on above date and the partners agreed that:

(i) Goodwill is to be valued at two year's purchase of the average profits of last four years. Profits for the years ending 31st March were : 2019 : Rs.14,400, 2020 : Rs.20,000, 2021: Rs.10,000 (Loss), 2022: Rs.15,600.

(ii) 5% provision for doubtful debts to be made on debtors.

(iii) Stock be appreciated by 10%.

(iv) Patents are valueless.

(v) Buildings be appreciated by 20%.

(vi) Sundry Creditors to be paid Rs.2,000 more than the book value.

Pass Journal entries and prepare Revaluation Account, Capital Accounts and the Balance Sheet of the new firm.

Ans.

JOURNAL ENTRIES

Date	Particulars		L.F.	Dr. (Rs.)	Cr. (Rs.)
April 1 2022	Reserve Fund A/c	Dr.		6,000	
	To A's Capital A/c				3,000
	To B's Capital A/c				1,800
	To C's Capital A/c				1,200
	(The transfer of Reserve Fund to Partner's Capital A/c-s in their old profit sharing ratio)				
	Workmen's Compensation Reserve A/c	Dr.		2,000	
	To A/s Capital A/c				1,000
	To B's Capital A/c				600
	To C's Capital A/c				400
	(The transfer of Workmen's Compensation Reserve to Partner's Capital A/cs in their old profit sharing ratio)				
	Revaluation A/c	Dr.		6,400	
	To Provision for Doubtful Debts A/c				400
	To Patents A/c				4,000
	To Sundry Creditors A/c				2,000
	(Decrease in the value of assets and increase in creditors)				
	Stock A/c	Dr.		4,000	
	Building A/c	Dr.		12,000	
	To Revaluation A/c				16,000
	(Increase in the value of Assets)				
	Revaluation A/c	Dr.		9,600	
	To A's Capital A/c				4,800
	To B's Capital A/c				2,880
	To C's Capital A/c				1,920
	(Profit on revaluation transferred to partner's Capital A/c)				
	A's Capital A/c	Dr.		3,000	
	B's Capital A/c	Dr.		1,800	
	C's Capital A/c	Dr.		1,200	
	To Goodwill A/c				6,000
	(Goodwill appearing in the books written off on C's retirement)				
	A's Capital A/c	Dr.		2,500	
	B's Capital A/c	Dr.		1,500	
	To C's Capital A/c				4,000
	(C's share of Goodwill adjusted to the accounts of continuing partners in their gaining ratio 5 : 3)				
	C's Capital A/c	Dr.		31,320	
	To C's Loan A/c				31,320
	(The Balance of C's Capital A/c transferred to C's loan A/c)				

Dr.   **REVALUATION ACCOUNT**   **Cr.**

Particulars		Rs.	Particulars	Rs.
To Provision for			By Stock A/c	4,000
Doubtful Debts A/c		400	By Building A/c	12,000
To Patents A/c		4,000		
To Sundry Creditors A/c		2,000		
To Profit transferred to				
A's Capital A/c	4,800			
B's Capital A/c	2,880			
C's Capital A/c	1,920	9,600		
		16,000		**16,000**

Dr.   **CAPITAL ACCOUNTS**   **Cr.**

Particulars	A	B	C	Particulars	A	B	C
	Rs.	Rs.	Rs.		Rs.	Rs.	Rs.
To Goodwill A/c	3,000	1,800	1,200	By Balance b/d	50,000	35,000	25,000
To C's Capital A/c	2,500	1,500		By Reserve			
To C's Loan A/c			31,320	Fund A/c	3,000	1,800	1,200
To Balance c/d	53,300	36,980		By Workmen's			
				Compensation			
				Reserve A/c	1,000	600	400
				By Revaluation A/c	4,800	2,880	1,920
				By A's Capital A/c			2,500
				By B's Capital A/c			1,500
	58,800	**40,.280**	**32,520**		**58,800**	**40,280**	**32,520**

BALANCE SHEET OF NEW FIRM (OF A AND B)

as at 1st April 2022

Liabilities		Rs.	Assets		Rs.
Sundry Creditors		12,000	Cash		2,000
C's Loan		31,320	Sundry Debtors	8,000	
Employee's Provident			Less: Provision for		
Fund		5,000	Doubtful Debts	400	7,600
Capitals:			Stock		44,000
A	53,300		Furniture		13,000
B	36,980	90,280	Buildings		72,000
		1,38,600			**1,38,600**

Working Notes:

(i) Calculation of Goodwill: Total profits of the last four years

= Rs.14,400 + Rs.20,000 – Rs.10,000 + Rs.15,600 = Rs.40,000

Average Profit = Rs.$\dfrac{40,000}{4}$ = Rs.10,000

Goodwill = 10,000 × 2 = Rs.20,000

(ii) In the absence of any information, the retiring partner's balance of Capital Accounts is transferred to his Loan Account.

(iii) Amount of Employee's Provident Fund belongs to the employees of the Firm. It will be paid to them on their retirement, hence it cannot be transferred to the Capital Accounts of partners.

Q.13. Ram, Shyam and Mohan were in partnership sharing profits and losses in the proportions of 3 : 2 : 1. On 1st April, 2022, Shyam retires from the firm. On that date their Balance Sheet was as follows:

Liabilities		Rs.	Assets		Rs.
Trade Creditors		30,000	Cash in Hand		90,000
Bills Payable		27,000	Debtors	1,60,000	
Expenses Owing		45,000	Less: Provision	10,000	1,50,000
Reserve Fund		1,05,000	Stock		1,20,000
Workmen's			Factory Premises		2,25,000
Compensation Reserve		48,000	Investments		80,000
Capitals:			Loose Tools		40,000
Ram	2,00,000				
Shyam	1,50,000				
Mohan	1,00,000	450,000			
		7,05,000			**7,05,000**

The terms were:

(i) Goodwill of the firm to be valued at 2 times of Average Super Profits of last three years. Taking into consideration the risk of the business, normal profits of the firm are estimated at Rs.5,00,000 every year. But actual profits of last three years ending 31st March were as 2020: Rs.6,00,000, 2021: Rs.5,50,000, 2022: Rs.5,75,000.

(ii) Expenses owing to be brought down to Rs.37,500.

(iii) Investments are revalued at Rs.72,000. Ram took over investments at this value.

(iv) Factory premises is to be revalued at Rs.2043,000; and Loose tools at Rs.36,000.

(v) Provision for Doubtful Debts to be increased by Rs.19,500.

(vi) Claim on account of Workmen's Compensation is Rs.18,000.

(vii) Shyam be paid Rs.50,000 in cash and balance due to him treated as a loan carry interest @ 6% per annum.

Show Journal entry for goodwill adjustment, prepare necessary ledger accounts and opening balance sheet of the continuing partners.

Ans.

JOURNAL ENTRY FOR GOODWILL

Date	Particulars		L.F.	Dr. (Rs.)	Cr. (Rs.)
	Ram's Capital A/c	Dr.		37,500	
	Mohan's Capital A/c	Dr.		12,500	
	To Shyam's Capital A/c				50,000
	(Shyam share of goodwill adjusted to the accounts of continuing partners in their gaining ration 3 : 1)				

Dr.   **REVALUATION ACCOUNT**   **Cr.**

Particulars	Rs.	Particulars		Rs.
To Investments	8,000	By Expenses owing A/c		7,500
To Loose Tools	4,000	By Factory Premises		18,000
To Provision for doubtful debts	19,500	By Loss transferred to:		
		Ram's Capital A/c	3,000	
		Shyam's Capital A/c	2,000	
		Mohan's Capital A/c	1,000	6,000
	31,500			**31,500**

Dr.   **Cr.**

CAPITAL ACCOUNTS

Particulars	Ram	Shyam	Mohan	Particulars	Ram	Shyam	Mohan
	Rs.	Rs.	Rs.		Rs.	Rs.	Rs.
To Revaluation A/c	3,000	2,000	1,000	By Balance b/d	2,00,000	1,50,000	1,00,000
To Shyam's Capital A/c	37,500	....	12,500	By Reserve fund A/c	52,500	35,000	17,500
To Investment A/c	72,000	....	....	By Workmen's Compensation Reserve A/c	15,000	10,000	5,000
To Cash A/c	....	50,000	....	By Ram's Capital A/c		37,500	
To Shyam's loan A/c	....	1,93,000	....	By Mohan's Capital A/c		12,500	
To Balance c/d	1,55,000						
	2,67,500	**2,45,000**	**1,22,500**		**2,67,500**	**2,45,000**	**1,22,500**

BALANCE SHEET

as at 1st April 2022

Liabilities		Rs.	Assets		Rs.
Trade Creditors		30,000	Cash in Hand		40,000
Bills Payable		27,000	Debtors	1,60,000	
Expenses Owing		37,500	Less: Provision	29,500	1,30,500

Liability for Workmen's			Stock		1,20,000
Compensation Claim		18,000	Factory Premises		24,3,000
Shyam's Loan		1,93,000	Loose Tools		36,000
Capitals:					
Ram	1,55,000				
Mohan	1,09,000				
		2,64,000			
		5,69,500			**5,69,500**

Working Note:

Calculation of Goodwill:

$$\text{Average profits of the past three years} = \text{Rs.}\frac{6,00,000+5,50,000+5,75,000}{3} = \text{Rs.}5,75,000$$

Super profits =Actual Profits – Normal Profits = Rs.5,75,000 – Rs.5,00,000 = Rs.75,000

Goodwill at 2 year's Purchase of Super Profits = Rs.75,000 × 2 = Rs.1,50,000

Q.14. M, N and G were partners in a firm sharing profits and losses in the ratio of 5 : 3 : 2. On 31.03.2016 their Balance Sheet was as under: [CBSE2015]

Balance Sheet of M, N and G as at 31.03.2016

Liabilities		Rs.	Assets		Rs.
Creditors		55,000	Cash		40,000
General Reserve		30,000	Debtors	45,000	
Capitals			Less: Provision	5,000	40,000
M			Stock		50,000
N	1,50,000		Machinery		1,50,000
G	1,25,000		Patents		30,000
	75,000	3,50,000	Building		1,00,000
			Profit & Loss A/c		25,000
		435,000			**435,000**

M retired on the above date and it was agreed that:

(i)   Debtors of Rs.2,000 will be written off as bad debts and a provision of 5% on debtors for bad and doubtful debts will be maintained.

(ii) Patents will be completely written off and stock, machinery and building will be depreciated by 5%.

(iii) An unrecorded creditor of Rs.10,000 will be taken into account.

(iv) N and G will share the future profits in the ratio of 2 : 3.

(v) Goodwill of the firm on M's retirement was valued at Rs.3,00,000.

Pass necessary Journal Entries for the above transactions in the books of the firm on M's retirement.

Ans.

JOURNAL

Date	Particulars	L.F.	Dr. (Rs.)	Cr. (Rs.)
2016 March 31	General Reserve A/c Dr.		30,000	
	To M's Capital A/c			15,000
	To N's Capital A/c			9,000
	To G's Capital A/c			6,000
	(General Reserve credited to all partners in 5 : 3 : 2)			
	M's Capital A/c Dr.		12,500	
	N's Capital A/c Dr.		7,500	
	G's Capital A/c Dr.		5,000	
	To Profit & Loss A/c			25,000
	(Accumulated loss debited to all partners in 5 : 3 : 2)			
	N's Capital A/c (Note 1) Dr.		30,000	
	G's Capital A/c Dr.		1,20,000	
	To M's Capital A/c			1,50,000
	(Adjustment for goodwill in the gaining ratio of 1 : 4)			
	Bad Debts A/c Dr.		2,000	
	To Debtors A/c			2,000
	(Bad Debts written off)			
	Provision for Bad Debts A/c Dr.		55,000	
	To Bad Debts A/c			2,000
	To Revaluation A/c (Note 2)			- 850
	(Excess provision credited to revaluation account)			
	Revaluation A/c Dr.		55,000	
	To Patents A/c			30,000
	To Stock A/c			2,500
	To Machinery A/c			7,500
	To Building A/c			5,000
	To Creditors A/c			10,000
	(Decrease in assets and increase in creditors)			
	M's Capital A/c Dr.		27,075	
	N's Capital A/c Dr.		16,245	
	G's Capital A/c Dr.		10,830	
	To Revaluation A/c			54,150
	(Transfer of loss on revaluation)			
	M's Capital A/c Dr.		2,75,425	
	To M's Loan A/c (Note 4)			2,75,425
	(Balance due to M transferred to his Loan A/c)			

Working Notes:

(i) Gaining Ratio:

$$N: \frac{2}{5} - \frac{3}{10} = \frac{4-3}{10} = \frac{1}{10}$$

$$G: \frac{3}{5} - \frac{2}{10} = \frac{6-2}{10} = \frac{4}{10}$$

Gaining Ratio = 1 : 4

(ii)   Rs.

Net Debtors: Rs.45,000 – Bad Debts Rs.2,000	= 43,000
Provision @ 5% on Rs.43,000	2,150
Less: Existing Provision : Rs.5,000 – Bad Debts Rs.2,000	= 3,000
Excess Provision Credited to Revaluation Account	850

(iii)

Dr.		REVALUATION ACCOUNT		Cr.
Particulars	**Rs.**	**Particulars**		**Rs.**
To Patents	30,000	By Provision for Bad Debts		850
To Stock	2,500	By Loss transferred to:		
To Machinery	7,500	M's Capital A/c	27,075	
To Building	5,000	N's Capital A/c	16,245	
To Creditors	10,000	G's Capital A/c	10,830	54,150
	55,000			**55,000**

(iv)

Dr.		M's Capital Account		Cr.
Particulars	**Rs.**	**Particulars**		**Rs.**
To Profit & Loss A/c	12,500	By Balance b/d		1,50,000
To Revaluation A/c (Loss)	27,075	By General Reserve A/c		15,000
To M's Loan A/c	2,75,425	By N's Capital A/c (Goodwill)		30,000
		By G's Capital A/c (Goodwill)		1,20,000
	3,15,000			**3,15,000**

Q.15. Anita, Gaurav and Sonu were partners in a firm sharing profits and losses in proportion to their capitals. Their Balance Sheet as at 31st March, 2019 was as follows: **[CBSE 2017]**

BALANCE SHEET OF ANITA, GAURAV AND SONU
as at 31st March, 2019

Liabilities		Rs.	Assets		Rs.
Capital A/cs			Land and Building		5,00,000
Anita	2,00,000		Investments		1,20,000
Gaurav	2,00,000		Debtors	1,50,000	

Sonu	1,00,000	5,00,000	Less: Provision for		
Investment			Doubtful Debts	10,000	1,40,000
Fluctuation Fund		40,000	Stock		1,00,000
General Reserve		30,000	Cash at Bank		1,70,000
Creditors		4,60,000			
		1,030,000			**1,030,000**

On the above date, Anita retired from the firm and the remaining partners decided to carry on the business. It was agreed to revalue the assets and reassess the liabilities as follows:

(i)   Goodwill of the firm was valued at Rs.3,00,000 and Anita's share of goodwill was adjusted in the capital accounts of the remaining partners, Gaurav and Sonu.

(ii) Land and Building was to be brought up to 120% of its book value.

(iii) Bad debts amounted to Rs.20,000. A provision for doubtful debts was to be maintained at 10% on debtors.

(iv) Market value of investments was Rs.1,10,000.

(v)   Rs.1,00,000 was paid immediately by cheque to Anita out of the amount due and the balance was to be transferred to her loan account which was to be paid in two equal annual installments along with interest @ 10% p.a.

Prepare the Revaluation Account, Partners' Capital Accounts and the Balance Sheet of the reconstituted firm on Anita's retirement.

Ans.

Dr.   **REVALUATION ACCOUNT**   **Cr.**

Particulars		Rs.	Particulars	Rs.
To Bad Debts* A/c		10,000	By Land and	
To Provision for Doubtful Debts A/c		13,000	Building A/c	1,00,000
[10/100 (Rs.1,50,000 – Rs.20,000)]				
To Gain transferred to:				
Anita's Capital A/c	30,800			
Gaurav's Capital A/c	30,800			
Sonu's Capital A/c	15,400	77,000		
		1,00,000		**1,00,000**

*Out of Bad Debts of Rs.20,000 Rs.10,000 is adjusted from existing Provision for Doubtful Debts and balance Rs.10,000 is debited to Revaluation Account.

Dr.   **Partner's Capital Accounts**   **Cr.**

Particulars	Anita (Rs.)	Gaurav (Rs.)	Sonu (Rs.)	Particulars	Anita (Rs.)	Gaurav (Rs.)	Sonu (Rs.)
To Anita's				By Balance b/d	2,00,000	2,00,000	1,00,000
Capital A/c	...	80,000	40,000	By General			
To Bank A/c	1,00,000	...	...	Reserve A/c	12,000	12,000	6,000
To Anita's				By Revaluation A/c	30,800	30,800	15,400

Loan A/c	2,74,800	...	...	By Gaurav's				
To Bal. c/d	...	1,74,800	87,400	Capital A/c (WN 1)	80,000	...	...	
				By Sonu's Capital A/c (WN 1)	40,000	...	...	
				By Investment Fluctuation Fund A/c (WN 2)	12,000	12,000	6,000	
	3,74,800	**2,54,800**	**1,27,400**		**3,74,800**	**2,54,800**	**1,27,400**	

Balance Sheet of Reconstituted firm as at 31st March, 2019

Liabilities		Rs.	Assets		Rs.
Capital A/cs:			Land and Building		6,00,000
Gaurav	1,74,800		Investments		1,10,000
Sonu	87,400	2,62,200	Debtors	1,30,000	
Anita's Loan		2,74,800	Less: Provision for	13,000	
Sundry Creditors		4,60,000	Doubtful Debts		1,17,000
			Stock		1,00,000
			Cash (Rs.1,70,000 – Rs.1,00,000)		70,000
		9,97,000			**9,97,000**

Working Notes:

(i) Anita's share of goodwill Rs.1,20,000 (Rs.3,00,000 × 2/5) to be adjusted between Gaurav and Sonu in their gaining ratio of 2:1.

(ii) Fall in the book value of investments Rs.10,000 (Rs.1,20,00 – Rs.1,10,000) is met through Investment Fluctuation Fund and balance of Investment Fluctuation Fund Rs.30,000 (Rs.40,000 – Rs.10,000) is distributed among the partners in their profit-sharing ratio, *i.e.*, 2:2:1.

Q.16. Mohan, Vinay and Nitya were partners in a firm sharing profits and losses in the proportion of 1/2, 1/3 and 1/6 respectively. On 31st March, 2018, their Balance Sheet was as follows:

Balance Sheet of Mohan, Vinay and Nitya as at 31st March, 2018

Liabilities		Rs.	Assets		Rs.
Creditors		48,000	Cash at Bank		31,000
Employees' Provident Fund		1,70,000	Bills Receivable		54,000
			Book Debts	63,000	
Contingency Reserve		30,000	Less: Provision for		
Capitals:			Doubtful Debts	2,000	61,000
Mohan	1,20,000		Plant and Machinery		1,20,000
Vinay	1,00,000		Land and Building		2,92,000
Nitya	90,000	3,10,000			
		5,58,000			**5,58,000**

Mohan retired on the above date and it was agreed that:

(i) Plant and Machinery will be depreciated by 5%.

(ii) An old computer previously written off was sold for Rs.4,000.

(iii)Bad debts amounting to Rs.3,000 will be written off and a provision of 5% on debtors for bad and doubtful debts will be maintained.

(iv)Goodwill of the firm was valued at Rs.1,80,000 and Mohan's share of the same was credited in his account by debiting Vinay's and Nitya's Accounts.

(v) The capital of the new firm was to be fixed at Rs.90,000 and necessary adjustments were to be made by bringing in or paying off cash as the case may be.

(vi)Vinay and Nitya will share future profits in the ratio of 3:2.

Prepare Revaluation Account, Partners' Capital Accounts and the Balance Sheet of the reconstituted firm.

Ans.

Dr.   **REVALUATION ACCOUNT**   **Cr.**

Particulars	Rs.	Particulars	Rs.
To Plant and Machinery A/c	6,000	By Bank A/c (Computer)	4,000
To Provision for Doubtful Debts:		By Loss transferred to	
Bad Debts 1,000		Partner's Capital A/cs:	
Provision for		Mohan 3,000	
Doubtful Debts 3,000	4,000	Vinay 2,000	
		Nitya 1,000	6,000
	10,000		**10,000**

Dr.   **Partner's Capital Accounts**   **Cr.**

Particulars	Mohan Rs.	Vinay Rs.	Nitya Rs.	Particulars	Mohan Rs.	Vinay Rs.	Nitya Rs.
To Mohan's	...	48,000	42,000	By Balance c/d	1,20,000	1,00,000	90,000
Capital A/c	3,000	2,000	1,000	By Contingency			
To Revaluation	2,22,000	...	...	Reserve A/c	15,000	10,000	5,000
A/c (Loss)	...	6,000	16,000	By Vinay's			
To Mohan's	...	54,000	36,000	Capital A/c	48,000	...	...
Loan A/c				By Nitya's			
To Bank A/c				Capital A/c	42,000	...	...
(Bal. Fig.)							
To Balance c/d							
(WN 3)							
	2,25,000	**1,10,000**	**95,000**		**2,25,000**	**1,10,000**	**95,000**

BALANCE SHEET OF THE RECONSTITUTED FIRM

as at 31st March, 2018

Liabilities	Rs.	Assets		Rs.
Creditors	48,000	Cash at Bank		13,000
Employees' Provident Fund	1,70,000	(Rs.31,000 + Rs.4,000 –		
Mohan's Loan A/c	2,22,000	Rs.6,000 – Rs.16000)		
Vinay's Capital A/c	54,000	Bills Receivable		54,000
Nitya's Capital A/c	36,000	Book Debts	63,000	
		Less: Bad Debts	3,000	
		Provision for		
		Doubtful Debts	3,000	57,000
		Plant and Machinery		1,14,000
		Land Building		2,92,000
	5,30,000			**5,30,000**

Working Notes:

(i) Calculation of Gaining Ratio (Gain of a Partner = New Profit Share – Old Profit Share):

$$\text{Vinay's Gain} = \frac{3}{5} - \frac{1}{3} = \frac{9-5}{15} = \frac{4}{15}; \quad \text{Nitya's Gain} = \frac{2}{5} - \frac{1}{6} = \frac{12-5}{30} = \frac{7}{30}$$

Gaining Ratio of Vinay nad Nitya = 4/15 : 7/30 = 8 : 7

(ii) Mohan's share of Goodwill = Rs.1,80,000 × 1/2 =Rs.90,000, which is contributed by Vinay and Nitya in their gaining ratio, *i.e.*, 8 : 7. Thus,

Vinay's contribution = Rs.90,000 × 8/15 = Rs.48,000

Nitya's contribution = Rs.90,000 × 7/15 = Rs.42,000

(iii) Calculation of Vinay's Capital and Nitya's Capital in New Firm:

Total capital of new firm = Rs.90,000 which is contributed by Vinay and Nitya in their new profit sharing ratio, *i.e.*, 3 : 2. Thus,

Vinay's capital in new firm = Rs.90,000 × 3/5 = Rs.54,000

Nitya's capital in new firm = Rs.90,000 x 2/5 = Rs.36,000

TOPIC 4 Death of a Partner

Summary

The accounting treatment in the event of the death of a partner is the same as that in the case of the retirement of a partner. Here, his claim is transferred to his executor's account and settled in the same manner as that of the retired partner.

The only major difference between the retirement and death of a partner is that retirement normally takes place at the end of the accounting period whereas death may occur on any day. Therefore, in case of death, his claim shall also include his share of profit or loss, interest on capital, interest on drawings (if any), from the beginning of the year to the date of death.

Accounting Treatment of Outgoing Partner's Share in Profit

1. Through Profit and Loss Suspense Account

    In case of Profit:

    Profit and Loss Suspense A/c Dr.

    To Deceased Partner's Capital A/c (Share of profit for the intervening period)

    In case of Loss:

    Deceased Partner's Capital A/c Dr.

    To Profit and Loss Suspense A/c (Share of loss for the intervening period)

2. Through Capital Transfer In case of Profit:

    Remaining Partner's Capital A/c's Dr.

    To Deceased Partner's Capital A/c In case of Loss:

    Deceased Partner's Capital A/c Dr.

To Remaining Partner's Capital A/c's The executors of deceased partner are entitled to the following:

1. The credit balance of deceased partner's capital account;

2. His share of goodwill;

3. His share of profit till the date of death;

4. His share of profit on revaluation of assets and liabilities;

5. His share of accumulated profits and reserves;

6. His interest on capital if partnership deed provides till the date of death;

7. His share of Joint Life Policy (if any);

8. His salary and commission due (if any);

The following deduction has to made from above.

1. His drawings, interest in drawings till the date of death;

2. His share of loss till the date of death;

3. His share of loss on revaluation of assets and liabilities. ,

4. His share of the reduction in the value of goodwill (if any).

Payment to the executors

1. When payment is made in full Executor's A/c Dr.

    To Bank A/c.

2. When payment is made in instalment The executor's are entitled to interest when the payment is made in instalment. If the deed is silent about this, then 6% p.a. should be given as per Section 37 of the Indian Partnership Act, 1932.

    When interest is due

    Interest A/c Dr.

    To Executor's A/c

    When instalment paid along with interest

    Executor's A/c Dr.

    To Cash/Bank A/c

Multiple Choice Questions   [1 Mark]

Q.1. An account opened to ascertain the loss or gain on reassessment of assets and liabilities at the time of death of a Partner is called

(a) Realization Account

(b) Executors Account

(c) Revaluation Account

(d) Deceased Partners capital account

Ans. (c)

Q.2. A, B and C are partners in a firm sharing profits and losses in the ratio of 2 : 2 : 1. On March, 31, 2018 C died. Accounts are closed on December 31st every year. The sales for the year 2017 was Rs.6,00,000 and the profits were Rs.60,000. The sales for the period for the period January 1, 2018 to March 31st 2018 were Rs.2,00,000. The share of deceased Partner in the current year's profit on the basis of sales is

(a) Rs.20,000   (b) Rs.8,000   (c) Rs.3,000   (d) Rs.4,000

Ans. (d)

Q.3. A, B and C were partners sharing profits and losses in the ratio of 2 : 2 : 1. Books are closed on 31st March every year. C died on November 5, 2018. Under the Partnership deed the executors of the deceased partner are entitled to his share of profit to the date of death calculated on the basis of last year's profit. Profit for the year ended 31st March, 2018 was Rs.2,14,000. C's share of profit will be

(a) Rs.28,000   (b) Rs.32,000   (c) Rs.28,800   (d) Rs.48,000

Ans. (c)

Q.4. On death of a Partner, the remaining partner(s) who have gained due to change in profit sharing ratio should compensate the

(a) Deceased partner only

(b) Remaining partners (who have sacrificed) as well as deceased partner

(c) Remaining partners only (who have sacrificed)

(d) None of the above

Ans. (b)

Q.5. Which account is opened to transfer deceased partner's share of profit to his capital account

(a) P&L Adjustment account   (b) P&L Appropriation account

(c) P&L Suspense account   (d) None of the above

Ans. (c)

Q.6. Kiran, Umesh and Aditya were in Partnership firm. Suddenly on October 31,2018, Kiran died. Amount payable to her on that date amounted to Rs.1,05,000. Rs.5000 was paid immediately and balance was paid in 4 equal annual instalments along with interest @ 12% p.a. starting from 31st October 2019. Calculate the interest due as on 31st March, 2019. Financial year was followed as accounting year by the firm.

(a) Rs.2,500   (b) Rs.3,000   (c) Rs.4,500   (d) Rs.3,750

Ans. (c)

Q.7. Karan, Aman and Girish were Partners with capitals of Rs. 3,00,000; Rs.2,50,000 and Rs.2,00,000 respectively as on 31st March, 2018. Aman died, partners decided to pay the entire amount to Aman's Executor, but they only had Rs.50,000 cash and rest of the amount was to be brought in by Karan and Girish in such a way that their future capital will be equal. Calculate the amount to be brought in by Karan and Girish.

(a) Rs.50,000 by Karan and Rs.1,50,000 by Girish

(b) Rs.50,000 by Girish and Rs.1,50,000 by Karan

(c) Rs.25,000 by Karan and Rs.1,25,000 by Girish

(d) Rs.25,000 by Girish and Rs.1,25,000 by Karan

Ans. (a)

Very Short Answer Type [1 Mark]

Q.8. Assertion (A): Unrecorded outstanding repair bill at time of death of partner is recorded on debit side of Revaluation a/c.

Reason (R): Increase in capital of partner is recorded on credit side of Capital account.

(a) Both Assertion and reason are true and reason is correct explanation of assertion.

(b) Assertion and reason both are true but reason is not the correct explanation of assertion.

(c) Assertion is true, reason is false.

(d) Assertion is false, reason is true.

Ans. (b)

Q.9. Assertion (A): Unrecorded assets at time of death of partner is recorded on credit side of Revaluation a/c.

Reason (R): Revaluation account is credited due to increase in liability.

(a) Both Assertion and reason are true and reason is correct explanation of assertion.

(b) Assertion and reason both are true but reason is not the correct explanation of assertion.

(c) Assertion is true, reason is false.

(d) Assertion is false, reason is true.

Ans. (c)

Short Answer Type - I [2 Marks]

Q.10. A,B and C are partners in 3:4:2 B wants to retire from the firm. The profit on revaluation on that date was Rs. 36,000. New ratio of A and C is 5: 3. Profit on revaluation will be distributed as;

Ans. A Rs. 12,000, B Rs. 16,000, C Rs. 8,000

Short Answer Type - II [3 Marks]

Q.11. How to calculate Deceased Partner share of profit?

Ans. (i) On the basis of last years profit (On Average Basis)

(ii) On the basis of sales.

Calculation of Profits/ Loss for the intervening Period is calculated by any one of the two methods given below:

(a) On Time Basis: In this method proportionally profit for the time period is calculated either on the basis of last year's profit or on the basis of average profits of last few years and then deceased partner's share is calculated based on his share of profits.

(b) On Turnover or Sales Basis: in this method the profits up to the date of death for the current year are calculated on the basis of current year's sales up to the date of death by using the formula. Profits for the current year up to the date of death = Sales of the current year up to the date of death/total sales of last year x Profit for the last year. Then from this profit the deceased partner's share of profit is calculated

Long Answer Type   [5 Marks]

Q.12. On 31st March, 2018 the Balance Sheet of P, Q and R who were partners in a firm, was as under:

Liabilities		Rs.	Assets	Rs.
Sundry Creditors		21,000	Buildings	26,000
Employee's Provident Fund		4,000	Investment	15,000
Employee's Compensation			Debtors	15,000
Reserve		8,000	Bills Receivable	6,000
Contingency Reserve		12,000	Stock	12,000
Capitals:			Cash	6,000
P	15,000			
Q	10,000			
R	10,000	35,000		
		80,000		**80,000**

The partnership deed provides that the profits be shared in the ratio of 2 : 1 : 1 and that in the event of death of any partner, his executors will be entitled to be paid out:

(a) The capital to his credit at the date of last Balance Sheet;

(b) His proportion of Reserve at the date of last Balance Sheet;

(c) His proportion of profits to the date of death based on the average profits of the last three completed years, plus 10%, and

(d) By way of goodwill, his proportion of the total profits for the three preceding years.

(e) The net profit for the last three years ending 31st March were:

2016	Rs.16,000
2017	Rs.16,000
2018	Rs.15,400

R died on 1st July 2018. He had withdrawn Rs.5,000 to the date of his death. The investments were sold at par and R's executors were paid off.

Prepare Partner's Capital Accounts, R's Executor's Account and Balance Sheet of the surviving partners P and Q.

Ans.

Dr.   **Partner's Capital Accounts**   **Cr.**

Particulars	P Rs.	Q Rs.	R Rs.	Particulars	P Rs.	Q Rs.	R Rs.
To R's Capital A/c (Share of Goodwill)	7,900	3,950	...	By Balance b/d	15,000	10,000	10,000
To Bank A/c (Drawings)	...	...	5,000	By Employee's Compensation Reserve	4,000	2,000	2,000
To R's Executors	...	...	22,936	By Contingency Reserve	6,000	3,000	3,000
To Balance c/d	17,100	11,050	...	By P & L Suspense A/c (See Note 1)	...	...	1,086
				By P's Capital A/c (Share of goodwill)	...	...	7,900
				By Q's Capital A/c (Share of goodwill)	...	...	3,950
	25,000	**15,000**	**27,936**		**25,000**	**15,000**	**27,936**

Dr.   **R's Executor's Account**   **Cr.**

Particulars	Rs.	Particulars	Rs.
To Bank A/c	22,936	By R's Capital A/c	22,936
	22,936		**22,936**

BALANCE SHEET OF P AND Q

as at 1st July 2018

Liabilities	Rs.	Assets	Rs.
Sundry Creditors	21,000	Buildings	26,000
Employee's Provident Fund	4,000	Debtors	15,000
Bank Loan	6,936	Bills Receivable	6,000
Capitals:		Stock	12,000
P 17,100		Profit & Loss Suspense A/c	1,086
Q 11,050	28,150		
	60,086		**60,086**

Working Notes:

(i)   Ascertainment of R's share of profit:

Total profits for the last three years = Rs.16,000 + Rs.16,000 + Rs.15,400

$$= Rs.47,400$$

$$\text{Average Profits} = \frac{Rs.47,400}{3} = Rs.15,800$$

$$\text{Profit (From 1}^{st}\text{ April 2018 to 1}^{st}\text{ July 2018)} = \text{Rs.}15,800 \times \frac{3}{12} = \text{Rs.}3,950$$

$$\text{R's share in Profit} = \text{Rs.}3,950 \times \frac{1}{4} = 987$$

$$\text{Add: 10\% of Rs.}987 = 99$$

$$= 1086$$

(ii) R's Share of Goodwill:

Total profits for the three preceding years= Rs.47,400

R's Share of goodwill = Rs.11,850, which is contributed by P and Q in the ratio of 2 : 1.

(iii) Calculation of Bank Loan: Rs.

Available Cash   6,000

(+) Received from sale of Investments   15,000
                                                                                   ———
                                                                                   21,000

(–) Withdrew by R to the date of his death (Drawings)   5,000
                                                                                   ———
                                                                                   16,000

(–) Amount required to pay off R's Executors Loan Required   22,936
                                                                                   ———
                                                                                   6,936

Alternatively, a Bank Account may be prepared to ascertain the amount of bank loan:

Dr.		**BANK ACCOUNT**		**Cr.**
Particulars	**Rs.**	**Particulars**	**Rs.**	
To Cash A/c	6,000	By R's Capital A/c (Drawings)	5,000	
To Investments A/c	15,000	By R's Executor's A/c	22,936	
To Bank Loan (Balancing Figure)	6,936			
	27,936		**27,936**	

Q.13. Khanna, Seth and Mehta were partners in a firm sharing profits in the ratio of 3 : 2 : 5. On 31.12.2018 the Balance Sheet of Khanna, Seth and Mehta was as follows:

Liabilities		Rs.	Assets	Rs.
Capitals:			Goodwill	300,000
Khanna	Rs.3,00,000		Land and Building	500,000
Seth	Rs.2,00,000		Machinery	170,000
Mehta	Rs.5,00,000	1,000,000	Stock	30,000
General Reserve		100,000	Debtors	120,000
Loan from Seth		50,000	Cash	45,000
Creditors		75,000	Profit and Loss Account	60,000
		1,225,000		**1,225,000**

On 14th March 2019 Seth died.

The partnership deed provided that on the death of a partner the executor of the deceased partner is entitled to:

(i) Balance in Capital Account;

(ii) Share in profits upto the date of death on the basis of last year's profit;

(iii) His share in profit/loss on revaluation of assets and re-assessment of liabilities which were as follows:

    (a) Land and Building was to be appreciated by Rs.1,20,000;

    (b) Machinery was to be depreciated to Rs.1,35,000 and Stock to Rs.25,000.

    (c) A provision of 2.5% for bad and doubtful debts was to created on debtors;

(iv) The net amount payable to Seth's executors was transferred to his loan account which was to be paid later.

Prepare Revaluation Account, Partners Capital Accounts and Seth's Executors A/c. Khanna and Mehta decided to continue the business keeping their capital balances in their new profit sharing ratio. Any surplus or deficit to be transferred to current accounts of the partners.

Ans.

Dr.   **REVALUATION ACCOUNT**   **Cr.**

Particulars	Rs.	Particulars	Rs.
To Machinery A/c	35,000	By Land & Building A/c	1,20,000
To Stock A/c	5,000		
To Provision for Doubtful Debts	3,000		
To Profit transferred to:			
Khanna's Capital A/c 23,100			
Seth's Capital A/c 15,400			
Mehta's Capital A/c 38,500	77,000		
	1,20,000		**1,20,000**

Dr.   **Partners's Capital Accounts**   **Cr.**

Particulars	Khanna Rs.	Seth Rs.	Mehta Rs.	Particulars	Khanna Rs.	Seth Rs.	Mehta Rs.
To Goodwill A/c	90,000	60,000	1,50,000	By Balance b/d	3,00,000	2,00,000	5,00,000
To P & L A/c	18,000	12,000	30,000	By General			
To P & L				Reserve	30,000	20,000	50,000
Suspense A/c	...	2,400	...	By Revaluation			
To Seth's				A/c Profit	23,100	15,400	38,500
Executor's A/c	...	1,61,000	...				
To Balance c/d	2,45,100	...	4,08,500				
	3,53,100	**2,35,400**	**5,88,500**		**3,53,100**	**2,35,400**	**5,88,500**

Dr.   **Seth's Executor's Accounts**   **Cr.**

Particulars	Rs.	Particulars	Rs.
To Seth's Executor's Loan A/c	2,11,600	By Seth's Capital A/c	1,61,000
		By Seth's Loan A/c	50,000
		By Interest on Seth's Loan[2]	600
	2,11,600		**2,11,600**

Working Notes:

(i) Calculation of Seth's Share in loss for 73 days:

$$= Rs.60,000^* \times \frac{73}{365} \times \frac{2}{10} = Rs.2,400$$

*Dr. Balance of Profit & Loss A/c shown in the Balance Sheet Rs.60,000 indicates loss of 2010. Seth's Share of loss upto the date of death on the basis of last years loss = Rs.2,400.

(ii) Interest on Seth's Loan $= 50,000 \times \dfrac{73}{365} \times \dfrac{6}{100} = 600$

(iii) Calculation of adjusted capitals of Khanna and Mehta in the new firm:

Khanna's Capital (Adjusted) = Rs.2,45,100

Mehta's Capital (Adjusted) = Rs.4,08,500

$$= 6,53,600$$

$$\text{Khanna's Capital} = Rs.6,53,600 \times \frac{3}{8} = Rs.2,45,100$$

$$\text{Mehta's Capital} = Rs.6,53,600 \times \frac{5}{8} = Rs.4,08,500$$

Since adjusted capitals are the same as shown by their Capital Accounts, there is no need of transferring any amount to their Current Accounts.

Q.14. Following is the Balance Sheet of Ram, Mohan and Sohan as at 31st March, 2020.

Liabilities		Rs.	Assets	Rs.
Capital A/cs			Tools	30,000
Ram	2,00,000		Furniture	1,80,000
Mohan	1,00,000		Stock	1,60,000
Sohan	1,00,000	4,00,000	Debtors	1,20,000
Workmen Compensation Reserve		75,000	Cash at Bank	80,000
Sundry Creditors		1,00,000	Cash in Hand	5,000
		5,75,000		5,75,000

(i)   Amount standing to the credit of his Capital Account.

(ii) Interest on capital which amounted to Rs.1,500.

(iii) His share of goodwill Rs.50,000.

(iv) His share of profits from the closing of last financial year till the date of death which was estimated at Rs.7,500.

Sohan's executors were paid Rs.14,000 on 1st July 2020 and the balance in two equal yearly installments from 30th June 2021 with interest @ 6% p.a.

Pass necessary Journal entries and draw up Sohan's Capital Account to be rendered to his executors and Sohan's Executors' Account till it is finally paid.

Ans.

JOURNAL

Date	Particulars	L.F.	Dr. (Rs.)	Cr. (Rs.)
2020 June 30	Profit & Loss Suspense A/c (Interest on Capital)　　Dr. 　To Sohan's Capital A/c (Interest credited to Sohan's Capital Account up to 30th June)		1,500	1,500
June 30	Ram's Capital A/c　　Dr. Mohan's Capital A/c　　Dr. 　To Sohan's Capital A/c (Sohan's share of goodwill credited to his Capital Account)		25,000 25,000	50,000
June 30	Profit & Loss Suspense A/c　　Dr. 　To Sohan's Capital A/c (Sohan's Share of profit credited)		7,500	7,500
June 30	Workmen Compensation Reserve A/c　　Dr. 　To Ram's Capital A/c 　To Mohan's Capital A/c 　To Sohan's Capital A/c (Workmen Compensation Reserve credited to Partners' Capital Accounts)		75,000	30,000 30,000 15,000
June 30	Sohan's Capital A/c　　Dr. 　To Sohan's Executors' A/c (Balance in Sohan's Capital Account transferred to Sohan's Executors' Account)		1,74,000	1,74,000
July 1	Sohan's Executor's A/c　　Dr. To Bank A/c (Amount paid to Sohan's Executors)		14,000	14,000

Dr.　　　　　　　　　　　**Sohan's Capital Account**　　　　　　　　　　**Cr.**

Date	Particulars	Rs.	Date	Particulars	Rs.
2020 June 30	To Sohan's Executor's A/c (Balancing Figure-Transfer)	1,74,000	2020 April 1	By Balance b/d	1,00,000
			April 30	By Profit & Loss Suspense A/c (Interest on Capital)	1,500
			June 30	By Ram's Capital A/c	25,000
			June 30	By Mohan's Capital A/c	25,000
			June 30	By Profit & Loss Suspense A/c	7,500
			June 30	By Workmen compensation Reserve A/c	15,000
		1,74,000			**1,74,000**

| Dr. | | | | Sohan's Executor's Account | Cr. |

Date	Particulars	Rs.	Date	Particulars	Rs.
2020			2020		
July 1	To Bank A/c	14,000	June 30	By Sohan's Capital A/c	1,74,000
2021			2021		
March 31	To Balance c/d	1,67,200	March 31	By Interest A/c	7,200
				[(Rs.1,74,000 – Rs.14,000) $\times$ 6/100 $\times$ 9/12]	
		1,81,200			1,81,200
2021			2021		
June 30	To Bank A/c	89,600	April 1	By Balance b/d	1,67,200
	(Rs.80,000 + Rs.7,200 + Rs.2,400)		June 30	By Interest A/c	2,400
				(Rs.1,60,000 $\times$ 6/100 $\times$ 3/12)	
2022			2022		
March 31	To Balance c/d	83,600	March 31	By Interest A/c	3,600
				(Rs.80,000 $\times$ 6/100 $\times$ 9/12)	
		1,73,200			1,73,200
2022			2022		
June 30	To Bank A/c	84,800	April 1	By Balance b/d	83,600
	(Rs.80,000 + Rs.3,600 + Rs.1,200)		June 30	By Interest A/c	1,200
				(Rs.80,000 $\times$ 6/100 $\times$ 3/12)	
		84,800			**84,800**

Notes:

1. The date of closing the accounts is 31st March and date of payment of installment is 30th June.

2. Total amount due to Sohan's Executors Rs.1,60,000 is payable in two equal annual installments. Therefore, yearly installment = Rs.1,60,000/2 = Rs.80,000 plus interest.

Chapter Practice

Multiple Choice Questions   [1 Mark]

Q.1. A,B and C were partners sharing profits in the ratio 5 : 3 : 2. B retired so A and C agreed to share future profits in ratio 3 : 2. Their gaining ratio would be :

(a) 5 : 2   (b) 3 : 2   (c) 1 : 2   (d) 2 : 10

Q.2. 'Gainning Ratio' means :

(a) Old Ratio – New Ratio   (b) New Ratio – Old Ratio

(c) Old Ratio – Sacrificing Ratio   (d) New Ratio – Sacrificing Ratio

Q.3. On retirement of a partner, goodwill will be credited to Capital A/c of :

(a) Retiring Partner (b) Remaining Partners   (c) All Partners   (d) None of the above

Q.4. If the executor's of the deceased partner are to be paid in installments, his legal heirs are entitled to interest at :

(a) Market Rate   (b) 6% p.a.   (c) 6 %   (d) None of these

Very Short Answer Type   [1 Mark]

Q.5. What is meant by retirement of a partner ?

Q.6. What entry is passed at the time of retirement of a partner for existing goodwill in Balance Sheet?

Q.7. Name the account which is opened to credit the share of profit of the deceased partner, till the time of his death to his Capital account.

Q.8. Why is Gaining Ratio calculated ?

Q.9. Give the journalentryto distribute 'Workmen Compensation Reserve' of Rs. 60,000 at the time of retirement of Pankaj, when no claim against it. The firm has three partners Kamal, Pankaj and Saras.

Q.10. Why are assets and liabilities revalued at the time of retirement of a partner?

Q.11. State two basis for determination of Profit from the date of last Balance Sheet to the date of death/retirement.

Short Answer Type - II   [3 Marks]

Q.12. Hanny, Pammy and Sunny are partners in the ratio of 3 : 2 : 1. Goodwill is appearing in the books at a value of Rs. 60,000. Pammy Retires and at the time of Pammy's Retirement goodwill is valued Rs.84,000. Hanny and Sunny decided to share future profits in the ratio of 2 : 1. Record the necessary journal entries.

Q.13. A B and C are partners in a firm whose books are closed on 31st March each year.A died on 30th June 2022 and according to the agreement the share of profit of a deceased partner up to the date of the death is to be calculated on the basis of the average profit for last five years . The net profits for last five years have been:

2018 Rs.14,000; 2019 Rs.18,000; 2020 Rs. 16,000; 2021 Rs.10,000(loss) and 2022 Rs.16,000

New profit ratio of B and C will be 3 : 2. Calculate A's share of profit up to date of death and pass necessary journal entry.

_Q.14. A, B and C were partners in a firm sharing profits in 3 : 2 : 1. Ratio. The firm close its books on 31st March every year.B died on 12-06-2022. On B's death his share of profits of the firm till the time of his death was to be calculated on the basis of previous year's profit which was 1,50,000. Calculate B's share of profit of the firm and Pass necessary journal entry of profit.

Long Answer Type   [5 Marks]

_Q.15. Arpit, Gopal and Tushar are partners in a firm sharing profits in the ratio of 2 : 3 : 4. On 31st March, 2022 Arpit retires and Gopal and Tushar decided to share future profits in the ratio of 2:1.Following balance appeared in their books on this date :

Profit and Loss (Dr.)	Rs.72,000
Employee's Provident Fund	Rs.1,50,000
Workmen Compensation Reserve	Rs.45,000
General Reserve	Rs.1,20,000

It is agreed that (i) Claim on account of Workmen Compensation is Rs. 18,000 and (ll) 25%of the General Reserve is to be transferred to Provision for Doubtful Debts. Pass necessary journal entries for adjustment of these items on retirement of Arpit .

_Q.16. Anil, Sunil and Kamal are partners sharing profits in the ratio of 5 : 3 : 2. Sunil retires and new ratio between Anil and Kamal is agreed 2 : 3. They also decided to record the effect of the following without affecting their book value :

General Reserve	Rs.1,20,000
Contingency Reserve	Rs.70,000
Profit and Loss A/c (Dr.)	Rs.30,000
Advertisement Suspense Account	Rs.10,000

Your are required to give the necessary single adjusting entry.

Q.17. Anshul, Aditya and Ankit are partners sharing profits in the ratio of 2 : 2 : 1. Anshul retires and after alladjustment relating to revaluation ,goodwill and accumulated profits the capital account of Aditya showed a credit balance of Rs. 1,40,000 and that of Ankit Rs.1,00,000 . It was decided to adjust the capitals of Aditya and Ankit in their profit sharing ratio. Calculate the new capitals of the partners and record necessary journal entry for bringing in or withdrawing cash.

Q.18. Amitabh, Dharmendra and Jitendra are partners in a firm . Amitabh retires from the firm on 01st April, 2018. On the date of retirement, Rs. 8,00,000 is due to him in all. It is agreed to pay him this amount in four yearly installmentsplus interest @ 10% p.a. Mukesh Books are closed on 31st March every year .

Prepare Amitabh's loan Account.

Q.19. Mukesh, Mahesh and Manish were partners in a firm sharing profits and losses n the ratio of 5 : 3 : 2. On 31st March 2022 their Balance Sheet was as under :

Liabilities	Amount		Assets	Amount	
Creditors		55,000	Cash		40,000
General Reserve		30,000	Debtors	45,000	
Capitals			Less: Provision	(5,000)	40000
Mukesh	1,50,000		Stock		50,000
Mahesh	1,25,000		Machinery		1,50,000
Manish	75,000	3,50000	Patents		30,000
			Building		1,00,000
			Profit and Loss A/c		25,000
		4,35,000			**4,35,000**

Mukesh retired on the above date and it was agreed that :

(l) Debtors of Rs.2,000 will be written off as bad debts and provision of 5% on debtors for bad and doubtful debts will be maintained.

(ll) Patents are valueless .Machinery and Building will be depreciated by 5%

(lll) An recorded creditor of Rs.10,000 will be taken in the books .

(IV)Mahesh and Manish will share the future profits in the ratio of 2 : 3.

(V) Goodwill of the firm on Mukesh's retirement was valued at Rs. 3,00,000.

Prepare Revaluation Account ,Partners Capital Account and New Balance Sheet

Q.20. Neena, Seena and Teena were partners in a firm sharing profit and losses in the ratio of 5 : 4 : 1. Their Balance Sheet As at 31st March 2022 was as bellow:

Liabilities	Amount		Assets	Amount
Capitals			Plant and Machinery	5,50,000
Neena	3,00,000		Stock	1,20,000
Seena	2,00,000		Debtor	1,30,000
Teena	1,00,000	6,00,000	Cash	40,000
Profit & LossA/c (2021-22)		1,50,000	Advertisement Expenditure	20,000
Sundry Creditors		1,10,000		
		8,60,000		**8,60,000**

Neena died on 30th June 2022. According to the partnership deed ,in addition to deceased partner's capital, the executors are entitled to :

(i) Interest on capital@ 10% p.a. and Salaries to Neena @ 36,000 p.a.

(ii) Her share in profits till the date of death on basis of average profits of two years. The profit for the year 2020-21 was Rs.50,000

(iii) His share in goodwill of the firm . Goodwill was to becalculated on the basis of two year's purchase of the average profit of the last two years.

(iv) Neena's withdrew Rs. 60,000 on 01st June ,2022

Prepare Neena's Capital Account which is to be rendered to his executor.

CHAPTER 5

Dissolution of the Partner

 Introduction, Settlement of Accounts

Summary

Dissolution of partnership firm is a process in which relationship between partners of firm is dissolved or terminated. If a relationship between all the partners of firm is dissolved then it is known as dissolution of firm. In case of dissolution of partnership firm, the firm ceases to exist. According to Section 39 of the Indian Partnership Act, 1932, the dissolution of partnership between all the partners of a firm is called "Dissolution of the Firm". A firm may be dissolved with the consent of all the partners or in accordance with a contract between the partners

Dissolution of Partnership:

(1) Change in existing profit sharing ratio among partners;

(2) Admission of a new partner;

(3) Retirement of a partner;

(4) Death of a partner;

(5) Insolvency of a partner;

(6) Completion of the venture, if partnership is formed for that; and

(7) Expiry of the period of partnership, if partnership is for a specific period of time.

Dissolution of a firm takes place in any of the following ways:

1. By Agreement (Section 40) According to Section 40 of the Indian Partnership Act, 1932, partners can dissolve the partnership by agreement and with the consent of all the partners. Partners can also dissolve the partnership based on a contract that has already been made.

2. Compulsory Dissolution (Section 41) An event can make it unlawful for the firm to carry on its business. In such cases, it is compulsory for the firm to dissolve. However, if a firm carries on more than one undertakings and one of them becomes illegal, then it is not compulsory for the firm to dissolve. It can continue carrying out the legal undertakings. Section 41 of the Indian Partnership Act, 1932, specifies this type of voluntary dissolution.

3. On the happening of certain contingencies (Section 42) According to Section 42 of the Indian Partnership Act, 1932, the happening of any of the following contingencies can lead to the dissolution of the firm:

   • Some firms are constituted for a fixed term. Such firms will dissolve on the expiry of that term.

   • Some firms are constituted to carry out one or more undertaking. Such firms are dissolved when the undertaking is completed.

- Death of a partner.
- Insolvency of a partner.

4. By notice of partnership at will (Section 43) According to Section 43 of the Indian Partnership Act, 1932, if the partnership is at will, then any partner can give notice in writing to all other partners informing them about his intention to dissolve the firm. In such cases, the firm is dissolved on the date mentioned in the notice. If no date is mentioned, then the date of dissolution of the firm is the date of communication of the notice.

5. Dissolution by Court: At the suit of a partner, the court may order a partnership firm to be dissolved on any of the following grounds:

   (a) when a partner becomes insane;

   (b) when a partner becomes permanently incapable of performing his duties as a partner;

   (c) when a partner is guilty of misconduct which is likely to adversely affect the business of the firm;

   (d) when a partner persistently commits breach of partnership agreement;

   (e) when a partner has transferred the whole of his interest in the firm to a third party;

   (f) when the business of the firm cannot be carried on except at a loss; or

   (g) when, on any ground, the court regards dissolution to be just and equitable.

Settlement of Accounts In Case Of Dissolution of Firm:

(a) Treatment of Losses Losses, including deficiencies of capital, shall be paid :

   (i) first out of profits,

   (ii) next out of capital of partners, and

   (iii) lastly, if necessary, by the partners individually in their profit sharing ratio.

(b) Application of Assets The assets of the firm, including any sum contributed by the partners to make up deficiencies of capital, shall be applied in the following manner and order:

   (i) In paying the debts of the firm to the third parties;

   (ii) In paying each partner proportionately what is due to him/her from the firm for advances as distinguished from capital (i.e. partner' loan);

   (iii) In paying to each partner proportionately what is due to him on account of capital; and

   (iv) The residue, if any, shall be divided among the partners in their profit sharing ratio.

Multiple Choice Questions   **[1 Mark]**

Q.1. New ratio is not to be calculated on:

   (a) Admission of a partner   (b) Retirement of a partner

   (c) Death of a partner   (d) Dissolution of a partnership

Ans. (d)

Q.2. On dissolution of a firm in which ratio profit and loss on realisation is distributed among the partners:
                                                   [CBSE Compartment 2017]

   (a) Capital ratio   (b) Profit sharing ratio

   (c) Equally   (d) In the ratio of amount due to each partner.

Ans. (b)

Q.3. Realisation account is a: [CBSE Sample Paper 2018]

    (a) Personal account   (b) Real account

    (c) Nominal account   (d) None of the above

Ans. (c)

Q.4. At the time of firm's dissolution credit balance of profit and loss account is credited to:

    (a) Realisation account   (b) Partners capital account

    (c) Cash account   (d) Profit and loss account

Ans. (b)

Q.5. On dissolution of a firm Goodwill appearing in the balance sheet is transferred to: [CBSE 2017]

    (a) Capital account of partners   (b) Cash account

    (c) Debit side of realisation account   (d) Credit side of realisation account

Ans. (c)

Q.6. Section 41 of partnership act 1932 deals with dissolution of a firm

    (a) By mutual agreement   (b) Compulsory dissolution

    (c) By notice   (d) By order of court

Ans. (b)

Q.7. Settlement of accounts in case of dissolution of partnership is dealt with which section of partnership act 1932?

    (a) Section 45   (b) Section 46

    (c) Section 47   (d) Section 48

Ans. (d)

Q.8. Court may order dissolution of partnership firm   [CBSE 2019]

    (a) When a partner has become of unsound mind   (b) When a partner is permanently incapacitated

    (c) When a partner is found guilty of misconduct   (d) All of the above

Ans. (d)

Q.9. Which of the following is paid first in case of dissolution of partnership firm?

    (a) Realisation expenses   (b) External liabilities

    (c) Secured loan   (d) Partner's loan

Ans. (a)

Q.10. When realisation expenses are to be borne by a partner, actual realisation expense is credited to:

    (a) Partners capital a/c   (b) Cash a/c

    (c) Realisation a/c   (d) None of the above

Ans. (d)

Very Short Answer Type   **[1 Mark]**

Q.11. At the time of admission partnership firm is dissolved if <u>business</u> is _______.

Ans. discontinued

Q.12. All the accounts are settled among partners and creditors at the time of _______ of a business. **[CBSE 2016]**

Ans. dissolution

Q.13. First of all _______ of the firms will be settled out of sources of the business.

Ans. liabilities

Q.14. Admission of a partner is termination of _______ and not a dissolution of _______ .

Ans. agreement, firm

Q.15. Court may also dissolve a firm, if a partner _______ a suit, that one of the partners is of _______ mind.

Ans. files, unsound

Q.16. Partners are liable to settle the account of accounts payable even from their _______ sources, if they are solvent.

Ans. personal

Q.17. If all partners mutually decide for the dissolution, it will be dissolution of the _______.

[CBSE Sample Paper 2017]

Ans. firm

Q.18. Assertion (A): the court may order to dissolve a partnership firm.

Reason (R): A partner repeatedly breaks the terms of agreement

(a) Both Assertion and reason are true and reason is correct explanation of assertion.

(b) Assertion and reason both are true but reason is not the correct explanation of assertion.

(c) Assertion is true, reason is false.

(d) Assertion is false, reason is true.

Ans. (a)

Q.19. Assertion (A): dissolution of firm means closing down of the partnership business

Reason (R): All the partners terminate their connections with the firm and the business of the firm is brought to an end. **[CBSE Sample Paper 2022]**

(a) Both Assertion and reason are true and reason is correct explanation of assertion.

(b) Assertion and reason both are true but reason is not the correct explanation of assertion.

(c) Assertion is true, reason is false.

(d) Assertion is false, reason is true.

Ans. (a)

Q.20. Assertion (A): A firm is dissolved compulsorily when all the partners or all but one partner, become insolvent.

Reason (R): Dissolution of partnership and dissolution of firm both are the same.

(a) Both Assertion and reason are true and reason is correct explanation of assertion.

(b) Assertion and reason both are true but reason is not the correct explanation of assertion.

(c) Assertion is true, reason is false.

(d) Assertion is false, reason is true.

Ans. (c)

Short Answer Type - I   [2 Marks]

Q.21. Define Dissolution of partnership firm.   [CBSE 2015]

Ans. As per 39 of the partnership act 1932, "Dissolution of the firm means dissolution of partnership among all the partners in the firm." Its means business of the firm ends. All the assets of the firm are disposed off and all outside Liabilities and partner capital are paid.

Q.22. Write Modes of dissolution of firm

Ans. (i) Dissolution by agreement

(ii) Compulsory Dissolution

(iii) On happening of an event like insolvency of a partner

(iv) Dissolution by notice

(v) Dissolution by court

Q.23. Name the accounts which are prepared at the time of dissolution of a firm.

Ans. (i) realization A/c

(ii) partner's capital A/c

(iii) partner's loan A/c

(iv) bank A/c

Q.24. Define Realisation Account.   [CBSE 2010]

Ans. It is nominal A/c opened at the time of dissolution of a firm to ascertain profit and loss from realization of assets and payment of outsider's liabilities which may be transferred to partner's capital A/c in the profit sharing ratio.

Q.25. Explain Settlements of Assets at the time of dissolution of a firm.

Ans. (a) Fictitious assets such as advertisement suspense, preliminary expenses etc, directly transferred to partner's capital A/c in their profit sharing ratio.

(b) Unrecorded assets must be realized and shown credit side of the realization A/c.

Q.26. Explain Settlement of Liabilities at the time of dissolution of a firm.   [CBSE 2013]

Ans. (a) All outside liabilities must be paid off even if nothing is stated for their payment.

(b) Unrecorded liabilities also paid through cash or settled by unrecorded assets or settling recorded assets.

(c) Contingent liabilities discounting of B/R become liability must be settled or paid.

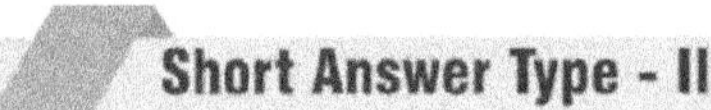

Short Answer Type - II   **[3 Marks]**

Analyses the case given below and answer the questions that follow:

The partnership firm of Vikram and Mohan located in Jorhat Assam a backward and rural area of northeast. The firm is producing tea and producing the product with the help of machinery and labour. This firm was dissolved on 1.3.2021 due to bad financial position.. According to the agreement Mr. Vikram had agreed to undertake the dissolution work for an agreed remuneration of Rs.2,000. Dissolution expenses were paid by Vikram.

Q.27. Who will bear the expenses of firm at dissolution?

    (a) Vikram   (b) Mohan   (c) Firm   (d) None of the above

Ans. (a)

Q.28. What will be the entry if payment made by partner Vikram?

    (a) Realisation A/c Dr To Bank A/c   (b) Realisation A/c Dr To Vikram's Capital A/c

    (c) No Entry   (d) Vikram's Capital A/c Dr To Bank A/c

Ans. (c)

Q.29. What will be the entry if expenses of dissolution if expenses is paid by firm Rs.2500?

    (a) Realisation A/c Dr 2500 To Bank A/c 2500

    (b) Realisation A/c Dr 2500 To Vikram's Capital A/c 2500

    (c) No Entry

    (d) Vikram's Capital A/c Dr 2500 To Bank A/c 2500

Ans. (d)

Q.30. What will be the entry if expenses of dissolution if expenses is paid by Mohan Rs.2000?

    (a) Realisation A/c Dr 2000 To Bank A/c 2000

    (b) Realisation A/c Dr 2000 To Vikram's Capital A/c 2000

    (c) Vikram's Capital A/c Dr 2000 To Mohan's Capital A/c 2000

    (d) Vikram's Capital A/c Dr 2000 To Bank A/c 2000

Ans. (c)

Q.31. Differentiate between Dissolution of partnership and Dissolution of firm.   **[CBSE 2009, 2015]**

Ans.

	Basis	**Dissolution of Partnership**	**Dissolution of firm**
1.	End of business	The business of the firm continue	The business of the Firm closed.
2.	Settlement of assets & liabilities	Assets and Liabilities are reassessed and new balance sheet is opened. Revaluation a/c is opened.	Assets are realized and liabilities are paid off. Realisation a/c is opened.
3.	Economic relationship	Economic relationship between the partners are changed	Economic relationship between the partners are to end.
4.	Closer of books and accounts	Books of accounts of the firm need not to be closed.	Books of accounts of the firm are closed.

Long Answer Type   **[5 Marks]**

Q.32. Explain SETTLEMENT OF ACCOUNTS at the time of dissolution of a firm.   **[CBSE Sample Paper 2016]**

Ans. As per section 48 of the partnership act 1932, the following rules shall apply.

    (i) Treatment of losses: losses including deficiencies of capital, shall be paid:-

        (a) first out of profit,

        (b) next out of capital and

        (c)if necessary, by the partners individually in the profit sharing ratio.

    (ii) Application of assets: Assets of the firm shall be applied in the following manner.

        (a)In paying firm's debts to the third party.

        (b)In paying each partner proportionately what is due to him on a/c of loan (i.e. partner's loan)

        (c)In paying each partner proportionately what is due to him on a/c of capital

        (d) The residue, if any shall be divided among the partners in their profit sharing ratio

Q.33. Pass the necessary journal entries on the dissolution of a firm in the following cases: **[CBSE 2011, 2022]**

    (a) Tanmay, a partner, was appointed to look after the process of dissolution at a remuneration of Rs.12,000 and he had to bear the dissolution expenses. Dissolution expenses Rs.11,000 were part by the Bharma.

Ans. (a) Realisations A/c   Dr. 12000

        To Tanmay's capital A/c   12000

        (Being remuneration allowed to partner to carry out dissolution)

    (b) Jay a partner was to look after the process of dissolution and for this work he was allowed a remuneration of Rs.7,000 agreed to bear all dissolution expenses. Actual expenses Rs.6000 were pound from firm's Bank A/c.

Ans. (i) Realisation A/c   Dr. 7000

        To Jay's capital A/c   7000

        (Being the remunerable all out to partner for bear realisation expenses)

    (ii) Jay' capital A/c   Dr. 6000

        To Bank A/c   6000

        (Being the expenses paid by firm on behalf partner)

    (c) Realisation expenses Rs.12000 born by the partner Deepa. These expenses were paid by Deepa by drawing cash from the firm. She was allowed commission Rs. 10,000 for process of dissolution.

Ans. (i) Realisation A/c   Dr. 10000

        To Deepa's capital A/c   10000

        (Being the commission paid for realisation expenses to Deepa)

    (ii) Deepa's capital A/c   Dr. 12000

        To cash A/c   12000

        (Being the cash is drawn for payment of realisation expenses by Deepa)

(d) Dev, a partner, agreed to do the work of dissolution for Rs.7500. He took away stock for his commission.

Ans. No Entry.

(e) A debtor of Rs. 8,000 already transferred to realization account agreed to pay the realization expenses of Rs.7,800 in full settlement.

Ans. No Entry.

(f) Realisation expenses amounted to Rs.15,000 out of this Rs. 12000 were to be born by 'A' a partner and the balance by firm.

Ans.   A's capital A/c   Dr. 12000

Realisation A/c   Dr. 3000

To Bank A/c   15000

(Being the payment of realization expenses)

TOPIC 2 Preparations of Accounts
[Realisation A/c, Partners Capitals A/c, Bank A/c]

Summary

Journal Entries on Dissolution of a Firm

1. For transfer of assets to Realization Account: (All assets excluding Cash/Bank, fictitious assets, accumulated losses are transferred to Realization Account)

   Realisation A/c   Dr.

   To Assets (Individually) A/c

2. For transfer of liabilities to Realization Account: (All outside liabilities are transferred to Realization Account) Note:

   (i)   Liabilities (individually)   Dr.

   To Realisation A/c

3. For sale of assets Bank A/c   Dr.

   To Realisation A/c

4. For an asset taken over by a partner

   Partner's Capital A/c   Dr.

   To Realisation A/c

5. For payment of liabilities

   Realisation A/c   Dr.

   To Bank A/c

6. For a liability which a partner takes responsibility to discharge

   Realisation A/c   Dr.

   To Partner's Capital A/c

7. For payment of realisation expenses

    (a) When some expenses are incurred and paid by the firm in the process of realisation of assets and payment of liabilities:

    Realisation A/c   Dr.

    To Bank A/c

    (b) When realisation expenses are paid by a partner on behalf of the firm:

    Realisation A/c Dr.

    To Partner's Capital A/c

    (c) When a partner has agreed to bear the realisation expenses:

    if payment of realisation expenses is made by the firm

    Partner's Capital A/c   Dr.

    To Bank A/c

8. For agreed remuneration to such partner who agrees to undertake the dissolution work. Realisation A/c   Dr.

    To Partner's Capital A/c

9. For realisation of any unrecorded assets including goodwill, if any

    Bank A/c Dr.

    To Realisation A/c

10. For settlement of any unrecorded liability

    Realisation A/c   Dr.

    To Bank A/c

11. For transfer of profit and   (Cr. Balance)

    loss on realisation

    (a) In case of profit on realisation

        Realisation A/c   Dr.

        To Partners' Capital A/c (individually) A/c

    (b) In case of loss on realisation

        Partners' Capital A/c   (Dr. Balance)

        (individually) Dr.

        To Realisation A/c

12. For settlement of loan by a firm to a partner:

    Bank A/c   Dr.

    To loan to partners A/c

13. For transfer of accumulated profits in the form of general reserve to partners' capital accounts in their profit sharing ratio:

    General Reserve A/c   Dr.

    To Partners' Capital A/c (individually)

14. For transfer of fictitious assets, if any, to partners' capital accounts in their profit sharing ratio:

    Partners' Capital A/c (individually)   Dr.

    To Fictitious Asset A/c

15. For payment of loans due to partners

    Partner's Loan A/c   Dr.

    To Bank A/c

FORMAT FOR REALISATION ACCOUNT

Particulars	Amount	Particulars	Amount
To Sundry Assets (Excluding Cash, Bank Fictitious assets, accumulated losses, debit balance of Partner's capital A/c and Loan to Partners)		By Sundry Liabilities A/c (Excluding Partner's Capital A/c, loan from Partners, Reserves and Accumulated Profit etc.)	
To Provsion (on liability)		By Specific Reserves (if required) By Provision (on assets)	
To Bank/Cash A/c (Payment of liabilities)		By Bank/Cash A/c (Assets realized)	
To Bank/Cash A/c (Payment of unrecorded liabilities)		By Bank/Cash A/c (Unrecorded Assets realized)	
To Bank/Cash A/c (Payment of Realization Exp.)		By partner's Capital/Current A/c (Assets taken over)	
To partner's Capital/Current A/c (For Discharge of liability)		By Partner's Capital/Current A/c (For distribution of Realization Loss)	
To Partner's Capital/Current A/c (For distribution of Realization Profit			

FORMAT FOR PARTNER'S CAPITAL ACCOUNT

Particulars	A	B	Particulars	A	B
To Balance b/d			To Balance b/d		
To profit and Loss			By Reserves		
To Advertisement			By Profit and Loss		
Suspense A/c			By WCR/IFF		
To Realization A/c			By Realization A/c		
(Assets taken over)			(Liabilities taken		
To Realization			By Realization A/c		
(Loss on Realization)			(Profit on Realization		
To Bank/Cash A/c			By Bank/Cash A/c		
(Excess cash paid			(Cash brought in)		

BANK/CASH ACCOUNT

Particulars	Amount	Particulars	Amount
To Balance b/d (opening balance)		By Realization A/c (Payment of liabilities)	
To Realization A/c (Assets Realized)		By Realization A/c (Payment of realization Exp.)	
To Partner's Capital A/c (Cash brought in)		By partner's Loan A/c (Amount of loan paid to the Partner)	
		By Partner's (Capital A/c (Final Cash paid to the partner)	

Multiple Choice Questions   [1 Mark]

Q.1. At the time of dissolution of partnership an unrecorded asset taken by X a partner is debited to:

(a) X capital account

(b) Realisation account

(c) Cash account

(d) None of the above

Ans. (a)

Q.2. On firm's dissolution which of the following account is prepared at the last?

(a) Realisation account   (b) Partners capital account

(c) Cash account partners   (d) Loan account

Ans. (c)

Q.3. On dissolution of a firm fictitious assets are transferred to:

(a) Credit side of partners capital account   (b) Debit side of realisation account

(c) Debit side of partners capital account   (d) Credit side of realisation account

Ans. (c)

Q.4. On dissolution of the firm amount received from sale of unrecorded asset is credited to:

(a) Partner's capital account   (b) Profit and loss account

(c) Cash account   (d) Realisation account

Ans. (d)

Q.5. On dissolution the balance of partners capital account appearing on the credit side of the balance sheet is transferred to: **[CBSE Sample Paper]**

(a) Debit side of realisation account   (b) Credit side of realisation account

(c) Debit side of partners capital account   (d) Credit side of partners capital account

Ans. (d)

Q.6. A, B and C are partners. The firm had given a loan of Rs. 20,000 to B. They decided to dissolve the firm. In the event of dissolution the loan will be settled by transferring it to the:

(a) Debit side of realisation account

(b) Transferring it to the credit side of realisation account

(c) Transfer it to the debit side of B's capital account

(d) B paying A and C privately

Ans. (c)

Q.7. In case of dissolution, total creditors of the firm were Rs.40,000; creditors worth Rs.10000 were given a piece of furniture costing Rs.8000 in full and final settlement. Remaining creditors allowed a discount of 10%. What will be the amount with which cash will be credited in the realisation account for payment to creditors:

[CBSE 2019]

(a) 28,000　　　　　　(b) 27,000　　　　　　(c) 20,000　　　　　　(d) 25,000

Ans. (b)

Q.8. In case of dissolution A one of the partner was paid only Rs.5000 for his loan to the firm which amounted to Rs.5500. Rs.500 will be recorded in which account and on which side:　　　　　　[CBSE 2015]

(a) Realisation account credit side　　　　　　(b) Realisation account debit side

(c) Loan account debit side　　　　　　(d) A's capital account credit side

Ans. (a)

Q.9. In case of dissolution of partnership there was no workmen compensation fund and firm had to pay Rs. 3000 as compensation to workers where will be this Rs. 3000 recorded in the books of accounts?

(a) Debit side of realisation account　　　　　　(b) Credit side of realisation account

(c) Debit side of partners capital account　　　　　　(d) Credit side of partners capital account

Ans. (a)

Q.10. At the time of dissolution total assets are worth Rs.3,00,000 and external liabilities are worth Rs.1,20,000. If assets realised 120% and realisation expenses paid were Rs.4,000, then profit/loss on realisation will be:

(a) Profit Rs. 60,000　(b) Loss Rs. 60,000　　　　(c) Loss Rs. 56,000　　　(d) Profit Rs. 56,000

Ans. (d)

Very Short Answer Type　　　　　　　　　　　　　　　　　　　　　　　[1 Mark]

Q.11. _______________ of partner will be paid off, before the settlement of partner's capital.

Ans. loan

Q.12. Assertion (A): On dissolution, goodwill account is transferred to Realisation Account.

Reason (R): Goodwill is an Asset which cannot be seen or touched.　　　　　　[CBSE 2020]

(a) Both Assertion and reason are true and reason is correct explanation of assertion.

(b) Assertion and reason both are true but reason is not the correct explanation of assertion.

(c) Assertion is true, reason is false.

(d) Assertion is false, reason is true.

Ans. (b)

Q.13. Assertion (A): At the time of Dissolution of Partnership Firm, The amount received from realisation of all the assets of the firm is used first of all to pay the external liabilities of the firm

Reason (R): As per the Partnership Act, outside liability should be paid first of all at the time of dissolution of partnership firm.

(a) Both Assertion and reason are true and reason is correct explanation of assertion.

(b) Assertion and reason both are true but reason is not the correct explanation of assertion.

(c) Assertion is true, reason is false.

(d) Assertion is false, reason is true.

Ans. (a)

Q.14. Assertion (A): On the dissolution of a firm the cash-in-hand is not transferred to Realisation Account

Reason (R): Realisation Account is Real Account.   **[CBSE Sample Paper 2021]**

(a) Both Assertion and reason are true and reason is correct explanation of assertion.

(b) Assertion and reason both are true but reason is not the correct explanation of assertion.

(c) Assertion is true, reason is false.

(d) Assertion is false, reason is true.

Ans. (c)

Q.15. Assertion (A): A partnership firm is deemed to be dissolved at the time of retirement of a Partnership firm.

Reason (R): Partnership firm lacks stability.

(a) Both Assertion and reason are true and reason is correct explanation of assertion.

(b) Assertion and reason both are true but reason is not the correct explanation of assertion.

(c) Assertion is true, reason is false.

(d) Assertion is false, reason is true.

Ans. (d)

Q.16. Assertion (A): the consent of all the partners is mandatory in dissolution.

Reason (R): dissolution by agreement.

(a) Both Assertion and reason are true and reason is correct explanation of assertion.

(b) Assertion and reason both are true but reason is not the correct explanation of assertion.

(c) Assertion is true, reason is false.

(d) Assertion is false, reason is true.

Ans. (b)

Q.17. Assertion (A): first of all the external liabilities and expenses are to be paid. Then, all loans and advances forwarded by the partners should be paid.

Reason (R): Define in partnership act 1932.

(a) Both Assertion and reason are true and reason is correct explanation of assertion.

(b) Assertion and reason both are true but reason is not the correct explanation of assertion.

(c) Assertion is true, reason is false.

(d) Assertion is false, reason is true.

Ans. (a)

Q.18. Assertion (A): Dissolution expenses paid by the firm on behalf of a partner is recorded on the debit side of realisation account.

Reason (R): Such expenses are a Non-business expense.

(a) Both Assertion and reason are true and reason is correct explanation of assertion.

(b) Assertion and reason both are true but reason is not the correct explanation of assertion.

(c) Assertion is true, reason is false.

(d) Assertion is false, reason is true.

Ans. (d)

Q.19. Assertion (A): On dissolution of firm, partners loan is transferred to realisation account.

Reason (R): Partners loan is an internal liability.

(a) Both Assertion and reason are true and reason is correct explanation of assertion.

(b) Assertion and reason both are true but reason is not the correct explanation of assertion.

(c) Assertion is true, reason is false.

(d) Assertion is false, reason is true.

Ans. (d)

Q.20. Assertion (A): Realisation account is prepared at the time of dissolution of partnership.

Reason (R): Realisation account records the cash release from sale of assets and amount paid to external liabilities.

(a) Both Assertion and reason are true and reason is correct explanation of assertion.

(b) Assertion and reason both are true but reason is not the correct explanation of assertion.

(c) Assertion is true, reason is false.

(d) Assertion is false, reason is true.

Ans. (d)

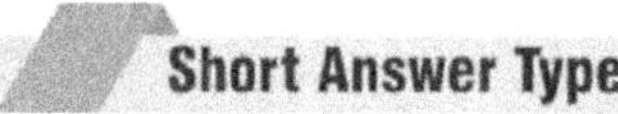

Short Answer Type - I   **[2 Marks]**

Q.21. Write the rules applicable while preparing Realisation account. **[CBSE 2014]**

Ans. I. for assets

    (i) Cash and Bank balance are not transferred to Realisation Account.

    (ii) Assets (tangible and intangible) are transferred to Realisation Account at their Gross Value .

    (iii) Fictitious Asset such as Debit balance of Profit and Loss Account or Advertisement Suspense Account etc. are not transferred to Realisation Account. These are directly debited to partners' capital accounts in their profit-sharing ratio.

II. for liabilities

    (i) Only third parties' liabilities/outsiders 'liabilities are transferred to Realisation A/c.

    (ii) Balance of Partner's Loan Account is not transferred to Realisation Account. Separate accounts are opened to settle such liabilities.

    (iii) Undistributed profits and reserves are also not transferred to Realisation A/c. These are directly credited to partners' capital accounts in their profit-sharing ratio.

Q.22. Distinction between Revaluation Account and Realisation Account.   [CBSE 2011, 2017]

Ans.

Basis of Difference	Revaluation Account	Realisation Account
Purpose	It is prepared to show assets and liabilities in the books at their revised values	It is prepared to ascertain profit or loss from sale of assets and repayment of Liabilities.
When to be prepared	It is prepared at the time of change in profit sharing ratio among the existing partner, admission, retirement and death of a partner.	It is prepared at the time of dissolution of a firm.
Preparation of Account	This account may be prepared at a number of times during the life of a firm.	This account is prepared once during the life of a firm.

Short Answer Type - II   [3 Marks]

Analyses the case given below and answer the questions that follow:

A and B were partners in a firm sharing profits in the ratio of 3 : 2. On 31st March, 2020, the balance sheet of the firm was as follows:

BALANCE SHEET

as at 31st March, 2020

Liabilities		Amount	Assets	Amount
Capital			Building	2,40,000
A	3,00,000		Stock	75,000
B	2,00,000	5,00,000	Debtors	80,000
Creditors		1,17,000	Cash	47,000
			Furniture	1,75,000
		6,17,000		**6,17,000**

The firm was dissolved on 1st April, 2011 and the assets and liabilities were settled

Q.23. Building was taken over by creditors as their full and final payment. How much amount will be debited to Realisation Account?

(a) Rs. 1,23,000   (b) NIL   (c) Rs. 1,33,000   (d) Rs. 1,43,000

Ans. (b)

Q.24. Furniture was taken over by B for cash payment at 5% less than the book value. The account Debited will be:

(a) Realisation A/c   (b) B's Capital A/c   (c) A's Capital A/c   (d) Cash A/c

Ans. (d)

Q.25. Debtors were collected by a debt collection agency at a cost of Rs.5,000. How much amount will be credited to Realisation Account?

(a) Rs. 80,000   (b) NIL   (c) Rs. 75,000   (d) Rs. 85,000

Ans. (c)

Q.26. B agreed to bear all realisation expenses. For this service, B is paid Rs.500. Actual expense on realisation amounted to Rs.1,000. Realisation A/c will be debited with

(a) Rs. 1500   (b) Rs. 500   (c) Rs. 3,000   (d) Rs. 1,000

Ans. (b)

Analyses the case given below and answer the questions that follow:

Raman and Suman were partners sharing profits in the ratio of 3 : 1. On 31st March, 2019, their balance sheet was as follows:

BALANCE SHEET

as at 31st March, 2019

Liabilities		Amount	Assets	Amount
Capital:			Land & Building	70,000
Raman	1,00,000		Machinery	60,000
Suman	80,000	1,80,000	Debtors	80,000
Creditors		70,000	Bank	60,000
Profit & Loss		20,000		
		2,70,000		**2,70,000**

The firm was dissolved on 1st April, 2011 and the assets and liabilities were settled.

Q.27. Creditors of Rs.50,000 took over land and building in full settlement of their claim. Remaining creditors were paid in cash. How much amount will be debited to Realisation Account?

(a) Rs.10,000   (b) NIL   (c) Rs.20,000   (d) Rs.40,000

Ans. (c)

Q.28. Machinery was sold at a depreciation of 30%. How much amount will be credited to Realisation Account?

(a) Rs.52,000   (b) Rs.62,000   (c) Rs.42,000   (d) Rs.72,000

Ans. (c)

Q.29. Expenses on realisation were Rs.1,700. The account Credited will be:

(a) Realisation A/c   (b) Partner's Capital A/c   (c) Revaluation A/c   (d) Bank A/c

Ans. (d)

Q.30. Profit and Loss A/c appearing on the liabilities side of the Balance Sheet will be transferred to

(a) Realisation A/c   (b) Partner's Capital A/c   (c) Revaluation A/c   (d) Bank A/c

Ans. (b)

Analyses the case given below and answer the questions that follow: [CBSE Guidelines]

Gopal, Mohan and Sohan were partners in a firm sharing in 2:2:1. On 31st March 2021, they decided to dissolve the firm. On the date following was their position:

BALANCE SHEET

(as on 31.3.2021)

Liabilities		₹	Assets		₹
Creditors		50,000	Cash at Bank		20,000
Gopal	1,10,000		S. Debtors	1,50,000	
Mohan	90,000		Less: Provision	10,000	140,000
Sohan	70,000	2,70,000	Stock		60,000
			Fixed Assets		1,00,000
		3,20,000			3,20,000

The assets and liabilities of settled as follows:

(i)   One of the creditors for ₹20,000 agreed to accept half of the stock in full settlement. Balance of the creditors were paid at a discount of 5%.

(ii) Remaining half of the stock was sold in the market at a profit of 331%. 3

(iii) All other assets realised at rupees ₹2,00,000.

(iv) Sohan was appointed to look after all the dissolution procedure and hence, he was allowed a remuneration of 15% on the cash realised to from sale of assets.

Q.31. What is the amount paid to creditors at the time of dissolution?

    (a) Rs.48,500   (b) Rs.30,000   (c) Rs.58,500   (d) Rs.28,500

Ans. (d)

Q.32. State the amount realised from sale of stock.

    (a) Rs.33,333   (b) Rs.40,000   (c) Rs.30,000   (d) Rs.33,000

Ans. (b)

Q.33. What is the amount of remuneration payable to Sohan?

    (a) Rs.36,000   (b) Rs.30,000   (c) Rs.6,000   (d) Rs.37,500

Ans. (a)

Q.34. What is the amount of gain or loss on realisation?

    (a) Rs.76,000 Gain   (b) Rs.76,000 Loss   (c) Rs.74,500 Gain   (d) Rs.74,500 Loss

Ans. (d)

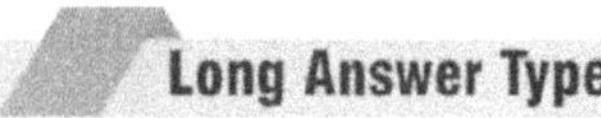 **Long Answer Type**   **[5 Marks]**

Analyses the case given below and answer the questions that follow:

X and Y were partners in a firm in equal ratio. Following was their balance sheet as on 31st March 2021:

[CBSE Sample Paper 2020]

BALANCE SHEET
(as on 31.3.2021)

Liabilities	₹	Assets	₹
Provision for DD	5,000	Cash at Bank	15,000
Creditors	45,000	S. Debtors	80,000
Mrs. Y's Loan	25,000	Stock	50,000
Capitals:		Machinery	75,000
X 1,00,000		Profit & Loss A/c	20,000
Y 65,000	1,65,000		
	2,40,000		**2,40,000**

They dissolve the firm on the above date and following agreements were decided upon:

(i) X took over a part of the stock at Rs. 18,000 being 10% less than its book value. Balance of the stock was taken over by Y at 75% of its book value less Rs. 2,500.

(ii) One of the creditors of Rs.20,000 agreed to accept a part of machine at an agreed valuation of Rs.25,000 being 25% more than its book value. Balance of the creditors were paid in full.

(iii) Balance of the machine and the debtors were realised at Rs.1,00,000.

Q.35. State the amount at which stock was taken over by Y:

    (a) Rs.30,000   (b) Rs.22,500   (c) Rs.20,000   (d) Rs.24,000

Ans. (c)

Q.36. What is the book value of the machine which was taken over by one of the creditors?

    (a) Rs.20,000   (b) Rs.25,000   (c) Rs.31,500   (d) None of the above

Ans. (a)

Q.37. State the treatment of balance in profit and loss account appears on the asset side.

    (a) Transfer to the credit side of partners' capital account

    (b) Transfer to the debit side of partners' capital account

    (c) Transfer to the credit side of realisation account

    (d) Transferred to the debit side of realisation account

Ans. (b)

Q.38. State the total amount paid to various external liabilities at the time of dissolution.

    (a) Rs.25,000   (b) Rs.55,000   (c) Rs.50,000   (d) Rs.20,000

Ans. (c)

Q.39. Gayatri and Gopal were partners in a firm sharing, profits and losses in the ratio of 2:3. On 31st March, 2020 their Balance Sheet was as follows: **[CBSE 2012]**

Liabilities	Amount (Rs.)	Assets		Amount (Rs.)
Creditors	80,000	Cash at Bank		20,000
Bank Overdraft	50,000	Debtors	55,000	
Gayatri's Brother's Loan	77,000	Less: Provision for		
Gopal's Loan	28,000	Doubtful Debts	2,000	53,000
Investment Fluctuation Fund	15,000	Stock		78,000
Capitals:		Investments		89,000
Gayatri 1,50,000		Buildings		2,50,000
Gopal 1,00,000	2,50,000	Profit and Loss A/c		10,000
	5,00,000			**5,00,000**

On the above date the firm was dissolved. The assets were realised and the liabilities were paid of as follows:

(a) Debtors of Rs.6,000 were proved bad.

(b) Gayatri agreed to pay off her brother's loan.

(c) One of the creditors for Rs.10,000 was paid only Rs.3,000 in full settlement of his account.

(d) Buildings were auctioned for Rs.1,80,000 and the auctioneer's commission amounted to Rs.8,000.

(e) Gopal took over part of stock at Rs.4,000 (being 20% less than the book value). Balance of the Stock was handed over to the remaining creditors in full settlement of their account.

(f) Investments realised Rs.9,000 less.

(g) Realisation expenses amounted to Rs.17,000 and were paid by Gopal.

Prepare Realisation Account, Partner's Capital Accounts and Bank Account.

Ans. Dr.   **REALISATION ACCOUNT**   Cr.

Particulars		Amount (Rs.)	Particulars		Amount (Rs.)
To Sundry Assets:			By Sundry Liabilities:		
Debtors	55,000		Provision for		
Stock	78,000		Doubtful Debts	2,000	
Investments	89,000		Creditors	80,000	
Buildings	250,000	4,72,000	Gayatri's Brother's		
To Gayatri's Capital			Loan	77,000	
A/c			Bank Overdraft	50,000	2,09,000
(Brother's Loan)		77,000	By Investment		
To Bank A/c:	3,000		Fluctuation Fund		15,000
Creditors	50,000	53,000	By Bank A/c:		
Bank Overdraft			Debtors	49,000	
To Gopal's Capital			Buildings	1,72,000	
A/c			Investments	80,000	3,01,000
(Realisation Exp.)		17,000	By Gopal's Capitla A/c		
			(Stock)		4,000

			By Partner's Capital A/c: (Loss)		
			Gayatri	36,000	
			Gopal	54,000	90,000
		6,19,000			**6,19,000**

Dr.   Partners' Capital Account   Cr.

Particulars	Gayatri (Rs.)	Gopal (Rs.)	Particulars	Gayatri (Rs.)	Gopal (Rs.)
To P & L A/c	4,000	6,000	By Balance b/d	1,50,000	1,00,000
To Realisation A/c	36,000	54,000	By Realisation A/c	77,000	17,000
To Realisation A/c	...	4,000			
To Bank A/c	187,000	53,000			
	2,27,000	**1,17,000**		**227,000**	**1,17,000**

Dr.   BANK ACCOUNT   Cr.

Particulars	Amount (Rs.)	Particulars	Amount (Rs.)
To Balance c/d	20,000	By Realisation A/c (Liabilities)	53,000
To Realisation A/c (Assets)	3,01,000	By Gopal's Loan A/c	28,000
		By Gayatri's Capital A/c	1,87,000
		By Gopal's Capital A/c	53,000
	3,21,000		**3,21,000**

Q.40. Rohit and Raghav were partners in a firm sharing profits and losses in the ratio of 3:2. On 31st March, 2018 their Balance Sheet was as follows: [CBSE 2015]

BALANCE SHEET OF ROHIT AND RAGHAV

as at 31st March, 2018

Liabilities	Amount (Rs.)	Assets	Amount (Rs.)
Trade Creditors	42,000	Bank	35,000
Employee's Provident Fund	60,000	Stock	24,000
Mrs Rohit's Loan	9,000	Debtors	19,000
Raghav's Loan	35,000	Furniture	40,000
Workmen's Compensation Fund	20,000	Plant	2,10,000
Investment Fluctuation Reserve	4,000	Investments	32,000
Capital:		Profit and Loss Account	10,000
Rohit 1,20,000	2,00,000		
Raghav 80,000			
	370,000		**370,000**

On the above date they decided to dissolve the firm.

(i) Rohit agreed to take over furniture at Rs.38,000 and pay off Mrs. Rohit's loan.

(ii) Debtors realised Rs.18,500 and plant realised 10% more.

(iii) Raghav took over 40% of the stock at 20% less that the book value. Remaining stock was sold at a gain of 10%.

(iv) Trade creditors took over investments in full settlement.

(v) Raghav agreed to take over the responsibility of completing dissolution at an agreed remuneration of Rs.12,000 and to bear realisation expenses. Actual expenses of realisation amounted to Rs.8,000.

Prepare Realisation Account.

Ans. Dr.	**REALISATION ACCOUNT**	**Cr.**

Particulars	Amount (Rs.)	Particulars	Amount (Rs.)
To Stock	24,000	By Trade Creditors	42,000
To Debtors	19,000	By Employees Provident Fund	60,000
To Furniture	40,000	By Mrs Rohit's Loan	9,000
To Plant	2,10,000	By Investment Fluctuation Reserve	4,000
To Investments	32,000	By Rohit's Capital A/c	38,000
To Rohit's Capital	9,000	By Bank:	
To Bank	60,000	Debtors 18,500	2,49,500
To Raghav's Capital	12,000	Plant 2,31,000	7,680
To Capitals:		By Raghav's Capital	15,840
Rohit 12,012		By Bank	
Raghav 8,008	20,020		
	4,26,020		**4,26,020**

Working Notes:

(i) Employees provident fund is a liability payable to employees of the firm.

(ii) Workmen's compensation fund is an accumulated profit.

(iii) Investment fluctuation reserve is a provision against investments.

(iv) Book value of plant	Rs.2,10,000

Add: 10%	Rs.21,000

Realised value of plant	Rs.2,31,000

	Rs.
(v) Book value of stock	24,000
40% of book value of stock	9,600
Less: 20%	1,920
Agreed value of stock taken over by Raghav	7,680
60% of book value of stock	14,400
Add: 10%	1,440
Realised value	15,840

Q.41. Musab, Jeeshan and Jafar were partners in a firm sharing profits in the ratio of 3:1:1. On 31st March, 2017, they decided to dissolve their firm. On that date their Balance Sheet was as follows:

BALANCE SHEET OF MUSAB, JEESHAN AND JAFAR

as at 31.03.2017

Liabilities	Amount (Rs.)	Assets		Amount (Rs.)
Creditors	11,500	Bank		6,000
Loan	3,500	Debtors	48,400	
Capital:		Less: Provision for		
Musab 50,000		Doubtful Debts	2,400	46,000
Jeeshan 25,000		Stock in Trade		16,000
Jafar 14,000	89,000	Furniture		2,000
		Sundry Assets		34,000
	1,04,000			**1,04,000**

It was agreed that:

(i) Musab was to take over Furniture at Rs.2,600 and Debtors amounting to Rs.40,000 at Rs.34,400 and the Creditors of Rs.10,000 were to be paid by him at this figure.

(ii) Jeeshan was to take over all the Stock in Trade Rs.14,000 and some of the other Sundry Assets at Rs.28,800 (being 10% less than book value).

(iii) Jafar was to take over the remaining Sundry Assets at 90% of the book value and assumed the responsibility for the discharge of the loan.

(iv) The remaining debtors were sold to a debt collecting agency for 50% of the book value. The expenses of dissolution Rs.600 were paid by Jafar.

Prepare Realisation Account, Bank Account and Partner's Capital Accounts.

Ans. Dr.   **REALISATION ACCOUNT**   **Cr.**

Particulars	Amount (Rs.)	Particulars		Amount (Rs.)
To Debtors	48,400	By Provision Doubtful Debts		2,400
To Stock	16,000	By Creditors		11,500
To Furniture	2,000	By Loan		3,500
To Sundry Assets	34,000	By Musab's Capital		
To Musab's Capital (creditors)	10,000	(2,600 + 34,400)		37,000
To Jafar's Capital (expenses)	600	By Jeeshan's Capital		
To Jafar's Capital (loan)	3,500	(14,000 + 28,800)		42,800
To Bank A/c (creditors)	1,500	By Bank		4,200
		By Jafar's Capital		1,800
		By Capitals:		
		Musab	7,680	
		Jeeshan	2,560	
		Jafar	2,560	12,800
	1,16,000			**1,16,000**

Dr.   Musab's Capital Account   **Cr.**

Particulars	Amount (Rs.)	Particulars	Amount (Rs.)
To Realisation A/c	37,000	By Balance b/d	50,000
To Realisation A/c	7,680	By Realisation A/c	10,000
To Bank A/c	15,320		
	60,000		**60,000**

Dr.   Jeeshan's Capital Account   **Cr.**

Particulars	Amount (Rs.)	Particulars	Amount (Rs.)
To Realisation A/c	42,800	By Balance b/d	25,000
To Realisation A/c	2,560	By Bank A/c	20,360
	45,360		**45,360**

Dr.   Jafar's Capital Account   **Cr.**

Particulars	Amount (Rs.)	Particulars	Amount (Rs.)
To Realisation A/c	1,800	By Balance b/d	14,000
To Realisation A/c	2,560	By Realisation A/c	600
To Bank A/c	13,740	By Realisation A/c	3,500
	18,100		**18,100**

Dr.   BANK ACCOUNT   **Cr.**

Particulars	Amount (Rs.)	Particulars	Amount (Rs.)
To Balance b/d	6,000	By Musab's Capital	15,320
To Realisation A/c	4,200	By Jafar's Capital	13,740
To Jeeshan's Capital	20,360	By Realisation A/c	1,500
	30,560		**30,560**

Working Notes: Rs.

(i) Book value of debtors as per B/S   48,400

     Less: Book value of debtors taken over by Musab   40,000

     Book value of debtors to be collected   **8,400**

$$\text{Money realised from debtors} = 8,400 \times \frac{50}{100} = \text{Rs.4,200}$$

(ii) Book value of Sundry Assets taken over by Jeeshan $= 28,800 \times \frac{100}{90} = \text{Rs.32,000}$

     Book value of Sundry Assets taken over by Jafar $= 34,000 - 32,000 = \text{Rs.2,000}$

Extra Questions Previous Year

Q.1. Ankit, Bobby and Kartik were partners in a firm sharing profits in the ratio 4:3:3. The firm was dissolved on 31-3-2018. Pass the necessary Journal entries for the following transactions after various assets (other than cash and bank) and third party liabilities had been transferred to Realisation Account:

     (i) The firm had stock of ₹80,000. Ankit took over 50% of the stock at a discount of 20% while the remaining stock was sold off at a profit of 30% on cost.

(ii) A liability under a suit for damages included in creditors was settled at ₹32,000 as against only ₹13,000 provided in the books. Total creditors of the firm were ₹50,000.

(iii) Bobby's sister's loan of ₹20,000 was paid off along with interest of ₹2,000.

(iv) Kartik's Loan of ₹12,000 was settled at ₹12,500.   **(CBSE Delhi 2019)**

Ans.

In the Books of Firm

JOURNAL

Date	Particulars		L.F.	Dr. (₹)	Cr. (₹)
(i)	Ankit Capital A/c	Dr.		32,000	
	Cash Bank A/c	Dr.		52,000	
	To Realisation A/c				84,000
	(Being half stock sold & half stock taken by April)				
(ii)	Realisation A/c	Dr.		69,000	
	To Cash/Bank A/c				69,000
	(Being creditor and contingent liabilities settled				
(iii)	Realisation A/c	Dr.		22,000	
	To Cash/Bank A/c				22,000
	(Being Body's sister's loan paid off along with interest)				
(iv)	Kartik's Loan A/c	Dr.		12,000	
	Realisation A/c	Dr.		500	
	To Cash Bank A/c				12,500
	(Being Kartik's loan paid off)				

Q.2. The firm of Manjeet, Sujeet and Jagjeet was dissolved on 31st March, 2018. It was agreed that Sujeet will take care of the dissolution related activities and will get 10% of the value of assets realised. Sujeet agreed to bear the realisation expenses. Assets realised ₹10,00,750 and realisation expenses were ₹ 90,000, which were paid from the firm's cash. ₹4,50,000 were paid to the creditors in full settlement of their claim.

Pass necessary journal entries for the above transactions in the books of the firm.

(CBSE Outside Delhi 2019)

Ans.

Books of Manjeet, Sujeet and Jagjeet

JOURNAL

Date	Particulars		L.F.	Dr. (₹)	Cr. (₹)
(a)	Bank A/c	Dr.		10,00,750	
	To Realisation A/c				10,00,750
	(assets realised)				
(b)	Realisation A/c	Dr.		1,00,075	
	To Sujeet's Capital A/c				1,00,075
	(10% of assets realised paid as remuneration)				

(c)	Sujeet's Capital A/c	Dr.		90,000	
	To Bank/Cash Capital A/c				90,000
	(realisation expense paid on behalf of Sujeet)				
(d)	Realisation A/c	Dr.		4,50,000	
	To Bank A/c				4,50,000
	(Creditors paid in full Settlement)				

Q.3. The firm of R, K and S was dissolved on 31.3.2019. Pass necessary journal entries for the following after various assets (other than cash and Bank) and the third party liabilities had been transferred to realisation account.

(i) K agreed to pay off his wife's loan of ₹6,000.

(ii) Total Creditors of the firm were ₹40,000. Creditors worth ₹10,000 were given a piece of furniture costing ₹8,000 in full and final settlement. Remaining creditors allowed a discount of 10%.

(iii) A machine that was not recorded in the books was taken over by K at ₹3,000 whereas its expected value was ₹5,000.

(iv) The firm had a debit balance of ₹15,000 in the profit and loss A/c on the date of dissolution.

(CBSE Sample Paper 2019-20)

Ans.

JOURNAL

Date	Particulars		L.F.	Dr. Amount (₹)	Cr. Amount (₹)
(i)	Realization A/c	Dr.		6,000	
	To K's Capital A/c				6,000
	(Being wife's loan discharged by the partner				
(ii)	Realization A/c	Dr.		27,000	
	To Bank A/c				27,000
	(Being balance creditor's paid at a discount of 10% after part payment through furniture				
(iii)	K's Capital Account	Dr.		3,000	
	To Realization A/c				3,000
	(Being unrecorded machine taken over by a partner)				
(iv)	R's Capital A/c	Dr.		5,000	
	K's Capital A/c	Dr.		5,000	
	S's Capital A/c	Dr.		5,000	
	To Profit and Loss A/c				15,000
	(Being debit balance of profit and Loss distributed amongst partners)				

Q.4. L and M were partners in a firm sharing profits in the ratio of 2 : 3. On 28.2.2016 the firm was dissolved. After transferring assets (other than cash) and outsider's liabilities to realisation account you are given the following information:

(i) A creditor of ₹1,40,000 accepted building valued at ₹1,80,000 and paid to the firm ₹40,000.

(ii) A second creditor for ₹30,000 accepted machinery valued at ₹28,000 in full settlement of his claim.

(iii) A third creditor amounting to ₹70,000 accepted ₹30,000 in cash and investments of the book value of ₹45,000 in full settlement of his claim.

(iv) Loss on dissolution was ₹4,000.

Pass necessary journal entries for the above transactions in the books of firm assuming that all payments were made by cheque.   **(CBSE Outside Delhi 2016)**

Ans.

In the Books L and M
JOURNAL

Date	Particulars		L.F.	Dr. (₹)	Cr. (₹)
(i)	Bank A/c	Dr.		40,000	
	To Realization A/c				40,000
	(Being building accepted by creditors and balance paid by him)				
(ii)	No Entry				
(iii)	Realization A/c	Dr.		30,000	
	To Bank A/c				30,000
	(Being cash paid to creditor)				
(iv)	L's Capital A/c	Dr.		1,600	
	M's Capital A/c	Dr.		2,400	
	To Realization A/c				4,000
	(Being loss on dissolution distributed to partners)				

Q.5. Pradeep and Rajesh were partners in a firm sharing profits and losses in the ratio of 3:2. They decided to dissolve their partnership firm on 31st March, 2018. Pradeep was deputed to realize the assets and to pay off the liabilities. He was paid ₹1,000 as commission for his services. The financial position of the firm on 31st March, 2018 was as follows:

Balance Sheet as at March 31, 2018

Liabilities	Amount (₹)	Assets		Amount (₹)
Creditors	80,000	Building		1,20,000
Mrs. Pradeep's Loan	40,000	Investment		30,600
Rajesh's loan	24,000	Debtors	34,000	
Investment Fluctuation Fund	8,000	Less: Provision for Doubtful Debts	4,000	30,000

			Bills Receivable	37,400
Capitals:			Bank	6,000
Pradeep	42,000		Profit and Loss A/c	8,000
Rajesh	42,000	84,000	Goodwill	4,000
		2,36,000		**2,36,600**

Following terms and conditions were agreed upon:

(i) Pradeep agreed to pay off his wife's loan.

(ii) Half of the debtor's realized ₹12,000 and remaining debtors were used to pay off 25% of the creditors.

(iii)Investment sold to Rajesh for ₹27,000

(iv) Building realized ₹1,52,000

(v) Remaining creditors were to be paid after two months, they were paid immediately at 10% p.a. discount

(vi) Bill receivables were settled at a loss of ₹1,400

(vii)Realization expenses amounted to ₹2,500

Prepare Realization Account.   (CBSE Sample Paper 2018-19)

Ans.

Dr.   **REALIZATION ACCOUNT**   **Cr.**

Particulars		Amount (₹)	Particulars		Amount (₹)
To building		1,20,000	By Provisions on Debtors		4,000
To Investment		30,600	By Creditors		80,000
To Debtors		34,000	By Mrs. Pradeep's Loan		40,000
To Bills Receivable		37,400	By Investment Fluctuation Fund		8,000
To Goodwill		4,000	By Bank A/c		
To Pradeep's Capital A/c		40,000	Debtors	12,000	
To Bank A/c (expenses)		2,500	Building	1,52,000	
To Bank A/c (creditors)		59,000	Bill Receievable	36,000	2,00,000
To Pradeep's Capital A/c		1,000	By Cash A/c		27,000
To Partner's Capital A/cs:					
Pradeep	18,300				
Rajesh	12,200	30,500			
		3,59,000			**3,59,000**

Working Notes:

Payment to creditors = (₹80,000 – ₹20,000) – {₹60,000 × (10/100) × (2/12)} = ₹60,000 – ₹1,000 = ₹59,000

* 1/2 mark each for transferring assets and liabilities to realization account.

Q.6. Parth and Shivika were partners in a firm sharing profits in the ratio of 3 : 2. The Balance Sheet of the firm on 31st March, 2014 was as follows:

Liabilities		(₹)	Assets	(₹)
Sundry Creditors		80,000	Bank	1,72,000
Shivika's sister's load		20,000	Debtors	27,000
Capitals:			Stock	50,000
Parth	1,75,000		Furniture	2,20,000
Shivika	1,94,000	3,69,000		
		4,69,000		4,69,000

On the above date the firm was dissolved. The assets were realized and the liabilities were paid off as follows:

(a) 50 % of the furniture was taken over by Parth at 20% less than book value. The remaining furniture was sold for ₹1,05,000.

(b) Debtors realised ₹26,000.

(c) Stock was taken over by Shivika for 29,000.

(d) Shivika's sister's loan was paid off along with an interest of ₹2,000.

(e) Expenses on realisation amounted to ₹5,000.

Prepare Realisation Acount, Partners' Capital Accounts and Bank Account.   [**Compartment Delhi 2015**]

Ans.

REALISATION A/C

Particulars	(₹)	Particulars		(₹)
To Stock	50,000	By Shivika's Sister Loan by Sundry Creditors		20,000
To Debtors	27,000	By Bank - assets realised:		80,000
To Furniture	2,20,000	Furniture	1,05,000	
To Bank (Sundry creditors)	80,000	Debtors	26,000	1,31,000
To Bank (Sister Loans + Interest	22,000	By Parth's Capital A/c (Furniture)		88,000
To Bank (Exp.)	5,000	By Shivika's Capital A/c (Stock)		29,000
		By Capital A/c: (Loss)		
		Parth	33,600	
		Shivika	22,400	56,000
	4,04,000			4,04,000

Dr.			Partner's Capital Accounts		Cr.

Particulars	Parth (₹)	Shivika	Particulars	Parth	Shivika
To Realisation A/c	88,000	–	By Balance b/d	1,75,000	1,94,000
To Realisation A/c	–	29,000			
To Realisation A/c	33,600	22,400			
To Bank A/c	53,400	142,600			
	1,75,000	1,94,000		1,75,000	1,94,000

Dr.			BANK ACCOUNT		Cr.
Particulars		**(₹)**	**Particulars**		**(₹)**
To Balance b/d		1,72,000	By Realisation (loan + interest)		22,000
To Realisation (assets realised)			By Realisation (creditors)		80,000
Furniture	1,05,000		By Realisation (expenses)		5,000
Debtors	26,000	1,31,000	By Parth's Capital A/c		53,400
			By Shivika's Capital A/c		1,42,600
		3,03,000			3,03,000

Q.7. E, F and G were partners in a firm sharing profits in the ratio of 2 : 2 : 1. On March 31,2017, their firm was dissolved. On the date of dissolution, the Balance Sheet of the firm was as follows:

Balance Sheet as at March 31, 2017

Liabilities		(₹)	Assets	(₹)
Capital			G's Capital	500
E	1,30,000		Profit and Loss Account	10,000
F	1,00,000	2,30,000	Land and Building	1,00,000
Creditors		45,000	Furniture	50,000
Outstanding Expenses		17,000	Machinery	90,000
			Debtors	36,500
			Bank	5,000
		2,92,000		2,92,000

F was appointed to undertake the process of dissolution for which he was allowed a remuneration of ₹5,000. F agreed to bear the dissolution expenses. Assets realized as follows:

(i) The Land & Building was sold for ₹1,08,900.

(ii) Furniture was sold at 25% of book value.

(iii) Machinery was sold as scrap for ₹9,000.

(iv) All the Debtors were realized at full value.

Creditors were payable on an average of 3 months from the date of dissolution. On discharging the Creditors on the date of dissolution, they allowed a discount of 5%.

Pass necessary Journal entries for dissolution in the books of the firm.   **(CBSE Sample Paper 2017-18)**

Ans.

Date	Particulars		L.F.	Dr. (₹)	Cr. (₹)
	Realisation Account	Dr.		2,76,500	
	To Land and Building Account				1,00,000
	To Furniture Account				50,000
	To Machinery Account				90,000
	To Debtors Account				36,500
	(Individual Assets accounts closed by transferring their balance to Realisation Account)				
	Creditors Account	Dr,		45,000	

Particulars		Dr.	Cr.
Outstanding Expenses Account	Dr.	17,000	62,000
To Realisation Account			
(Individual External Liabilities Accounts closed by transferring their balances to Realisation Account)			
Bank Account	Dr.	1,66,900	
To Realisation Account			1,66,900
(Assets realized and debtors collected)			
Realisation Account	Dr.	59,750	
To Bank Account			59,750
(Creditors paid at a discount of 5% and payment of outstanding expenses)			
Realisation Account	Dr.	5,000	
To F's Capital Account			5,000
(Remuneration paid to F for undertaking dissolution process			
E's Capital Account	Dr.	44,940	
F's Capital Account	Dr.	44,940	
G's Capital Account	Dr.	22,470	
To Realisation Account			1,12,350
(Loss on Realisation transferred to partners' Capital Accounts)			
E's Capital Account	Dr.	4,000	
F's Capital Account	Dr.	4,000	
G's Capital Account	Dr.	2,000	
To Profit and Loss Account			10,000
(Profit and Loss Account transferred to partners' Capital Accounts)			
Bank Account	Dr.	24,970	
To G's Capital Account			24,970
(Final payment received from G)			
E's Capital Account	Dr.	81,060	
F's Capital Account	Dr.	56,060	
To Bank Account			1,37,120
(Final payment made to E and F)			

Chapter Practice

Multiple Choice Questions   [1 Mark]

Q.1. Out of the proceeds received from sale of assets on dissolution of partnership firm .... will be paid first.

    (a) Partners loan   (b) Partners Capital A/c   (c) Outside Creditors   (d) Partners Current A/c.

Q.2. On dissolution of partnership firm ,unrecorded assets when realized are credited to :

    (a) Revaluation A/c (b) Realisation A/c   (c) Partners Capital A/c (d) None of these

Q.3. Which account is closed at the last during the course of dissolution of partnership firm :

    (a) Realisation A/c (b) Partners Capital A/c   (c) Partners Capital A/c (d) Cash/BankA/c

Q.4. Basically Realisation account is a :

    (a) Personal A/c   (b) Nominal A/c   (c) Real A/c   (d) None of these

Q.5. Which of the following item is not transferred to Realisation Account:

    (a) Partner's Loan A/c   (b) General Reserve

    (c) Deferred Revenue Exp.   (d) All These

Very Short Answer Type   [1 Mark]

Q.6. Indentify a situation under which the court may order for dissolution of a partnership firm.

Q.7. How is dissolution of partnership different from dissolution of partnership firm ?

Q.8. Why Realisation Account is prepared ?

Short Answer Type - I   [2 Marks]

Q.9. Why Partner's loan Account is not transferred to Realisation account ?

Q.10. When an assets is taken over by a partner why is his capital debited ?

Q.11. On dissolution of firm,what entry passed for payment of an unrecorded liability ?

Short Answer Type - II   [3 Marks]

Q.12. What entry passed when an assets is given to a Creditor in full settlement of his dues ?

Q.13. How would you treat Employees Provident Fund shown on liability side of Balance Sheet, at the time of Dissolution of partnership firm and why?

Q.14. On dissolution of a firm, Creditors are Rs.70,000; Partners Capital is Rs.1,20,000 ;Cash balance is Rs.10,000. Other assets realized Rs.1,50,000. What will be Profit/Loss in the realization Account.

Q.15. Creditors amounting Rs.80,000 are transferred to Realisation Account. What entry will be passed on their payment if Rs. 10,000 of the creditors are not to be paid and remaining creditors agreed to accept 20% less amount ?

Q.16. Write the circumstances under which a firm is dissolved.

Q.17. What accounting record is made on dissolution of partnership firm ?

Q.18. State occasion for the dissolution of firm on court's orders.

Long Answer Type   [5 Marks]

Q.19. Deep, Danish and Deny started business on April 01, 2021 with Capital of Rs. 1,00,000; Rs. 80,000 and Rs. 60,000 respectively sharing profit and loss in the ratio of 4:3:3. For the year ending 31st March 2022, the suffered a loss of Rs. 50,000. Each of the partner withdrew Rs. 10,000 during the year.

On 31st March 2022, the firm was dissolved, the creditors of the firm stood at Rs. 24,000 on that date and cash in hand Rs.4,000. The assets realized Rs.2,99,500 and creditors were paid Rs.23,500 in full settlement of their claims.

Prepare Realisation Account and show your working clearly.

Q.20. Rajesh and Yogesh were partners in a firm sharing profit and losses in the ratio of 2:3. Their Balance Sheet was as follows :

Liabilities		Amount	Assets		Amount
Creditors		80,000	Cash		20,000
Bank Overdraft		50,000	Debtors	55,000	
Rajesh's Wife's Loan		77,000	Less : Provision	2,000	53,000
Yogesh's Loan		28,000	Stock		78,000
Investment Fluctuation Fund		15,000	Investment		89,000
Capital:			Building		2,50,000
Rajesh	1,50,000		Profit and Loss A/c		10,000
Yogesh	1,00,000	2,50,000			
		5,00,000			5,00,000

On the above date ,the firm was dissolved. The assets were realized and liabilities were paid off as follows:

(a) Debtors of Rs. 6,000 were bad

(b) Rajesh agreed to pay off his wife's loan

(c) One of the creditor for Rs.10,000 was paid only Rs.3,000 in full settlements of his account.

(d) Building were auctioned for Rs.1,80,000 and the auctioneer's commission amounted to Rs. 8,000

(e) Yogesh took over part of stock at Rs.4,000 (being 20% less than the book value). Balance of the stock was handed over to the remaining creditors in full settlement of their account.

(f) Investments realized Rs. 9,000 less.

(g) Realisation expenses amounted Rs .17,000 and were paid by Yogesh.

Prepare necessary accounts on dissolution of the firm.

Q.21. Vijay, Vikas and Viswas were partners in firm in the ratio of 1:2:2. Their Balance Sheet on 31st March 2022 was as follows :

Liabilities	Amount	Assets	Amount
Sundry Creditors	14,000	Land and Building	47,000
Bills Payable	1,000	Office Equipment	8,000
Bank Overdraft	12,000	Stock	56,000
Vikas's Loan	18,000	Sundry Debtors	18,000
Workmen Compensation Fund	20,000	Investment	15,000
Capitals		Cash	16,000
Vijay's 19,000			
Vikas 38,000			
Vishwas 38,000	95,000		
	1,60,000		**1,60,000**

Partners agreed to dissolve the firm on that date. You are given the following information about dissolution:

(a) Investments realized at Rs. 9,000

(b) Office equipment was accepted by creditor for Rs.7,000 in full settlement. The remaining creditors   were paid in full by cash.

(c) Assets realized as follows :

Land & Building Rs. 1,20,000 and Stock Rs. 40,000. Sundry Debtors Rs 15,000 were accepted by Vikas in full settlement of his loan.

(d) Other liabilities were paid in full.

(e) There was a claim against Workmen Compensation amounting Rs. 5,000

(f) Dissolution expenses amounted to Rs. 3,000

Prepare Realisation Account, Partners Capital Account and Cash account

CHAPTER 6

Accounting for Share Capital

 Introduction, Issue of Share of Par, At Premium, Consideration Other than Cash

Summary

A company form of organisation is the third stage in the evolution of forms of organisation. Its capital is contributed by a large number of persons called shareholders who are the real owners of the company. A company usually raises its capital in the form of shares (called share capital) and debentures (debt capital.)

Features of a Company

1. **Body Corporate:** A company is formed according to the provisions of Law enforced from time to time.

2. **Separate Legal Entity:** A company has a separate legal entity which is distinct and separate from its members. It can hold and deal with any type of property. It can enter into contracts and even open a bank account in its own name.

3. **Limited Liability:** The liability of the members of the company is limited to the extent of unpaid amount of the shares held by them. In the case of the companies limited by guarantee, the liability of its members is limited to the extent of the guarantee given by them in the event of the company being wound up.

4. **Perpetual Succession:** The company being an artificial person created by law continues to exist irrespective of the changes in its membership. A company can be terminated only through law

5. **Common Seal:** The company being an artificial person, cannot sign its name by itself. Therefore, every company is required to have its own seal which acts as official signatures of the company. Any document which does not carry the common seal of the company is not binding on the company.

6. **Transferability of Shares:** The shares of a public limited company are freely transferable. The permission of the company or the consent of any member of the company is not necessary for the transfer of shares.

Types of Companies:

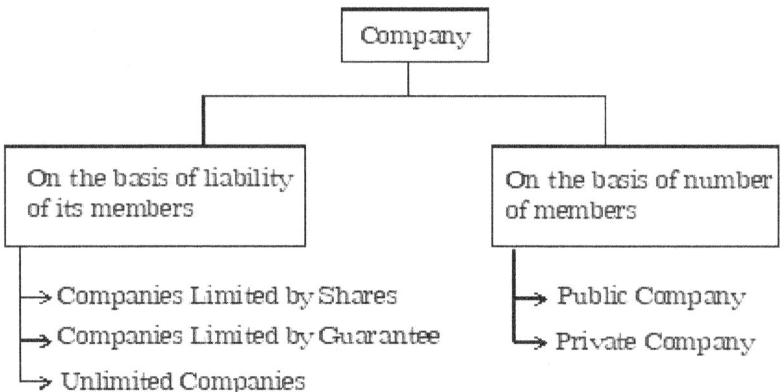

1. **Companies Limited by Shares:** In this case, the liability of the members is limited to the extent of the nominal value of shares held by them.

2. **Companies Limited by Guarantee:** In this case, the liability of its members is limited to the extent of the guarantee given by them in the event of the company being wound up.

3. **Unlimited Companies:** When there is no limit on the liability of its members, such Companies are called unlimited companies.

4. **Public Company:** A Public Company means a company that is not a Private Company.

5. **Private Company:** A Private Company is one which by its Articles of Association:

    1. Restricts the right to transfer its shares;

    2. Limits the number of its members to fifty;

    3. Prohibits any invitation to the public to subscribe for any shares in or debentures of the company.

Share Capital of a Company: Every company should have capital in order to finance its activities. The company raises this capital by issue of share because it does not have capital of its own being an artificial person. Thus, the total capital of the company is divided into shares, therefore, it is called share capital.

Categories of Share Capital:

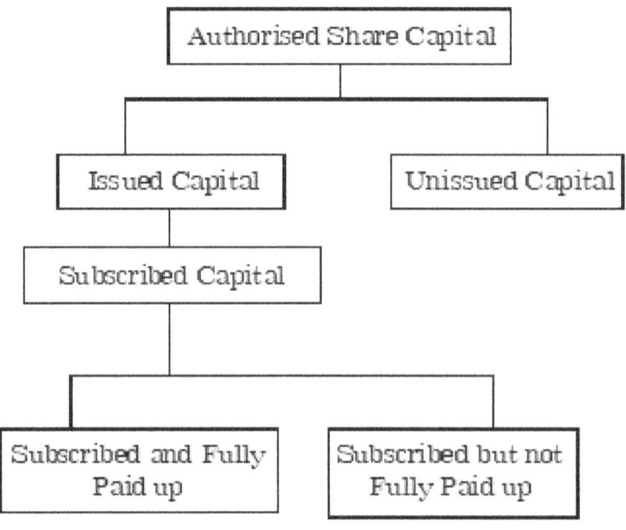

1. **Authorised Capital:** An Authorised Capital refers to that amount that is stated in the Memorandum of Association as the share capital of the company. It is the maximum amount with which the company is registered and which it is authorized to raise from the public by the issue of shares. The amount is also called the registered or nominal capital.

2. **Issued Capital:** It is that part of the authorised capital which is actually issued to the public for subscription including the shares allotted to vendors and the signatories to the company's memorandum. The authorised capital which is not offered for public subscription is known as 'unissued capital'. Unissued capital may be offered for public subscription at a later date.

3. **Subscribed Capital:** It is that part of the issued capital which has been actually subscribed by the public. When the shares offered for public subscription were subscribed fully by the public, in such a case the issued capital and subscribed capital would be the same.

4. **Called-up Capital:** It is that part of the subscribed share capital which the company actually demands from the share-holders. The company may decide to call the entire amount or part of the face value of the shares.

5. **Paid-up Capital:** It means the total amount paid up or credited as paid upon the subscribed capital. Some of the shareholders may fail to pay the amount due from them on account of a call which is termed as "call-in-arrears" or "unpaid capital".

6. **Uncalled Capital:** That portion of the subscribed capital that has not been called up is called uncalled capital. The company may collect this amount at any time when it needs further funds.

7. **Reserve Capital:** Sometimes a company, by means of a special resolution, decides that a certain portion of its uncalled capital shall not be called up during its existence and it would be available in the event of winding up of the company. Such a portion of uncalled capital is termed as 'reserve capital'.

Nature and Classes of Shares

Shares, refer to the units into which the total share capital of a company is divided. Thus, a share is a fractional part of the share capital and forms the basis of ownership interest in a company. The persons who contribute money through shares are called shareholders.

1. **Preference shares :** According to Section 43 of The Companies Act, 2013, a preference share is one, which fulfils the following conditions :

    (a) That it carries a preferential right to dividend to be paid either as a fixed amount payable to preference shareholders or an amount calculated by a fixed rate of the nominal value of each share before any dividend is paid to the equity shareholders.

    (b) That with respect to capital it carries or will carry, on the winding up of the company, the preferential right to the repayment of capital before anything is paid to equity shareholders.

2. **Equity Shares:** According to Section 43 of The Companies Act, 2013, shares which do not enjoy any preferential right in the payment of dividend or repayment of capital, are termed as equity/ordinary shares. The equity shareholders are entitled to share the distributable profits of the company after satisfying the dividend rights of the preference share holders.

    The equity share capital may be:

    (i) with voting rights; or

    (ii) with differential rights as to voting, dividend or otherwise in accordance with such rules and subject to such conditions as may be prescribed in the Articles of Association of the company.

Issue of Shares

The important steps in the procedure of share issue are:

1. **Issue of Prospectus:** The company first issues the prospectus to the public. Prospectus is an invitation to the public that a new company has come into existence and it needs funds for doing business. It contains complete information about the company and the manner in which the money is to be collected from the prospective investors.

2. **Receipt of Application:** When prospectus is issued to the public, prospective investors intending to subscribe the share capital of the company would make an application along with the application money. and deposit the same with a scheduled bank as specified in the prospectus. The company has to get minimum subscription within 120 days from the date of the issue of the prospectus. If the company fails to receive the same within the said period, the company cannot proceed for the allotment of shares and application money should be returned within 130 days of the date of issue of prospectus.

3. **Allotment of Shares:** If minimum subscription has been received, the company may proceed for the allotment of shares after fulfilling certain other legal formalities. Letters of allotment are sent to those whom the shares have been alloted, and letters of regret to those to whom no allotment has been made. When allotment is made, it results in a valid contract between the company and the applicants who now became the shareholders of the company.

Accounting Treatment of Issue Shares

1. Terms of Issue of Shares

(i)   Issue of shares at par When shdares are issued at their face value, the shares are said to have been issued at par. i.e. issue price and face value are same.

(ii) Issue of shares at premium When shares are issued at a value that is higher than the face value of the shares, the shares are said to have been issued at premium, i.e. issue price is more than face value.

2. Utilisation of Securities Premium Reserve Section 52 (2) of the Companies Act, 2013 restrict the use of the amount received as premium on securities for the following purposes

(i)   In purchasing its own shares (buy back) (Section 77A).

(ii)   Issuing fully paid bonus shares to the members (Section 78).

(iii) Writing-off preliminary expenses of the company (Section 78).

(iv) Writing-off the expenses of, or the commission paid or discount allowed on any issue of securities or debentures of the company (Section 78).

(v)   Providing for the premium payable on the redemption of any redeemable preference shares or of any debentures of the company (Section 78).

Accounting entries for issue of Shares at Premium

i.   For receipt of Application money:

Bank A/c ...Dr. [amount received on application including premium]

   To Shares Application A/c

ii.   For Allotment of Shares:

Shares Application A/c ...Dr. [application money on shares allotted]

   To Share Capital A/c [amount paid towards share capital]

   To Securities Premium Reserve A/c [amount of premium received with application money]

iii.   For Amount due on Allotment:

   Shares Allotment A/c …Dr. [amount due on shares allotted]

      To Share Capital A/c [amount paid towards share capital]

      To Securities Premium Reserve A/c [amount due towards premium]

iv.   For receipt of Allotment money: Bank A/c …Dr. [amount received on shares allotted]

   Calls-in-Arrears A/c …Dr. [amount not received against allotment money]

      To Shares Allotment A/c

v.   For first call being due:

   Shares First Call A/c …Dr. [amount payable on first call]

      To Share Capital A/c [amount paid towards share capital]

      To Securities Premium Reserve A/c [amount due to towards premium]

vi.   For receipt of first call:

   Bank A/c …Dr. [amount received on first call]

   Calls-in-Arrears A/c …Dr. [amount not received towards first call money due]

      To Shares First Call A/c

Accounting Treatment:

1.   **On Application:** The amount of money paid with various instalment represents the contribution to share capital and should ultimately be credited to share capital.

   Bank A/c Dr.

      To Share Application A/c

   (Amount received on application for   shares @ Rs. _______ per share)

2.   **On Allotment:** When minimum subscription has been received and certain legal formalities on the allotment of shares have been duly compiled with, the directors of the company proceed to make the allotment of shares.

The journal entries with regard to allotment of shares are as follows:

1.   For Transfer of Application Money

   Share Application A/c Dr.

      To Share Capital A/c

   (Application money on ______ Shares allotted/ transferred to Share Capital)

2.   For Money Refunded on Rejected Application

   Share Application A/c Dr.

      To Bank A/c

   (Application money returned on rejected application for ___shares)

3.   For Amount Due on Allotment

   Share Allotment A/c Dr.

      To Share Capital A/c

4.   For Adjustment of Excess Application Money

Share Application A/c Dr.

    To Share Allotment A/c

(Application Money on __Shares @ Rs__per shares adjusted to the amount due on allotment).

5.   For Receipt of Allotment Money Bank A/c Dr.

    To Share Allotment A/c

(Allotment money received on ___Shares @ Rs. — per share Combined Account)

Combined Account: Sometimes a combined account for share application and share allotment is kept in the books of a company under the name Share Application and Allotment Account.

1.   For Receipt of Application and Allotment

Bank A/c Dr.

    To Share Application and Allotment A/c

[Total Amount Received on Application]

(Money received on applications for shares @ Rs. per share)

2.   Transfer of Application money and Allotment Amount Due

Share App. and Allotment A/c   Dr.

    To Share Capital [No. of share Allotted (Application money per share + Allotment Amount per share)]

(Transfer of application money to share capital for the amount due on allotment of shares @ Rs. – per share)

3.   Money Refunded on Rejected Applications

Share App. and Allotment A/c Dr.

    To Bank A/c [No. of share Rejected App. money per share]

(Application money returned on the rejected application for....share)

4.   Receipt of Balance Allotment money

Bank A/c   Dr.

    To Share Application and Allotment A/c

(Balance of Allotment money received)

> **NOTE:** Shares of a company are issued either at par or at a premium. Shares are to be issued at par when their issue price is exactly equal to their nominal value according to the terms and conditions of issue. When the shares of a company are issued more than its nominal value (face value), the excess amount is called premium

Issue of Shares for Consideration other than cash

If a company purchases some assets from vendors, in exchange it can issue fully paid shares to them whereby the latter agrees to accepts it. Thus, no cash is received for the issue of shares. These shares can also be issued either at par, at a premium, or at a discount. The number of shares to be issued will depend on the price at which shares are issued and the amount payable to the vendor. To find out the number of shares to be issued to the vendor will be calculated as follows:

No. of Shares to be issued = Amount Payable / Issue Price

(a)   On purchase of assets:

Assets A/c   Dr.

To Vendor's A/c

(Assets Purchased)

(b) Shares can be issued to vendors in any manner out of the following:

1.   At Par:

Vendor's A/c Dr.

To Share Capital A/c

2.   At Premium:

Vendor's A/c Dr.

To Share Capital A/c

To Securities Premium A/c

3.   At discount:

Vendor's A/c Share Discount A/c

To Share Capital A/c

Multiple Choice Questions   [1 Mark]

Q.1. The part of un-called capital, to be called only in the liquidation of a company is called:

(a) Un-reserved Capital   (b) Reserve Capital

(c) Capital Reserve   (d) Calls-in Arrears

Ans. (b)

Q.2. Company can utilise securities premium for: [CBSE 2018]

(a) Writing off loos incurred on revaluation of asset   (b) Issuing fully paid bonus shares

(c) Paying divided   (d) Writing off trading loss

Ans. (b)

Q.3. Maximum limit of premium on shares is :

(a) 32%   (b) 20%   (c) No limit   (d) 100%

Ans. (c)

Q.4. When nominal (face) value of a share is called up by the company but as some shareholders did not pay the money, the shares are forfeited. The share capital is shown in the balance sheet (notes) of a company under the following heading:

(a) Subscribed and fully paid up   (b) Subscribed but not fully paid up

(c) Subscribed and called up   (d) Subscribed but not called up

Ans. (a)

Q.5. Devi Ltd purchased the sundry assets of M/s Ambani Industries for Rs.28,60,000 payable in fully paid shares of Rs.100 each. State the number of shares issued to vendor when issued at premium of 10%.

(a) 28,000 (b) 31,778 (c) 28,600 (d) 26,000

Ans. (d)

Q.6. The subscribed share capital of Atul Ltd is Rs.1,00,00,000 of Rs.100 each. There were no calls in arrear till the final call was made. The final call made was paid on 97,500 shares. The calls in arrear amounted to Rs.87,500. The final call on share :   [**CBSE 2009**]

(a) Rs.20 (b) Rs.35 (c) Rs.25 (d) Rs.45

Ans. (b)

Q.7. These shares which in addition to the fixed preference dividend, carry a right to participate in the surplus profits, if any, after dividend at a stipulated rate has been paid to the equity share holders are called:

(a) Participating preference shares (b) Convertible preference shares

(c) Redeemable preference shares (d) Cumulative preference shares

Ans. (a)

Q.8. Arora Limited was formed with share capital of Rs.50,00,000 divided into 50,000 shares of Rs.100 each. 9,000 shares were issued to the vendor as fully paid for purchase consideration of a furniture acquired. 30,000 shares were allotted in payment of cash on which Rs.70 per share was called and paid. State the amount of subscribed capital: [**CBSE Compartment 2011**]

(a) Rs.50,00,000 (b) Rs.30,50,000 (c) Rs.30,00,000 (d) Rs.20,00,000

Ans. (c)

Q.9. Faltu Limited invited application for 2,00,000 shares of Rs.10 each. These shares were issued at premium of Rs.11 each which was allowed at the time of allotment. All money was called and duly received except on 10,000 shares on which only application money of Rs.3 per share was received.

The company forfeited all the shares. 7000 of forfeited share where re-issued at Rs.13 per share. State the amount of securities premium to be shown under the head -Reserve and surplus.

(a) Rs.20,00,000 (b) Rs.11,11,000 (c) Rs.8,11,000 (d) Rs.21,11,000

Ans. (d)

Q.10. On Equity Shares dividend is proposed by the Board of Directors every year but rate of dividend is fixed on: [**CBSE Sample Paper**]

(a) Debentures (b) Equity Shares (c) Loan to outsiders (d) Preference Shares

Ans. (d)

Q.11. Capital included in the liabilities of a company is called:

(a) Authorised Capital (b) Issued Capital

(c) Subscribed Capital (d) Paid-up Capital

Ans. (d)

Q.12. If vendors are issued fully paid shares of Rs. 1,25,000 in consideration of net assets of Rs. 1,50,000, the balance of Rs. 25,000 will be credited to:

(a) Statement of Profit & Loss   (b) Goodwill Account

(c) Security Premium Reserve Account   (d) Capital Reserve Account

Ans. (c)

Q.13. A Co. has issued 6,000 equity shares of Rs. 10 each at par and called up amount Rs. 6 per share. The remaining part of capital is termed as   **[CBSE 2017]**

(a) Called up Capital   (b) Paid up Capital

(c) Uncalled Capital   (d) Subscribed Capital

Ans. (c)

Q.14. Reserve Capital is not a part of:

(a) Authorised Capital   (b) Subscribed Capital

(c) Unsubscribed Capital   (d) Issued Share Capital

Ans. (c)

Q.15. Match the following:

(a) Cumulative Pref. Share   (i) Repaid after some time

(b) Participating Pref. Share   (ii) Converts into equity shares

(c) Redeemable Pref. shares   (iii) Dividend accumulates if not paid

(d) Convertible Pref. shares   (iv) Gets share in urplus profit

The correct match is:

(a) a-ii ,b-i, c-iii, d-iv   (b) a-iii, b-iv, c-i, d-ii   (c) a-iii, b-iv, c-ii ,d-i   (d) a-ii, b-iv, c-iii, d-i

Ans. (b)

Very Short Answer Type   [1 Mark]

Q.16. Arrange the following in proper sequence as types of "Share Capital"

Ans. Issued, Subscribed, Called–up, Paid-up

Q.17. Share application amount is in the nature of Real account

Ans. False

Q.18. Out of total face value, liability of a shareholder is limited to …………… value of the share allotted to him.

Ans. Called up

Q.19. Share allotment account is a ………………

Ans. personal account

Q.20. The portion of the authorised capital which can be called up only on the liquidation of the company is called.......

[CBSE 2013]

Ans. Reserve capital

Q.21. G Ltd acquired assets worth 7,50,000 from H Ltd. by issue of shares of Rs.100 at a premium of 25%. The number of shares to be issued by G Ltd. to settle the purchase.

Ans. 6,000 shares

Q.22. Maximum amount that can be collected as premium as a percentage of face value. ......

Ans. Unlimited

Q.23. Assertion (A): Equity shares are those shares which are not preference shares.

Reason (R): Equity shares are the least issued class of shares and carries the minimum risks and rewards of the business.   **[CBSE Guidelines]**

(a) Both Assertion and reason are true and reason is correct explanation of assertion.

(b) Assertion and reason both are true but reason is not the correct explanation of assertion.

(c) Assertion is false, reason is true.

(d) Assertion is true, reason is false.

Ans. (d)

Q.24. Assertion (A): Preliminary expenses are not shown in balance sheet.

Reason (R): preliminary expenses are written off in the same year.

(a) Both Assertion and reason are true and reason is correct explanation of assertion.

(b) Assertion and reason both are true but reason is not the correct explanation of assertion.

(c) Assertion is false, reason is true.

(d) Assertion is true, reason is false.

Ans. (a)

Short Answer Type - I   [2 Marks]

Q.25. Define a Company.

Ans. A Company is an artificial person created by law, having separate entity with a perpetual succession and a common seal.

Q.26. Write Characteristics of a company.   **[CBSE Compartment 2017]**

Ans. (i) A company has a separate legal entity which is distinct and separate from its members.

(ii) It has perpetual existence

(iii)It has its own common seal.

(iv)Shares of a company are transferrable subject to certain conditions.

(v) The liability of the members of the company is limited to the extent of unpaid amount of the shares held by them.

Short Answer Type - II
[3 Marks]

Q.27. Write Types of company. [CBSE 2013, 2018]

Ans. On the basis of the number of members, companies can be divided as follows:

(i) **Public Company:** A company which is not a private company and which is not a subsidiary of a private company.

(ii) **Private Company:** A private company is one which by its articles-Restricts the right to transfer its shares, must have at least 2 persons, except in case of one person company and limits the number of its members to 200 (excluding its employees)

(iii) **One Person Company (OPC):** The companies Act, 2013, defines OPC as a "company which has only one person as a member". Rule 3 of the companies (Incorporation) Rules, 2014, provides that: Only a natural person being an Indian Citizen and resident in India can form one person company, (b) It cannot carry ot nonbanking financial investment activities (c) Its paid up share capital is not more than Rs.50 Lakhs (d) Its average annual turnover of three years does not exceed Rs. 2 Crores.

Q.28. Explain Issue of Shares for Consideration other than cash.

Ans. If a company purchases some assets from vendors, in exchange it can issue fully paid shares to them whereby the latter agrees to accepts it. Thus, no cash is received for the issue of shares. These shares can also be issued either at par, at a premium, or at a discount. The number of shares to be issued will depend on the price at which shares are issued and the amount payable to the vendor.

Q.29. Write a short note on Issue of shares at premium (Sec 52). [CBSE 2019]

Ans. The Money received on premium is transferred to Security Premium Reserve (SPR) account and the amount received on SPR can be utilized for the following purpose: (Section 52)

(i) Issue of fully paid bonus shares to the shareholders

(ii) Write off preliminary expenses of the company

(iii) Writing off securities issue expenses commission paid discount on issue of securities.

(iv) For providing the premium payable on redemption of Redeemable preference shares or debentures of the company.

(v) For Buy back of its own shares as per Secion 68.

Q.30. Rohit Ltd. purchased machinery from Rohan Ltd., for Rs.3,50,000. An amount of Rs.73,500 was paid by the means of a bank draft under cash discount of 2% and for the balance due Rohit Ltd. issued equity shares of Rs.10 each at a premium of 10%. Journalise the above transactions in the books of the company.

Ans.

JOURNAL OF ROHIT LTD.

Date	Particulars		L.F.	Dr. (Rs.)	Cr. (Rs.)
	Machinery A/c	Dr.		3,50,000	
	To Rohan Ltd.				3,50,000
	(For Machinery purchased on credit)				
	Rohan Ltd. (73,500 ÷ 98/100)	Dr.		75,000	
	To Discount Received A/c				1,500

To Bank A/c					73,500
(For payment made under cash discount)					
Rohan Ltd.	Dr.		2,75,000		
To Equity Share Capital A/c					
(25,000(s) × Rs.10)					2,50,000
To Securities Premium Reserve A/c					
(25,000(s) × Rs.1)					25,000
(For issue of shares at premium, *i.e.* Rs.2,75,000/11 = 25,000 shares)					

Long Answer Type　　　　　　　　　　　　　　　　[5 Marks]

Q.31. Describe share capital and its types.　　　　　　　　　　**[CBSE 2010, 2016]**

Ans. Share Capital: Capital raised by issue of shares is called share capital.

(a) Authorised Capital: It is also called as Nominal or registered capital. It is the Maximum amount of or Capital a company can issue. It is stated in the memorandum of Association.

(b) Issued Capital: This is part of authorized capital which is offered to public for subscription. It cannot exceed authorized capital.

(c) Called Up Capital: It is the amount of nominal values of shares that has been called up by the company for payment by the subscriber towards the share.

(d) Paid Up Capital: It is part of called up capital that the members of company or shareholders have paid.

(e) Reserve Capital: It is part or portion of uncalled share capital of an unlimited company which can be called only in case of winding up of the company.

Q.32. Explain the treatment when a company may purchase the assets as well as take over the liabilities of another concern.

Ans. Sometimes a company may purchase the assets as well as take over the liabilities of another concern. It happens usually in case of purchase of the whole business of the other concern. In such a situation, the purchase consideration will be equal to the value of net assets (Assets-Liabilities) taken over, and if the whole amount of the consideration is paid by issue of shares, the journal entry will be:

JOURNAL

Date	Particulars		L.F.	Dr. (Rs.)	Cr. (Rs.)
	Sundry Assets A/c	Dr.			
	To Sundry Liabilities A/c				
	To Vendor's A/c				
	(For purchase of the				
	vendors' business)				

In case of the whole business being taken over if the purchase consideration is more than the amount of the net assets taken over, the difference (excess) will be treated as value of goodwill and it will be debited to Goodwill Account while passing the journal entry for the purchase of vendor's business. But if it is the other way round, i.e. the purchase consideration is less than the value of the net assets taken over the difference will be credited to Capital Reserve Account.

Q.33. Raman Limited purchased building from Saini Limited for Rs.6,00,000. 10% amount was paid in cash and the remaining is to be paid through the issue of shares of Rs.100 each (a) at par (b) at 20% premium.

Pass necessary journal entries in the books of Raman Limited.   [CBSE 2020]

Ans. (a) When shares are issued at par, i.e.at Rs.100

Number of shares to be issued = Amount Payable/Issue Price = (Rs.6,00,000 –Rs.60,000)/Rs.100 = 5,400

(b) When shares issued at premium of 20%, i.e.at Rs.120 (Rs.100 face value + Rs.20 premium)

Number of shares to be issued = Amount Payable/Issue Price = Rs.5,40,000/Rs.120 = 4,500

JOURNAL

Date	Particulars		L.F.	Dr. (Rs.)	Cr. (Rs.)
	Building A/c	Dr.		6,00,000	
	To Saini Limited				6,00,000
	(Being building purchased)				
	When shares are issued at par:				
	Saini Limited	Dr.		6,00,000	
	To Bank A/c				60,000
	To Share Capital A/c				5,40,000
	(Being 10% paid in cash and for the balance 5,400 shares issued at par)				
	When shares are issued at premium of 20%:				
	Saini Limited	Dr.		6,00,000	
	To Bank A/c				60,000
	To Share Capital A/c				4,50,000
	To Securities Premium Reserve A/c				90,000
	(Being 4,500 shares issued at Rs.120 per share)				

Q.34. A Ltd. acquired assets of Rs.20 lakh and took over creditors of Rs.2 Lakh from B Ltd. A Ltd. issued shares of Rs.100 each at par as purchase consideration.

Ans.

JOURNAL

Date	Particulars		L.F.	Dr. (Rs.)	Cr. (Rs.)
	Sundry Assets A/c	Dr.		2,000,000	
	To Sundry Creditors A/c				2,00,000
	To B Ltd.				1,800,000
	(Being business purchased from B Ltd.)				
	B Ltd.	Dr.		1,800,000	
	To Share Capital A/c				1,800,000
	(For issue of 18,000 shares of Rs.100 each at par)				

Q.35. Manoj Ltd. took over the assets of Rs.3,90,000 and Liabilities of Rs.40,000 of Roshan Ltd. for a consideration of Rs.4,00,000. 20% was paid by a cheque and the balance by issue of fully paid equity shares of Rs.100 each at a premium of 60%. Show necessary journal entries for these transactions in the books of Manoj Ltd.

Ans.

Date	Particulars		L.F.	Dr. (Rs.)	Cr. (Rs.)
(i)	Assets A/c	Dr.		3,90,000	
	Goodwill A/c	Dr.		50,000	
	To Liabilities A/c				40,000
	To Roshan Ltd.				4,00,000
	(Being assets and liabilities of Roshan Ltd. taken over)				
(ii)	Roshan Ltd.	Dr.		4,00,000	
	To Bank A/c				80,000
	To Equity share Capital A/c				2,00,000
	To Securities Premium				
	Reserve A/c				1,20,000
	(Being 20% payment made to Roshan Ltd. by cheque and balance settled by issue of equity shares at a premium of 60%)				

Q.36. Dainik India Ltd. took over the assets of Rs.14,00,000 and liabilities of Rs.4,00,000 from Patrika Ltd. for a purchase consideration of Rs.9,19,000. Dainik India Ltd. issued a promissory note of Rs.17,000 payable after 60 days in favour of Patrika Ltd. and the balance amount was paid by issue of equity shares of Rs.100 each at a premium of Rs.25 per share. Pass necessary Journal entries for the above transactions.

Ans.

JOURNAL

Date	Particulars		L.F.	Dr. (Rs.)	Cr. (Rs.)
	Sundry Assets	Dr.		1,400,000	
	To Sundry Liabilities A/c				4,00,000
	To Patrika Ltd. A/c				9,19,000
	To Capital Reserve A/c				81,000
	(Being Assets & Liabilities acquired)				
	Patrika Ltd. A/c	Dr.		9,19,000	
	To Bills Payable A/c				17,000
	To Equity Share Capital A/c				721,600
	To Securities Premium Reserve A/c				1,80,400
	(Being promissory note issued and equity shares issued at a premium)				

TOPIC 2 Over Subscription, Under Subscription, Calls in Arrears, Calls in Advance

Summary

Calls on Share: Two points are important regarding the Calls on shares.

1.   The call amount should not exceed 25% of the face value of shares.

2.   There must be an internal dynamics of keeping at least some months between the making of two calls unless otherwise provided by the Articles of Association of the company.

Accounting Treatment:

i.   Call Amount Due

   Share Call A/c   Dr. [No. of shares × Call Amount per share]

      To Share Capital A/c

   (Call money due on – Shares @ Rs. – per share)

ii.   Receipt of Call Amount

   Bank A/c Dr.

   To Share Call A/c

   (Call money received)

Calls in arrears:

When any shareholder fails to pay the amount due on allotment or on any of the calls, such amount is known as 'Calls in Arrears'/'Unpaid Calls'.

Accounting Treatment:

Calls in Arrears A/c Dr.

To Share Allotment Account A/c

To Share Call Account A/c

(Calls in arrears brought into account)

Calls in Advance:

Sometimes shareholders pay a part or the whole of the amount of the calls not yet made. The amount so received from the shareholders is known as "Calls in Advance". The amount received in advance is a liability of the company and should be credited to Call in Advance Account.

Accounting Treatment:

Bank A/c Dr.

To Call-in-Advance A/c

(Amount received on Call-in-Advance)

On the due date of the calls, the amount of 'Calls in Advance' is adjusted by the following entry : Calls in Advance A/c Dr.

To Particular Call A/c

(Calls in advance adjusted with the call money due)

As calls in advance are a liability to the company and it is under an obligation if provided by the Articles of Association, to pay interest on such amount. In case, the articles are silent then Table 'A' shall be applicable, according to which interest @ 6% p.a. may be paid.

1. Interest due

    Interest on Calls-in-Advance A/c Dr.

    To Sundry Shareholder's A/c [Amount of Interest due for payment]

    (Interest due on Calls-in-Advance)

2. Payment of Interest

    Sundry Shareholder's A/c Dr.

    To Bank A/c [Amount of Interest paid]

    (Interest paid on Calls-in-Advance)

Over subscription:

When Shares are issued to the public for subscription through the prospectus by well-managed and financially strong companies, it may happen that applications for more shares are received than the number of shares offered to the public, such a situation is said to be a case of oversubscription.

In such a condition, three alternatives are available to the directors to deal with the situation:

(1) they can accept some applications in full and totally reject the others;

(2) they can make a pro-rata allotment to all; and

(3) they can adopt a combination of the above two alternatives which happens to be the most common course adopted in practice.

Accounting Treatment:

1. If the excess applicants are totally refused for allotment, the application money received on these shares refunded.

    Capital A/c   [No. of Share Alloted × Application per share]

       To Bank A/c   [No. of Share Received × Application Amount per Share]

    (i)   Bank A/c   Dr. [No. of Application Received × Application money per Share]

              To Share Application A/c

           (Money received on application

           for–Share @ Rs.–per share)

    (ii)   Share Application A/c   Dr. [Application money Received]

              To Share Capital A/c   [No. of Share Alloted × Application per share]

                 To Bank A/c   [No. of Share Received × Application Amount per Share]

2. If the applicants are made partial allotment (or pro-rata allotment):

    The directors can as well opt to make a proportionate distribution of shares available for allotment among the applicants of shares. The proportion is determined by the ratio which the number of shares to be allotted to bear to the number of shares applied for. This is called 'pro-rata allotment.

    Generally, excess application money received on these shares is adjusted towards the amount due on allotment or call.

(i)   Bank A/c   Dr. [No. of Application Received × Application Amount Per Share]

        To Share Application A/c

        (Application money received on– Shares @ Rs. – per share)

(ii)   Share Application A/c   Dr. [Application money Received]

            To Share Capital A/c [No. of Share Alloted × Application Amount per share]

            To Share Allotment A/c [Excess Application Money]

Transfer of application money to share capital and excess application money credited to share allotment.)

(iii)   Bank A/c   Dr. [No. of Share Alloted × Allotment Amount per Share]

            To Share Capital A/c

        (Amount due on the Allotment of - Share @ Rs. - Per Share)

(iv)   Bank A/c   Dr. [Amount per Share due – Excess Application Money]

            To Share Allotment A/c

This is a combination of two alternatives described above as thus:

(a)   Application for some shares are rejected outright, and

(b)   pro-rata allotment is made to the applicants of a remaining number of shares.

Thus, money on the rejected applications is refunded and excess application money due to pro-rata distribution is adjusted towards the amount due on the allotment of shares allotted.

(i)   Bank A/c   Dr. [No. of Share Applied for × Application Amount per Share]

        To Share Application A/c

        (Money received on application for – Share @ Rs. – per share)

(ii)   Share Application A/c   Dr. [Application money Received]

        To Share Capital A/c   [No. of Share Alloted × Application Amount per Share]

        To Share Allotement A/c   [Excess Application Money due to Pro-rata Allotment]

        To Bank A/c   [No. of Share Rejected × Application Amount Per Share]

Transfer of application money to share capital, excess application amount credited to share allotment and money refunded on rejected application)

(iii)   Share Allotment A/c   Dr. [No. of Share Allotted × Allotment Amount per Share]

            To Share Capital A/c

        (Amount due on the Allotment of – Share @ Rs. – Per Share)

(iv)   Bank A/c   Dr. [Allotment Amount due – Excess Application Money]

        Share Allotment A/c

        (Allotment money received after adjusting the amount already received as excess application money)

Under Subscription:

Under subscription is a situation where number of shares applied for is less than the number for which applications have been invited for subscription.

Issue of Shares at a Premium:-When shares are issued at an amount more than the face value of a share, they are said to be issued at a premium. The difference between the issue price and the face value of the Share is called the premium.

It can be used only for the following five purposes:

(a)   to issue fully paid bonus shares to the extent not exceeding unissued share capital of the company;

(b)   to write-off preliminary expenses of the company;

(c)   to write-off the expenses of, or commission paid, or discount allowed on any securities of the company; and

(d)   to pay premium on the redemption of preference shares or debentures of the company.

(e) Purchase of its own shares (i.e., buy back of shares).

When Shares are issued at a premium, the journal entries are as follows:

(a)   Premium Amount called with Application money

   (i)   Bank A/c   Dr. [Total Application Money + Premium Amount]

            To Share Application A/c

   (Money received on the application for- Shares @ Rs. - per share including premium)

   (ii)   Share Application A/c   Dr. [Amount Received]

               To Share Capital A/c [No. of Share Applied for × Application Amount per share]

            To Securities Premium A/c [No. of share applied for × Premium Amount per share]]

   (Transfer of application money to share capital and premium accounts)

(b)   Premium Amount called with Allotment money

   (i)   Share Allotment A/c   Dr. [No. of Share Alloted × Allotment & Premium money per share]

               To Share Capital A/c [No. of Share Alloted × Allotment Amount per share]

            To Securities Premium A/c [No. of Share Alloted × Premium Amount per share]

   (Amount due on allotment of shares @ Rs. - per share including premium)

   (ii)   Bank A/c   Dr.

            To Share Allotment A/c

   (Allotment money received including premium)

Multiple Choice Questions   [1 Mark]

Q.1. A shareholder allotted to whom 9,000 shares of Rs. 10 per share failed to pay first & final of Rs. 2 per share. Rs. 18,000 to be recorded in the books of company with ....

   (a) Dr. to Calls in Arrears A/c

   (b) Dr. to Share Forfeiture A/c

   (c) Cr. To Calls in Arrears A/c

   (d) Cr. To Share Forfeiture A/c

Ans. (a)

Q.2. Amount of money not received out of called up capital is :   [CBSE 2016]

   (a) Added to share capital   (b) Subtracted from share capital

   (c) Shown as current liabilities   (d) Shown as current asset

Ans. (b)

Q.3. Following amounts were payable on issue of shares by a company : Rs. 3 on application, Rs.3 on allotment, Rs.2 on first call and Rs.2 on final call. X holding 500 shares paid only application and allotment money whereas Y holding 400 shares did not pay final call. Amount of calls in arrear will be:

(a) 3,800   (b) 2,800   (c) 1,800   (d) 6,200

Ans. (b)

Q.4. E Ltd. had allotted 10,000 shares to the applicants of 14,000 shares on pro-rata basis, application money on another 6000 shares was refunded. The amount payable on the application was Rs.2. Sush applied for 420 shares. The number of shares allotted to him will be:

(a) 60 shares   (b) 340 shares   (c) 320 shares   (d) 300 shares

Ans. (d)

Q.5. A company issued 4,000 equity shares of rupees 10 each at par payable as under:

On application rupees 3, on allotment rupees 2; on first call rupees 4 and on final call rupees 1 per share. Applicants were received for 16,000 share. Application for 6,000 shares were rejected and pro-rata allotment was made to the applicants for 10,000 shares. How much amount will be received in cash on first call, when excess application money is adjusted towards amount due on allotments and calls:

[CBSE Compartment 2018]

(a) Rupees 6.000   (b) Nil   (c) Rupees 16,000   (d) Rupees 10,000

Ans. (a)

Q.6. A company issued 4000 equity shares of rupees 50 each at par payable as under:

On application rupees 20%, on allotment 40%; on first call 10%; on final call-balance Applications were received for 10,000 shares. Allotment was made pro-rata. How much amount will be received in cash on allotment?

(a) Rupees 6,000   (b) Nil   (c) Rupees 16,000   (d) Rupees 20,000

Ans. (d)

Q.7. Tanmay Ltd had allotted 20,000 shares to the applicants of 24,000 shares on pro rata basis. The amount payable on application is Rs.2. Harsh applied for 450 shares. The number of shares allotted and the amount carried forward for adjustment against allotment money due from him is:

(a) 150 shares, Rs.375   (b) 375 shares, Rs.150

(c) 400 shares, Rs.100   (d) 300 shares, Rs.300

Ans. (b)

Q.8. If a shareholder does not pay his dues on allotment, for the amount due, there will be

[CBSE Sample Paper 2017]

(a) credit balance in the Shares Allotment Account

(b) debit balance in the Share forfeiture Account

(c) credit balance in the Shares forfeiture Account

(d) debit balance in the Shares Allotment Account

Ans. (d)

Q.9. If applicants for 80, shares were allotted 60,000 shares on pro-rata basis, the shareholder who was allotted 1,200 shares must have applied for:

(a) 900 Shares   (b) 3,600 Shares   (c) 1,600 Shares   (d) 4,800 Shares

Ans. (c)

Q.10. A company invited applications for 1,00,000 shares and it received applications for 1,50,000 shares. Application for 30,000 shares were rejected and the remaining shares were allotted on prorate basis. How many shares an applicant for 3,000 shares will be allotted: **[CBSE 2008]**

(a) 2,500 Shares   (b) 3,600 Shares   (c) 45,00 Shares   (d) 2,000 Shares

Ans. (a)

Very Short Answer Type   [1 Mark]

Q.11. According to the below given information the final call per share is Rs.22.

The subscribed capital of a company is Rs.80,00,000 and the nominal value of the share is Rs.100 each. There were no calls in arrear till the final call was made. The final call made was paid on 77,500 shares only. The balance in the calls in arrear amounted to Rs.55,000.

Ans. True

Q.12. Harshita limited has an Authorised capital of Rs.1,00,00,000 divided into 1,00,000 equity shares of Rs.100 each. If offered 90,000 equity shares Rs.10 each at a premium of Rs.8. The public applied for 81,000 equity shares. Till 31st March 2018, Rs.17 (including premium) was called. An applicant holding 5000 shares did not pay first call of Rs.2 per share.

As per the above given information:

.... is the amount of Share capital to be shown in the balance sheet of the company.

Ans. 7,19,000

Q.13. Assertion (A): Minimum subscription is the minimum amount which must be subscribed by the public.

Reason (R): Minimum subscription has been fixed at 80% of the issued amount.   **[CBSE Guide Lines]**

(a) Both Assertion and reason are true and reason is correct explanation of assertion.

(b) Assertion and reason both are true but reason is not the correct explanation of assertion.

(c) Assertion is false, reason is true.

(d) Assertion is true, reason is false.

Ans. (d)

Q.14. Assertion (A): Calls - in arrear is the amount which has not been called by the company but has been paid by the shareholders.

Reason (R): Calls - in arrear will be shown as a deduction from the subscribed but not fully paid up capital.

(a) Both Assertion and reason are true and reason is correct explanation of assertion.

(b) Assertion and reason both are true but reason is not the correct explanation of assertion.

(c) Assertion is false, reason is true.

(d) Assertion is true, reason is false.

Ans. (c)

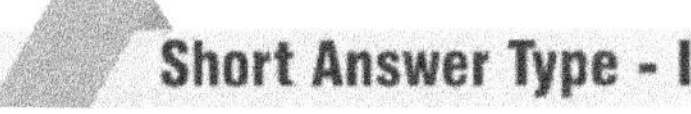

Short Answer Type - I   [2 Marks]

Q.15. Define Under Subscription.   [CBSE 2011]

Ans. Under subscription is a situation where number of shares applied for is less than the number for which applications have been invited for subscription

Q.16. Write the meaning of Minimum Subscription.   [CBSE 2019]

Ans. It is the minimum amount stated in the prospectus that must be subscribed by the public before and allotment of any security is made.

Short Answer Type - II   [3 Marks]

Q.17. Describe Over subscription.   [CBSE Compartment Paper 2015]

Ans. When Shares are issued to the public for subscription through the prospectus by well-managed and financially strong companies, it may happen that applications for more shares are received than the number of shares offered to the public, such a situation is said to be a case of oversubscription. In such a condition, three alternatives are available to the directors to deal with the situation:

(i) They can accept some applications in full and totally reject the others;

(ii) They can make a pro-rata allotment to all; and

(iii) They can adopt a combination of the above two alternatives which happens to be the most common course adopted in practice.

Q.18. What is the meaning of Calls in arrear.

Ans. Any Amount which has been called or demanded by company from shareholders but not paid by the shareholder till the last date mentioned in call letter is called as call in arrears, Company can charge interest on this rate mentioned in Article of Association or 10% p.a. as per Table F)

Q.19. What is the meaning of Calls in advance?

Ans. Any Amount paid in excess of what they have asked to pay is called as call in advance. Interest is paid on this at rate mentioned in Article of Association or 12% p.a. as per Table F

Long Answer Type   [5 Marks]

Q.20. Premier Tools Ltd. invited applications for issuing 2,00,000 equity shares of Rs.10 each at a premium of Rs.2 per share. The amount was payable as follows:

On application - Rs.5 per share (including premium) On allotment-3 per share

On first and final call - Balance

Applications were received for 2,50,000 shares. Applications for 10,000 shares were rejected and pro-rata allotment was made to the remaining applicants. Over payments received on application were adjusted towards sums due on allotment.

All calls were made and duly received except allotment and first and final call from Naveen who applied for 7,200 shares. His shares were forfeited. Half of the forfeited shares were reissued for Rs.48,000 as fully paid.

Pass the necessary journal entries for the above transactions in the books of Premier Tools Ltd. Open calls in arrears account wherever required.   [CBSE 2020]

Ans.

In the books of Premier Tools Ltd.

JOURNAL

Date	Particulars		L.F.	Dr. Amount (Rs.)	Cr. Amount (Rs.)
	Bank A/c	Dr.		1,250,000	
	To Equity Share Application A/c				1,250,000
	(Being application money received on Rs.2,50,000 shares)				
	Equity Share Application A/c	Dr.		1,250,000	
	To Equity Share Capital A/c				6,00,000
	To Securities Premium Reserve A/c				4,00,000
	To Equity Share Allotment A/c				2,00,000
	To Bank A/c				50,000
	(Being Application money transferred to share capital, securities premium reserve, share allotment and the balance refunded)				
	Equity Share Allotment A/c	Dr.		6,00,000	6,00,000
	To Equity Share Capital A/c				
	(Being allotment money due)				
	Bank A/c	Dr.		3,88,000	
	Calls in arrears A/c	Dr.		12,000	
	To Equity Share Allotment A/c				4,00,000
	(Being allotment money received)				
	Equity Share First and Final Call A/c	Dr.		8,00,000	
	To Equity Share Capital A/c				8,00,000
	(Being first and final call money due)				
	Bank A/c	Dr.		7,76,000	
	Calls in Arrears A/c	Dr.		24,000	
	To Equity Share First and Final Call A/c				8,00,000
	(Being call money received)				
	Equity Share Capital A/c	Dr.		60,000	
	To Share Forfeited A/c				24,000
	To Calls in Arrears A/c				36,000
	(Being 6,000 shares forfeited)				
	Bank A/c	Dr.		48,000	
	To Equity Share Capital A/c				30,000
	To Securities Premium Reserve A/c				18,000
	(Being 3,000 shares reissued)				

Share forfeited A/c	Dr.	12,000	
To Capital Reserve A/c			12,000
(Being gain on reissue of shares transferred to capital reserve)			

Q.21. Sudershan Ltd. invited applications for 1,00,000 equity shares of Rs.10 each. The shares were issued at a premium of Rs.5 per share. The amount was payable as follows:

On Application and Allotment Rs.8 per share (including premium Rs.3)

Balance on the first and final call.

The allotment was made to the applicants on the following basis:

(i) Applicants for 80,000 shares were allotted 60,000 shares;

(ii) Applicants for 60,000 shares were allotted 40,000 shares; and

(iii) Applicants for 10,000 shares were allotted nil.

X, who belonged to the first category and was allotted 300 shares, failed to pay the first call money.

Y, who belonged to the second category and was allotted 200 shares also failed to pay the first call money. Their shares were forfeited. The forfeited shares were reissued @ Rs.12 per share fully paid up. Pass the necessary Cash Book and Journal entries in books company. **[CBSE 2015]**

Ans.

Dr.   **CASH BOOK**   **Cr.**

Particulars	Rs.	Particulars	Rs.
To Equity Share Application and Allotment A/c	1,200,000	By Equity Share Application and Allotment A/c	80,000
To Equity Share First and Final Call A/c	378,100	By Balance c/d	1,504,000
To Equity Share Capital A/c (500 (s) × Rs.10)	5,000		
To Securities Premium Reserve A/c (500 (s) × Rs.2)	1,000		
	1,584,100		**1,584,100**

	JOURNAL OF SUDERSHAN LTD.				
Date	Particulars		L.F.	Dr. (Rs.)	Cr. (Rs.)
	Equity Share Application and Allotment A/c	(Rs.12,00,000 – Rs.80,000) Dr.		1,120,000	
	To Equity Share Capital A/c	[(1,00,000 (Share) × Rs.5)]			5,00,000
	To Securities Premium Reserve A/c	[(1,00,000 (Share) × Rs.3)]			3,00,000
	To Calls in Advance A/c	((i) Rs.1,60,000 + (ii) Rs.1,60,000)]			3,20,000
	(For share application and allotment money adjusted)				

Equity Share First & Final Call A/c　(Rs.1,00,000 (s) × Rs.7)　Dr.			7,00,000	
To Equity Share Capital A/c　(Rs.1,00,000 (s) × Rs.5)				5,00,000
To Securities Premium Reserve　(Rs.1,00,000 (s) × Rs.2) A/c				2,00,000
(For share first & final call money due including premium)				
Calls in Advance A/c　　　　　　　　　　　　　　　　Dr.			3,20,000	
To Equity Share First & Final Call A/c				3,20,000
(For calls in advance adjusted)				
Equity Share Capital A/c　　　[500 (share) × Rs.10]　Dr.			5,000	
Securities Premium Reserve A/c　[500 (share) × Rs.2]　Dr.			1,000	
To Equity Share First & Final　(Rs.1,300 + Rs.600) Call A/c				1,900
To Share Forfeiture A/c　　　(Balancing Figures)				4,100
(For 500 shares forfeited for non-payment of call money)				
Share Forfeiture A/c　　　　　　　　　　　　　　　　Dr.			4,100	
To Capital Reserve A/c				4,100
(For the balance of share forfeiture transferred to capital reserve)				

Working Note:

Calculation of share First and Final Call money received:	Rs.	Rs.
Category (i): Call due for 60,000 shares @ Rs.7	4,20,000	
Less: Calls in Advance adjusted	(1,60,000)	
Net amount due for 60,000 shares	2,60,000	
Less: Calls not received for 300 shares, i.e.:		
Rs.2,60,000 60,000(s) × 300(s)	(1,300)	2,58,700
Category (ii): Call due for 40,000 shares @ Rs.7	2,80,000	
Less: Calls in Advance on these shares	(1,60,000)	
Net amount due for 40,000 shares	1,20,000	
Less: Calls not received for 200 shares i.e.,		
Rs.1,20,000 40,000(s) × 200(s)	(600)	1,19,400

Q.22. On 1st April 2017, Mayank Ltd. was formed with an authorised capital of Rs.25,00,000 divided into 50,000 equity shares of Rs.50 each. The company issued prospectus inviting applications for 45,000 shares. The issue price was payable as under:

On Application　　　　　- Rs.15

On Allotment　　　　　- Rs.20

On call　　　　　　　　- Balance Amount

The issue was fully subscribed and the company allotted shares to all the applicants. The company did not make the call during the year.

Show the following:

(a) Share capital in the Balance Sheet of the company as per revised Schedule III, Part I of the companies Act, 2013.

(b) Also prepare 'Notes to Accounts' for the same.   [CBSE 2018]

Ans.

Balance Sheet of Mayank Ltd. (An Extract)

as at 31st March 2018

Particulars	Note No.	Rs.
1. Equity and Liabilities		
(i) Shareholder's Funds		
(a) Share Capital	1	1,575,000

Notes to Accounts:

Particulars	Rs.
(1) Share Capital:	
Authorised Capital:	
50,000 equity shares of Rs.50 each	2,500,000
Issued Capital:	
45,000 equity shares of Rs.50 each	2,250,000
Subscribed Capital:	
Subscribed but not fully paid up	
45,000 equity shares of Rs.35 called up	1,575,000

TOPIC 3 Forfeiture, Reissue, Complete Numericals of Shares

Summary

Forfeiture of Shares

If a shareholder fails to pay allotment money or call money on his share as called upon by the company, his shares may be forfeited by giving due notice and following the procedure specified in the Articles of Association in this behalf. This is known as forfeiture of shares.

To forfeit a share means to cancel the allotment to the defaulting shareholders and to treat the amount already received thereon as forfeited to the company.

Accounting Treatment

1. Forfeiture of Shares issued at par

     Share Capital A/c   Dr. [Amount Called-up]

     To Share Forfeiture A/c   [Amount Paid]

     To Share Allotment A/c   [Amount unpaid]

     and/or

     To Share Call/Calls

Note: In case 'Calls-in-Arrears' A/c is maintained by a company, 'Call-in-Arrears' A/c would be credited in the above instead of 'Share Allotment' and/or 'Share Call or Calls' A/c.

The balance on the Share Forfeited A/c is shown in addition to the total paid capital of the company under the heading 'Share Capital' on the liabilities side of the Balance Sheet till the forfeited shares are reissued.

2. Forfeiture of Shares issued at a Premium:

    (a) If Premium has not been paid by the Shareholders:

    Share Capital A/c Dr. (Amount Called up Premium)

    Securities Premium A/c Dr. (Premium amount)

    To Share Allotment A/c (Amount unpaid)

    To Share Call/Calls A/c (Amount unpaid)

    To Share Forfeiture A/c (Amount paid)

    (For Share forfeited)

    (b) If Premium has been paid by the shareholder:

    Share Capital A/c Dr. (Amount Called up Premium)

    To Share Allotment A/c Dr. (Premium amount)

    To Share Call/Calls A/c (Amount unpaid)

    To Share Forfeiture A/c (Amount paid)

    (For Share forfeited)

3. Forfeiture of Shares issued at a discount:

    Share Capital A/c Dr. (Amount Calledup + Discount)

    To Discount on Issue of Share A/c (Discount on forfeited share)

    To Share Allotment A/c (Amount unpaid)

    To Share Call/Calls A/c (Amount unpaid)

    To Share Forfeiture A/c (Amount paid)

    (Forfeiture of Shares and discount on issue adjusted)

Re-Tissue of Forfeited Share:

The director of a company has the authority to re-issue the shares once forfeited. These forfeited shares are reissued at par, at a premium, or at a discount, the amount of the discount does not exceed the amount paid on such shares by the original shareholder but in case of shares originally issued at discount, the maximum permissible discount will be the amount paid on such shares by the original shareholder plus the amount of original discount.

Accounting Treatment:

1. For Forfeited Shares reissued at Par:

    Bank A/c Dr.

    To Share Capital A/c

2. For Forfeited Shares reissued at Premium:

    Bank A/c Dr.

    To Share Capital A/c

    To Securities Premium A/c

3. For Forfeited Shares reissued at Discount:

Bank A/c Dr.

Share Forfeiture A/c Dr. (Discount Allowed)

To Share Capital A/c

Multiple Choice Questions   [1 Mark]

Q.1. If a share of Rs.10 on which Rs.8 has been called and Rs.6 is paid is forfeited, the Share Capital Account should be debited with:

(a) Rs.8   (b) Rs.6   (c) Rs.10   (d) Rs.2

Ans. (a)

Q.2. Which one of the following is not a part of subscribed capital:

(a) Equity shares issued to vendor   (b) Preference shares of convertible type

(c) Forfeited shares   (d) Bonus shares

Ans. (c)

Q.3. Zee Ltd issued 15,000 equity shares of Rs.20 each at a premium of Rs.5 payable Rs.5 on application, Rs.10 on allotment (including premium) and the balance on first and final call. The company received applications for 22,500 shares and allotment was made pro rata. Bittoo to whom 1,200 shares were allotted, failed to pay the amount due on allotment. All his shares were forfeited after the call was made. The forfeited shares were reissued to Dheeraj at par. Assuming that no other bank transactions took place, the bank balance of the company after the above transactions is: **[CBSE 2016]**

(a) Rs.6,85,000   (b) Rs.3,60,500   (c) Rs.3,78,000   (d) Rs.6,34,000

Ans. (c)

Q.4. A company forfeited 3,000 shares of Rs.10 each (which were issued at par) held by Kishore for nonpayment of allotment money of Rs.5 per share. The called up value per share was Rs.8. On forfeiture, the amount debited to share capital:

(a) Rs.30,000   (b) Rs.24,000   (c) Rs.15,000   (d) Rs.6,000

Ans. (b)

Q.5. Jio limited issued shares of Rs.100 each at a premium of 10%. Mr. Harsh purchased 500 shares and paid Rs.20 on application but did not pay the allotment money of Rs.30. If the company forfeited his 30% shares, the forfeiture account will be credited by: **[CBSE Compartment 2018]**

(a) Rs.4500   (b) Rs.3500   (c) Rs.1650   (d) Rs.3000

Ans. (d)

Q.6. Career launcher Limited forfeited 200 shares Rs.10 each who had applied for 500 shares, issued at a premium of 10% for nonpayment of final call of Rs.3 per share. Out of these 100 shares were issued as fully paid up for Rs.15. The profit on reissue is:

(a) Rs.700   (b) Rs.6400   (c) Rs.300   (d) Rs.400

Ans. (a)

Q.7. When shares are forfeited, the Share Capital Account is debited with:

(a) Nominal value of Shares

(b) Market value of Shares

(c) Called-up value of Shares

(d) Paid-up value of Shares

Ans. (c)

Q.8. On a share of Rs. issued at a premium of Rs.2 on which whole amount is called-up and Rs.7 is received, is forfeited the share capital account is debited by:

(a) Rs.7   (b) Rs.12   (c) Rs.10   (d) Rs.16

Ans. (a)

Q.9. A company forfeited 3,000 shares of Rs.10 each (which were issued at par) held by Kishore for non-payment of allotment money of Rs.5 per share. The called up value per share was Rs.8. On forfeiture, the amount debited to share capital:

(a) Rs.30,000   (b) Rs.24,000   (c) Rs.15,000   (d) Rs.6,000

Ans. (b)

Q.10. A company forfeited 4000 shares of Rs.10 each on which application money of Rs.3 has been paid. Out of these 2000 shares were reissued as fully paid up and Rs.4,000 has been transferred to capital reserve. Calculate the rate at which these shares were reissued: **[CBSE Sample Paper]**

(a) Rs.10 per share   (b) Rs.9 per share   (c) Rs.11 per share   (d) Rs.8 per share

Ans. (b)

Q.11. A forfeited share can: **[CBSE 2019]**

(a) Not be re-issued at discount

(b) Re-issued at a maximum discount of 10%

(c) Be re-issued at a maximum discount equal to the amount in share forfeiture account.

(d) None of the above

Ans. (c)

Q.12. Vimal Ltd. forfeited a share of Rs.50 issued at a premium of 20% for non-payment of first call of Rs.15 per share and final call of Rs.5 per share. At what minimum price it can be reissued: **[CBSE 2017]**

(a) Rs.50   (b) Rs.30   (c) Rs.40   (d) Rs.20

Ans. (d)

Q.13. The Directors of Vina Ltd. forfeited 70,000 Equity Shares of Rs. 10 each, Rs. 10 called up, for non-payment of final call of Rs. 1 per share. Half of the forfeited shares were reissued at Rs. 20 per share fully paid up. On reissue of forfeited shares, the following amount will be transferred to the Capital Reserve Account:

(a) Rs.70,000   (b) Rs.1,40,000   (c) Rs.6,30,000   (d) Rs.3,15,000

Ans. (d)

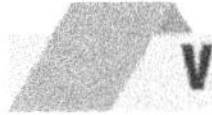 **Very Short Answer Type** [1 Mark]

Q.14. Loss of re-issue should not exceed the .... amount.

Ans. forfeited

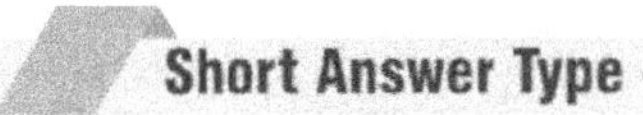 **Short Answer Type - I** [2 Marks]

Q.15. Define Capital Reserve. [CBSE 2014]

Ans. It is capital profit not available for distribution as dividend. It is represented in balance sheet of company as Reserves and Surplus under the heading Shareholders eraser's Funds.

Short Answer Type - II [3 Marks]

Q.16. Define Forfeiture of Shares. [CBSE Compartment Paper 2016]

Ans. If a shareholder fails to pay allotment money or call money on his share as called upon by the company, his shares may be forfeited by giving due notice and following the procedure specified in the Articles of Association in this behalf. This is known as forfeiture of shares. To forfeit a share means to cancel the allotment to the defaulting shareholders and to treat the amount already received thereon as forfeited to the company

Q.17. Define Re-issue of Forfeited Share.

Ans. The director of a company has the authority to re-issue the shares once forfeited. These forfeited shares are reissued at par, at a premium, or at a discount, the amount of the discount does not exceed the amount paid on such shares by the original shareholder but in case of shares originally issued at discount, the maximum permissible discount will be the amount paid on such shares by the original shareholder plus the amount of original discount.

Q.18. Prithvi Ltd. forfeited 500 equity shares of Rs.100 each for the non payment of first call of Rs.30 per share. The final call of Rs.10 per share was not yet made. The forfeited shares were reissued for Rs.65,000 fully paid up. Pass necessary journal entries in the books of the company. [CBSE 2012]

Ans.

JOURNAL

Date	Particulars			L.F.	Dr. (Rs.)	Cr. (Rs.)
	Share Capital A/c	(500 × Rs.90)	Dr.		45,000	
	To Share First Call A/c	(500 × Rs.30)				15,000
	To Share Forfeiture A/c	(500 × Rs.60)				30,000
	(500 shares forfeited for non-payment of first call)					
	Bank A/c		Dr.		65,000	
	To Share Capital A/c	(500 × Rs.100)				50,000
	To Securities Premium Reserve A/c					15,000
	(500 shares reissued at premium)					
	Share Forfeited A/c		Dr.		30,000	
	To Capital Reserve A/c					30,000
	(Profit on reissue of forfeited shares transferred to Capital Reserve)					

Q.19. Shravan Ltd. forfeited 800 equity shares of Rs.100 each for the non-payment of first call of Rs.30 per share. The final call of Rs.20 per share was not yet made. Out of the forfeited share, 400 were reissued at the rate of Rs.105 per share fully paid up. Pass necessary journal entries in the books of Shravan Ltd. for above transactions.

Ans.

JOURNAL

Date	Particulars			L.F.	Dr. (Rs.)	Cr. (Rs.)
	Share Capital A/c	(800 × Rs.80)	Dr.		64,000	
	To Share First Call A/c	(800 × Rs.30)				24,000
	To Share Forfeited A/c					40,000
	(For forfeiture of 800 shares for non-payment of first call)					
	Bank A/c	(400 × Rs.105)	Dr.		42,000	
	To Share Capital A/c	(400 × Rs.100)				40,000
	To Securities Premium Reserve A/c	(400 × Rs.5)				2,000
	(Reissued of 400 forfeiture shares)					
	Share Forfeiture A/c		Dr.		20,000*	
	To Capital Reserve A/c					20,000
	(Profit on 400 share transferred to Capital Reserve)					

Note. Profit on 800 forfeited shares = Rs.40,000

$$\text{Profit on 400 shares} = \text{Rs.}40{,}000 \times \frac{400}{800} = \text{Rs.}20{,}000$$

Less: loss on reissue of shares = Nil

Transfer to Capital Reserve A/c = Rs.20,000*

Q.20. Abhay Ltd. forfeited 300 shares of Rs.10 each Rs.8 called up on which he had paid application and allotment money of Rs.5 per share. Out of these, 100 shares were reissued at Rs.6 per share. Journalise.   **[CBSE 2020]**

Ans.

JOURNAL

Date	Particulars			L.F.	Dr. (Rs.)	Cr. (Rs.)
	Share Capital A/c	(300 × Rs.8)	Dr.		2,400	
	To Calls in Arrears A/c	(300 × Rs.3)				900
	To Share forfeiture A/c	(300 × Rs.5)				1,500
	(Forfeiture of 300 shares of Rs.8 called up)					
	Bank A/c	(100 × Rs.6)	Dr.		600	
	Share Forfeiture A/c	(100 × Rs.8)	Dr.		200	
	To Share Capital A/c					800
	(Reissue of 100 shares @ Rs.6, Rs.8 called up)					
	Share Forfeiture A/c		Dr.		300*	
	To Capital Reserve A/c					300
	(Profit on reissue of 100 shares trans. To Capital Reserve)					

Notes:

(i) Profit on forfeiture of 300 shares = Rs.1,500

So profit on 100 shares $= Rs.\dfrac{1500 \times 100}{300} = Rs.500$

Less: loss on reissue of shares	200
Profit on reissue	**300***

(ii) Reissue of shares at Rs.6 but Rs.8 called & paid up.

Q.21. Which value has been affected by forfeiting above mentioned shares just after the share first call. Suggest a better alternative.

Ans. (i) The forfeiture of shares just after the share first call is legal but not a wise and fair decision of the company. The small investors will be discouraged to apply in the public issues of companies. Share forfeiture will result in loss of capital invested by them

(ii) Better alternative would be to give sufficient time to defaulting shareholders to make the payment of arrears along with the share final call. Company can forfeit the share if still the default continues. This will give them fair chance to arrange money and pay the calls in arrears.

Long Answer Type   [5 Marks]

Q.22. Dhawan Ltd. issued 10,000 shares of Rs.10 each payable Rs.2 on application, Rs.3 on allotment, Rs.3 on first call and balance on final call. Rishi was allotted 100 shares. Give journal entries related to forfeiture of shares in the following alternative cases: **[CBSE Sample Paper]**

Case I: Rishi failed to pay allotment money and his shares were forfeited.

Case II: Rishi failed to pay allotment money and first call and his shares were forfeited.

Case III: Rishi failed to pay both the calls and his shares were forfeited.

Ans.

JOURNAL

Date	Particulars		L.F.	Dr. (Rs.)	Cr. (Rs.)
Case I	Share Capital A/c (100 × Rs.5) Dr.			500	
	To Share Allotment A/c (100 × Rs.3)				300
	To Share Forfeiture A/c (100 × Rs.2)				200
	(For forfeiture of 100 shares for non-payment of allotment money)				
Case II	Share Capital A/c (100 × Rs.8) Dr.			800	
	To Share Allotment A/c (100 × Rs.3)				300
	To Share First Call A/c (100 × Rs.3)				300
	To Share Forfeiture A/c (100 × Rs.2)				200
	(For 100 shares forfeited due to non-payment of allotment & first call)				
Case III	Share Capital A/c (100 × Rs.10) Dr.			1,000	
	To Share First Call A/c (100 × Rs.3)				300
	To Share Second & Final Call A/c (100 × Rs.2)				200
	To Share Forfeiture A/c (100 × Rs.5)				500
	(For forfeiture of shares due to non-payment of both the calls)				

Q.23. Barinder Ltd. forfeited 200 shares of Rs.10 each, Rs.7 called up for non-payment of first call of Rs.2. Out of these 100 shares were issued as per maximum discount permissible as per law.   **[CBSE 2019]**

Ans.

JOURNAL

Date	Particulars			L.F.	Dr. (Rs.)	Cr. (Rs.)
	Share Capital A/c	(200 × Rs.7)	Dr.		1,400	
	To Share First Call A/c	(200 × Rs.2)				400
	To Share Forfeiture A/c					1,000
	(Forfeiture of 200 shares)					
	Bank A/c		Dr.		200*	
	Share Forfeiture A/c		Dr.		500	
	To Share Capital A/c	(100 × Rs.7)				700
	(For reissue of 100 shares @ Rs.2 each)					

Notes.

(i) Profit on 200 forfeited shares = Rs.1,000

$$\text{So profit on 100 shares} = \text{Rs.1,000} \times \frac{100}{200} = \text{Rs.500}$$

(ii) 100 shares were reissued @ Rs.7 called up = Rs.700

    Maximum permissible loss on 100 shares = Rs.500

    So reissue price must be = Rs.200*

Q.24. C Ltd. forfeited 500 shares of Rs.10 each, Rs.8 called up for non-payment of first call of Rs.3 per share. Company reissued 200 shares at Rs.8 fully paid up and also reissued 100 shares at Rs.9 per share Rs.8 paid up

Ans.

JOURNAL

Date	Particulars			L.F.	Dr. (Rs.)	Cr. (Rs.)
	Share Capital A/c	(500 × Rs.8)	Dr.		4,000	
	To Share First Call A/c	(500 × Rs.3)				1,500
	To Share Forfeiture A/c					2,500
	(Forfeiture of 500 shares for non-payment of first call)					
	Bank A/c	(200 × Rs.8)	Dr.		1,600	
	Share Forfeiture A/c		Dr.		400	
	To Share Capital A/c	(200 × Rs.10)				2,000
	(Reissue of 200 shares fully paid up @ Rs.8)					
	Bank A/c	(100 × Rs.9)	Dr.		900	
	To Share Capital A/c	(100 × Rs.8)				800
	To Securities Premium Reserve A/c	(100 × Rs.1)				100
	(Reissue of 200 shares fully paid up @ Rs.8)					

Share Forfeiture A/c	Dr.		1,100	
To Capital Reserve A/c				1,100*
(Transfer of profit on 300 shares to Capital Reserve)				

Notes.

(i) Profit on 500 forfeiture shares   = Rs.2,500

So profit on 300 reissued shares $\left\{\dfrac{2,500 \times 300}{500}\right\}$ = Rs.1,500

Less: loss on reissue of 200 shares   400

Balance   1,100

Less: loss on reissue of 100 shares   Nil

Profit transferred to Capital Reserve   **1,100***

Q.25. Concept Stationary Ltd. invited applications for issuing 3,00,000 shares of Rs.10 each at a premium of Rs.3 per share. The amounts were payable as follows:

On application and allotment - Rs.7 per share

On first and final call - Balance (including premium of Rs.3)

Applications were received for 4,00,000 shares and allotment was made as follows:

(i) To applicants for 80,000 shares - 80,000 shares.

(ii) To applicants for 40,000 shares - nil

(iii) Balance of the applicants were allotted shares on pro-rata basis.

Excess money received with applications was adjusted towards sums due on first and final call.

Amit, who belonged to category (i) and was allotted 4,000 shares and Veni, who belonged to category (iii) and was allotted 4,400 shares failed to pay the first and final call money. Their shares were forfeited. The forfeited shares were re-issued at Rs.7 per share fully paid-up.

Pass necessary journal entries for the above transactions in the books of the company.   [CBSE 2017]

Ans.   **In the books of Concept Stationery Ltd.**
JOURNAL

Date	Particulars		L.F.	Dr. (Rs.)	Cr. (Rs.)
	Bank A/c	Dr.		2,800,000	
	To Share Application and Allotment A/c				2,800,000
	(Being application and allotment money received on 4,00,000 shares)				
	Share Application & Allotment A/c	Dr.		2,800,000	
	To Share Capital (3,00,000 × 7)				2,100,000
	To Calls in Advance A/c				4,20,000
	To Bank A/c (40,000 × 7)				2,80,000
	(Being application and Allotment money transferred to share capital, call and the balance refunded)				

Share First and Final Call A/c	Dr.		1,800,000	
To Share Capital A/c				9,00,000
To Securities Premium Reserve A/c				9,00,000
(Being first and final call due including premium)				
Bank A/c	Dr.		1,338,000	
Calls in Arrears A/c	Dr.		42,000	
Calls in Advance A/c	Dr.		4,20,000	
To share First Call A/c				1,800,000
(Being first and final call received)				
Or				
Bank A/c	Dr.		1,338,000	
Calls in Advance A/c	Dr.		4,20,000	
To Share First Call A/c				1,758,000
(Being first and final call money received)				
Share Capital A/c	Dr.		40,000	
Securities Premium Reserve A/c	Dr.		12,000	
To Share Forfeited A/c				28,000
To Share First Call A/c				24,000
(Being 4,000 shares of Amit forfeited)				
Or				
Share Capital A/c	Dr.		40,000	
Securities Premium A/c	Dr.		12,000	
To Share Forfeited A/c				28,000
To Calls in Arrears A/c				24,000
(Being 4,000 shares of Amit forfeited)				
Share Capital A/c	Dr.		44,000	
Securities Premium Reserve A/c	Dr.		13,200	
To Share Forfeited A/c				39,200
To Share First and Final Call/Calls in				
Arrears A/c				18,000
(Being 4,400 shares of Veni Forfeited)				
Or				
Combined entry for forfeited can also be				
passed as follows:	Dr.		84,000	
Share Capital A/c	Dr.		25,200	
Securities Premium Reserve A/c				
To Shares forfeiture A/c				67,200
To Calls in Arrear/Share First and Final				
Call A/c				42,000
(Being 8,400 shares forfeited)				

Bank A/c	Dr.	58,800	
Share forfeiture A/c	Dr.	25,200	
To Share Capital A/c			84,000
(Being all the forfeited shares reissued @ Rs.7 per share fully paid up)			
Share Forfeiture A/c	Dr.	42,000	
To Capital Reserve A/c			42,000
(Being gain on reissue of shares transferred to capital reserve)			

TOPIC 4 Concept of Private Placement, ESOP

Summary

Concept of Private Placement of Shares as per Section 42 of the Companies Act, 2013:

i.   As per Section 42 of the Companies Act, 2013, Private Placement means any offer of the securities or invitation to subscribe securities to a select group of persons by a company (other than by way of public offer) through issue of private placement offer letter and which satisfies the conditions specified in this section.

ii. In simple terms, securities offered to the selective group of persons by issuing private placement offer is known as the Private Placement of Shares. There are conditions specified by Companies Act, 2013 that are to be fulfilled for offering such private placement of shares.

- Conditions to be fulfilled for offering Private Placement of Shares: Conditions have been prescribed for the following points:

  i.   Limit on offers:

- Invitation to subscribe securities shall be made in a financial year to persons not exceeding 50 in number or such higher number as may be prescribed.

- Also, the maximum number of persons to whom offer of Private Placement can be made is prescribed as 200.

- For this purpose, Qualified Institutional buyers and employees of the company offered securities under a scheme of employees stock option is excluded.

  ii. Previous/Earlier offers: Such offer or invitation shall not be made unless the allotments with respect to any offer or invitation made earlier have been completed or that offer or invitation has been withdrawn or abandoned by the company.

  iii. Subscription Amount: Amount of subscription should not be less than ` 20, 000. Any amount payable towards subscription of securities shall be paid through cheque or bank draft or any other banking instrument but not by cash.

  iv. Allotment: Condition with respect to allotment prescribes that the company shall allot its securities within 60 days from the date of receipt of application money. In case the company is not able to allot securities within 60 days, it shall refund the application money within 15 days from the day of completion of 60 days.

  v.   Application money received: Any amount received towards application of securities shall be kept in a separate bank account and shall be utilised for: a. adjustment against allotment of securities; or b. repayment of money against which the company is not able to allot securities.

vi. Offers: Offer for such securities shall be made only to such persons whose names are recorded by the company before the invitation to subscribe.

vii. Filing with Registrar of Companies: It is necessary to file complete information with the Registrar of Companies within 30 days of the circulation of offer for private placement.

viii. Public Advertisement: No public advertisement or use of any media, marketing or distribution channels or agents to inform the public at large about the offer.

Concept of Employees Stock Option Plan (ESOP):

i. It is a category of Sweat Equity which is a wider term than ESOP and includes issue of shares to promoters as remuneration for their contribution towards incorporating the company and other related services.

ii. It is an option granted to the employees and employee directors of a Company to subscribe the company's shares at a price that is lower than the market price (fair value) of the share.

iii. It is an option and not an obligation for the employees and employee directors. Therefore, they may or may not exercise the option.

iv. It is necessary to fulfil the prescribed conditions to issue such stock options.

Terms associated with Employees Stock Option Plan (ESOP):

i. Grant: It is the option given to the Employees to subscribe to the share of the company.

ii. Grant Date: It is the date at which the enterprise and its employees agree to the terms of Employees Stock Option Plan (ESOP).

iii. Vesting: It is the process by which the employee is given the right to apply for shares of the company against ESOP.

iv. Vesting Date: It is date when all the specified vesting conditions are satisfied by the employee and therefore, becomes entitled to receive the shares.

v. Vesting Period: It is the period between the grant date and the date on which all the specified vesting conditions of an Employee Stock Option Plan are to be satisfied.

vi. Exercise: It is an application by the employee for issue of shares against the option vested in him in pursuance of the Employees Stock Option Plan (ESOP).

vii. Exercise Period: It is the period after vesting within which the employee should exercise the right to apply for shares against the option vested in him in pursuance of the Employees Stock Option Plan (ESOP).

viii. Exercise Price: It is the price payable by the employee for exercising the option granted in pursuance of the Employees Stock Option Plan.

ix. Value of Option: It is the difference between the market price and the issue price of the security.

Conditions to issue stock options:

i. shares issued are of the same class of shares already issued;

ii. such issue is authorised by a special resolution passed by the company;

iii. such resolution specifies all possible details of the number of shares, consideration, market price, and class or classed of employees or directors to whom such shares are to be issued;

iv. at the date of issue, not less than 1 year has been elapsed since the date on which the company had commenced business; and

v. all the regulations prescribed by SEBI with respect to such issue have been duly complied with

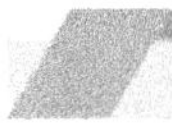 **Multiple Choice Questions**

[1 Mark]

Q.1. Rajan Limited issued 50,000 shares at a price lower than the nominal value of the share. The shares issued are called:

(a) Sweat equity shares

(b) Redeemable Preference shares

(c) Equity shares

(d) Bonus shares

Ans. (a)

Q.2. An issue of shares which is not a public issue but offered to be a selected group of persons is called:

(a) Public offer

(b) Private placement of shares

(c) Initial public offer

(d) None of these

Ans. (b)

 **Short Answer Type - II**

[3 Marks]

Q.3. Write a short note on Private Placement of Shares [Section-42]:

Ans. When Shares are offered by the company the company to a selected group of persons, not to the public through public offer, it is called private placement of shares. This is an issue of shares to institutional investors or some selected group of persons subject to prior approval of existing shareholders. There is no need of issuing formal prospectus and it is cost and time saving method of raising capital

Long Answer Type

[5 Marks]

Q.4. Explain EMPLOYEE STOCK OPTION PLAN/SCHEME.

Ans. Employee stock option plan scheme or sweat equity share refers to option granted by any company to its employees to subscribe its shares at a price lesser than market price. It is employees' right to exercise or not to exercise the option, it is not an obligation on the employees to subscribe it. The difference between the market price and issue price is an expense for the company and this is accounted over the vesting period on proportionate basis on straight line basis.

Objectives/Significance of ESOP

(i) It helps in creating a long term wealth for the employees.

(ii) It motivates the employees to have a higher participation in the company

(iii) It helps the company to attract efficient employees and keep them retained on long term basis

Some Important Terms Related with ESOP

Grant date: The date at which the company and its employees agree to the conditions of ESOP.

Vesting Period: Period between Grant date and the date on which all the conditions are fulfilled.

Exercise Period: Period within which employees have to exercise the option granted under ESOP.

Exercise Price: Price to be paid by the employee on exercising the options.

Extra Questions (Previous Year)

Q.1. Sundram Ltd purchased furniture for Rs 3,00,000 from Ravindram Ltd, Rs 1,00,000 were paid by drawing a promissory note in favour of Ravindram Ltd. The balance was paid by issue of equity shares of Rs 10 each at a premium of 25%. Pass journal entries in the books of Sundram Ltd.   **(All India 2012)**

Ans.

JOURNAL

Date	Particulars		L.F.	Amount (Dr.)	Amount (Cr.)
	Furniture A/c	Dr.		3,00,000	
	To Ravindram Ltd.				3,00,000
	(Being Furniture purchased)				
	Ravindram Ltd	Dr.		3,00,000	
	To Bills Payable A/c				1,00,000
	To Equity Share Capital A/c (16,000 × 10)				1,60,000
	To Securities Premium Reserve A/c (16,000 × 25)				40,000
	(Being payment made by issuing of a promissory note of Rs. 1,00,000 and 16,000 equity shares @ Rs.10 per share at a premium of 25%)				

$$\text{Number of shares to be issued to Ravindram Ltd.} = \frac{2,00,000}{10+2.5}$$

$$= 16,000 \text{ shares}$$

Q.2. SSP Ltd forfeited 300 shares of Rs. 10 each issued at a premium of Rs. 2 per share for the non-payment of allotment of Rs 4 per share (including premium). The first and final call of Rs. 3 per share has not been made yet, 50% of forfeited shares were re-issued at Rs 8 per share fully paid-up. Pass necessary journal entries for the forfeiture and re-issue of shares.   **(Delhi 2011)**

Ans.

JOURNAL

Date	Particulars		L.F.	Amount (Dr.)	Amount (Cr.)
	Share Capital A/c (300 × 7)	Dr.		2,100	
	Securities Premium Reserve A/c (300 × 2)	Dr.		600	
	To Forfeited Shares A/c (300 × 5)				1,500
	To Share Allotment A/c (300 × 4)				1,200
	(Being 300 shares forfeited for the non-payment of allotment of Rs.4 each including premium)				
	Bank A/c (150 × 8)	Dr.		1,200	
	Foreited Shares A/c (150 × 2)	Dr.		300	
	To Share Capital A/c (150 × 2)				1,500
	(Being re-issue of 150 shares @ Rs.8 per share as fully paid-up				

Foreited Shares A/c	Dr.		450	
To Capital Reserve A/c (W.N)				450
(Being balance of forfeited shares account transferred to capital reserve)				

Working Note

Amount of 50% forfeited shares = $1,500 \times \dfrac{150}{300}$ = Rs.750

Amount of forfeited shares transferred to capital reserve = 750 – 300 = Rs.450

Q.3. TAG Ltd forfeited 400 shares of Rs 10 each issued at a premium of Rs 1 per share for the non-payment of allotment of Rs. 4 per share (including premium). The first and final call of Rs. 3 per share has not been made yet. 50% of forfeited shares were re-issued at Rs. 8 per share fully paid-up. Pass necessary journal entries for the forfeiture and re-issue of shares. **(All India 2011)**

Ans.

JOURNAL

Date	Particulars	L.F.	Amount (Dr.)	Amount (Cr.)
	Share Capital A/c (400 × 7) Dr.		2,800	
	Securities Premium Reserve A/c (400 × 1) Dr.		400	
	To forfeited Shares A/c (400 × 4)			1,600
	To Share Allotment A/c (400 × 4)			1,600
	(Being 400 shares forfeited for the non-payment of allotment of Rs.4 each including premium)			
	Bank A/c (200 × 8) Dr.		1,600	
	Forfeited Shares A/c (200 × 2) Dr.		400	
	To Share Capital A/c (200 × 10)			2,000
	(Being re-issue of 200 shares @ Rs.8 per share as fully paid-up)			
	Forfeited Shares A/c Dr.		400	
	To Capital Reserve A/c (WN)			400
	(Being balance of forfeited shares account transferred to capital reserve)			

Working Note:

Amount of 50% forfeited shares = $1,600 \times \dfrac{200}{400}$ = Rs.800

Amount of forfeited shares transferred to capital reserve = 800 – 400 = Rs.400

Q.4. SSS Ltd has a paid-up share capital of % 60,00,000 and a balance of Rs. 15,00,000 in the securities premium account. The companies management do not want to carry over this balance. State the purpose for which this balance can be utilised.   **(Delhi 2010)**

or

State the purposes for which the securities premium can be utilised under Section 52 (2) of the Companies Act, 2013.   **(All India 2009)**

Ans. According to Section 52 (2) of the Companies Act, 2013, SSS Ltd can utiiise the securities premium of Rs. 15,00,000, only for the following purposes

(i) Issuing fully paid bonus shares to the members.

(ii) Writing off the preliminary expenses of the company.

(iii) Writing off the expenses of or the commission paid or the discount allowed on any issue of securiities or debentures of the company.

(iv) Providing for the premium payable on the redemption of any redeemable preference shares or any debentures of the company.

(v) In purchasing its own shares (Buy back).

Q.5. On 1.1.2016 the first call of Rs. 3 per share became due on 1,00,000 equity shares issued by Kamini Ltd. Karan a holder of 500 shares did not pay the first call money. Arjun a shareholder holding 1000 shares paid the second and final call of Rs. 5 per share along with the first call.

Pass the necessary journal entry for the amount received by opening 'Calls-in-arrears' and 'Calls-in- advance' account in the books of the company.   **(CBSE Outside Delhi 2016)**

Ans.

JOURNAL

Date	Particulars	L.F.	Dr. (Rs.)	Cr. (Rs.)
	Bank A/c Dr.		3,03.500	
	Call in Arrears A/c Dr.		1,500	
	To Share IstCall A/c			3,00,000
	To Call in Advance A/c			5,000
	(Being amount received on 1st call)			

Q.6. Bliss Products Ltd. registered with capital of Rs.90,00,000 divided into 90,000 equity shares of Rs.100 each. The company issued prospectus inviting applications for 50,000 equity shares of Rs.100 each payable as Rs. 20 on application, Rs.30 on allotment, Rs.20 on first call and balance on second call.

Applications were received for Rs.40,000 shares. Raman to whom 1600 shares were allotted failed to pay final call money and these shares were forfeited. Of the forfeited shares, 600 shares were reissued to Sukhman, credited as fully paid for Rs.90 per share.

Present the Share Capital as per Schedule III of Companies Act, 2013.   **(CBSE Sample Paper 2019-20)**

Ans.

Extract of Balance Sheet of Bills Products Ltd.

As at_________

Particulars	Note No.	Amount Current Year	Amount Previous Year
I. Equity and Liabilities			
1. Shareholder's Fund			
a. Share Capital	1	3,970,000	

Note No.	Parituclar		Amount (Rs.)
1	Share Cpaital		
	Authorized Capital		9,000,000
	90,000 Equity shares of Rs. 100 each		
	Issued Capital		
	50,000 Equity shares of Rs.100 each		5,000,000
	Subscribed Capital		
	Subscribed and Fully Paid Capital		
	39,000 Equity shares of Rs.100 each	3,900,000	
	Add: Forfeited Shares (1,000, of Rs.70 each)	70,000	3,900,000

Q.7. Drumbeats Ltd. had a prosperous shoe business. They were manufacturing shoes in India and exporting to Italy. Being a socially aware organization, they wanted to pay back to the society. They decided to not on supply free shoes to 50 orphanages in various parts of the country but also give employment to children from those orphanages who were above 18 years of agc. In order to meet the fund requirements, they decided to raise 50,000 equity shares of Rs.50 each and 40,000. 9% debentures of Rs.40 each. Pass the necessary journe entries for issue to shares and debentures. **(CBSE Sample Paper 2015, Modified)**

Ans.

JOURNAL

Date	Particulars		L.F.	Dr. (Rs.)	Cr. (Rs.)
	Bank A/c	Dr.		2,500,000	
	To Share Application and Allotment A/c				2,500,000
	(Being the amount of application money received on 50,000 shares @ Rs.50 per share)				
	Share Application and Allotment A/c	Dr.		2,500,000	
	To Share Capital A/c				2,500,000
	(Being the amount transferred to share capital)				
	Bank A/c	Dr.		1,600,000	
	To 9% Debentures Application and Allotment A/c				1,600,000
	(Being the amount received on 9% Debenture application and allotment on 40,000 Debentures @ Rs.40 per debentures)				

9% Debentures Application and Allotment A/c	Dr.		1,600,000	
To 9% Debentures A/c				1,600,000
(Being the amount transferred to Debentures A/c)				

Q.8. Prayuj Ltd. forfeited 2,000 shares of Rs.10 each, fully called up, on which they had received only Rs. 14,000. 50 of the forfeited shares were reissued for Rs.9 per share fully paid up.

Pass necessary journal entries for forfeiture and re-issue of shares. Also prepare share forfeited account.

(Compt. Delhi 2017)

Ans.

Books of the Prayuj Ltd.
JOURNAL

Date	Particulars		L.F.	Dr. (Rs.)	Cr. (Rs.)
	(i) Share Capital A/c	Dr.		20,000	
	To Forfeited Shares A/c				14,000
	To Calls in arrear A/c				6,000
	(2,000 shares of Rs.10 each forfeited for non payment of Rs.6,000)				
	(ii) Bank A/c	Dr.		450	
	Forfeited Shares A/c	Dr.		50	
	To Share Capital A/c				500
	(50 of the forfeited shares reissued for Rs.9 per share)				
	(iii) Forfeited Shares A/c	Dr.		300	
	To Capital Reserve A/c				300
	(Gain on reissue of shares transferred to capital Reserve A/c)				

Q.9. EF Ltd. invited applications for issuing 80,000 equity shares of Rs.50 each at a premium of 20%. The amount was payable as follows:

On Application : Rs.20 per share (including premium Rs.5)

On Allotment : Rs.15 per share (including premium Rs.5)

On First Call : Rs.15 per share

On Second and Final call : Balance amount

Applications for 1,20,000 shares were received. Applications for 20,000 shares were rejected and pro-rata allotment was made to the remaining applicants.

Seema, holding 4,000 shares failed to pay the allotment money. Afterwards the first call was made. Seema paid allotment money along with the first call. Sahaj who had applied for 2,500 shares failed to pay the first call money. Sahaj's shares were forfeited and subsequently reissued to Geeta for Rs.60 per share, Rs.50 per share paid up. Final call was not made.

Pass necessary journal entries for the above transactions in the books of EF Ltd. by opening calls-in-arrears account.

(CBSE Delhi 2019)

Ans.

In the Books of Firm Journal Entries (EF Ltd.)

Date	Particulars		L.F.	Dr. (Rs.)	Cr. (Rs.)
	Bank A/c	Dr.		2,400,000	
	To Equity Share Application A/c				2,400,000
	(Being application amount received)				
	Equity Share Application A/c	Dr.		24,000,000	
	To Equity Share Capital A/c				1,200,000
	To Bank A/c				4,00,000
	To Equity Share Allotment A/c				4,00,000
	To Security Premium Reserve A/c				4,00,000
	(Being application amount adjusted)				
	Equity Share Allotment A/c	Dr.		1,200,000	
	To Equity Share Capital A/c				8,00,000
	To Security Premium Reserve A/c				4,00,000
	(Being allotment amount due)				
	Bank A/c	Dr.		7,60,000	
	Calls in Arrear A/c	Dr.		40,000	
	To Equity Share Allotment A/c (12,00,000 – 4,00,000)				8,00,000
	(Being allotment amount received)				
	Equity Share I Call A/c	Dr.		1,200,000	
	To Equity Share Capital A/c				1,200,000
	(Being first call amount due)				
	Bank A/c	Dr.		1,210,000	
	To Equity Share I Call A/c				1,200,000
	To Calls in Arrear A/c (40,000 – 30,000)				10,000
	(Being first call amount received)				
	(Equity Share Capital A/c (2,000 × 40)	Dr.		80,000	
	To Share Forfeiture A/c				50,000
	To Calls in Arrear A/c				30,000
	(Being share forfeited)				
	Bank A/c (2000 × 60)	Dr.		1,20,000	
	To Equity Share Capital A/c (2,000 × 50)				1,00,000
	To Security Premium Reserve A/c				20,000
	(Being Share Reissued)				
	Share Forfeiture A/c	Dr.		50,000	
	To Capital Reserve A/c				50,000
	(Being Forfeiture amount Transferred to Capital Reserve)				

Q.10. S Ltd. invited applications for issuing 1,00,000 equity shares of Rs.10 each. The shares were issued at a premium of Rs.5 per share. The amount was payable as follows :

On Application and Allotment - Rs.8 per share (including premium Rs.3)

On the First and Final call - Balance including premium

Applications for 1,50,000 shares were received. Applications for 10,000 shares were rejected and pro-rata allotment was made to the remaining applicants on the following basis :

(I) Applicants for 80,000 shares were allotted 60,000 shares, and

(II) Applicants for 60,000 shares were allotted 40,000 shares.

Excess amount received on application and allotment was to be adjusted against sums due on call. X, who belonged to the first category and was allotted 300 shares, failed to pay the first and final call money. Y, who belonged to the second category and was allotted 200 shares, also failed to pay the first and final call money. Their shares were forfeited. The forfeited shares were reissued @ Rs.12 per share as fully paid-up.

Pass necessary cash book and journal entries for the above transactions in the books of the company.

(CBSE Outside Delhi 2019)

Ans.

Dr.   **CASH BOOK**   **Cr.**

Receipts	L.F.	Amount (Rs.)	Payment	L.F.	Amount (Rs.)
To Share Application & Allotment A/c		1,200,000	By Share Application & Allotment A/c		80,000
To Share I & Final Call A/c		378,100	By Balance c/d		1,504,100
To Equity Share Capital A/c		5,000			
To Securities Premium Reserve A/c		1,000			
		1,584,100			**1,584,100**

Books of S Ltd.

JOURNAL

Date	Particulars		L.F.	Dr. Amt. (Rs.)	Cr. Amt. (Rs.)
(i)	Equity Share Application & Allotment A/c	Dr.		1,120,000	
	To Equity Share Capital A/c				5,00,000
	To Securities Premium Reserve A/c				3,00,000
	To Calls in Advance A/c				3,20,000
	(Being application & Allotment money transferred				
(ii)	Equity Share First & Final Call A/c	Dr.		7,00,000	
	To Equity Share Capital A/c				5,00,000
	To Securities Premium Reserve A/c				2,00,000
	(Being share first & Final Call money due)				

(iii)	Calls in arrear A/c	Dr.		1,900	
	Call in Advance A/c	Dr.		3,20,000	
	To Equity Share First & Final Call A/c				3,21,900
	(Calls in Advance Adjusted and amount not received transferred to Calls-in-arrear A/c				
	OR				
	Calls in Advance A/c	Dr.		3,20,000	
	To Equity Share First & Final Call A/c				3,20,000
	(Calls in Advance adjusted on first and final call)				
(iv)	Equity Share Capital A/c	Dr.		1,14,900	
	Securities Premium Reserve A/c	Dr.			1,14,900
	To Shares Formatted A/c				
	To Call in Arrear A/c				
	(Being shares forfeited)				
(v)	Shares Forfeited A/c	Dr.		4,100	
	To Capital Reserve A/c				4,100
	(Gain on reissue of forfeited Shares transferred to Capital Reserve)				

(a) X Ltd. forfeited 10 shares of Rs.10 each, Rs. 7 called up on which the shareholder had paid application and allotment money of Rs. 5 per share. Out of these, 8 shares were re-issued to Y for ? 8 per share at ? 8 per paid up per share. Record the journal entries for forfeiture and reissue of shares by opening call in arrear, call in advance account.

(b) L ltd forfeited Mr M's shares who has applied for 600 shares and was allotted 400 shares failed to pay allotment money of Rs. 4 per share including premium of Rs. 2 on which he had paid application money of Rs. 2 only. Pass necessary journal entries for forfeiture of shares by opening call in arrear, call in advance account.

(c) Crown Ltd forfeited 50 shares of Rs.10 each, for non-payment of final call money of Rs. 3 per share. Out of these 20 shares were reissued to Taj at Rs.8 per share. Record the journal entries for forfeiture and reissue of shares assuming that the company maintains call in arrear, call in advance account.

(CBSE Sample Paper 2019-20)

Ans. (a)

Date	Particulars		L.F.	Amount (Rs.)	Amount (Rs.)
	Equity Share Capital A/c	Dr.		70	
	To Equity Share Forfeited A/c				50
	To Calls in Arrears A/c				20
	(Being forfeiture of 10 shares executed)				
	Bank A/c	Dr.		64	
	To Share Capital A/c				64
	(Being eight shares reissued to Y as Rs.8 per share paid up for Rs.8 per share)				

Equity Share Forfeited A/c	Dr.		40	
To Capital Reserve A/c				40
(Being gain on reissue of forfeited shares transferred to Capital Reserve)				

(b)

Date	Particulars	L.F.	Amount (Rs.)	Amount (Rs.)
	Equity Share Capital A/c	Dr.		1,600	
	Security Premium A/c	Dr.		800	
	To Equity Share Forfeited A/c				1,200
	To Calls in Arrears A/c				1,200
	(Being Mr. M's Shares forfeited)				

(c)

Date	Particulars	L.F.	Amount (Rs.)	Amount (Rs.)
	Equity Share Capital A/c	Dr.		500	
	To Share Forfeited A/c				350
	To Calls in Arrears A/c				150
	(Being 50 shares forfeited for nonpayment of calls)				
	Bank A/c	Dr.		160	
	Share Forfeited A/c	Dr.		40	
	To Share Capital A/c				200
	(Being 20 shares reissued for Rs. 8 per share)				
	Share Forfeited A/c	Dr.		100	
	To Capital Reserve A/c				100
	(Being gain on reissue of forfeited shares transferred to Capital Reserve)				

Q.11. Venus Ltd' was registered with an authorised capital of Rs. 40,00,000 divided into 4,00,000 equity shares of 10 each. 70,000 of these shares were issued as fully paid to 'M/s. Star Ltd.' for building purchased from them. 2,00,000 shares were issued to the public and the amounts were payable as follows:

On Application - Rs. 3 per share

On Allotment - Rs. 2 per share

On First Call - Rs. 2 per share

On Second and Final Call - Rs. 3 per share

The amounts received on these shares were as follows:

On 1,00,000 shares - Full amount called

On 60,000 shares - Rs. 1 per share

On 30,000 shares - Rs. 5 per share

On 10,000 shares - Rs. 3 per share

The directions forfeited 10,000 shares on which only Rs. 3 per share were received. These shares were reissued at Rs. 12 per share fully paid. Pass necessary journal entries for the above transactions in the books of 'Venus Ltd'.   **(CBSE Compt. 2019)**

Ans.

Building A/c	Dr.	7,00,000	
To M/s Star Ltd.			7,00,000
(Being building purchased from M/s Star Ltd.)			
M/s Star Ltd.	Dr.	7,00,000	
To Equity Share Capital A/c			7,00,000
(Being 70,000 shares issued as fully paid to Star Ltd. for payment of building purchased)			
Bank A/c	Dr.	6,00,000	
To Equity Share Application A/c			6,00,000
(Being application money received on 2,00,000 shares)			
Equity Share Application A/c	Dr.	6,00,000	
To Equity Share Capital A/c			6,00,000
(Being application money transferred to share capital)			
Equity Share Allotment A/c	Dr.	4,00,000	
To Equity Share Capital A/c			4,00,000
(Being Allotment money received on 2,00,000 shares)			
Bank A/c	Dr.	380,000	
To Equity Share Allotment A/c			380,000
(Being allotment money received)			
Bank A/c	Dr.	3,80,000	
Calls in arrears A/c	Dr.	20,000	
To Equity Share Allotment A/c			4,00,000
(Being Allotment money received)			
Equity Share First Call A/c	Dr.	4,00,000	
To Equity Share Capital A/c			4,00,000
(Being First call money due on 2,00,000 shares)			

Bank A/c	Dr.	3,20,000	
To Equity Share First call A/c			3,20,000
Being first call money received)			
Bank A/c	Dr.	3,20,000	
Calls in arrears A/c	Dr.	80,000	4,00,000
To Equity Share First call A/c			
(Being first call money received)			

Equity Share Second and First call A/c	Dr.	6,00,000	
To Equity Share Capital A/c			6,00,000
(Being First call money due on 2,00,000 shares)			
Bank A/c	Dr.	3,00,000	
To Equity Share Second and Final call A/c			3,00,000
(Being first call money received)			
Bank A/c	Dr.	3,00,000	
Calls in arrear A/c	Dr.	3,00,000	
To Equity Share Second and Final call A/c			6,00,000
(Bing first call money received)			
Equity Share Capital A/c		1,00,000	
To Share Forfeiture A/c			30,000
To Equity Share Allotment A/c			20,000
To Equity Share First call A/c			20,000
To Equity Share Second and Final call A/c			20,000
(Being First call money due on 2,00,000 shares)			
OR			
Equity Share Capital A/c	Dr.	1,00,000	
To Share Forfeiture A/c			30,000
To Calls in Arrears A/c			70,000
(Being shares Forfeited)			
Bank A/c	Dr.	1,20,000	
To Equity Share Capital A/c			1,00,000
To Securities Premium Reserve A/c			20,000
(Being share reissued for Rs. 12 per share fully paid)			
Share Forfeiture A/c	Dr.	30,000	
To Capital Reserve A/c			30,000
(Being balance in Share forfeiture Account transferred to capital reserve)			

Chapter Practice

Multiple Choice Questions [1 Mark]

Q.1. A Company is created by :

(a) Special act of the Parliament

(b) Company Act

(c) Investors

(d) Members

Q.2. Shareholders receive from the company :

(a) Interest

(b) Commission

(c) Profit

(d) Dividend

Q.3. A company can not issue :

(a) Redeemable Equity Share

(b) Redeemable Preference Shares

(c) Redeemable Debentures

(d) Fully Convertible Debentures

Q.4. Reserve Capital is also known by :

(a) Capital Reserve

(b) Called up Capital

(c) Subscribed Capital

(d) None of the above

Q.5. Share Application Account is in the nature of :

(a) Real Account

(b) Personal Account

(c) Nominal Account

(d) None of the above

Q.6. On Issue of shares Premium is:

(a) Profit

(b) Income

(c) Revenue Receipt

(d) Capital Profit

Q.7. Interest on calls in arrears is charged according to Table F at

(a) 6 % p.a.

(b) 10% p.a.

(c) 5% p.a.

(d) 12% p.a.

Q.8. Forfeiture of shares result in the reduction of :

(a) Subscribed Capital

(b) Authorised Capital

(c) Reserve Capital

(d) Fixed Capital

Q.9. Discount allowed on re-issue of Forfeited shares is debited to :

(a) Share Capital a/c

(b) Share Forfeited A/c

(c) General Reserve A/c

(d) Share Discount A/c

Q.10. The balance of forfeited shares A/c after re-issue of forfeited shares is transferred to :

    (a) Statement of Profit & Loss   (b) Share Capital A/c

    (c) Capital Reserve A/c   (d) General Reserve A/c

Very Short Answer Type   [1 Mark]

Q.11. Give the meaning of 'Registered Capital' of a company ?

Q.12. What are Preliminary Expenses ?

Q.13. What should be the minimum time interval between two consecutive share calls ?

Q.14. How is 'Calls –in –Advance' shown in the Balance Sheet of a Company?

Q.15. Can a company declare dividend out of its securities Premium Reserve ?

Q.16. What is the maximum amount of discount at which forfeited share can be issued ?

Short Answer Type - I   [2 Marks]

Q.17. What is meant by Private placement of shares?

Q.18. What is meant by Employee Stock Option Plan ?

Q.19. State any three purposes for which Securities Premium can be utilized ?

Q.20. Ramesh Ltd took over Assets of Rs. 25,00,000 and liabilities of 6,00,000 of Ravi ltd Ramesh ltd paid the purchase consideration by issuing 10,000 equity shares of Rs.100 each at a premium of 10% and 11,00,000 by Bank Draft.

    Calculate purchase consideration and pass necessary Journal Entries in the books of Ramesh Ltd.

Q.21. Narendra Ltd .purchased a running business from Ashok Traders for a sum of Rs.15,00,000 payable Rs.3,00,000 by cheque and for the balance, it issued equity shares of Rs. 100 each at a premium of 20%.

    The assets and   Liabilities consisted of the following :

Plant and Machinery		Rs.4,00,000
Building	Rs.6,00,000	
Stock		Rs.5,00,000
Sundry Debtors	Rs.3,00,000	
Sundry Creditors	Rs.2,00,000	

    Record necessary journal entries in the books of Narendra ltd.

Q.22. On 01.01.2022, Rajendra Info Ltd. Received in advance for the first call of Rs. 2 per share on 10,000 equity Shares. The first call was due on 15.02.2022.

    Journalise the above transaction and transfer the advance to first call account by opening a call in advance A/c.

Q.23. Mahesh Chemical Ltd. Forfeited 500 equity shares of Rs. 100 each fornon payment of first call of Rs. 30 per share. The final call of Rs. 10 per share was not yet made the forfeited shares were reissued for Rs. 65,000 fully paid up. Pass necessary journal entries in the books of the company.

Q.24. Manoj Pipes Ltd. Forfeited 800 equity shares of Rs. 100 each for non payment of first call of Rs 30 per share. The final call of Rs. 20 per share was not yet made. Out of the forfeited shares, 400 were reissued at the rate Of 105 per share fully paid up. Pass necessary journal entries in the books of Manoj Ltd. For above transactions.

Long Answer Type   [5 Marks]

Q.25. Vishnu Agro Ltd. Issued 40,000 equity shares of Rs. 10 each at a premium of Rs. 2 per share payable as under:

On Application Rs. 2 per share

On Allotment Rs. 5 per share(including premium)

On First and Final Call Rs. 5 per share

Application were receivedfor 60,000 shares. Allotment was made on pro-rata bass to all the applicants. Money overpaid on applications was applied towards sum due on allotment.

Sandeep to whom 1,000 shares were allotted failed to pay allotment and call money.

Vineet to whom applied for 3,000 shares ,failed to pay the final call.

The shares of Sandeep and Vineet were subsequently forfeited after the first and final call was made.

2,000 of the forfeited shares were reissued shares @ Rs. 8 per share fully paid up. The reissued shares include all ofSaneep,s shares.

Pass necessary journal entries in the books of the Company.

Q.26. Badri Publications Ltd. Issued 2000 shares of Rs.10 each at a premium of Rs. 2 per share, payable Rs.2 on Application; Rs. 5 on allotment (including premium); Rs. 3 on first call and Rs 2 on final call.

Application were received for 3,000 shares and pro-rata allotment was made among applicants for 2,400 shares. Money overpaid was adjusted on sum due on allotment.

Vandana who was allotted 40 shares failed to pay allotment and first call and her shares were forfeited. Sanjana holding 60 shares failed to pay two calls and her shares were forfeited after final call. Of the forfeitedshares 80 were reissued as fully paid up at Rs 8 per shares, the whole of Vandana's share were included Record the above transactions in Cash Book and in journal of the company

CHAPTER 7

Issue and Redemption of Debentures

TOPIC 1 Introduction, Issue of Debentures

Summary

Meaning of Debentures:

The word 'debenture' has been derived from a Latin word 'debere' which means to borrow. Debenture is a written instrument acknowledging a debt under the common seal of the company. It contains a contract for repayment of principal after a specified period or at intervals or at the option of the company and for payment of interest at a fixed rate payable usually either half-yearly or yearly on fixed dates.

Bond: Bond, like debenture, is an acknowledgment of debt issued under the seal of a company and signed by an authorized signatory.

Distinction between Shares and debentures:

Ownership: A 'share' represents ownership of the company whereas a debenture is only acknowledgement of Debt. A share is a part of the owned capital whereas a debenture is a part of borrowed capital.

Return: The return on shares is known as dividend while the return on debentures is called interest. The rate of return on shares may vary from year to year depending upon the profits of the company but the rate of interest on debentures is prefixed. The payment of dividend is an appropriation of profits, whereas the payment of interest is a charge on profits and is to be paid even if there is no profit.

Repayment: Normally, the amount of shares is not returned during the life of the company, whereas, generally, the debentures are issued for a specified period and repayable on the expiry of that period.

Voting Rights: Shareholders enjoy voting rights whereas debenture holders do not normally enjoy any voting right.

Security: Shares are not secured by any charge whereas the debentures are generally secured and carry a fixed or floating charge over the assets of the company.

Convertibility: Shares cannot be converted into debentures whereas debentures can be converted into shares if the terms of issue so provide, and in that case these are known as convertible debentures.

Types of Debentures:

1. **Security point of view**

   (a) **Secured/Mortgage Debentures:** Secured Debentures are those which are secured either on a particular asset or on all the assets of the company in general.

   (b) **Unsecured/Naked Debentures:** Unsecured Debentures do not have a specific charge on the assets of the company.

Tenure point of view:

   (a) **Redeemable Debentures:** Redeemable debentures are those that will be repaid by the company at the end of a specified period during the existence of the company.

   (b) **Irredeemable Debentures:** Irredeemable debentures are those that are not repayable during the lifetime of the company

3. **Mode of Redemption point of view:**

   (a) **Convertible Debentures:** Convertible debentures are those the holder of which is given an option of exchanging the amount of their debenture for equity shares after a specified period.

   These are of two types:

   1. Fully Convertible Debentures (FCD) are those debentures where the whole amount is to be converted into equity shares.

   2. Partly Convertible Debentures (PCD) are those debentures where only a part of the amount of debenture is convertible into equity shares.

   (b) **Non-Convertible Debentures:** The debentures which cannot be converted into shares or in any other securities are called non-convertible debentures.

4. **From Coupon Rate Point of view:**

   (a) **Specific Coupon Rate Debentures:** These debentures are issued with a specified rate of interest, which is called the coupon rate. The specified rate may either be fixed or floating. The floating interest rate is usually tagged with the bank rate.

   (b) **Zero Coupon Rate Debentures:** These debentures do not carry a specific rate of interest. In order to compensate the investors, such debentures are issued at substantial discount and the difference between the nominal value and the issue price is treated as the amount of interest related to the duration of the debentures.

5. **Registration point of view:**

   (a) **Registered Debentures:** Registered debentures are those which are payable to the persons whose name appears in the Register of Debenture holders. These can be transferred only by executing a transfer deed.

   (b) **Bearer Debentures:** Bearer debentures are those which are payable to the bearer thereof. These can be transferred merely by delivery. Interest is paid to the persons who produced the interest coupon attached to such debenture.

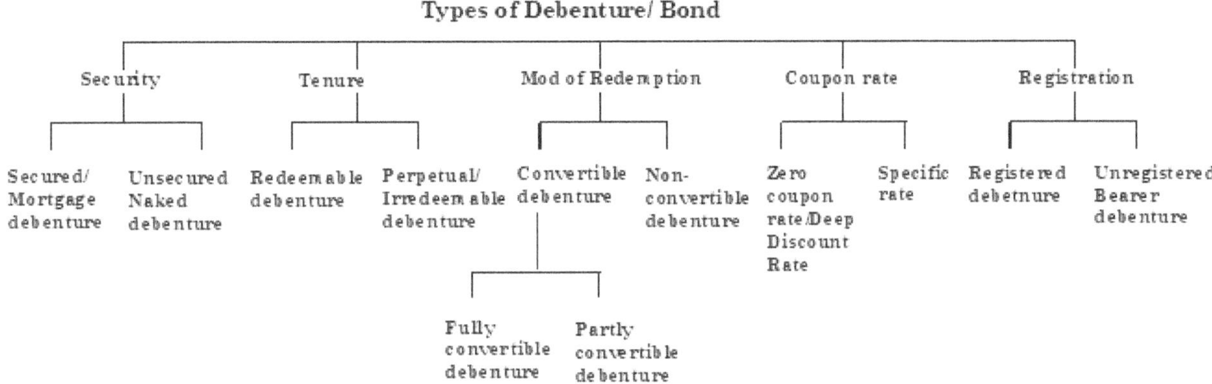

Issue of Debentures:

The procedure for the issue of debentures is the same as that for the issue of shares. The intending investors apply for debentures on the basis of the prospectus issued by the company. The company may either ask for the entire amount to be paid on application or by means of instalments on application, on allotment and on various calls. Debentures can be issued at par, at a premium or at a discount. They can also be issued for consideration other than cash or as a collateral security.

Issue of Debentures at Par: Debentures are said to have been issued at par when the issue price is equal to their face value.

1. If the debenture amount is received in one installment (lump sum).

    a. On receipt of the money

      Bank A/c   Dr. [With the total money received on application]

        To Debentures Application & Allotment A/c

    b. On making the allotment

      Debenture Application & Allotment A/c   Dr.   [At the time of allotment]

        To Debenture A/c

2. If the debenture amount is received in instalments

    a. On receipt of Application money

      Bank A/c   Dr. [With the money received on application]

        To Debenture

        Application A/c

    b. On Acceptance of Applications

      Debenture Application A/c   Dr.   [With application money received on debenture

        To Debenture A/c   alloted]

    c. On making Allotment money due

      Debenture Allotment A/c   Dr.   [With allotment money due]

        To Debenture A/c

    d. On Receipt of Allotment money

      Bank A/c   Dr.   [With allotment money received]

        To Debenture

        Allotment A/c

e. On making the First Call

Debenture First Call A/c   Dr.[With allotment money received]

    To Debentures A/c

f. On receipt of First Call money

Bank A/c   Dr.[With the first call money received]

    To Debenture First Call A/c

Issue of Debentures at a Discount: When the debentures are issued at less than the face value, it is said to be issued at discount. Discount on issue of debenture is a capital loss and is shown on the assets side of the Balance Sheet under the head "Miscellaneous Expenditure" till it is written off.

Accounting Treatment:

On the issue of debentures at a discount

Debenture Allotment A/c   Dr.

Discount of Issue of Debenture A/c   Dr.

To Debenture A/c

Issue of Debentures at Premium:A debenture is said to have been issued at a premium when the price charged is more than the face value of debenture. Premium on Issue of Debenture represents a capital receipt and should be transferred to Securities Premium A/c. It can be used for writing off capital losses and fictitious assets. This account is shown on the liabilities side of the Balance Sheet under the head of 'Reserves & Surplus'.

Accounting Treatment:

On Issue of Debenture at Premium

Debenture Allotment A/c   Dr.

To Debenture A/c

To Securities Premium A/c

Over Subscription: When the number of debentures applied for is more than the number of debentures offered to the public, the issue is said to be oversubscribed. The excess money received on oversubscription may be retained for adjustment towards allotment and respective calls when the amount is payable in Instalments or excess money will be refunded.

Multiple Choice Questions [1 Mark]

Q.1. Debentures which are transferable by mere delivery are

(a) Registered debentures

(b) First debentures

(c) Bearer debentures

(d) Second debentures

Ans. (c)

Q.2. Premium received on issue of debentures may be utilised for writing off:

(a) Premium allowed on redemption of debentures (b) Writing off preliminary expenses

(c) Writing off discount allowed on issue of shares (d) All of the above

Ans. (d)

Q.3. A company can issue debentures

   (a) For cash   (b) As a collateral security

   (c) For consideration other than cash   (d) Any of the above

Ans. (d)

Q.4. When the number of debentures applied is less than number of debentures offered to public the issue is said to be:

   (a) Over subscribed   (b) Under subscribe

   (c) Fully subscribed   (d) None of the above

Ans. (b)

Q.5. Maximum limit on premium on issue of debentures is

   (a) 10%   (b) 20%   (c) 15%   (d) No limit

Ans. (d)

Q.6. Debentures that do not carry any charge or security on assets of the company are known as:

   (a) Secured debentures   (b) Unsecured debentures

   (c) Convertible debentures   (d) Registered debentures

Ans. (b)

Q.7. Debenture is:

   (a) Written instrument acknowledging a debt written by its holder.

   (b) An oral acknowledgement of debt by a company

   (c) A written instrument acknowledging a debt written by its company

   (d) None of these

Ans. (c)

Very Short Answer Type   [1 Mark]

Q.8. _____________________Debentures are not secured with a specific asset rather they are secured on all the assets of the company in general.

Ans. floating

Assertion Reason Type Questions

Q.9. Assertion (A): Issue price of debentures can be collected in lump sum or in instalments.

Reason (R): when Issue price is payable in lump sum, the amount received on application is credited to "Debentures Application and Allotment Account".

   (a) Both Assertion (A) and Reason (R) are true and reason is correct explanation of assertion.

   (b) Assertion (A) and Reason (R) both are true but reason is not the correct explanation of assertion.

   (c) Assertion (A) is true, Reason (R) is false.

   (d) Assertion (A) is false, Reason (R) is true.

Ans. (b)

Q.10. Assertion (A): Debenture holder gets interest at the stated rate whether the company earns profit or not

Reason (R): interest on debenture is treated as an appropriation of profit.

(a) Both Assertion (A) and Reason (R) are true and reason is correct explanation of assertion.

(b) Assertion (A) and Reason (R) both are true but reason is not the correct explanation of assertion.

(c) Assertion (A) is true, Reason (R) is false.

(d) Assertion (A) is false, Reason (R) is true.

Ans. (c)

Q.11. Assertion (A): A Company may allot debentures to the promoters for rendering services for incorporating the Company

Reason(R): Incorporation Expenses are written off in the year they are incurred.

(a) Both Assertion (A) and Reason (R) are true and reason is correct explanation of assertion.

(b) Assertion (A) and Reason (R) both are true but reason is not the correct explanation of assertion.

(c) Assertion (A) is true, Reason (R) is false.

(d) Assertion (A) is false, Reason (R) is true.

Ans. (a)

Q.12. Assertion (A): 10,000, 11% debentures of Rs.100 each are issued on 1st April 2020 redeemable on 31st December 2022. These debentures will be shown as Short term Borrowings under the head Current liabilities in the Balance Sheet as at 31st March2021

Reason (R): when debentures are issued and are due for redemption within 12 months or within the period of operating cycle from the date of Balance Sheet they are treated as Short term borrowings.

(a) Both Assertion (A) and Reason (R) are true and reason is correct explanation of assertion.

(b) Assertion (A) and Reason (R) both are true but reason is not the correct explanation of assertion.

(c) Assertion (A) is true, Reason (R) is false.

(d) Assertion (A) is false, Reason (R) is true.

Ans. (a)

Q.13. Assertion (A): Debentures are liability

Reason (R): Debentures are shown on the asset side of the balance sheet.

(a) Both Assertion (A) and Reason (R) are true and reason is correct explanation of assertion.

(b) Assertion (A) and Reason (R) both are true but reason is not the correct explanation of assertion.

(c) Assertion (A) is true, Reason (R) is false.

(d) Assertion (A) is false, Reason (R) is true.

Ans. (c)

Q.14. Assertion: Debentures carry voting rights

Reason: Debentures are the creditors of the company.

(a) Both Assertion (A) and Reason (R) are true and reason is correct explanation of assertion.

(b) Assertion (A) and Reason (R) both are true but reason is not the correct explanation of assertion.

(c) Assertion (A) is true, Reason (R) is false.

(d) Assertion (A) is false, Reason (R) is true.

Ans. (d)

Q.15. Assertion (A): zero coupon bonds are issued without specified rate of interest.

Reason (R): it is type of bond which is similar to the debenture and being issued by the government.

(a) Both Assertion (A) and Reason (R) are true and reason is correct explanation of assertion.

(b) Assertion (A) and Reason (R) both are true but reason is not the correct explanation of assertion.

(c) Assertion (A) is true, Reason (R) is false.

(d) Assertion (A) is false, Reason (R) is true.

Ans. (a)

Q.16. Assertion (A): redeemable debentures are those debentures which will be repaid by the company either in lump-sum at the end of a specified period or by instalments during the lifetime of the company.

Reason (R): Irredeemable debentures are repayable only at the time of liquidation of the company.

(a) Both Assertion (A) and Reason (R) are true and reason is correct explanation of assertion.

(b) Assertion (A) and Reason (R) both are true but reason is not the correct explanation of assertion.

(c) Assertion (A) is true, Reason (R) is false.

(d) Assertion (A) is false, Reason (R) is true.

Ans. (b)

Q.17. Assertion (A): a debenture issued by a company in the form of a certificate, which is a written acknowledgement of debt taken by the company.

Reason (R): a debenture is a part of the loan and as such, the debenture holders re the creditors of the company.

(a) Both Assertion (A) and Reason (R) are true and reason is correct explanation of assertion.

(b) Assertion (A) and Reason (R) both are true but reason is not the correct explanation of assertion.

(c) Assertion (A) is true, Reason (R) is false.

(d) Assertion (A) is false, Reason (R) is true.

Ans. (a)

Q.18. Assertion (A): Issue of debenture does not result in dilution of interest of equity shareholders.

Reason (R): Debenture holders have voting rights.

(a) Both Assertion (A) and Reason (R) are true and reason is correct explanation of assertion.

(b) Assertion (A) and Reason (R) both are true but reason is not the correct explanation of assertion.

(c) Assertion (A) is true, Reason (R) is false.

(d) Assertion (A) is false, Reason (R) is true.

Ans. (a)

Q.19. Assertion (A): Debentures saves income tax.

Reason (R): Interest on debenture is tax deductible expenditure.

(a) Both Assertion (A) and Reason (R) are true and reason is correct explanation of assertion.

(b) Assertion (A) and Reason (R) both are true but reason is not the correct explanation of assertion.

(c) Assertion (A) is true, Reason (R) is false.

(d) Assertion (A) is false, Reason (R) is true.

Ans. (a)

Q.20. Assertion: Debenture holders do not enjoy any voting right.

    Reason: A debenture holder just lends money but does not become an owner of the company with the purchase of debentures

    (a) Both Assertion (A) and Reason (R) are true and reason is correct explanation of assertion.

    (b) Assertion (A) and Reason (R) both are true but reason is not the correct explanation of assertion.

    (c) Assertion (A) is true, Reason (R) is false.

    (d) Assertion (A) is false, Reason (R) is true.

Ans. (a)

Q.21. Assertion: Debenture holders are the owners of the company

    Reason: Debenture holders do not have the voting right.

    (a) Both Assertion (A) and Reason (R) are true and reason is correct explanation of assertion.

    (b) Assertion (A) and Reason (R) both are true but reason is not the correct explanation of assertion.

    (c) Assertion (A) is true, Reason (R) is false.

    (d) Assertion (A) is false, Reason (R) is true.

Ans. (b)

Q.22. Assertion: Debenture is a written acknowledgement of debt taken by the company

    Reason: A debenture is generally secured by a charge on the assets of the company.

    (a) Both Assertion (A) and Reason (R) are true and reason is correct explanation of assertion.

    (b) Assertion (A) and Reason (R) both are true but reason is not the correct explanation of assertion.

    (c) Assertion (A) is true, Reason (R) is false.

    (d) Assertion (A) is false, Reason (R) is true.

Ans. (a)

Q.23. Assertion (A): A Debenture is issued by a company in the form of a certificate, which is written acknowledgement of debt taken by the company

    Reason (R): It contains a contract for repayment of principal sum at specific date

    (a) Both Assertion (A) and Reason (R) are true and reason is correct explanation of assertion.

    (b) Assertion (A) and Reason (R) both are true but reason is not the correct explanation of assertion.

    (c) Assertion (A) is true, Reason (R) is false.

    (d) Assertion (A) is false, Reason (R) is true.

Ans. (b)

Q.24. Assertion (A): Debentures are presented under non-current liabilities in the balance sheet of a company.

    Reason (R): Debenture is a written acknowledgement of a long term debt taken by the company from the public (investors)

    (a) Both Assertion (A) and Reason (R) are true and reason is correct explanation of assertion.

    (b) Assertion (A) and Reason (R) both are true but reason is not the correct explanation of assertion.

    (c) Assertion (A) is true, Reason (R) is false.

    (d) Assertion (A) is false, Reason (R) is true.

Ans. (a)

Q.25. Assertion (A): Debenture holder are not the owner of the company.

Reason (R): Debenture is a part of borrowed capital

(a) Both Assertion (A) and Reason (R) are true and reason is correct explanation of assertion.

(b) Assertion (A) and Reason (R) both are true but reason is not the correct explanation of assertion.

(c) Assertion (A) is true, Reason (R) is false.

(d) Assertion (A) is false, Reason (R) is true.

Ans. (c)

Q.26. Assertion (A): Debenture holders are the creditor of company carrying a fixed rate of interest.

Reason (R): Debentures are short term loans taken from public.

(a) Both Assertion (A) and Reason (R) are true and reason is correct explanation of assertion.

(b) Assertion (A) and Reason (R) both are true but reason is not the correct explanation of assertion.

(c) Assertion (A) is true, Reason (R) is false.

(d) Assertion (A) is false, Reason (R) is true.

Ans. (c)

Q.27. Assertion (A): The bank account is debited with the money is received from debentures.

Reason (R): Bank being a real account need to be debited when something comes in.

(a) Both Assertion (A) and Reason (R) are true and reason is correct explanation of assertion.

(b) Assertion (A) and Reason (R) both are true but reason is not the correct explanation of assertion.

(c) Assertion (A) is true, Reason (R) is false.

(d) Assertion (A) is false, Reason (R) is true.

Ans. (a)

Short Answer Type - I   [2 Marks]

Q.1. Define Debenture.   [CBSE 2011, 2013]

Ans. Sec 2(30) of companies Act, 2013 defines debenture as "Debenture includes debenture stock, bond or any other instrument of a company evidencing a debit, whether constituting a charge on the company's assets or not".

It is a document issued by a company under its common seal acknowledging the debt and it also contains the terms of repayment of debt and payment of interest at a specified rate.

Q.2. What is meant by a bond?   [Compartment 2014]

Ans. Bond is an instrument of acknowledgement of debt, but it does not carry a pre-determined rate of interest.

Q.3. Why would an investor prefer to invest partly in shares and partly in the debentures of a company?

[All India; Delhi 2009]

Ans. An investor would prefer to invest partly in shares and partly in debentures to have high return as well as to reduce the risk.

Short Answer Type - II   [3 Marks]

Q.1. Name the various types of Debentures .

Ans. (i) On the basis of Security: Secured, Unsecured

(ii) On the basis of Record: Registered , Bearer

(iii) On the basis of Priority: First , Second

(iv) On the basis of Redemption: Redamble, Irredeemable

(v) On the basis of Coupen rate: Specific, Zero

(vi) On the basis of Convertibility: Convertible, Nonconvertible

Q.2. Differentiate between Share and Debenture .

Ans. (i) Ownership : Shareholder are the owners of company.

Debenture holder are the lenders of company.

(ii) Form of Return :Share holders get Dividend.

Debenture holders get Interest

(iii) Voting Right: Shareholder have the voting right .

Debentures holder do not have voting right.

Q.3. Explain various conditions of Issue of debentures.

Ans. Debentures may be issued:

- For "Cash" (At Par, Premium or Discount)

- For "Consideration other than Cash"

- As "Collateral Security"

Issue of Debentures for Cash

Just like shares, debentures may be issued either at par or at a premium or at a discount. company may either require the amount for debentures to be paid in lumpsum instalment. The accounting entries to be passed are also same as in the case of issue of shares.

"Consideration other than Cash" When Debentures are issued for purchase of asset.

Sundry Assets A/c   Dr.

To Vendor

(Asset bought)

Vendor A/c   Dr.

To % Debentures A/c

(Payment made by — % Debentures)

Issue of Debentures as Collateral Security

Collateral Security: Collateral security means security provided to lender in addition to the principal security. It is a subsidiary or secondary security. The lender will have a right over such debentures only when company fails to pay the loan amount and the principal security is exhausted. No interest is paid on the debentures issued as collateral security because company pays interest on loan.

(i) **First method:** No journal entry to be made in the books of accounts of the company for debentures issued as collateral security. A note of this fact is given in this case.

(iii) **Second method:** Entry to be made in the books of accounts of the company. A journal entry is made on the issue of debentures as a collateral security; Debentures Suspense is debited because no cash is received for such issue Following journal will be made

Debenture Suspense A/c   Dr.

     To % Debentures A/c

(Being the issue of Debentures of Rs........ issued as collateral security)

Q.4. Pass necessary journal entries for the following transaction-issued 60,000, 9% debentures of Rs 75 each at a premium of Rs 25 per debenture. **[Delhi 2008]**

Ans. **JOURNAL**

Date	Particulars		LF	Amt (Dr)	Amt (Cr)
	Bank A/c (60,000 × 100)	Dr		6,000,000	
	To Debenture Application and Allotment A/c				6,000,000
	(Being application money received)				
	Debenture Application and allotment A/c	Dr		6,000,000	
	To 9% Debentures A/c (60,000 × 75)				4,500,000
	To Securities Premium Reserve A/c (60,000 × 25)				1,500,000
	(Being application and allotment money transferred to				
	debentures and security premium reserve)				

Q.5. Garvit Ltd. invited applications for issuing 3,000, 11% Debentures of 100 each at a discount of 6%. The full amount was payable on application. Applications were received for 3,600 debentures. Applications for 600 debentures were rejected and the application money was refunded. Debentures were allotted to the remaining applicants.

Pass the necessary journal entries for the above transactions in the books of Garvit Ltd.

[CBSE Delhi 2019]

Ans. **BOOK OF GARVIT LTD.**

Date	Particulars		LF	Dr. (Rs.)	Cr. (Rs.)
	Bank A/c	Dr.		3,38,400	
	To Debenture Application & Allotment A/c				3,38,400
	(Being debenture application money received)				
	Debenture Applicatkon & Allotment A/c	Dr.		3,38,400	
	Discount on issue of Debetnure A/c	Dr.		18,000	
	To 11% Debenture A/c				3,00,000
	To Bank A/c				56,400
	(Being application money transferred)				

Q.6. Z Ltd. Invited application for 5,000, 8% Debentures of Rs.100 each at a premium of 2%, Rs.40 were payable on Application and balance on allotment. Applications were received for 4,800 shares and accepted in full. All money duly received. Journalise the transactions. **[CBSE 2016]**

Ans.

Date	Particulars		L.F.	Debit (Rs.)	Credit (Rs.)
	Bank A/c			1,92,000	
	To Debentures Application A/c				1,92,000
	(Being the application money Received on 4800 Debentures @ Rs. 40 per Debentures)				
	Debentures application A/c	Dr.		1,92,000	
	To Debentures A/c				1,92,000
	(Being the transfer of application Money to 8% debentures account)				
	Debentures Allotment A/c			2,97,600	
	To 8% Debentures A/c				2,88,000
	To Security Premium Reserve A/c				9600
	(Being the allotment money due on 4,800 debentures @ Rs. 60 and premium of Rs. 2 Share)				
	Bank A/c	Dr.		2,97,600	
	To Debentures Allotment A/c	Dr.			2,97,600
	(Being the application Money received)				

Q.7. ABC Limited issued Rs. 10,000, 12% debentures of Rs. 100 each payable Rs. 30 on application and remaining amount on allotment. The public applied for 9,000 debentures which were fully allotted, and all the relevant allotment money was duly received. Give journal entries in the books of ABC Ltd. **[NCERT]**

Ans.

Books of ABC Limited

JOURNAL

Date	Particulars		L.F.	Debit Amount (Rs.)	Credit Amount (Rs.)
	Bank A/c	Dr.		2,70,000	
	To 12% Debenture Application A/c				
	(Application money on 9,000 debentures received)				2,70,000
	12% Debenture Application A/c	Dr.		27,0,000	
	To 12% Debenture A/c				2,70,000
	(Application money transferred to debentures Account on allotment				
	12% Debenture Application A/c	Dr.		6,30,000	
	To 12% Debenture A/c				6,30,000
	(Amount due on 9,000 debentures on allotment @ Rs. 70 per debenture)				
	Bank A/c	Dr.		6,30,000	
	To 12% Debenture allotment A/c				6,30,000
	(Amount received on allotment)				

Q.8. TV Components Ltd., issued 10,000, 12% debentures of Rs 100 each at a discount of 5% payable as follows: On application Rs 40 On allotment Rs 55 Show the journal entries including those for cash, assuming that all the instalments were duly collected.

Ans.   BOOKS OF TV COMPONENTS LTD. JOURNAL

Date	Particulars		L.F.	Debit Amount (Rs.)	Credit Amount (Rs.)
	Bank A/c	Dr.		4,00,000	
	To 12% Debenture Application A/c				4,00,000
	(Receipt of application money @ Rs. 30 per debenture)				
	12% Debenture Application A/c	Dr.		4,00,000	
	To 12% Debenture A/c				4,00,000
	(Transfer of application money to debenture account)				
	12% Debenture Allotment A/c	Dr.		5,50,000	
	Discount on issue of Debentures A/c			50,000	6,00,000
	To 12% Debenture A/c				
	(Allotment money due on debentures)				
	Bank A/c	Dr.		5,50,000	
	To 12% Debenture allotment A/c				5,50,000
	(Receipt of allotment money on debentures)				

Q.9. XYZ Industries Ltd., issued 2,000, 10% debentures of Rs 100 each, at a premium of Rs 10 per debenture payable as follows:

On application Rs 50

On allotment Rs 60

The debentures were fully subscribed and all money was duly received. Record the journal entries in the books of a company.   [CBSE 2014]

Ans.   Books of XYZ Industries Limited

JOURNAL

Date	Particulars		L.F.	Debit Amount (Rs.)	Credit Amount (Rs.)
	Bank A/c	Dr.		1,00,000	
	To 10% Debenture Application A/c				1,00,000
	(Application money Rs. 50 per debentures received)				
	10% Debenture Application A/c	Dr.		1,00,000	
	To 10% Debenture A/c				1,00,000
	(Transfer of application money)				
	To debenture A/c				
	10% Debenture Allotment A/c	Dr.		1,20,000	
	To 10% Debentures A/c				1,00,000
	To Securities Premium A/c				20,000
	(Allotment money due on debentures including the premium)				

Bank A/c Dr.		1,20,000	
To 10% Debenture Allotment A/c			1,20,000
(Allotment money received)			

Q.10. X Ltd. invited applications for issuing 1000,9% debentures of Rs. 100 each at a discount of 6%. Applications for 1,200 debentures were received. Pro-rata allotment was made to all the applicants. Pass necessary Journal Entries for the issue of debentures assuming that the whole amount was payable with applications.

[Delhi 2017]

Ans.

Books of the firm

JOURNAL

Date	Particulars		L.F.	Dr. (Rs.)	Cr. (Rs.)
2016	Bank A/c	Dr.		1,12,800	
Jan 1	To 9% Debenture Application and Allotment A/c				1,12,800
	(Being application money received for 1,200 debentures @ Rs.94 each				
	9% Debenture Application and Allotment A/c	Dr.		1,12,800	
	Discount on Issue od Debentures A/c	Dr.		6,000	
	To 9% Debenture A/c				1,00,000
	To Bank A/c				18,800
	Being 1000 9% debentures allotted on pro-rata basis)				
	Statement of profit and Loss				
	To discount on issue of debentures A/c	Dr.		6,000	
	(Being loss on issue of debentures written off)				6,000

Long Answer Type

[5 Marks]

Q.1. Read the passage given below and answer questions.

Sushi Ltd. Is a manufacturer of heavy machines in a town of Kota. It follows high standards of environment safety in the process of manufacturing. The company runs a school to provide quality education and a medical centre to address health issues of the resident of the resident of that area. The company is doing well and is going to start new manufacturing unit in Indore creating livelihood for people, especially those from disadvantage section of the society. To raise fund company decided to issue 50,000 shares of Rs. 100 each at par and 80,000, 10% debentures of Rs. 100 at 95, repayable at Rs. 105. [Kerala board]

(i) Total Fund raised by the company:

    (a) 50,000   (b) 1,30,00,000   (c) 1,26,00,000   (d) 80,00,000

Ans. (c)

(ii) When debentures are allotted, 10% debenture account is:

    (a) Debited with Rs. 80,00,000   (b) Credited with Rs. 80,00,000

    (c) Debited With Rs. 76,00,000   (d) Credited with Rs. 76,00,000

Ans. (b)

(iii) Loss on issue of debenture:

    (a) 4,00,000   (b) 80,000

    (c) 8,00,000   (d) None of the above

Ans. (c)

(iv) The values which the company wants to communicate to the society.

    (a) Welfare of employees   (b) Environmental awareness

    (c) Employment in backward areas   (d) All these

Ans. (d)

Q.2. Read the passage given below and answer questions.

Nikhil Technologies Ltd. issued 5,000; 9% Debentures of Rs.100 each at a premium of Rs.20 payable as follows:

(i) Rs.40 including premium of Rs.10 on application

(ii) Rs.40 including premium of Rs.10 on allotment

(iii) Balance as first and final call. Applications were received for 5,000 debentures and allotment was made to all the applicants. All the calls were made, and amounts received.

(i) What is the total interest payable on the debentures issued?

    (a) Rs.1,20,000   (b) Rs.45,000   (c) Rs.4,50,000   (d) Rs.4,500

Ans. (b)

(ii) What amount of the money received in application is transferred to the securities premium reserve account?

    (a) 5,00,000   (b) 50,000   (c) 1,00,000   (d) 5,000

Ans. (b)

(iii) The amount of money received during application is:

    (a) Rs.2,00,000   (b) Rs.1,50,000   (c) Rs.20,00,000   (d) Rs.2,50,000

Ans. (a)

(iv) The is the balance amount per debenture to be received at the first and final call is:

    (a) Rs.20   (b) Rs.40   (c) Rs.30   (d) Rs.10

Ans. (b)

Q.3. Harsh Industries Ltd., issued 2,000, 10% debentures of Rs.100 each at a premium of Rs.10 per debenture payable as follows:

On application   Rs.50

On allotment   Rs.60

The debentures were fully subscribed and all money was duly received. Record the journal entries in the books of a company. Show how the amounts will appear in the balance sheet.

Ans. **Books of Harsh Industries Limited**

JOURNAL

Date	Particulars		L.F.	Debit Amount (Rs.)	Credit Amount (Rs.)
	Bank A/c	Dr.		1,00,000	
	To 10% Debenture Application A/c				1,00,000
	(Application money Rs.50 per debenture received)				
	10% Debenture Application A/c	Dr.		1,00,000	
	To 10% Debentures A/c				1,00,000
	(Transfer of application money to debenture account)				
	10% Debenture Allotment A/c	Dr.		1,20,000	
	To 10% Debenture A/c				1,00,000
	To Securities Premium Reserve A/c				20,000
	(Allotment money due on debentures including the premium)				
	Bank A/c	Dr.		1,20,000	
	To 10% Debenture Allotment A/c				1,20,000
	(Allotment money received)				

Harsh Industries Limited

BALANCE SHEET

Particulars	Note No.	Amount (Rs.)
I. Equity and Liabilities		
Shareholders' Funds		
Reserve and Surplus	1	20,000
Non-current Liabilities		
Long-term borrowings	2	2,00,000
		2,20,000
II. Assets		
Current assets		2,20,000
Cash and cash equivalents		2,20,000

Notes to Accounts:

Sr. No.	Particulars	Amount (Rs.)
1.	Reserve and Surplus	
	Securities Premium Reserve	20,000
2.	Long-term borrowings	
	2,000, 10% debentures of Rs.10 each	2,00,000
3.	Cash and cash equivalents	
	Cash at bank	2,20,000

Q.4. Z Ltd. purchased machinery from K Ltd. Z Ltd paid K Ltd as follows:

(i) By issuing 5,000 equity shares of Rs. 10 each at a premium of 30%.

(ii) By issuing 1000, 8% Debentures of Rs. 100 each at a discount of 10%.

(iii) Balance by giving a promissory note of Rs. 48,000 payable after two months.

Pass necessary journal entries for the purchase of machinery and payment to K Ltd. in the books of Z Ltd.

[Delhi 2017]

Ans.　　　　　　　　　　**Z LTD. JOURNAL**

Date	Particulars		L.F.	Dr. (Rs.)	Cr. (Rs.)
(i)	Machinery A/c	Dr.		2,03,000	
	To K Ltd.				203,000
	(Being machinery purchased from K Ltd.)				
(ii)	K Ltd	Dr.		65,000	
	To Equity Share Capital A/c				50,000
	To Securities Premium Reserve A/c				15,000
	(Being 5,000 equity shares of Rs. 10 each issued at 30% premium)				
(iii)	K Ltd.	Dr.		90,000	
	Discount on Issue of Debentures A/c	Dr.		10,000	
	To 8% Debentures A/c				1,00,000
	(Being 1,000 8% debentures of Rs.100 each issued at 10% discount)				
(iv)	K Ltd.	Dr.		48,000	
	To Bills Payable A/c				48,000
	(Being balance payment made by giving two months' promissory note)				
	Statement of Profit Loss				
	To Discount on issue of debentures A/c	Dr.		10,000	10,000
	(Being discount on issue of debentures written off)				

Q.5. Vishwas Ltd. issued 2,000; 9% Debentures of Rs. 100 each payable as follows:

Rs. 25 on application; Rs. 25 on allotment and Rs. 50 on first and final call.

Applications were received for all the debentures along with the application money did allotment was made . Call money was also received on the due date.

Pass necessary Journal entries in the books of the company.

Ans. **Books of Vishwas Ltd.**

JOURNAL

Date	Particulars	L.F.	Debit Amount Rs	Credit Amount Rs
	Bank A/c Dr.		50,000	
	To 9% Debenture Application A/c			50,000
	(Debenture application money received for 2,000 debentures at Rs 25 each)			
	9% Debenture Application A/c Dr.		50,000	
	To 9% Debenture A/c			50,000
	(Debenture application money transferred to 9% Debentures A/c)			
	9% Debenture Allotment A/c Dr.		50,000	
	To 9% Debentures A/c			50,000
	(Debenture allotment money due on 2,000 Debentures at Rs 25 each)			
	Bank A/c Dr.		50,000	
	To 9% Debenture Allotment A/c			50,000
	(Debenture allotment money received)			
	9% Debenture First and Final Call A/c Dr.		1,00,000	
	To 9% Debentures A/c			1,00,000
	(Debenture first and final call money due on 2,000 debentures at Rs 50 each)			
	Bank A/c Dr.		1,00,000	
	To 9% Debenture First and Final Call A/c			1,00,000
	(Debenture first and final call received)			

Q.6. *A* Ltd. issued 2,000; 9% Debentures of Rs. 100 each on the following terms:

Rs. 20 on applications; Rs. 20 on allotment; Rs. 30 on first call; Rs. 30 on final call.

The public applied for 2,400 debentures. Applications for 1,800 debentures were accepted in full. Applications for 400 debentures were allotted 200 debentures and applications for 200 debentures were rejected. Pass necessary Journal entries.

Ans.

Books of A Ltd.

JOURNAL

Date	Particular	L.F.	Debit Amount Rs	Credit Amount Rs
	Bank A/c Dr.		48,000	
	To 9% Debenture Application A/c			48,000
	(Debenture application money received for 2,400 debentures at Rs 20 each)			
	9% Debenture Application A/c Dr.		48,000	
	To 9% Debentures A/c			40,000
	To 9% Debentures Allotment A/c			4,000
	To Bank A/c			4,000
	(Debenture application money transferred to 9% Debenture account for 2,000 Debenture, adjusted to Debenture Allotment account for 200 Debentures and money refunded for 200 debentures)			
	9% Debenture Allotment A/c Dr.		40,000	
	To 9% Debentures A/c			40,000
	(Debenture allotment money due on 2,000 debentures at Rs 20 each)			
	Bank A/c Dr.		36,000	
	To 9% Debentures Allotment A/c			36,000
	(Debenture allotment money received)			
	Debenture First Call A/c Dr.		60,000	
	To 9% Debentures A/c			60,000
	(Debenture first call money due on 2,000 9% debenture at Rs 30 each)			
	Bank A/c Dr.		60,000	
	To Debenture First Call A/c			60,000
	(Debenture first call money received)			
	Debenture Final Call A/c Dr.		60,000	
	To 9% Debentures A/c			60,000
	(Debentures final call money due on 2,000 9% Debentures at Rs 30 each)			
	Bank A/c Dr.		60,000	
	To Debenture Final Call A/c			60,000
	(Debenture final call received on 2,000 9% Debenture at Rs 30 each)			

Q.7. Narain Laxmi Ltd. invited applications for issuing 7,500; 12% Debentures of Rs. 100 each at a premium of Rs. 35 per debenture. The full amount was payable on application. Applications were received for 10,000 Debentures. Allotment was made to all the applications on pro rata.

Pass necessary Journal entries for the above transactions in the books of Narain Laxmi Ltd.

Ans. **In the Books of Narain Laxmi Ltd.**

JOURNAL

Date	Particulars	L.F.	Debit Amount Rs	Credit Amount Rs
	Bank A/c (10,000 debentures × 135) Dr.		1,350,000	
	To Debenture Application and Allotment A/c			1,350,000
	(Application money received on 10,000 12% debenture)			
	Debenture Application and Allotment A/c Dr.		1,350,000	
	To 12% Debentures A/c			7,50,000
	To Securities Premium Reserve A/c			2,62,500
	To Bank A/c			3,37,500
	(7,500; 12% Debentures of Rs 100 each issued at a premium of Rs 35 and excess money refunded)			

Q.8. Raj Ltd . issued 5,000; 8% Debentures of Rs. 100 each at a premium of 5% payable as follows:

Rs.10 on application; Rs. 20 along with premium on allotment and balance on first and final call. Pass necessary Journal entries.

Ans: **Books of Raj Ltd.**

JOURNAL

Date	Particulars	L.F.	Debit Amount Rs	Credit Amount Rs
	Bank A/c Dr.		50,000	
	To 8% Debenture Application A/c			50,000
	(Debenture application money received for 5,000 debentures at Rs 10 each)			
	8% Debenture Application A/c Dr.		50,000	
	To 8% Debentures A/c			50,000
	(Debenture application money transferred to 8% Debentures A/c)			
	8% Debenture Allotment A/c Dr.		1,00,000	
	To 8% Debentures A/c			75,000
	To Securities Premium A/c			25,000
	(Debenture allotment due on 5,000 8% Debentures at Rs 20 including premium of Rs 5)			
	Bank A/c Dr.		1,00,000	

To 8% Debentures Allotment A/c			1,00,000
(Debenture allotment money received)			
8% Debentures First and Final Call A/c	Dr.	3,75,000	
To 8% Debenture A/c			3,75,000
(Debenture first and final call due on 5,000 Debentures at Rs 75 each)			
Bank A/c	Dr.	3,75,000	
To 8% Debenture First and Final Call A/c			3,75,000
(Debenture first and final call received)			

TOPIC 2 Issue of Debentures other than Cash, Colletral Security

Summary

Issue of Debentures for Consideration Other than Cash: When the company purchases some assets (including services) and instead of making the payment to the supplier in the form of cash, issues its fully paid debentures, such issue of debentures is called the Issue of Debentures for Consideration Other than Cash. Such debentures can be issued at par, a premium, or at a discount.

(a)   On Purchase of Business

   Sundry Assets A/c   Dr. [With the agreed value of assets]

    To Sundry Liabilities A/c   [With the agreed value of Liabilities]

    To Vendor's A/c   [With Purchase consideration]

If the purchase consideration is greater than the value of the net assets acquired (i.e., the difference between the agreed value of the assets taken over and the agreed value of liabilities taken over), the difference is treated as a capital loss which should be debited to Goodwill A/c.

  Sundry Assets A/c   Dr. [Agreed value of assets taken over]

  Goodwill A/c   Dr. [Excess of purcahse consideration over the value of net assets]

  To Sundry Liabilities A/c   [Agreed value of liabilities]

  To vendors A/c   [Purchase consideration]

        Or

If the amount of the purchase consideration is lower than the value of the net assets acquired, the difference is treated as a capital profit which should be credited to Capital Reserve A/c.

  Sundry Assets A/c   Dr. [Agreed value of assets taken over]

  To Sundry Liabilities A/c   [Agreed value of liabilities]

  To Vendor's A/c   [Purchase considerations]

  To Capital Reserve A/c   [Excess of value of net assets over purchase considerations]

(b)   On the issue of Debentures

  1. At par

  Vendor's A/c Dr.

    To Debentures A/c

2. At Premium

   Vendor's A/c Dr.

       To Debentures A/c To Securities Premium A/c

3. At a Discount Vendor's A/c

   Discount on Issue of Debentures A/c

       To Debentures A/c

   No. of Debentures issued

   Issue Price of a Debenture:

Issue of Debentures as Collateral Security: When a company takes a loan from a bank or any other party and gives some additional security in the shape of debentures, the debentures are said to be issued as collateral security. In such a case, the lender has the absolute right over the debentures unless and until the loan is repaid. On repayment of the loan, the lender is legally bond to release the debenture forthwith.

In case the loan is not repaid by the company on the due date, the lender has the right to retain these debentures and realize them. The holder of such debentures is entitled to interest only on the amount of loan, but not on the debentures.

Debentures issued as collateral security can be dealt with in two ways in the books.

1.   No accounting entry is required to be shown in the books at the time of issue of such debentures, but a footnote to the fact that the loan has been secured by the issue of debentures is appended.

2.   If it is desired that such an issue of debentures is to be recorded in the books, the following entries are recorded:

   (a) On the issue of Debentures as Collateral Security

       Debentures Suspense A/c Dr.

       To Debentures A/c

   (b) On repayment of the loan

       Debentures A/c Dr.

Multiple Choice Questions   [1 Mark]

Q.1. Excess value of net assets over purchase consideration at the time of purchase of business is credited to:

   (a) General reserve   (b) Capital reserve   (c) Vendor's account   (d) Goodwill account

Ans. (b)

Q.2. ABC took over the assets of Rs.7,60,000 and liabilities of Rs.80,000 of Y limited for purchase consideration of Rs.5,85,000 payable by the issue of 12% debentures of Rs.100 each at a discount of 10%. The number of debentures to be issued is:

   (a) 6600   (b) 6500   (c) 4500   (d) 5400

Ans. (b)

Q.3. Debentures issued as collateral security will be________ to debenture suspense account:

   (a) Debited   (b) Credited

   (c) Sometimes debited and sometimes credited (d) None of these

Ans. (a)

Q.4. Collateral security means ___________ security:

(a) Primary   (b) Secondary   (c) Government   (d) Valuable

Ans. (b)

Q.5. A ltd took over the assets of Rs.6,60,000 and liabilities of Rs.80,000 of B Ltd for an agreed purchase consideration of Rs.6,00,000 payable 10% in cash and the balance by issue of 15% debentures of Rs.100 each at 10% discount. The number of debentures to be issued is:

(a) 6600   (b) 5400   (c) 6000   (d) 4500

Ans. (c)

Q.6. Gaurav Ltd. purchased machinery costing Rs.1,71,000. It was agreed that the purchase consideration be paid by issuing 12% debentures of Rs.100 each. Assume debentures have been issued at a discount of 10%. No. of debentures issued to vendor are:

(a) 1500   (b) 1900   (c) 2000   (d) 2100

Ans. (b)

Q.7. A company purchased sundry assets of Rs.10,00,000 and liabilities of Rs. 50,000 from another company for purchase consideration of 12,00,000. Amount transfer to vendor account will be:

(a) 2,00,000   (b) 12,50,000   (c) 12,00,000   (d) 8,50,000

Ans. (c)

Q.8. Devika Ltd took over assets of Rs.12,00,000 and creditors of Rs.2,40,000 from Arora ltd. Devika ltd. Issued 8% debenture of Rs.100 each at a premium of 20% as purchase consideration the amount credited to debentures a/c will be Rs._________

(a) 8,00,000   (b) 12,00,000   (c) 4,00,000   (d) 6,00,000

Ans. (a)

Very Short Answer Type   [1 Mark]

Q.9. If X ltd purchased plant worth Rs5 lakh from Y ltd but agreed to issue 5250 10% Debentures of Rs100 each to Vendor. The difference in the amount will be adjusted in ___________ account.

Ans. goodwill

Assertion Reason Type Questions

10. Assertion (A): Debentures can be issued as a collateral security

Reason (R): The amount of loan can be realized in full with the help of collateral security during default.

(a) Both Assertion (A) and Reason (R) are true and reason is correct explanation of assertion.

(b) Assertion (A) and Reason (R) both are true but reason is not the correct explanation of assertion.

(c) Assertion (A) is true, Reason (R) is false.

(d) Assertion (A) is false, Reason (R) is true.

Ans. (a)

Q.11. Assertion (A): Collateral security means secondary security in addition to principal security.

Reason (R): Debentures can be issued as a collateral security by the companies in case principal security fall short.

(a) Both Assertion (A) and Reason (R) are true and reason is correct explanation of assertion.

(b) Assertion (A) and Reason (R) both are true but reason is not the correct explanation of assertion.

(c) Assertion (A) is true, Reason (R) is false.

(d) Assertion (A) is false, Reason (R) is true.

Ans. (a)

Short Answer Type - I   [2 Marks]

Q.1. A Ltd. Took over the assets of Rs.560000 and creditors of Rs.80000 from S Ltd. A Ltd issued 8% debentures of Rs.20 each at a premium of 20% as purchase consideration to S Ltd.

(i) Calculate amount of purchase consideration

(a) Rs.5,80,000   (b) Rs.3,80,000   (c) Rs.6,80,000   (d) Rs.4,80,000

Ans. (d)

(ii) Calculate the number of debenture issued by Ltd. A.

(a) 20000   (b) 30,000   (c) 40,000   (d) 10,000

Ans. (a)

Q.2. What is meant by 'Issue of Debentures as Collateral Security' ?   **[CBSE Outside Delhi 2019]**

Ans. Debenture issued as secondary security/additional security over and above the primary security is known as Issue of Debentures as Collateral Security.

Q.3. When the company issues debentures to the lenders as an additional/secondary security, in addition to other assets already pledged/ some primary security. What does such issue of debentures is called?

[CBSE 2018]

Ans. Issue of debentures as collateral security.

Q.4. Explain the concept of Collateral Security.

Ans. Collateral security" means additional security to the main obligation in a contract. A company may issue its debentures in addition to the Primary Security when it takes loan from bank or any financial institution. It is called 'issue of debentures as collateral security'. The lender may take possession only if company is not able to repay the loan amount and the principal security is exhausted. In such a case company pays interest on loan, thus no interest will be paid on the debentures issued as collateral Security.

Q.5. What is meant by issue of debentures for consideration other than cash?

Ans. When a company does not have sufficient Cash to acquire the fixed Assets for the business or Company is not able to meet its obligations, in such a case a company may offer and allot its debentures to the outsiders in lieu of cash. This is known as issue of debentures for consideration other than cash. For example Machinery is purchased and debentures are issued to Vendor instead of paying cash.

Q.6. What is meant by issue of debentures as 'Purchase Consideration'?

Ans. When a company purchases some assets but do not make the payment in cash to vendor, instead of paying cash to vendor, company issues fully paid debentures for the same amount, is called debentures issued for purchase consideration.

Short Answer Type - II   [3 Marks]

Q.1. B Ltd. Purchased assets of the book value of Rs.1045000 from C Ltd. It was agreed that the purchase consideration be paid by issuing 14% debentures of Rs.100 each. Calculate no. of debentures issued if it is issued

(i) At par

(a) 11,450   (b) 12,450   (c) 10,450   (d) 15,450

Ans. (c)

(ii) At a discount of 5%

(a) 11,000   (b) 12,000   (c) 13,000   (d) 14,000

Ans. (a)

(iii) At a premium of 10%

(a) 7,500   (b) 8,500   (c) 6,500   (d) 9,500

Ans. (d)

Q.2. Varun Ltd. was a profit making organisation. They decided to expend their business. So Varun Ltd. took over Assets of Rs.10,00,000 and liabilities of Rs.1,80,000 of Cayns Ltd. for Rs.7,60,000 .Varun Ltd. issued 9% Debentures of Rs.100 each at a discount of 5% in full satisfaction of the purchase consideration in favour of Cayns Ltd. On the basis of above paragraph answer question no 18 to 20

(i) What will be the amount of Capital Reserve

(a) Rs.1,00,000   (b) Rs.80,000   (c) Rs.60,000   (d) Rs.40,000

Ans. (c)

(ii) What will be the number of Debentures to be issued to Cayns Ltd?

(a) 7,600   (b) 8,000   (c) 10,000   (d) None of the above

Ans.   (b)

(iii)In the above case from where amount of discount on issue of Debentures will be written off

(a) Capital Reserve   (b) Securities Premium Reserve

(c) Statement of profit and Loss   (d) None of the above

Ans. (a)

Q.3. K K Limited obtained a loan of[1] 10,00,000 from State Bank of India @ 9% interest. The company issued Rs. 15,00,000, 9% debentures of Rs.100/- each, in favour of State Bank of India as collateral security. Pass necessary Journal entries for the above transactions:

(i) When company decided not to record the issue of 9% Debentures as collateral security.

(ii) When company decided to record the issue of 9% Debentures as collateral security.

(CBSE Sample Paper 2018-19, 2017-18)

Ans.

K.K Limited

JOURNAL

Date	Particulars		L.F.	Dr. Amount (Rs.)	Cr. Amount (Rs.)
(i)	Bank Account	Dr.		1,000,000	
	To Bank Loan Account				1,000,000
	Obtained loan from State Bank of India @ 9%)				
(ii)	Bank Account	Dr.		1,000,000	
	To Bank Loan Account				1,000,000
	(Obtained loan from State Bank of India @ 9%)				
	Debenture Suspense Account	Dr.		1,500,000	
	To 9% Debenture Account				1,500,000
	(Issued 9% Debentures as collateral security in favour of State bank of India)				

Q.4. Meghnath Limited took a loan of Rs. 1,20,000 from a bank and deposited 1,400, 8% debentures of Rs. 100 each as collateral security along with primary security worth Rs. 2 Lakhs. Company again took a loan of Rs. 80,000 after two months from a bank and deposited 1,000, 8% debentures of Rs. 100 each as collateral security. Record necessary journal entries.

Ans.

Journal Entries in the Books of Meghnath Limited

Date	Particulars		L.F.	Dr. (Rs.)	Cr. (Rs.)
	Bank A/c	Dr.		1,20,000	
	To Bank Loan A/c				1,20,000
	(Being loan taken from bank against 1400, 8% debentures of Rs. 100 each as collateral security along with primary security worth Rs.2 Lakh)				
	Debentures Suspense A/c	Dr.		80,000	
	To Bank Loan A/c				80,000
	(Being loan taken from bank against 1000, 8% debentures of Rs.100 each as collateral security)				

Q.5. B. Ltd. purchased assets of the book value of Rs. 4,00,000 and took over the liability of Rs. 50,000 from Mohan Bros. It was agreed that the purchase consideration settled at Rs. 3,80,000 be paid by issuing debentures of Rs. 100 each.

What journal entries will be made in the following three cases, if debentures are issued: (a) at par; (b) at a discount of 10%, (c) at a premium of Rs. 10%. It was agreed that a fraction of debentures be paid in cash.

Ans.   Journal Entries in the Books of B. Ltd.

Date	Particulars		L.F.	Dr. (Rs.)	Cr. (Rs.)
	Sundry Assets A/c	Dr.		4,00,000	
	Goodwill A/c (B/F.)	Dr.		30,000	
	To Sundry Liabilities A/c				50,000
	To Mohan Bros. A/c				3,80,000
	(Being purchase of business of Mohan Bros. for consideration to be paid in debentures)				
	(i) Payment in Debentures issued at par:				
	Mohan Bros. A/c (3,800 × 100)	Dr.		3,80,000	
	To Debenture A/c				3,80,000
	(Being issue of 3,800 debentures of Rs.100 each issued at par i.e. 3,80,000 , 10 = 3,800 debenture)				
	(ii) Payment in Debentures issued at 10% premium:				
	Mohan Bros. A/c	Dr.		3,80,000	
	To Debenture A/c (3454 × 100)				3,45,000
	To Security Premium A/c (3454 × 10)				34,540
	To Cash A/c (B.F.)				60
	Being issue of 3454 debentures of Rs. 100 each at a presmum of 10% to Mohan Bros. i.e. 380000 , 110 = 3454				
	(iii) Payment in Debentures issued at 10% discount:				
	Mohan Bros. A/c	Dr.		3,80,000	
	Discount on Issue of Debenture A/c (4220 × 10)	Dr.		42,220	
	To Debenture A/c				4,22,200
	To Cash A/c				20
	(Being issue of 4,222 debentures of Rs. 100 each at a discount of 10% to Mohan Bros. i.e., 3,80,000 , 90 = 4,222 debentures)				
	Statement of Profit and Loss	Dr.		42,220	
	To Discount on issue of debentures A/c				42,220
	(Being discount on issue of debentures written off)				

Q.6. Zee Ltd. Took over the following assets and liabilities of business of Usha Ltd. Assets : Machinery-Rs. 1,00,000, Furniture Rs.1,80,000 Stock Rs. 20,000 Liabilities-Creditors Rs. 80,000

The purchases price was agreed at Rs. 1,08,000. This is to settle by issue of 12%

Debentures at premium of 20% pass necessary Journal entries.

Ans.

JOURNAL

Date	Particulars	L.F.	Debit (Rs.)	Credit (Rs.)
	Machine A/c Dr.		1,00,000	
	Furniture A/c Dr. Dr.		1,80,000	
	Stock A/c Dr.		20,000	
	To Creditors A/c			80,000
	To Capital Reserve A/c (B/F)			1,12,000
	To Usha Co. Ltd.			1,08,000
	(Being the purchases of Business)			
	Usha Co. Ltd		1,08,000	
	To 12% Debentures A/c			90,000
	To Security Premium A/c			18,000
	(Being issue of 900 Dentures of Rs. 100 each at premium of 20%)			

Calculations Net assets = Total assets-liabilities = Rs.3,00,000 – Rs.80,000 = Rs.2,20,000 Capital reserve = Net assets – Purchases consideration = Rs.2,20,000 – Rs.1,08,000 = Rs.1,12,000

Q.7. Sangam Woollens Ltd', Ludhiana, are the and exporters of garments. The company decided to distribute free of cost woollen garments to 10 villages of lahual and spiti district of Himachal Pradesh. The company also decided to employ 50 young persons from these villages in its newly established factory. The company issued 40,000 equity shares of' 10 each and 1,000 9% debentures of'100 each to the vendors for the purchase of machinery of' 5,00,000.

Pass necessary Journal Entries.   **(Delhi 2015, Modified)**

Ans.

Books of Sangam Woollens Ltd
JOURNAL

Date	Particulars	L.F.	Dr. (Rs.)	Cr. (Rs.)
(i)	Machinery A/c Dr.		5,00,000	
	To Vendors A/c			5,00,000
	(For purchase of machinery)			
(ii)	Vendors A/c Dr.		5,00,000	
	To Equity Share Capital A/c			4,00,000
	To 9% Debentures A/c			1,00,000
	(For issue of equity shares and debentures at par)			
	OR			
	Vendors A/c Dr.		4,00,000	
	To Equity Share Capital A/c			4,00,000
	(For issue of equity shares)			
	Vendors A/c Dr.		1,00,000	
	To 9% Debentures A/c			1,00,000
	(For issue of debentures at par)			

Long Answer Type   [5 Marks]

Q.1. Bee ltd purchased the following assets of See ltd. Land and building of Rs.55,00,000 at Rs.75,00,000; Furniture Rs.20,00,000; and Machinery Rs.30,00,000. The purchase consideration was Rs.1,00,00,000. Payment of Rs.10,00,000 was made through cheque and remaining amount by issue of 9% debentures of Rs.100 each at a premium of 20%

    (i) According to Companies Act 2013, what is the maximum rate of premium at which debentures can be issued?

        (a) 10%   (b) 15%

        (c) 20%   (d) Maximum limit not specified

Ans. (d)

    (ii) Amount credited to Capital Reserve A/c is

        (a) 25,00,000   (b) 20,00,000   (c) 15,00,000   (d) 10,00,000

Ans. (a)

    (iii) What is the number of debentures to be issued?

        (a) 65,000   (b) 70,000   (c) 75,000   (d) 80,000

Ans. (c)

    (iv) Securities premium reserve A/c is to be credited with————

        (a) 10,00,000   (b) 15,00,000   (c) 20,00,000   (d) 25,00,000

Ans. (b)

Q.2. ABC decided to acquire the running business of Y ltd, so it took over the assets of Rs.6,60,000 and liabilities of Rs.80,000 of Y limited for a purchase consideration of Rs 5,85,000 payable by the issue of 12% debentures of Rs100 each at a discount of 10%.

    (i) Goodwill A/c will be debited with

        (a) 10,000   (b) 15,000   (c) 5,000   (d) 8,000

Ans. (c)

    (ii) Discount on issue of debenture is written off, in the year debentures are allotted, in the following sequence-

        (a) Securities premium reserve, capital reserve, statement of Profit and loss

        (b) Securities premium reserve, statement of Profit and loss, capital reserve

        (c) Capital reserve, securities premium reserve, statement of Profit and loss

        (d) Statement of Profit and loss, capital reserve, securities premium reserve

Ans. (a)

    (iii) The number of debentures to be issued is:

        (a) 6600   (b) 6500   (c) 4500   (d) 5400

Ans. (b)

    (iv) 12% Debentures Account is credited with

        (a) 6,50,000   (b) 7,00,000   (c) 6,00,000   (d) 7,50,000

Ans. (a)

Q.3. Devika Ltd. Engaged in manufacturing of Lab equipment In Delhi, During COVID pandemic demand of equipment rapidly Increased and the company decided to take loan of Rs. 40,00,000 from IDBI Bank to provide sufficient supply of equipment in market. The company took loan from IDBI bank of Rs.40,00,000 and placed debentures for Rs. 50,00,000 as collateral security. The company provide free covid testing kit, Sanitizers and masks for backward villages.

(i) Entry for Recording of debentures as collateral Security:

    (a) Bank A/c   Dr. To debenture A/c

    (b) Bank Loan A/c   Dr. To Debenture A/c

    (c) Debenture   Dr. To Debenture A/c

        suspense A/c

    (d) Bank A/c   Dr. To Bank Loan A/c

Ans. (c)

(ii) Entry for Loan obtained from IDBI Bank

    (a) IDBI Bank A/c   Dr. To Bank Loan A/c

    (b) Debenture A/c   Dr. To Bank Loan A/c

    (c) Bank Loan A/c   Dr. To IDBI Bank A/C

    (d) Bank Loan A/c   Dr. To Debenture A/c

Ans. (a)

(iii) In context of above case Bank loan from IDBI shown in balance sheet as:

    (a) Under head non-current liabilities and sub head long term borrowings

    (b) Under Head current assets and sub head cash and cash equivalents

    (c) Both (a) and (b)

    (d) None of the above

Ans. (a)

(iv) Which of following statement is not true about in context of above case:

    (a) Company empowering backward village

    (b) Debentures of Rs.50,00,000 are shown in balance sheet as long-term borrowings

    (c) Debenture suspense account is shown as deduction from debenture account in Notes to accounts of balance sheet

    (d) None of the above

Ans. (b)

Q.4. Tanmay Ltd. took over Assets of Rs.6,00,000 and Liabilities of Rs. 40,000 of Arora Ltd. at an agreed value of Rs. 6,30,000. Tanmay Ltd. issued 10% Debentures of [1] 100 each at a discount of 10% to Arora Ltd. in full satisfaction of the price. Tanmay Ltd. writes off any capital losses incurred during a year, at the end of that financial year.

(i) In which account is the difference between the assets and liabilities taken over and the payment made be transferred to?

    (a) General Reserve   (b) Capital reserve

    (c) Goodwill   (d) DRR

Ans. (c)

(ii) As Tanmay Ltd. writes off the capital losses where will the discount on issue of debentures be transferred to?

    (a) Statement of P/L   (b) General Reserve

    (c) Capital Reserve   (d) DRR

Ans. (a)

(iii) What is the amount of discount given to Arora Ltd. on the issue of debentures?

    (a) 60,000   (b) 70,000   (c) 75,000   (d) 50000

Ans. (b)

(iv) What is the Purchase consideration payable to Arora Ltd.?

    (a) 7,00000   (b) 6,00000   (c) 6,30,000   (d) 5,60,000

Ans. (c)

Q.5. XYZ Ltd. Issued 30,000 10% debentures of Rs.500 each to public on 1st June 2018 for 10 years. The company had issued 10,000 9% debentures of Rs.200 at premium of 25% to AB Ltd against a machine purchased from him. The company had taken a loan of Rs.20,00,000 for which 15,000 8% debentures of Rs.100 was issued to bank as collateral security.

(i) Which of the following journal entry will be made for issue of debentures as collateral security

    (a) Loan A/c   Dr

            To 8% Debentures A/c

    (b) Bank A/c   Dr

            To 8% Debentures A/c

    (c) Debentures Suspense A/c   Dr

            To 8% Debentures A/c

    (d) Bank A/c   Dr

            To Loan A/c

Ans. (c)

(ii) On which date the above debentures will be redeemed?

    (a) 31st December, 2028   (b) 31st March 2028

    (c) 31st May, 2028   (d) 31st July 2028

Ans. (c)

(iii) What is the cost of Machine purchased from AB Ltd.

    (a) Rs.15,00,00   (b) Rs.20,00,000

    (c) Rs.25,00,000   (d) Rs.30,00,000

Ans. (c)

(iv) As per the case above, which method of issue of debentures was not undertaken by XYZ Ltd.

    (a) Issue of debentures for cash

    (b) Issue of debentures for consideration other than cash

    (c) Issue of debentures as collateral security

    (d) Issue of debentures on the point of view of redemption

Ans. (d)

Q.6. Devi Ltd. issued 10,000, 8% debentures of Rs.100 each at a premium of 10% on 01.04.2016. It purchased sundry assets of the value of Rs.2,50,000 and took over the liabilities of Rs.60,000 and issued 8% debentures at a discount of 5% to the vendor. On the same date, it took loan from the Bank for Rs.1,00,000 and issued 8% debentures as Collateral Securities. Record the relevant journal entries in the books of Devi Ltd. and prepare the extract of balance sheet on 31.03.2017. Ignore interest.

Ans.

In the books of Devi Ltd.

JOURNAL ENTRIES

Date	Particulars		L.F.	Dr. (Rs.)	Cr. (Rs.)
2016	Bank A/c	Dr.		1,100,000	
April 01	To Debenture Application and Allotment A/c				1,100,000
	(For application money received on 10,000 8% debentures @ Rs.100 each along with 10% premium)				
April 01	Debenture Application and Allotment A/c	Dr.		1,100,000	
	To 8% Debentures A/c				1,000,000
	To Securities Premium Reserve A/c				1,00,000
	(For application money accepted and transferred to debentures and securities premium reserve)				
April 01	Sundry Assets A/c	Dr.		2,50,000	
	To Sundry Liabilities A/c				60,000
	To Vendor A/c				1,90,000
	(For sundry assets and liabilities taken over)				
	Vendor A/c	Dr.		1,90,000	
	Discount on Issue of 8% Debentures A/c	Dr.		10,000	
	To 8% Debentures A/c (2,000 (d) x Rs.100)				2,00,000
	(For 2,000 debentures issued at 5% discount)				
	[Number of debentures issued = Rs.1,90,000/Rs.95				
	= 2000 debentures]				
April 01	Bank A/c	Dr.		1,00,000	
	To Bank Loan A/c				100,000
	(For loan taken from Bank)				
	Debentures Suspense A/c	Dr.		1,00,000	
	To 8% Debentures A/c				1,00,000
	(For 10,000, 8% debentures of Rs.100 each issued as collateral security)				
	Securities Premium Reserve A/c	Dr.		10,000	
	To Discount on issue of Debenture A/c				10,000
	(For discount on issue of debenture written off)				

BALANCE SHEET OF DEVI LTD.

as at 31st March 2017

Particulars	Note No.	Amount (Rs.)
I. EQUITY AND LIABILITIES		
Shareholder's Funds:		
Reserve and Surplus	1	90,000
Non-current Liabilities:		
Long-term Borrowings	2	1,300,000
Current Liabilities		
Trade Payables		60,000
Total		1,450,000
II. ASSETS		
Non-current Assets:		
Fixed Assets		250,000
Current Assets		
Cash and Cash Equivalents (Bank)		1,200,000
Total		1,450,000

Note to Accounts:

Sr. No.	Particulars		(Rs.)
1	Reserves and Surplus:		
	Securities Premium Reserve	1,00,000	
	Less: Discount on Issue of Debentures	10,000	90,000
2	Long-term Borrowings		
	Bank Loan	1,00,000	
	8% Debentures		
	Issued to Public: 10,000 Debentures of Rs.100 each	1,000,000	
	Issued to Vendors: 2,000, 8% Debentures of Rs.100 each	2,00,000	1,300,000
	Issued to Bank as collateral security: 10,000, 8%		
	Debentures of Rs.100 each	(1,00,000)	Nil
	Less: Debentures Suspense A/c	1,00,000	1,300,000

TOPIC 3 Interest on Debentures, Write off Discount/Loss on Issue of Debentures

Summary

Interest on Debentures: Interest on debentures is a charge against the profits of the company and is payable irrespective of the fact whether there are profits or not. It is calculated on the face value of the debenture. According to Income-tax Act, 1961, the company must deduct income tax at the prescribed rate from the gross amount of interest payable on debenture before the annual amount is paid to debenture holders. Accounting Treatment:

1. For Interest due

    Debentures Interest A/c   Dr.   [With the amount of Gross Interest]

    To Income Tax Payable A/c   [With the tax deducted at source]

    To Dependent holder A/c   [with the interest payable to debenture holder]

2. For Payment of Interest

    Debenture holder A/c Dr.

    To Bank A/c

3. On Closing of Debenture Interest A/c

    Profit and Loss A/c Dr.

    To Debenture Interest A/c

4. For Payment of Income Tax to Government

    Income Tax Payable A/c Dr.

    To Bank A/c

Writing off Discount/Loss on Issue of Debentures: The discount/ loss on the issue of debentures is a capital loss and therefore must be written off during the lifetime of debentures. The discount/loss on the issue of debentures is shown under the head "Miscellaneous Expenditure" on the assets side of the Balance Sheet. Section 78 of the Companies Act, 1956 permits the utilization of Securities Premium for writing off the discount/loss on the issue of the debenture.

Entry is following:

Security Premium A/c Dr.

To Discount/Loss on Issue of Debenture A/c

In case there are no capital profits or if the capital profits are not adequate, the amount of such discount/loss can be written off by utilizing the revenue profits.

There are two methods, which can be used to write off the Discount/Loss on the issue of debentures:

(a) **Fixed Installment Method:** When the debentures are redeemed at the end of a specified period, the total amount of discount should be written off in equal installments of a fixed amount over the period.

(b) **Fluctuating Installment Method:** When debentures are repaid by annual drawings or installments, the discount is written off in the ratio of debentures outstanding before redemption. The amount of discount, in this method, goes on reducing every year as a greater amount is used in the initial years than the later years. This method is also known as the Reducing Instalment Method.

Multiple Choice Questions   [1 Mark]

Q.1. When debentures are issued at par and redeemable and premium the loss on such an issue is debited to:

(a) Profit and loss account

(b) Debenture application and allotment account

(c) Loss on issue of debentures account

(d) Discount on issue of debentures account

Ans. (c)

Q.2. When debentures are issued at discount and redeemable at a premium which one of the following account is debited at the time of issue?

(a) Debentures account

(b) Premium on redemption of debentures account

(c) Loss on issue of debentures account

(d) None of these

Ans. (c)

Q.3. XYZ limited issued 4000, 12% debentures of Rs100 each at a premium of 5% the total amount of interest for one year will be:

(a) 48,000   (b) 58,000   (c) 50,000   (d) 50,400

Ans. (a)

Q.4. ABC limited issues 10,000 9% debentures of 100 each at a premium of 5% payable at a premium of 10%, the loss on issue of debentures account will be debited to by:

(a) Rs.10,00,000   (b) Rs.1,00,000   (c) Rs.10,50,000   (d) Rs.1,05,000

Ans. (b)

Q.5. Interest on debenture is calculated on:

(a) Its face value   (b) Its issue price   (c) Its book value   (d) Its cost price

Ans. (a)

Q.6. 10% debenture issued at Rs105 is repayable at Rs110, the face value of debenture being Rs100. Calculate the amount of loss on redemption of debentures:

(a) 10   (b) 5   (c) 15   (d) 25

Ans. (a)

Q.7. Debenture interest: [CBSE 2009]

(a) Is payable only in case of profits

(b) Accumulates in case of losses are inadequate profits

(c) Is payable irrespective of profit or loss

(d) None of the above

Ans. (c)

Q.8. If debentures are issued at par and redeemed at a premium then which account will be debited by the amount of premium on debentures.   [CBSE 2013]

(a) Discount on issue of debentures

(c) Premium on redemption of debentures

(c) Profit and loss account

(d) Loss on issue of debentures

Ans. (d)

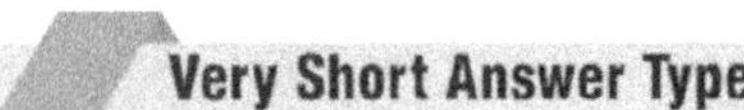

[1 Mark]

Fill in the blanks:

Q.9. Interest on debentures is paid on the ______________ of Debentures.

Ans. Face value

Q.10. ______________ is the rate at which interest is payable on Debentures.

Ans. coupon rate

Q.11. If X ltd issued 1,000; 10% Debentures of Rs.100 each at a discount of 5% but redeemable after 4 years at a premium of 6%, loss on issue of Debentures a/c will be debited by ______________.

Ans. Rs.11,000

Q.12. Alfa Ltd. issued 20,000, 8% debentures of Rs.10 each at par. The debentures are redeemable at a premium of 20% after 5 years. The amount of loss on redemption of debentures should be:

[CBSE COMPARTMENT 2016]

Ans. Rs.40,000

Q.13. Discount or loss on issue of debentures is a ______________

Ans. Capital loss

Assertion Reason Type Questions

Q.14. Assertion (A): Interest on debentures must be paid irrespective of profit or loss

Reason (R): Interest on debenture is a charge against the profit of the company.

(a) Both Assertion (A) and Reason (R) are true and reason is correct explanation of assertion.

(b) Assertion (A) and Reason (R) both are true but reason is not the correct explanation of assertion.

(c) Assertion (A) is true, Reason (R) is false.

(d) Assertion (A) is false, Reason (R) is true.

Ans. a

Q.15. Assertion (A): Discount or loss on issue of debentures must be written off before such debentures are redeemed.

Reason (R): Discount or loss on issue of debenture is a capital loss.

(a) Both Assertion (A) and Reason (R) are true and reason is correct explanation of assertion.

(b) Assertion (A) and Reason (R) both are true but reason is not the correct explanation of assertion.

(c) Assertion (A) is true, Reason (R) is false.

(d) Assertion (A) is false, Reason (R) is true.

Ans. b

Q.16. Assertion (A): a debenture holder is entitled to interest at the fixed rate.

Reason (R): interest payable on debentures is transferred to general reserve.

(a) Both Assertion (A) and Reason (R) are true and reason is correct explanation of assertion.

(b) Assertion (A) and Reason (R) both are true but reason is not the correct explanation of assertion.

(c) Assertion (A) is true, Reason (R) is false.

(d) Assertion (A) is false, Reason (R) is true.

Ans. c

Q.17. Assertion (A): If debentures of Rs.100, issued for Rs.95 and is redeemable at 105, then loss on issue debentures will be Rs.10

Reason (R): Both on discount of issue and premium on redemption are capital losses and combined into one account

(a) Both A and R are individually true, and R is correct explanation of A

(b) Both A and R are individually true, and R is not the correct explanation of A.

(c) A is true but R is False.

(d) Both A and R are False.

Ans. a

Q.18. Assertion (A): If debentures of Rs.100, issued for Rs.95 and is redeemable at 105, then loss on issue debentures will be Rs.5

Reason (R): Premium on redemption of debentures is not capital loss.

(a) Both A and R are individually true, and R is correct explanation of A

(b) Both A and R are individually true, and R is not the correct explanation of A

(c) A is true but R is False.

(d) Both A and R are False.

Ans. d

Q.19. Assertion (A): Balance in debenture interest accounts transferred to statement of profit and loss at end of the year.

Reason (R): Interest on debentures is a charge against profit earned by the company

(a) Both A and R are individually true, and R is correct explanation of A

(b) Both A and R are individually true, and R is not the correct explanation of A

(c) A is true but R is False.

(d) Both A and R are False.

Ans. (a)

Q.20. Assertion (A): XYZ Ltd. Issued 10,000, 10% debentures of Rs. 100 each. During the first year of issue the company suffers a huge loss. Therefore, the payment on debentures on due date, the company obtained a loan from bank.

Reason (R): If profit not available for payment of interest on debentures, the company repay the interest by taking loan only

(a) Both A and R are individually true, and R is correct explanation of A

(b) Both A and R are individually true, and R is not the correct explanation of A.

(c) A is true but R is False.

(d) Both A and R are False.

Ans. (a)

Q.21. Assertion (A): Sarita Pvt. Ltd. issued 15% 10,000 debentures at par @ Rs. 100 per debenture. The company suffered a loss but still the directors of the company paid interest on debentures.

Reason (R): Interest on debenture is a charge against profits and therefore, its payment is not subject to the earning of profit.

(a) Both Assertion (A) and Reason (R) are true and reason is correct explanation of assertion.

(b) Assertion (A) and Reason (R) both are true but reason is not the correct explanation of assertion.

(c) Assertion (A) is true, Reason (R) is false.

(d) Assertion (A) is false, Reason (R) is true.

Ans. (a)

Q.22. Assertion (A): The 'discount on debentures' issuance is charged to 'Securities Premium Account' and is reflected as an asset.

Reason (R): The 'discount on debentures' issuance is noted as a capital loss side as a fictitious asset. Hence, has to be written off during the years of its issue.

(a) Both Assertion (A) and Reason (R) are true and reason is correct explanation of assertion.

(b) Assertion (A) and Reason (R) both are true but reason is not the correct explanation of assertion.

(c) Assertion (A) is true, Reason (R) is false.

(d) Assertion (A) is false, Reason (R) is true.

Ans. (c)

Q.23. Assertion (A): Discount or loss on issue of debentures is written off from securities premium reserve or capital reserve.

Reason (R) It is a capital loss so it must be written off, first from capital profit.

(a) Both Assertion (A) and Reason (R) are true and reason is correct explanation of assertion.

(b) Assertion (A) and Reason (R) both are true but reason is not the correct explanation of assertion.

(c) Assertion (A) is true, Reason (R) is false.

(d) Assertion (A) is false, Reason (R) is true.

Ans. a

Q.24. Assertion (A): Interest on debenture must be paid whether the company has earned any profit or not

Reason (R): Interest on debenture is an appropriation of profit of the company.

(a) Both Assertion (A) and Reason (R) are true and reason is correct explanation of assertion.

(b) Assertion (A) and Reason (R) both are true but reason is not the correct explanation of assertion.

(c) Assertion (A) is true, Reason (R) is false.

(d) Assertion (A) is false, Reason (R) is true.

Ans. d

Q.25. Assertion (A): Sarita private limited issued 15% 10000 at par @ Rs.100 per debenture. The company suffered a loss but still the director of company paid interest on debentures

Reason (R): Interest on debenture is a charge against profit and therefore its payment is not subject to earning of profit.

(a) Both Assertion (A) and Reason (R) are true and reason is correct explanation of assertion.

(b) Assertion (A) and Reason (R) both are true but reason is not the correct explanation of assertion.

(c) Assertion (A) is true, Reason (R) is false.

(d) Assertion (A) is false, Reason (R) is true.

Ans. (a)

Q.26. Assertion (A): The discount on debentures issuance is charge to security premium account and is reflected as an asset.

Reason (R): The discount on debenture issue of debenture is noted as a capital loss hence has to be written off during the year of its issue.

(a) Both Assertion (A) and Reason (R) are true and reason is correct explanation of assertion.

(b) Assertion (A) and Reason (R) both are true but reason is not the correct explanation of assertion.

(c) Assertion (A) is true, Reason (R) is false.

(d) Assertion (A) is false, Reason (R) is true.

Ans. (d)

Short Answer Type - I [2 Marks]

Q.27. Explain treatment of interest on debentures. [CBSE 2015]

Ans. Interest on Debentures is calculated at a fixed rate on its face value and is usually payable half yearly. Interest on debentures is to be paid even company is suffering from loss because it is charge against profit. Income Tax is deducted from interest before payment to debenture holders. It is called T.D.S. (Tax deducted at source).

JOURNAL ENTRIES

1. Debenture's Interest A/c Dr. (Gross Interest)

    To Debenture holder A/c (Net interest)

    To Income Tax Payable A/c (Income Tax deducted)

2. When interest is paid

    Debenture holder A/c Dr. (With Interest)

    To Bank A/c

3. On payment of Income Tax to Government

    Income Tax Payable A/c Dr.

    To Bank A/c

4. On transfer of Interest on debentures to Statement of Profit and Loss

    Statement of Profit & Loss A/c Dr.

    To Debenture Interest A/c

Q.28. Describe Writing off Discount or Loss on issue of Debentures.   **[CBSE SAMPLE PAPER]**

Ans. Discount or Loss on issue of Debentures, being Loss for a company, is to be written off by the company as early as possible but within the tenure of the debentures. Discount or Loss on issue of Debentures should be written off by a company by using write of the entire discount or loss in the same year itself as finance cost (As per AS-16)

Short Answer Type - II   [3 Marks]

Read the passage given below and answer questions.

29. X Ltd. was in need of short term requirement of funds. And there was depression in the Capital market. Mr.Y the finance manager wanted to issue shares. But Z Sr. manager finance advised him in place of issuing equity share, they should issue debentures. Due to Capital market conditions. So company issued 10,000, 8% Debentures of Rs.100 each at a discount of 10% and redeemable at a premium of Rs.10 per share amount was payable in along with application. Debenture Applications received were for 11,000, 8% Debentures.

    1. State the amount of loss on issue of Debentures

        (a) Rs.1,00,000   (b) Rs. 2,00,000   (c) Rs.1,50,000   (d) Rs. 50,000

Ans. (b)

    2. What type of securities investors prefer during depression

        (a) Preference Shares (b) Equity Shares   (c) Debentures   (d) None of the above

Ans. (c)

    3. Name the account from which loss on issue of debentures will be written off

        (a) Statement of Profit and Loss   (b) Capital Reserve Account

        (c) Securities Premium Reserve Account   (d) All of the above

Ans. d

Long Answer Type   [5 Marks]

Q.30. Read the cases and answer the following questions   **[CBSE 2012]**

    Consider the following cases:

    (i) Issued 2000, 12% debentures of Rs 100 each at a discount of 2%, redeemable at par

    (ii) Issued 2000, 12% debentures of Rs 100 each at par but redeemable at 5% premium

    (iii) Issued 2000, 12% debentures of Rs 100 each at a discount of 2%, redeemable at a premium of 5%

    (iv) Issued 2000, 12% debentures of Rs 100 each at a premium of 5%, redeemable at a premium of 10%

    1. What is the amount debited to bank at the time of issue (case i)?

        (a) 200000   (b) 198000   (c) 197000   (d) 196000

Ans. (d)

    2. The amount debited to "Loss on issue of debentures a/c" in case ii……….

        (a) 10000   (b) 5000   (c) 15000   (d) 20000

Ans. (a)

3. The amount debited to "Loss on issue of debentures a/c" in case iii…….

    (a) 10000   (b) 12000   (c) 14000   (d) 16000

Ans. (c)

4. The amount debited to "Loss on issue of debentures a/c" in case iv………

    (a) 5000   (b) 10000   (c) 15000   (d) 20000

Ans. (d)

Read the passage given below and answer the following questions.

Q.31. A company issued debentures of the face value Rs 10,00,000 at a discount of 6% on 1st April 2012. These debentures are redeemable by annual drawings of Rs 2,00,000 made on 31st march each year. The directors decided to write off discount based on debentures outstanding each year.

1. Amount of discount to be written off on 31st march 2013

    (a) 20000   (b) 15000   (c) 25000   (d) 10000

Ans. (a)

2. Amount of discount to be written off on 31st march 2014

    (a) 12000   (b) 14000   (c) 16000   (d) 18000

Ans. (c)

3. Amount of discount to be written off on 31st march 2015

    (a) 8000   (b) 10000   (c) 12000   (d) 14000

Ans. (c)

4. Amount of discount to be written off on 31st march 2016

    (a) 5000   (b) 6000   (c) 7000   (d) 8000

Ans. (d)

Q.32. On 01.04.2016, Arora Ltd. issued Rs.20,00,000, 6% debentures of Rs.100 each at a discount of 4%, redeemable at a premium of 5% after three years. The amount was payable as follows:

On application Rs.50 per debenture,

Balance on allotment.

Record the necessary journal entries for issue of debentures.   **[CBSE 2015]**

Ans.   **JOURNAL ENTRIES OF ARORA LTD.**

Date	Particulars		L.F.	Dr. (Rs.)	Cr. (Rs.)
	Bank A/c	Dr.		1,000,000	
	To Debenture Application A/c				1,000,000
	(For application money received on 20,000, 6% debentures @ Rs.50 each)				
	Debenture Application A/c	Dr.		1,000,000	
	To 6% Debentures A/c				1,000,000
	(For application accepted and debentures issued)				
	Debentures Allotment A/c	Dr.		9,20,000	

Loss on Issue of Debentures A/c	Dr.	1,80,000	
To 6% Debentures A/c			1,000,000
To Premium on Redemption of Debentures A/c			1,00,000
(For allotment money due issued of discount and re-payable at premium)			
Bank A/c	Dr.	9,20,000	
To Debentures Allotment A/c			9,20,000
(For allotment money received)			

TOPIC 4 Redemption of Debentures

Summary

Redemption of Debentures: Redemption of debentures means repayment of the loan due on debentures to debenture holders. According to Section 117 C (3) of the Companies Act 1956, the debentures should be redeemed in accordance with the terms and conditions of their issue/offer documents. The date, the terms, and the conditions are generally stated in the debenture certificate itself or in the trust deed.

On the due date or happening of the circumstances so specified, the company becomes liable to pay the principal amount to the debenture holder. A company may purchase its own debenture which then stands cancelled

Redemption of Debentures: Redemption of debentures means repayment of the loan due on debentures to debenture holders. According to Section 117 C (3) of the Companies Act 1956, the debentures should be redeemed in accordance with the terms and conditions of their issue/ offer documents. The date, the terms, and the conditions are generally stated in the debenture certificate itself or in the trust deed.

On the due date or happening of the circumstances so specified, the company becomes liable to pay the principal amount to the debenture holder. A company may purchase its own debenture which then stands cancelled.

Methods of the Redemption of Debentures: The various methods of redemption of debentures are as under:

1. Payment in Lump-Sum

2. Payment in Instalments

3. Purchase in Open Market

4. Conversion of existing Debenture into Shares or New Debentures.

1. **Payment in Lump Sum:** It means debentures can be redeemed by paying the debenture holders in one lump sum at the expiry of the agreed time or earlier at the option of the company. In this case, the time of repayment is known in advance and thus the company can plan its financial resources accordingly.

2. **Payment in Instalments:** It means the redemption is made in annual installments. The amount of installment is worked out by dividing the total amount of debentures by the number of years it is to last. The number of debentures to be redeemed each year are selected by lottery. Thus, it is also known as drawing by lottery or draw of lots.

3. **Purchase in Open Market:** A company, if authorized by its Articles of Association, can purchase its own debenture in the open market. Debentures so purchased may be canceled and it means the debentures have been paid.

4. **Conversion of Existing Debentures into Shares or New Debentures:** It means the debenture holder can exchange their debenture either for shares or new debentures of the company and the debentures which carry such right are called convertible debentures.

Sources of funds for Redemption of Debentures: The redemption of debentures can be done either out of capital or out of profits.

(a) **Redemption of Debenture out of Capital:** In this case, profits of the company are not utilized for the redemption of debentures, so the assets of the company are reduced by the amount paid. Normally the profits are transferred to Debenture Redemption Reserve for redemption. In case no profits have been transferred to Debenture Redemption Reserve and debentures are redeemed on the due date, it is regarded as redemption out of the capital. It is, however, presumed that the company has adequate funds to redeem the debentures.

Accounting Treatment:

(a) If debentures are to be redeemed at par

    1. On debentures becoming due

       Debentures A/c Dr.

       To Debenture- holder A/c

    2. On Redemption Debenture holder A/c Dr.

       To Bank A/c

(b) If debentures are to be redeemed at a premium

    1. On debentures becoming due

       Debentures A/c Dr.

       Premium on Redemption of

       Debenture A/c Dr.

       To Debentureholder A/c

    2. On Redemption Debentureholder A/c Dr.

       To Bank A/c

(b) **Redemption of Debentures out of Profits:** Redemption of debentures out of profits means the amount equal to that utilized for repayment to debenture holders is transferred from Profit and Loss Appropriation A/c to a newly opened A/c called 'Debenture Redemption Reserve A/c' (DRR). The portion of the profits set aside may either be retained in the business or maybe invested.

Clarifications regarding Debenture Redemption Reserve:

The Department of Company Affairs, Government of India, vide their circular No. 9/2002, dates 18.04.2002 has issued the following clarifications regarding the creation of Debenture Redemption Reserve (DRR):

(a) No DRR is required for debentures issued by All India Financial Institutions, by RBI and, Banking Companies for both public as well as privately placed debentures.

(b) No DRR is required in case of privately placed debentures.

(c) Section 117c will apply to debentures issued and pending to be redeemed and, therefore, DRR will also be created for debentures issued prior to 13.12.2000 and pending redemption.

(d) Section 117c will apply to the non-convertible portion of debentures issued whether they are fully or partly paid.

Journal Entries:

1. Debenture A/c To Debenture holders A/c

2. Debenture holder A/c To Bank A/c

3. Profit and Loss Appropriation A/c To Debenture Redemption Reserve A/c

Redemption Of Debentures

DRR A/c appears on the liability side of the Balance Sheet, under the head "Reserves and Surplus". The balance in DRR A/c increases with each redemption. When all the debentures are redeemed, the DRR A/c is closed by transferring its balance to General Reserve A/c.

Redemption by Purchase in the Open Market: A company, if authorized by its Articles of Association, can redeem its own debenture by purchasing them in the open market.

If a company purchases its own debenture for the purpose of immediate cancellation, the purchase and cancellation of such debenture are called, redemption by purchase in the open market.

Accounting Treatment:

(In case of Profits)

(a) On purchase of own debentures for immediate cancellation.

   Debenture A/c Dr.

   To Bank A/c

   To Profit on Cancellation of Debenture A/c

(b) On transfer of Profit on Redemption

   Profit on Cancellation of Debenture A/c Dr.

   To Capital Reserve A/c

   (In case of Loss)

(a) On purchase of own debenture for immediate cancellation.

   Debenture A/c Dr.

   Loss on Cancellation

   of Debenture A/c Dr.

   To Bank A/c

(b) On transfer of Loss on Redemption

   Profit and Loss A/c Dr.

   To Loss on Cancellation of Debenture A/c

Redemption by Conversion: Sometimes, at the time of issue of debentures, a company gives the convertible debenture holders the privilege that they can get their debentures converted into shares or new debentures after the expiry of a specified period. Whenever debenture is redeemed by conversion, the debenture holders have to.; apply for the same. The new shares or debentures may be issued at par, discount, or a premium.

No DRR is required in case of convertible debentures because no funds are required for redemption.

If debentures to be converted were issued at discount, the issue price of the share must be equal to the amount actually received from debentures. If this rule is not followed, it would be a violation of section 79 of the Companies Act, 1956.

Accounting Treatment:

(i) For the amount due to debenture holders

1.

   (a) If Redemption at par

   Debentures A/c Dr.

   To Debentureholder A/c

    Or

    If Redemption at a premium

    Debentures A/c Dr.

    Securities Premium A/c Dr.

    To Debentureholder A/c

(b) For discharging obligation by issuing shares or debentures

    Debentureholder A/c Dr.

    To Equity Share Capital

        Or

    To Debentures A/c (New)

Sinking Fund Method: The amount required for the redemption of debentures is generally large and the date of redemption is known to the company. Thus, it is prudent for a company to make arrangements to ensure the availability of adequate funds for the redemption of debenture at the end of the stipulated period for which debentures are issued. Hence, it is better for the company to set aside every year a part of divisible profits and to invest the same outside the business in marketable securities.

Debenture Redemption Sinking Fund A/c will be created every year to provide means for the redemption of debentures. The company sets aside every year a certain sum of money out of its profits and invests the same along with the interest that may be earned on an investment. The investment is sold when debentures fall due for redemption. The amount available from the sale of investment is utilized for the redemption of debentures.

Accounting Treatment:

I.   At the end of First Year

  (a) For setting aside the amount out of Profit

    Profit & Loss Appropriation A/c Dr. [With the amount of profit set aside]

    To Debenture Redumption Fund A/c

  (b) For Investing the amount set aside

    Debenture Redumption Fund Dr. [With the amount of investment made]

    Investment A/c

    To Bank A/c

II.   At the end of the second year and subsequent years other than the last year.

  (a) For Receiving the Interest on Investments made

    Bank A/c   Dr. [With the amount

    To Interest on of interest received]

    Debentures

    Redumption Fund

    Investment A/c

  (b) For the transfer of Interest on Deb. Red. Fund Investment to DRF A/c

    The interest of Deb. Red

    Fund Investment A/c Dr.

    To Debenture Redemption Fund A/c

(c) For Setting aside the number of profits

Profit and Loss Dr. [With the amount

Appropriation A/c of Profit set aside]

To Debenture Redemption FundA/c

(d) For Investing the amount set aside along with interest received.

Deb. Red. Fund Investment A/c Dr.

ToBank A/c

III.   At the end of last year

(a)   For Receiving the Interest on Investment made

Bank A/c Dr.

To Interest on Deb. Red. Fund Investment A/c

(b)   For the transfer of Interest on Deb. Red. Fund Investment to DRF A/c

Interest in Deb. Red.

Fund Investment A/c Dr.

To Deb. Red. Fund A/c

(c)   For setting aside the number of profits

Profit & Loss

Appropriation A/c Dr.

To Deb. Red. Fund A/c

(d)   For Realising the Investment made

Bank A/c Dr. [With the sale

To Deb. Red. Fund proceeds]

Investment A / c

(e)   For the transfer of profit/loss on realization of Deb. ReRed. Fund Investments

In ase of profit

Deb. Red. Fund   Dr. [With the amount] of profit]

Investment A/c

To Deb. Red. Fund A/c

                        or

In case of Loss

Deb. Red. Fund A/c   Dr. [With the amount of Loss]

To Deb. Red. Fund

Investment A/c

(f) For the amount due to debenture holders

Debenture A/c Dr.

To Debentureholders A/c

(g) For redemption

Debenture holders A/c

To Bank A/c

(h) For the transfer of the balance, if any, Discount on Issue of Debentures A/c/Loss on Issue of Debenture A/c

Deb. Red. Fund. A/c Dr.

To Discount on Issue of Debentures A/c,

To Loss on Issue of Debentures A/c

1.   For the transfer of an amount from the Deb. Red. Fund A/c to General Reserve:

(a) If some of the Debentures are redeemed

Deb. Red. Fund A/c   Dr. [With the nominal value of Debentures redeemed]

To Deb. Red. Reserve

(b) If all the Debentures are redeemed

Deb. Red. Fund A/c   Dr. [With the balance

To General   Left in Deb. Red.

Reserve A/c   Fund A/c]

Multiple Choice Questions   [1 Mark]

Q.1. What is the nature of premium on redemption of debenture account

(a) Real account   (b) Nominal account   (c) Personal account   (d) None of the above

Ans. (c)

Q.2. If debentures of Rs. 50,000 are issued at par but redeemable at a premium of 10%. By what principle of accounting, the loss on issue of debentures account will be debited with Rs. 5,000 while passing the issue entry?

(a) Principle of Revenue recognition   (b) Principle of Materiality

(c) Principle of Conservatism/Prudence   (d) Principle of Full Disclosure

Ans. (c)

Q.3. X Ltd. has issued 10,000 6% debentures of Rs. 100 each. The company decided to redeem half of its debentures at 10% premium. There was a balance of Rs. 3,40,000 in Debenture redemption reserve. As per SEBI guidelines what amount still need to be transferred to Debenture redemption reserve account out of profits.

(a) Rs.6,60,000   (b) Rs.1,60,000   (c) Rs.5,50,000   (d) Rs.2,75,000

Ans. (b)

Q.4. The rules regarding transfer of DRR to general reserve is mentioned in

(a) Companies Ac 2013

(b) Rule 18(7) (c) of Companies Rule 2014

(c) Section 71(4) of Companies (Share Capital and Debentures) Rules, 2014

(d) All of the above

Ans. (a)

Q.5. Debenture redemption reserve is created

(a) Before redemption starts   (b) At the closure of previous accounting year

(c) Before 30th April of the current year   (d) All the above

Ans. (a)

Q.6. Premium on redemption of debentures is a   **[CBSE Compartment]**

(a) Liability account (b) Asset Account   (c) Expense Account   (d) None of these

Ans. (a)

Q.7. In case the question is silent, DRR is created on the nominal value of outstanding redeemable debentures to the extent of

(a) 25%   (b) 15%   (c) More than 25%   (d) Any of the above

Ans. (a)

Q.8. Debentures cannot be redeemed at

(a) Premium   (b) Discount   (c) More than 10% premium   (d) At Par

Ans. (b)

Q.9. If debentures are issued at par and redeemed at a premium then which account will be debited by the amount of premium on debentures.

(a) Discount on issue of debentures   (b) Premium on redemption of debentures

(c) Profit and loss account   (d) Loss on issue of debentures

Ans. (d)

Q.10. The provisions of the Companies Act 2013 in respect of redemption of debentures are to protect the interest of

(a) Debenture holders   (b) Creditors

(c) Share holders   (d) Bankers

Ans. a

Q.11. Best Company Ltd decides to redeem 10000, 10% debentures of Rs.100 each on 30th June 2018. The Company shall invest in specified securities on or before

(a) 30th April 2017   (b) 30th April 2016   (c) 30th June 2017   (d) 30th April 2018

Ans. (d)

Q.12. Amount is set aside to Debenture redemption reserve (DRR) by   **[CBSE 2018]**

(a) All the Companies

(b) All companies except banking companies

(c) All Companies except All India Financial Institutions

(d) All Companies except Banking Company and all India Financial Institutions regulated by RBI

Ans. (d)

Q.13. Amount is not set aside to Debenture redemption reserve if

    (a) The debentures are not convertible

    (b) The debentures are partly convertible

    (c) The debentures are fully convertible.

    (d) None of these

Ans. (c)

Q.14. Premium payable on redemption of debentures is in the nature of

    (a) Liability Account   (b) Asset Account

    (c) Expense Account   (d) None of these

Ans. a

Q.15. Once the debentures are redeemed, amount of debenture redemption reserve is transferred to **[CBSE 2011]**

    (a) Capital Reserve   (b) Balance in Profit and loss account

    (c) General Reserve   (d) Capital Redemption reserve

Ans. (a)

Q.16. G Limited has outstanding 10000 8% debentures of Rs.100 each that are redeemable at a premium of Rs.10. Out of these 5000 debentures are to be redeemed on 31st December 2018 Debenture redemption Investment should be

    (a) 75,000   (b) 82,500   (c) 1,50,000   (d) 1,65,000

Ans. (a)

Q.17. Global savings Bank is to redeem 40000 10% debentures of Rs.100 each on 31st December 2018.How much amount should it invest in specified securities?

    (a) 6,00,000   (b) 10,00,000   (c) 5,00,000   (d) Nil

Ans. d

Q.18. H Limited has outstanding 10,000, 8% debentures of Rs.100 each that are redeemable at a premium of Rs.10 each. Out of these 5000 debentures are to be redeemed on 31st December 2018. Denture redemption investment should be

    (a) 75,000   (b) 82,500   (c) 1,50,000   (d) 1,65,000

Ans. a

Q.19. Amount is not invested in debenture redemption Investment if   **[CBSE Sample paper]**

    (a) Debentures are not convertible

    (b) The debentures are partly convertible

    (c) The debentures are fully convertible

    (d) None of the above

Ans. (c)

Very Short Answer Type   [1 Mark]

Fill in the Blanks

Q.20. Debentures are redeemed setting aside 25% of the nominal value of debentures to Debenture Redemption Reserve.It is redemption out of _______________

Ans. Profit and Capital

Q.21. Amount to be set aside to ___________before redemption of debentures.

Ans. DRR

Q.22. Debenture Redemption Investment should be made _____________30th April of the year in which debentures re redeemed.

Ans. On or before

Q.23. Discount or loss on issue of debentures is a _______________

Ans. Capital loss

Q.24. Once the debentures re redeemed, amount of DRR is transferred to _____________

Ans. General Reserve

State True of False

Q.25. Debenture Redemption Investment is made by companies required to set aside amount to Debenture redemption Reserve.

Ans. True

Q.26. Debenture redemption reserve may be set aside by a company out of any reserve.

Ans. False

Q.27. Surplus cannot be transferred to Debenture Redemption Reserve.

Ans. False

Q.28. Debenture Redemption Investment can be used by the Company for any purpose after the debentures have been redeemed.   **[CBSE 2009 Compartment]**

Ans. True

Q.29. General Reserve can be transferred to Debenture Redemption Reserve.

Ans. True

Q.30. **Assertion (A):** Debentures are redeemable.

   Reason (R): It is a type of liability which must be minimized.

   (a) Both Assertion (A) and Reason (R) are true and reason is correct explanation of assertion.

   (b) Assertion (A) and Reason (R) both are true but reason is not the correct explanation of assertion.

   (c) Assertion (A) is true, Reason (R) is false.

   (d) Assertion (A) is false, Reason (R) is true.

Ans. (b)

Q.31. Assertion (A): X ltd. Issued 10,000 12% debentures of Rs.100 at a premium of Rs.20 per debentures for 5 years. At least Rs.2,00,000 must be invested in DRI before redemption of these debentures.

Reason (R): As per SEBI regulations an amount equal to 15% of debentures to be redeemed must be invested in DRI before redemption of these debentures.

(a) Both Assertion (A) and Reason (R) are true and reason is correct explanation of assertion.

(b) Assertion (A) and Reason (R) both are true but reason is not the correct explanation of assertion.

(c) Assertion (A) is true, Reason (R) is false.

(d) Assertion (A) is false, Reason (R) is true.

Ans. (b)

Short Answer Type - I   [2 Marks]

Q.32. Write the Meaning of Redemption of debentures.

Ans. Redemption of debentures means repayment of the due amount of debentures to the debenture holders. It may be at par or at premium. Time of Redemption (a) At maturity: - When repayment is made at the date of maturity of debentures which is determined at the time of issue of debentures. (b) Before maturity: If articles of association and terms of issue mentioned in prospectus allows, then a company can redeem its debentures before maturity date.

Q.33. Explain methods of redemption of debentures.   [CBSE 2019]

Ans. Redemption Methods

(1) **Redemption in Lump-sum:** When redemption is made at the expiry of a specific period, as per the terms of issue.

(2) **Redemption by draw of lots**: In this method a certain proportion of debentures are redeemed each year, the debenture for which repayment is to be made is selected by draw of lots. Sometimes company purchase's the debentures at more than the redeemable value due to the following reasons: 1. To maintain the solvency ratio. 2. To utilize the surplus money or funds which are lying idle with the company. 3. When rate of interest on debentures is more than the current market rate of interest on debentures in the industry.

Q.34. Explain sources of redemption of debentures.   [CBSE 2017]

Ans. Sources of Redemption of Debentures

1. Proceeds from fresh issue of Share Capital or Debentures.

2. From accumulated profit.

3. Proceeds from sale of fixed assets.

4. A company may purchase its own debentures out of its surplus funds.

Q.35. Explain Redemption out of capital and out of profit.   [CBSE 2010, 2016]

Ans. 1. Redemption out of capital

When a company has not used its reserve or accumulated profit for redemption of its debentures, it is called redemption out of capital, So company using this method have not transferred its profit to DRR A/c. But as per Companies Act, 2013 it is necessary for a company to transfer 25% amount of nominal value of debentures to be redeemed in DRR A/c before redemption of debentures commences.

2. Redemption out of profit

Redemption out of profit means that adequate amount of profits are transferred to DRR A/c from Balance in Statement of Profit & Loss A/c before the redemption of debenture commences. This reduces the amount available for dividends to shareholders.

Debenture Redemption Reserve (DRR): Section 71 (4) of the Companies Act, 2013 requires the company to create DRR out of the profits available for dividend and the amount credited in DRR shall not be utilizes for any purpose except redemption. Rule 18(7) of Companies (Share Capital and Debentures) Rules, 2014 requires every Company to create DRR of an amount equal to 25% of the value of outstanding debentures. Exemption to Create DRR a) NBfc registered with RBI b) All India financial institutions (AIfs) regulated by RBI and Banking companies (for both public as well as privately placed debentures) c) Financial institutions other than All India finance Companies registered with RBI d) Housing finance Companies registered with National Housing Bank. DRR is required for publicly issued debentures by the above three classes of companies, not for privately placed. e) Any other Company (Whether listed or unlisted), DRR to be created for Public and Private placed debentures. Debenture Redemption Investment

As per Rule 18(7)(c), every company required to create/maintain DRR shall invest or deposit before 30th April in specified securities a sum which shall not be less than 15% of the amount of debentures maturing for payment during the year ending 31st March of the next year. Specified securities for Debenture Redemption Investment 1. In deposits with any scheduled bank, free from any charge or lien. 2. In unencumbered securities of central or any state Government. 3. In unencumbered securities mentioned in clause (a) to (d) and (ee) of section 20 of Indian Trusts Act, 1882. 4. In unencumbered bonds issued by a company which is notified under sec 20 (f) of Indian Trust Act, 1882.

Short Answer Type - II　　　　　　　　　　　　　　　　　　　　[3 Marks]

Q.36. Read the passage given below and answer questions.

Career Launcher Ltd issued 15,000 11% debentures of Rs.200 each at premium of 25% on 1 November 2018 redeemable after 6 years on premium of Rs.10 each. Give the answer of following question.

1. What journal entry will be passed for receipt of amount of the above debentures?

    (a) Bank A/c　　　　　　　　　　　　　　Dr

        To 11% Debentures Application A/c

    (b) Bank A/c　　　　　　　　　　　　　　Dr

        To 11% Debenture Application & Allotment A/c

    (c) Debenture Application A/c　　　　　　Dr

        To Bank A/c

    (d) Bank A/c　　　　　　　　　　　　　　Dr

        To 11% Debenture Application & Allotment A/c

        To Security Premium Reserve A/c

Ans. (b)

2. Debentures are issued for in the above case:

    (a) Cash　　　　　　　　　　　　　　(b) Consideration other than cash

    (c) Collateral security　　　　　　　　(d) for conversion

Ans. (a)

3. How much amount will be debited on loss on issue of these debentures.

    (a) Rs.1,00,000/=   (b) Rs.1,50,000   (c) Rs.2,00,000/   (d) Rs.4,50,000

Ans. (d)

4. On which dates interest will be credited to debentures holders every year against these debentures?

    (a) 31st March and 31st December   (b) 30th April and 31st October

    (c) 30th June and 31st December   (d) 1st May and 1st November

Ans. (b)

Long Answer Type [5 Marks]

Q.37. Give journal entries for issue of debentures in each of the following cases of the following cases of the face value of a debenture is Rs.100. **[CBSE 2012,2018]**

    (i) 200, 9% debentures issued at 100 repayable at Rs.100.

    (ii) 200, 9% debentures issued at Rs.110 repayable at Rs.100.

    (iii) 200, 9% debentures issued at Rs.95 repayable at Rs.100.

    (iv) 200, 9% debentures issued at Rs.100 repayable at Rs.105.

    (v) 200, 9% debentures issued at Rs.98 redeemable at Rs.105.

    (vi) 200, 9% debentures issued at Rs.105 redeemable at Rs.107.

Ans.

JOURNAL ENTRIES FOR ISSUE

Date	Particulars		L.F.	Dr. (Rs.)	Cr. (Rs.)
(i)	Bank A/c	Dr.		20,000	
	To Debenture Application and Allotment A/c				20,000
	(For debenture application money received)				
	Debentures Application and Allotment A/c	Dr.		20,000	
	To 9% Debentures A/c				20,000
	(For debenture application money adjusted)				
(ii)	Bank A/c	Dr.		22,000	
	To Debenture Application and Allotment A/c				22,000
	(For debenture application money received including premium)				
	Debenture Application and Allotment A/c	Dr.		22,000	
	To 9% Debentures A/c				20,000
	To Securities Premium Reserve A/c				2,000
	(For debenture application money adjusted)				
(iii)	Bank A/c	Dr.		19,000	
	To Debenture Application and Allotment A/c				19,000
	(For debenture application money received excluding discount)				
	Debenture Application and Allotment A/c	Dr.		19,000	
	Discount on Issue of Debenture A/c	Dr.		1,000	
	To 9% Debentures A/c				20,000
	(For debenture application money adjusted)				

(iv)	Bank A/c	Dr.		20,000	
	To Debentures Application and Allotment A/c				20,000
	(For debenture application money received)				
	Debenture Application and Allotment A/c	Dr.		20,000	
	Loss on Issue of Debentures A/c	Dr.		1,000	
	To 9% Debentures A/c				20,000
	To Premium on Redemption of Debentures A/c				1,000
	(For debenture application money and premium on redemption adjusted)				
(v)	Bank A/c	Dr.		19,600	
	To Debenture Application and Allotment A/c				19,600
	(For debenture application money received)				
	Debenture Application and Allotment A/c	Dr.		19,600	
	Less on Issue of Debentures A/c (400 + 1,400)	Dr.		1,400	
	To 9% Debentures A/c				20,000
	To Premium on Redemption of Debentures A/c				1,000
	(For debenture application money, discount and premium on redemption adjusted)				
(vi)	Bank A/c	Dr.		21,000	
	To Debenture Application and Allotment A/c				21,000
	(For debenture application money received)				
	Debenture Application and Allotment A/c	Dr.		21,000	
	Loss on Issue of Debentures A/c	Dr.		1,400	
	To 9% Debentures A/c				20,00
	To Securities premium Reserve A/c				1,000
	To Premium on Redemption of Debentures A/c				1,400
	(For debenture application money and premium on redemption adjusted)				

Q.38. Pass necessary journal entries and prepare 9% Debentures Account for the issue of 7,500, 9% Debentures of Rs.50 each at a discount of 6%, redeemable at a premium of 10%.

Ans.

JOURNAL

Date	Particulars		L.F.	Dr. (Rs.)	Cr. (Rs.)
	Bank A/c	Dr.		3,52,500	
	To Debenture Application and Allotment A/c				3,52,500
	(For application money received for 7,500, 9% debentures @ Rs.50 each at a discount of 6%)				
	Debenture Application and Allotment A/c	Dr.		3,52,000	
	Loss on Issue of Debentures A/c	Dr.		60,000	
	To 9% debentures A/c				3,75,000
	To Premium on Redemption of Debentures A/c				37,500
	(For 7500, 9% debentures of Rs.50 each issued at a discount of 6% redeemable at a premium of 10%)				
	Statement of Profit and Loss A/c	Dr.		60,000	
	To Loss on issue of Debenture A/c				60,000
	(Being Loss on issue of debentures written off)				

Dr.   **9% Debentures A/c**   **Cr.**

Date	Particulars	Amount (Rs.)	Date	Particulars	Amount (Rs.)
	To Balance c/d	3,75,000		By Debentures Application and Allotment A/c	3,52,500
				By Loss on Issue of Debentures A/c	22,500
		3,75,000			**3,75,000**

Chapter Practice

Multiple Choice Questions   [1 Mark]

Q.1. Debentures which are transferable by mere delivery are :

    (a) Registered Debentures   (b) First Debentures

    (c) Bearer Debentures   (d) Second Debentures

Q.2. When debentures issued at par and are redeemable at a premiumthe loss on such an issued debited to

    (a) Profit & Loss A/c   (b) Debenture Allotment A/c

    (c) Loss on Issue of Debenture A/c   (d) Discount on Issue of Debentures A/c

Q.3. Lata Ltd .took over the assets of Rs.7,60,000 and liabilities of Rs. 80,000 of Krisna Ltd. for an agreed purchase consideration of Rs.5,85,000 payable by issue of 12% Debentures of Rs. 100 each at 10%discount. The number of debentures to be issued is :

    (a) Rs. 6,600   (b) Rs. 6,500   (c) Rs. 4,500   (d) Rs. 5,400

Q.4. Madhu Ltd. Issued 4,000 ,12% Debenture of Rs.100 each at a premium of 5% redeemable at a premium of 10% . The total amount of interest for one year will be :

    (a) 48,000   (b) 50,400   (c) 58,000   (c) 50,000

Q.5. A company can issue debentures

    (a) For Cash   (b) As a collateral Security

    (c) For Consideration other than cash   (d) Any of the above

Very Short Answer Type   [1 Mark]

Q.6. Give the meaning of 'Debentures'.

Q.7. What is meant by Bond ?

Q.8. How can a debenture be categorised from the point of view of security ?

Q.9. What is the maximum limit of discount on issue of debentures ?

Q.10. What is nature of Premium of Redemption of Debentures Account ?

Long Answer Type   [5 Marks]

Q.11. Explain meaning and any two points of difference between Equity shares and Debentures.

Q.12. Veena Prakashan ltdpurchased a running business of Vasudha oils for a sum of Rs. 12,00,000.

Veena Prakashan Ltd. paid Rs. 60,000 by drawing a bills Payable in favour of Vasudha Oils, Rs. 1,90,000 through Bank draft and balance by issue of 8% debentures of Rs. 100 each at a discount of 5%. The assets and liabilities of Vasudha ltd consisted of Fixed valued at Rs. 17,30,000 and Trade Payables at Rs.3,20,000

You are required to pass necessary journal entries in the books of Veena Prakashan Ltd.

Q.13. Abhiyank Ltd. Took a loan of Rs. 15,00,000 from State Bank Of India against the security of tangible assets. In addition to principal security, it issued 10,000 ,11% debentures of Rs. 100 each as collateral security.

Pass necessary journal entries for the above transactions ,if the company decided to record the issue of 11% debentures as collateral security and show the presentation in the Balance Sheet of Abhiyank Ltd.

Q.14. Priyank ?. Computer Ltd. Appointed marketing expert Mr. Shobhik as the C E O of the company, with a target to penetrate their roots in the rural regions. Mr. Shobhik discussed the ways and means to achievetarget of the company with financial, production and marketing departmental heads and asked the finance manager to prepare the budget. After reviewing the suggestions given by all the departmental heads, the finance manager proposed requirement of additional fund of Rs. 52,50,000. Priyank Ltd. Is a zero debt company. To avail the benefits of financial leverage ,the finance managerproposed to include debt in the capital structure. After deliberation, on April. 01.2022 the board of directors had decided to issue 6% Debentures of Rs.100 each to public at a premium of 5%, redeemableafter 5 years at Rs.110 pershare.

You are required to answer the following questions :

(a) Calculate the numbers of debentures to be issued to raise additional funds.

(b) Pass Journal entry for the allotment of debentures

(c) Pass Journal entry to write off loss on issue of debentures.

(d) Calculate the amount of annual fixed obligation associated with debentures.

(e) Prepare loss on issue of Debentures Account.

Q.15. Pass the necessary journal entries for 'Issue of Debenture' for the following :

(a) Rashi ltd. Issued 750. 12% Debentures of Rs. 100 each at a discount of 10% redeemable at a premium of 5%

(b) Bhavik Ltd issued 800, 9% debentures of Rs. 100 each at a premium of Rs. 20 per Debenture Redeemable at a premium of Rs. 10 per Debenture.

Q.16. On 01.04.2021, Soniya Ltd. Issued 500, 9% Debentures of Rs 50 each at a discount of 4% redeemable at a of5% after three years.

Pass necessary Journal entries for the issue of debentures and debenture interest for the year ended 31.03.2022. Assuming that interest is payable on 30 th September and 31st March and rate of tax deductedat sources (TDS) is 10%. The company closes its books on 31st March every year.

Q.17. On 01st April 2016, Manan Ltd. Issued Rs.1,00,000, 9 % Debentures at a Discount of 6%. These debentures are to be redeemable equally spreaded over 5annual instalments . Show Discount of Issue of DebenturesAccount for 5 years.

Q.18. Anshul Ltd.issued Rs. 10,00,000, 8% Debentures at a discount of 10 % on 01.04.2017, redeemable in 4 equal annual instalments starting from 31st March 2019. The securities Premium ReserveA/c shows a   balance of 30,000. Compute amount of discount to be written off each year andprepare Discount on Issue of debenture Account for 5 years

CHAPTER 8

Financial Statements of A Company

 Introduced

Summary

Terms Introduced in the Chapter

1. Financial Statements

2. Statement of profit and loss

3. Balance Sheet

Meaning of Financial Statements:

Financial statements are the basic and formal annual reports through which the corporate management communicates financial information to its owners and various other external parties which include investors, tax authorities, government, employees, etc.

OR

The statements which are prepared to ascertain the profit earned or loss suffered and position of assets and liabilities at a particular date are known as financial statements. These are the final product of accounting process.

Nature of Financial Statement:

1. **Recorded facts:** Financial statements are prepared on the basis of facts in the form of cost data recorded in accounting books. The original cost or historical cost is the basis of recording transactions. The figures of various accounts such as cash in hand, cash at bank, trade receivables, fixed assets, etc., are taken as per the figures recorded in the accounting books

2. **Accounting conventions:** Certain accounting conventions are followed while preparing financial statements. The convention of valuing inventory at cost or market price, whichever is lower, is followed. The valuing of assets at cost less depreciation principle for balance sheet purposes is followed. The convention of materiality is followed in dealing with small items like pencils, pens, postage stamps, etc. These items are treated as expenditure in the year in which they are purchased even though they are assets in nature

3. **Postulates:** Financial statements are prepared on certain basic assumptions (pre-requisites) known as postulates such as going concern postulate, money measurement postulate, realisation postulate, etc. Going concern postulate assumes that the enterprise is treated as a going concern and exists for a longer period of time. So the assets are shown on historical cost basis.

4. **Personal Judgements:** Under more than one circumstance, facts and figures presented through financial statements are based on personal opinion, estimates and judgements. The depreciation is provided taking into consideration the useful economic life of fixed assets.

Objective of financial statement

(i)   Financial statements provide the information about the earning capacity of the business.

(ii)   Financial statements provide the information about the economic resources and obligation of an enterprise.

(iii) Financial statements also provide the information about the cash flows.

(iv)   Financial statements supply the information useful for judging the management's ability to utilise the resources of business effectively.

(v)   Financial statements have to report the activities of the business organisation affecting the society, which is important in its social environment.

Users of Financial Statements

(i)   Owners including shareholders and investors

(ii)   Debenture holders and financial institutions (bankers)

(iii) Creditors

(iv)   Management

(v)   Employees

(vi)   Government, tax authorities and regulators

Limitations of financial Statements:

1.   Qualitative elements are ignored

2.   Historical records

3.   Price level changes are ignored

4.   Aggregate information

5.   Different accounting practices

6.   Historical records

Types of Financial Statements:

The financial statements generally include two statements:

i.   balance sheet and

ii.   statement of profit and loss

Balance sheet:

It may be defined as a statement of assets and liabilities of the company, at a particular date. It must exhibit a true and fair view of the financial position at the close of the year. It is prepared and presented in the form prescribed in Schedule III Part I of the Companies Act, 2013, and is broadly divided into two parts, (i) Equity and liabilities (ii) Assets.

Format of balance sheet(As per schedule vi)

Balance Sheet as at 31st March, 20...

Particulars	Note No.	Figure as at the end of current reporting period	Figure as at the end of previous reporting period
I. **Equity and Liabilities**			
1. Shareholder's Funds			
(a) Share Capital			
(b) Reserves and Surplus			
(c) Money received against share warrants			
2. Share Application money pending allotment			
3. Non-current Liabilities			
(a) Long term borrowings			
(b) Defered tax liabilities (net)			
(c) Other long term liabilities			
(d) Long term provisions			
4. Current Liabilities			
(a) Short-term borrowings			
(b) Trade payables			
(c) Other current liabilties			
(d) Short-term provisions			
Total			
II. **Assets**			
1. Non-Current Assets			
(a) Fixex Assets			
(i) Tangible assets			
(ii) Intangible assets			
(iii) Capital work-in-progress			
(iv) Intangible assets under development			
(b) Non-current investments			
(c) Deferred tax assets (net)			
(d) Long-term loans and advances			
(e) Other non-current assets			
2. Current Assets			
(a) Current investments			
(b) Inventories			
(c) Trade receivables			
(d) Cash and cash equivalents			
(e) Short term loans and advances			
(f) Other current assets			
Total			

1. **Shareholders Fund:** The shareholders' funds are sub-classified on the face of the balance sheet.

   (a) Share Capital

   (b) Reserves and Surplus

   (c) Money received against Share Warrants

2. **Share Capital:** Disclosures relating to share capital are to be given in notes to accounts

3. **Reserve and Surplus:**

   They can be classified as:

   (i) Capital Reserve

   (ii) Capital Redemption Reserve

   (iii) Securities Premium Reserve

   (iv) Debenture Redemption Reserve

   (v) Revaluation Reserve

   (vi) Share Options Outstanding Account

   (vii) Other Reserves (Specifying nature and purpose)

   (viii) Surplus: Balance in statement of profit and loss; disclosing allocations and Appropriation such as dividend, bonus shares, transfer to/from reserve, etc

4. **Money Received against share warrants:** It is the amount received by the company which are converted into shares at a specified date on a specified rate. The instrument issued against the amount so received as share warrants. Money received against share warrants' to be disclosed as a separate line item under 'shareholder's fund'.

5. **Current and Non-current Classification:** The classified balance sheet in terms of current and non-current assets and current and non-current liabilities have been introduced. Thecriteria for defining current assets and liabilities has been clearly spelled out with non-current assets and liabilities being the residual items.

   Current/Non-current distinction An item is classified as current:

   - if it is involved in entity's operating cycle or,

   - is expected to be realised/settled within twelve months or,

   - if it is held primarily for trading or,

   - is cash and cash equivalent or,

   - if entity does not have on unconditional rights to defer settlement of liability for atleast 12 months after the reporting period,

   - Other assets and liabilities are non-current

6. **Share application money pending allotment:** Share application money not exceeding the issued capital and to the extent non-refundable shall be classified as non-current. It will be shown on this face of balance sheet as share application money pending allotment.

7. **Borrowings:** Total borrowings are categorised into long-term borrowings, short-term borrowings and current maturities to long-term debt.

8. Deferred tax assets/liabilities are always non – current.

9. Trade payables Sundry creditors have been replaced with the term Trade payables and are classified as current and non-current. Trade payables to be settled beyond 12 months from the date of balance sheet or beyond the operating cycle are classified under "other long-term liabilities" with Note to Account.

10. **Proposed Dividend:** Board of Directors propose the dividend after the annual accounts for the year have been prepared. Annual General Meeting of the shareholders is held thereafter meaning it is held in the next financial year.

11. **Provisions:** The amount of provision settled within 12 months from balance sheet date or within operating cycle period from date of its recognition is classified as short term provisions and shown under current liabilities on the face of balance sheet.

12. **Fixed assets:** There is no change in the treatment of fixed assets. Both tangible and intangible assets are non-current

13. **Investments:** are also classified into current and non-current categories. Investments expected to realise within twelve months are considered as current investments under current assets

14. **Inventories:** are always treated as current

15. Trade receivables Trade receivables realised beyond twelve months from reporting date/ operating cycle starting from the date of their recognition are classified as "Other non-current assets" under the head non-current assets with Note to Accounts.

16. Cash and cash equivalent It is always current however, amounts which qualify as cash and cash equivalents as per AS-3 is shown here. The supremacy is accorded to AS over Schedule III, cash and cash equivalents are to the disclosed in accordance to the prescribed standard.

Profit and Loss Statement:

The title of 'profit and loss account' is charged to statement of profit and loss. If shows the net result of business operations. Its form is prescribed in Schedule III, Part II of the Companies Act, 2013.

FORMAT OF P/L STATEMENT

Particulars	Note No.	Figure as at the end of current reporting period	Figure as at the end of previous reporting period
I Revenue from operations			
II Other income			
III Total Revenue (I + II)			
IV Expenses:			
Cost of materials consumed			
Purchases of stock-in-trade			
Changes in inventories of finished goods			
Work-in-progress and stock-in-trade			
Employee benefits expense			
Finance costs			
Depreciation and amortisation expense			
Other expenses			
Total expenses			
V Profit before extraordinary items and tax (III-IV)			
VI Exceptional items			
VII Profit before extraordinary items and tax (V-VI)			

VIII	Extraordinary items		
IX	Profit before tax (VII-VIII)		
X	Tax expense:		
	(1) Current tax		
	(2) Deferred tax		
XI	Profit/(Loss) for the period from continuing operation (IX-X)		
XII	Profit/(Loss) from discontinuing operations		
XIII	Tax expense of discontinuing operations		
XIV	Profit/(Loss) from discontinuing operations (after tax) (XII-XIII)		
XV	Pfofit/(Loss) for the period (XI+XIV)		
XVI	Earnings per equity share:		
	(1) Basic		
	(2) Diluted		

Multiple Choice Questions

[1 Mark]

Q.1. Calls-in-advance appears in Company's Balance Sheet under the head:

(a) Current liabilities

(b) Share capital

(c) Long term Borrowings

(d) Reserves and Surplus

Ans. (a) Current liabilities

Q.2. 11% Debentures redeemable within 12 months of the date of balance sheet will be shown under:

[CBSE 2011]

(a) Short term borrowings

(b) Short term provisions

(c) Other current liabilities

(d) Trade payables

Ans. (c) Other current liabilities

Q.3. Bills receivables appears in a company balance sheet under sub head:

(a) Current investments

(b) Trade receivables

(c) Inventories

(d) Cash and cash equivalents

Ans. (b) Trade receivables

Q.4. The financial statements of a business enterprise include: [CBSE 2010]

(a) Balance sheet

(b) Statement of Profit and loss

(c) Cash flow statement

(d) All of the above

Ans. (d) All of the above

Q.5. Interest accrued on investments is shown in company's Balance Sheet under the main head ………. .

[CBSE 2008]

(a) Non-current investments   (b) Current assets

(c) Other current assets   (d) Other Non-current assets

Ans. (b) Current assets

Q.6. Expenses allowed on issue of shares appears in a Company's Balance Sheet under:

(a) Share Capital   (b) Current Liability

(c) Unamortized Expenditure   (d) Contingent Liability

Ans. (b) Current Liability

Q.7. Which of the following is not required to be prepared under the Companies Act?

(a) Statement of Profit and Loss

(b) Balance Sheet

(c) Report of Director's and Auditor's

(d) Funds Flow Statement

Ans. (d) Funds Flow Statement

Q.8. 'Loose Tools' appear in the company's Balance Sheet under the head/sub-head:

(a) Inventory

(b) Non-Current Assets

(c) Other Current Assets

(d) Stores and Spare Parts

Ans. (a) Inventory

Q.9. …………….. appear in a Company's Balance Sheet under the Sub-head Short-term Provision.

[CBSE Sample Paper 2018]

(a) Interest Accrued but not due on Borrowings

(b) Provision for Tax

(c) Unpaid Dividend

(d) Calls in Advance

Ans. (b) Provision for Tax

Q.10. Under which heading the item 'Bills discounted but not yet matured' will be shown in the Balance Sheet of a company?

(a) Current Liability

(b) Current Assets

(c) Contingent Liabilities

(d) Unamortized Expenditure

Ans. (c) Contingent Liabilities

Q.11. Match the items given in Column I with the headings/subheadings (Balance sheet) as defined in Schedule III of Companies Act 2013.

	Column I		**Column II**
(i)	Loose Tools	(a)	Intangible Fixed Assets
(ii)	Patents	(b)	Other Current Assets
(iii)	Prepaid Insurance	(c)	Long term Borrowings
(iv)	Debentures	(d)	Inventories
(v)	Machinery	(e)	Tangible Fixed Assets

Choose the correct option:

(a) (i)-(a), (ii)-(b), (iii)-(d), (iv)-(c), (v)-(e)

(b) (i)-(d), (ii)-(a), (iii)-(b), (iv)-(c), (v)-(e)

(c) (i)-(d), (ii)-(a), (iii)-(b), (iv)-(e), (v)-(c)

(d) (i)-(e), (ii)-(d), (iii)-(a), (iv)-(b), (v)-(c)

Ans. (b) (i)-(d), (ii)-(a), (iii)-(b), (iv)-(c), (v)-(e)

Q.12. A company has an operating cycle of eight months. It has accounts receivables amounting to Rs.1,00,000 out of which Rs.60,000 have a maturity period of 11 months. How would this information be presented in the balance sheet?

(a) Rs.40,000 as current assets and Rs.60,000 as non-current assets.

(b) Rs.60,000 as current assets and Rs.40,000 as non-current assets.

(c) Rs.1,00,000 as non-current assets.

(d) Rs.1,00,000 as current assets.

Ans. (d) Rs.1,00,000 as current assets.

Q.13. Which of the following is not a part of Finance Cost (in statement of profit and loss)?

[CBSE 2016]

(a) Bank Charges (b) Interest Paid on Debentures

(c) Interest Paid on Public Deposits (d) Loss on Issue of Debentures

Ans. (a) Bank Charges

Q.14. The balance sheet shows the financial position of an enterprise [CBSE 2018]

(a) over a period of time (b) during a period of time

(c) for a period of time (d) at a point of time

Ans. (d) at a point of time

Q.15. Name the item out of the following which is shown as short-term provision:

(a) Provision for tax (b) Interest accrued but not due

(c) Employees' provident fund (d) Interest accrued and due

Ans. (a) Provision for tax

Q.16. Match group I with group II and select the correct answer using the codes given below the lists:

[CBSE 2020]

	Group I (Parties)		Group II (Interest in financial analysis)
1.	Investors	A.	Interested to regulate the activities of the company and to set suitable taxation policy and other acts.
2.	Suppliers and Creditors	B.	Interested to get better returns in terms of dividend and interest on their investment.
3.	Government	C.	Interested to know regarding repayment of their dues in time.
4.	Management	D.	Interested in the overall financial performance and financial position of the enterprise.

Codes

	1	2	3	4		1	2	3	4
(a)	B	A	D	C	(b)	D	B	A	C
(c)	A	B	D	C	(d)	B	C	A	D

Ans. (d)

Q.17. Calls-in-advance and interest payable thereon is shown in the balance sheet as   [CBSE 2013]

    (a) Shareholders' funds   (b) Other non-current liabilities

    (c) Other current liabilities   (d) Trade payables

Ans. (c) Other current liabilities

Q.18. Surplus, i.e., balance in statement of profits & loss is shown in the balance sheet as

    (a) Share capital   (b) Reserves and surplus.

    (c) Other long – term liabilities.   (d) Current liabilities

Ans. (b) Reserves and surplus.

Q.19. In a company balance sheet, debit (negative) balance of statement of profit & loss is shown under

[CBSE 2019]

    (a) Non-current liabilities   (b) Current liabilities

    (c) Non- current assets.   (d) Reserves and surplus.

Ans.   (d) Reserves and surplus.

Q.20. Match group I with group II, and select the correct answer using the codes given below the lists:

[CBSE Sample Paper]

	Group I		Group II
1.	Interest accrued on investment	A.	Current Liabilities- short-term borrowings.
2.	Bank Overdraft	B.	Intangible assets
3.	Trade Mark	C.	Current Assets-inventories.
4.	Stores and Spares	D.	Current Assets- other Current Assets

Codes

        1   2   3   4   1   2   3   4
(a) C   B   D   A   (b) D   C   B   A
(c) D   A   B   C   (d) D   A   C   B

Ans. (c)

Q.21. Trade payable of a company, whose operating cycle is 18 months, is expected to be paid in 24 months, will be classified as   **[CBSE 2009]**

  (a) Current liabilities.   (b) Non- current liabilities

  (c) Either (a) or (b).   (d) None of these.

Ans. (b) Non- current liabilities

Q.22. Cash and cash equivalents does not include   **[CBSE 2010]**

  (a) Cheques.   (b) Balance with banks.

  (c) Bank deposits with more then 12 month maturity. (d) Inventories

Ans. (d) Inventories

Q.23. In a company balance sheet provision for employees benefits to be settled within 12 month is shown under   **[CBSE 2013]**

  (a) Non- current liabilities   (b) Current liabilities

  (c) Non- current assets.   (d) Current assets.

Ans. (b) Current liabilities

Q.24. Out of the following items, identify which is not shown in the note to accounts on other expenses:

  (a) Courier expenses   (b) Internet expenses

  (c) Rent for factory   (d) Wages

Ans. (d) Wages

Q.25. Under which of the following head/ sub head is forfeited shares presented in the balance sheet of a company?   **[CBSE 2012]**

  (a) Reserves and surplus   (b) Share capital

  (c) Other long term liabilities   (d) Other current liabilities

Ans. (b) Share capital

Read the following statements – Assertion (A) and Reason (R). Choose one of the correct alternatives given below :

Q.26. Assertion (A): Certain accounting conventions like conventions of consistency, conservatism, full disclosure, etc, are followed while preparing financial statement.

  Reason (R): Use of accounting convention makes the financial statement comparable, simple and realistic.
                                                                                          [CBSE Guidelines]

  (a) Both Assertion and reason are true and reason is correct explanation of assertion.

  (b) Assertion and reason both are true but reason is not the correct explanation of assertion.

  (c) Assertion is true, reason is false.

  (d) Assertion is false, reason is true.

Ans. (a)

Q.27. Assertion (A): The management uses accounting information to arrive at various decision like determination of selling price, cost controls investment in to new ventures, etc.

Reason (R): The management has the responsibility to safeguard the customer's investment and increase its value by managing the business efficiently.

(a) Both Assertion and reason are true and reason is correct explanation of assertion.

(b) Assertion and reason both are true but reason is not the correct explanation of assertion.

(c) Assertion is true, reason is false.

(d) Assertion is false, reason is true.

Ans. (d)

Q.28. Assertion (A): The bank charges charged by the bank are included in finance cost.

Reason (R): Bank charges are an expense not incurred in connection with raising fiancé but for availing the services of the bank.

(a) Both Assertion and reason are true and reason is correct explanation of assertion.

(b) Assertion and reason both are true but reason is not the correct explanation of assertion.

(c) Assertion is true, reason is false.

(d) Assertion is false, reason is true.

Ans. (c)

Q.29. Assertion (A): Bills receivable are shown as trade receivables in the balance sheet of the company.

Reason   (R): Debtors and bills received forms the part of trade receivables.

(a) Both Assertion and reason are true and reason is correct explanation of assertion.

(b) Assertion and reason both are true but reason is not the correct explanation of assertion.

(c) Assertion is true, reason is false.

(d) Assertion is false, reason is true.

Ans. (a)

Q.30. Assertion (A): Balance Sheet of a Company is prepared according to the going concern concept.

Reason (R): Balance Sheet of a Company is based on absolute facts but is influenced by personal judgements.

[CBSE 2021 Sample Paper]

(a) Both (A) and (R) are correct and (R) is the correct reason of (A).

(b) Both (A) and (R) are correct but (R) is not the correct reason of (A).

(c) Only (R) is correct.

(d) Both (A) and (R) wrong.

Ans. (b)

Q.31. Assertion (A): Balance Sheet of a Company is prepared under two broad heads i.e. (*i*) Equity & Liabilities and (*ii*) Assets.

Reason (R): In a Company's Balance Sheet, Equity & Liabilities are shown in first part and Assets in the second part.

(a) Both (A) and (R) are true, but (R) is not the correct explanation of (A).

(b) Both (A) and (R) are correct and (R) is the correct explanation of (A).

(c) Both (A) and (R) are false.

(d) (A) is true, but (R) is false.

Ans. (b)

Very Short Answer Type   [1 Mark]

Q.32. Name any two items that can be disclosed under 'Long-term Borrowings'.

Ans. (i) Bonds/Debentures;

     (ii) Term-Loans

Q.33. How will you treat Bank Overdraft and Cash Credit in the Balance Sheet of a Company?

[CBSE 2018]

Ans. These will be treated as 'Short term borrowings'.

Q.34. Give the meaning of 'Long-term Provisions'.   [CBSE 2009]

Ans. Provisions for which the related claims are expected to be settled beyond twelve months or an operating cycle are classified as Long-term Provisions.

Q.35. If Operating Cycle is 12 months and payment is received in 15 months, how will you classify the asset?

Ans. Non Current Asset

Q.36. How will you show the following items in the Balance Sheet of a Company:

     (i) Calls in Arrears

     (ii) Calls in Advance

Ans. (i) Calls in Arrears: It is deducted from the subscribed but not fully paid capital.

     (ii) Calls in Advance: It is shown under the head 'Current Liabilities' under sub-head 'Other Current Liabilities'.

Fill in the blanks.

Q.37. Capital Reserve is created out of ……… profits.

Ans.   Capital

Q.38. Trade receivables include both Debtors and ………. .   [CBSE 2012]

Ans. Bills Receivable

Q.39. Employee benefit expenses mainly include ………. .

Ans. Salary

True/False.

Q.40. Securities Premium Reserve is shown under Share Capital head.

Ans. False

Q.41. A balance Sheet is prepared for a particular period and not on a particular date.

Ans. False

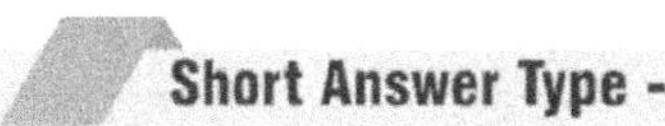 **Short Answer Type - I** [2 Marks]

Q.42. Under what heads the following items on the assets side of the Balance Sheet of a Company will be presented: [CBSE 2016]

(i) Sundry Debtors

(ii) Patents and Trade Marks

(iii) Shares in D.C.M. Limited

(iv) Bills Receivable

(v) Advances recoverable in cash within the operating cycle

(vi) Prepaid Insurance

(vii) Work-in-Progress

Ans.

S. No.	Items	Heading	Sub-heading (if any)
(i)	Sundry Debtors	Current Assets	Trade Receivables
(ii)	Patents and Trade Marks	Non-Current Assets	Fixed Assets-Intangible Assets
(iii)	Shares in D.C.M. Ltd.	Non-Current Assets	Non-Current Investments
(iv)	Bills Receivable	Current Assets	Trade Receivables
(v)	Advances Recoverable in Cash within the operating cycle	Current Assets	'Short-term Loans and Advances'
(vi)	Prepaid Insurance	Current Assets	Other Current Assets
(vii)	Work-in-Progress	Current Assets	Inventories

Q.43. State under which major headings and sub-headings the following items will be presented in the balance sheet of a company as per Schedule III of the Companies Act 2013. [CBSE 2013]

(i) Calls in Advance

(ii) Accrued Interest on Calls in Advance

(iii) Provision for Retirement Benefits

(iv) Stores and Spares

(v) Capital Work in Progress

(vi) Design

(vii) Securities Premium Reserve

Ans.

S. No.	Items	Heading	Sub-heading (if any)
(i)	Calls in Advance	Current Liabilities	Other Current Liabilities
(ii)	Accrued Interest on Calls in Advance	Current Liabilities	Other Current Liabilities
(iii)	Provision for Retirement Benefits	Non Current Liabilities	Long-term Provisions
(iv)	Stores and Spares	Current Assets	Inventory
(v)	Capital Work in Progress	Non Current Assets	Fixed Assets-Tangible
(vi)	Design	Non Current Assets	Fixed Assets-Intangible
(vii)	Securities Premium Reserve	Shareholder's Funds	Reserve and Surplus

Q.44. Under which head the following items of a non-financial company will be shown: [CBSE 2016]

(i) Sales

(ii) Sale of Scrap

(iii) Dividend received

(iv) Interest earned

(v) Profit on sale of fixed asset and

(vi) Profit on sale of investments

Ans. Revenue from Operations: Sales and Sale of Scrap.

Other Income: Dividend received, Interest earned, Profit on sale of fixed asset and Profit on sale of investments.

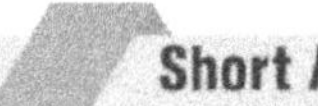
Short Answer Type - II   **[3 Marks]**

Q.45. Compute Revenue from Operations, other Income and Total Revenue for a financial company from the following particulars: [CBSE Sample Paper]

	Rs.
Interest on loans given	40,00,000
Fees received for arranging loans	5,00,000
Miscellaneous Income	15,000
Profit on sale of Building	2,00,000
Profit on sale of Investments	1,20,000

Ans.

	Particulars	Rs.	Rs.
I.	**Revenue from Operations:**		
	Interest on loans given	4,000,000	
	Fees received for arranging loans	5,00,000	
	Profit on sale of investments	120,000	4,620,000

II.	Other Income:		
	Miscellaneous Income	15,000	
	Profit on sale of Building	2,00,000	2,15,000
	Total Revenue (I + II)		4,835,000

Q.46. Operating Cycle and the period when payment is received is given below:

How will you classify the asset?

Particulars	(i)	(ii)	(iii)	(iv)	(v)	(vi)
Operating Cycle (Months)	10	10	10	15	15	20
Expected Period when payment is received (Months)	9	12	14	14	18	18

Ans. (i) Current; (ii) Current; (iii) Non-Current;

(iv) Current; (v) Non-Current; (vi) Current.

Q.47. How would you show the following items in a Company's Balance Sheet as at 31st March, 2022:

[CBSE Compartment 2015]

Particulars	Rs.
Public Deposits	4,00,000
Outstanding Expenses	10,000
Calls in Advance	25,000
Provision for Employee Benefits (maturing within 12 months)	20,000
Provision for Taxation	1,50,000

Ans. Non Current Liabilities: Rs.

Long term Borrowings   4,00,000

Current Liabilities:

Other Current Liabilities   35,000   (Outstanding Exp. + Calls in Advance)

Short term Provisions   1,70,000

(Provision for Employee Benefits + Provision for Taxation

Long Answer Type   [5 Marks]

Q.48. How will you show the following items in the Balance Sheet of a Company:

(i) Calls in Arrears

(ii) Calls in Advance

(iii) Forfeited Shares

(iv) Debenture Sinking Fund

(v) Contingent Liability

Ans. (i) Calls in Arrears: It is deducted from subscribed but not fully paid Capital.

(ii) Calls in Advance: It is shown under the head 'Current Liabilities' under sub-head 'Other Current Liabilities'.

(iii) Forfeited Shares: It is added to 'Subscribed Capital' under the head 'Shareholder's Funds'.

(iv) Debenture Sinking Fund: It is shown under the head 'Reserves and Surplus' on the equities and liabilities side.

(v) Contingent Liability: It appears in notes to accounts below the balance sheet.

Q.49. Under which major headings and subheadings will the following items be presented in the Balance Sheet of a company as per Schedule III, Part I of the companies Act, 2013?

[CBSE 2014]

(i) Interest accrued and due on debentures

(ii) Accrued interest on calls in advance

(iii) Interest due on calls in arrears

(iv) Premium on redemption of debentures

(v) Plant and Machinery

(vi) Trade marks

(vii) Provident Fund

Ans.

S. No.	Items	Major Head	Sub-head
(i)	Interest accrued and due on debentures.	Current Liabilities	Other Current Liabilities
(ii)	Accrued Interest on Calls in advance.	Current Liabilities	Other Current Liabilities
(iii)	Interest due on calls in arrears.	Current Liabilities	Other Current Liabilities
(iv)	Premium on redemption of debentures.	Non Current Liabilities	Other Non Current Liabilities
(v)	Plant and Machinery	Non Current Assets	Fixed Assets-Tangible
(vi)	Trade marks	Non Current Assets	Fixed Assets-Intangible
(vii)	Provident Fund	Non Current Liabilities	Long-term Provision

Q.50. Under which major head of the Statement of Profit and Loss of a Company following items will appear:

[CBSE Sample Paper 2020]

(i) Bonus

(ii) Revenue from Services rendered

(iii) Internet Expenses

(iv) Materials Purchased

(v) Discount on Issue of Debentures written off

(vi) Goodwill Amortized

Ans.

	Item	Major Head
(i)	Bonus	Employee Benefit Expenses
(ii)	Revenue from Services rendered	Revenue from Operations
(iii)	Internet Expenses	Other Expenses
(iv)	Materials Purchased	Cost of Materials Consumed
(v)	Discount on Issue of Debentures written off	Finance Costs
(vi)	Goodwill Amortized	Depreciation and Amortization Expenses

Q.51. Under which of the heads will the following items be shown, while preparing the Balance Sheet of a company, as per provisions of Companies Act, 2013, as contained in Schedule III?   **[CBSE 2013]**

Ans.

	Rs.
Preliminary Expenses	1,40,000
Discount on Issue	10,000
8% Debentures with maturity period in current financial year	1,90,000
Stock-in-Trade	40,000
Cash at Bank	35,000
Bills Receivable	12,000
Goodwill	20,000
Loose Tools	12,000
Horses and Carts	22,000
Motor Truck	75,000
Provision for Taxation	6,000
Sundry Creditors	30,000

	Items	Heading	Sub-heading (if any)
1.	Preliminary Expenses	Not shown in the Balance Sheet as these expenses are written off in the same year.	
2.	Discount on Issue of Debentures	Not shown in the Balance Sheet as these expenses are written off in the same year.	
3.	8% Debentures with maturity period in current financial year	Current Liabilities	Other Current Liabilities
4.	Stock-in-Trade	Current Assets	Inventories
5.	Cash at Bank	Current Assets	Cash and Cash Equivalents
6.	Bills Receivable	Current Assets	Trade Receivables
7.	Goodwill	Non-Current Assets	Fixed Assets-Intangible Assets
8.	Loose Tools	Current Assets	Inventories
9.	Horses and Carts	Non-Current Assets	Fixed Assets-Tangible Assets
10.	Motor Truck	Non-Current Assets	Fixed Assets-Tangible Assets
11.	Provision for Taxation	Current Liabilities	Short-term Provisions
12.	Sundry Creditors	Current Liabilities	Trade Payables

Chapter Practice

Multiple Choice Questions [1 Mark]

Q.1. As per the company act, 2013, Balance Sheet of the Company can be drawn in :

  (a) Vertical Format   (b) Horizontal Format

  (c) Either (a) or (b)   (d) As per wishes of Directors

Q.2. Which of the following is not the sub head of Non-Current Liabilities:

  (a) Long Term Borrowings   (b) Trade Payable

  (c) Deferred Tax Liabilities   (d) Long-Term Provisions

Q.3. Share Forfeited A/c is added in Notes to Accounts to Balance Sheet in :

  (a) Called-up Capital   (b) Issued Capital

  (c) Subscribed Capital   (d) Capital Reserve

Q.4. Securities Premium Reserve is shown on Equity and Liabilities side of Balance Sheet under the head :

  (a) Share Capital   (b) Reserve & Surplus

  (c) Long Term Provisions   (d) Short Term Provisions

Q.5. Which of the following is not a component of Short-Term Provisions ?

  (a) Provision for Tax   (b) Proposed Dividend

  (c) Provision for warranty   (d) Provision for bad debts

Very Short Answer Type [1 Mark]

Q.6. What is 'Operating Cycle' ?

Q.7. How are the assets and liabilities of a Company usually marshaled ?

Q.8. Define Trade Payable ?

Q.9. Name the major heads of items shown under Equity And Liabilities part of Balance Sheet of a Company ?

Q.10. List any three items of Reserve and Surplus as per Schedule lll of Companies Act, 2013.

Q.11. Give main heading of items shown under Non- current Liabilities.

Q.12. How is the preliminary Expenses treated in Balance Sheet of a Company ?

Q.13. What is meant by Revenue from Operations ?

Q.14. What is Meant by 'Finance Cost'?

Q.15. Give four examples of other expenses .

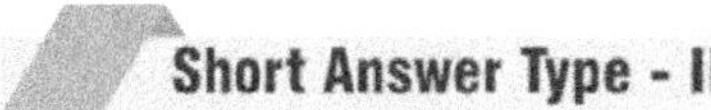

Short Answer Type - II   [3 Marks]

Q.16. What is meant by 'Financial Statement of Company ?

Q.17. What is Characteristics of Financial Statements?

Q.18. Under which major heading and sub headings will the following items shown in the Balance Sheet of a Company As per Schedule III Part I of the companies Act, 2013 :

    (i) Net loss as shown by Statement of Profit and Loss

    (ii) Capital Redemption Reserve

    (iii)Bonds/Debentures issued by the Company

    (iv)Unpaid Dividend

    (v) Buildings

    (vi)Raw Material

Q.19. Under what headings will you show the following items in the Balance Sheet of a Company :

    (i) Balances with Bank

    (ii) Investment in Debenture

    (iii)Outstanding Salaries

    (iv)Authorised Capital

    (v) Acceptances / Bills Payables

    (vi)Provision for Tax

Q.20. On April 01, 2021, Laxmi Agro Ltd. Issued 10,000; 12% debentures of Rs. 100 each at a discount of 20%., redeemable after 5 years. The company decided to write off discount on issue of such debentures on March 31, 2022.

Show the items in the Balance Sheet of the Company as at 31st March 2022

Analysis of Financial Statements

 Meaning of Analysis of Financial Statements

Summary

Meaning of Financial Statement

It is the systematic numerical representation of the relationship of one financial fact with the other to measure the profitability, operational efficiency, solvency and the growth potential of the business. The term 'financial analysis' includes both 'analysis and interpretation'.

Significance of Analysis of Financial Statements

Financial analysis is the process of identifying the financial strengths and weaknesses of the firm by properly establishing relationships between the various items of the balance sheet and the statement of profit and loss.

Financial analysis is useful and significant to different users in the following ways:

1. **Finance manager:** Financial analysis focusses on the facts and relationships related to managerial performance, corporate efficiency, financial strengths and weaknesses and creditworthiness of the company. A finance manager must be well-equipped with the different tools of analysis to make rational decisions for the firm. The tools for analysis help in studying accounting data so as to determine the continuity of the operating policies, investment value of the business, credit ratings and testing the efficiency of operations. The techniques are equally important in the area of financial control, enabling the finance manager to make constant reviews of the actual financial operations of the firm to analyse the causes of major deviations, which may help in corrective action wherever indicated.

2. **Top management:** The importance of financial analysis is not limited to the finance manager alone. It has a broad scope which includes top management in general and other functional managers. Management of the firm would be interested in every aspect of the financial analysis.

3. **Trade payables:** Trade payables, through an analysis of financial statements, appraises not only the ability of the company to meet its short-term obligations, but also judges the probability of its continued ability to meet all its financial obligations in future. Trade payables are particularly interested in the firm's ability to meet their claims over a very short period of time. Their analysis will, therefore, evaluate the firm's liquidity position.

4. **Lenders:** Suppliers of long- term debt are concerned with the firm's longterm solvency and survival. They analyse the firm's profitability over a period of time, its ability to generate cash, to be able to pay interest and repay the principal and the relationship between various sources of funds (capital structure relationships). Long-term lenders analyse the historical financial statements to assess its future solvency and profitability.

5. **Investors:** Investors, who have invested their money in the firm's shares, are interested about the firm's earnings. As such, they concentrate on the analysis of the firm's present and future profitability. They are also interested in the firm's capital structure to ascertain its influences on firm's earning and risk. They also evaluate the efficiency of the management and determine whether a change is needed or not. However, in some large companies, the shareholders' interest is limited to decide whether to buy, sell or hold the shares

6. **Labour unions:** analyse the financial statements to assess whether it can presently afford a wage increase and whether it can absorb a wage increase through increased productivity or by raising the prices.

Objectives of Analysis of Financial Statements:

(i)   Judging the operational efficiency of the business.

(ii)   Measuring the profitability.

(iii)   Measuring short-term and long-term financial position.

(iv)   Indicating the trend of achievements.

(v)   Assessing the growth potential of the business.

(vi)   Inter-firm comparison

Limitations of Financial Analysis:

1. Financial analysis does not consider price level changes.

2. Financial analysis may be misleading without the knowledge of the changes in accounting procedure followed by a firm.

3. Financial analysis is just a study of reports of the company.

4. Monetary information alone is considered in financial analysis while non-monetary aspects are ignored.

5. The financial statements are prepared on the basis of accounting concept, as such, it does not reflect the current position

Tools of Analysis of Financial Statements:

1. **Comparative Financial Statements:** Are used to compare the items of income statement i.e. profit and loss account and position statement i.e. balance sheet for ascertaining the trend of the performance and profitability of an enterprise are known as comparative financial statements. It usually applies to the two important financial statements, namely, balance sheet and statement of profit and loss prepared in a comparative form.

FORMAT OF COMPARATIVE BALANCE SHEET

Comparative Balance Sheet as at...

Particulars	Previous Year (Rs.)	Current Year (Rs)	Absolute Change (Increase of Decrease (Rs)	Percentage Change (Increase or Decrease) (%)
I. Equity and Liabilities				
1. Shareholder' Funds				
(a) Share Capital				
(i) Equity Share Capital	....	....	....	....
(ii) Preference Share Capital	....	....	....	....
(b) Reserves and Surplus	....	....	....	....

2. Non-current Liabilities				
(a) Long-term Borrowings	....	....	....	....
(b) Long-term Provisions	....	....	....	....
3. Current Liabilities				
(a) Short-term Borrowings	....	....	....	....
(b) Trade Payables	....	....	....	....
(c) Other Current Liabilities	....	....	....	....
(d) Short-term Provisions	....	....	....	....
Total	....	....	....	....
II. **Assets**				
1. **Non-current Assets**				
(a) Fixed Assets	....	....	....	....
(i) Tangible Assets	....	....	....	....
(ii) Intangible Assets	....	....	....	....
(b) Non-current Investments	....	....	....	....
(c) Long-term Loans and Advances	....	....	....	....
2. **Current Assets**				
(a) Current Investments	....	....	....	....
(b) Inventories	....	....	....	....
(c) Trade Receivables	....	....	....	....
(d) Cash and Cash Equivalents	....	....	....	....
(e) Short-term Loans and Advances	....	....	....	....
(f) Other Currents Assets	....	....	....	....
Total	....	....	....	....

2. **Common Size Statements:** These are the statements which indicate the relationship of different items of a financial statement with a common item by expressing each item as a percentage of that common item. Common size statements are useful, both, in intra-firm comparisons over different years and also in making inter-firm comparisons for the same year or for several years. This analysis is also known as 'Vertical analysis.

Particulars	Absolute Amounts		Percentage of Balance Sheet Total	
	Previous Year (Rs.)	Current Year (Rs)	Previous Year (Rs.)	Current Year (Rs)
(1)	(2)	(3)	(4)	(5)
I. **Equity and Liabilities**				
1. **Shareholder' Funds**				
(a) Share Capital				
(i) Equity Share Capital	....	....	....	....
(ii) Preference Share Capital	....	....	....	....
(b) Reserves and Surplus	....	....	....	....
2. **Non-current Liabilities**				
(a) Long-term Borrowings	....	....	....	....
(b) Long-term Provisions	....	....	....	....
3. **Current Liabilities**				
(a) Short-term Borrowings	....	....	....	....

(b) Trade Payables	....	....	....	....
(c) Other Current Liabilities	....	....	....	....
(d) Short-term Provisions	....	....	....	....
Total	....	....	100	100
II. **Assets**				
1. **Non-current Assets**				
(a) Fixed Assets	....	....	....	....
(i) Tangible Assets	....	....	....	....
(ii) Intangible Assets	....	....	....	....
(b) Non-current Investments	....	....	....	....
(c) Long-term Loans and Advances	....	....	....	....
2. **Current Assets**				
(a) Current Investments	....	....	....	....
(b) Inventories	....	....	....	....
(c) Trade Receivables	....	....	....	....
(d) Cash and Cash Equivalents	....	....	....	....
(e) Short-term Loans and Advances	....	....	....	....
(f) Other Currents Assets	....	....	....	....
Total	....	....	100	100

3. **Ratio Analysis:** The mathematical expression that shows the relationships between various groups of items contained in the financial statements is known as ratio analysis.

4. **Cash Flow Statement:** It shows the inflows and outflows of cash and cash equivalents of an enterprise by classifying cash flows into operating, investing and financing activities during a particular period and analysing the reasons for changes in balance of cash between the two balance sheets dates.

Multiple Choice Questions [1 Mark]

Q.1. Which analysis is considered as static?

(a) Horizontal Analysis

(b) Vertical Analysis

(c) Internal Analysis

(d) External Analysis

Ans. (b) Vertical Analysis

Q.2. Main objective of analysis of financial statements is [CBSE 2019]

(a) To know the financial strength

(b) To make a comparative study with othe firms

(c) To know the efficiency of management

(d) All of the above

Ans. (d) All of the above

Q.3. For whom the analysis of financial statements is not significant? [CBSE 2008]

(a) Investor

(b) Government

(c) Ambassador of India

(d) Company's Employee

Ans. (c) Ambassador of India

Q.4. Which of the following is not a limitation of analysis of financial statements?

(a) Affected by personal bias   (b) Inter firm comparative study possible

(c) Lack of Qualitative Analysis   (d) Ignores price level changes

Ans. (b) Inter firm comparative study possible

Q.5. Which of the following statements are false?					**[CBSE Sample Paper]**

(i) When all the comparative figures in a balance sheet are stated as percentage of the total, it is termed as horizontal analysis.

(ii) When financial statements of sevcral years are analysed, it is termed as vertical analysis.

(iii) Vertical analysis is also termed as time series analysis.

Choose from the following options:

(a) Both (i) and (ii)   (b) Both (i) and (iii)   (c) Both (ii) and (iii)   (d) All three (i), (ii), (iii)

Ans. (d) All three (i), (ii), (iii)

Q.6. Feature of financial analysis is to present the data contained in financial statements in

(a) Easy form   (b) Convenient and rational groups

(c) Comparable form   (d) All of the above

Ans. (d) All of the above

Q.7. Analysis of Financial Statements is significant:					**[CBSE 2010]**

(a) For Creditors   (b) For Managers   (c) For Employees   (d) For all of the above

Ans. (d) All of the above

Q.8. Main limitation of analysis of financial statements is

(a) Affected by window dressing   (b) Difficulty in forecasting

(c) Do not reflect changes in price level   (d) All of the above

Ans. (d) All of the above

Q.9. Which of the following is not an objective of Analysis of Financial Statements:

(a) To judge the financial health of the firm.

(b) To judge the short-term and long-term liquidity position of the firm.

(c) To judge the reasons for change in the profitability of the firm.

(d) To judge the variations in the accounting practices of the business followed by different enterprises

Ans. (d) All of the above

Q.10. Which of the following are the tools of Vertical Analysis?					**[CBSE 2018]**

(i) Ratio Analysis

(ii) Comparative Statements

(iii) Common Size Statements

(a) Only (iii)   (b) Both (i) and (iii)   (c) Both (i) and (ii)   (d) Only (i)

Ans. (b) Both (i) and (iii)

Q.11. While preparing common –size balance sheet, each item of balance sheet is expressed as % of

(a) Non- current assets. (b) Current assets.

(c) Non- current liabilities. (d) Total assets.

Ans. (d) Total assets.

Q.12. Which analysis is considered as dynamic? **[CBSE Compartment 2018]**

(a) Horizontal analysis (b) Vertical analysis

(c) Internal analysis (d) External analysis

Ans. (a) Horizontal analysis

Q.13. Comparison of values of one period with those of same period with the another firm is

(a) Intra –firm comparison. (b) Inter-firm comparison

(c) Pattern comparison. (d) Trend comparison.

Ans. (b) Inter –firm comparison.

Q.14. Management is interested in financial analysis since: **[CBSE Sample Paper 2016]**

(a) It provides information about the overall financial performance of the enterprise.

(b) It provides information about the financial position of the enterprise.

(c) It provides information about the financial performance and financial position of the enterprise as a whole and its various divisions.

(d) None of the above.

Ans. (c) It provides information about the financial performance and financial position of the enterprise as a whole and its various divisions.

Q.15. Comparison of financial statement of an enterprise for two or more accounting periods is known as

[CBSE 2020]

(a) Intra – firm analysis(b) Time series analysis (c) Trend analysis. (d) All of the above.

Ans. (d) All of the above

Q.16. Match column I with column II and select the correct answer using the codes given below the lists:

Colum I	**Colum II**
A. Horizontal analysis	1. Conducting for one accounting period
B. Vertical analysis	2. Comparison of financial statement of an enterprise for two or more accounting periods
C. Intra – firm	3. Conducted for two or analysis is more accounting periods.
D. Inter- firm analysis	4. Comparison of financial statement of two or more enterprise for the same accounting period.

Codes:

(a) A-4, B-3, C-2, D-1 (b) A-3, B-1, C-2, D-4

(c) A-3, B-2, C-4, D-1 (d) A-2, B-3, C-4, D-1

Ans. (b)

Q.17. Feature of financial analysis is to present the data contained in financial statements in

(a) Easy form

(b) Convenient and rational groups

(c) Comparable form

(d) All of the above

Ans. (d) All of the above

Q.18. Which Analysis is based on one year's data?   [CBSE 2015]

(a) Horizontal Analysis

(b) Vertical Analysis

(c) Cash Flow Statement

(d) Dividend Analysis

Ans. (b) vertical Analysis

Q.19. Financial Analysis becomes significant because it   [CBSE 2016]

(a) Ignores price level changes

(b) Measures the efficiency of business

(c) Lacks qualitative analysis

(d) Is effected by personal bias

Ans. (b) Measures the efficiency of business

Q.20. When bad position of the business is tried to be depicted as good it is known as

(a) Personal bias

(b) Price level changes

(c) Window dressing

(d) All the above

Ans. (c) Window dressing

Q.21. Financial Analysis becomes useless because it

(a) Measures the profitability

(b) Measures the solvency

(c) Lacks qualitative analysis

(d) Makes a comparative study

Ans. (c) Lacks qualitative analysis

Q.22. Intra – Firm Analysis is also known as :   [CBSE 2011]

(a) Cross- section Analysis

(b) Trend analysis

(c) Dividend decision Analysis

(d) Debt Analysis

Ans. (b) Trend analysis

Q.23. Inter – Firm Analysis is also known as :

(a) Cross- section Analysis

(b) Trend analysis

(c) Dividend decision Analysis

(d) Debt Analysis

Ans. (a) Cross- section Analysis

Read the following statements – Assertion (A) and Reason (R). Choose one of the correct alternatives given below :

Q.24. Assertion (A): With the help of financial analysis, short term lenders are interested in knowing the liquidity of the company.

Reason (R): With the help of financial analysis, investors assess the profitability of the Company.

[CBSE Guide Lines]

In the context of the above two statements, which of the following is correct?

Codes:

(a) Both (A) and (R) are correct and (R) is the correct reason of (A).

(b) Both (A) and (R) are correct but (R) is not the correct reason of (A).

(c) Only (R) is correct.

(d) Both (A) and (R) are wrong.

Ans. (b)

Q.25. Assertion (A): Intra-firm analysis means comparing the financial data of the same firm for two or more accounting periods.

Reason (R): Inter-firm analysis means comparing the financial data of two or more enterprises for the same accounting period.

In the context of the above two statements, which of the following is correct?

Codes:

(a) Both (A) and (R) are true, but (R) is not the correct explanation of (A).

(b) Both (A) and (R) are true and (R) is the correct explanation of (A).

(c) Both (A) and (R) are false.

(d) (A) is false, but (R) is true.

Ans. (a)

Q.26. Assertion (A): Financial analysis is a systematic process of analyzing the financial statements for presenting them in a understandable form for the purpose of decision making.

Reason (R): Various tools for analysing the financial statements are Comparative Statements, Common-size Statements, Accounting Ratios, Cash Flow Statement etc.

In thee context of the above two statements, which of the following is correct?

Codes:

(a) Both (A) and (R) are correct and (R) is the correct reason of (A).

(b) Both (A) and (R) are correct but (R) is not the correct reason of (A).

(c) Only (R) is correct.

(d) Both (A) and (R) are wrong.

Ans. (b)

Q.27. Assertion (A): Quality of management and staff, firm's ability to develop new products, customer satisfaction etc. are ignored in financial analysis.

Reason (R): Since financial statements do not record qualitative elements of the business and consider only those items which can be measured in terms of money, financial analysis also ignores qualitative factors.

In the context of the above two statements, which of the following is correct?

Codes:

(a) (A) and (R) both are correct and (R) correctly explains (A).

(b) Both (A) and (R) are correct but (R) does not explain (A).

(c) Both (A) and (R) are incorrect.

(d) (A) is correct but (R) is incorrect.

Ans. (a)

Q.28. Assertion(A): The objective of financial statement analysis is to measure the earning capacity and financial strength of a business and to facilitate comparative study.

Reason (R): Financial statements of a company are to be prepared as per format prescribed in Schedule III of the Indian Companies Act, 2013.

(a) Both Assertion (A) and Reason (R) are true and Reason (R) is the correct explanation of Assertion(A)

(b) Both Assertion (A) and Reason (R) are true, but Reason (R) is not the correct explanation of Assertion (A)

(c) Assertion(A) isfalse, butReason (R) istrue

(d) Assertion(A)istrue,butReason(R)isfalse

Ans. (a)

Q.29. Assertion(A): Invertical analysis financial statements for a single year orona particular date are reviewed and analyzed with the help of proper devices like ratios.

Reason (R): Such type of analysis is based on data of a single year. As such it is also called static an alysis.

(a) Both Assertion (A) and Reason (R) are true and Reason (R) is the correct explanation of Assertion (A)

(b) Both Assertion (A) and Reason (R) are true, but Reason (R) is not the correct explanation of Assertion (A)

(c) Assertion(A) is false, but Reason (R) is true

(d) Assertion (A) is true, but Reason (R) is false

Ans. (a)

Q.30. Assertion (A): Financial analysis suffer from the limitation of ignoring price level changes.

Reason (R): Financial analysis is based upon financial statements which do not show price level changes because all items in financial statements are recorded at coast and value of money in the latest year is not the same as it was in the previous years.

In the context of the above two statements, which of the following is correct?

Codes:

(a) (A) and (R) both are correct and (R) correctly explains (A).

(b) Both (A) and (R) are correct but (R) does not explain (A).

(c) Both (A) and (R) are incorrect.

(d) (A) is correct but (R) is incorrect.

Ans. (a)

Q.31. Assertion (A): Dince financial analysis is strictly based upon financial statements, there is no scope of effect of personal ability and bias of analyst on such analysis.

Reason (R): Financial analysis suffers from personal ability and bias of analyst because analysis is based on financial statements.

In the context of the above two statements, which of the following is correct?

Codes:

(a) Both (A) and (R) are correct and (R) is the correct reason of (A).

(b) Both (A) and (R) are correct but (R) is not the correct reason of (A).

(c) Only (R) is correct.

(d) Both (A) and (R) are wrong.

Ans. (c)

Q.32. Assertion (A): Tools for financial analysis include Comparative Statements, Common-size Statements, Balance Sheet, Statement of Profit & Loss etc.

Reason (R): Tools for financial analysis include Comparative Statements, Common-size Statements and Balance Sheet.

In the context of the above two statements, which of the following is correct?

Codes:

(a) Both (A) and (R) are correct and (R) is the correct reason of (A).

(b) Both (A) and (R) are correct but (R) is not the correct reason of (A).

(c) Only (R) is correct.

(d) Both (A) and (R) are wrong.

Ans. (d)

Very Short Answer Type   [1 Mark]

Fill in the blanks.

Q.33. When financial statements for a single year are analyzed, it is called ……………analysis.   [CBSE 2011]

Ans. Vertical

Q.34. When financial position of an enterprise is tried to be shown better than the actual, it is called …………….. .

Ans. Window dressing

Q.35. Vertical analysis is also known as ………….. analysis.   **[CBSE Compartment 2012]**

Ans. Static

Q.36. Analysis of financial statements measure …………….. capacity.

Ans. Earnings

Q.37. …………….. are interested in knowing the firm's ability to meet its short term liabilities.

Ans. Short term creditors

State whether the following statements are True or False.

Q.38. Financial analysis is helpful to the investors in ascertaining the profitability of the company.

Ans. True

Q.39. Financial analysis is not affected by window dressing.   [CBSE 2019]

 Ans. False

Q.40. Financial Analysis considers price level changes.

 Ans. False

Q.41. With the help of financial analysis, short term lenders can know about the liquidity of the company.

[CBSE 2009]

 Ans. True

Q.42. Financial analysis is used only by the creditors.

 Ans. False

Q.43. Financial Analysis removes the limitations of financial statements.

 Ans. False

Short Answer Type - I   [2 Marks]

Q.44. What is meant by 'Financial Analysis'?   [CBSE 2008, 2016]

 Ans. Financial analysis is a systematic process of classifying the data into simple groups and making a comparison of various groups with one another to pin-point the strong points and weaknesses of the business.

Q.45. What is Horizontal Analysis?   [CBSE 2014]

 Ans. When financial statements for a number of years are analyzed, the analysis is called horizontal analysis. Such analysis is mostly in the form of 'Comparative financial statements'.

Q.46. List any two uses of analyzing the financial statements.

 Ans. (i) Helpful in taking investment decisions.

 (ii) Helpful in taking credit decisions.

Short Answer Type - II   [3 Marks]

Q.47. How can the financial strength of a business enterprise be judged?

 Ans. The financial strength of a business enterprise can be judged on the basis of

 (i) its earning capacity, *i.e.*, profitability, and

 (ii) its ability to repay the loans and pay dividends.

Q.48. Explain how Financial Statements Analysis ignores qualitative elements?

 Ans. The qualitative elements like quality of management, quality of labour force, public relations etc. are ignored while carrying out the Analysis of Financial Statements.

Q.49. What is Vertical Analysis?   [CBSE Compartment 2016]

 Ans. When financial statements for a single year are analysed, the analysis is called vertical analysis. The items in the financial statement are expressed as a percentage to total and the total is taken as equivalent to 100. Statements containing such analysis are termed as 'Common Size Statements'.

Q.50. State the interest of tax authorities in the analysis of financial statements.

Ans. (i) To judge whether the financial statements have been prepared in accordance with the legal provisions.

(ii) To judge whether various types of taxes have been paid appropriately.

Q.51. How is 'window dressing' a limitation of Financial Statement Analysis?   **[CBSE 2019]**

Ans. Window dressing refers to the manipulation of accounts to conceal vital facts and presentation of the 'Financial Statements' in a way so as to show a position better than what it actually is. On account of such a situation financial analysis may give false information to the users.

Q.52. How is analysis of financial statements useful for the Top Management?

Ans. Analysis of financial statements is useful for management in measuring the solvency, profitability and capital structure of the firm.

Chapter Practice

Multiple Choice Questions   [1 Mark]

Q.1. Features of financial analysis is to present the data contained in financial statements in :

    (a) Easy Form   (b) Convenient and rational group

    (c) Comparable form   (d) all of the above

Q.2. Which analysis is considered as dynamic:

    (a) Horizontal Analysis   (b) Vertical Analysis

    (c) Internal Analysis   (d) External Analysis

Q.3. Financial analysis becomes significant because it :

    (a) Ignores price level changes   (b) Measures the efficiency of business

    (c) Lacks qualitative analysis   (d) Is effected by personal bias

Q.4. Financial analysis become useless because it:

    (a) Measures the profitability   (b) Measures the Solvency

    (c) Lacks qualitative Analysis   (d) Makes a comparative study

Q.5. Parties interested in financial analysis are :

    (a) Investors   (b) Government

    (c) Financial Institutions   (d) All of the above

Very Short Answer Type   [1 Mark]

Q.6. What is meant by analysis of financial statements?

Q.7. State any one objective of Financial Statement Analysis ?

Q.8. What is Horizontal Analysis of Financial Statements ?

Q.9. What is intra –firm Analysis of Financial Statements ?

Q.10. Name tools of analysis of financial statements.

Q.11. Why is public interested in analysing financial analysis ?

Q.12. What is meant by Inter –firm comparison ?

Q.13. Name four users of Financial Statement Analysis.

Q.14. How is analysis of financial statements useful for Top Management?

Short Answer Type - I   [2 Marks]

Q.15. State briefly any three objectives of 'Analysis of Financial Statements.

Q.16. State three essential features of financial analysis.

Long Answer Type   [5 Marks]

Q.17. Explain the below limitations of Financial Analysis :

1. Affected by window –dressing
2. Do not reflect changes in Price Level
3. Different Accounting Policies
4. Difficulty in forecasting
5. Lack of Qualitative Analysis

Accounting Ratios

 Introduction, Liquidity Ratios

Summary

Meaning of Accounting Ratios:

Ratio It is an arithmetical expression of relationship between two related or interdependent items. Accounting Ratios It is a mathematical expression that shows the relationship between various items or groups of items shown in financial statements. When ratios are calculated on the basis of accounting information, they are called accounting ratios.

Objectives of Ratio Analyis:

(i) To know the areas of an enterprise which need more attention.

(ii) To know about the potential areas which can be improved on.

(iii) Helpful in comparative analysis of the performance.

(iv) Helpful in budgeting and forecasting.

(v) To provide analysis of the liquidity, solvency, activity and profitability of an enterprise.

(vi) To provide information useful for making estimates and preparing the plans for future.

Advantages of Ratio Analysis:

(i) It is useful in analysis of financial statements.

(ii) Helps in simplifying accounting figures.

(iii) Useful in judging the operating efficiency of business.

(iv) Helps in identification of problem areas.

(v) Helpful in comparative analysis.

Limitations of Ratio Analysis

(i) Accounting ratios ignore qualitative factors.

(ii) Absence of universally accepted terminology.

(iii) Ratios are affected by window-dressing.

(iv) Effects of inherent limitations of accounting.

(v) Misleading results in the absence of absolute data.

(vi) Price level changes ignored.

(vii) Affected by personal bias and ability of the analyst.

Types of Ratios:

There is a two way classification of ratios: (1) traditional classification, and (2) functional classification. The traditional classification has been on the basis of financial statements to which the determinants of ratios belong. On this basis the ratios are classified as follows:

1. **Statement of Profit and Loss Ratios:** A ratio of two variables from the statement of profit and loss is known as statement of profit and loss ratio. For example, ratio of gross profit to revenue from operations is known as gross profit ratio. It is calculated using both figures from the statement of profit and loss.

2. **Balance Sheet Ratios:** In case both variables are from the balance sheet, it is classified as balance sheet ratios. For example, ratio of current assets to current liabilities known as current ratio. It is calculated using both figures from balance sheet.

3. **Composite Ratios:** If a ratio is computed with one variable from the statement of profit and loss and another variable from the balance sheet, it is called composite ratio. For example, ratio of credit revenue from operations to trade receivables (known as trade receivables turnover ratio) is calculated using one figure from the statement of profit and loss (credit revenue from operations) and another figure (trade receivables) from the balance sheet

4. **Liquidity Ratios:** To meet its commitments, business needs liquid funds. The ability of the business to pay the amount due to stakeholders as and when it is due is known as liquidity, and the ratios calculated to measure it are known as 'Liquidity Ratios'. These are essentially short-term in nature.

   They can be classified as:

   i. **Current ratio:** Current ratio is the proportion of current assets to current liabilities. It is expressed as follows: Current Ratio = Current Assets: Current Liabilities or Current Assets / Current Liabilities.

   Current assets include current investments, inventories, trade receivables (debtors and bills receivables), cash and cash equivalents, short-term loans and advances and other current assets such as prepaid expenses, advance tax and accrued income, etc.

   Current liabilities include short-term borrowings, trade payables (creditors and bills payables), other current liabilities and short-term provisions

   ii. **Liquid ratio/Quick ratio/Acid test ratio:** This ratio establishes relationship between liquid assets and current liabilities and is used to measure the firm's ability to pay the claims of creditors immediately. This ratio is a better indicator of liquidity and 1 : 1 is considered to be ideal.

$$\text{Liquid Ratio/Quick Ratio/Acid Test Ratio} = \frac{\text{Liquid Assets or Quick Assets}}{\text{Current Liabilities}}$$

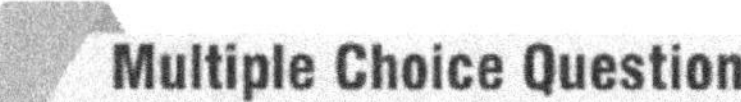

Multiple Choice Questions   [1 Mark]

Q.1. The two basic measures of operations efficiency of a company are:

(a) Inventory turnover ratio and working capital turnover ratio

(b) Liquid ratio and operating ratio

(c) Liquid ratio and current ratio

(d) Gross profit margin and net profit margin.

Ans. (a)

Q.2. Match **List I** (Accounting Ratios) with **List II** (Formulae) and select the correct answer using the codes given below the lists:

List I	List II
A. Current ratio	1. Credit from operations Average trade receivables
B. Return on investment	2. Profit before interest and tax Interest on long – term debt
C. Interest coverage ratio	3. Net profit before interest, Tax and divided Capital employed
D. Trade receivables turnover ratio	4. Current assets Current liabilities

Codes:

(a) A-1, B-3, C-2, D-4   (b) A-4, B-2, C-3, D-1

(c) A-4, B-3, C-2, D-1   (d) A-3, B-2, C-1, D-4

Ans. (c)

Q.3. Two basic measures of liquidity are: [CBSE 2009]

(a) Inventory turnover and Current ratio

(b) Current ratio and Quick ratio

(c) Gross Profit ratio and operating ratio

(d) Current ratio and average Collection period

Ans. (b)

Q.4. A transaction involving decrease in both current ratio and quick ratio is

(a) Sale of non- current asset for cash.

(b) Sale of stock –in trade at loss.

(c) Cash payment of a current liability.

(d) Purchase of stock –in trade on credit.

Ans. (d)

Q.5. Stock is considered as a liquid asset as anytime it can be converted into cash immediately.

(a) True   (b) False   (c) Both   (d) None of the above

Ans. (b)

Q.6. The ideal level of current ratio is

    (a) 4 : 2   (b) 2 : 1   (c) Both (a) and (b)   (d) None of the above

Ans. (c)

Q.7. A transaction involving increase in both current ratio and quick ratio:

    (a) Purchase of stock- in – trade for cash   (b) Sale of stock at loss

    (c) Cash payment of non- current liability   (d) Sale of non- current asset for cash

Ans. (d)

Q.8. Current ratio is:

    (a) Solvency Ratio   (b) Liquidity ratio   (c) Activity Ratio   (d) Profitability Ratio

Ans. (b)

Q.9. Current Ratio is :

    (a) Liquid Assets/Current Assets   (b) Fixed Assets/Current Assets

    (c) Current Assets/Current Liabilities   (d) Liquid assets/Current Liabilities

Ans. (c)

Q.10. Liquid Assets do not include:

    (a) Bills Receivable   (b) Debtors   (c) Inventory   (d) Bank balance

Ans. (c)

Q.11. Ideal Current Ratio is:

    (a) 1 : 1   (b) 1 : 2   (c) 1:3   (d) 2:1

Ans. (d)

Q.12. Working Capital is the: **[CBSE 2020]**

    (a) Cash and Bank Balance

    (b) Capital borrowed from Banks

    (c) Difference between Current Assets and Current Liabilities

    (d) Difference between Current Assets and Fixed assets

Ans. (c)

Q.13. Current assets include only those assets which are expected to be realized within......

    (a) 3 months   (b) 6 months   (c) 1 year   (d) 2 years

Ans. (c)

Q.14. If the liquid ratio of a company is 1.5:1, then the company purchased goods of Rs. 50,000. It will

                                                    [CBSE Sample Paper]

    (a) Decrease in liquid ratio   (b) Increase in liquid assets

    (c) Decrease in current liability   (d) Increase in liquid ratio

Ans. (a)

Q.15. Liquidity ratios are expressed in

    (a) Pure ratio form

    (b) Percentage

    (c) Rate or time

    (d) None of the above

Ans. (a)

Q.16. Liquid ratio is also known as

    A) Quick ratio

    B) Acid test ratio

    C) Working capital ratio

    D) Stock turnover ratio

    (a) A and B   (b) A and C   (c) B and C   (d) C and D

Ans. (a)

Q.17. Current ratio is stated as a crude ratio because

    (a) It measures only the quantity of current assets

    (b) It measures only the quality of current assets

    (c) Both (a) and (b)

    (d) None of the above

Ans. (c)

Q.18. Collection of debtors

    (a) Decreases current ratio

    (b) Increases current ratio

    (c) Has no effect on current ratio

    (d) None of the above

Ans. (a)

Q.19. The most precise test of liquidity is

    (a) Quick ratio

    (b) Current ratio

    (c) Absolute Liquid ratio

    (d) None of the above

Ans. (c)

Q.20. Higher the ratio, the more favorable it is, doesn't stand true for

    (a) Operating ratio

    (b) Liquidity ratio

    (c) Net profit ratio

    (d) Stock turnover ratio

Ans. (a)

Q.21. Liquid assets is determined by

    (a) Current assets – stock - Prepaid expenses

    (b) Current assets + stock + prepaid expenses

    (c) Current assets + Prepaid expenses

    (d) None of the above

Ans. (a)

Read the following statements – Assertion (A) and Reason (R). Choose one of the correct alternatives given below :

Q.22. Assertion (A): Personal bias can be reflected in ratio analysis.

Reason (R): Different people may interpret the same ratio in different ways, which affects its trust ability.

[CBSE guideline]

(a) Both Assertion and reason are true and reason is correct explanation of assertion.

(b) Assertion and reason both are true but reason is not the correct explanation of assertion.

(c) Assertion is true, reason is false.

(d) Assertion is false, reason is true.

Ans. (a)

Q.23. Assertion (A): Inventories and prepaid expenses are not considered as quick assets.

Reason (R): Inventories take some time before it is converted in to cash while prepaid expenses can be converted into cash .

(a) Both Assertion and reason are true and reason is correct explanation of assertion.

(b) Assertion and reason both are true but reason is not the correct explanation of assertion.

(c) Assertion is true, reason is false.

(d) Assertion is false, reason is true.

Ans. (d)

Q.24. Assertion (A): Current ratio is computed to asses the short –term financial position of the enterprise.

Reason (R): Current ratio explains the relation between long- term assets and currents liabilities of a business.

(a) Both Assertion and reason are true and reason is correct explanation of assertion.

(b) Assertion and reason both are true but reason is not the correct explanation of assertion.

(c) Assertion is true, reason is false.

(d) Assertion is false, reason is true.

Ans. (d)

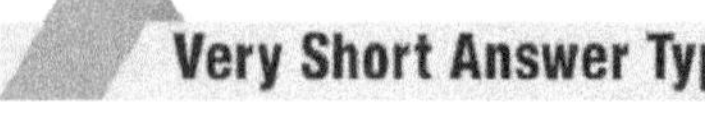
Very Short Answer Type   **[1 Mark]**

State whether the following statement are True or False:

Q.25. Current ratio improves with increase in sales at profit.

Ans. True

Q.26. The four classification of ratio analysis are liquidity ratio, fixed asset ratio, Profitability ratio and efficiency ratio.

Ans. True

Q.27. Liquid ratio is also known as acid test ratio.

Ans. True

Q.28. A loose tool is a part of Inventory while calculating current Ratio.

Ans. True

Fill in the blanks with appropriate word:

Q.29. An ideal Quick Ratio is ……………

Ans. 1 : 1

Q.30. ……………is the process of determining and interpreting numerical relationship between figures of the financial statements.

Ans. Ratio Analysis

Q.31. How will you asses the liquidity or short term financial position of a business ?

Ans. Short term financial position of the business is assessed by calculating current ratio and liquid ratio.

Q.32. Why Liquidity ratios are calculated?

Ans. Liquidity Ratios are calculated to know short term solvency position.

Q.33. List two Ratios which are included in liquidity Ratios

Ans. Current Ratio, Quick Ratio

Q.34. Current Ratio is also known as?

Ans. working capital Ratio

Q.35. Quick Ratio is also called as ?   [CBSE 2019]

Ans. Acid test Ratio or Liquid Ratio

Q.36. Write formula for working capital Ratio.

Ans. Working capital Ratio = Current assets-Current liabilities.

Short Answer Type - I   [2 Marks]

Q.37. Define Ratio Analysis.   [CBSE 2008, 2016]

Ans. Ratio Analysis: It is a technique of analysis of financial statements to conduct a quantitative analysis of information in a company's financial statements. "Ratio analysis is a study of relationship among various financial factors in a business."

Q.38. In how many ways a Ratio may be expressed?

Ans. There are four ways to express the ratio:

    1. Pure   2. Times   3. %   4. Fraction

Q.39. Give two objectives of Ratio Analysis.

Ans. 1. To find out the weak areas of business

    2. To help in formulation of plans for future

Q.40. List two uses of Accounting Ratios.   [CBSE Compartment 2-18]

Ans. 1.To Analyse the financial statements

2. To simplify the Accounting Data

Q.41. Write two limitations of Accounting Ratios.   [CBSE Sample Paper]

Ans. 1.   Ignoring Price level changes

2. Ignoring qualitative aspect

Q.42. Current ratio of Arora Ltd. Is 1.5 at present, In future it want to improve this ratio to 2:1. Suggest any two accounting transaction for improving the current ratio.

Ans. 2 (i) Payment of current liabilities (ii) Issue of share capital etc.

Q.43. State one transaction which results in an increase in ' liquid ratio 'and no change in 'current ratio'.

[CBSE 2018]

Ans. Sale of stock at cost price.

Q.44. Why stock is excluded from liquid assets ?

Ans. (i) because there is uncertainty whether it will be sold or not.

(ii) It will take time before it is converted into debtors' and cash.

Q.45. Quick ratio of a company is 1.5 :1 . state giving reason whether the ratio will improve, decline or not change on payment of dividend by the company.

Ans. Quick ratio will improve as both the liquid assets and current liabilities will decrease by the same Amount.

Q.46. What are current Assets?   [CBSE 2016]

Ans. Assets which may be converted into cash or cash equivalent within, 12 months from the date of Balance sheet or operating cycle.

Q.47. What are current liabilities?

Ans. Liabilities which are to be paid within 12 months from the date of Balance sheet or operating cycle.

Q.48. Give examples of current liabilities?

Ans. Short term borrowing (including Bank overdraft), trade payables (Bills payables and sundry creditors), other current liabilities.

Q.49. What are liquid Assets?   [CBSE 2015]

Ans. These assets which can be converted into cash or cash equivalents within short period of time.

Q.50. Give examples of Liquid Assets

Ans. Current investments, trade receivables, cash and cash equivalents, short term loans and advances.

Short Answer Type - II   [3 Marks]

Q.51. Quick ratio is 1.8:1, current ratio is 2.7:1 and current liabilities are Rs. 60,000. Determine value of stock.

[CBSE Sample Paper]

Ans. Rs. 54,000

Q.52. Current assets are Rs. 10,00,000, inventories Rs. 5,00,000, working capital Rs. 6,00,000. Calculate current ratio.

Ans. 2.5 : 1

Q.53. If current ratio of a firm is 2.5:1 and its current assets are Rs. 4,00,000. Its working capital will be.

Ans. Rs. 6,00,000

Q.54. A Company's liquid assets are Rs.5,00,000 and its current liabilities are Rs.3,00,000. Thereafter, it paid Rs.1,00,000 to its trade payables. Quick ratio will be.

Ans. 2:1

Q.55. A Company's Quick Ratio is 1.5:1; Current Liabilities are Rs. 2,00,000 and Inventory is Rs.1,80,000. Current Ratio will be: **[CBSE 2011]**

Ans. 2.4 : 1

Q.56. Current ratio is 2:1 current assets = Rs. 82,000. What will be current liabilities?

Ans. Rs. 41,000

Q.57. Current ratio 1.5 : 1, Working capital Rs. 30,000. What will be the current liabilities and Current assets? **[CBSE Compartment]**

Ans. Current assets = 90,000

Current Liabilities = 60,000

Q.58. Find the value of current liabilities and current assets if Current Ratio is 2.5:1. Liquid Ratio is 1.2:1 and the value of inventory of the firm is Rs. 78,000.

Ans. Current Assets = Rs. 1,50,000;

Current liabilities = Rs. 60,000

Q.59. Current Ratio is 3.5. Working Capital is Rs. 90,000. Calculate the amount of Current Assets and Current Liabilities. **[CBSE2016]**

Ans. Current Assets =1,26,000

Current liabilities = 36,000

Q.60. Sushi Limited has current ratio 4.5:1 and quick ratio 3:1; if the inventory is Rs. 36,000, calculate current liabilities, Liquid assets and current assets. **[CBSE 2008]**

Ans. Current Assets = 1,08,000.

Current Liabilities = 24,000

Liquid assets = 72,000

Q.61. Current liabilities of a company are Rs. 75,000. If current ratio is 4:1 and liquid ratio is 1:1, calculate value of current assets, liquid assets and inventory.

Ans. Inventory = 2,25,000

Current assets = 3,00,000

Liquid assets = 75,000

Q.62. Devika Ltd. has inventory of Rs. 20,000. Total liquid assets are Rs. 1,00,000 and quick ratio is 2:1. Calculate current ratio.

Ans. Current Ratio = 2 : 4 : 1

Current assets = 1,20,000

Current liabilities = 50,000

Q.63. Current Assets Rs. 2,00,000; Inventories Rs. 1,00,000; Working Capital Rs. 1,20,000; Calculate Current Ratio.

[CBSE 2019]

Current liabilities = Current Assets – Working Capital

Rs. 2,00,000 – Rs. 1,20,000 = Rs. 80,000

Current Ratio = Current Assets/ Current liabilities

= Rs. 2,00,000/Rs. 80,000

Ans. = 2.5 : 1

TOPIC 2 Solvency, Turnover, Profitability Ratios

Summary

Solvency Ratios:

Solvency of business is determined by its ability to meet its contractual obligations towards stakeholders, particularly towards external stakeholders, and the ratios calculated to measure solvency position are known as 'Solvency Ratios'. These are essentially long-term in nature.

They can be classified as:

i. **Debt-Equity Ratio:** Debt-Equity Ratio measures the relationship between long-term debt and equity

Debt-Equity Ratio = Long "term Debts / Shareholders' Funds

where:

Shareholders' Funds (Equity) = Share capital + Reserves and Surplus + Money received against share warrants + Share application money pending allotment

Share Capital = Equity share capital + Preference share capital

Working Capital = Current Assets – Current Liabilities

Significance: This ratio measures the degree of indebtedness of an enterprise and gives an idea to the long-term lender regarding extent of security of the debt. A low debt equity ratio reflects more security. A high ratio, on the other hand, is considered risky as it may put the firm into difficulty in meeting its obligations to outsiders.

ii. **Debt to Capital Employed Ratio:** The Debt to capital employed ratio refers to the ratio of long-term debt to the total of external and internal funds (capital employed or net assets).

Significance: Like debt-equity ratio, it shows proportion of long-term debts in capital employed. Low ratio provides security to lenders and high ratio helps management in trading on equity.

Debt to Capital Employed Ratio = Long-term Debt/Capital Employed (or Net Assets)

Notes: Capital employed = Shareholders' funds + Long-term debts (or Non-current liabilities)

Alternatively, Capital employed = Net assets = Total assets – Current liabilities

or = Non-current assets + Net working capital

Significance: Like debt-equity ratio, it shows proportion of long-term debts in capital employed. Low ratio provides security to lenders and high ratio helps management in trading on equity.

Debt to Capital Employed Ratio can also be computed in relation to total assets.

Debt to Capital Employed Ratio = Total debts / Total assets

Total debts = Long-term debts + Current liabilities Total assets = Non-current assets + Current assets (or shareholders' funds + long-term debts + current liabilities).

iii.　**Proprietary Ratio:** Proprietary ratio expresses relationship of proprietor's (shareholders) funds to net assets.

Proprietary Ratio = Shareholders', Funds/Capital employed (or net assets)

Significance: Higher proportion of shareholders funds in financing the assets is a positive feature as it provides security to creditors. This ratio can also be computed in relation to total assets instead of net assets (capital employed)

iv.　**Total Assets to Debt Ratio:** This ratio measures the extent of the coverage of long-term debts by assets.

Significance: This ratio primarily indicates the rate of external funds in financing the assets and the extent of coverage of their debts are covered by assets.

Total assets to Debt Ratio = Total assets / Long-term debts

v.　**Interest Coverage Ratio:** This ratio expresses the relationship between net profit before interest and tax and interest payable on long-term debts. The ideal coverage ratio is 6 to 7 times.

$$\text{Interest Coverage Ratio} = \frac{\text{Net profit before Interest and Tax}}{\text{Interest on Long} - \text{term Debts}}$$

Significance: It reveals the number of times interest on long-term debts is covered by the profits available for interest. A higher ratio ensures safety of interest on debts.

vi.　**Fixed Assets Turnover Ratio:**

It reflects relationship between net revenue from operations and net fixed assets of the business. Higher turnover means better activity and profitability.

Fixed Assets Turnover ratio = Net Revenue from Operations Net Fixed Assets

Significance: High turnover of fixed assets is a good sign and implies efficient utilisation of resources resulting in higher liquidity and profitability in the business.

vii.　**Net Assets Turnover Ratio (or Capital Employed Turnover Ratio)**

It reflects relationship between net revenue from operations and net assets (capital employed) in the business. Higher turnover means better activity and profitability.

Net Assets Turnover ratio (or Capital Employed Turnover Ratio) = Net Revenue from Operations Capital Employed (or Net Assets)

Significance: High turnover of net assets (or capital employed) is a good sign and implies efficient utilisation of resources resulting in higher liquidity and profitability in the business.

Activity (or Turnover) Ratios: These ratios indicate the speed at which, activities of the business are being performed. The activity ratios express the number of times assets employed, or, for that matter, any constituent of assets, is turned into sales during an accounting period. Higher turnover ratio means better utilisation of assets and signifies improved efficiency and profitability, and as such are known as efficiency ratios.

They can be classified as:

i.　**Stock turnover ratio or Inventory turnover ratio:** The ratio indicates the number of times the stock is turned in sales during the accounting period, i.e. it measures how fast the stock is moving through the firm and generating sales.

Inventory Turnover Ratio = Cost of Revenue from Operations / Average Inventory

Significance: It studies the frequency of conversion of inventory of finished goods into revenue from operations. It is also a measure of liquidity. It determines how many times inventory is purchased or replaced during a year. Low turnover of inventory may be due to bad buying, obsolete inventory, etc., and is a danger signal. High turnover is good but it must be carefully interpreted as it may be due to buying in small lots or selling quickly at low margin to realise cash. Thus, it throws light on utilisation of inventory of goods.

ii. **Trade Receivables or Debtors turnover ratio:** It indicates economy and efficiency in the collection of amount due from debtors.

Trade Receivable Turnover ratio = Net Credit Revenue from Operations / Average Trade Receivable

Significance: The liquidity position of the firm depends upon the speed with which trade receivables are realised. This ratio indicates the number of times the receivables are turned over and converted into cash in an accounting period. Higher turnover means speedy collection from trade receivable. This ratio also helps in working out the average collection period. The ratio is calculated by dividing the days or months in a year by trade receivables turnover ratio.

iii. **Trade payables or Creditors turnover ratio:** It indicates the speed with which the amount is being paid to creditors. The higher the ratio, the better it is.

$$\text{Creditors/Payables Turnover Ratio} = \frac{\text{Net Credit Purchases}}{\text{Average Payables}}$$

Net Credit Purchases = Credit Purchases – Purchase Return

Significance: It reveals average payment period. Lower ratio means credit allowed by the supplier is for a long period or it may reflect delayed payment to suppliers which is not a very good policy as it may affect the reputation of the business. The average period of payment can be worked out by days/ months in a year by the Trade Payable Turnover Ratio

iv. **Net Assets or Capital Employed Turnover Ratio:** It reflects relationship between revenue from operations and net assets (capital employed) in the business. Higher turnover means better activity and profitability.

Net Assets or Capital Employed Turnover ratio = Revenue from Operation/ Capital Employed

Significance : High turnover of capital employed, working capital and fixed assets is a good sign and implies efficient utilisation of resources. Utilisation of capital employed or, for that matter, any of its components is revealed by the turnover ratios. Higher turnover reflects efficient utilisation resulting in higher liquidity and profitability in the business.

Profitability Ratios: It refers to the analysis of profits in relation to revenue from operations or funds (or assets) employed in the business and the ratios calculated to meet this objective are known as 'Profitability Ratios'.

They can be classified as:

i. **Gross Profit Ratio:** Gross profit ratio as a percentage of revenue from operations is computed to have an idea about gross margin.

Gross Profit Ratio = Gross Profit / Net Revenue of Operations × 100

Significance: It indicates gross margin on products sold. It also indicates the margin available to cover operating expenses, non-operating expenses, etc. Change in gross profit ratio may be due to change in selling price or cost of revenue from operations or a combination of both. A low ratio may indicate unfavourable purchase and sales policy. Higher gross profit ratio is always a good sign.

ii. **Operating Ratio:** It is computed to analyse cost of operation in relation to revenue from operations.

Operating Ratio = (Cost of Revenue from Operations + Operating Expenses) / Net Revenue from Operations × 100

Operating expenses include office expenses, administrative expenses, selling expenses, distribution expenses, depreciation and employee benefit expenses etc.

Cost of operation is determined by excluding non-operating incomes and expenses such as loss on sale of assets, interest paid, dividend received, loss by fire, speculation gain and so on.

iii.	**Operating Profit Ratio:** It is calculated to reveal operating margin. It may be computed directly or as a residual of operating ratio.

Operating Profit Ratio = 100 – Operating Ratio

Significance: Operating ratio is computed to express cost of operations excluding financial charges in relation to revenue from operations. A corollary of it is 'Operating Profit Ratio'. It helps to analyse the performance of business and throws light on the operational efficiency of the business. It is very useful for inter-firm as well as intra-firm comparisons. Lower operating ratio is a very healthy sign.

iv.	**Net Profit Ratio:** Net profit ratio is based on all inclusive concept of profit.

Net Profit Ratio = Net profit/Revenue from Operations × 100

Significance: It is a measure of net profit margin in relation to revenue from operations. Besides revealing profitability, it is the main variable in computation of Return on Investment. It reflects the overall efficiency of the business, assumes great significance from the point of view of investors.

v.	**Return on investment/Capital employed:** It establishes the relationship between net profit before interest, tax and preference dividend and capital employed (equity + debts).

Return on Investment (or Capital Employed) = Profit before Interest and Tax/ Capital Employed × 100

Significance: It measures return on capital employed in the business. It reveals the efficiency of the business in utilisation of funds entrusted to it by shareholders, debenture-holders and long-term loans

vi.	**Return on Shareholders' Funds:** It helps the shareholder's in assessing whether their investment in the firm generates a reasonable return or not.

This ratio is very important from shareholders' point of view in assessing whether their investment in the firm generates a reasonable return or not. It should be higher than the return on investment otherwise it would imply that company's funds have not been employed profitably.

Return on Shareholders' Fund = Profit after Tax Shareholders' Funds × 100

vii.	**Earnings per Share The ratio is computed as:**

EPS = Profit available for equity shareholders/Number of Equity Shares

This ratio is very important from equity shareholders point of view and also for the share price in the stock market. This also helps comparison with other to ascertain its reasonableness and capacity to pay dividend.

viii.	**Book Value per Share This ratio is calculated as :**

Book Value per share = Equity shareholders' funds/Number of Equity Shares

Equity shareholder fund refers to Shareholders' Funds – Preference Share Capital. This ratio is again very important from equity shareholders point of view as it gives an idea about the value of their holding and affects market price of the shares.

ix.	**Dividend Payout Ratio:** This refers to the proportion of earning that are distributed to the shareholders.

Dividend Payout Ratio = Dividend per share / Earnings per share

x.	**Price / EarningRatio:**

The ratio is computed as –

	P/E Ratio = Market Price of a share/earnings per share

Multiple Choice Questions [1 Mark]

Q.1. Which of the following is not correct?

(a) Equity = capital employed +debt.

(b) Equity = share capital + reserves and surplus

(c) Debt = long –term borrowing + long –term provisions.

(d) Working capital= current assets- current liabilities.

Ans. (a)

Q.2. Harshita Ltd. has a proprietary ratio of 25% to maintain this ratio at 30% management may

(a) Increase equity.   (b) Reduce debt.

(c) Either increase equity or reduce debt.   (d) Increase current assets.

Ans. (c)

Q.3. Fixed Assets Rs.5,00,000; Current Assets Rs.3,00,000; Equity Share Capital Rs.4,00,000; Reserve Rs.2,00,000; Long –term debts Rs.40,000.Proprietory Ratio will be: **[CBSE 2015]**

(a) 75%   (b) 80%   (c) 125%   (d) 133%

Ans. (a)

Q.4. If Debt equity ratio exceeds ……………., it indicates risky financial position.

(a) 1 : 1   (b) 2 : 1   (c) 1 : 2   (d) 3 : 1

Ans. (b)

Q.5. Equity Share Capital Rs.20,00,000; Reserves Rs.5,00,000; Debentures Rs.10,00,000; Current Liabilities Rs.8,00,000. Debt-equity ratio will be:

(a) 0.4 : 1   (b) 0.32 : 1   (c) 0.72 : 1   (d) 0.5 : 1

Ans. (a)

Q.6. On the basis of following data, the Debt-Equity Ratio of a Company will be: Equity Share Capital Rs.5,00,000; General Reserve Rs.3,20,000; Preliminary Expenses Rs.20,000; Debentures Rs.3,20,000; Preliminary Expenses Rs.20,000; Debentures Rs.3,20,000; Current Liabilities Rs.80,000. **[CBSE Sample Paper]**

(a) 1 : 2   (b) 0.52 : 1   (c) 0.4 : 1   (d) 0.37 : 1

Ans. (c)

Q.7. On the basis of the following information received from a firm, its Proprietory Ratio will be:

Fixed Assets Rs.3,30,000; Current Assets Rs.1,90,000; Preliminary Expenses Rs.30,000; Equity share Capital Rs.2,44,000; Preference Share capital Rs.1,70,000; Reserve Fund Rs.58,000.

(a) 70%   (b) 80%   (c) 85%   (d) 90%

Ans. (c)

Q.8. If opening inventory is Rs. 1,20,000, cost of revenge from operations is Rs. 10,00,000 and inventory turnover ratio is 5 times then closing inventory will be

(a) Rs. 3,20,000.   (b) Rs. 2,80,00.   (c) Rs. 1,60,000.   (d) Rs. 4,00,000.

Ans. (b)

Q.9. Opening Inventory Rs.1,00,000; Closing Inventory Rs.1,50,000; Purchases Rs.6,00,000; Carriage Rs.25,000; wages Rs.2,00,000. Inventory Turnover Ratio will be: **[CBSE 2012]**

(a) 6.6 Times   (b) 7.4 Times   (c) 7 Times   (d) 6.2 Times

Ans. (d)

Q.10. Revenue from Operations Rs.2,00,000; Inventory Turnover ratio 5; Gross Profit 25%. Find out the value of Closing Inventory, if Closing Inventory is Rs.8,000 more than the Opening Inventory.   **[CBSE 2019]**

(a) Rs.38,000   (b) Rs.22,000   (c) Rs.34,000   (d) Rs.26,000

Ans. (c)

Q.11. Total revenue from operations Rs.9,00,000; Cash revenue from operations Rs.3,00,000; Debtors Rs.1,00,000; B/R Rs.20,000. Trade Receivables Turnover Ratio will be: **[CBSE Compartment 2017]**

(a) 5 Times   (b) 6 Times   (c) 7.5 Times   (d) 9 Times

Ans. (a)

Q.12. Trade receivable turnover ratio 5 times, average trade receivables Rs. 60,000. Calculate net credit revenue from operations.

(a) Rs. 3,00,000   (b) Rs. 2,00,000   (c) Rs. 12,000   (d) Rs.2,40,000

Ans. (a)

Q.13. If cash sales is Rs. 2,00,000 and credit sales is 20% of total sales. Calculate amount of credit sales.

(a) Rs. 50,000   (b) Rs. 2,50,000   (c) Rs. 16,000   (d) Rs. 3,00,000

Ans. (a)

Q.14. If average inventory is Rs. 30,000 and closing inventory is Rs. 20,000 more than the opening, what will be the value of closing inventory?   **[CBSE 2015]**

(a) Rs. 10,000   (b) Rs. 20,000   (c) Rs. 30,000   (d) Rs. 40,000

Ans. (d)

Q.15. If credit revenue from operation is Rs. 7,00,000. Cash revenue operations is Rs. 1,00,000. Cost of revenue from operations is Rs. 6,40,000, then gross profit ratio will be   **[CBSE Sample paper]**

(a) 15%   (b) 18%   (c) 25%   (d) 20%

Ans. (d)

Q.16. If revenue from operation is 2,50,000 and gross profit ratio is 25% the amount of gross profit will be

(a) Rs. 60,000   (b) Rs. 62,500   (c) Rs. 80,000   (d) Rs. 50,000

Ans. (b)

Q.17. Revenue from operations Rs. 9,00,000, gross profit 25% on cost ,operating expenses Rs. 90,000, operating ratio will be

(a) 100%   (b) 50%   (c) 90%   (d) 10%

Ans. (c)

Q.18. A firm's credit revenue from operations is Rs.3,60,000, cash revenue from operations is Rs.70,000. Cost of revenue from operations is Rs.3,61,200. Its gross profit ratio will be:

(a) 11% (b) 15% (c) 18% (d) 16%

Ans. (d)

Q.19. Revenue from Operations Rs.6,00,000; Gross Profit 20%; Office Expenses Rs.30,000; Selling Expenses Rs.48,000. Calculate operating ratio.   **[CBSE 2018]**

(a) 80% (b) 85% (c) 96.33% (d) 93%

Ans. (d)

Q.20. While calculating Earnings per share, if both equity and preference share capitals are there, then

(a) Preference share is deducted from the net profit (b) Equity share capital is deducted from the net profit

(c) Both (a) and (b) (d) None of the above

Ans. (a)

Q.21. Return on equity capital is calculated on basis of:

(a) Funds of equity shareholders (b) Equity capital only

(c) Either (a) or (b) (d) None of the above

Ans. (c)

Q.22. Overall Profitability ratios are based on

(a) Investments (b) Sales (c) Both (a) and (b) (d) None of the above

Ans. (a)

Q.23. Which of the following is expenses ratio?

A) Administrative expenses ratio

B) Selling and Distribution expenses ratio

C) Factory expenses ratio

D) Finance Expenses ratio

(a) A, B and D (b) A, C and D (c) A, B and C (d) A, B, C, D

Ans. (d)

Q.24. Operating ratio is calculated by

(a) (Operating Cost / Gross sales) × 100 (b) (Operating Cost / Gross sales) × 100

(c) (Operating cost / Net sales) × 100 (d) None of the above

Ans. (c)

Q.25. Net operating profit ratio determines

(a) Overall efficiency of the business, working efficiency of the management

(b) Working efficiency of the management, overall efficiency of the business

(c) Overall efficiency of the external market, working efficiency of the internal management

(d) None of the above

Ans. (b)

Q.26. Gross Profit ratio should be adequate to cover

(a) Selling expenses

(b) Administrative expenses

(c) Dividends

(d) All of the above

Ans. (d)

Q.27. Assertion (A): The debt to equity ratio will increase at the time of issue of equity shares for cash.

Reason (R): Issue of equity shares will increase the shareholder's funds but the long-term debts will remain the same. [cbse guideline]

(a) Both Assertion and reason are true and reason is correct explanation of assertion.

(b) Assertion and reason both are true but reason is not the correct explanation of assertion.

(c) Assertion is true, reason is false.

(d) Assertion is false, reason is true.

Ans. (c)

Very Short Answer Type   [1 Mark]

State whether the following statement are True or False:

Q.28. Solvency refers to the ability of the enterprise to meet its current obligations.

Ans. True

Q.29. Lower the Gross Profit Ratio, higher will be the profitability of a company.

Ans. False

Q.30. Shareholders 'funds are also known as net worth.   [CBSE 2009]

Ans. True

Q.31. A short term borrowing is a part of capital employed.

Ans. False

Q.32. Net worth is also known as Share capital.

Ans. False

Q.33. Solvency refers to the ability of the enterprise to meet its current obligations.

Ans. False

Q.34. Purchase of goods will increase the cost of Revenue from operations.   [CBSE 2012]

Ans. True

Q.35. State one transaction which result in a decrease in 'debt-equity ratio 'and no change in ' current Ratio'.

[CBSE Sample Paper]

Ans. Conversion of debentures into shares.

Q.36. How does ratio analysis becomes less effective when the price level changes?

Ans. Accounting ratios are calculated from financial statements, which are down on the basis of historical Cost as recorded in the book of accounts .

Q.37. Indicate which ratio a shareholders would use who is examining his portfolio and wants to decide Whether he should hold or sell his shareholdings?

Ans. Total Assets to Debt Ratio.

Q.38. Indicate which ratio would be used by a Long-Term creditor who is interested in determining whether his claim is adequately secured?

Ans. Debt-Equity-Ratio

Q.39. What will be the Operating profit, If operating Ratio is 78%?   **[CBSE 2011]**

Ans. 100 – 78 = 22%

Q.40. The Debaters turnover Ratio of a company is 6 times. State with reasons whether the ratio will Improve, decrease, or not change due to increases in the value of closing stock by Rs. 50,000?

Ans. No change because it will neither affect net credit sales nor average receivable.

Q.41. What will be the impact of 'Issue of shares against the purchase of fixed assets'on a debt Equity ratio of 1:1?

[CBSE Compartment Paper]

Ans. Debt-equity ratio will decrease because the Long-term loans remain unchanged whereas the Shareholders funds are increased by the amount f share capital issued .

Q.42. Assuming that the Debt Equity Ratio is 2:1. State giving reason, whether the ratio will improve, decline or will have no change in case bonus shares allotted to equity shareholders by Capitalizing profits.

Ans. Debt equity ratio will not change as the total amount of shareholders' funds will remain same.

Q.43. A company has a loan of Rs.15,00,000 as part of its capital employed. The interest payable on Loan is 15% and the ROI of the company is 25%. The rate of income tax is 60%. what is the Gain to shareholders due to the loan raised by the company?

Ans. Net gain to shareholders Rs.60,000.

Q.44. What do you mean by solvency Ratios?   **[CBSE 2014]**

Ans. Those ratios which show whether the business will be able to pay its long term commitment/ payments on time.

Q.45. How can we calculate debt?

Ans. Debt = long term borrowings + long term provisions

OR

= Total Debt-current liabilities

Q.46. How to deal with debit balance of statement of P&L account?

Ans. It is to be deducted from equity / shareholders' funds

Q.47. What are long term provisions?

Ans. Provisions for those liabilities to be paid after 12 months from the date of balance sheet or after operating cycle.

Q.48. Give examples of longterm provisions?

Ans. Employees benefit expenses like provision for gratuity, provision for warranty.

Q.49. Return on Proprietors funds is also known as:

Ans. Return on Shareholders' Investment

Q.50. Debt-equity ratio is a sub-part of which category of ratios?

Ans. Long-term solvency ratio

Q.51. What are the other names of Activity ratios?

Ans. Activity Ratios are also known as performance Ratios/ turnover Ratios.

Q.52. Working capital turnover ratio can be determined by:

Ans. (Cost of goods sold / Working capital)

Q.53. Debtors Turnover ratio is also known as

Ans. Trade Receivables turnover ratio

Q.54. Stock velocity establishes a relationship between

Ans. Cost of goods sold in a given period and the average amount of inventory held during that period .

Q.55. Net Profit ratio is calculated by

Ans. (Net Profit / Net sales) × 100

Q.56. Give examples of non-operating incomes

Ans. Interest received, dividend received, profit on sale of fixed assets.

Q.57. Give examples of non-operating expenses

Ans. Interest on long term loans, loss on sale of non-current assets.

## Short Answer Type - I	[2 Marks]

Q.58. Calculate Debt-Equity ratio from the following information: Total equity Rs.2,50,000, Total Debt Rs. 5,00,000

Ans. Debt Equity ratio = Debt / Equity

Debt Equity Ratio = 2 : 1

Q.59. Calculate proprietary ratio: if share capital Rs. 5,00,000, reserve & surplus Rs. 2,00,000 and general reserve Rs. 1,00,000 and total assets Rs. 21,00,000.

Ans. 0.33 : 1

Q.60. Rs.2,00,000 is the cost of goods sold, inventory turnover 8 times, stock at the beginning is 1.5 Times more than the stock at the end. Calculate the value of opening & closing stock. **[CBSE 2019]**

Ans. Closing stock = Rs.14,285.

Opening stock = Rs.35,715.

Q.61. From the given information, calculate the stock turnover ratio: sales Rs.5,00,000, Gross Profit 25% on cost , opening stock was $1/3^{rd}$ of the value of closing stock. Closing stock was 30% Of sales.

Ans. Stock turnover Ratio = 4 times

Q.62. Calculate cost of goods sold from the following information: Sales Rs.12,00,000, Sales Returns Rs.80,000, operating expenses Rs.1,82,000, operating ratio 92%.

Ans. Cost of goods sold =Rs.8,48,400.

Q.63. If sales is Rs 10,00,000, sales returns is Rs 50,000, Profit Before Tax is Rs 2,00,000, Income tax is 40%, Net profit ratio is

Ans. 12.63%

Q.64. If sales is Rs 5,00,000 and net profit is Rs 1,20,000 Net Profit ratio is **[CBSE 2017]**

Ans. 24%

Q.65. Determine Operating ratio, if operating expenses is Rs 60,000, Sales is Rs 9,40,000, Sales Return is Rs 40,000 and Cost of net goods sold is Rs 6,60,000.

Ans. 80%

Q.66. What will be the Gross Profit if, total sales is Rs. 2,60,000, cost of net goods sold is Rs 2,00,000 and sales return is Rs 10,000?

Ans. 20%

Q.67. From the following information. Calculate Debt-equity Ratio: Equity Share Capital 1,50,000 Preference Share capital 1,00,000 Reserves and Surplus 1,50,000 Long-term Borrowings 6,00,000 Long-term Provisions 2,00,000

Ans.　　　　　　　　　　　　　Debt = Long-term Borrowings + Long-term Provisions

$$= Rs.\ 6,00,000 + Rs.\ 2,00,000 = Rs.\ 8,00,000$$

Equity = Equity Share Capital + Pref. Share Capital + Reserves & Surplus

$$= Rs.\ 1,50,000 + Rs.\ 1,00,000 + Rs.\ 1,50,000 = Rs.\ 4,00,000$$

$$\text{Debt-Equity Ratio} = \frac{\text{Debt}}{\text{Equity}} = \frac{Rs.\ 8,00,000}{Rs.\ 4,00,000} = 2{:}1$$

Q.68. Tanmay ltd. has a liquid ratio of 1.5 : 1. Its Net working Capital is Rs. 1,20,000 and its inventories are Rs 80,000. Total Assets Rs. 3,80,000. Total Debt Rs. 2,80,000. Calculate Debt-Equity Ratio.

Ans.　　　　　　　　　$\text{Debt-Equity Ratio} = \dfrac{\text{Debt}}{\text{Equity}} = 2 : 1$

Q.69. From the following information, calculate Proprietory Ratio: Share Capital Rs. 2,50,000 Reserves & Surplus Rs. 1,50,000 Non-current Assets Rs. 11,00,000 Current Assets Rs. 5,00,000. **[CBSE compartment paper]**

Ans.
$$\text{Proprietary ratio} = \frac{\text{Equity}}{\text{Total assets}} \times 100$$

$$= \frac{\text{Rs. } 4,00,000}{\text{Rs. } 16,00,000} \times 100 = 25\%$$

Q.70. P ltd has a long term loan Rs. 10,00,000. Interest on the loan for the year is Rs. 1,25,000 and its profit before interest and tax is Rs. 5,00,000. Calculate Interest coverage ratio.

Ans.
$$\text{Interest coverage ratio} = \frac{\text{EBIT}}{\text{Fixed int. charges}}$$

$$\text{Interest coverage ratio} = \frac{5,00,000}{1,25,000} = 4 \text{ times.}$$

Q.71. Calculate the amount of opening stock and closing stock from the following figures:

Average Debt collection period 4 month stock turnover ratio 3 times. Average Debtors Rs.1,00,000 Cash sales being 25% of total sales Gross profit ratio 25% stock at the end was 3 Times that in the beginning.

Ans. Opening stock Rs. 50,000.

Closing stock Rs. 1,50,000.

Q.72. Determine Debtors turnover ratio if, closing debtors is Rs 40,000, Cash sales is 25% of credit sales and excess of closing debtors over opening debtors is Rs 20,000.

Ans. 4 times

Q.73. Determine stock turnover ratio if, Opening stock is Rs 31,000, Closing stock is Rs 29,000, Sales is Rs 3,20,000 and Gross profit ratio is 25% on sales.

Ans. 8 times

Q.74. Determine Working capital turnover ratio if, Current assets is Rs 1,50,000, current liabilities is Rs 1,00,000 and Cost of goods sold is Rs 3,00,000.

Ans. 6 times

Q.75. Cost of goods sold/Revenue from operations Rs. 9,00,000 Inventories in the beginning Rs. 2,00,000 Inventories at the end Rs. 2,50,000. **[CBSE 2013]**

Ans.
$$\text{Inventory turnover ratio} = \frac{9,00,000}{2,25,000} = 4 \text{ times}$$

Q.76. Calculate Trade receivable or Debtors turnover ratio and Average collection period.

Credit revenue from operation for the year is Rs. 12,00,000, Debtors Rs. 1,00,000; Bills receivable Rs. 1,00,000.

Ans.
$$\text{Debtors turnover ratio} = \frac{12,00,000}{2,00,000} = 6 \text{ times}$$

$$\text{Average collection period} = \frac{\text{No. of days in a year}}{\text{Trade receivable ratio}} = \frac{365}{6}$$

$$= 61 \text{ days approx.}$$

Q.77. Closing Trade Payables Rs. 45,000, Net Purchases Rs. 3,60,000, Cash Purchases Rs. 90,000, Reserve for Discount on Closing Trade Payables Rs. 5,000. Calculate the Creditors Turnover Ratio.

Trade payables/Creditors turnover ratio Net credit purchases/avg accounts payables

$$\text{Creditors Turnover Ratio} = \frac{(\text{Rs. } 3,60,000 - \text{Rs. } 90,000)}{\text{Rs. } 45,000} = 6 \text{ times}$$

$$\text{Average Payment Period} = \frac{12 \text{ months}}{\text{Creditors turnover ratio}} = 2 \text{ months}$$

Q.78. Calculate Working capital turnover ratio from the following:

Cost of revenue from operations Rs. 3,00,000 Current Assets Rs. 2,00,000 Current liabilities Rs. 1,50,000

$$\text{Working capital turnover ratio} = \frac{\text{Working Capital}}{\text{Net sales}} = \frac{3,00,000}{50,000}$$
$$= 6 \text{ times.}$$

Q.79. Calculate Gross Profit Ratio: Revenue from operations – Rs. 6,00,000 Gross profit 25% on cost.

[CBSE Sample Paper]

Ans.
$$\text{Gross Profit Ratio} = \frac{\text{Gross profit}}{\text{Net sales}} \times 100$$

Let the cost = Rs.100 Gross profit = Rs. 25 Revenue from operations =Rs.125

$$\text{Cost of revenue from operations} = \frac{100}{125} \times 6,00,000 = 4,80,000$$
$$\text{Gross Profit} = 6,00,000 - 4,80,000 = 1,20,000$$
$$\text{Gross Profit Ratio} = \frac{1,20,000}{6,00,000} \times 100 = 20\%$$

Q.80. Revenue from operations Rs. 6,00,000, Operating Cost Rs. 5,10,000. Cost of Revenue from operations Rs. 4,00,000. Calculate Operating Profit Ratio. **[CBSE 2020]**

Ans.
$$\text{Operating Profit Ratio} = \frac{\text{Operating Profit}}{\text{Net Sales}}$$
$$\text{Operating Profit} = \text{Rs. } 6,00,000 - 5,10,000 = \text{Rs. } 90,000$$
$$\text{Operating Profit Ratio} = \frac{\text{Rs. } 90,000}{\text{Rs. } 6,00,000} \times 100 = 15\%$$

Q.81. From the following information calculate operating ratio Cost of revenue from operation = Rs. 6,00,000 Operating expenses = Rs. 40,000 Revenue from operation = Rs. 8,20,000 Revenue return from operations = Rs. 20,000

Ans.
$$\text{Operating ratio} = \frac{\text{Operating cost}}{\text{Net sales}}$$
$$\text{Operating ratio} = \left(6,00,000 + \frac{40,000}{8,00,000} \right) \times 100 = 80\%$$

Q.82. Revenue from Operations Rs. 10,00,000, Gross Profit Ratio 25%, Operating Ratio 90%, Operating Rs. 1,00,000, Non-operating Expenses Rs. 5,000, Non-operating income Rs 55,000. Calculate Net Profit Ratio.

Ans.
$$\text{Operating Profit Ratio} = 100 - \text{Operating Ratio} = 100 - 90\% = 10\%$$

$$\text{Operating Profit} = \text{Rs. } 10,00,000 \times \frac{10}{100} = \text{Rs. } 1,00,000$$

$$\text{Net Profit} = \text{Operating Profit} + \text{Non-operating Incomes} - \text{Non-Operating Expenses}$$

$$= \text{Rs. } 1,00,000 + \text{Rs. } 55,000 - \text{Rs. } 5,000 = \text{Rs. } 1,50,000$$

$$\text{Net Profit Ratio} = \frac{\text{Rs. } 1,50,000}{\text{Rs. } 10,00,000} \times 100 = 15\%$$

Q.83. Calculate Debt to Capital Employed Ratio by the following information:

Long-term Debt 5,00,000

Capital Employed or Net Assets 20,00,000.

Ans. $\text{Debt to Capital Employed Ratio} = \dfrac{\text{Total debts}}{\text{Total assets}}$

$$= \frac{5,00,000}{20,00,000} = 0.25 : 1$$

Here, Debt to Capital Employed ratio is less than half which indicates reasonablefunding by debt and adequate security of debt

Long Answer Type   [5 Marks]

Q.84. (a) Calculate return on Investment from the following information: **[CBSE Sample Paper]**

Net profit after Tax	Rs.6,50,000.
12.5% convertible debentures	Rs 8,00000.
Income Tax	50%.
Fixed Assets at cost	Rs.24,60,000.
Depreciation reserve	Rs.4,60,000.
Current Assets	Rs. 15,00,000.
Current Liabilities	Rs. 7,00,000.

(b) Profit before interest and tax(PBIT) Rs.2,00,000, 10% preference shares of Rs.100 each.Rs.2,00,000, 2,0000 equity shares of Rs. 10 each, Rate of tax @ 50% calculate earning per Share(EPS).

Ans. (a)   Net profit before interest = Rs.14,00,000

Capital employed = Rs. 28,00,000

Return on investment = 50%.

(b)   Earning per share = Rs. 4.

Q.85. From the following information calculate Return on Investment

Net profit after interest and tax	Rs. 1,20,000
Tax	Rs. 1,20,000
Net fixed Assets	Rs. 5,00,000
Long term trade investment	Rs. 50,000
Current assets	Rs. 2,20,000
12% debentures	Rs. 4,00,000
Equity share capital	Rs. 50,000
10% preference share capital	Rs. 50,000

Reserve and surplus	Rs. 1,00,000
Current liability	Rs. 1,70,000

Ans. Return on Investment or Return on Capital Employed = EBIT $\times$ 100 Capital Employed

Return on Investment = 1,20,000 + 1,20,000 + 48,000 = 2,88,000

5,00,000 + 50,000 + 50,000 = 6,00,000

$$= \frac{2,88,000}{6,00,000} \times 100 = 48\%$$

Q.86. From the following calculate :

(a) Net Profit Ratio

(b) Operating Profit Ratio

Revenue from operations Rs. 2,00,000 Gross Profit Rs. 75,000 Office Expenses Rs. 15,000 Selling Expenses Rs. 26,000 Interest on Debentures Rs. 5,,000 Accidental Losses Rs. 12,000 Income from Rent Rs. 2,500 Commission received Rs. 2,000

Ans. Net profit ratio = 10,75%

Operating profit ratio = 18%

Q.87. Calculate following ratios from the following information:

    i. Current Ratio

   ii. Acid – Test Ratio

  iii. Operating Ratio

  iv. Gross Profit Ratio

Current Assets Rs. 35000 Current Liabilities Rs. 17,500 Inventory Rs. 15,000 Operating Expenses Rs. 20,000 Revenue from Operaions Rs. 60,000 Cost of revenue from Operations Rs. 30,000

Ans. i. Current Ratio 2 : 1,

   ii. Acid – Test Ratio 1.14 : 1,

  iii. Operating Ratio 83.3%,

  iv. Gross Profit Ratio 50%

Q.88. Calculate Net Assets Turnover ratio (or Capital Employed Turnover Ratio) and

Fixed Assets Turnover ratio by following information:

Share Capital	7,00,000
Reserves and Surplus	4,00,000
Long-term Debts	4,00,000
Net Revenue from Operations	45,00,000
Fixed assets	22,50,000

Ans. Capital Employed (or Net Assets) = Share Capital + Reserves and Surplus + Long-term Debts

= 7,00,000 + 4,00,000 + 4,00,000 = 15,00,000

Net fixed assets = 22,50,000

Net Assets Turnover ratio (or Capital Employed Turnover Ratio)

$$= \frac{\text{Net Revenue from Operations}}{\text{Capital Employed (or Net Assets)}}$$

$$= \frac{45,00,000}{15,00,000} = 3 \text{ times}$$

$$\textbf{Fixed Assets Turnover ratio} = \frac{\text{Net Revenue from Operations}}{\text{Net Fixed Assets}}$$

$$= \frac{45,00,000}{22,50,000} = 2 \text{ times}$$

Note: Net Assets (or capital employed) turnover ratio is analysed by two turnover ratios:

(i) Fixed Assets Turnover Ratio

(ii) Working Capital Turnover Ratio

Q.89. On the basis of the following information, calculate

(i) Debt equity ratio (ii) Working capital turnover ratio   [CBSE 2013]

Information	Amount (Rs.)
Cash revenue from operations	4,000,000
Credit revenue from operations	2,000,000
Cost of revenue operations (Cost of goods sold)	3,500,000
Other current assets	8,00,000
Current liabilities	4,00,000
Paid-up share capital	1,700,000
6% loan from bank	1,00,000
Debenture redemption reserve	3,00,000
Closing inventory	1,00,000

[Delhi 2012]

Ans. (i)

$$\text{Debt Equity Ratio} = \frac{\text{Long-term Debts or Loans}}{\text{Shareholders' Fund}}$$

$$\text{Debt equity ratio} = \frac{4,00,000}{20,00,000}$$

Debt equity ratio = 0.2 : 1

Working Note

Long-term Debts = 6% Debentures + 9%

Loan = 3,00,000 + 1,00,000 = Rs.4,00,000

Shareholder's Funds = Paid-up Share Capital + Debenture Redemption Reserve

= 17,00,000 + 3,00,000 = Rs.20,00,000

(ii) $$\text{Working Capital Turnover Ratio} = \frac{\text{Cost of Revenue from Operations}}{\text{Working Capital}}$$

$$= \frac{35,00,000}{5,00,000} = 7 \text{ times}$$

Working Note

$$\text{Working Capital} = \text{Current Assets} - \text{Current Liabilities}$$
$$= 9,00,000 - 4,00,000 = \text{Rs}.5,00,000$$
$$\text{Current Assets} = \text{Other Current Assets} + \text{Closing Stock}$$
$$= 8,00,000 + 1,00,000 = \text{Rs}.9,00,000$$
$$\text{Current liabilities} = \text{Rs}.4,00,000$$

Q.90. (i) A business has a current ratio of 3 : 1 and quick ratio of 1.2 : 1. If the working capital is Rs. 1,80,000. Calculate the total current assets and value of inventory.

(ii) From the given information calculate the inventory turnover ratio. Revenue from operations (Sales) Rs 2,00,000, gross profit 25% on cost, inventory at the beginning is 1/3 of the inventory at the end which was 30% of sales. **(Delhi 2010; All India 2010)**

Ans. (i)

$$\text{Working Capital} = \text{Current Assets} - \text{Current Liabilities}$$
$$\text{Current ratio} = 3 : 1$$
$$\text{Therefore, working capital} = 3 - 1 = 2$$
$$\text{If working capital} = 2, \text{ current assets} = 3$$
$$\text{If working capital} = 1,80,000$$
$$\text{Current assets} = 1,80,000 \times \frac{3}{2} = \text{Rs. } 2,70,000$$
$$\text{Current Liabilities} = \text{Current Assets} - \text{Working Capital}$$
$$\text{Current liabilities} = 2,70,000 - 1,80,000 = \text{Rs}.90,000$$
$$\text{Quick Ratio} = \frac{\text{Current Assets} - \text{Inventory}}{\text{Current Liabilities}}$$
$$1.2 = \frac{2,70,000 - \text{Inventory}}{90,000}$$
$$- \text{Inventory} = (1.2 \times 90,000) - 2,70,000$$
$$- \text{Inventory} = 1,08,000 - 2,70,000$$
$$\text{Inventory} = \text{Rs}.1,62,000$$

or

$$\text{Let current liabilities} = \text{Rs}.x$$
$$\text{Curent Ratio} = \frac{\text{Current Assets}}{\text{Current Liabilities}} = \frac{3}{1}$$
$$\therefore \quad \text{Current assets} = 3x$$
$$\text{Quick Ratio} = \frac{\text{Liquid Assets}}{\text{Current Liabilities}} = \frac{1.2}{1}$$
$$\therefore \quad \text{Liquid assets} = 1.2 \, x$$
$$\text{Working capital} = \text{Rs}.1,80,000$$
$$\text{Current assets} - \text{Current liabilities} = 1,80,000$$
$$3x - x = 1,80,000$$
$$2x = 1,80,000$$
$$\text{Current liabilities } x = \text{Rs. } 90,000$$

$$\text{Current assets} = 3x$$

$$= 3 \times 90,000 = Rs.2,70,000$$

$$\text{Liquid assets} = 1.2x$$

$$= 1.2 \times 90,000 = 1,08,000$$

$$\text{Inventory} = \text{Current Assets} - \text{Liquid Assets}$$

$$= 2,70,000 - 1,08,000 = Rs.1,62,000$$

(ii) $\text{Invenstory Turnover Ratio} = \dfrac{\text{Cost of Revenue from Operations}}{\text{Average Inventory}} = \dfrac{1,60,000}{40,000}$

$$\text{Inventory turnover ratio} = 4 \text{ times}$$

Working Note

$$\text{Cost of revenue from operations} = 2,00,000 \times \frac{100}{100+25} = Rs.\ 1,60,000$$

$$\text{Closing inventory} = 2,00,000 \times \frac{30}{100} = Rs.60,000$$

$$\text{Opening inventory} = 60,000 \times \frac{1}{3} = Rs.20,000$$

$$\text{Average inventory} = \frac{20,000+60,000}{2}$$

$$= Rs.40,000$$

Q.91. (a) X Ltd. has a current ratio of 3.5 : 1 and quick ratio of 2 : 1. If excess of current assets over quick assets represented by Inventory is 24,000 calculate current assets and current liabilities.

(b) From the following information calculate Inventory Turnover Ratio.

Revenue from Operations: 4,00,000

Average Inventory : 55,000.

The rate of Gross Loss on revenue from Operations was 10%.

(CBSE Sample paper Delhi 2016, 2017)

Ans. (a) $\text{Current Ratio} = 3.5 : 1$

$$\text{Quick Ratio} = 2 : 1$$

$$\text{Let Current Liabilities} = x$$

$$\text{Current Assets} = 3.5x \text{ and Quick Assets} = 2x$$

$$\text{Inventory} = \text{Current Assets} - \text{Quick Assets}$$

$$24,000 = 3.5x - 2x$$

$$24,000 = 1.5x$$

$$x = Rs.16,000$$

$$\text{Current Assets} = 3.5x = 3.5 \times Rs.16,000 = Rs.56,000$$

Verification: Current Ratio = Current Assets : Current Liabilities

$$= Rs.56,000 : Rs.16,000$$

$$= 3.5 : 1$$

$$\text{Quick Ratio} = \text{Quick Assets} : \text{Current Liabilities}$$

$$= Rs.32,000 : Rs.16,000 = 2 : 1$$

(b) Revenue from Operations = Rs.4,00,000

Gross Loss = 10% of Rs.4,00,000 = Rs.40,000

Cost of Revenue from Operations = Revenue from Operation + Gross Loss

$$= \text{Rs. } 4,00,000 + \text{Rs.}40,000$$

$$= \text{Rs. } 4,40,000$$

$$\text{Inventory Turnover Ratio} = \frac{\text{Cost of Goods Sold}}{\text{Average Inventory}} = \frac{\text{Rs. } 4,40,000}{\text{Rs. } 55,000}$$

$$= 8 \text{ times}$$

Chapter Practice

Multiple Choice Questions   [1 Mark]

Q.1. Accounting ratio is a numerical relation between accounting variables of ....

(a) Income Statement

(b) Balance Sheet

(c) Financial Statements

(d) Income Statement or Balance Sheet

Q.2. Ratio may be expressed in .... form.

(a) Ratio   (b) Rate

(c) Percentage   (d) All Above

Q.3. .... turnover ratio is considered good as signifies use of resources.

(a) Lower   (b) Higher

(c) Average   (d) Medium

Q.4. Ratio Analysis is useful to :

(a) Shareholders   (b) Financial Institutions

(c) Creditors   (d) All above

Q.5. If capital employed of a company is Rs. 10,00,000; Total Debts Rs. 8,00,000 and its Current liabilities Is Rs. 3,00,000 , then its Debt Equity Ratio will be:

(a) 1 : 1   (b) 8:10

(c) 5 : 10   (d) None of these

Very Short Answer Type   [1 Mark]

Q.6. What is Ratio Analysis ?

Q.7. What is meant by Short-term Solvency Ratio ?

Q.8. What is the standard ratio for Current Ratio And Liquid Ratio ?

Q.9. In Debt Equity Ratio ,what does equity stands for ?

Q.10. What is meant by Average Holding Period and what does it represent ?

Q.11. How the 'earning capacity of a business' is assessed by Financial Statement Analysis?

Q.12. What is Operating Cost ?

Q.13. What does activity ratio show?

Q.14. What is Return on Investment Ratio ?

Q.15. State one transaction which result in an increase in 'Liquid Ratio' and no change in 'Current Ratio.

Q.16. What will be the impact of Cash Paid to Trade Payables on a Current Ratio of 2 : 1? State the reason.

Q.17. The quick ratio of a company is 0.5:0.75.Will cash sales of Rs.5,000 increase, decrease or not change the ratio? Give reason in support of your answer.

Q.18. The Debt Equity Ratio of X Ltd. Is 1:2. What is effect of conversion of debentures into preference share on this ratio ?

Q.19. What is the accounting treatment of 'Stores and Spares' when the company will calculate its Inventory Turnover Ratio ?

Q.20. What will be the operating profit ratio, if operating ratio is 83.64 % ?

Short Answer Type - I [3 Marks]

Q.21. 'Accounting ratio ignore qualitative factors and are also not comparable if different firms follow Different accounting policies' Comment.

Q.22. Current Assets of a company are Rs. 17,00,000. Its current ratio is 2.5 and liquid ratio is 0.95. Calculate Current Liabilities and Inventory.

OR

The Current ratio of A Ltd., is 4.5 : 1 and liquid ratio is 3 : 1. Inventories is Rs.3,00,000. What are the Current Liabilities.?

Q.23. Compute (i) Debt-Equity Ratio n(ii) Total Assets to Debt Ratio from the following data :

Total Debts	Rs. 5,50,000
Total Assets	Rs. 10,00,000
Current Liabilities	Rs. 2,00,000

Q.24. Compute Interest Coverage ratio from the following details :

(i)	10% Debentures	Rs. 4,00,000
(ii)	8% Loan from Bank	Rs.3,00,000
(iii)	9% Public Deposit	Rs. 2,00,000
(iv)	Net Profit after	50%
(v)	Tax Rs.	2,05,000

Q.25. Cost of Revenue from operation = Rs. 3,00,000; Inventory Turnover ratio = 6 Times

Find out the value of Opening Inventory, if opening inventory is Rs.10,000 less than the closing Inventory.

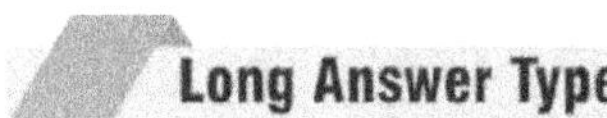

[5 Marks]

Q.26. Compute Trade Receivable Turnover Ratio from the following information :

Cost of Revenue from Operations = Rs. 4,00,000 Gross Profit on Cost = 25%

Cash Revenue from Operations 20% of total revenue from operations

Opening Trade Receivables = Rs. 70,000 : Closing Trade Receivables = Rs.90,000

Q.27. From the following information related to Friends Ltd.

Calculate :

(a) Return On Investment

(b) Total Assets To Debt Ratio.

Fixed Assets Rs. 75,00,000; Current Assets Rs.40,00,000 ; Current Liabilities Rs.27,00,000; 12% Debentures Rs. 80,00,000 and Net Profit before Interest and Tax Rs. 14,50,000

Q.28. From the following details given below ,calculate the followings ratios :

(i) Gross Profit Ratio

(ii) Stock Turnover Ratio

(iii) Operating Ratio

Revenue from Operations (Sales) Rs.1,50,000

Cost of revenue from operations Rs.1,20,000

Opening Stock Rs. 29,000,

Closing Stock Rs. 31,000,

Debtors Rs. 16,000, Operating Expenses Rs. 16,000

Cash Flow Statement

 Introduction, Cash and Cash Equivalent, Operating Activity

Summary

Cash Flow Statement Cash flow statement is a statement showing the changes in financial position of a business concern during different intervals of time in terms of cash and cash equivalents. The Revised Accounting Standard-3 has made it mandatory for all listed companies to prepare and present a cash flow statement along with other financial statements on annual basis.

Objectives of Cash Flow Statement :

(i)Useful in short-term financial planning.

(ii)Useful inefficient cash management.

(iii)Helpful in formulation of business policies.

(iv)Assists in preparation of cash budget.

(v)Used for assessment of cash flow from various activities, viz operating, investing and financing activities.

Cash and cash equivalents: As per AS-3, 'Cash' comprises cash in hand and demand deposits with banks, and Cash equivalents means short-term highly liquid investments that are readily convertible into known amounts of cash and which are subject to an insignificant risk of changes in value.

Cash Flows: 'Cash Flows' implies movement of cash in and out due to some non-cash items. Receipt of cash from a non-cash item is termed as cash inflow while cash payment in respect of such items as cash outflow.

Classification of Business Activities Accounting Standard-3(Revised) requires that the changes resulting in inflows and outflows of cash and cash equivalents will be classified into following three activities:

(i)Cash flow from operating activities.

(ii)Cash flow from investing activities.

(iii)Cash flow from financing activities.

1. **Cash Flow From Operating Activities:** Operating activities are the activities that constitute the primary or main activities of an enterprise. Cash flows from operating activities are primarily derived from the main activities of the enterprise. They generally result from the transactions and other events that enter into the determination of net profit or loss.

Cash Inflows from operating activities	Cash Outflows from operating activities
I. Cash receipts from sale of goods and the rendering of services.	I. Cash payments to suppliers for goods and services.
II. Cash receipts from royalties, fees, commissions and other revenues	II. Cash payments to and on behalf of the employees
	III. Cash payments to an insurance enterprise for premiums and claims, annuities, and other policy benefits
	IV. Cash payments of income taxes unless they can be specifically identified with financing and investing activities

Cash Flows from Operating Activities:

Operating activities are the main source of revenue and expenditure in an enterprise. Therefore, the ascertainment of cash flows from operating activities is of prime importance.

    i. **Direct Method:** The direct method provides information which is useful in estimating future cash flows.

    ii. **Indirect Method:** Indirect method of ascertaining cash flow from operating activities begins with the amount of net profit/loss.

1. As per AS-3, (Revised), under the indirect method, net cash flow from operating activities is determined by adjusting net profit or loss for the effects of:

    1. Non-cash items are to be added back. Non-cash items like

        (a) Depreciation

        (b) Goodwill has written off

        (c) Patents and Copyrights are written off

        (d) Appropriation to General Reserve

        (e) Interim dividend

        (f) Deferred taxes etc.

    2. All other items for which the cash effects are investing or financing cash flows. The treatment of such items depends upon their nature. All investing and financing incomes are to be deducted from the number of net profits while all such expenses are to be added back.

    3. Changes in current assets and liabilities during the period. An increase in current assets and a decrease in current liabilities are to be deducted while the increase in current liabilities and a decrease in current assets are to be added up.

CASH FLOWS FROM OPERATING ACTIVITIES (INDIRECT METHOD)

	Rs	Rs.
(A) Net Profit before Taxation and Extraordianry Items		×××
Adjustment For Non-cash and Non-Operating Items		
(B) **Add:**		
– Depreciation	×××	
– Goodwill written off	×××	
– Preliminary Expenses written off	×××	

	– Discount on Issue of Shares and Debentures written off	×××	
	– Patents and Trademarks written off	×××	
	– Interest on Borrowings and Debentures (For Finance (Co.)	×××	
	– Loss on Sale Fixed Assets etc.	×××	×××
			×××
(C)	**Less:**		
	– Interest Income (For Finance (Co.)	×××	
	– Dividend Income (For Finance Co.)	×××	
	– Rental Income	×××	
	– Profit on Sale of Fixed Assets etc.	×××	×××
(D)	**Operating Profit before Working Capital Changes (A + B – C)**		×××
(E)	**Add:**		
	– Decrease in Current Assets	×××	
	– Increase in Current Liabilities	×××	×××
			×××
(F)	**Less:**		
	– Increase in Current Assets	×××	
	– Decrease in Current Liabilities	×××	×××
(G)	**Cash Flow from Operation (D + E – F)**		×××
(H)	**Less:** Income Tax Paid		×××
(I)	Cash Flow from Operations before Extraordinary Items		×××
	Add/Less: Extraordinary Items		×××
	Net Cash Flow from Operating Activities		×××

Multiple Choice Questions [1 Mark]

Q.1. Divided received by financial enterprise is shown in cash flow statement under

(a) Operating activities   (b) Investing activities   (c) Financing activities   (d) General activity

Ans. (a)

Q.2. Payment of income tax is shown as [CBSE 2014]

(a) Operating activity   (b) Investing activity   (c) Financing activity   (d) General activity

Ans. (a)

Q.3. Which of the following is not a part of cash and cash equivalents?

(a) Inventories   (b) Current investments (c) Short- term deposits   (d) Marketable securities

Ans. (a)

Q.4. Tanmay Ltd. has balance in provision for tax account of Rs. 50,000 and Rs. 75,000 as on 31st march, 2021 and 2022 respectively. It made a provision for tax during the of Rs. 65,000. The amount of tax paid during the year was

(a) Rs. 50,000   (b) Rs. 60,000   (c) Rs. 40,000   (d) Rs. 75,000

Ans. (c)

Q.5. Soham Ltd: is a financing company. Under which activities will the amount of interest paid on a loan settled in the current year be shown? [CBSE 2017]

    (a) Investing activities   (b) Financing activities

    (c) Both investing and financing activities   (d) Operating activities

Ans. (d)

Q.6. Which of the following transaction will not result in to flow of cash?

    (a) Issue of equity share of Rs.1,00,000.   (b) Purchase of machinery of Rs. 1,75,000.

    (c) Redemption of 90% debentures of Rs. 3,50,000.   (d) Cash deposited into bank Rs. 15,000.

Ans. (d)

Q.7. While preparing cash flow statement match the following activities :

Group A	Group B
1. Payment of cash for purchase of debentures by a financing company	A. Financing activity
2. Purchase of goodwill	B. Investing activity
3. Dividend paid by manufacturing company	C. Operating activity

Select the correct answer using the codes given below :

    (a) 1-C, 2-A, 3-B   (b) 1-B, 2-A, 3-C

    (c) 1-A, 2-B, 3-C   (d) 1-C, 2-B, 3-A

Ans. (d)

Q.8. In cash flow statement, match the following activities:

Group A	Group B
1. Receipt of dividend	(A) Financing activities
2. Purchase and sale of securities by a finance company	(B) Investing activities
3. Buy –back of own shares	(C) Operating activities

    (a) 1-B, 2-A, 3-C   (b) 1-B, 2-C, 3-A

    (c) 1-A, 2-C, 3-B   (d) 1-A, 2-B, 3-C

Ans. (b)

Q.9. Gain on sale of tangible current asset is an

    (a) Operating activity   (b) Investing activity

    (c) Financing activity   (d) Cash and Cash Equivalents

Ans. (a)

Q.10. Interest collected by an automobile company selling a car on instalment basis will be classified as

    (a) Investing activity   (b) Operating activity

    (c) Financing activity   (d) Cash and cash equivalents

Ans. (b)

Q.11. A decrease in outstanding expense would result in [CBSE Sample Paper]

    (a) Decrease in cash balance   (b) Increase in cash balance

    (c) Unaltered   (d) Would change the current liabilities.

Ans. (d)

Q.12. Pick the odd one out

    (a) Long term borrowings   (b) Reserves and surplus

    (c) Share capital   (d) Public deposits.

Ans. (b)

Q.13. Expenses paid in advance at the end of the year are i……..in ……ii activities while preparing cash flow statement

    (a) Added, Operating   (b) Subtracted, Operating

    (c) Added, Investing   (d) Subtracted, Investing

Ans. (a)

Q.14. Gain on sale of tangible non current asset is an

    (a) Operating activity   (b) Investing activity

    (c) Financing activity   (d) Cash and Cash Equivalents

Ans. (a)

Q.15. Which of the following shall be considered as an outflow of cash in cash flow statement.

    (a) Decrease in Public Deposits   (b) Issue of share capital

    (c) Increase in accounts payable   (d) Decrease in accounts receivables.

Ans. (a)

Q.16. Which of the following transactions would not create a cash flow?

    (a) A company purchased some of its own stock from a stockholder

    (b) Amortization of a patent

    (c) Payment of a Cash Dividend

    (d) Sale of equipment at book value

Ans. (b)

Q.17. Bank Overdraft and cash credit are to be treated as:

    (a) Cash Equivalents   (b) Non-Current Liabilities

    (c) Investing Activity   (d) Short Term Borrowings

Ans. (d)

Q.18. Declaration of Final Dividend would result in –

    (a) Outflow in Financing activities.   (b) Outflow in Operating activities.

    (c) Inflow in Operating activities.   (d) No Flow of cash.

Ans. (d)

Q.19. Which of the following transactions would result in neither cash inflow nor outflow of cash and cash equivalents.

[CBSE 2018]

    (a) Issue of share capital   (b) Issue of bonus shares

    (c) Redemption of debentures   (d) Trade receivable realized.

Ans. (b)

Q.20. Cash from operation is equal to :

    (a) Net Profit + Increase in Current Assets

    (b) Net Profit + Decrease in Current Liabilities

    (c) Operating Profit + Adjustment of Current Assets and Current Liabilities

    (d) All of the above

Ans. (b)

Q.21. Cash Flow Statement is related to:

    (a) AS-3   (b) AS-6   (c) AS-9   (d) AS-12

Ans. (b)

Q.22. Net Profit during the year Rs. 1,00,000 Debtors in the beginning the year of Rs. 30,000 Debtors at the end of the year Rs.36,000 What is the amount of cash from operating activities ?   **[CBSE Sample Paper]**

    (a) Rs. 30,000   (b) Rs. 94,000   (c) Rs. 1,06,000   (d) Rs. 1,66,000

Ans. (b)

Q.23. Cash deposit with the bank with a maturity date after two months belongs to which of the following while preparing Cash Flow Statement?

    (a) Investing Activities   (b) Financing Activities

    (c) Cash and Cash Equivalents   (d) Operating Activities

Ans. (c)

Q.24. If net profit is Rs. 35,000 after writing off good will Rs. 6,000 and loss on sale of furniture Rs. 1,000, cash flow from operating activities will be :   **[CBSE 2009]**

    (a) Rs. 35,000   (b) Rs. 42,000   (c) Rs. 29,000   (d) Rs. 28,000

Ans. (b)

Q.25. Which activity comes under 'Operating Activities'?

    (a) Purchase of Land   (b) Issue of Debentures

    (c) Proceeds from Issuance of Equity Shares   (d) Cash Sales

Ans. (d)

Q.26. Net Profit during the year Rs. 50,000 Debtors in the beginning the year of Rs. 15,000 Debtors at the end of the year Rs. 18,000 What is the amount of cash from operating activities?   **[CBSE Compartment]**

    (a) Rs. 15,000   (b) Rs. 47,000   (c) Rs. 53,000   (d) Rs. 83,000

Ans. (b)

Q.27. An example of cash flow from operating activity is :

    (a) Purchase of own debenture   (b) Sale of fixed assets.

    (c) Interest paid on term-deposits by a bank   (d) Issue of equity share capital

Ans. (c)

Q.28. Which of the following statements are false?

    (A) Old Furniture written off doesn't affect cash flow.

    (B) Cash flow statement is a substitute for cash account.

    (C) Appropriation of retained earnings is not shown in Cash flow statement.

    (D) Net cash flow during a period can never be negative.

    (a) A, B, C   (b) B, C, D   (c) C, D, A   (d) All are true

Ans. (b)

Q.29. As per Accounting Standard-3, Cash Flow is classified into   **[CBSE 2014]**

    (a) Operating activities and investing activities

    (b) Investing activities and financing activities

    (c) Operating activities and financing activities

    (d) Operating activities, financing activities and investing activities

Ans. (d)

Read the following statements – Assertion (A) and Reason (R). Choose one of the correct alternatives given below: **[CBSE Guidelines]**

Q.30. For the following two statement of Assertion (A) and Reasoning (R) indicate the correct code:

    Assertion (A): Cash Flow Statement are historical in nature.

    Reasoning (R): It is prepared from Statement of Profit and Loss and Balance sheet, which are historical in nature.

    (a) Both A and R are true and R is the correct explanation of A.

    (b) Both A and R are true, but R is not the correct explanation of A.

    (c) A is true ,but R is false.

    (d) A is false ,but R is true.

Ans. (a)

Q.31. For the following two statement of Assertion (A) and Reasoning (R) indicate the correct code:

    Assertion (A): Operating Activities are the principal revenue producing activities.

    Reasoning (R): It results in change of the size and composition of the owners capital.

    (a) Both A and R are true and R is the correct explanation of A.

    (b) Both A and R are true, but R is not the correct explanation of A.

    (c) A is true, but R is false.

    (d) A is false, but R is true.

Ans. (c)

Q.32. For the following two statement of Assertion (A) and Reasoning (R) indicate the correct code:

Assertion (A): While preparing Cash Flow Statement, Cash withdrawn from bank result in no flow cash.

Reasoning (R): There is no change in Cash and Cash Equivalents.

(a) Both A and R are true and R is the correct explanation of A.

(b) Both A and R are true, but R is not the correct explanation of A.

(c) A is true, but R is false.

(d) A is false, but R is true

Ans. (a)

Q.33. For the following two statement of Assertion (A) and Reasoning (R) indicate the correct code:

Assertion (A): Discount received on making payment to suppliers would result in inflow of cash.

Reasoning (R): Discount received on payment to suppliers does not involve cash.

(a) Both A and R are true and R is the correct explanation of A.

(b) Both A and R are true, but R is not the correct explanation of A.

(c) A is true, but R is false.

(d) A is false, but R is true

Ans. (d)

Q.34. Assertion: Loss due to earthquake' is an extraordinary item (loss)

Reason: For calculating net profit before taxation and extraordinary items, it will be added back.

(a)Both Assertion and reason are true and reason is correct explanation of Assertion.

(b)Assertion and reason both are true but reason is not the correct explanation of Assertion.

(c) Assertion is true, Reason is false.

(d) Assertion is false, Reason is true.

Ans. (a)

Q.35. Assertion: A cash flow statement provides information about the historical changes in cash and cash equivalents.

Reason: Cash means short-term highly liquid investments that are readily convertible into known amounts of cash.

(a) Both Assertion and reason are true and reason is correct explanation of assertion.

(b) Assertion and reason both are true but reason is not the correct explanation of assertion.

(c) Assertion is true, reason is false.

(d) Assertion is false, reason is true.

Ans. (c)

Q.36. Assertion: Cash Flows' implies movement of cash and cash equivalents (in and out).

Reason: Sale proceeds from sale of machinery are cash inflow & purchase of machinery by paying cash is cash outflow.

(a) Both Assertion and reason are true and reason is correct explanation of assertion.

(b) Assertion and reason both are true but reason is not the correct explanation of assertion.

(c) Assertion is true, reason is false.

(d) Assertion is false, reason is true.

Ans. (a)

Q.37. Assertion: The primary objective of cash flow statement is to provide useful information about cash flows (inflows and outflows) of an enterprise during a particular period under various heads, i.e., operating activities, investing activities and financing activities.

Reason: Cash flow statement is a substitute of Statement of Profit and Loss account.

(a) Both Assertion and reason are true and reason is correct explanation of assertion.

(b) Assertion and reason both are true but reason is not the correct explanation of assertion.

(c) Assertion is true, reason is false.

(d) Assertion is false, reason is true.

Ans. (c)

Very Short Answer Type   [1 Mark]

Fill in the Blanks

Q.38. The basis of Cash Flow Statement is __________

Ans. Cash basis

Q.39. Debentures issued for consideration other than cash are not shown in the Cash Flow Statement because__________ is not received against the issue.

Ans. Cash

Q.40. Loss on issue of debentures written off is shown by way of deduction from__________of the debentures.

Ans. Face value

State True of False

Q.41. Gratuity paid to a retiring employee is an Operating activity.

Ans. True

Q.42. Why is the cash flow statement not a suitable judge of profitability ?

Ans. Cash Flow statement is prepared on cash basis of accounting but profit is calculated on accrual basis. So cash flow statement is not a judge of profitability.

Q.43. Under which accounting standard , cash flow statement is prepared ?

Ans. Under accounting standard-3(Revised).

Q.44. Why do we add back depreciation to net profit while calculating cash flow from operating activities.

[CBSE 2012]

Ans. Depreciation reduces the net profit without reducing the cash balance as it is a non-cash item.

Q.45. How will you classify loans given by Birla Finance Ltd.? While preparing cash flow statement.

Ans. As Operating Activities.

Q.46. How will you classify deposits by customers in HDFC Bank while preparing cash flow statement.

[CBSE 2016]

Ans. As Operating Activities.

Q.47. What are the two methods which can be employed to calculate net cash flow from operating activities?

Ans. Direct Method and Indirect Method.

Q.48. Why is specific disclosure of cash flow from financing activities important while preparing cash flow statement?

[All India 2014]

Ans. Separate disclosure of cash flows arising from financing activities is important because it is useful in predicting claims on future cash flows by providers of funds (both capital and borrowings) to the enterprise.

Q.49. Why is a cash flow statement prepared?   [Delhi 2010 C]

Ans. A cash flow statement provides information about the historical changes in cash and cash equivalents of an enterprise by classifying cash flows into operating, investing and financing activities between the dates of two balance sheets.

Q.50. Give the meaning of cash.   [All India 2014; Delhi 2011]

Ans. 'Cash flow' implies inflow and outflow of cash and cash equivalents. Receipt of cash from an item other than cash and cash equivalents is termed as 'cash inflow' while cash payment in respect of such item is termed as 'cash outflow'.

Q.51. What is meant by cash equivalents?   [All India 2014, 2011; Delhi 2014, 2011 C]

Ans. Cash equivalents mean short-term highly liquid investments that are readily convertible into known amount of cash and which are subjected to an insignificant risk of change in value.

Q.52. What is meant by 'cash from operating activities'?   [Delhi 2013]

Ans. 'Cash from operating activities' are the principal revenue producing activities of the enterprise and other activities that are not investing or financing activities.

Short Answer Type - I   [2 Marks]

Q.1. Normally, what should be the maturity period for a short-term investment from the date of its acquisition to be qualified as cash equivalents?   [All India 2017]

Ans. Maximum maturity period is 90 days or 3 months for a short term investment from the date of its acquisition to be qualified as cash equivalents.

Q.2. State the primary objective of preparing a cash flow statement.   [CBSE 2015]

Ans. The primary objective of cash flow statement is to find out the inflows and outflows of cash and cash equivalent from Operating, Investing and Financing Activities.

Q.3. 'Cash advances and loans' made by financial enterprises will be shown under which type of activity while preparing cash flow statement? Give reason in support of your answer.   [CBSE 2018]

Ans. Operating activity.

Q.4. Given salary expenses Rs 40,000, Outstanding in the beginning of the year: Rs 5,000 and outstanding at the end of the year Rs 10,000. Cash outflow on salary will be:

Ans. Rs 35000

Q.5. Which items are considered as cash or cash equivalent?

Ans. (a) Cash on hand

(b) Demand deposit

(c) Short term marketable securities

Q.6. Give the meaning of 'Cash Equivalents' for the purpose of preparing Cash Flow Statement.

(CBSE Delhi 2019)

Ans. "Cast equivalents" means short term highly liquid investments that are readily convertible into known amount of cash & which are subject to an in significant risk of changes in value.

For Ex-short term marketable securities.

The primary purpose of the statement of cash flows is to provide information about cash receipt, cash payments, and the net change in cash resulting from the operating, investing and financing activities of a company during the period.

Q.7. State the primary objective of preparing Cash Flow Statement.   **(CBSE 2019 Compt.)**

Ans. The primary objective of preparing Cash Flow Statement is to provide useful information about cash inflows and outflows of an enterprise during a particular period.

Q.8. State whether the following will increase, decrease or have no effect on cash flow from operating activities while preparing 'Cash Flow Statement' :

 (i) Decrease in outstanding employees benefits expenses by Rs.3,000

 (ii) Increase in prepaid insurance by Rs.2,000.   **(Compt. Delhi 2017)**

Ans. (i) Decrease

(ii) Decrease

Short Answer Type - II   [3 Marks]

Q.1. Which items are to be added to net profit after tax and extraordinary items to reach to net profit before tax and extraordinary items?   **[CBSE Sample Paper]**

Ans. (A) Provision for tax made during the year

(B) Proposed dividend made during the year

(C) Interim dividend

(D) Transfer to General reserves and other reserves

Q.2. What is meant by 'cash equivalents' while preparing cash flow statement?   **[CBSE 2014 & 2016]**

Ans. Cash equivalent are short term highly liquid investment that are readily convertible into known amounts of cash and which are subject to an insignificant risk of change in value.

Q.3. Short term investments are not considered while preparing cash flow statement. Why?   [CBSE 2017]

Ans. Short term investments or current investments or marketable securities are a part of cash and cash equivalents. Therefore they are not considered under any of the three activities (operating, investing and financing).

Q.4. Net increase in working capital other than cash and cash equivalent will increase, decrease or not change cash flow from operating activities. Give reasons in support of your answer.   [CBSE 2017]

Ans. Net increase in working capital means that the decrease in current assets and increase in current liabilities is more than the increase in current assets and decrease in current liabilities. So the net effect is increase in cash flow from operating activities.

Q.5. From the following particulars, what will be the amount of provision for tax made during the year?

	Provision for Taxation
31.3.2011	50,000
31.3.2012	40,000

The Company paid taxes Rs 45,000 for the year 2011-2012.

Ans. Rs 35,000

Q.6. Anand Ltd. arrived at a net income of Rs. 5,00,000 for the year ended March 31,2007. Depreciation for the year was Rs.2,00,000. There was a gain of Rs. 50,000 on assets sold which was credited to profit and loss account. Bills Receivables increased during the year Rs. 40,000 and Bills Payables also increased by Rs. 60,000. Compute the cash flow from operating activities by the indirect approach.   [CBSE 2008]

Ans. Cash Flow from Operating Activities for the year ending 31st March, 2007

Particulars	Details	(Rs.)
Net Income for the year		5,00,000
Add: Depreciation		(50,000)
Operating Profit before working capital changes		6,50,000
Less: Increase in Bills Receivable		(40,000)
Add: Increase in Bills Payable		60,000
Net Cash Inflow from Operating Activities		6,70,000

Q.7. X Ltd. Made a profit of Rs. 1,00,000 after considering the following items:

    1. Depreciation of fixed assets   Rs. 20,000

    2. Writing off preliminary expenses   Rs. 10,000

    3. Loss on sale of furniture   Rs. 1,000

    4. Provision of Taxation   Rs. 1,60,000

    5. Transfer to General reserve   Rs. 14,000

    6. Profit on sale of Machinery   Rs. 6,000

The following additional information is available to you:

Particulars	31.03.2014 Rs.	31.03.2015 Rs.
Debtors	24,000	30,000
Creditors	20,000	30,000
Bills Receivables	20,000	17,000
Bill Payables	16,000	12,000
Prepaid Expenses	400	600

Calculate Cash Flow from Operating Activities. [CBSE 2016]

Ans. Calculation of Net Profit before Tax and Extra-ordinary items:

Net Profit (Given) Rs. 1,00,000

Add: Provision for Taxation Rs. 1,60,000

Transfer to general reserve Rs. 14,000

Net Profit before Tax and Extra-ordinary item Rs. 2,74,000

Long Answer Type [5 Marks]

Q.1. State advantages of preparing cash flow statement. [CBSE 2009, 2016]

Ans. Advantages of cash flow statement

I. It helps in short term financial planning by providing information about sources and application of cash and cash equivalent for a specific period.

II. It helps in efficient cash management as it gives information relating to surplus and deficit of cash.

III. It facilitates comparative study by enabling comparison of actual cash flow with budgeted cash flows.

IV. It helps investors and creditors evaluating management decisions by providing information relating to company's investing and financing activities.

V. It helps in deciding how much dividend should be paid as it provides information about availability of cash and cash equivalents

Q.2. From the following information find the cash generated from operations:

Operating Profit before working capital changes 1,00,000

Depreciation on fixed assets 15,000

Loss on sale of Furniture 5,000

Interest paid 13,000

Dividend received 33,000

Increase in debtors 8,000

Decrease in stock 7,000

Increase in creditors 4,000

Ans. 1,00,000 + (15,000 + 5,000 + 13,000 + 7,000 + 4,000) – (8,000 + 33,000)

= 1,00,000 + 44,000 – 31000

= Rs 1,03,000

Q.3. Devika Ltd. made a profit of 1,00,000 after considering the following items:

Depreciation of fixed assets 20,000

Writing off preliminary expenses 10,000

Loss on sale of furniture 1,000

Provision of Taxation 1,60,000

Transfer to General reserve 14,000

Profit on sale of Machinery 6,000

The following additional information is available to you:

Particulars	31.03.2019 (Rs.)	31.03.2020 (Rs.)
Debtors	24,000	30,000
Creditors	20,000	30,000
Bills Receivables	20,000	17,000
Bills Payables	16,000	12,000
Prepaid Expenses	400	600

Calculate Cash Flow from Operating Activities.

Ans. [I] Calculation of Net Profit before Tax and Extra-ordinary items:

Net Profit (Given)   1,00,000

Add: Provision for Taxation   1,60,000

Transfer to general reserve   14,000

Net Profit before Tax and Extra-ordinary item 2,74,000

[II]Cash flow from Operating Activities

Net Profit Before Tax and 2,74,000

Extra-ordinary Item

Adjustment for non-cash and non-operating items:

Add: Depreciation on fixed assets 20,000

Preliminary expenses written off 10,000

Loss on sale of furniture 1,000 +31,000

Less: Profit on sale on machinery 6000 (6,000)

Operating Profit before working capital changes 2,99,000

Adjustment for Working Capital Changes

Add: Increase in creditors 10,000

Decrease in Bills Receivables 3,000 + 13,000

Less: Increase in Debtors 6,000

Increase in prepaid Expenses 200

Decrease in Bills Payable 4,000 (10,200)

Cash generated from operation 3,01,800

before Tax

Less: Income tax Paid   (1,60,000)

Ans. Net Cash inflow from Operating Activities 1,41,800

Q.4. The following is the Profit and Loss Account of Yamuna Limited:

STATEMENT OF PROFIT AND LOSS OF YAMUNA LTD.
for the year ended March 31, 2013

	Particular	Note No.	(Rs)
(i)	Revenue from Operations		1,000,000
(ii)	Expenses		
	Cost of Materials Consumed	1	50,000
	Purchases of Stock-in-trade		5,00,000
	Other expenses	2	3,00,000
	Total expenses		8,50,000
(iii)	Profit before tax (i – ii)		1,50,000

Additional Informations:

(i) Trade receivables decrease by Rs. 30,000 during the year.

(ii) Prepaid expenses increase by Rs. 5,000 during the year.

(iii) Trade payables decrease by Rs. 15,000 during the year.

(iv) Outstanding expenses payable increased by Rs. 33.000 during the year.

(v) Other expenses included depreciation off 25,000.

Compute net cash provided by operations for the year ended March 31, 2014 by the indirect method.

[CBSE 2014]

Ans.

CASH FROM OPERATION
for the year ended March 31, 2013

	Particular	Dr. (Rs.)	Cr. (Rs)
	Net Profit for the year	1,50,000	
Add:	Depreciation	25,000	
	Operating Profit before Working Capital Changes		1,75,.000
Add:	Increase in Current Liabilities and decrease in Current Assets		
	Decrease in Trade Debtors	30,000	
	Increase in Outstanding Expenses	33,000	
	Decrease in Stock		63,000
			2,38,000
Less:	Decrease in Current Liabilities increase in Current Assets		
	Increase in Prepaid Expenses	(5,000)	
	Decrease in Trade Creditors	(15,000)	(20,000)
	Net Cash from Operating Activities		2,18,000

Q.5. From the following Balance Sheet of Dreams Converge Ltd as at 31.3.2018 and 31.3.2017; Calculate Cash from operating activities. Showing your workings clearly.   **[CBSE SP 2019-20]**

Ans.

Particulars	Note No.	31.3.2019 (Rs.)	31.3.2018 (Rs.)
I. Equity and Liability:			
1. Shareholder's Fund:		7,00,000	5,00,000
a. Share Capital			
b. Reserve and Surplus		3,50,000	2,00,000
2. Non-Current Liabilities:			
Long Term Borrowings		50,000	100,000
3. Current Liabilities:			
a. Trade Payables		1,22,000	1,05,000
b. Short term Provisions (Provision for tax)		50,000	30,000
Total		**1,272,000**	**935,000**
II. Assets:			
1. Non Current Assets:			
a. Fixed Assets:			
i. Tangible Assets	1	5,00,000	5.00,000
ii. Instangible Assets	2	95,000	1,00,000
b. Non-current Investments		1,30,000	Nil
2. Current Assets:			
a. Inventory		1,30,000	55,000
b. Trade Receivable		1,47,000	80,000
c. Cash and Cash Equivalents		3,00,000	2,00,000
Total		**1,272,000**	**935,000**

Note No.	Particulars	31.3.2018 (Rs)	31.3.2017 (Rs)
1	**Tangible Assets:**		
	Machinery	2,80,000	2,00,000
	Accumulated depreciation	(1,00,000)	(80,000)
		1,80,000	**1,20,000**
2	Equipments	3,20,000	3,80,000
	Intangible Assets:	5,00,000	5,00,000
	Goodwill	95,000	1,00,000

Additional Information:

L Machinery of the book value of 80,000 (accumulated depreciation Rs. 20,000) was sold at a loss of Rs. 18,000.

CASH FLOW STATEMENT AS PER AS 3 (REVISED)

Particulars	Details	Amount (Rs.)
Cash from Operating Activity		
Net Profit Before Tax		
Profit during the year	1,50,000	
Add: Transfer to Reserve	50,000	2,00,000
Add: Non Cash Non-Operating Expenses		
Depreciation provided	40,000	
Loss on Sale of Assets	18,000	
Goodwill Amortised	5,000	63,000
Less: Non-Operating Incomes		
Operating Profit before Working Capital		2,63,000
Add: Increase in Trade Payable	17,000	17,000
		2,80,000
Less: Increase in Inventory	(75,000)	
Increase in Trade Receivable	(67,000)	(1,42,000)
Cash From Operating Activities before Tax		1,38,000
Less: Tax Paid		(30,000)
Cash From Operating Activities After Tax		1,08,000

Dr.   **MACHINERY A/C**   Cr.

Particulars	Amount (Rs.)	Particulars	Amount (Rs.)
To Balance b/d	2,00,000	By Accumulated Depreciation	20,000
To Bank A/c	1,80,000	By Loss on sale of Fixed Asset	18,000
(Purchases)		By Bank A/c (Sale)	62,000
		(80,000 – 18,000)	2,80,000
		By Balance c/d	
	3,80,000		3,80,000

Dr.   **ACCUMULATED DEPRECIATION A/C**   Cr.

Particulars	Amount (Rs.)	Particulars	Amount (Rs.)
To Machinery A/c	20,000	To Balance c/d	80,000
To Balance c/d	1,00,000	By Statement of Profit and loss account	40,000
	1,20,000		1,20,000

TOPIC 2 Financing, Investing Activities, Complete Questions

Summary

Cash flow from investing activities: Investing activities are the acquisition and disposal of long-term assets and other investments not included in cash equivalents. Investing activities relate to purchase and sale of long-term assets or fixed assets such as machinery, furniture, land and building, etc.

	Cash Outflows from investing activities:	Cash Inflows from Investing Activities
I.	Cash payments to acquire fixed assets including intangibles and capitalised research and development	Cash receipt from disposal of fixed assets including intangibles
II.	Cash payments to acquire shares, warrants or debt instruments of other enterprises other than the instruments those held for trading purposes.	Cash receipt from the repayment of advances or loans made to third parties (except in case of financial enterprise).
III.	Cash advances and loans made to third party (other than advances and loans made by a financial enterprise wherein it is operating activities)	Cash receipt from disposal of shares, warrants or debt instruments of other enterprises except those held for trading purposes
		Interest received in cash from loans and advances.
		Dividend received from investments in other enterprises.

Cash From Financing Activites: Financing activities are activities that result in changes in the size and composition of the owners' capital (including preference share capital in case of a company) and borrowings of the enterprise.

Cash Inflows from financing activities	Cash Outflows from financing activities
Cash proceeds from issuing shares (equity or/and preference).	Cash repayments of amounts borrowed
Cash proceeds from issuing debentures, loans, bonds and other short/ long-term borrowings.	Interest paid on debentures and long-term loans and advances
	Dividends paid on equity and preference capital.

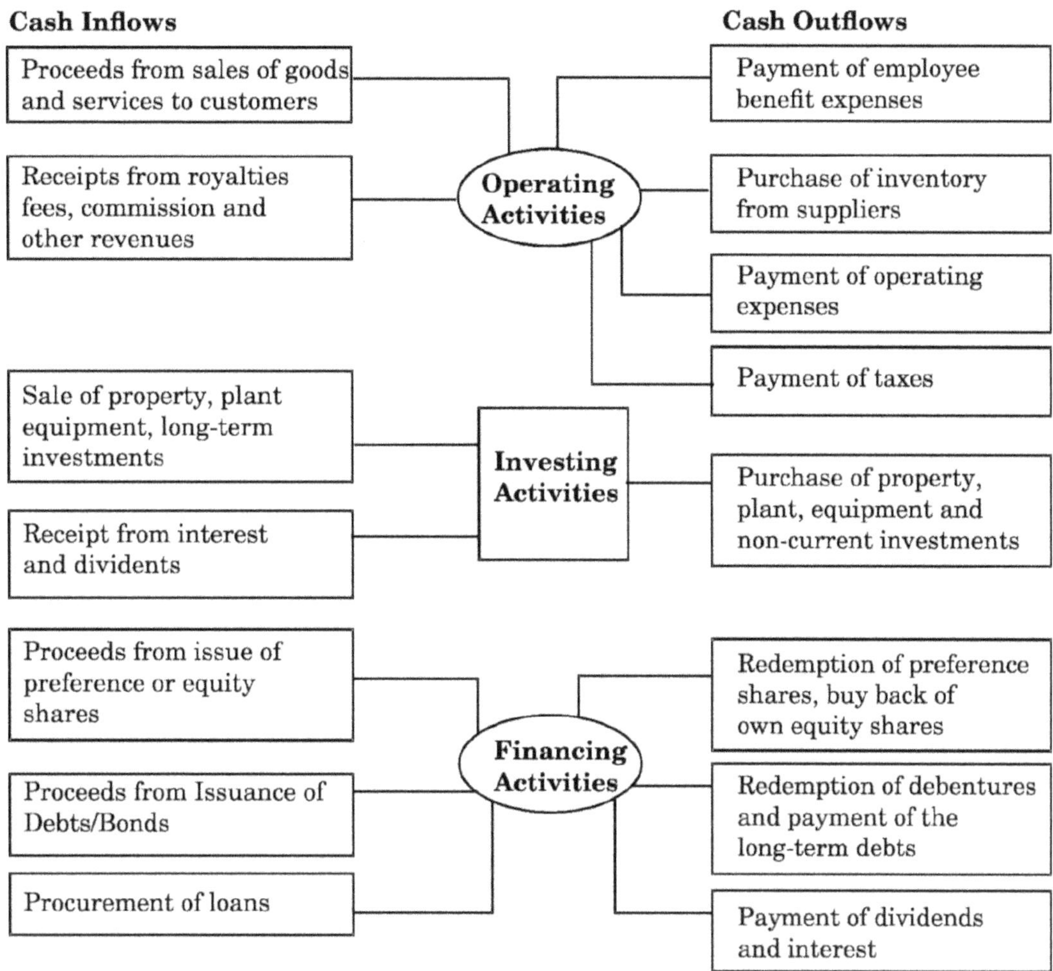

Treatment of Some Peculiar Items:

1. **Extraordinary items:** Extraordinary items are non-recurring in nature and hence cash flows associated with extraordinary items should be classified and disclosed separately as arising from operating, investing or financing activities.

2. **Interest and Dividend:** In case of a financial enterprise (whose main business is lending and borrowing), interest paid, interest received and dividend received are classified as operating activities while dividend paid is a financing activity.

3. **Taxes on Income and Gains:** AS-3 requires that cash flows arising from taxes on income should be separately disclosed and should be classified as cash flows from operating activities unless they can be specifically identified with financing and investing activities.

4. **Non-cash Transactions:** As per AS-3, investing and financing transactions that do not require the use of cash or cash equivalents should be excluded from a cash flow statement.

Cash Flow from Investing Activities:

Investing activities are the acquisition and disposal of long terms assets and other investments not included in cash equivalent. Accordingly, cash inflow and outflow relating to fixed assets, shares, and debentures of other enterprises, advances, and loans to third parties and their repayments are shown separately under investing activities in the Cash Flow Statement.

CASH FLOW FROM INVESTING ACTIVITIES

– Sale of Fixed Assets	×××	
Add:		
– Sale of Invetments	×××	
– Sale of Intangible Assets	×××	
– Interest and Dividend Received (Non finance Co.)	×××	
– Rent Income	×××	×××
Less:		
– Purchase of Fixed Assets/ Intangible Assets	×××	
– Purchase of Investments	×××	×××
		×××
Add/Less: Extraordinary Items		×××
		×××
Net Cash Flow from Investing Activities		×××

Cash Flows from Financing Activities:

The Financing Activities of an enterprise are those activities that result in a change in size and composition of owners capital and borrowing of the enterprise. It includes separate disclosure of proceeds from the issue of shares or other similar instruments, issue of debentures, loans, bonds, other short-term or long-term borrowings, and repayment of amounts borrowed. It is useful in predicting claims on future cash flows by providers of funds (both capital and borrowings to the enterprise.)

Cash Flow from Financing Activities

Issue of Shares		×××
Add:		
– Issue of Debentures	×××	
– Long Term Loan and Advances	×××	×××
		×××
Less:		
– Repayment of Loan etc.	×××	
– Dividend paid (Final, Interim)	×××	
– Redemption of Debenture, Preference Share	×××	
– Interest on Debenture and Loan	×××	×××
Add/Less:		
– Extraordinary Items		×××
		×××
– Net Cash Flow from Investing Activities		×××

FORMAT OF CASH FLOW STATEMENT

Particulars	Details	Amount
I. Cash Flow from Operating Activities		
(A) Net Profit before Tax Taxation and Extraordinary Items		
Adjustment for Non-cash and Non-operating Items		
(B) Add: Items to be Added		
(C) Less: Items to be Deducted		
(D) Operating Profit before Working Capital changes (A + B – C)		...
(E) Add: ↓ in CA and in CL		
(F) Less: in CA and ↓ in CL		
(G) Cash generated from Operations (D + E – F)		...
Less: Income Tax Paid (Net of Tax Refund received)		(...)
Cash Flow before Extraordinary Items		
Extraordinary Items (+/–)		...
(H) Net Cash from (or used in) Operating Activities		...
II. Cash Flow from Investiong Activities		
Proceeds from Sale of Fixed Assets		...
Purchase of Fixed Intangible Assets		(...)
Extraordinary Items (+/–)		...
(I) Net Cash from (or used in) Investing Activities		
III. Cash Flow from Financing Activities		
Proceeds from Issue of Shares or Debentures		...
Proceeds from Other Long-term Borrowings		...
Repayment of Loan		(...)
Redemption of Shares or Debentures		(...)
Bank Overdraft		...
Extraordinary Items (+/–)		...
(J) Net Cash from (or used in) Financing Activities		...
IV. Net /↓ in Cash & Cash Equivalents (I + II + III)		...
Add: Cash & Cash Equivalents in the beginning of the year		...
V. Cash & Cash Equivalents at the end of the year		...

Q.1. Divided paid by a finance company is shown as cash outflow under

  (a) Operating activities

  (b) Investing activity

  (c) Financing activity

  (d) Cash and cash equivalent.

Ans. (c)

Q.2. Which of the following is shown under financing activity?   [CBSE 2010]

  (a) Interest paid

  (b) Commission received

  (c) Cash received against sale of goods

  (d) Cash paid for purchase of goods.

Ans. (a)

Q.3. Arora Ltd. Purchased furniture for Rs.20,00,000 paying 60% by issue of equity shares of Rs. 10 each and the balance by a cheque. This transaction will result in

  (a) Cash used in investing activities Rs. 20,00,000.

  (b) Cash generated from financing activities Rs. 12,00,000

  (c) Increase in cash and cash equivalents Rs. 8,00,000.

  (d) Cash used in investing activities Rs. 8,00,000.

Ans. (d)

Q.4. Aradhya Ltd a stock broker, purchased 5,000 shares of Tata housing Ltd. It is

  (a) Operating activity.   (b) Investing activity

  (c) Financing activitiy.   (d) General activity

Ans. (b)

Q.5. Dividend received by Covid Pharma Limited will be a i.)........for the organization .and will be classifies as ii.)........activity.

  (a) Inflow, investing (b) Inflow, financing   (c) Outflow, financing   (d) Inflow, Operating

Ans. (a)

Q.6. If a machine whose original cost is Rs. 40,000 having accumulated depreciation Rs. 12,000, were sold for Rs. 34,000 then while preparing Cash Flow Statement its effect on cash flow will be :   **[CBSE Sample Paper]**

  (a) Cash flow from financing activities Rs. 34,000

  (b) Cash flow from financing activities Rs. 6,000

  (c) Cash flow from investing activities Rs. 34,000

  (d) Cash flow from investing activities Rs. 6,000

Ans. (c)

Q.7. If 6% Pref. share capital Rs. 2,00,000 were redeemed at a premium of 5%, while preparing Cash Flow Statement its effect on cash flow will be :

(a) Cash used from financing activities Rs. 2,12,000

(b) Cash received from financing activities Rs. 2,12,000

(c) Cash used (Payment) from financial activities Rs. 2,10,000

(d) Cash used (Payment) from financial activities Rs. 2,00,000

Ans. (c)

Q.8. If the amount of goodwill is Rs. 40,000 at the beginning of a year and Rs. 48,000 at the end of that year then while preparing cash flow statement its effect on cash flow will be :   **[CBSE Compartment 2015]**

(a) Cash used (Payment) in Investing Activities Rs. 8,000

(b) Cash received from operating activities Rs. 8,000

(c) Cash used (Payment) from Operating Activities Rs. 8,000

(d) Cash used (Payment) from Financial Activities Rs. 8,000

Ans. (a)

Q.9. Devika India Ltd. has given you the following information:

Machinery as on April 01, 2016 50,000;

Machinery as on March 31, 2017 60,000;

Accumulated Depreciation on April 01, 2016 25,000;

Accumulated Depreciation on March 31, 2017 15,000;

During the year, a Machine costing Rs. 25,000 with Accumulated Depreciation of Rs. 15,000 was sold for Rs. 13,000.

Calculate cash flow from Investing Activities on the basis of the above information.

(a) 48000   (b) (48,000)   (c) 22,000   (d) (22,000)

Ans. (d)

Q.10. Long-term Loans on 1st April, 2016 Rs. 2,00,000;

Long-term Loans on 31st March, 2017 Rs.2,50,000 ;

During the year, the company repaid a loan of Rs. 1,10,000.

Loan obtained during the year...............

(a) 50,000   (b) 1,60,000   (c) (1,60,000)   (d) None of the above

Ans. (b)

Q.11. If a machine whose original cost is Rs. 40,000 having accumulated depreciation Rs. 12,000, were sold for Rs. 34,000 then while preparing Cash Flow Statement its effect on cash flow will be :   **[CBSE Sample Paper]**

(a) Cash flow from financing activities Rs. 34,000

(b) Cash flow from financing activities Rs. 6,000

(c) Cash flow from investing activities Rs. 34,000

(d) Cash flow from investing activities Rs. 6,000

Ans. (c)

Q.12. If the amount of goodwill is Rs. 40,000 at the beginning of a year and Rs. 48,000 at the end of that year then while preparing cash flow statement its effect on cash flow will be :

    (a) Cash used (Payment) in Investing Activities Rs. 8,000

    (b) Cash received from operating activitiesRs. 8,000

    (c) Cash used (Payment) from Operating Activities Rs. 8,000

    (d) Cash used (Payment) from Financial Activities Rs. 8,000

Ans. (a)

Q.13. How will you deal increase in the balance of 'Securities Premium Reserve' while preparing a Cash Flow Statement?   **[CBSE 2017]**

    (a) Cash Flow from Operating Activities   (b) Cash Flow from Investing Activities

    (c) Cash Flow from Financing Activities   (d) Cash Equivalent

Ans. (c)

Q.14. How will you treat Bank Overdraft in a Cash Flow Statement?

    (a) Cash Flow from Operating Activities'   (b) Cash Flow from Investing Activities

    (c) Cash Flow from Financing Activities   (d) Cash Equivalent

Ans. (c)

Q.15. In case of other enterprises cash flow arising from interest paid should be classified as cash flow from _________ while dividends and interest received should be stated as cash flow from _____.

    (a) Operating activities, financing activities   (b) Financing activities, investing activities

    (c) Investing activities, operating activities   (d) None of the above

Ans. (b)

Q.16. Which of the following transactions would result inflow of cash: **[CBSE 2016]**

    (a) Cash withdrawn from Bank for office use.

    (b) Purchase of machinery worth Rs. 2,00,000 and issued shares in consideration thereof.

    (c) Sale of furniture for Rs. 3,000 to Mr. Mohan.

    (d) Cash received from Debtors Rs. 6,000

Ans. (d)

Read the following statements – Assertion (A) and Reason (R). Choose one of the correct alternatives given below: **[CBSE Guidelines]**

Q.17. For the following two statement of Assertion (A) and Reasoning (R) indicate the correct code:

    Assertion (A): Redemption of Debentures would result in outflow of cash.

    Reasoning (R): It is payment and thus, decreases cash.

    (a) Both A and R are true and R is the correct explanation of A.

    (b) Both A and R are true, but R is not the correct explanation of A.

    (c) A is true, but R is false.

    (d) A is false, but R is true.

Ans. (a)

Q.18. Assertion: Cash proceeds from short-term borrowings is classified as cash inflow from operating actives

Reason: Transactions related to long-term investment are investing activates.

(a) Both Assertion and reason are true and reason is correct explanation of assertion.

(b) Assertion and reason both are true but reason is not the correct explanation of assertion.

(c) Assertion is true, reason is false.

(d) Assertion is false, reason is true.

Ans. (d)

Q.19. Assertion: Increase in share capital is inflow under financing activity

Reason: It increases shareholder's fund

(a) Both Assertion and reason are true and reason is correct explanation of assertion.

(b) Assertion and reason both are true but reason is not the correct explanation of assertion.

(c) Assertion is true, reason is false.

(d) Assertion is false, reason is true

Ans. (b)

Very Short Answer Type   [1 Mark]

Q.20. Patents purchased and completely amortized in the year of purchase is added under _________and shown as an outflow under_________

Ans. Operating,Investingactivitiy

Q.21. Purchase of securities by a non- finance company is _________

Ans. Investing activity

Q.22. Issue of Bonus shares is shown as a financing activity.

Ans. False

Q.23. Shares issued to promoters in consideration of their services are shown as a financing activity. **[CBSE 2011]**

Ans. False

Q.24. Operating activities are principal revenue producing activities of an enterprise and those activities that are not investing or financing activities.

Ans. True

Q.25. Buy Back of shares is an extraordinary item for Financing activity

Ans. True

Q.26. Where will you show purchase of computer in cash flow statement?

Ans: As Outflow under Investing Activities.

Q.27. Give two examples of 'Significant non cash transactions'.

Ans. Give any two examples-

    (i) Acquisition of fixed asset by issue of debentures or shares.

    (ii) Conversion of debentures into shares.

Q.28. How will you classify loans given by Tata Manufacturing Company.

Ans. Classified as Financing Activities.

Q.29. A company receives a dividend of Rs. 2 Lakhs on its investment in other company's share will it be Cash inflow from operating or investing activities in case of a.

    (i) Finance Company,

    (ii) Non-Finance Company.

Ans. It will be operating activities in case of a finance company and investing activities in case of Non-Financing Company.

Q.30. How are various activities classified as per AS-3 (Revised) ? **[CBSE 2018]**

Ans. (i) Operating Activities.

    (ii) Investing Activities.

    (iii) Financing Activities.

Q.31. Cash flow from operating Activities + Cash flow from Investing Activities + Cash flow from Financing Activities =.........

Ans. ...= Net Increase /Decrease in cash and Cash Equivalents

Q.32. Agrawal Ltd. Engaged in the business of manufacturing shoes invested Rs.40,00,000 in the shares of a Car manufacturing Company. state whether the dividend received on this investment will Be cash flow from operating activities or Investing activities.

Ans. Investing Activities

Q.33. ToddlerToys Ltd. Purchased a machinery of Rs.20,00,000 for manufacturing toys. State whether the cash flow due to the purchase of machinery will be cash flow from operating activities, Investing activities or Financing activities ?

Ans. Investing Activities

Q.34. When can 'Receipt of Dividend' be classified as an operating activity Rs. State. Also give reason in support of your answer. **[CBSE Delhi 2019]**

Ans. Receipt of dividend can be an operating activity for a financial company as it is a principal revenue generating activity.

Q.35. What is meant by 'Financing Activities' for preparing Cash Flow Statement? **[CBSE 2019 Compt.]**

Ans. Financing activities are the activities that result in change in capital or borrowings of the enterprise.

Q.36. What is mean by investing activities for preparing Cash Flow Statement? **[CBSE 2019 Compt.]**

Ans. Investing activities (as per AS-3) are the acquisition and disposal of long term assets and other investments not included in cash equivalents.

Q.37. Under which type of activity will you classify 'Rent received' while preparing cash flow statement?

[CBSE Sample Paper 2018-19]

Ans. Rent received is inflow of cash from Investing Activities.

Q.38. P P Limited is Share Broker Company. G G Limited is engaged in manufacturing of packaged food. P P Limited purchased 5,000 equity shares of Rs. 100 each of Savita Limited. G G Limited also purchased 10,000 equity shares of Rs. 100 each of Savita Limited.

For the purpose of preparing their respective Cash Flow Statements, under which category of activities the purchase of shares will be classified by P P Limited and G G Limited?   [CBSE Sample Paper 2017-18]

Ans. (a) For P P Limited: Operating Activity

(b) For G G Limited: Investing Activity

Short Answer Type - I   [2 Marks]

Q.1. What is meant by 'cash flow from investing activities?   [CBSE compartment]

Ans. Cash flow from investing activities means inflows and outflows of cash and cash equivalents from sale or acquisition of fixed assets and non-current investment.

Q.2. J. K. Ltd purchased machinery on deferred payment basis. During the year ended 31-03-2016 the company paid an instalment of Rs.4,00,000 which included interest of Rs.40,000. While preparing cash flow statement, under which type of activities will this payment be classified? Also, mention the amount involved in each activity.

Ans. Payment of Rs.3,60,000 will be shown under cash outflows from investing activities. Payment of Rs.40,000 will be shown under cash outflows from financing activities

Q.3. The patents of X Ltd. increased from Rs.3,00,000 in 2013 14 to Rs.3,50,000 in 2014-15. What will be its treatment while preparing cash flow statement for the year ended 31st March, 2015.   [Sample paper -2017]

Ans. It will be taken as purchase of patents of Rs.50,000 and will be shown under cash from investing activities an outflow of cash.

Q.4. List any two investing activities which result in outflow of cash.   [AI-2017]

Ans. (i) Purchase of fixed assets

(ii) Purchase of investment

Q.5. ABC Ltd had investment of Rs. 68,000 as on 31.3.2013 and investment of Rs. 56,000 as on 31.3.2019. During the year ABC Ltd sold 40% of its investments being held in the beginning of period at a profit of Rs. 16,800. Determine cash flow from investing activities.

Ans. Rs 28,800

Q.6. Cheques and drafts in hand' are not considered while preparing cash flow statement. Why?   [Delhi 2017]

Ans. Cheques and Drafts in hand are not considered while preparing cash flow statements as they are part of cash and cash equivalents only.

Short Answer Type - II [3 Marks]

Q.1. Why is separate disclosure of cash flows from investing activities important? State. [AI-2014 &16]

Ans. The separate disclosure of cash flows from investing activities is important because the cash flows represent the extent to which expenditure have been made for resources intended to generate future income and cash flows by way of investing activities.

Q.2. Payment of receipt of interest and dividend is classified as which type of activity while preparing cash flow statement? [2017]

Ans. Payment of interest and dividend is classified as Financing Activity.

Receipt of interest and dividend is classified as Investing Activity.

Q.3. From the following information, the outflow of cash for the purchase of machinery will be:

Written down value of machinery as on 1.4.2011 - Rs. 5,00,000

Written down value of machinery as on 31.3.2012 -Rs.7,00,000

Depreciation on machinery charged during the year Rs. 60,000

Machinery having book value Rs. 25,000 sold for Rs. 20,000

Ans. Rs. 2,85,000

Q.4. From the following information find out the inflow of cash

Office Equipment

31st March, 2014 60,000

31st March, 2013 1,00,000

Additional Information:

Depreciation for the year 2013-14 is Rs. 7,000, Purchase of office Equipment during the year Rs. 10,000 Part of Office Equipment sold at a profit of Rs 6,000

Ans. Rs 49,000

Q.5. From the following information find out the cash flow from financing activities.

Liabilities

Proposed Dividend

31st March 2013 20,000

31st March 2014 15,000

Additional Information:

Equity Share Capital raised 3,00,000 10% Debentures Redeemed 1,00,000 Preference Share capital Redeemed 50,000. Interim Dividend paid during the year 20,000

Ans: Rs 1,00,000

Q.6. From the following information find out the inflow of cash

	31st March, 2015	31st March, 2014
Plant and Machinery Account	Rs.6,00,000	Rs. 4,50,000
Accumulated Depreciation	Rs.1,60,000	Rs 1,00,000

Additional Information:

Depreciation for the year 2014 15 is Rs. 80,000. During the year Machinery was Purchased for Rs 2,50,000 and a part of asset was sold at a profit of Rs. 40,000. **[CBSE 2015]**

Ans. Rs 1,20,000.

Q.7. State the category of the following items for a financial as well as non-financial company (i) Dividend received (ii) Dividend paid (iii) Interest paid (iv) Interest received **[CBSE 2013, 2019]**

Ans.

	Financial Company	**Non-Financial Company**
Dividend received	Operating activity	Investing activity
Dividend paid	Financing activity	Financing activity
Interest paid	Operating activity	Financing activity
Interest received	Operating activity	Investing activity

Q.8. From the following particulars, calculate cash flows from investing activities: **[CBSE 2015]**

	Purchased (Rs.)	**Sold (Rs)**
Plant	4,40,000	50,000
Investments	1,80,000	1,00,000
Goodwill	2,00,000	–
Patents	–	1,00,000

Interest received on debentures held as investment Rs. 60,000.

Dividend received on shares held as investment Rs. 10,000.

A plot of land had been purchased for investment purposes and was let out for commercial use and rent received Rs. 30,000.

Ans.

CASH FLOW FROM INVESTING ACTIVITIES

	(Rs.)	**(Rs.)**
Inflows of Cash:		
Sale of Plant	50,000	
Sale of Investment	1,00,000	
Sale of Patent	1,00,000	
Interest on Debentures	6,000	
Dividend on Shares	10,000	
Rent from Land	30,000	2,96,000
Outflows of Cash:		
Purchase of Plant	(4,40,000)	
Purchase of Investment	(1,80,000)	
Purchase of Goodwill	(2,00,000)	(8,20,000)
Net Inflow from Investment Activity		5,24,000

Q.9. From the following information, calculate Cash Flow from Investing and Financing Activities

	2012 (Rs.)	2013 (Rs.)
Machine at cost	5,00,000	9,00,000
Accumulated Depreciation	3,00,000	4,50,000
Equity Share Capital	2,800,000	3,500,000
Bank Loan	1,250,000	7,50,000

In year 2013, machine costing Rs. 2,00,000 was sold at a profit of Rs. 1,50,000. Depreciation charged on machine during the year 2013 amounted to Rs. 2,50,000.   [CBSE 2013]

Ans.

Dr.   ACCUMULATED DEPRECIATION A/C   Cr.

Particulars	(Rs.)	Particulars	(Rs.)
To Machinery (Bal. Figure)	1,00,000	To Balance b/d	3,00,000
To Balance c/d	4,50,000	By P & L A/c (Current Year Dep.)	2,50,000
	5,50,000		**5,50,000**

Dr.   MACHINERY A/C   Cr.

Particulars	(Rs.)	Particulars	(Rs.)
To Balance b/d	5,00,000	By Acc. Depreciation	1,00,000
To P & L A/c (Profit on Sale)		By Bank (Sale of Machinery)	2,50,000
	1,50,000		
		(Rs.2,00,000 – Rs.1,00,000 + Rs. 1,50,000	
To Bank (Purchase of Mach.)	6,00,000	By Balance c/d	9,00,000
	1,250,000		**1,250,000**

Cash from Investing Activities:	
Sale of Machinery	2,50,000
Less: Purchase of Machinery	(6,00,000)
Net Cash Lost in Investing Activities	(3,50,000)
Cash from Financing Activities:	
Issue of Shares	7,00,000
Less: Repayment of Bank Loan	(5,00,000)
Net Cash Flow from Fianancing Activities	2,00,000

Q.10. For each of the following transactions, calculate the resulting cash flow and state the nature of cash flow viz., operating, investing and financing.

(a) Acquired machinery for Rs. 2,50,000 paying 20% drawn and executing a bond for the balance payable.

(b) Paid Rs. 2,50,000 to acquire shares in Informa Tech, and received a dividend of Rs. 50,000 after acquisition.

(c) Sold machinery of original cost Rs. 2,00,000 with an accumulated depreciation of Rs. 1,60,000 for Rs. 60,000.

Ans.

(a) **Investing Activity:**

Outflow	=	Rs.2,50,000 Machinery Purchase)
Less	=	Rs.2,00,000 (Bond)
Net Outflow	=	Rs.50,000 (20% of Rs.2,50,000)

(b) **Investing Activity:**

Outflow	=	Rs.2,50,000 (Machinery Purchase)
Less: Inflow claims	=	Rs.50,000 (Dividend)
Net Outflow	=	Rs.2,00,000

(c) **(i) Investing Activity:**

Inflow	=	Rs.60,000 (Sale of Machinery)

(ii) **Operating Activity:**

Rs. 20,000 will be deducted (profit sale of machinery), while calculating cash from operating activities due to non-operating profit.

Q.11. Calculate Cash Flows from Investing Activities from the following information:

S.No.	Particulars	31st March 2015 (Rs.)	31st March 2014 (Rs.)
1.	Investments in land	1,600,000	6,00,000
2.	10% Long term Investments	2,50,000	4,00,000
3.	Plant and Machinery	3,00,000	2,00,000
4.	Goodwill	80,000	15,000

Additional Information:

A machine costing Rs.40,000 (depreciation provided thereon Rs. 12,000) was sold for X 35,000. Depreciation charged during the year was Rs. 60,000. **(Compt. Delhi 2017)**

Cash flows From Investing Activities

Particulars	Details (Rs.)	Amount (Rs.)
B. Cash Flows from investing Activities:		
Purchase of Land	(10,00,0000)	
Sale of Long-Term Investments	1,50,000	
Interest on Long-Term Investments	40,000	
Purchase of Plant and Machinery	(1,88,000)	
Sale of Plant and Machinery	35,000	
Purchase of Goodwill	(65,000)	
Net Cash used in investing activities		(10,88,,000)

Notes:

PLANT AND MACHINERY A/C

Particulars	(Rs.)	Particulars	(Rs.)
To Balance b/d	2,00,000	By Cash A/c	35,000
To Statement of P/L	7,000	By Depreciation A/c	60,000
To Cash A/c (Bal Figure) (Purchase)	3,46,000	By balance c/d	3,00,000
	3,95,000		**3,95,000**

Q.1. Explain Investing Activities, Financing Activities of cash flow statement.

Ans. **[I]Cash Flow from Investing Activities:**

Investing activities are those activities which are related to the acquisition (buying) and disposal (selling) of fixed assets and investment (other than cash equivalents). It also includes income from fixed assets and investment like rent received, interest received on investment, dividend received on investment in shares and mutual funds.

Inflows of Cash: (Plus items)

Cash Received from sale of Fixed Assets.

Cash Received from sale of Investment. Excluding Marketable Securities

Cash Received from sale of intangible Assets like Patents.

Interest Received, Dividend Received, Rent Received

Outflows of Cash (minus items)

Cash paid for purchase of intangible Fixed assets like goodwill, patents and copy rights

Cash paid for purchase of fixed assets.

Cash paid for purchase of investment. Excluding Marketable Securities.

[II] Cash Flow from Financing Activities:

Financing activities are those activities that result in the change in size and composition of the share capital (equity and preference) and borrowed fund of the business enterprises. Generally cost related to these funds are also included in financing activities like interest paid on loans and debentures and dividend paid on equity and preference share capital.

Inflows of Cash: (Plus items)

1. Proceeds from Issue of equity shares capital.

2. Proceeds from Issue of preference share capital.

3. Proceeds from taking long-term loan and issue of debentures.

4. Proceeds from Bank Overdraft and Cash credit.

Outflows of Cash (minus items)

1. Amount paid for repayment of long-term loan.

2. Redemption of Preference share capital in cash.

3. Redemption of Debenture in cash.

4. Buy back of Equity shares (Extra-Ordinary Item)

5. Payment of Bank Overdraft and Cash Credits.

6. Interest paid on long term loan and debentures

7. Final Dividend paid.

8. Interim dividend paid.

9. Dividend paid on Preference Shares

Q.2. The Extaract of the Balance Sheet of a company's as follows :   **[CBSE 2020]**

Balance Sheet (Extract)

As on 31st March 2020 & 2021

Assets	31.03.2020	31.03.2021
Plant	40,000	50,000

Additional Information:

(i) Plant costing Rs. 25,000 (accumulated Depreciation Rs 8,000) was sold for Rs 12,000.

(ii) Depreciation on Plant charged during the year was Rs.25, 000.

Answer the following on the basis of above information:

(I) The above activity will be classified as:

  (a) Operating activity

  (b) Investing activity

  (c) Financing activity

  (d) None of the above

Ans. (b)

(II) What will be the final cash flow/used from the activity classified in above question:

  (a) Rs. 52, 000

  (b) Rs. 12,000

  (c) Rs. 40,000

  (d) Rs. 64,000

Ans. (c)

(III)While preparing working note, The Depreciation charged during the year will be shown on:

  (a) Dr. side of plant A/c

  (b) Cr. Side of plant A/c

  (c) It will get not be shown any where

  (d) The difference of 'Depreciation charged during the year' and 'Accumulated depreciation' will be shown on Dr. side of Plant A/c.

Ans. (a)

(IV)What is the amount of Profit/Loss on sale of Plant and where will it be shown?

  (a) Profit of Rs. 5,000, Add in Operating activity

  (b) Loss of Rs. 5,000, Less in Operating activity

  (c) Profit of Rs. 5000, Less in Operating activity

  (d) Loss of Rs. 5,000, Add in Operating activity

Ans. (a)

Q.3. Following particulars are taken from the Balance Sheets of C.L. Ltd., as on 31ˢᵗ March 2017 and 2018:

Particulars	Note No.	31.03.18 Rs.	31.03.17 Rs.
I.　EQUITY AND LIABILITIES			
1. Shareholder's Funds			
(a) Share Capital		1,400,000	1,000,000
(b) Reserves and Surplus (Balance in			
Statement of Profit and Loss)		5,00,000	4,00,000
2. Non-Current Liabilities			
Long-term Borrowings (9% Public Deposits)		6,00,000	2,00,000
3. Current Liabilities			
Short-term Provisions (Provision for Tax)		80,000	60,000
Total		2,580,000	1,660,000
II.　ASSETS			
1. Non-Current Assets			
Fixed Assets			
(a) Tangible Assets (Machinery)		1,600,000	9,00,00
(b) Intangible Assets (Goodwill)		1,40,000	2,00,000
2. Current Assets			
(a) Inventories		2,50,000	2,00,000
(b) Trade Receivable		5,00,000	3,00,000
(c) Cash and Cash Equivalents		90,000	60,000
Total		2,580,000	1,660,000

Prepare a Cash Flow Statement after taking into account the following adjustments:

(a) The company paid interest of Rs.45,000 on its Public Deposits.

(b) Depreciation provided on machinery during the year Rs.2,00,000.

Ans.

CASH FLOW STATEMENT OF C.L. LTD.

for the year ending 31st March 2018

Sr. No.	Particulars	Details Rs.	Amount Rs.
A.	Cash Flows from / (used in) Operating Activities:		
	Profit before Tax	1,80,000	
	Add: Depreciation on machinery	2,00,000	
	Interest on public deposits	45,000	
	Goodwill written off	60,000	
	Operating Profit before Working Capital Changes	4,85,000	
	Less: Increase in Inventories	(50,000)	
	Increase in Trade Receivables	(2,00,000)	
	Cash generated from Operating Activities	235,000	
	Less: Tax paid	(60,000)	
	Net Cash from Operating Activities	1,75,000	17,5,000

B.	Cash Flows from / (used in) Investing Activities:		
	Machinery purchased (16,00,000 + 2,00,000 – 9,00,000)	(9,00,000)	
	Net Cash used in Investing Activities	(9,00,000)	(9,00,000)
C.	Cash Flows from / (used in) Financing Activities:		
	Issue of Share Capital	4,00,000	
	9% Public Deposits raised	4,00,000	
	Interest paid	(45,000)	
	Net Cash from Financing Activities	7,55,000	7,55,000
D.	Net Increase in Cash and Cash Equivalents (A + B + C)		30,000
E.	Cash and Cash Equivalents – Opening Balance		60,000
F.	Cash and Cash Equivalents – Closing Balance (D + E)		90,000

Q.4. Statement of Profit and Loss of Arora Ltd.is as follows, calculate Cash Flow from Operating Activities from the following information: **[CBSE 2015]**

STATEMENT OF PROFIT AND LOSS OF ARORA LTD.

for the year ended March 31, 2018

Particulars		Amount
I. Revenue from Operations		50,000
II. Add: Other Incomes-Profit on sale of Machinery	2,000	
Income Tax Refund	3,000	5,000
III. Total Revenue from Operations (I + II)		55,000
IV. Less: Expenses:		
(a) Employee Benefit Expenses		
(b) Depreciation and Amortisation		25,000
Depreciation on fixed tangible assets	5,000	
Goodwill written off	2,000	7,000
(c) Other Expenses:		
Office Rent	10,000	
Loss on Sale of Equipment	3,000	13,000
Total Expenses (a + b + c)		(45,000)
V. Profit Before Tax (III – IV)		10,000
VI. Less: Provision for Taxation		(8,000)
VIII. Profit After Tax (V-VI)		2,000

Additional Information:

Particulars	31.03.2018 Rs.	01.04.2017 Rs.
Provision for Taxation	13,000	10,000
Outstanding Rent	2,500	2,000
Trade Payables	25,000	21,000
Trade Receivables	21,000	15,000
Inventories	22,000	25,000

Ans. (i) Calculate of missing figures:

Dr.   PROVISION FOR TAXATION A/C   **Cr.**

Particulars	Rs.	Particulars	Rs.
To Bank A/c (Income Tax paid	5,000	By Balance b/d	10,000
during the year-Bal. Fig.)	13,000	By Statement of Profit and	8,000
To Balance c/d	18,000	Loss (Current year's	18,000
		provision)	

(ii) Statement of Cash Flows From Operating Activities

Particulars	Details Rs.	Total Rs.
Profit before Tax	10,000	
Less: Income Tax refund	3,000	7,000
Adjustments for:		
Add: Depreciation on Fixed tangible assets	5,000	
Goodwill written off	2,000	
Loss on sale of Equipment	3,000	
Less: Profit on sale of Machinery	(2000)	
Operating Profit before Working Capital changes	15,000	
Add: Decrease in Inventories	3,000	
Increase in Trade Payables	4,000	
Increase in Outstanding Rent	500	
Less: Increase in Trade Receivables	(6,000)	
Cash generated from Operating Activities	16,500	
Less: Income Tax paid	(5,000)	
	11,500	
Add: Income Tax refund	3,000	
Net Cash from Operating Activities	14,500	14,500

Q.5. Cash flow from operating activities of Devika Ltd. For the year ended 31.03.2019 was Rs.18,000. The Balance Sheet along with notes to accounts of Devika Ltd. As at 31.03.2019 is given below:

DEVIKA LIMITED

Balance Sheet as at 31st March 2019

Particulars	Note No.	31.03.2019 Rs.	31.03.2018 Rs.
I. EQUITY AND LIABILITIES			
1. Shareholder's Funds:			
(a) Share Capital		1,800,000	1,000,000
(b) Reserves and Surplus	1	50,000	40,000
2. Non-Current Liabilities:			
Long-term Borrowings	2	1,00,000	4,00,000
3. Current Liabilities:			
Short-term Provisions	3	2,50,000	3,60,000
Total		2,200,000	1,800,000

II. ASSETS			
1. Non-Current Assets:			
Fixed Assets:			
(i) Tangible assets	4	1,400,000	1,000,000
(ii) Intangible assets	5	180,000	70,000
2. Current Assets:			
(a) Current Investments		30,000	1,90,000
(b) Trade Receivables		2,90,000	3,10,000
(c) Cash and Cash Equivalents		3,00,000	2,30,000
Total		2,200,000	1,800,000

Notes to Accounts:

S. No.	Particulars	31.03.2019 (Rs.)	31.03.2018 (Rs.)
1.	Reserves and Surplus	50,000	40,000
	Surplus (Balance in statement of Profit and Loss)	50,000	40,000
2.	Long term Borrowings	1,00,000	4,00,000
	8% debentures	1,00,000	4,00,000
3.	Short-term Provisions	2,50,000	3,60,000
	Provision for tax	2,50,000	3,60,000
4.	Tangible Assets		
	Plant and Machinery	1,520,000	1,090,000
	Less: Accumulated depreciation	(1,20,000)	(90,000)
		14,00,000	10,00,000
5.	Intangible Assets		
	Goodwill	1,80,000	70,000
		1,80,000	70,000

You are given the following additional information:

(a) A machinery of the book value of Rs.40,000 (depreciation provided thereon Rs.12,000) was sold at a loss of Rs.6,000)

(b) 8% debentures were redeemed on 1st July 2018.

Prepare Cash Flow Statement.

Ans.

CASH FLOW STATEMENT OF DEVIKA LTD.
For the year ended 31st March, 2019

S. No.	Particulars	Details (Rs.)	(Rs.)
A.	Cash Flow from Operating Activities: (given)		18,000
B.	Cash Flow from Investing Activities:		
	Purchase of goodwill	(1,10,000)	
	Purchase of Plant and Machinery	(4,82,000)	
	Sale of Plant and Machinery	34,000	5,58,000

C.	Cash Flow from Financing Activities:			
	Issue of Share Capital		8,00,000	
	Redemption of Debentures		(3,00,000)	
	Interest paid on Debentures		(14,000)	4,86,000
D.	Net decrease in Cash and Cash Equivalents (A + B + C)			(90,000)
E.	Add: Cash and Cash Equivalents (Opening)			4,20,000
F.	Cash and Cash Equivalents (Closing)			(3,30,000)

Working Note:

Dr.   **PLANT AND MACHINERY A/C**   **Cr.**

Particulars	(Rs.)	Particulars	(Rs.)
To Balance b/d	1,090,000	By Accumulated Depreciation A/c	12,000
To Bank A/c (Bal. Fig.)	4,82,000	By Statement of Profit and Loss	6,000
		By Bank A/c	34,000
		By Balance c/d	1,520,000
	1,572,000		**1,572,000**

Dr.   **ACCUMULATED DEPRECIATION A/C**   **Cr.**

Particulars	(Rs.)	Particulars	(Rs.)
To Plant & Machinery A/c	12,000	By Balance b/d	90,000
To Balance c/d	**1,20,000**	By Statement of Profit and Loss	42,000
	1,32,000		**1,32,000**

Q.6. From the following Balance Sheet of Kiero Ltd. and the additional information as on 31-3-2018, prepare a Cash Flow Statement: **[CBSE Delhi 2019]**

KIEOR LTD

Balance Sheet as at 31st March, 2018

Particulars	Note No.	31-3-2018 (Rs.)	31-3-2017 (Rs.)
I. Equity and liabilities:			
(1) Shareholder's Funds:			
(a) Share Capital	1	7,90,000	5,80,000
(b) Reserve and Surplus		4,60,000	1,20,000
(2) Non-current Liabilities:	2		
Long-term borrowings		5,00,000	3,00,000
(3) Current Liabilities:			
(a) Short-term borrowings	3	1,15,000	42,000
(b) Short-term borrowings	4	1,18,000	46,000
Total		1,983,000	1,088,000

	Assets:			
II.	(1) Non-current Assets:			
	Fixed Assets:	5	9,80,000	6,35,000
	(i) Tangible	6	2,68,000	1,70,000
	(ii) Intangible			
	(3) Current Assets:		1,40,000	70,000
	(a) Current Investments		4,40,000	1,50,000
	(b) Trade Inventories		1,55,000	63,000
	(c) Cash & Cash Equivalents			
	Total		**1,983,000**	**1,088,000**

Note to Accounts:

Note No.	Particulars	31.3.2018 (Rs.)	31.3.2017 (Rs.)
1.	**Reserved and Surplus**		
	Surplus (Balance in Statement of Profit & Loss	3,20,000	60,000
	General Reserve	1,40,000	60,000
		4,60,000	1,20,000
2.	**Long-term borrowings:**		
	12% Debentures	5,00,000	3,00,000
		5,00,000	3,00,000
3.	**Short-term borrowings:**		
	Bank Overdraft	1,15,000	42,000
		1,15,000	42,000
4.	**Short-term provisions:**		
	Provision for tax	1,18,000	46,000
		1,18,000	46,000
5.	**Tangible Assets:**		
	Plant and Machinery	1,100,000	7,50,000
	Less: Accumulated Depreciations	(1,20,000)	(1,15,000)
		9,80,000	6,35,000
6.	**Intangible Assets:**		
	Goodwill	2,68,000	1,70,000
		2,68,000	(1,70,000)

Additional Information:

12% debentures were issued on 1st September, 2017.

CASH FLOW STATEMENT

Particulars	Amount (Rs.)	Amount (Rs.)
Net profit as per P&L A/c	2,60,000	
Add: General Reserve	80,000	
Provision for tax	1,18,000	
Net profit before tax and extraordinary items	4,58,000	
Add: Depreciation	5,000	
Interest on debenture	50,000	
Operating profit before working capital changes	5,13,000	
Add: Decrease in C/A. and Increase in C.L	NIL	
Less: Increase in C.A and decrease in C.L		
Increase in Trade Receivable	(2,90,000)	
Cash Generated from operations	2,23,000	
Less: Tax paid	(46,000)	1,77,000
A. Cash Flow from operating activities		
Purchase of Plant and Machinery	(3,50,000)	
Purchase of Goodwill	(98,000)	(4,48,000)
B. Cash used in investing activities		
Bank overdraft	73,000	
Issue of shares capital	2,10,000	
Issue of debentures	2,00,000	
Payment of interest on debenture	(50,000)	4,33,000
C. Cash flow from financing activities		
A + B + C		
Net increase in cash and cash equivalents		1,62,000
Add: Opening Cash and Cash equivalents		
(63,000 + 70,000)		1,33,000
Closing Cash and Cash equivalents		
(1,55,000 + 1,40,000)		2,95,000

Q.7. From the following Balance Sheets of Vishva Ltd., prepare Cash Flow Statement as per AS – 3 (revised) for the year ending 31st March, 2018

Particulars	Note No.	31.3.2018 (Rs.)	31.3.2017 (Rs.)
I. Equity and Liabilities:			
(i) **Shareholder's Funds:**			
(a) Share Capital		1,02,000	84,000
(b) Reserves and Surplus	1	36,000	22,560

		2	60,000	48,000
(ii) **Non-current Liabilities**				
(a) Long-term borrowings		2	60,000	48,000
(iii) **Current Liabilities**				
(a) Short term Borrowings		3	10,000	5,000
(b) Trade Payable			28,800	36,000
(c) Short term provision		4	16,800	18,000
Total			**2,53,600**	**2,13,560**
II. **Assets**				
(i) **Non-current Assets:**				
(a) Fixed Assets:				
Tangible Assets		5	1,18,800	1,32,000
(ii) **Current Assets:**				
(a) Inventories			61,800	45,600
(b) Trade Receivables		6	33,600	27,600
(c) Cash and Cash Equivalents			39,400	8,360
Total			**2,53,600**	**2,13,560**

NOTES TO ACCONTS

Note No.	Particular	31.3.2018 (Rs.)	31.3.2017 (Rs.)
1.	**Reserve and Surplus**		
	Balance in Statement of Profit & Loss	15,600	5,760
	General Reserve	20,400	16,800
		36,000	**22,560**
2.	**Long Term Borrowings**		
	10% Debentures	60,000	48,000
		60,000	**48,000**
3.	**Short-term Borrowings**		
	Bank Overdraft	10,000	5,000
		10,000	**5,000**
4.	**Short-term Provisions**		
	Provision for Income Tax	16,800	18,000
		16,800	**18,000**
5.	**Tangible assets**		
	Land and Building	96,000	97,200
	Plant and Machinery	22,800	34,800
		1,18,800	**1,32,000**

6.	Trade Receivables		
	Debtors	19,200	24,000
	Bills Receivables	14,400	3,600
		33,600	27,600

Additional Information:

(a) Tax paid during the year 2017-18 Rs.4,400

(b) Depreciation on plant charged during the year 2017-18 was Rs.14,400

(c) Additional debentures were issued on March 31, 2018   [CBSE Sample Paper 2018-19]

Ans.

VISHVA LTD

Cash Flow Statement for the year ended on 31st March, 2018

Particulars	Details	Amount (Rs.)
I. **Cash flow from Operating Activities**		
Net profit before tax and Extraordinary Itmes (W.N.I)		26,640
Adjustment for Non cash and Non operating Expenses		
Add: Interest on Debentures	4,800	
Depreciation on Land and Building	1,200	
Depreciation on Plant and Machinery	14,400	20,400
Operating profit before working capital changes		47,040
Add: Increase in Current Liability and decrease in Current Assets Debtors	4,800	4,800
Less: Decrease in Current Liability and increase in Current Assets		
Trade Payables	(7,200)	
Inventories	(16,200)	
Bill Receivables	(10,800)	(34,200)
Cash Flow from Operating Activities before payment of Tax		
Less: Tax paid		
Cash Flow from Operating Activities before payment of Tax		
Less: Tax paid		17,640
		(14,400)
Cash flow from Operating Activities		3,240
II. **Cash flow from investing activities**		
Purchase of Plant and Machinery		(2,400)
Cash used in Investing Activity		(2,,400)
III. **Cash flow from financing activities**		
Issue of Equity Shares	18,000	
10% Debentures raised	12,000	
Interest on Debentures Paid	(4,800)	
Proceeds from Bank Overdraft	5,000	30,200
Cash flow from financing activities		

IV.	Increase in Cash and Cash Equivalent (I + II + III)	31,040
V.	Operating Cash and cash Equivalents	8,360
	Closing Cash and Cash Equivalents (IV + V)	**39,400**

Working Notes:

Calculation of Net Profit before Tax and Extraordinary items

Surplus i.e. Balance in Statement of Profit and Loss	9,840
Add: Transfer to General Reserve	3,600
Add: Provision for Tax	13,200
Net profit before tax and Extraordinary Item	26,640

Dr. **PROVSION FOR INCOME TAX ACCOUNT** **Cr.**

Particulars	Amount (Rs.)	Particulars	Amount (Rs.)
To Bank A/c (Tax Paid)	14,400	By Balance b/d	18,000
To Balance C/d	16,800	By Profit and Loss A/c	13,200
	31,200		**31,200**

Dr. **PROVSION FOR INCOME TAX ACCOUNT** **Cr.**

Particulars	Amount (Rs.)	Particulars	Amount (Rs.)
To Bank A/c (Tax Paid)	14,400	By Balance b/d	18,000
To Balance C/d	16,800	By Profit and Loss A/c	13,200
	31,200		**31,200**

Q.8. Following is the Balance Sheet of R.S. Ltd as at 31st March. 2016:

R.S. Ltd Balance Sheet as at 31.1.2015

Particulars	Note No.	31.3.2016 (Rs.)	31.3.2015 (Rs.)
I. **Equity and Liabilities:**			
(i) **Shareholder's Liabilities:**			
(a) Share Capital		9,00,000	9,00,000
(b) Reserves and Surplus	1	2,50,000	1,00,000
(ii) **Non-current Liabilities**			
Long-term borrowings	2	4,50,000	3,50,000
(iii) **Current Liabilities**			
(a) Short-term borrowings	3	1,50,000	75,000
(b) Short-term provisions	4	2,00,000	1,25,000
Total		1,950,000	1,350,000

II.	Assets:			
	(i) **Non-current Assets:**			
	(a) Fixed Assets:			
	Tangible	5	1,465,000	9,15,000
	Intangible	6	1,00,000	1,50,000
	(b) Non-Current Investments		1,50,000	1,00,000
	(ii) **Current Assets:**			
	(a) Current Investments		40,000	70,000
	(b) Inventories	7	1,22,000	72,000
	(c) Cash and Cash Equivalents		73,000	43,000
	Total		**1,950,000**	**1,350,000**

NOTE TO ACCOUNTS

Note No.	Particulars	31.3.2016 (Rs.)	31.3.2015 (Rs.)
1.	**Reserves and Surplus**		
	(Surplus i.e. Balance in Statement of Profit and Loss)	250,000	100,000
		2,50,000	**1,00,000**
2.	**Long-term borrowings:**		
	12% Debentures	4,50,000	3,50,000
		4,50,000	**3,50,000**
3.	**Short-term borrowings:**		
	Bank overdraft	1,50,000	75,000
		1,50,000	**75,000**
4.	**Short-term provisions:**		
	Provision for Tax	2,00,000	1,25,000
		2,00,000	**1,25,000**
5.	**Tangible Assets:**		
	Machinery	1,675,000	1,055,000
	Accumulated Depreciation	(2,10,000)	(1,40,000)
		1,465,000	**9,15,000**
6.	**Intangible Assets:**		
	Goodwill	1,00,000	1,50,000
		1,00,000	**1,50,000**
7.	**Inventories:**		
	Stock in trade	1,22,000	72,000
		1,22,000	**72,000**

Additonal Information:

(i) Rs. 1,00,000,12% Debenures were issued on 31.3.2016.

(ii) During the year a piece of machinery costing Rs. 80,000, on which accumulated depreciation was Rs. 40,000, was sold at a loss of Rs. 10,000.

Prepare a Cash Flow Statement. **(Delhi 2017, Modified)**

Ans:

CASH FLOW STATEMENT OF RS LTD

For the year ended 31st March 2016 as per AS-3 (Revised)

Particulars	Details (Rs.)	Amount (Rs.)
(A) **Cash Flows From Operating Activities:**		
Net profit before tax & extraordinary items (note 1)	3,50,000	
Add: Non cash and non-operating charges		
Goodwill Written off	50,000	
Depreciation on machinery	1,10,000	
Interest on debentures	42,000	
Loss on sale of machinery	10,000	
Operating profit before working Capital changes	562,000	
Less: Increase in Current Assets		
Increase in inventories	(50,000)	
	5,12,000	
Less Tax Paid	(1,25,000)	
Net Cash generated from Operating Activities		3,87,000
(B) **Cash Flows From Investing Activities**		
Purchase of machinery	(7,00,000)	
Sale of machinery	30,000	
Purchase of non current investments	(50,000)	
Net cash used in investing activities		(7,20,000)
(C) **Cash Flows From Financing Activities**		
Issue off Shares capital	2,00,000	
Issue of 12% debentures	1,00,000	
Interest on debentures paid	(42,000)	
Bank overdraft raised	75,000	
Net Cash flow from fnancing activities		3,33,000
Net increase/decrease in cash & cash equivalents (A + B + C)		NIL
Add: Opening balance of cash and cash equivalents current investments	70,000	
Cash and Cash Equivalents	43,000	1,13,000
Closing balance of cash and cash equivalents		
Current Investments	40,000	
Cash and Cash Equivalents	73,000	1,13,000

Notes:

Calculation of Net Profit Before Tax	
Net profit as per statement of Profit & Loss	1,50,000
Add: Provsion for Tax	2,00,000
Net Profit before tax & extraordinary items	350,000

MACHINERY A/C

Particulars	(Rs.)	Particulars	(Rs.)
To Balance b/d	1,055,000	By Cash A/c	30,000
To Cash A/c (Bal figure)	7,00,000	By Statement of P/L	10,000
(Purchase)		By Accumulated Depreciation A/c	40,000
		By Balance c/d	1,675,000
	1,755,000		1,755,000

ACCUMULATED DEPRECIATION A/C

Particulars	(Rs.)	Particulars	(Rs.)
To Machinery A/c	40,000	By Balance c/d	1,40,000
To Balanc c/d	2,10,000	By Statement of P/L (Bal figure)	1,10,000
	2,50,000		2,50,000

Note: Treatment of Proposed Dividend has been done as per AS4 revised previous year's dividend has been taken as dividend approved and paid.

Q.9. From the following Balance Sheet of Ajanta Limited as on March 31,2017, prepare a Cash Flow Statement:

Date	Particulars	Note No.	31.3.2017 (Rs.)	31.3.2016
I.	**Equity and Liabilities:**			
	(i) Shareholder's Funds			
	(a) Equity Sgare Caoutak		1,000,000	10,00,00
	(b) Reserves and Surpuls	1	2,40,000	120,000
	(ii) Non-current Liabilities			
	Long-term borrowwings-9% Devebtyres		3,20,000	240,000
	(iii) Current Liabilities			
	(a) Trade Payables	2	1,80,000	240,000
	(b) Otther Current Liabilities	3	1,80,000	160,000
	Total		1,920,000	1,760,000
II.	**Assets**			
	(i) Non-current Assets:			
	(a) Fixed Assets:			
	Tangible Assets	4	1,340,000	1,200,000
	(b) Non-Current Investments	5	2,40,000	1,60,000

				31.3.2017	31.3.2016
(ii) **Current Assets:**					
(a) Inventories				1,20,000	1,60,000
(b) Trade Receivables				1,60,000	1,60,000
(c) Cust and Cush Equivalents				60,000	80,000
		Total		1,920,000	1,760,000

NOTES TO ACCOUNTS

Note No.	Particulars	31.3.2017 (Rs.)	31.3.2016 Rs.
1.	**Reserves and Surplus**		
	General Reserve	1,20,000	1,20,000
	Balance in Statement of Profit & Loss	1,20,000	....
		2,40,000	**1,20,000**
2.	**Trade Payable**		
	Creditors	1,40,000	1,20,000
	Bills Payable	40,000	1,20,000
		1,80,000	**2,40,000**
3.	**Other Current Liabilities**		
	Outstanding Rend	1,80,000	1,60,000
		1,80,000	**1,60,000**
4.	**Tangible Assets**		
	Plant & Machinery	1,490,000	1,330,000
	Accumulated Depreciation	(1,50,000)	(1,00,0000)
		1,340,000	**1,200,000**
5.	**Non-Current Investments**		
	Shares in XYZ Limited	2,40,000	1,60,000
		2,40,000	**1,60,000**

Additional Information:

(a) During the year 2016-17, a machinery costing Rs.50,000 and accumulated depreciation thereon Rs. 15,000 was sold for Rs.32,000.

(b) 9% Debentures Rs. 80,000 were issued on April 1, 2016.   **[CBSE Sample Paper 2017-18]**

Ans.

AJANTA LIMITED

CASH FLOW STATEMENT

For the year ended 31st March, 2014

	Particulars			Amount (Rs.)
I.	**Cash flow from Operating Activities**			
	Surplus: Balance in the Statement of Profit & Loss			
	Adjustment for Non-Cash and Non-Operating Items		1,20,000	

	Depreciation	65,000	
	Loss on sale on Machinery	3,000	
	Interest on Debentures	28,800	
	Operating Profit before changes in working capital		96,800
Add:	Decrease in Current Assets and Increase in Current Liabilities		2,16,800
	Inventories	40,000	
	Outstanding Rent	20,000	
	Creditors	20,000	
Less:	Increase in Current Assets and Decrease in Current Liabilities		
	Bills Payable		(80,000)
			(2,16,800)
Cash Flow from Operating Activities			2,16,800
II.	**Cash flow from investing activities**		(2,40,000)
	Purchase of Machinery		32,000
	Sale of Machinery		(80,000)
	Purchase of Shares in XYZ Limited		(2,88,000)
Cash Flow from Investing Activities			(2,88,000)
III.	**Cash flow from investing activities**		80,000
	Issue of 9% Debentures		(28,800)
	Interest on Debentures		51,200
	Cash flow from financing activities		51,200
	Net Cash Flow		(20,000)
	Add: Opening balance of Cash and Cash Equivalents		80,000
	Closing Balance of Cash and Cash Equivalents		60,000

PLANT & MACHINERY ACCOUNT

Particulars	Amount (Rs.)	Particulars	Amount (Rs.)
To Balance b/d	1,300,000	By Bank Account	32,000
To Bank Acount	2,40,000	By Accumulated Depreciation Account	15,000
		By Statement of Profit & Loss	3,000
		By Balance c/d	1,490,000
	180,000		1,540,000

ACCUMULATED DEPRECIATION ACCOUNT

Particulars	Amount (Rs.)	Particulars	Amount (Rs.)
To Plant & Machinery Account	15,000	By Balance b/d	1,00,000
To Balance c/d	1,50,000	By Statement of Profit & Loss	65,000
	1,65,000		1,65,000

Q.10. From the following balance sheet of JN Ltd as on 31st March, 2010 and 2011, prepare a cash flow statement.

Particulars	Note No.	31st March 2010 (Rs.)	31st March 2011 (Rs.)
I.　Equity and Liabilities			
1. Shareholder's Funds			
Equity Share Capital		6,00,000	9,00,000
Reserves and Surplus (Surplus, i.e, Balance in statement of profit and loss		1,50,000	3,00,000
2. Current Liabilities			
Short-term Borrowings (Bank loan)		3,00,000	1,50,000
Trade Payables (Creditors)		90,000	67,500
Short-term Provisions	1	1,80,000	1,95,000
Total		1,320,000	1,612,500
II.　Assets			
1. Non-current Assets			
Fixed Assets	2	9,75,000	9,62,500
Non-current Investments		–	1,12,500
2. Current Assets			
Trade Receivables (Debtors)		3,00,000	3,82,500
Inventories (Stock)		15,000	22,500
Cash and Cash Equivalents (Cash)		30,000	1,32,500
Total		1,320,000	16,12.500

Notes of Account

Particulars	31st March, 2010 (Rs.)	31st March, 2011 (Rs.)
1.　**Short-term Provisions**		
Provision for Tax	60,000	1,05,000
Proposed Dividend	1,20,000	90,000
	1,80,000	1,95,000
2.　**Fixed Assets**		
Tangible (Building)	90,000	9,00,000
Intangible (Patents)	75,000	62,500
	9,75,000	9,62,500

Additional Information

During the year a building having book value Rs. 1,25,000 was sold at a loss of Rs. 8,000 and depreciation charged on building was Rs. 20,000.　　　　　　　　　　　　**[Delhi 2012; Modified]**

Ans.

CASH FLOW STATEMENT

for the year ended 31st March, 2011

Particulars		Amount (Rs.)
A. **Cash Flow from Operating Activities**		
Net Profit before Tax Extraordinary Items [WN(i)]		3,45,000
(+) **Adjustment for**		
Depreciation on Building	20,000	
Patents Written-off	12,500	
Loss on Sale of Building	8,000	40,500
Operating Profit before Working Capital Changes		38,5,500
(−) Increase in Current Assets and Decrease in Current Liabilities		
Increase in Debtors	(82,500)	
Increase in Stock	(7,500)	
Decrease in Creditors	(22,500)	(1,12,500)
Cash from Operating Activities		2,73,000
(−) Income Tax Paid		(60,000)
Net Cash Flow from Operating Activities		2,13,000
B. **Cash Flow from Inesting Activities**		
Proceeds from Sale of Building	1,17,000	
Purchase of Building	(1,45,000)	
Purchase of Investment	(1,,12,500)	
Net Cash Used in Investing Activities		(1,40,500)
C. **Cash Flow from financing Activities**		
Proceeds from Issue of Shares	3,00,000	
Repayment of Bank Loan	(1,50,000)	
Divided Paid	(1,20,000)	
Net Cash Flow from Financing Activities		30,000
Net Increase in Cash and Cash Equipment		1,02,500
(+) Cash and Cash Equipments at the Beginning of Period		30,000
Cash and Cash Equipments at the End of Period		1,32,500

Working Note

(i)   **Net Profit before Tax and Extraordinary Items**

Particulars	Amt (Rs.)
Net Profit for the Year	1,50,000
(+) Provision for Tax	1,05,000
Proposed Dividend	90,000
	3,45,000

Q.11. From the following information prepare a 'cash flow statement' for Ronak Ltd. Balance sheet of Ronak Ltd as at 31st March, 2011 and 2012.

	Paticulars	Note No.	31st March 2011 (Rs.)	31st March 2012 (Rs.)
I.	**Equity and Liabilities**			
	1. Shareholders' Funds			
	(a) Equity Share Capital		2,50,000	3,50,000
	(b) Reserves and Surplus		40,000	5,000
	2. Non-current Liabilities			
	Long-term Borrowings (12% Debentures)		60,000	1,00,000
	3. Current Liabilities			
	Trade Payables		1,50,000	1,25,000
	Total		5,00,000	5,80,000
II.	**Assets**			
	1. Non-current Assets			
	(a) Fixed Assets		2,00,000	2,80,000
	(b) Non-current Investments		1,00,000	1,00,000
	2. Current Assets			
	(a) Trade Receivables		1,50,000	1,60,000
	(b) Cash and Cash Equivalents		30,000	40,000
	(c) Other Current Assets (Prepaid expenses)		20,000	–
	Total		5,00,000	5,80,000

Notes to Accounts

	Particular	31st March, 2011 (Rs.)	31st March, 2012 (Rs.)
1.	**Reserves and Surplus**		
	Surplus, i.e. Balance in Statement of Profit and Loss	40,000	(20,000)
	Securities Reserve	–	25,000
		40,000	5,000

Additional Information

(i) Debentures were issued on 1st April, 2011.

(ii) During the year a machine included in fixed assets costing Rs 1,20,000 was purchased and another machine of the book value of Rs 30,000 was sold at a loss of Rs 2,000.   **(Delhi 2012; Modified)**

Ans.

CASH FLOW STATEMENT

for the year ended 31st March, 2012

Particular		Amt (Rs.)
A.	**Cash Flow from Operating Activities**	
	Net Loss During the year	(60,000)
	(+) Adjustments for	
	Depreciation of Fixed Assets (WN) 10,000	
	Loss on Sale of Fixed Asets 2,000	
	Interet on Debentures (Rs.1,00,000 × 12/100) 12,000	44,000
	Operating Profit before Working Capital Changes	(16,000)
	(+) Decrease in Current Assets and Increase is Current Liabilities	
	Decrease in Prepaid Expenses	20,000
	(–) Increase in Current Assets and Decrease is Current Liabilities	
	(–) Increase in Trade Receivables (10,000)	
	Decrease in Trade Payables (25,000)	(35,000)
	Net Cash Used in Operating Activities	(51,000)
B.	**Cash Flow from Investing Activities**	
	Sales of Fixed Assets (W/N) 28,000	
	Purchase of Fixed Assets (1,20,000)	
	Net Cash Used in Investing Activities	(92,000)
C.	**Cash Flow from Financing Activities**	
	Cash Proceeds from Issue of Shares (Rs.1,00,000 + Rs.25,000) 1,25,000	
	Proceeds from Issue of Debentures 40,000	
	Interest Paid on Debentures (12,000)	
	Net Cash Flow from Financing Activities	1,53,000
	Net Increase in Cash and Cash Equivalents (A + B + C)	10,000
	(+) Cash and Cash Equivalents at the Beginning of the Year	30,000
	Cash and Cash Equivalents at the End of the year	40,000

Working Note

Dr.   **FIXED ASSETS ACCCOUNT**   Cr.

Particulars	Amt (Rs.)	Particulars	Amt (Rs.)
To Balance b/d	2,00,000	By Bank A/c (Sale)	28,000
To Bank A/c (Purchase)	1,20,000	BY Statement of Profit and Loss (Loss)	2,000
		By Depreciation A/c(Balancing Figure)	10,000
		By Balance c/d	2,80,000
	3,20,000		3,20,000

Chapter Practice

Multiple Choice Questions   [1 Mark]

Q.1. Cash Flow Statement is prepared for financial planning of……………………..

    (a) Long range   (b) Medium range   (c) Short range   (d) Very long range

Q.2. Which of the following is not application of cash?

    (a) Increase in Debtors   (b) Increase in Inventories

    (c) Increase in Bills Payables   (d) Increase in Prepaid Expenses

Q.3. Cash deposit with the bank, with a maturity date after two months belongs to which of the following in the Cash flow statement :

    (a) Investing Activities   (b) Financing Activities

    (c) Cash and cash equivalents   (d) Operating Activities

Q.4. An Investment normally qualifies as cash and cash equivalents only when from the date of acquisition it has a Short maturity period of :

    (a) One month or less   (b) Three months or less

    (c) Three month or more   (d) One year or less

Q.5. Issue of Debenture for consideration other than cash is shown under which activity ?

    (a) Operating Activity   (b) Investing Activity

    (c) Financing Activity   (d) None of the above

Very Short Answer Type   [1 Mark]

Q.6. Under which Accounting Standard Cash Flow Statement is prepared ?

Q.7. What is meant by term 'Cash Flow' ?

Q.8. State why Cash Flow Statement is not a substitute for Income Statement ?

Q.9. A company receive a dividend of Rs. 2 Lakhs on its investment in other company's shares. Will it be Cash inflow from operating or investing activities in case of a

    (i) Finance co.

    (ii) Non-Finance Co

Q.10. State giving reason, whether issue of share for consideration other than cash will result into inflow, outflow or no flow of cash.

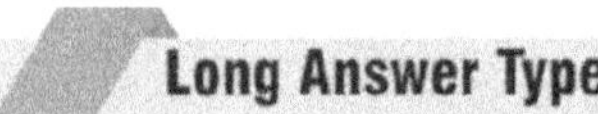

Long Answer Type   **[5 Marks]**

Q.11. From the following information of Anshika Ltd., calculate Cash Flow from Financing Activities:

Particulars	31.03.2022	31.03.2021
Equity Share Capital	30,00,000	20,00,000
12% Debentures	-------	3,00,000
10% Debentures	5,00,000	-------
Bank Overdraft	80,000	1,00,000

Additional Information:

(a) During the year 2021-22, Anshika Ltd. Issued bonus shares in ratio of 2:1 by capitalizing reserve.

(b) 12% Debentures were redeemed on 01st July 2021 and new 10% Debentures were issued on the same date at a discount of 5%

(c) Proposed Dividend on equity share capital for previous year ended 31st March 2021 was paid @ 8%

(d) Interest paid on Bank Overdraft Rs.10,000

Q.12. Following information calculate the amount of Cash Flows from Investing Activities :

Particulars	31.03.2021	31.03.2022
Plant and Machinery NonCurrentInvestments	8,50,000	10,00,000
Land (At Cost)	40,000	1,00,000
	2,00,000	1,00,000

Additional Information:

(a) Depreciation charged on Plant And Machinery was Rs.50,000

(b) Plant and Machinery with a book value of Rs. 60,000 was sold for Rs. 40,000

(c) Land was sold at a gain of Rs .60,000

OR

From the following particulars of Bharat Gas Limited, calculate Cash Flow from Investing Activities:

Particulars	31.03.2021	31.03.2022
Goodwill	1,00,000	3,00,000
Patents	2,80,000	1,60,000
Machinery	1,020,000	1,240,000
10% Long Term Investment	60,000	1,60,000
Investment in Land	1,00,000	1,00,000
Shares of Tata Motors	1,00,000	1,00,000

Additional Information :

(1) Patent were written off to the extent of Rs. 40,000 and some Patent were sold at a profit of Rs.20,000

(2) A Machine costing Rs. 1,40,000 (Depreciation provided thereon Rs.60,000) was sold for Rs.50,000. Depreciation charged during the year was Rs 1,40,000

(3) On March ,31,2022,10% Investment were purchased for Rs. 1,80,000 and some Investment were Sold at a profit of Rs. 20,000. Interest on Investment was received on March 31,2022

(4) Tata Motors Ltd. Paid dividend @ 10% on its shares.

(5) A Plot of Land was purchased out of surplus fund for investment purposes and let out for commercial use and rent received Rs 30,000.

Q.13. Following are the Balance Sheet of Abhideep ltd. For two years .Prepare a Cash Flow Statement:

Particulars	Note no	31.03.2022	31.03.2021
I. EQITY AND LIABILITIES :			
(1) Shareholder's Fund :			
(a) Share Capital		3,00,000	2,00,000
(b) Reserve and Surplus		80,000	30,000
(2) Non –Current Liabilities			
Long –Term Borrowings			75,000
(3) Current Liabilities			
(a) Short-Term Borrowings		25,000	37,000
(b) Trade Payables		1,50,000	96,000
(c) Short –term Provision (Provision for Tax)		15,000	12,000
TOTAL			
		5,70,000	4,50,000
		==========	========
II. ASSETS			
(1)Non –Current Assets			
Fixed Assets		3,40,000	3,00,000
(2) Current Assets			
(a) Current Investment (Short –term Investment)		30,000	20,000
(b) Inventories		90,000	60,000
(c)Trade Payables		97,000	65,000
(d) Cash & Bank Balance		13,000	5,000
TOTAL			
		5,70,000	4,50,000
		==========	=======

Notes	Particulars	31.03.2022	31.03.2021
1.	Long –Term Borrowings (15% Loan)	– –	75,000
2.	Short –Term Borrowings (Bank Overdraft)	**25,000**	37,000
3.	Fixed Assets :		
	Plant & Machinery	4,50,000	3,50,000
	Less : Accumulated Depreciation		
		60,000	50,000
		3,40,000	3,00,000

Additional Information :

1.	Contingent liability	31.03.2022	31.03.2021
	Proposed Dividend	30,000	20,000
2.	Loan was repaid on 01st April 2021		

PART II

CHAPTER 1

Overview of Computerised Accounting System

Summary

Introduction

In modern business accounting transactions are processed through computers. Usage of computers and Information Technology (IT) enables a business to quickly, accurately and timely access the information that helps in decision-making. This sharpens the competitive edge and enhances profitability.

The Computerised Accounting System (CAS) has the following components:

Procedure : A logical sequence of actions to perform a task.

Data : The raw fact (as input) for any business application.

People : Users. Hardware : Computer, associated peripherals, and their network.

Software : System software and Application software.

Computerised Accounting System

Computerised Accounting System refers to the processing of accounting transaction through the use of hardware and software in order to produce accounting records and reports.

CAS takes accounting transactions as inputs that are processed through Accounting **Software to generate the following reports:**

- Day books/Journals
- Ledger
- Trial Balance
- Position Statement (Balance Sheet)
- Statement of Profit and Loss (Profit and Loss Account)

Basic flow of Accounting Transaction

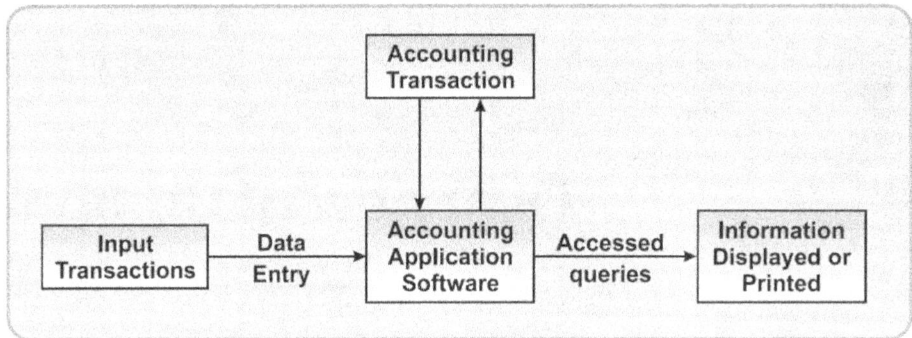

Data and Information

Various elements (items) of accounting transactions are essentially the data items, which are processed through an accounting software to generate different sets of information in the form of accounting reports such as journals, ledger, etc. A data-item (data element) is the smallest named unit of data in the information system. In accounting, a transaction consists of four data elements, such as name of account, accounting code, date of transaction and amount

Components of CAS

The manual system of accounting is traditionally most popular method of keeping records of financial transactions of an organisation. Financial statements are the end products of the accounting process, which are prepared in accordance with Generally Accepted Accounting Principles (GAAP).

The accounting cycle means the processes involved in identifying, measuring and communicating the information.

The basic phases of the cycle are as follows:

- Business transactions are analysed.
- The transactions are recorded in the journal.
- Journal entries are posted to the ledger accounts.
- A trial balance is prepared from balances of accounts.
- Accounts are reviewed and the necessary adjustments made.
- Adjustments are posted in the ledger to prepare adjusted trial balance.
- Adjusted trial balance is used to prepare the balance sheet and profit and loss account.
- Financial Statements are prepared from the finally adjusted ledger and balancing the accounts.

Salient Features of Computerised Accounting System (CAS)

1. **Simple and Integrated**:

   Computerised accounting system is designed to integrate all the business operations such as sales, finance, purchase, etc.

2. **Accuracy and speed**:

   Computrised Accounting system provides data entry forms for fast and accurate data entry of the transactions.

3. **Scalability**:

   The system can cope easily with the increase in the volume of business transactions. The software can be used for any size and type of the organisation.

4. **Security**:

   This system is highly secured and the data and information can be kept confidential.

5. **Reliability**:

   Computerised accounting system makes sure that the critical financial information is accurate, controlled and safe from data corruption.

   Grouping of Accounts

   The increase in the number of transaction changes the volume and size of the business. Therefore it becomes necessary to have proper classification of data. The basic classifications of different accounts embodied in a transaction are resorted through accounting equation.

Accounting Equation

The modern accounting is based on double-entry system, which implies equality of assets and equities (liabilities and capital), i.e.

$$A = E$$

Where $\qquad$ $E = L + C$

Now $A = L + C$ Where A = Assets

$$E = \text{Equities}$$

$$C = \text{Capital}$$

$$L = \text{Liabilities}$$

Thus, $\qquad$ Assets = Liabilities + Capital

In this equation the Liabilities means claims on the firm by creditors and the Capital means claims of owners. The claims of owners keep on changing due to success (profit) or failure (loss) of the firm. This is reflected by the income statement, which provides the summary of income and expenses of business for a given accounting period. Keeping this in view, the **above equation can be re-written as**:

Assets = Liabilities + Capital + (Revenues – Expenses)

Each component of the above equation can be divided into groups of accounts as follows:

EQUITY AND LIABILITIES § Shareholder's Funds

- Share Capital
- Reserves and Surplus
- Money Received against Share Warrents
- Share Application Money Pending Allotment
- Non-Current Liabilities
- Long Term Borrowings
- Deferred Tax Liabilities (net)
- Other Long Term Liabilities
- Long Term Provisions s Current Liabilities
- Short Term Borrowings
- Trade Payables
- Other Current Liabilities
- Short Term Provisions

Assets

1. Non-Current Assets

   Fixed Assets

   Tangible Assets

   Intangible Assets

   Capital Work-in-Progress

   Intangible Assets Under Development

   Fixed Assets held for Sales

   Non Current Investments

   Deferred Tax Assets (net)

   Long Term Loans and Advances

   Other Non-Current Assets

2. Current Assets

   - Current Investments
   - Inventories
   - Trade Receivables
   - Cash and Cash Equivalents
   - Short Term Loans and Advances
   - Other Current Assets

3. REVENUES

   - Sales
   - Other Income

4. EXPENSES

   - Material Consumed
   - Salary and Wages
   - Manufacturing Expenses
   - Depreciation
   - Administrative Expenses
   - Interest
   - Selling and Distribution Expenses

Codification of Accounts

Giving a numerical number or alphabet or both to a particular account for identification is known as codification of accounts.

1. **Types of Codes:**

   (a) Sequential codes:

   Here numbers or alphabets are assigned in consecutive order. These codes are applied primarily to source documents such as cheques, invoices, etc.

(i) Name of customers:

Code	Accounts
CU001	Akhil
CU002	Fijo
CU003	Joshy

(ii) Name of suppliers:

Code	Accounts
001	ABC Ltd
002	PQR Ltd
003	XYZ Ltd

(b) Block Codes:

In Block codes, a range of numbers is alloted to a particular account group. Here, numbers within a range follow sequential coding scheme.

Room Numbering System of a Lodge

Code	Accounts group (group of Ledgers)
100 – 199	Rooms in First Floor
200 – 299	Rooms in Second Floor
300 – 399	Rooms in Third Floor

Coding of Dresses

Code		Accounts group (group of Ledgers)
HS400 – HS 499	-	Half Sleve Shirts
FS500 – FS 599	-	Full Sleve Shirts
MI 600 – MI 699	-	Mens Inner wares

(c) Mnemonic codes:

A mnemonic code consists of alphabets or abbreviations as symbols to codify an account.

Code	Name of Accounts
1) SLR	Salary Account
2) BOD	Bank Overdraft
3) INV	Inventroy
Code	**Name of Accounts**
1) TSR	Thrissur
2) TVM	Thiruvananthapuram
3) DLH	Delhi

Using Software of CAS

- There are two basic activities in using software of CAS – One time activities and recurring activities.

- One time activities include creation of Organisation details, accounting year, type of ledger (also called "creation of master files"), etc.

- While recurring activities include entry of transactions and generation of reports.

- The transactions are recorded on the basis of Cash Vouchers, Bank Vouchers, Purchase Vouchers, Sales Vouchers, Journal Vouchers, etc. Reports include generation of Day books, Ledgers, Trial Balance, Statement of Profit and Loss, Position Statement and Cash Flow Statement

Security Features of CAS Software

Every accounting software ensures data security, safety and confidentiality by providing the features like Password Security, Data Audit and Data Vault.

1. **Password Security**:

   Password is the key to allow the access to the system. Computerised accounting system protects the unauthorised persons from accessing to the business data. Only authorised person, who is supplied with the password, can enter to the system.

2. **Data Audit**:

   It enables one to know as to who and what changes have been made in the original data there by helping and fixing the responsibility of the person who has manipulated the data and ensures data integrity.

3. **Data Vault**:

   Software provides additional security through data encryption. Encryption means scrambling the data so as to make its interpretation impossible.

   Advantages of Computerised Accounting System (CAS)

   1. Financial reports can be prepared in time.

   2. Alterations and additions in transactions are easy and gives the changed result in all books of accounts instantly.

   3. It ensures effective control over the system.

   4. Economy in the processing of accounting data.

   5. Confidentiality of data is maintained.

   6. The closing balance of one financial year is automatically carried forward to next financial year.

   Limitations of Computerised Accounting System

   1. Faster Obsolescence of technology necessitates frequently upgradation in accounting software.

   2. Data may be lost or corrupted due to power interruption.

   3. Un programmed reports can not be generated.

   4. Alterations in transactions are easy. This reduces the reliability of accounting work.

   5. Work with CAS is expensive.

Accounting Information System (AIS)

Accounting Information System (AIS) and its various subsystems may be implemented through Computerised Accounting System (CAS). Such system of AIS are described below.

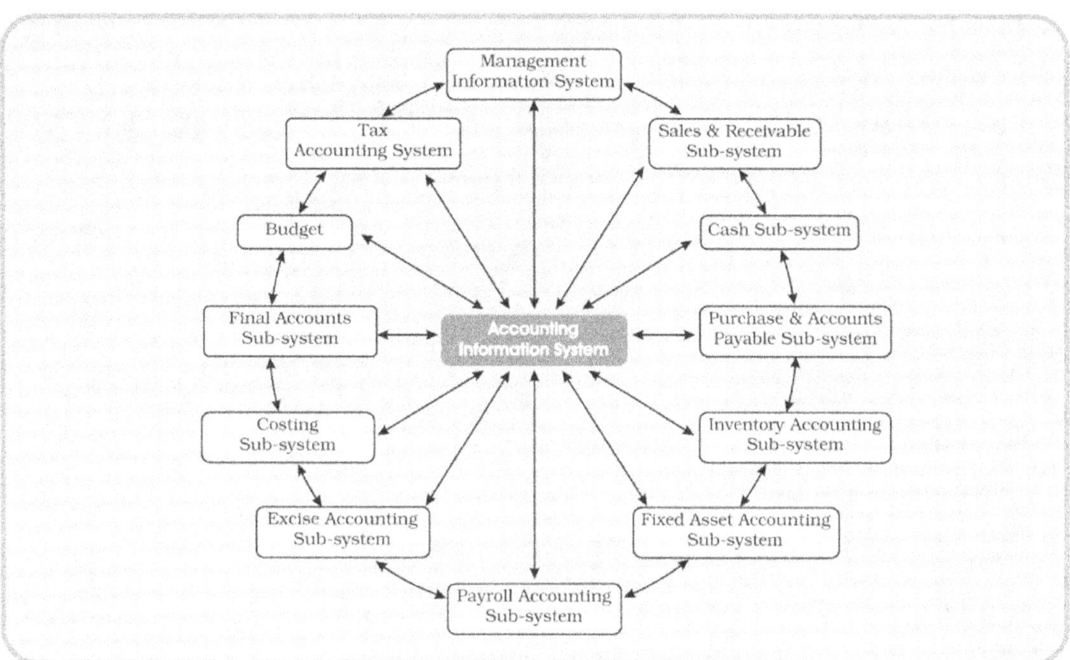

1. **Cash and Bank subsystem**: Receipts and payments of cash.

2. **Sales and Accounts Receivable sub system**: Maintaining of sales and Receivables ledgers.

3. **Inventory subsystem**: Purchase and sale of goods. Specifying the price, quantity, and date.

4. **Purchase and Accounts Payable sub system**: Maintaining of purchase and payable ledgers.

5. **Pav Roll Accounting sub system**: Payment of salaries and wages.

6. **Fixed Assets Accounting sub system**: Purchases, additions, sale and usage of fixed assets.

7. **Expense Accounting sub system**: Various types of expenses.

8. **Tax Accounting sub system**: Deals with GSTIN, Income Tax etc.

9. **Final Accounts sub system**: Preparation of final accounts.

10. **Costing sub system**: Ascertainment of cost of goods produced.

11. **Budget sub system**: Preparation of budgets.

12. **Management information sub system (MIS)**: Preparation of reports that are vital for management decision making

Multiple Choice Questions [1 Mark]

Q1. The components of computerised accounting system are

(a) Data, Report, Ledger, software, Hardware

(b) Software, Hardware, People, Procedure, Data

(c) Data, Coding, Procedure, Objective, Output

(d) People, Procedure, Hard ware, software

Ans. (b) Software, Hardware, People, Procedure, Data

Q2. Grouping of Accounts means the classification of data from:

    (a) Assets, Capital, and Liabilities   (b) Assets, Capital, Liabilities, Revenues & Expenses

    (c) Assets, Owners equity, Revenue & Expenses   (d) Capital, Liabilities, Revenues, & Expenses

Ans. (b) Assets, Capital, Liabilities, Revenues & Expenses

Q3. Codification of Accounts required for the purpose of:

    (a) Hierarchical relationship between groups and components

    (b) Data processing faster and preparing of final accounts

    (c) Keeping data and information secured

    (d) None of the above

Ans. (a) Hierarchical relationship between groups and components

Q4. Method of codification should be

    (a) Such that it leads to grouping of accounts

    (b) An identification mark

    (c) Easy to understand and leads to grouping of accounts

    (d) None of the above

Ans. (c) Easy to understand and leads to grouping of accounts

Q5. Final account subsystem in Accounting Information System (AIS) deals with

    (a) Preparation of budgets   (b) Preparation of Pay Roll

    (c) Preparation of Final Accounts   (d) None of the above

Ans. (c) Preparation of Final Accounts

Q6. Pick the odd one out

    (a) Password security   (b) Data Audit

    (c) Data Bank   (d) Data vault

Ans. (c) Data Bank

Q7. The need of codification is

    (a) Easy to process data   (b) Keeping proper records

    (c) The generation of block codes   (d) The encryption of data

Ans. (d) The encryption of data

Q8. _______________ deals with generation and processing of reports that are vital for management decision-making.

    (a) Management Information system   (b) Data bank

    (c) CAS   (d) RAM

Ans. (a) Management Information system

Q9. Advantages of CAS include:

(a) Speed

(b) Efficiency

(c) arithmetic accuracy

(d) all of the above

Ans. (d) All of the above

Q10. The Computerised Accounting System refers to :

(a) Printing of Balance Sheet and Profit and Loss Accounts using computer;

(b) Processing of accounting transaction through computer and produce records and reports;

(c) Processing of accounting related data and printing reports;

(d) None of the above.

Ans. (b) Processing of accounting transaction through computer and produce records and reports;

Q11. The components of Computerised Accounting System refers to :

(a) Business transactions are analysed, transactions recorded, prepare trial balance, preparation of balance sheet and profit and loss account;

(b) From data entry to preparation of final statements;

(c) Transformation of manual accounting system to CAS;

(d) None of the above.

Ans. (a) Business transactions are analysed, transactions recorded, prepare trial balance, preparation of balance sheet and profit and loss account

Q12. Method of Codification should be :

(a) Such that it leads to grouping of accounts

(b) An identification mark.

(c) Easy to understand, cryptic, and leads to grouping of accounts

(d) None of the above

Ans. (c) Easy to understand, cryptic, and leads to grouping of accounts

Very Short Answer Type   [1 Mark]

Q1. Name the components of Computerised accounting system ?

Ans. The Computerised Accounting System (CAS) has the following components:

(a) Procedure

(b) Data

(c) People

(d) Hardware

(e) Software

Q2. What reports are generated accounting software ?

Ans. CAS takes accounting transactions as inputs that are processed through Accounting Software to generate the following reports:

- Day books/Journals
- Ledger
- Trial Balance
- Position Statement (Balance Sheet)
- Statement of Profit and Loss (Profit and Loss Account)

Q3. Define transaction ?

Ans. The transaction is a record of inflow and outflow of resources.

Q4. In the equation Asset = Liabilities + capital : what does liabilities mean?

Ans. In the equation the Liabilities means claims on the firm by creditors.

Q5. What do you mean by Revenue ?

Ans. Revenue means inflow of resources, which results from the sale of goods or services in the normal course of business and increase in capital. Expenses imply consumption of resources in generating revenues

Q6. State the security features of CAS ?

Ans. security features of CAS are :

- Password Security
- Data Audit
- Data Vault

Q7. What is the full form of AIS ?

Ans. ACCOUNTING INFORMATION SYSTEM is the full form of AIS .

Q8. What are the purpose of cash and bank sub -system ?

Ans. cash and bank sub -system deals with the receipt and payment of cash both physical cash and electronic fund transfer.

Q9. What is costing sub -system ?

Ans. costing sub- system generates information about changes in the cost that takes place during the period under review.

Q10. State two limitations of CAS ?

Ans. Following are the limitation of CAS software:

1. Faster obsolescence of technology necessitates investment in shorter period of time.
2. Data may be lost or corrupted due to power interruptions.

Q11. What is encryption ?

Ans. Encryption ensures security of data even if it lands in wrong hands, because the receiver of data will not be able to decode and interpret it.

Short Answer Type - I
[2 Marks]

Q1. Define Data

Ans. Data is raw, unorganised facts that need to be processed. Data can be something simple and useless until it is organised.

When data is processed, organised, structured or presented in a given context so as to make it useful, it is called information. A computer is an information processing machine. Computers process data to produce information

Q2. Write down any two features of computerised accounting system

Ans. Features of computerised accounting system:

1. **Simple and Integrated**:

   Computerised accounting system is designed to integrate all the business operations such as sales, finance, purchase, etc.

2. **Accuracy and speed**:

   Computerised Accounting system provides data entry forms for fast and accurate data entry of the transactions

Q3. What are the account groups of Trading Account under Computerised Accounting System?

Ans. • Sales account

- Purchase account

- Direct Expenses Account

- Direct Incomes Account

Q4. Complete the Table

Name of Account – Account group in financial Account

Sundry Debtors – Balance sheet, Asset side

1. Indirect Income _______________________

2. Current Liabilities _______________________

3. Stock in hand _______________________

4. Sales Account _______________________

Ans. 1. Profit & Loss Account, Credit side

2. Balances Sheet, Liability side

3. Balance Sheet, Asset side

4. Trading Account, Credit side

Q5. What are mnemonic codes ?

Ans. A mnemonic code consists of alphabets or abbreviations as symbols to codify a piece of information. SJ for "Sales Journals", HQ for "Head Quarters" are examples of mnemonic codes.

Q6. What is a password security ?

Ans. Password Security: Password is a mechanism, which enables a user to access a system including data. The system facilitates defining the user rights according to organisation policy. Consequently, a person in an organisation may be given access to a particular set of a data while he may be denied access to another set of data.

Q7. Write 3 advantages of CAS ?

Ans. 3 advantages of CAS are :-

1. Timely generation of reports and information in desired format.

2. Efficient record keeping.

3. Ensures effective control over the system.

Q8. What are sequential codes?

Ans. In Sequential Code, numbers and/or letters are assigned in consecutive order. These codes are applied primarily to source documents such as cheques, invoices, etc

Q9. . Internal manipulation of accounting records is much easier in computerized accounting than in manual accounting. How?   **(CBSE 2017)**

Ans. Internal manipulation of accounting records is much easier in computerized accounting due to the following:

i.   Defective logical sequence at the programming stage

ii. Prone to hacking

Short Answer Type - II   [3 Marks]

Q1. A computerised accounting software is developed for a company. In Ledger Group, Expenses are divided in to direct expenses and indirect expenses. All the possible expenses of the company are listed under these two sub headings. Appropriate identification numbers are assigned to each such items.

1. Identify the concepts referred to this context

2. Give explanations to each.

Ans. 1. Grouping of Accounts and codification of Accounts

2. Grouping of accounts means classifying the ledger accounts and organizing them under major heads of accounts

The process of assigning codes to account groups and ledger groups is called codification of accounts.

Q2. What are the advantages of computerised Accounting System?

Ans. • Financial reports can be prepared in time

• Alterations and additions in transactions are easy and gives the changed result in all books of accounts instantly

• It ensures effective control over the system

• Economy in the processing of accounting data

• Confidentiality of data is maintained

• The closing balance of one financial year is automatically carried forward to next financial year

Q3. Create an accounting hierarchy for the following ledger account:

- Cash-in-hand
- Provisions for Tax
- Land and Buildings
- Bank Account (Current)
- Trade Investments
- Investments in Govt. Securities
- Deposits with Bank
- Duties and Taxes
- Sundry Debtors

Ans.
- **Fixed assets:** Land & Building Investment in Govt. Securities
- **Current assets:** Cash in hand Trade Investments
- **Bank:** Bank a/c (Current), Deposits with bank
- **Sundry debtors:** Sundry debtors
- **Loans & advances:** Provision for Tax
- **Duties and Taxes:** Duties of Taxes

Q4. Distinguish between Data Audit and Data Vault

Ans. Security Features of Computerised Accounting Software

1. **Data Audit:**

   It enables one to know as to who and what changes have been made in the original data there by helping and fixing the responsibility of the person who has manipulated the data and ensures data integrity.

2. **Data Vault:**

   Software provides additional security through data encryption. Encryption means scrambling the data so as to make its interpretation impossible.

Q5. What is the activity sequence of computerised Accounting information processing model?

Ans.
- Collect data
- Organise data
- Communicate Accounting Information

Q6. Akarsh, your class mate, argues that computerised Accounting System suffers some drawbacks

1. Do you agree with this?
2. Give your justification

Ans.
1. I agree
2. Limitations of CAS.

- Faster Obsolescence of technology necessitates frequently upgradation in accounting software.
- Data may be lost or corrupted due to power interruption.
- Un programmed reports can not be generated
- Alterations in transactions are easy. This reduces the reliability of accounting work.
- Work with CAS is expensive.

Q7. What are the different components of computerised Accounting System?

Ans. Components of computerised Accounting System:

- **Procedure:** A logical sequence of actions to perform a task.
- **Data:** The raw fact for any business operation.
- **People:** Users of computerised accounting system
- **Hardware:** The physical components of a computer.
- **Software:** A set of programmes to do a work.

Q8. The generation of ledger accounts is not a necessary condition for making trial balance in a computerized accounting system. Explain.   **(CBSE 2018)**

Ans. In computerized accounting system, every day business transactions are recorded with the help of computer software. Logical scheme is applied for codification of account and transaction. Every account and transaction is assigned a unique code. The grouping of accounts is done from the first stage. The hierarchy of ledger accounts is maintained and the data is transferred into Ledger accounts automatically by the computer. In order to produce ledger accounts the stored transaction data is processed to appear as classified so that same is presented in the form of report. The preparation of financial statements is independent of producing the trial balance.

9. Computerisation of accounting data on one hand stores voluminous data in a systematic and organized manner whereas on the other hand suffers from threats of vulnerability and manipulations. Discuss the security measures you would like to employ for securing the data from such threats.   **(CBSE 2017)**

Ans. Every accounting software ensures data security, safety and confidentiality. Therefore every, software should provide for the following:

- **Password Security:** Password is a mechanism, which enables a user to access a system including data. The system facilitates defining the user rights according to organization policy. Consequently, a person in an organization may be given access to a particular set of a data while he may be denied access to another set of data.
- **Data Audit:** This feature enables one to know as to who and what changes have been made in the original data thereby helping and fixing the responsibility of the person who has manipulated the data and also ensures data integrity. Basically, this feature is similar to Audit Trial.
- **Data Vault:** Software provides additional security through data encryption.

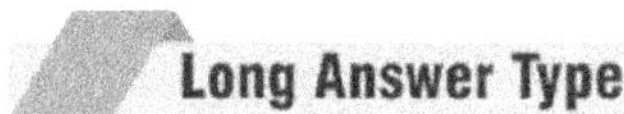 **Long Answer Type** [5 Marks]

Q1. What do you mean by AIS? What are the different subsystems of AIS?

Ans. Accounting Information System (AIS):

Accounting Information System (AIS) and its various subsystems may be implemented through the Computerised Accounting System (CAS). Such system of AIS are described below.

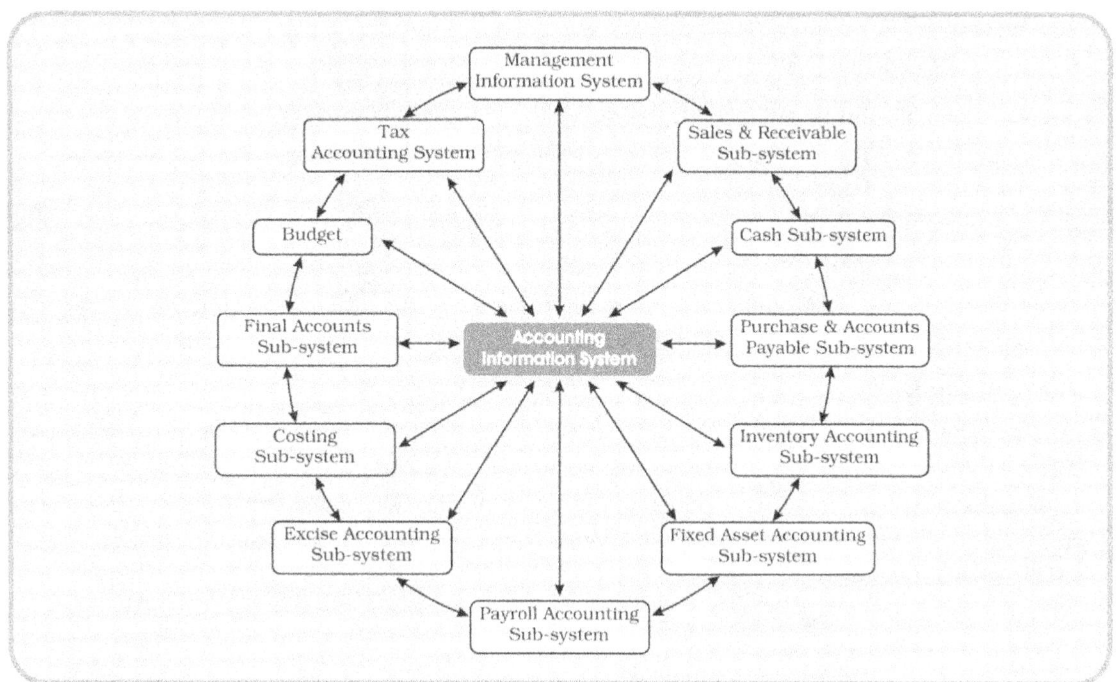

1. **Cash and Bank subsystem:**

    Receipts and payments of cash

2. **Sales and Accounts Receivable sub system:**

    Maintaining of sales and Receivables ledgers.

3. **Inventory sub system:**

    Purchase and sale of goods, Specifying the price, quantity, and date.

4. **Purchase and Accounts Payable Sub system:**

    Maintaining of purchase and payable leadgers.

5. **Pav Roll Accounting sub System:**

    Payment of salaries and wages.

6. **Fixed Assets Accounting Sub system:**

    Purchases, additions, sale and usage of fixed assets.

7. **Expense Accounting sub system:**

    Various types of expenses.

8. **Tax Accounting Sub system:**

   Deals with GSTIN, Income Tax etc.

9. **Final Accounts sub system:**

   Preparation of final accounts.

10. **Costing sub system:**

    Ascertainment of cost of goods produced.

11. **Budget sub system:**

    Preparation of budgets.

12. **Management information sub system (MIS):**

    Preparation of reports that are vital for management decision making.

Q2. Write a short note on CAS ?

Ans. Computerised Accounting System refers to the processing of accounting transaction through the use of hardware and software in order to produce accounting records and reports. CAS takes accounting transactions as inputs that are processed through Accounting Software to generate the accounting reports.

Components Of CAS:

The manual system of accounting is traditionally most popular method of keeping records of financial transactions of an organisation. Financial statements are the end products of the accounting process, which are prepared in accordance with Generally Accepted Accounting Principles (GAAP). The accounting cycle means the processes involved in identifying, measuring and communicating the information. The basic phases of the cycle are as follows:

- Business transactions are analysed.
- The transactions are recorded in the journal.
- Journal entries are posted to the ledger accounts.
- A trial balance is prepared from balances of accounts.
- Accounts are reviewed and the necessary adjustments made.
- Adjustments are posted in the ledger to prepare adjusted trial balance.
- Adjusted trial balance is used to prepare the balance sheet and profit and loss account.
- Financial Statements are prepared from the finally adjusted ledger and balancing the accounts.

Q.3. Enumerate the basic requirements of computerized accounting system for a business organization.

(CBSE 2018)

Ans. The computerized accounting is one the database-oriented applications wherein the transaction data is stored in well-organized database. The user operates on such database using the required interface and also takes the required reports by suitable transformations of stored data into information. Therefore, the fundamentals of computerized accounting include all the basic requirements of any database-oriented application in computers.

Accounting framework : It is the application environment of the computerized accounting. A healthy accounting framework in terms of accounting principles, coding and grouping structure is a pre-condition for any computerized accounting system.

Operating procedure: A well-conceived and designed operating procedure blended with suitable operating environment of the enterprise is necessary to work with the computerized accounting system.

Q.4. What are the phases in an accounting cycle?

Ans. Financial statements are the end products of the accounting process, which are prepared in accordance with Generally Accepted Accounting Principles (GAAP). The accounting cycle means the processes involved in identifying, measuring and communicating the information. The basic phases **of the cycle are as follows**:

- Business transactions are analysed.

- The transactions are recorded in the journal.

- Journal entries are posted to the ledger accounts.

- A trial balance is prepared from balances of accounts.

- Accounts are reviewed and the necessary adjustments made.

- Adjustments are posted in the ledger to prepare adjusted trial balance.

- Adjusted trial balance is used to prepare the balance sheet and profit and loss account.

- Financial Statements are prepared from the finally adjusted ledger and balancing the accounts

Chapter Practice

Multiple Choice Questions [1 Mark]

1. Grouping of Accounts means the classification of data from:
   - (a) Assets, Capital, and Liabilities
   - (b) Assets, Capital, Liabilities, Revenues & Expenses
   - (c) Assets, Owners equity, Revenue & Expenses
   - (d) Capital, Liabilities, Revenues, & Expenses

2. Pick the odd one out
   - (a) Password security
   - (b) Data Audit
   - (c) Data Bank
   - (d) Data vault

3. Which among the following deals with generation of reports that are vital for management decision making?
   - (a) Costing sub system
   - (b) Pay Roll Accounting Sub system
   - (c) Budget Sub System
   - (d) Management Information System

4. Codification of Accounts required for the purpose of :
   - (a) Hierarchical relationship between groups and components
   - (b) Data processing faster and preparing of final accounts
   - (c) Keeping data and information secured
   - (d) None of the above.

5. The need of Codification is :
   - (a) The Encryption of data
   - (b) The Generation of mnemonic code
   - (c) To secure the accounts, reports, etc.
   - (d) Easy to process data, keeping proper records

6. What are internal controls designed to do?
   - (a) safeguard assets and optimise the use of resource
   - (b) only achieve maximum revenue
   - (c) only safeguard assets
   - (d) only ensure accurate accounting records

Very Short Answer Type [1 Mark]

7. Name 5 pillars on which computerised accounting rests ?

8. What is meant by computerised accounting ?

9. State the importance of encryption ?

10. What is meant by revenue ?

11. What all are recorded in expense accounting sub-system?

Short Answer Type - I   [2 Marks]

12. Define Data

13. What is the activity sequence of computerised Accounting information processing model?

14. Explain costing sub- system ?

15. What is coding?

16. Define the term transaction and elaborate with the help of examples how the transaction will be shown in chart of accounts by hierarchical grouping?

Short Answer Type - II   [3 Marks]

17. Discuss any 3 salient features of computerised accounting system **?**

18. Write a short note on Management Information System (MIS) ?

19. State the limitations of computerised accounting system ?

Long Answer Type   [5 Marks]

20. Differentiate between Data and Information.

21. Explain the following in reference with Accounting Information System:

CHAPTER 2

Spreadsheet

Summary

Spreadsheet – Meaning

Spreadsheet application is a computer program that allows to record, calculate and compare numerical or financial data. Using a spreadsheet program. We can store a lot of data in the worksheet and also arrange and analyse the data by using different functions and formulae for meaningful object.

It is used to establish relationship between two or more sets of data. Libre Office Calc, MS Office Excel, Open Office Spreadsheet etc. are examples of spreadsheet software.

Features of Spreadsheet

1. A spreadsheet is a configuration of rows and columns.
2. A spreadsheet is also known as worksheet.
3. Spreadsheet application allows to enter (ie., add) and process data.
4. It makes quick and easy financial and numerical analysis of data.
5. The data stored in the spreadsheet can be converted into graphs, charts etc.
6. It can be used to store, arrange and filter data.

Basic concept of Spread Sheet

(a) **Workbook:**

   A file in spreadsheet is known as a workbook. A work book is a collection of a number of work sheets.

(b) **Work sheets:**

   The work area which consists of rows and columns in a spreadsheet is called worksheet. By default three worksheets – sheet-1, sheet-2, sheet-3 are available in work book.

(c) **Active work sheet:**

   The worksheet which is available to the user for carrying out operations is called active work sheet. The name of the active worksheet will be shown in bold letters in the Sheet Tab at bottom of work sheet.

(d) **Sheet Tab:**

   It shows the name of the work sheet at bottom left of the screen. Additional sheets can be added by clicking on the right hand side of the sheet Tab.

(e) Rename:

The Sheet-1, Sheet-2, and Sheet-3 etc. can be renamed by right clicking the mouse over the worksheet and selecting "Rename" option.

(f) Rows:

Rows are the horizontal vectors in the worksheet. These are numbered numerically from Top to Bottom.

(g) Columns:

Columns are vertical vectors in the worksheet. These are referred by alpha characters from left to right such as A, B, C, …, AA, AB, AC …etc.

(h) Cell:

The intersection of a row and a column is called a cell. A cell is identified by a **combination of an alpha – numeric character eg**: A1, B6, C10, etc. This alpha numeric character is called cell address. Hence each cell has a unique address.

    (i) Active cell:

When we start Libre Office Calc, the pointer (cursor) points the first cell ie., A1, and this cell is called the active cell. The active cell is distinguished by a dark box called cell pointer. We can move the cell pointer by using the arrow keys UP, DOWN, LEFT and RIGHT.

    (j) Cell Reference:

A cell reference identifies location of a cell or group of selected cells in spreadsheet.

    (i) Types of Cell References:

    1. **Relative Cell references:**

By default cell reference is relative; which means that as a formula or function is copied and pasted to other cells, the cell references in the formula or function change to reflect the new location.

    2. **Absolute Cell reference:**

The absolute cell reference consist of the column letter and row number surrounded by dollar ($) signs. Eg $A$5. An absolute cell reference is used when we want a cell reference to stay fixed on a specific cell.

    3. **Mixed cell reference:**

It is a combination of relative and absolute cell references that holds either row or column constant when the formula or function is copied to another location.

(k) Inserting Rows and Columns:

We can add or delete Rows and Columns in a spreadsheet. To add column, click at the column header (right click on the mouse) there we get an option to add column.

Likewise, we can add rows. To delete the column, click the column header (right click on the mouse) there we get an option to delete column. Likewise we can remove rows.

(l) Ranges:

Range is a group of adjacent cells that forms a rectangular area. A range is specified by giving the address for first cell in range and the last cell in the rage, **eg**: range starting from A10 to A20 is written asA10:A20 where colon (:) is the range operator.

(m)Spreadsheet navigation:

We can move around a worksheet through four arrow keys. ie;

- Left arrow key

- Right arrow key
- Up arrow key
- Down arrow key

The mouse can also be used for navigation in spreadsheet except data entry. Some common operations/ navigations are listed below:

Movement	Key stroke (Press Key)
One cell up	Up arrow key/Shift+Enter key
One cell down	Down arrow key/ Enter key
One cell right	Right arrow key/Tab key
One cell left	Left arrow key/Shift + Tab key
Top of sheet (Cell A1)	Ctrl + Home Key
Move to last cell containing data	Ctrl + End Key
Move to beginning of the Row	Home Key or Ctrl+ Left arrow key
Move to last filled cell in column	End key

(n) Labels:

A descriptive information for rows or columns in the form of a text, or a special character is called Label.

Eg: Name, Roll No, Address

(o) Formula:

The formula means a mathematical calculation on a set of cells. The formula must start with an = (equal to) sign. When a cell contains a formula, it often contains reference to other cells.

Eg: = Basic pay + DA + HRA.

Spreadsheet Functions

Functions

A function is a special key word which can be entered into a cell in order to perform and process the data which is appended within brackets. There is a function button f(x) on the formula bar.

When we click on it, function offers assistance through Function Wizard. Alternatively we can enter the function directly into the formula bar. A function is a build in set of formulae which starts with an 'equal to sign' (=).

Eg =SUM (), =AVERAGE (), =COUNT() etc.

There are twelve different categories of functions available in LibreOffice Calc. Important functions are

- Date and Time Function
- Financial Function
- Logical Function
- Mathematical Function
- Look Up and Reference Function
- Statistical Function

Date and Time Functions

These functions are used for inserting, editing and manipulating date and time. "Date" must be entered with quotation marks. Libre Office Calc internally handleds a date/time value as a numerical value. The most commonly used **Date and Time Functions are:**

1.   **TODAY ():**

     It is the function for today's date in the worksheet. This helps to update the date value when we reopen the spreadsheet or modify the values of the document.

     Syntax: =TODAY()

2.   **NOW ():**

     It is the function for today's date and present time. This helps to update the date and the time value when the cell value is modified.

     Syntax: =NOW()

3.   **YEAR ():**

     It helps to update the year for the given date value

     Syntax: = YEAR (Date value) or = YEAR ("Date")

4.   **. MONTH ():**

     It helps to update the month for the given date value. The month is recorded as an integer between 1 and 12.

     Syntax: =MONTH("date") or =MONTH (date value)

5.   **DAY ():**

     It helps to update the day of the given date value. The day is recorded as an integer between 1 and 31

     Syntax: = DAY("Date") or = DAY (date value)

6.   **DATEVALUE ():**

     This function converts the given date into the corresponding date number. By default 31/12/1899 has the value as 1.

     Syntax: =DATEVALUE ("Date")

7.   **DATE ():**

     This function calculates a date specified by year, month, day and displays it in the cell's formatting.

     Syntax: = DATE (Year; Month; Day)

Mathematical Functions

The following mathematical functions are very useful in business applications.

1.   **SUM ():**

     This function adds all the numbers in a range of cells. The AutoSum (S) button can also be used directly for summation of values from cells.

     Syntax:=SUM (number 1, number 2,.......)

2.   **SUM IF ():**

     It returns the sum of the cells as per a given criteria.

     Syntax: = SUMIF (range, "criteria", sum_range) where

     •   Range is the range of cells to evaluate.

- Criteria defines which cells will be added.
- Sum_range, is the range from which values are summed.

3. **ROUND ():**

   This function rounds a number to specified number of digits or decimal places.

   Syntax: = ROUND (Number, Count)

4. **ROUNDUP():**

   Rounds a number up, away from zero without considering the value next to the rounding digit.

   Syntax: = ROUNDUP (Number, Count)

5. **ROUNDDOWN ( ):**

   Rounds a number down towards zero without considering the value next to the rounding digit.

   Syntax: = ROUNDDOWN (Number, Count)

Statistical Functions

Statistical function operates on a set of data and give summarised results. Libreoffice Calc provides a number of statistical functions. They are

1. **COUNT ():**

   This function used to count the number of cells in a range contains numbers only.

   Syntax :=COUNT(Value 1, Value2,…)

   or := COUNT (Range)

2. **COUNTA():**

   This function used to count the number of ceils In a range contains any value. It will count number, text, time, date, logical values, error code, etc. In other words, this function counts the number of cells that are not empty in a range.

   Syntax: = COUNTA (Value 1, Value 2….) or = COUNTA (Range)

3. **COUNTBLANK():**

   This function in LibreOffice Calc count the number of empty cells in the given range. It is the opposite function of COUNTA.

   Syntax: =COUNTBLANK (Range)

4. **COUNTIF():**

   This function counts the number of cells within a given range that meet the criteria or condition.

   Syntax: COUNTIF (Range, Criteria)

5. **ROWS():**

   This function returns the number of rows in a reference or array.

   Syntax = ROWS (Array)

   Where Array is the reference or named area whose total number of rows is to be determihed.

6. **Columns ():**

   This function returns the number of columns in an array or reference

   Syntax: = COLUMNS (Array)

   Where Array is the reference to a cell range whose total number of columns is to be found.

   Text Manipulation Function

There are two types of Text Manipulation Functions in LibreOffice Calc. They are

1. **TEXT ( ):**

   This function converts a number or I numerical value into text according to a defined format.

   Syntax: TEXT (Number, Format)

   This function is useful in situations to display numbers in a more readable format.

2. **CONCATENATE ( ):**

   This function is used to combines several text strings in different cells into one string.

   Syntax:=CONCATENATE ("Text 1 ", "….."," Text n")

Logical Functions

Logical functions are used for comparison and checking a test condition. The major logical functions are IF, AND and OR.

1. **IF ():**

   This function is used to test a condition. When the condition is TRUE, then first action is taken. When it is FALSE, then the second action is taken.

   Syntax: IF (Test, Then value, Otherwise value)

2. NESTED IF ()

   Libre Office Calc allows to include one function inside another function. It is called nesting of functions. The IF function can be nested, when you have multiple condition to meet.

   Syntax: =IF (Test_1, Then value_1, If (Test_2, Then value _2, If (______)))

3. **AND ():**

   This function gives only a TRUE or FALSE answer.

   Syntax: =AND (Logical value 1, Logical value 2,…)

4. **OR ():**

   Returns TRUE if atleast one argument is TRUE. This function returns the value FALSE, If all the arguments have the logical value FALSE

   Syntax: = OR (Logical value 1, Logical value 2,…)

   Spreadsheet Reference Functions

The important spreadsheet reference functions are

1. **LOOKUP () functions:**

   The LOOKUP function returns a value either from a one-row or one-column **range or from an array. The lookup function has two syntax forms:** Vector form and Array form.

   The vector form of LOOUP looks in a one-row or one-column range (known as a vector) for a value, and then returns a value from the same position in a second one-row or one-column range.

   The array form of LOOKUP looks in the first row or column of an array for the specified value, and then returns a value from the same position in the last row or column of the array.

   - LOOKUP (Vector from)

     Syntax: =LOOKUP (search criterion, Search vector, Result vector)

   - LOOKUP (Array form)

     =(LOOKUP (lookup_value, array)

2. **VLOOK UP ():**

   VLOOK UP is the vertical LOOKUP function. Use VLOOK UP to search the first column (columns are vertical) of a block of data and return the value from another column in the same row.

   Syntax: = VLOOKUP (Search criterion; Array; Index; Sort Order)

3. **HLOOKUP ( ):**

   It is the Horizontal LOOKUP function, searches for a value in the first row of a table array and returns the corresponding value in ' the same column from another row of the same table array.

   Syntax: -HLOOKUP (search criteria; index; sorted)

Financial Functions

The major financial functions of LibreOffice Calc are discussed below:

1. **ACCRINT ():**

   This function returns the accrued interest for a security that pays periodic interest.

   Syntax:= ACCRINT(Issue, First_nterest, settlement, rate, Par, frequency, basis, calc_method)

2. **CUMIPMT():**

   This function returns the cumulative interest paid between two periods.

   Syntax: = CUMIPMT (Rate, NPER, PV, S, E, Type)

3. **PV():**

   This function is used to calculate the amount of money needed to be invested at a fixed rate today, to receive a specific amount, over a specified number of periods.

   Syntax: = PV (Rate, NPER, Pmt, FV, Type)

4. **PMT ():**

   PMT function calculates the equal periodic payment for an annuity with constant interest rates.

   Syntax: = PMT (Rate, NPER, PV, FV, Type)

5. **FV():**

   This function calculates the future value of an investment based on periodic, constant payment and a constant interest rate.

   Syntax: = FV (RATE, NPER, PMT, PV, TYPE)

6. **RATE ():**

   This function returns the interest rate per period of an annuity.

   Syntax: = RATE (NPER, PMT, PV, FV, Type, Guess)

7. **NPV ():**

   This function calculates the net present value of an investment by using a discount rate and a series of future payments (negative values) and income (positive values)

   Syntax:- NPV(Rate, Value 1, Value 2,....)

   Data Entry, Text Management, and Cell Formatting:-

   In any computerised business application, the basic requirement is to input data, which may be either for processing or to update various data elements. In both the cases, data should be correct, accurate and should be in proper format.

Data Entry

1. **The data fill options**:

   The 'fill' command can be used to fill data into worksheet cells. To fill quickly in several types of data series, we select cells and drag the fill handle (A fill handle is the small black square in the lower-right corner of the selection). When we point to the fill handle, the pointer changes to + symbol.

2. **Import/Copy Data from other sources**:

   This method will transfer data into required cells by copying or importing an external file to calc sheet.

3. **Data validation**:

   This is a feature to define restrictions on type of data entered into a cell. We can configure data validation rules for cells data that will not allow users to enter invalid data. There may be warning messages when users tries to type wrong data in the cell.

4. **Data Formatting**

   Formatting of spread sheets makes easier to read and understand the important information. On the Ribbon there are several tools and shortcuts to format spreadsheets effectively. Some of them are explained below.

   1. **Number formatting**:

      Number formatting includes adding percent symbols (%), commas(,), decimal **places (.), and currency signs (?) date (dd/mm/yyyy), time (HH:** mm), scientific values and as well as some special formats to a spreadsheet.

   2. **Currency**:

      If we enter a financial value with the currency sign, calc assigns a currency format to the cell along with the entry.

   3. **Dates**:

      If we enter the date, that follows one of the built-In Calc number formats, such as 01/06/2018 or 01 June 2018, the program assigns a Date format that follows the pattern of the date.

   4. **Changing cell colours**:

      Select the range to format. From the Toolbar, select format and click on cells to display format cells dialog box and choose background tab. The back ground tab provide Background colourforthe cell. Select the desired colour from the colour pallets. Then click OK to make necessary changes.

   5. **Create a custom cell border**:

      We can create a cell style that includes a custom border, and can apply to that cell style when we want to display the custom border around selected cells.

      - Select the properties option on the side bar (Right)
      - Click cell appearance
      - We can modify cell border properties

   6. **Conditional formatting**:

      We can apply conditional formatting to a cell range, a table, or a Pivot Table report. A conditional format changes the appearance of a cell range based on a condition or criteria. If the condition is true, the cell range is formatted based on that condition; if the condition is false, the cell range is not formatted based on that condition.

Changing The Alignment Of Data In Cells

There are several options to change the alignment of text (Data) in cells.

1. **Text Formatting:**

   We can format the text in the cell in the following way.

   - The font style can be changed
   - The font size can be changed
   - If we need bold letters, Italics, or underlined, choose from appropriate field.
   - The back ground colour can be changed
   - The text alignment in the cell either is left, right, center or justify
   - The position in the cell ie., Top, Center or Bottom of the cell can be selected.
   - The borders to the cell can choose from the appropriate field.
   - Different types of borders can be given in the field.

     All these actions are also given in property windows appears on the right of the work sheet.

2. **Merging a range of cells:**

   Merged cells are' a single cell that is created by combining two or more selected cells. When two or more adjacent horizontal or vertical cells are merged, the cells become one large cell and displayed across multiple columns or rows. The contents of cell appear in the centre of the merged cell.

3. **Split a merged cell:**

   Select the merged cell which we want to split into two. When we select a merged cell, the merge and centre button also appears selected in the Alignment group on the Home Tab. Click merge and centre.

4. **Formatting a table:**

   There are predefined table styles or quick styles that we can use to quickly, format a table. Select cells where the Table hasto be inserted. Then select the format option in the menu bar, in the dropdown menu select the auto format. We can select the predefined table format.

5. **Headers and Footers:**

   In calc spreadsheet, headers and footers are lines of text that are printed at the top (Header) and bottom (footer) of each page in the menu bar. They contain descriptive text such as titles, dates, and / or page numbers and are used to add information to a printed spreadsheet. These options are available under insert option in the menu bar.

Output Reports

We can print entire or partial worksheets and work books, one at a time, or several at once.

1. **Page set Up:**

   We can customize our output Report by editing the page set up option.

2. **Print Out:**

   Before Printing, we have to verify print preview which gives an idea about how the print out may come. The modification can be done by this verification.

3. **Defining the Print:**

   By default, Libre Office Calc prints all data on the current worksheet. The print area can be customized/ defined by using Dialog Box option.

4. **Preparation of reports using Pivot Tables**:

A Pivot Table is a way to present information in a report format. A PivotTable report provides enhanced layout, attractive and formatted report with improved readability. There are two types of data table.

- One-Variable Data Table
- Two-Variable Data Table

The one variable Data Table allows us to identify a single decision variable in our model and see how changing the values for that variable affect the values calculated by one or more formulas in our model.

The two variable Data table allows us to Specify two decision variables and a variety of inputs and only a single formula.

Advantages of Pivot Table (Report)

A PivotTable report is an interactive way to quickly summarise large amounts of data. Use a PivotTable report to analyse numerical data in depth and to **answer unanticipated questions about data. A PivotTable report designed for**:

i. Querying large amounts of data in user-friendly ways. Sub totalling and aggregating numeric data, summarising data by categories and subcategories, and creating custom calculations and formulas.

ii. Expanding and collapsing levels of data to focus on results, and providing from details to the summary of data for areas of interest.

iii. Moving rows to column or columns to rows (or "pivoting") to see different summaries of the source data.

iv. Filtering, sorting, grouping, and conditionally formatting the most useful and the interesting subset of data to enable us to focus on the information that we want.

v. Presenting concise, attractive, and annotated online or printed reports.

vi. The use of a PivotTable report is to analyse related totals, when we have a long list of figures to sum and to compare several facts about each figure

Common Error Codes (Messages) in spreadsheets

Spreadsheets provides some messages for errors of miscalculation, incorrect use of functions, invalid cell references, and values, and other user initiated mistakes. Some of the error codes/messages are given below.

Error Message	Error Code	Explanation of the error
1. ###	N/A	When numerical value entered in a column in not enough to display the contents
2. #DIV/0!	532	When a number is divided by zero
3. #NAME	525	When a calc does not recognize the Text in formula
4. #REF!	524	When a formula refers to a cell that is not valid
5. #VALUE!	519	When a wrong argument is given in a formula
6. #NUM!	503	When a calculation resulted in an overflow of the defined value range

Multiple Choice Questions   [1 Mark]

1) The horizontal tabs in MS-Excel 2007 are known as?

   (a) Ribbon   (b) Tabs

   (c) Menu   (d) Options

2) In Excel Rows are denoted by _______ and columns are denoted by_______

   (a) Numbers, numbers   (b) Alphabet, numbers

   (c) Numbers, alphabet   (d) Alphabet, alphabet

3) Where is formula bar situated?

   (a) Beside name box   (b) Above the column header

   (c) Below the ribbon   (d) All of these

4) Which of the following cannot be calculated in autosum?

   (a) Sum   (b) Average

   (c) Max/Min   (d) Countif

5) Which one is not one of the format of cell?

   (a) Special   (b) Char

   (c) General   (d) Number

6) From which tab can you do conditional formatting of cell?

   (a) Format   (b) Insert

   (c) Home   (d) Cell

7) From where can we add header and footer in excel?

   (a) Page layout   (b) Home

   (c) Insert   (d) View

8) From where can you print the spreadsheet?

   (a) File   (b) Office button

   (c) Home   (d) Print tab

9) Where can you find Pivot table?

   (a) Data tab   (b) Chart Tab

   (c) Insert Tab   (d) Format tab

10) The Reason of ###### error is ___________

   (a) Reference is wrong   (b) Division by zero

   (c) Column not wide enough   (d) Not an error

Very Short Answer Type   **[1 Mark]**

1) Give syntax of ACCRINT function with arguments

Ans. ACCRINT (issue, first_interest, settlement, rate, par, frequency, basis, calc_method)

2) Default number of sheets in worksheet

Ans. 3

3) How is cell address defined?

Ans. For example, the cell having address as G8 correspond to 8th row under G column. Each cell thus has a unique identification called as cell address.

4) What is shortcut to go to the cell at the intersection of the last row and last column containing data?

Ans. CTRL + END keys

5) What is shortcut to go to the beginning of the row?

Ans. HOME key

6) What are labels?

Ans. Labels (text) are descriptive data such as names, months and usually include alphabetic characters. Excel aligns text to the left side of the cell.

7) Which symbol at the start indicates a formula?

Ans. = (EQUALS TO SIGN)

8) Give names and syntax of Text manipulation functions

Ans. TEXT (value, format_text)

CONCATENATE (text1, text2,...)

9) Give the syntax of PMT function

Ans. = PMT(rate, nper, pv, [fv], [type])

10) Which handle helps the auto fill function?

Ans. Fill handle

11) What are functions? Where we use them?

Ans. A function is a built in set of formulas which starts with an = "equal to sign" such as = Function Name(Data). The data (or argument in proper terminology) includes a range of cells. The spreadsheet gives considerable power and flexibility in entering and editing information, setting up calculations with formula and functions.

12) What types of files have extension as .csv?

Ans. Text files in which the values are separated by commas(csv- comma separated values)

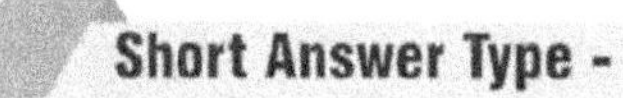

Short Answer Type - I
[2 Marks]

1) Explain what-if scenario and its uses?

Ans. A what-if scenario is used to generate a number of alternatives to examine the cause (if) and effect (what). Thus, it helps in analysing the impact of changes due to variations in one or more input values. Taking the above example, if all the other values are kept same, one can see how different rates of interest and different periods of compounding would affect the Compound Interest and the Maturity Amount to be received

2) Explain the Auto sum and functions included in it ?

Ans. AutoSum () function is the most basic and one of the common user functions. It is used to get the addition of various numbers or the contents of various cells. On the ribbon the AutoSum () button can be use directly for summation of values from cells. The AutoSum function also includes other series based functions such as AVERAGE, MIN, MAX and COUNT.

3) Explain in detail how the if function works, its arguments and output scenarios?

Ans. This function can be evoked from formula tab on the ribbon. This function returns one value if a specified condition evaluated to TRUE and **another value if it evaluates to FALSE. An IF function has the following format**: IF (logical_test, value_if_true, value_if_false). Now if the logical test gets tested true then function will return value_if_true and if it is tested false then it returns value_if_false.

4) List the round functions and the difference in their outputs

Ans. ROUND is the function to rounds a number to specified number of **digits. The syntax of this function is as follows**: ROUND (number, num_digits)

ROUNDUP (number, num_digits) which rounds a number up, away from 0 (zero)

ROUNDDOWN (number, num_digits) which rounds a number down, toward zero.

5) Explain the use of lookup functions and name them with their syntax?

Ans. look up functions helps us to find specific information in large data tables such as an inventory list of parts or a large employee contact list.

LOOKUP (lookup_value, array)

VLOOKUP (lookup_value, table_array, col_index_num, range_lookup)

HLOOKUP(lookup_value, table_array, row_index_num, range_lookup)

6) From where can you import data in excel and which kind of files can be imported?

Ans. In data tab you have a section of get external data. From here you can import various data files of different formats. These data files may be either in text files or non-text files format. Text files can be directly read using a text editor such as Note pad in MS Windows. These files often have extension .txt but can have other extensions (such as .csv known as Comma Separated Values text file), easily read into Excel.

7) Name and explain the types of error alert?

Ans. Warning or Stop as per the severity and accuracy requirement for data where.

   (i) Information: displays a message but will prevent entry of invalid data.

   (ii) Warning: displays a warning message but will not prevent entry of invalid data.

   (iii)Stop: will prevent invalid entry of data

8) Explain number formatting with any 3 types of formats?

Ans. Number formatting: Number formatting includes adding per cent symbols (%), commas (,), decimal places, and currency signs ($,etc), date, time, scientific values and as well as some special formats to a spreadsheet.

Currency: If we enter a financial value complete with the dollar/ currency sign and two decimal places, Excel assigns a Currency format to the cell along with the entry.

Percentages: If we enter a value representing a percentage as a whole number followed by the per cent sign without any decimal places, Excel assigns to the cell the percentage format that follows this pattern along with the entry.

Dates: If we enter a date (dates are values, too) that follows one of the built-in Excel number formats, such as 16-04-2009 or 16- Apr-2009 the program assigns a Date format that follows the pattern of the date.

9) Explain uses of conditional formatting?

Ans. Conditional formatting helps to answer these questions by making it easy to highlight interesting cells or ranges of cells, emphasise unusual values, and visualise data by using data bars, colour scales, and icon sets. A conditional format changes the appearance of a cell range based on a condition (or criteria). If the condition is true, the cell range is formatted based on that condition; if the conditional is false, the cell range is not formatted based on that condition

10) How to merge cells in excel?

Ans. Select two or more adjacent cells that we want to merge.

1. On the Home tab, in the Alignment group, click Merge and Centre. (Or button).

2. The cells will be merged in a row or column, and the cell contents will be centered in the merged cell. To merge cells without centering, click the arrow next to Merge and Centre, and then click Merge Across or Merge Cells. The cell address of merge cells will be the address of lower active cell.

3. To change the text alignment in the merged cell, select the cell; click any of the alignment buttons in the Alignment group on the Home tab.

11) How to split the merged cells in excel?

Ans. Split a merged cell :

1. Select the merged cell.

2. When we select a merged cell, the Merge and Centre button also appears selected in the Alignment group on the Home tab.

3. To split the merged cell, click Merge and Centre. The contents of the merged cell will appear in the upper-left cell of the range of split cells

12) Explain #N/A error. Also give reasons and correcting this error.

Ans. error occurs when a value is not available to a function or formula. 1. Optionally, click the cell that displays the error, click the button that appears, and then click Show Calculation Steps if it appears. Reasons and Solutions a. Missing data, and #N/A or NA() has been entered in its place. b. Giving an inappropriate value for lookup function as an argument such functions may be HLOOKUP, VLOOKUP, MATCH or LOOKUP. c. Using these lookup functions to locate the value in an unsorted table. d. Using an argument in the array formula that is not in the same number of rows or columns as the range that contains the array formula

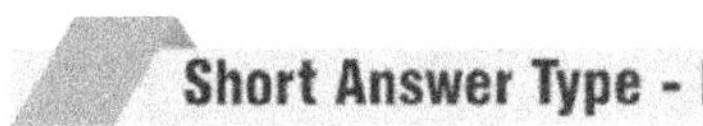

Short Answer Type - II   **[3 Marks]**

1) What is cell reference? What are its types?

Ans. A cell reference identifies the location of a cell or group of cells in the spreadsheet also referred as a cell address. Cell references are used in formulas, functions, charts, other Excel commands and also refer to a group or range of cells.

- Ranges are identified by the cell references of the cells in the upper left (cell A1) and lower right (cell E2).

- By default cell reference is relative; which means that as a formula or function is copied and pasted to other cells, the cell references in the formula or function change to reflect the new location

- The other cell reference is absolute cell reference which consists of the column letter and row number surrounded by dollar ($) signs e.g. $C$4. An absolute cell reference is used when we want a cell reference to stay fixed on specific cell, which means that when a formula or function is copied and pasted to other cells, the cell references in the formula or function do not change

- A mixed reference is also a cell reference that holds either row or column constant when the formula or function is copied to another location e.g., $C4 or C$4.

2. How to name a cell or cell range?

Ans. The steps are for defining Name Ranges are as follows:

1. Select the cell(s) which are to be).

2. Click on the ribbon on formula tab.

3. Select Define Name option on the ribbon and click it.

4. This will provide a dialogue box will be opened to click Define Name (another option Apply Names is for previously created Range Names to select) This will display a dialogue box as New Name

    Click OK on the New Name dialogue box which returns to the spreadsheet.

3) Explain in detail count function along with its variants?

Ans. This function counts the number of cells that contain numbers and counts numbers within the list of arguments.

COUNT is use to get the number of the entries in a number field (including date also) i.e. in a range or array of numbers.

The syntax for COUNT is COUNT (value1, value2…..,)

where value1, value2, … are 1 to 255 arguments that can be a variety of different types of data(logical values represented in numbers, numbers, dates, or text representation of numbers), but only numbers are counted.

Arguments that are error values or text that cannot be translated into numbers are ignored. If an argument is an array or reference, only numbers in that array or reference are counted. Empty cells, logical values, text, or error values in the array or reference are ignored. COUNTA function will be count logical values, text, or error values of cells within a range that meet the given criteria; in this function the Range is one or more cells to count, including numbers or names, arrays, or references that contain numbers. The blank cells and text values are ignored. Computerised Accounting System Criteria are the form of a number, expression, cell reference, or text that defines which cells will be counted.

4. You had started your own online business to sale and find out the sales **for the first week is as follows:**

Monday Rs.120.45

Tuesday Rs.187.43

Wednesday Rs.106.87

Thursday Rs.143.69

Friday Rs.117.52

Saturday Rs.87.93

Sunday Rs.92.12

Use a function to work out how much you earned, on average, each day.

Ans. The function will be : =ave(1st cell that contains amount, 2nd cell that contains amount,......, last cell that contains amount)

5. Explain HLOOKUP function in detail ?

Ans. The HLOOKUP function (short name of Horizontal Lookup), searches for a value in the first row of a table array and returns the corresponding value in the same column from another row of the same table array.

The syntax for HLOOKUP is as follows:

HLOOKUP(lookup_value, table_array, row_index_num, range_lookup)

where

- Lookup_value – The value to search for in the first row of the table array.
- Table_array – Two or more rows of data. The values in the first row of the table_array are the values searched for the lookup_value. These values can be text, numbers, or logical values. Uppercase and lowercase texts are equivalent.
- Row_index_num – The row number in table_array from which the corresponding value must be returned. A row_index_num of 2 returns the value in the second column in table_array; a row_index_num of 3 returns the value in the third column in table_array, and so on.
- Range_lookup – A logical value that specifies whether we want HLOOKUP to find an exact match or an approximate match. If set to "FALSE", a corresponding value will be returned only if an exact match is found. If set to "TRUE", the nearest match will be considered if an exact one is not found

6. Write the steps to freeze the formula using Paste Special command.?

Ans. Steps to Freeze The Formula Using Paste Special Command Are:

(a) Select the cell (s) that contains the formula

(b) Click on Home Tab and select Copy symbol. to click, this will copy the values and formulas of the cells

(c) Click on Paste tab and select Paste Special .

(d) In the Paste Special box , under paste select the radio button next to Values and click OK . This will permanently remove the formula from the workbook

7. Explain FPV function in detail with example

Ans. FV This function returns the future value of an investment based on periodic, constant payment and a constant interest rate .

The syntax of the function is :

FV (rate, nper, pmt, pv, type)

where

Rate is the interest rate per period.

Nper is the total number of payment periods in an annuity.

Pmt is the payment made each period; it cannot change over the life of the annuity. Typically, pmt contains principal and interest but no other fees or taxes. If pmt is omitted, then include the pv value in the argument.

Pv is the present value, or the lump-sum amount that a series of future payments is worth right now. If pv is omitted, it is assumed to be 0 (zero), and then include the pmt value in the argument. Type is the number 0 or 1 and indicates when payments are due.

If type is omitted, it is assumed to be 0.

8. Explain the following functions:

(a) **TODAY ():-** is the function for today's date in the blank worksheet. TODAY – Returns the serial number of the current date. The serial number is the date-time code used by Excel for date and time calculations. Times are represented as fractions of a day.

(b) **DAY(serial_number) function:-** It returns the day of a date as an integer ranging from1 to 31.

(c) **DATEVALUE (date_text) :-** converts a date in the form of text to a serial number

9. Explain pivot table and its advantages

Ans. A Pivot Table is a powerful tool to calculate, summarize, and analyze data. Moreover, it lets you gain insights and trends from your data. A pivot table is a table of statistics that summarizes the data of a more extensive table (such as from a database, spreadsheet, or business intelligence program). This summary might include sums, averages, or other statistics, which the pivot table groups together in a meaningful way.

Advantages are :

Easy to use

Pivot tables are simple to use. The drag and drop feature makes it very user friendly. With just a few click one can easily summarize complex data into meaningful insight. The columns can also be re-arranged as per requirement.

Ability to perform Data Analysis

With the help of excel pivot tables, you can handle large data set in one go. You can manipulate data in a way to spot recurring patterns or trends. Further, this will help in forecasting and Decision Making.

Summarize and Organize Data

Another benefit is the ability to make quickly summarize the data in an easy manner. Enabling preparation of concise summary out of thousands of rows and columns of unorganized data. You can also group data based on date or other fields based as per data. Grouping makes the Pivot informative and helpful to analyze. Users can also label the headers as per needs.

Quick Report Creation

Another important feature of excel pivot tables is that it helps to create efficient reports. This saves you time as it reduces redundancy and takes a step closer to automation.

Connect to External Source

One of the best advantage of Pivot table is the capability to pull from external sources.

10. Explain the following terms :-

(a) Value rule: The value rule according to computer scientist Alan Kay Alan KayAlan Kay implies in spreadsheet. It states that a cell's value relies solely on the formula that user has typed into the cell. The formula may rely on the value of other cells, but those cells are likewise restricted to user-entered data or formulas.

(b) What if Scenario: It is used to generate a number of alternatives to examine the cause (if) and effect (what). Thus, it helps in analysing the impact of changes due to variations in one or more input values.

(c) Array: Used to build single formulas that produce multiple results or that operate on a group of arguments that are arranged in rows and columns. An array range shares a common formula; an array constant is a group of constants used as an argument.

(d) Array for Array forArray formula: A formula that performs multiple calculations on one or more sets of values, and then returns either a single result or multiple results. Array formulas are enclosed between braces { } and are entered by pressing CTRL+SHIFT+ENTER.

(e) A logical value (true or false) outcome: is the comparison of data values or results of arithmetic expressions compared with another data values or results of another arithmetical expressions using logical operator.

Long Answer Type [5 Marks]

1) Explain all the logical functions in detail with syntax, arguments, outputs and example?

Ans. 1. AND function gives only a TRUE or FALSE answer. To determine whether the output will be TRUE or FALSE, the AND function evaluates at least one mathematical expression located in another cell in the spreadsheet.

The syntax for the AND function is:

= AND (logical-1, logical-2, ... logical-255)

where logical-1 , logical-2 , ... - refers to the cell reference that is being checked. Up to 255 logical values can be entered into the function.

Returns TRUE if all its arguments evaluate to TRUE;

returns FALSE if one or more arguments evaluate to FALSE.

2. Discuss IF function and nested IF functions giving example? **(NCERT)**

Ans. The IF function is one of the foremost useful functions present in Excel because it allows the users to form logical comparisons between a specific value and the expected value of the user.

- An IF function or statement can have two results. The first result is when the comparison of the user is 'True' and the second result is when the user's comparison is 'False'.

  IF function is used when the user needs to test for one condition or wants to make a simple comparison of a value or a fact.

  Example: =IF(Something is True, then do something, if not do something else)

  =IF(C4<8000,"Yes","No")

- "=IF(…) is called the IF functions.

- "C4<8000" is the condition that is evaluated by IF function. It checks whether the value of cell address C4 (subtotal) is less than 8,000.

- "Yes", this is the value that will be displayed by the function if the value of C4 is less than 8,000.

- "No", this is the value that will be displayed by the function if the value of C4 is greater than 8,000.

  The nested IF function is used when the user needs to test for more than one condition. The nested IF functions means an IF function within another IF function and the user can nest multiple IF statements together in one formula only.

  Example: =IF(D1="Saturday","Time to rest",IF(D1="Friday","Party well","to do list")).

- "=IF(…) is called the main IF function.

- "=IF(…,IF(…))" the second IF function is called the nested one. It provides further evaluation when the main IF function turned out to be false.

- "D1=Saturday" is the condition evaluated by the main IF function. It checks whether the value of cell address D1 shows Saturday.

- "Time to rest", this is the value that the main IF function will display if the result of D1 turns out to be Saturday.

- "D1=Friday" is condition evaluated by the nested IF function. It checks if the value of cell address D1 shows Friday, if not Saturday.

- "Party well", this is the value that the nested IF function will display if the D1 gives result as Friday instead of Saturday.

3. Explain data validation through dropdown in detail with steps?

Ans. Data validation is a feature to define restrictions on type of data entered into a cell. We can configure data validation rules for cells data that will not allow users to enter invalid data, There may be warning messages when users tries to type wrong data in the cell. The messages also guide users to what input is expected for the cell, and instructions to correct any errors.

The different methods for data validation are as follows:

Create a Drop down List – By this option pre-defined items names list is referred and restrict the users to select accordingly

4. Explain any 5 errors with their causes and corrections ?

Ans. **(a) Correct a ##### error** : This error occur when a column is not wide enough, or a negative date or time is used. Reason: The column is not wide enough to display the content

(b) Correct a #DIV/0! Error : This error occurs when a number is divided by zero (0).

1. Optionally, click the cell that displays the error, click the button that appears, and then click Show Calculation Steps if it is appears.

   Reasons

(A) Entering a formula that contains explicit division by zero (0) — for example, = 5/0.

(B) Using the cell reference to a blank cell or to a cell that contains zero as a divisor.

(C) Correct a #N/A error: This error occurs when a value is not available to a function or formula.

1. Optionally, click the cell that displays the error, click the button that appears, and then click Show Calculation Steps if it appears.

   Reasons and Solutions

   (a) Missing data, and #N/A or NA() has been entered in its place.

   (b) Giving an inappropriate value for lookup function as an argument such functions may be HLOOKUP, VLOOKUP, MATCH or LOOKUP.

(c) Using these lookup functions to locate the value in an unsorted table.

(d) Using an argument in the array formula that is not in the same number of rows or columns as the range that contains the array formula.

(D) **Correct a #NAME? Error** : This error occurs when Excel doesn't recognize text in a formula.

Reasons:

(a) The EUROCONVERT function without the Euro Currency Tools add-in being loaded.

(E) Correct #NULL! Error This error occurs when we specify an intersection of two areas that do not intersect. The intersection operator is a space between references.

Chapter Practice

Multiple Choice Questions [1 Mark]

1. Which function will be used to calculate the interest portion of on installment of loan :
   - (a) PPMT
   - (b) IPMT
   - (c) FAPM
   - (d) None of these

2. Which formula to be used to get the sum total of cell A1, A2 and A3 :
   - (a) SUM = (A1 + A2 + A3)
   - (b) SUM = (A1, A2, A3)
   - (c) = SUM (A1 : A3)
   - (d) None of these

3. Which of the following coordinates excel work book :
   - (a) Workbook
   - (b) Worksheet
   - (c) Chart
   - (d) Worksheet and chart

4. In windows at which place do we type values and formulae :
   - (a) In title toolbar
   - (b) Through smart screen menu command
   - (c) In formula bar
   - (d) In standard bar

5. Data or formula can be copied by :
   - (a) Through cut, copy, paste command on the edit menu
   - (b) Through smart screen menu command
   - (c) Through buttons of standard toolbar
   - (d) All of the above

Q6. Which function automatically totals a column or row of Values?
   - (a) TOTAL
   - (b) ADD
   - (c) SUM
   - (d) AVG

Very Short Answer Type [1 Mark]

Q7. Define one-variable Table and Two-variable tables?

Q8. How many ways Data Entry is possible in Spread Sheet?

Q9. Each cell value can either be an independent (basic) value or it may be derived on the basis of ______________.

Q10. Define Pivot Table?

Q11. What is Wrap Text feature of Excel, Merging of Cells and what will be the cell address of merged cells?

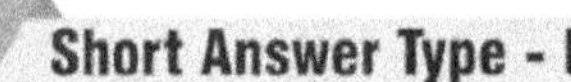

Short Answer Type - I   **[2 Marks]**

12. What is spreadsheet?

13. Write the syntax of PPMT function.

14. What is called cell and row?

15. Match the following

A	B
1. Rows	1. Intersection of a row & a column
2. Columns	2. Numerical numbers from top to bottom
3. Cell	3. Unique identification code of a cell
4. Cell address	4. Alpha characters from left to right

16. Give a short note on
   1. Work book
   2. Work sheet

Short Answer Type - II   **[3 Marks]**

Q17. Explain the basic elements of M.S. Excel.

Q18. Describe the key features of the spreadsheet.

Q19. Explain the importance of spreadsheet in Accountancy.

Long Answer Type   **[5 Marks]**

Q20. Define the following
   1. Cell
   2. Range
   3. Worksheet
   4. Workbook

Q21. What are the different spreadsheet reference functions in Libre Office Calc?

Use of Spreadsheet in Business Applications

Summary

Business Applications

The following accounting applications are done with the help of a spreadsheet

- Payroll Accounting
- Asset Management
- Loan Repayment

Pay Roll Accounting

Payroll is a statement prepared to show the detailed salary calculation of employees. It contains Basic

Pay, Dearness Allowance, Travelling Allowance, Provident Fund Contribution, ESI Premium, etc. The computation of salary payment is based on the number of days an employee has worked, rate per grade, rate of allowances and deductions to be made therefrom.

1. **Preparation of Salary Bill**:

   The preparation of salary bill should provide for the following:

   - Maintaining payroll related data such as Employee No., Name, attendance, Basic Pay, DA, and other allowances, deductions to be made, etc.

   - **Periodic Payroll Computations:** It includes the calculation of various earnings and deductions.

   - Preparation of salary statement and employee's salary slip.

   - **Generation of advice to bank:** It contains the net salary to be transferred to individual bank account of employees and other salary related statutory payments such as provident fund, tax, etc.

2. **Pay Roll Components**:

   The following elements are important for salary computation and its payment.

   Earnings:

   - **Basic Pay (BP):** It is the pay in the pay scale

   - **Grade Pay (GP):** It is the pay to be added to the basic pay according to the designation.

   - **Dearness Pay (DP):** Portion of dearness allowance merged with Basic Pay

   - **Dearness allowance (DA):** Compensation for erosion in the purchasing power of wage earner due to Price rise.

- **House Rent Allowance (HRA):** An amount paid as rent of residential accommodation.
- **Transport Allowance (TA):** It is an amount to faclitate commuting to the palace of work.

Deductions:

- **Professional TAX:** Statutory deduction levied by State Government.
- **Provident Fund (PF):** It is a statutory deduction under provident Fund Act. It is deducted from salary as a part of social security.
- **Tax Deducted at Source (TDs):** Monthly deduction towards income Tax liability of an employee.
- **Recovery of Loan instalment:** An amount deducted on account of any loan taken up by employee.

Elements Used in Payroll Calculation

Basic Pay Earned (BPE) – Basic Pay Earned of an employee is the Basic Pay calculated with reference to Number of Effective Days present (NOEDP) during the month.

BPE = BP * NOEDP/NODM

Dearness Allowance (DA) – DA = BPE * (Applicable Rate of DA for the Month)

House Rent Allowance (HRA) – HRA = BPE * (Applicable Rate of HRA for the Month)

Transport Allowance (TRA) – TRA = (Fixed Amount) or (On Percentage Basis)

Total Earnings (TE) – It is the aggregate of all the above earning elements.

Thus, TE = BPE + DA + HRA + TRA

Provident Fund (PF) : This can be calculated as

PF = BPE * PF Rate PF = BPE * PF

Rate Tax Deduction at Source (TDS) : It is usually a fixed amount deducted every month on account of TDS. In the last quarter of a year, the investment details, which are permissible for tax deduction, are received from employees to compute the quarterly and yearly income tax liability more accurately.

Recovery of Loan Instalments (LOAN) : It is a fixed amount to be deducted on account of Loan Installment as part of loan recovery.

Total Deductions (TD) : It is the total of all the above deductions.

Thus, TD = PF + TDS + LOAN

3. **Net Salary Calculation:**

Step 1: Calculate Gross salary by using the given formula.

Step 2: Calculate Total Deduction by using the following formula.

Total Deduction = Professional Tax + Provident Fund + Tax deducted at source + Loan Recovery + Any other deductions.

Step 3: Calculate net salary by the given formula

Net Salary = Gross salary – Total Deduction.

Asset Accounting

Assets are resources of the organisation. Assets which are used in the business for more than one year, called Fixed assets. The value of Fixed assets may be reduced due to depreciation. The gradual and permanent diminution in the value of assets due to wear and tear is called depreciation.

Computerised Asset Accounting

- Assets are classified into the following categories:
- Goodwill
- Land: Free-hold land and Lease-hold land
- Building: Factory building, Office building, and Residential building
- Plant and Machinery
- Furniture and Fixtures
- Vehicles
- Capital work in progress
- Others

The depreciation on fixed assets is provided to recognise the cost of the asset consumed during an accounting period since the life of such assets extends beyond single accounting year.

Total amount of Depreciation – Acquisition cost – Salvage value.

1. **Methods of calculation of depreciation**:
   - Straight Line Method (SLM)
   - Written Down Value Method (WDV)

Straight Line Method

Under this method a fixed amount is deducted from the value of an asset year after year on account of depreciation and debited to profit and loss account. This method is also called Fixed Instalment method, or Original Cost method. Under this method value of asset will be reduced to zero.

Depreciation = cost of the asset – Scrap Value Life of the asset

1. Cost of the asset/Acquisition cost = Purchase Price + Other expenses directly related with the asset (ie., carriage inward, freight, installation, renewal or reparis, Pre operating expenses).

2. **Scap value / salvage value**: It is the value of an asset which is realisable at the end of its useful life. Salvage value is the estimated residual value of depreciable asset or property at the end of its economical or useful life.

3. The depreciation under straight line method is computed by using the built in LibreOffice calc function SLN.

   Written Down Value Method (WDV)

   This method is also known as Diminishing balance method or Reducing balance method. Under this method, a fixed percentage is written off every year on the book value of the asset at the beginning of the year. Here the amount of depreciation goes on decreasing and there fore, the book value of asset will not become zero after its working life.

   Amount of depreciation = Written Down Value of asset × Rate of depreciation

1. This method is also called Declining Balance (DB) method and uses the LibreOffice Calc function DB to compute the depreciation.

   Loan Repayment Schedule:

   Loan is a sum of borrowed money for a specified period at a pre-specified rate of interest. The loan is repaid through a number of periodic repayment instalments over the loan repayment period.

LibreOffice Calc function PMT is used to calculate loan repayment schedule. The parameters of the function PMT are as follows.

Parameter   Explanation

Rate   –   Interest rate

N per   –   Total number of payments for the loan

Pv   –   Present Value (Loan amount)

Fv   –   Future Value, which is taken as Zero, is the balance at the end of the loan period

Type   –   Whether payment is made at the beginning (Value = 1) or at the end (Value = 0) of the period

Multiple Choice Questions   [1 Mark]

1. Which of the following arguments in a financial function represents the total number of payments? **(NCERT)**

    (a) FV.   (b) PV.

    (c) Nper.   (d) Rate.

2. **What category of functions is used in this formula**: =PMT(C10/12,C8,C9,1)

    (a) Logical.   (b) Financial.

    (c) Payment.   (d) Statistical.

3. Which formula would result in TRUE if C4 is less than 10 and D4 is less than 100?

    (a) =AND(C4>10, D4>10).   (b) =AND(C4>10, C410, D4<100).

    (c) =AND(C4>10, D4<100).   (d) =AND(C4<100).

4. Which of these is not an argument of the IF function?

    (a) Logical_test.   (b) Value_if_false.

    (c) Value_when_false.   (d) Value_if_true.

5. In what cell is the Rate for PMT function where = PMT (C8, C9, C10, C11, C12)?

    (a) C8.   (b) C9.

    (c) C10.   (d) C12.

6. When Extend Selection is active, what is the keyboard shortcut for selecting all data up to and including the last row?

    (a) [Ctrl]+[Down Arrow].   (b) [Ctrl]+[Home].

    (c) [Ctrl]+[Shift].   (d) [Ctrl]+[Up Arrow].

7. Under .... method of depreciation, the asset account will be reduced to zero.

    (a) Fixed Instalment method   (b) Reducing installment

    (c) Depreciation Fund Method   (d) Revaluation method

Ans. (a) Fixed Instalment Method

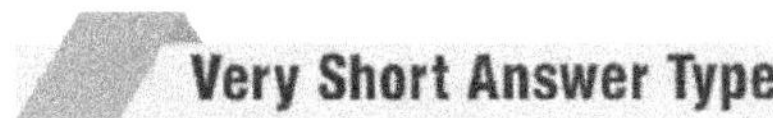 **Very Short Answer Type**   **[1 Mark]**

1. What is meant by PV ?

Ans. PV, one of the monetary capacities, figures the current estimation of a credit or a speculation, in view of a steady financing cost. ... Utilize the Excel Formula Coach to track down the current worth (advance sum) you can bear, in light of a set regularly scheduled installment.

2. What is professional tax?

Ans. It is a statutory deduction according to the legislature of the State Government

3. How is provident fund calculated?

Ans. Provident fund can be calculated as PF = BPE * PF Rate

4. State the advantage of using template ?

Ans. The advantage of preparing the template is that as a user puts in the values in the spreadsheet, the calculated results are shown correspondingly.

5. How to do you calculate Total Amount of Depreciation?

Ans. Total Amount of Depreciation = Acquisition Cost – Salvage Value (Over Life of the Asset)

6. Name the different method to calculate depreciation ?

Ans. The different method to calculate depreciation are :-

(a) Straight line method

(b) Written down value method

7. What is the salvage value of asset ?

Ans. The salvage value of an asset is the value, which is realisable at the end of its useful life.

8. If the cost of asset is 10000, Scrap value at the end of 10 years will be 2000, what will be the amount of annual depreciation?

Ans. Depreciation = 10000−2000 / 10

i.e., 800

9. Develop the command to calculate the Group Insurance Premium and Tax Deducted at source (TDS) by using the 'IF' function.

Rate of GI Rs. 200/-. for BP below Rs. 10,000/- and for others Rs. 300/- assuming that BP of employee is given in cell F2

Ans. = IF (B2 < 10000,200,300)

10. Give some examples for PayRoll components.

Ans. •   Basic Pay

•   Dearness Allowance

•   House Rent Allowance

•   Provident Fund

•   Professional Tax

•   ESI

Short Answer Type - I　　　　　　　　　　　　　**[2 Marks]**

1. If an investment of Rs. 1,000 is made today, ascertain its Future Value (FV) after 2 years if the rate of interest is taken as 10%?

Ans. FV = I x (1 + (R + T)

FV= 1000 X (1 + (0.10 + 2)

= 12000

It is concluded that the future value of investment Rs. 1000 at the rate of 10% after two years will be 1200

2. Classify the assets under computerised asset accounting.

Ans. Assets are classified into the following categories:

- Goodwill
- Land: Freehold and leasehold
- Building: Factory, office & residential building
- Plant & Machinery
- Furniture and fixtures
- Vehicles
- Work in progress (Capital)
- Other assets

3. List out common Payroll components regarding salary computation and its payment.

Ans. Earnings:

1. Basic pay
2. DearnessAllowances
3. House Rent Allowances
4. Transport Allowances
5. Other allowances.

Deductions:

- Provident Fund
- Professional Tax
- Tax deducted at source
- E.S.I. Premium

4. What are the common accounting applications done with the help of spreadsheet ?

Ans. • Payroll Accounting
- Asset Management
- Loan Repayment Schedule

5. Write the formula in spreadsheet to find the Professional Tax in cell B2 where annual income is given in cell A2. Profession Tax is 5% for income in between Rs. 100000 and Rs.200000 and 8% for income more than Rs. 2,00,000. No tax for income below Rs. 1,00,000.

Ans. = IF(B2 > 200000, B2*8%, IF(B2>100000, B2*5%,))

6. Write command to calculate state life Insurance Premium (SLI) of employee using the 'IF' function.

   Condition

   Premium Rs. 350/- below Basic Pay of Rs. 25000 and for others Rs. 450/- (BP is given in cell A3)

Ans. = IF(A3 < 25000, 350, 450)

7. Aman took a industrial loan of Rs. 300000, repayable in 4 years (equal monthly installments). The annual rate of interest is 10%. Assuming that the installments are paid at the end of each month. Find out the amount of monthly installments. Use PMT Function.

Ans. Procedure: Step 1 – Open a blank work sheet in LibreOffice Calc.

   Application → Office → Libre Office Calc.

   Step 2 – Enter the following data in appropriate cells.

	A	BG
1	Rate	10%
2	NPer (instalments)	4
3	PV	300000
4	FV	0
5	Type	0
6	Montly instalments	= PMT(B1/12, B2*12, B3, B4, B5)

Output: Monthly Installments= -7608.78

8. How can you define loan ?

Ans. Loan is a sum of borrowed money (termed as principal amount) for a specified period at a pre-specified rate of interest. The loan is repaid through a number of periodic (usually monthly) repayment instalments over the loan repayment period.

Short Answer Type - II   [3 Marks]

1. Mr. Kumar wants to take a housing loan of Rs. 2,00,000 repayable in 60 equal monthly installments over the next 5 years. Assuming that the installments are paid in the beginning of each month.

Ans.

   Step 1 – Open blank work sheet in LibreOffice Calc. Applications → Office → Libre Office Calc.

   Step 2 – Enter the following data in appropriate cells

A	B
Rate	12%
Nper (installments)	60
Pv	2,00,000
Fv	0
Type	1
Monthly installments	= PMT (B1/12,B2,B3,B4,B5)

Output

   Monthly installments = -4,404.84

2. Basic Pay, Dearness Allowance, House Rent allowance, Professional Tax, Provident fund contribution are given to prepare the PayRoll statement. Give the equation to calculate Net Salary.

   - Gross salary = Basic Pay + Dearness Allowance + House Rent Allowance

   - Total Deduction = Professional Tax + Provident fund contribution

   - Net Salary = Gross Salary – Total Deduction

Ans. Net Salary Calculation:

Step 1 – Calculate Gross salary by using the given formula.

Gross salary /Gross Pay = Basic Pay + Grade Pay + Dearness Pay+ Dearness Allowance + House Rent Allowance + Any other Earnings.

Step 2 – Calculate Total Deduction by using the following formula.

Total Deduction = Professional Tax+ Provident Fund + Tax deducted at source + Loan Recovery + Any other deductions

Step 3- Calculate net salary by the given formula.

Net Salary = Gross salary – Total Deduction

3. Write the parameters of the function PMT ?

Ans. Rate Interest rate per period for the loan

   - Nper Total number of payments for the loan. Its unit (e.g. year) should match with the unit of the interest rate.

   - Pv Present value, i.e. the loan amount

   - Fv Future value, which is taken as 0, is the balance at the end of the loan perio

   - Type Whether payment is made at the beginning (value=1) or at the end (value=0) of the period

4. **Solve the following for loan repayment schedule :**

   - A bank has given loan of Rs. 1, 00,000 to a customer for the purchase of a Plasma TV on April 1, 2007 @ 10% interest rate for a period of two years. The loan is to be repaid in 24 monthly instalments.

   - Ajay has been sanctioned the bank loan of Rs. 2, 50,000 for the purchase of a car on May 15, 2008. The loan carries the rate of interest @ 11% and it is to be repaid in 36 monthly instalments.

Ans.

Happy Banking Corp.						
Loan Repayment Schedule						
Loan Amt	**Loan Disbursement Date**	**Period of Loan (in Yrs)**	**Rate of Interest**	**Future Value**	**Yearly Instalment Amount**	**Monthly Instalment**
100000	01-Apr-07	2	10%	0.00	52380.95	4365.08
250000	15-May-08	3	11%	0.00	92165.11	7680.43

5. Explain written down value method with its parameters ?

Ans. Written Down Value (WDV) method uses the current book value as the base for computing the depreciation for the next period. It is also called Declining Balance (DB) method and uses the Excel function DB to compute the depreciation.

   - **Cost Initial:** cost of the asset

- **Salvage :** Salvage value
- **Life :** Life (in years) of the asset
- **Period :** Period (in years) for which the depreciation is calculated
- **Month :** No. of months in the 1st year

6. Name the contents of the salary bill ?

Ans. The preparation of salary bill should provide for the following :

- Maintaining payroll related data such as Employee No., Name, Attendance, Basic Pay, applicable Dearness and other Allowances, deductions to be made.
- **Periodic payroll computations:** the payroll computation includes the calculation of various earning and deduction heads, which are to be derived from basic values (such as basic salary, number of days under leave without pay (LWP) and unauthorised absence, etc) as per the formulae.
- Preparation of salary statement and employees salary slips
- **Generation of advice to bank:** It contains the net salary to be transferred to individual bank account of employees and other salary related statutory payments such as provident fund, tax, etc.

7. From the following particulars prepare a payroll of employees of a firm by using spreadsheet

- DA – 40% of basic pay
- HRA – 8% of basic pay
- Contribution to PF – 10% of basic pay.

Ans.
- DA = Basic pay *40%
- HRA = Basic pay *8%
- PF = Basic pay *10%
- Gross Pay = Basic Pay + DA + HRA
- Net Pay = Gross pay – PF

1. Write the difference between straight line method and written down value method ?

Ans.

Basis of comparison	Straight line method	Written down value method
Calculation of depreciation	It is calculated on original cost.	It is calculated on written down value of the assets.
Value of asset	Completely written off in this method of depreciation.	Not completely written off in this method.
Amount of depreciation	Initially lower.	Initially higher.
Annual depreciation charge	Remains fixed during the useful life.	Reduces every year.
Impact of repairs and depreciation on profit and loss a/c	Increasing trend	Remains constant.

2. Describe the two basic methods of depreciation. What functions of Excel are used for computation of depreciation?   **(NCERT)**

Ans. Depreciation can be calculated by two methods, namely;

1. **Straight Line Method(SLM)**: Under this method, depreciation is computed on the original cost of the asset. It is the default method as it is the simplest method to calculate depreciation.

2. **Written Down Value Method(WDV)**: This method is also called the Diminishing Balance method. Under this method, depreciation is calculated on the written down value of the asset i.e. it uses the current book value of the asset to calculate depreciation for the next period.

   Excel uses SLN and DB functions to compute depreciation according to Straight Line Method and Diminishing Balance Method respectively.

   Syntax of SLN function is = SLN(cost, salvage value, life)

   Syntax of DB function is = DB(cost, salvage value, life, period, months in first year)

3. Explain the importance of absolute and relative addresses. What is the basis of using relative address and absolute address?

Ans. The importance of relative and absolute cell address is explained below:

- Relative cell address- It is helpful when you need to use the same formula for different values entered in different cells. You need not enter the formula for every calculation, rather you can use relative cell address in one formula and then can drag the fill handle over the cells you wish to fill. In simple words, it is used when you need to repeat the same calculation across multiple rows and columns, thereby saving your time and effort.

   Example- If you copy the formula = A2+A3 from cell A4 and paste it to the cell B4, it will automatically change the formula to =B2+B3.

- Absolute cell address- It is used when you do not want a cell address to change when filling cells. You fix it by using a dollar($) sign before the row and column.

   Example- If you copy the formula =$A$2+$A$3 from cell A4 and paste it to the cell B4, it will remain as it is i.e. =$A$2+A.

4. Prepare the payroll of Amal Bros, for the month of January 2016.

Name	Basic Pay	PF Loan
Jaizal Grace	7750	1100
Haizal Rose	7300	540
Joshwin Zian	6000	600
Anlino Zinan	5100	0

- DA – 36% of Basic Pay
- HRA – Rs 500
- CCA – 6% of Basic pay

Deduction:

1. PF subscription – 8% of BP.

2. Group insurance premium Rs. 200 below basic pay Rs. 6000 and for others Rs. 350.

3. Tax deducted at source 10% of Gross Pay for employees below gross pay of Rs. 10000 arid for others 20%. Also, find out the total salary payable to employees for the month.

Procedure:

Step 1 – Open a blank work sheet in LibreOffice Calc

Step 2 – Enter the following details in the following cells.

	A	B	C	D	E	F	G	H
1	Name	Baisc pay	DA	HRA	CCA	Gross Salary	PF	PF Loan
2	Jaizal Grace	7750		500				1100
3	Haizal Rose	7300		500				540
4	Joshwin ZIan	6000	500					600
5	Anlino Zinan	5100		500				0

	I	J	K	L
1	GIP	TDS	Total Deduction	Net Salary

Step 3 – Enter the following formula in the respective cell

Cell	Formula
C2	= B2 * 36%
E2	= B2 * 6%
F2	= SUM(B2: E2)
G2	= B2 * 8%
12	= IF(B2 < 6000, 200, 350)
J2	= IF(F2 < 10000, F2 * 10%, F2 * 20%)
K2	= SUM(G2: J2)
L2	= F2 – K2

Step 4 – Copy the formula down up to the last employee.

Output:

Name of Employee	Net Salary
Jaizal Grace	7134
Haizal Rose	7218.80
Joshwin Zian	6688
Anlino Zinan	6359.80

5. Prepare a Pay Roll statement of Viswanath Enterprises from the table given below and additional information.

No.	Employee Name	Designation	Basic pay	LIC	TDS
1	Kumar	Manager	22000	1600	1000
2	Balu	Accountant	18000	650	500
3	Meera	Clerk	12000	300	400
4	Nayana	Clerk	13500	-	200
5	Ouseph	Clerk	11500	-	200
6	Premnath	Peon	7000	280	200

1. DA is provided at 90% of Basic Pay

2. **HRA:** Rs. 500 for manager, 400 for accountant and 200 for others.

3. PF is deducted @ 20% on Basic + DA

Procedure:

Step 1 – Open a blank worksheet in LibreOffice Calc.

Step 2 – Enter the following text/formula in respective cells

	A	B	C	D	E	F
1	No.	Name	Designation	B.P	DA	HRA
2	1	Kumar	Manager	22000		
3	2	Balu	Accountant	18000		
4	3	Meera	Clerk	12000		
5	4	Nayana	Clerk	13500		
6	5	Ouseph	Clerk	11500		
7	6	Premnath	Peon	7000		

	G	H	I	J	K	L
1	Gross Salary	PF	LIC	TDS	Total Deduction	Net Salary
2			1600	1000		
3			650	500		
4			300	400		
5			-	200		
6			-	200		
7			280	200		

Step 3 – Enter the given details

Cell	Formula
E2	= D2 * 90%
F2	= IF(C2 = "Manager", 500, IF(C2 = "Accountant", 400, 200))
G2	= SUM (D2: F2)
H2	= SUM(D2: E2) * 20%
K2	= SUM(H2: J2)
L2	= G2 – K2

Step 4 – Copy the formula down up to the last employee.

Output:

No	Employee Name	Net Salary
1	Kumar	31340
2	Balu	26610
3	Meera	17740
4	Nayana	20520
5	Ouseph	17480
6	Premnath	10360

Chapter Practice

1. Which of the following options in a financial function indicates the interest for a period?

   (a) FV   (b) PV

   (c) N per   (d) Rate

2. .... is the statement prepared to show detailed salary calculation

   (a) Employee Job Card   (b) Payroll

   (c) Loan Repayment Schedule   (d) All of the above

3. .... calculates the monthly installment of loan amount

   (a) Loan Repayment Schedule   (b) Loan analysis sheet

   (c) Loan card   (d) both a and b

4. Under .... method of depreciation, the asset account will be reduced to zero.

   (a) Fixed Instalment method   (b) Reducing installment

   (c) Depreciation Fund Method   (d) All of the above

5. The .... of an asset is the value, which is realisable at the end of its useful life

   (a) Depreciation   (b) Scrap value

   (c) Written down value   (d) Acquisition cost

6. Odd one out

   (a) Basic Pay   (b) Grade Pay

   (c) House Rent Allowance   (d) Provident Fund

7. __________ is a statutory deduction deducted monthly towards income tax liability of an employee

8. Gross Salary – Total Deduction = _______

9. Decrease in the value of fixed assets is called ....

10. If the cost of asset is 20000, Scrap value at the end of 10 years will be 4000, what will be the amount of annual depreciation?

11. Rate of Depreciation under straight line Method = ...

Short Answer Type - I   [2 Marks]

Q12. What are the different methods for calculating depreciation on fixed Assets?

Q13. Why is FV taken as Zero (0) in the PMT calculation?

Q14. Write the command to calculate the State Life Insurance (SLI) Premium of an Employee using the 'IF' function. **The condition is:** SLI Premium Rs. 250 for basic pay below Rs. 10,000/- for others Rs.500/- (**Hint:** Basic pay (BP) is given the cell B3)

Q15. What is a provident fund ?

Q16. How can you calculate NOEDP?

Short Answer Type - II   [3 Marks]

Q17. Give some examples for Pay Roll components.

Q18. Basic Pay, Dearness Allowance, House Rent allowance, Professional Tax, Provident fund contribution are given to prepare the Pay Roll statement. Give the equation to calculate Net Salary.

- Gross salary = Basic Pay + Dearness Allowance + House Rent Allowance
- Total Deduction = Professional Tax + Provident fund contribution
- Net Salary = Gross Salary – Total Deduction

Q19. List down the Parameters of the function PMT

Long Answer Type   [5 Marks]

Q20. The column headings of payroll to be prepared through Libre Office Calc is given below.

Cell	A1	B1	C1	D1	E1	F1	G1
content	Name	BP	DA (20% of BP)	HRA (5% of BP)	Gross Pay	TDs (10% of GP)	Net Pay

1. Write the formula to calculate DA, HRA, Gross pay, TDS and Net pay of Jexin Jose the first employee, in the second row of the worksheet.
2. Give the command to fill the calculation automatically for the remaining '10' employees in the firm.

21. Which built in function of LibreOffice Calc can be used to compute monthly instalments of repayment of loan? Give the parameters of this function.

CHAPTER 4

Graphs and Charts for Business Data

Summary

Graphs and Charts

Graphs and Charts are pictorial representation of data, which has at least two dimensional relationship. Graphs, has two axes X and Y. X axis is usually horizontal while Y axis is vertical. Graphs/ Charts allow you to present information contained in the worksheet in a graphic **format. Excel offers many types of charts including**: Column, Line, Pie, Bar, Area, Scatter and more. To view the charts available click the Insert Tab on the Ribbon.

A pie chart represents multiple sub-groups of single variable. A bar diagram depicts two or more variables.

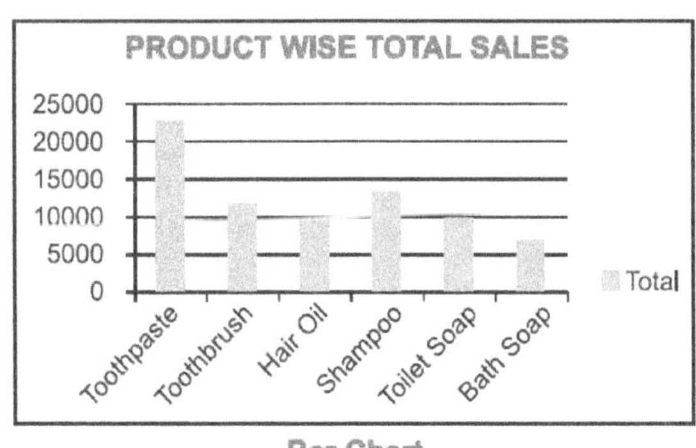

Bar Chart

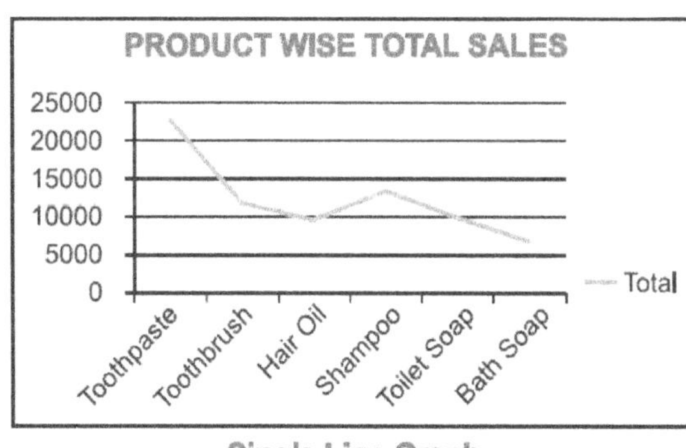

Single Line Graph

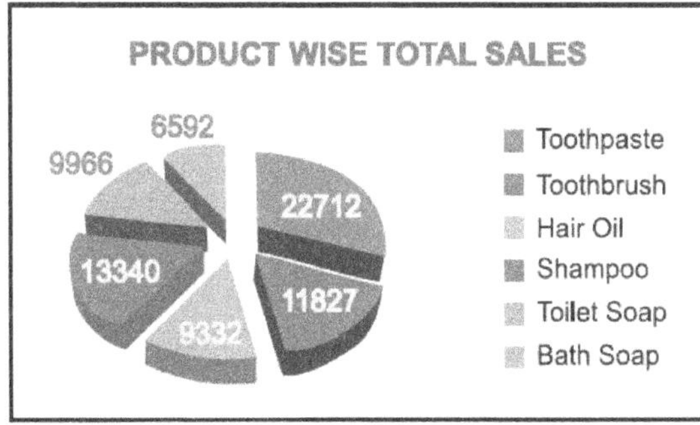

Pie Chart

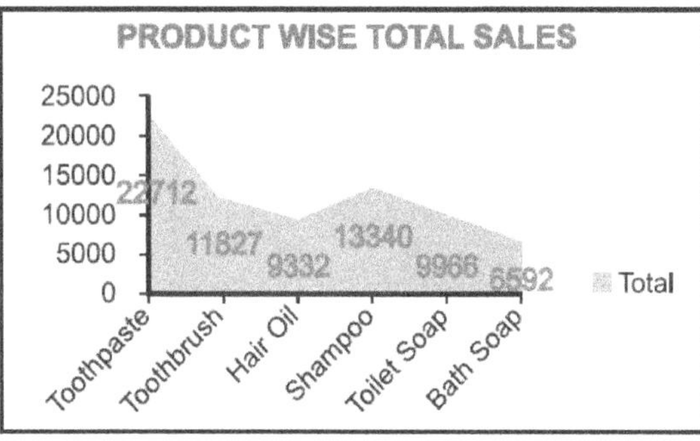

Area Chart

Different Types of Charts Used

Using Charts/Graphs tools in Excel

1. **Create a Chart To create a chart:**
   - Select the cells that contain the data you want to use in the chart
   - Click the Insert tab on the Ribbon
   - Click the type of Chart you want to create

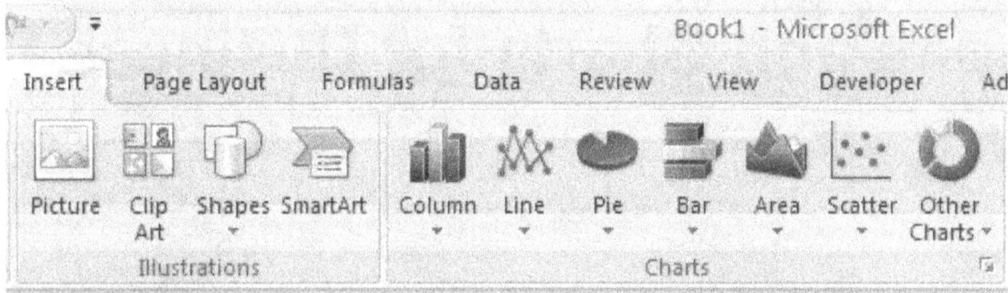

2. **Modify a Chart**

   Once you have created a chart you can do several things to modify the chart. To move the chart:
   - Click the Chart and Drag it to another location on the same worksheet, or
   - Click the Move Chart button on the Design tab
   - Choose the desired location (either a new sheet or a current sheet in the workbook)

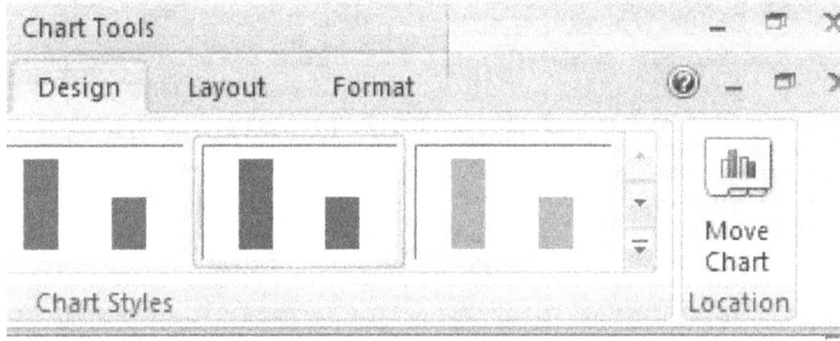

3. **To change the data included in the chart:**
   - Click the Chart
   - Click the Select Data button on the Design tab

4. **To reverse which data are displayed in the rows and columns**
   - Click the Chart
   - Click the Switch Row/Column button on the Design tab

5. **To modify the labels and titles:**
   - Click the Chart On the Layout tab,
   - click the Chart Title or the Data Labels button Change the Title and click Enter

Elements of a Chart/Graph

A chart/graph are a pictorial presentation of data.

Chart/Graph Elements are

1. **The chart area**: The entire chart including all elements.

2. **The plot area**: In a 2-D chart, the area is bounded by the X and Y axes. In a 3-D chart, the area is bounded by the three (X, Y and Z) axes.

3. **The data points**: Individual values plotted in a chart and represented by bars, columns, lines, pie or various other shapes are called data markers. Data markers of the same colour constitute a data series. The data series are related data points that are plotted in the chart/ graph. Each data series in a chart is shown in a unique colour or pattern or both. Its identification is given by the legend. There may be more than one data series in a chart/graph.

4. **The horizontal (category) and vertical (value) axis**: The x-axis is usually the horizontal line which contains categories (independent values or categories) and y-axis is usually the verticals which contains data (dependent values).

5. **The legend**: It is an identifier of a piece of information shown in the chart/graph. The legends are assigned to the data series or different categories in a chart .

6. **A chart and axes titles**: Descriptive text for chart title (6-A) and axis title (6-B) .

7. **A data label**: This provides additional information about a data marker to identify the details of data point in a data series.

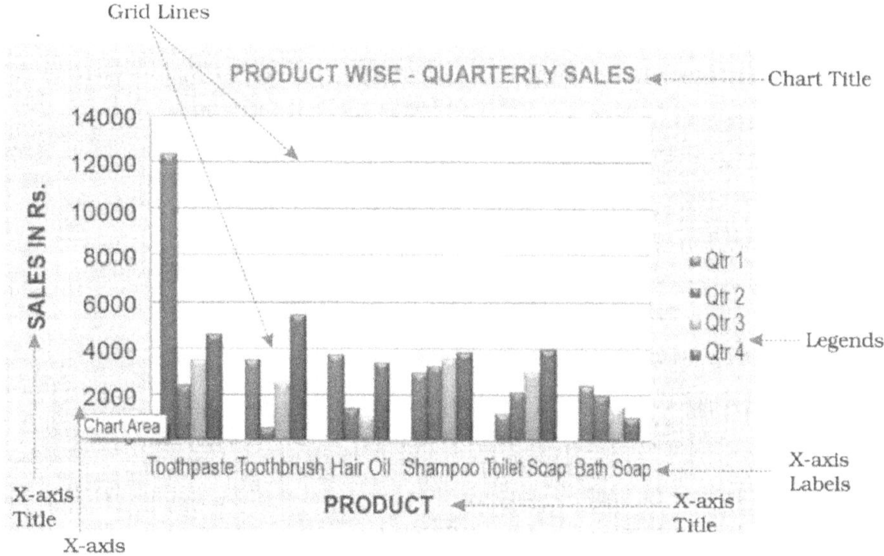

Formatting of Chart

The elements of a chart such as plot area, X-axis, Y-axis, data, titles, labels, legends and gridline can be formatted and edited as per the requirement. Click anywhere in the chart. This will display the Chart Tools, adding the Design, Layout, and Format tabs. Using Design option we can change the look of a chart. In the Design dialog box, we can click to change chart type, chart layouts and chart styles. One of the options provide for 2-d chart to swap the column data to row data and row data to column data.

The Steps are As Follows

In a chart click the chart element to change, or do the following to select the chart element from a list of chart elements:

1. Click anywhere in the chart. This will display the Chart Tools, adding the Design, Layout, and Format tabs.

2. On the Design tab, in the Data group, click the arrow the Switch Row/Column box.

Changing The Format of a Selected Chart Element

In the same chart, click the chart element to change, or do the following to select the chart **element from a list of chart elements**:

1. Click anywhere in the chart. This will display the Chart Tools, adding the Design, Layout, and Format tabs

2. On the Format tab, in the Current Selection group, click the arrow next to the Chart Elements box, and then select the chart element which requires to format.

3. On the Format tab, in the Current Selection group, click the Format Selection.

4. Format dialog box, click a category, and then select the formatting options

Changing the Shape Style

- On the Format tab, in the Shape Styles group, do one of the following:

- To see all available shape styles, click the More button.

- To apply a pre- defined shape style, in the shape style box, click the style that we want.

- To apply a different shape fill, click Shape Fill, and then do one of the following:

- To use a different fill Colour, under Theme Colours or Standard Colours, left click the select Colour. To remove the Colour from the selected chart element, click No Fill.

- To use a fill Colour that is not available under Theme Colours or Standard colours click More Fill Colours. In the Colours dialog box, specify the Colour that we want to use on the Standard or Custom tab, and then click OK. Custom fill Colours are added under Recent Colours can also be used

Changing the Shape Outline

- To apply a different shape outline, click Shape Outline, and then do one of the following:

- To use a different outline Colour, under Theme Colours or Standard Colours, click the Colour to use.

  To remove the outline Colour from the selected chart element, click No Outline. If the selected element is a line, the line will no longer be visible on the chart.

- To use an outline Colour that is not available under Theme Colours or Standard Colours click More Outline Colours. In the Colours dialog box, specify the Colour that to use on the Standard or Custom tab, and then click OK. Custom outline Colours are added under Recent Colours can be used again

- To change the weight (thickness) of a line or border, click Weight option, and then select the line that we wish to use. For additional line style or border style options, click on More Lines, and then click the line style or border style options.

- To use broken line (dash–dash) or border, click Dashes, and then click the dash type to use. For additional dash-type options, click on More Lines, and then click the selected dash.

- To add arrows to lines, click Arrows, and then click the arrow style for borders cannot be used. For additional arrow style or border style options, click More Arrows, and then click the arrow setting.

Changing the Text Format

To format the text in chart elements, we can use regular text formatting options, or we can apply a WordArt format.

1. Click the chart element that contains the text to format.

2. **Right-click the text or select the text to format, and then do one of the following**: Click the formatting options that we want on the Mini toolbar. On the Home tab, in the Font group, click the formatting buttons that we want to use. To use WordArt styles to format text use chart elements in the following steps:

    1. In a chart, click the chart element that contains the text to be changed, or do the following to select the chart element from a list of chart elements:

    2. Click anywhere in the chart.

    3. This displays the Chart Tools, adding the Design, Layout, and Format tabs.

    4. On the Format tab, in the Current Selection group, click the arrow next to the Chart Elements box, and then select the chart element that is to be formated.

    5. **On the Format tab, in the WordArt Styles group, do one of the following**: To see all available WordArt styles, click the More button.

We get options for Text related formatting

- Text Fill
- Text Outline
- Shadow
- 3-DFormat
- 3-D Rotation
- Text Box

Changing the Layout of the Chart Element

In the same chart, click the chart element to change, or do the following to select the chart **element from a list of chart elements**:

1. On the Layout tab, we can insert different Clip Arts, Picture, data labels, grids etc.

2. In the Format dialog box, click a category, and then select the formatting options.

Change the Chart Type

A chart can be changed to another type of chart to get different look and purpose. This is the easiest method to change from column chart or bar chart to Pie chart because

Only One Data Series is Used to Plot

The plotted data values are positive.

The data values are not equal to zero also

Steps for creating a Pie Chart

1. Enter the data in a worksheet.

2. Select the data from two (consecutive) columns only.

3. Select the chart type Pie from the ribbon.

4.   Under Pie types select 3-D Pie option

5.   Click the plot are of Pie chart this displays the Chart Tools, adding the Design, Layout, and Format tabs.

6.   On the Design tab, in the Chart Layouts group, select the layout to use.

7.   On the Design tab, in the Chart Styles group, click the chart style.

8.   On the Format tab, in the Shape Styles group, click Shape Effects, and then click Bevel.

9.   Click 3-D Options, and then under Bevel, click the Top and Bottom bevel options.

10. In the Width and Height boxes for Top and Bottom bevel options, type the point size.

11. Under Surface, click Material, and then click the material option.

12. Click Close.

13. On the Format tab, in the Shape Styles group, click Shape Effects, and then click Shadow.

14. Under Outer, Inner, or Perspective, click the shadow option.

15. To rotate the chart for a better perspective, select the plot area, and then on the Format tab in the Current Selection group, click Format Selection.

16. Under Angle of first slice, drag the slider to the degree of rotation that you want, or type a value between 0 (zero) and 360 to specify the angle of the first slice to appear, and then click Close.

17. Click the chart area of the chart.

18. On the Format tab, in the Shape Styles group, click Shape Effects, and then click Bevel.

19. Under Bevel, select the bevel option.

20. To use theme colors that are different from the default theme that is applied the **workbook, do the following**:

     a.   On the Page Layout tab, in the Themes group, click Themes.

     b.   Under Built-in, click the theme to use.

Resizing of Chart/Graph

Resizing of the chart means changing size of the chart as desired. This option can be used independently for the fonts, title, legends easily. The first step is to select the chart by clicking the left button of the mouse. Move the cursor on the corners or middle of the borders of the chart/graph which will provide the figure (the cursor will take the shape of a two headed arrow). By pressing the left button, and drag/ pull as desired to resize the chart

Advantages in Using Graphs/Charts

1.   **Help to Explore** : Many times we would like to see if there is a relationship between variables. Suppose that we wanted to determine if there is a relationship between: a country's GNP and the infant mortality rate, between age and between genders. It may be quicker and easier to create a chart immediately to see the possible relationship of variables to one another, rather than paging through raw data.

2.   **Help to Present** : We want to provide information in as little time as possible. Graphing plays a key role. It seems that there is no longer any time to sit and read a newspaper in order to find out what is going on. However, newspapers, such as The Economics Times and India Today magazines (which were early users of charting techniques), seem to understand this phenomena and provide graphs to convey and sum up ideas that they are making in their articles.

3.   **Help to Convince** : The same way that a graph can be used to present and explore different characteristics of data, it can also be used to convince. Graphs have the ability to take large amounts of information and make them into exhibitions that are easily used to persuade.

2D - 3D Charts/Graphs

To create graphs we use data which are plotted in two dimensional (2D) format (X- axis and Y-axis)

- Horizontal dimension is X-axis(contains categories)
- Vertical dimension is Y-axis(contains data)

  When we plot the data on 2-D type of graph; the known value goes on the X-axis (independent) and derived (dependent variable) value on Y-axis.

  2-D types of graphs/charts are line graphs, bar, area, surface column (horizontal or vertical), multiple line charts, radar chart, XY (scatter) or bubble chart. The 2-D Charts typically have **two axes (axis:** A line bordering the chart plot area used as a frame of reference for measurement. The Y axis is usually the vertical axis and contains data. The X-axis is usually the horizontal axis and contains categories.) that are used to measure and categorise data: a vertical axis (also known as derived value axis or Y axis), and a horizontal axis (also known as category axis or X axis).

  Sometimes graphs/charts can be prepared with three dimensional (3-D) effects. 3-D charts have a third axis, the depth axis (also known as series axis or Z axis), so that data can be plotted along the depth of a chart. In this type the third dimension is represented by Z-axis

  Doughnut:- charts display data in rings, where each ring represents a data series.

  Doughnut Chart:- Doughnut Chart Exploded Doughnut Much like exploded pie charts, exploded doughnut charts display the contribution of each value to a total while emphasising individual values, but they can contain more than one data series

Multiple Choice Questions   [1 Mark]

1) Which is the least dimension for which a graph can be made?

   (a) 3   (b) 4

   (c) 2   (d) 1

2) Where do you get option of making graph or chart in Excel?

   (a) Home tab   (b) Design tab

   (c) View tab   (d) Insert tab

3) Which is not one of the element of chart?

   (a) Bar   (b) Chart area

   (c) Data points   (d) Legend

4) Which is not one of the chart formatting tab?

   (a) Design   (b) Layout

   (c) Format   (d) View

5) Which is not a type of chart?

   (a) Cake   (b) Doughnut

   (c) Bar   (d) Column

6) Pie chart don't have more than _________ categories:

(a) Ten   (b) Twenty Five

(c) Seven   (d) Three

7) The 2D graph using _________ , __________ axes and in 3D graph _______ axis is also used.

(a) Category, value, vertical   (b) Horizontal, vertical, depth

(c) Category, value, series   (d) b and c both

8) Column charts are useful for ___________________:

(a) Showing data changes over a period of time   (b) Illustrating comparisons among items

(c) Both a and b   (d) None of the above

Very Short Answer Type   [1 Mark]

Define the following:

1) Graph

Ans. A graph is a pictorial representation of data, which has at least 2 dimensional relationship

2) Legend

Ans. It is an identifier of a piece of information shown in the chart/graph. The legends are assigned to the data series or different categories in a chart

3) Data points

Ans. Individual values plotted in a chart and represented by bars, columns, lines, pie or various other shapes are called data markers. Data markers of the same colour constitute a data series. The data series are related data points that are plotted in the chart/ graph. Each data series in a chart is shown in a unique colour or pattern or both. Its identification is given by the legend. There may be more than one data series in a chart/graph

4) Vertical and Horizontal axes

Ans. The x-axis is usually the horizontal line which contains categories (independent values or categories) and y-axis is usually the verticals which contains data (dependent values).

5) Data label

Ans. This provides additional information about a data marker to identify the details of data point in a data series

6) Chart area

Ans. The entire chart including all elements

7) Plot area

Ans. In a 2-D chart, the area is bounded by the X and Y axes. In a 3-D chart, the area is bounded by the three (X, Y and Z) axes.

8) Chart and axis titles

Ans. Descriptive text for chart title and axis title

9) 5 types of charts

Ans. Bar, column, pie, line, area, scatter, doughnut

10) 2D – 3D charts

Ans. When we plot the data on 2-D type of graph; the known value goes on the X-axis (independent) and derived (dependent variable) value on Y-axis. To represent the volume we require three parameters height (Y-axis), length (X-axis) and breadth (Z-axis) we need 3-D graph.

Short Answer Type - I [2 Marks]

1) Explain types of doughnut charts?

Ans. Doughnut charts display data in rings, where each ring represents a data series..

2) Mention basic steps of using charts in excel

Ans. First select the data for graph -> go to insert tab -> select the chart type -> format it

3) Why do we use graphs and charts?

Ans. graph is a pictorial representation of data, which has at least 2 dimensional relationship

For ease and enhancing of clarity, present the data properly, visualization is better than in table.

4) What is the importance of charts and graphs in business?

Ans. Chart and graphs covey lots of business information in a visual format

Different business Data variables plotted in charts and graphs show the trend of the business in an easy way

5) Define charts, graphs and how they are useful in business decisions?

Ans. · A chart is a representation of data in graphical form, in which the data is represented or presented by symbols, such as bars in a bar chart, lines in a line chart, or slices in pie charts. It can represent tabular numeric data, functions or some kinds of quality structure and provides different info.

- Whereas a graph is a pictorial representation or a diagram that represents data or values in an organized manner. The graph often represents the relationship between two or more things.
- Both graphs and charts are useful in making business decisions as these help in easy visualization of any trends present in data.

A graph or a chart both are different forms of presentation of data in simplified organized manners, which helps in making efficient business decisions as these norms helps in comparison and also make the information so much easier to digest and understand.

6) Describe about data series, legend, and data labels?

Ans. Data series is the column or the rows of the numbers which are entered into the worksheet and then plotted into the chart like the quarterly list of the profits of the business.

- Data labels are the static part of the chart or other layout, legends are useful in identifying the same set of the data series, whereas the data series are the excel grounded worksheet, which has the numbers of rows and columns.
- Legend is defined as the space which is located on the chart in the plotted area. It has the keys of the legend that are connected to the data source.

7) What are the advantages of using Graph/ Chart?

Ans. Advantages in using Graph/Chart:

- It summarises a large data set in visual form
- Charts or graphs can clarify trends better than do tables.
- It helps to estimate key values at a glance
- It shows each data category in a frequency distribution.
- It permits a visual check of the accuracy and reasonableness of calculations
- The charts and graphs allow the investigator to draw a valid conclusion.

8) How to use word Art styles to format text.

Ans. • Step 1: Click in the chart element that contains text to be changed.
- Step 2: Click on the format.
- Step 3: Click on word Art styles.
- Step 4: Choose suitable options related to text formating like text fill, text outlines, shadow, etc.

Short Answer Type - II   [3 Marks]

1) Explain in detail any 4 elements of chart

Ans. **(a)** **Legend**: It is an identifier of a piece of information shown in the chart/graph. The legends are assigned to the data series or different categories in a chart

(b) **Data points**: Individual values plotted in a chart and represented by bars, columns, lines, pie or various other shapes are called data markers. Data markers of the same colour constitute a data series. The data series are related data points that are plotted in the chart/ graph. Each data series in a chart is shown in a unique colour or pattern or both. Its identification is given by the legend. There may be more than one data series in a chart/graph

(c) **Axes**: The x-axis is usually the horizontal line which contains categories (independent values or categories) and y-axis is usually the verticals which contains data (dependent values).

(d) **Data label**: This provides additional information about a data marker to identify the details of data point in a data series

2) Explain formatting of chart?

Ans. The elements of a chart such as plot area, X-axis, Y-axis, data, titles, labels, legends and gridline can be formatted and edited as per the requirement. Click anywhere in the chart. This will display the Chart Tools, adding the Design, Layout, and Format tabs. Using Design option we can change the look of a chart. In the Design dialog box, we can click to change chart type, chart layouts and chart styles. One of the options provide for 2-d chart to swap the column data to row data and row data to column data.

The steps are as follows:

In a chart click the chart element to change, or do the following to select the chart element from a list of chart elements:

(1) Click anywhere in the chart. This will display the Chart Tools, adding the Design, Layout, and Format tabs.

(2) On the Design tab, in the Data group, click the arrow the Switch Row/Column box.

(3) Write steps of creating pie chart

Ans. 1. Enter the data in a worksheet.

2. Select the data from two (consecutive) columns only.

3. Select the chart type Pie from the ribbon.

4. Under Pie types select 3-D Pie option

5. Click the plot are of Pie chart this displays the Chart Tools, adding the Design, Layout, and Format tabs.

6. On the Design tab, in the Chart Layouts group, select the layout to use.

7. On the Design tab, in the Chart Styles group, click the chart style.

8. On the Format tab, in the Shape Styles group, click Shape Effects

(4) Write advantages of using graph and charts

Ans. Help to Explore: Many times we would like to see if there is a relationship between variables. Suppose, that we wanted to determine if there is a relationship between: a country's GNP and the infant mortality rate, between age and between genders. It may be quicker and easier to create a chart immediately to see the possible relationship of variables to one another, rather than paging through raw data.

Help to Present: We want to provide information in as little time as possible. Graphing plays a key role. It seems that there is no longer any time to sit and read a newspaper in order to find out what is going on. However, newspapers, such as The Economics Times and India Today magazines (which were early users of charting techniques), seem to understand this phenomenon and provide graphs to convey and sum up ideas that they are making in their articles.

Help to Convince: The same way that a graph can be used to present and explore different characteristics of data, it can also be used to convince. Graphs have the ability to take large amounts of information and make them into exhibitions that are easily used to persuade

(5) List out the steps to Rotate a chart.

Ans. • Step 1. Select the plot area of the chart.

• Step 2. Click on the format tab.

• Step 3. Click on format selection.

• Step 4. Click on 3D Rotation and type a value of angle between 0° to 360° and then click close

• Step 5. Click on the chart area of the chart and click on format tab.

• Step 6. Click on shape effects and then click on Bevel and select a bevel option.

(6) How can we change the format of a selected chart element?

Ans. • Step 1. Click anywhere in the chart.

• Step 2. Click format

• Step 3. Click format selection

• Step 4. Select a category (Fill border, style, etc)

• Step 5. Select formatting options

(7) What is pie chart and what are percentage values means in pie chart?

Ans. • A pie chart is a special type of chart in which data is displayed with the help of pie slices where each slice of the pie is relative to the size of that category in the group which is being represented by that particular pie slice. In other words, a pie chart represents data in a circular graph and the pieces of graph are proportional to the fraction of the whole in each class of category.

- A pie chart is a type of chart which is used to depict the relative share of the different elements contained in a piece of data. The data is represented in a circular graph and the slices of pie are proportional to the fraction of the whole in each class of category.

- The percentage values in a pie chart mean the relative values or share of the different elements such as the size of the total sales in each quarter where the whole pie displays the sum of all the percentage values of total sales in each quarter which equals to 100%.

(8) Prepare a Pie chart and Column chart for the 10 different plots areas 5, 7, 8, 9, 8, 10, 4, 6, 7 and 3 hectares respectively.   **(NCERT)**

Ans.

Pie Chart:

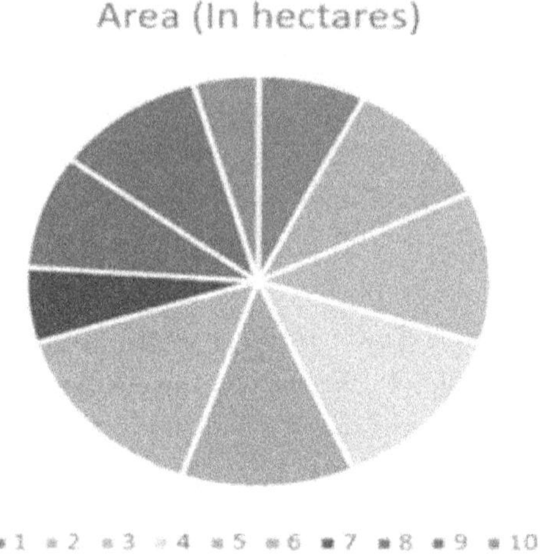

Column chart:

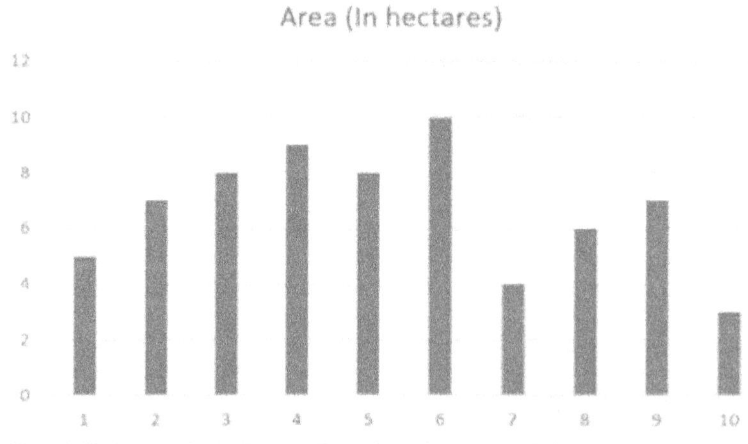

9) Draw a Column chart for the following data.   (NCERT)

Marks	0–20	21–40	41–60	61–80	81–100	Total
Number of Students	113	180	350	232	125	1000

Ans. Column chart refers to the graphical representation of the data to show the comparison between the two categories or things. One axis represents the categories which is being compared and the other axis shows the data values. In the above figure, x axis shows the marks and y axis shows the number of students who obtains the marks in between the 0–20,21–40,41–60,61–80 and 81–100

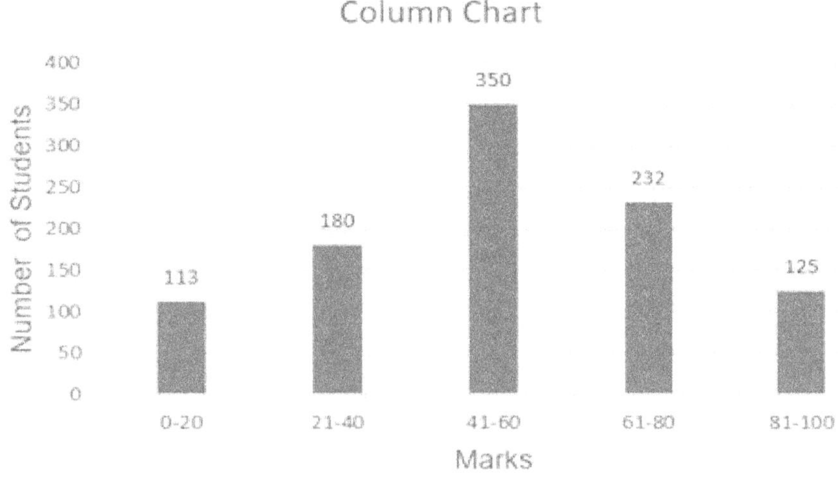

Long Answer Type   [5 Marks]

1. What are the difference between 2D charts and 3D charts

Ans.

2D Chart	3D Chart
(a) The chart represents business data with just two dimensions	(a) The chart represents business data with three dimensions
(b) The two dimensions are length and height (No width)	(b) The Three dimensions are Length and Height and width (or depth)
(c) There are X-axis and Y-axis	(c) There is X-axis, Y-axis is and Z-axis
(d) The shape of the chart may be in the form of Rectangle, Square, Triangle, Polygon, etc	(d) The shape of the chart may be Cylinder, Cube, Pyramid, etc

2. Write the steps to change the shape style ?

Ans. 1. On the Format tab, in the Shape Styles group, do one of the following:

- To see all available shape styles, click the More button.
- To apply a pre- defined shape style, in the shape style box, click the style that we want.

- To apply a different shape fill, click Shape Fill, and then do one of the following:
- To use a different fill Colour, under Theme Colours or Standard Colours, left click the select Colour.
- To remove the Colour from the selected chart element, click No Fill.
- To use a fill Colour that is not available under Theme Colours or Standard Colours click More Fill Colours. In the Colours dialog box, specify the Colour that we want to use on the Standard or Custom tab, and then click OK. Custom fill Colours are added under Recent Colours can also be used.
- To fill the shape with a picture, click Picture. In the Insert Picture dialog box, click the picture to use, and then click Insert.
- To use a gradient effect for the selected fill Colour, click Gradient, and then under Variations, click the gradient style to be used. For additional gradient styles, click More Gradients, and then in the Fill category, click the gradient options that to use.
- To use a texture fill, click Texture, and then click the texture to use.

3. Write the steps to create a pie-chart?

Ans. 1. Enter the data in a worksheet.

2. Select the data from two (consecutive) columns only.

3. Select the chart type Pie from the ribbon.

4. Under Pie types select 3-D Pie option

5. Click the plot are of Pie chart this displays the Chart Tools, adding the Design, Layout, and Format tabs.

6. On the Design tab, in the Chart Layouts group, select the layout to use.

7. On the Design tab, in the Chart Styles group, click the chart style.

8. On the Format tab, in the Shape Styles group, click Shape Effects, and then click Bevel

9. Click 3-D Options, and then under Bevel, click the Top and Bottom bevel options.

10. In the Width and Height boxes for Top and Bottom bevel options, type the point size.

11. Under Surface, click Material, and then click the material option.

12. Click Close.

13. On the Format tab, in the Shape Styles group, click Shape Effects, and then click Shadow.

14. Under Outer, Inner, or Perspective, click the shadow option.

15. To rotate the chart for a better perspective, select the plot area, and then on the Format tab in the Current Selection group, click Format Selection

16. Under Angle of first slice, drag the slider to the degree of rotation that you want, or type a value between 0 (zero) and 360 to specify the angle of the first slice to appear, and then click Close.

17. Click the chart area of the chart.

18. On the Format tab, in the Shape Styles group, click Shape Effects, and then click Bevel.

19. Under Bevel, select the bevel option.

20. To use theme colors that are different from the default theme that is applied the workbook, do the following:

   (a) On the Page Layout tab, in the Themes group, click Themes.

   (b) Under Built-in, click the theme to use.

4. Quarterly sales of a product are given below. Draw a bar diagram/bar chart

Ist Quarter	25,600
IInd Quarter	33,400
IIIrd Quarter	28,700
IVth Quarter	40,400

Ans. Procedure:

Step 1 – Open a new blanks worksheet in LibreOffice Calc

Step 2 – Enter the above data as follows.

	A	B
1	Period	Sales
2	Ist Quarter	25,600
3	IInd Quarter	33,400
4	IIIrd Quarter	28,700
5	IVth Quarter	40,400

Step 3 – Select the range A1: B5 which is to be shown in the chart:

Step 4 – Click on Insert menu → Click on Chart → Chart wizard Click on Bar chart → Finish

Output:

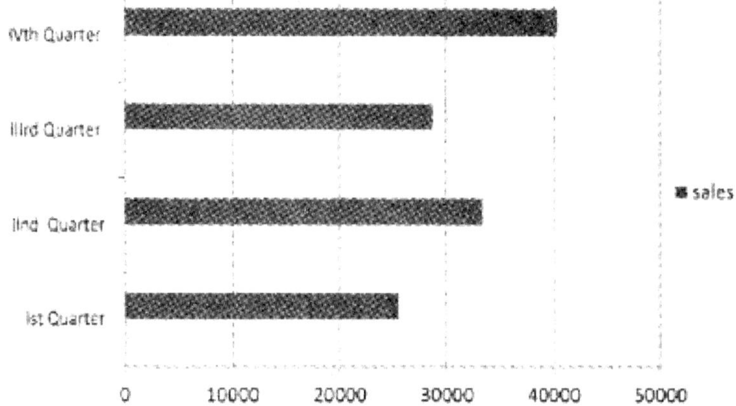

Chapter Practice

Multiple Choice Questions [1 Mark]

1. _______ Chart is similar to the column chart, with the difference being that the data series are displayed horizontally

    (a) Line chart

    (b) Pie chart

    (c) Bar chart

    (d) Area chart

2. Chart / Graph has at least _____________ dimenstional relationship

    (a) Two   (b) Three

    (c) Four   (d) Five

3. _____________ is a pictorial representation of data, which has at least two dimensional relationships.

    (a) Graph   (b) Chart

    (c) Diagram   (d) All the above

4. The change the location of a chart, right click the chart and select.

    (a) Chart Type   (b) Source Data

    (c) Move here   (d) Chart Options

5. Give a suitable name to the diagram

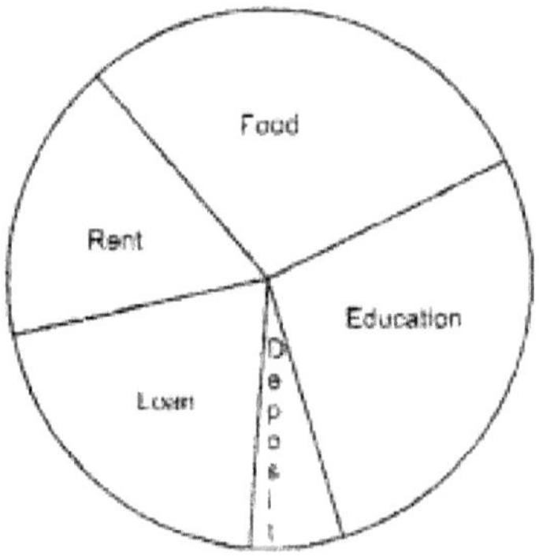

    (a) Bar chart   (b) Single line graph

    (c) Pie chart   (d) Area Chart

6. Which chart element details the data values and categories below the chart?

    (a) Data point.   (b) Data labels.

    (c) Data marker.   (d) Data table

 [1 Mark]

7. Name the different chart formats?

8. What is the importance of charts and graphs in business?

9. identify the type of a graph?

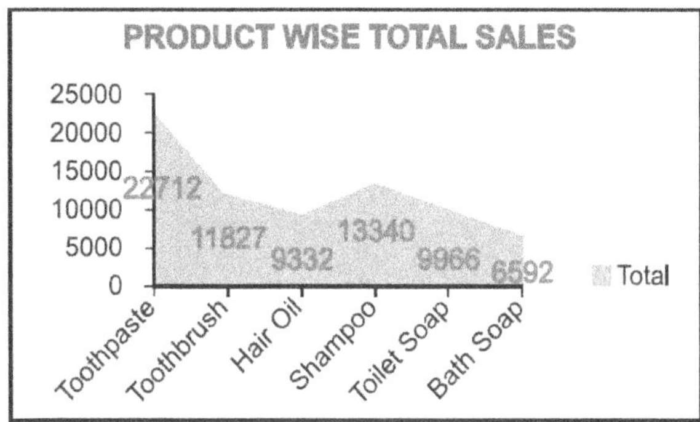

10. Define resizing of chart/Graph?

11. Give some examples of 2-D graphs ?

 [2 Marks]

12. Differentiate between Chart area and Chart wall?

13. Identify the type of chart

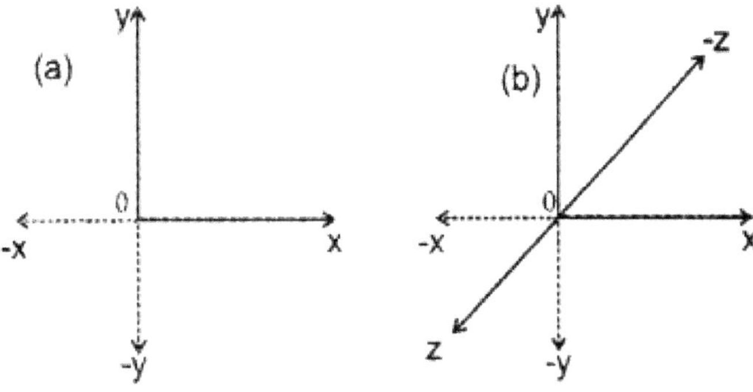

14. What is a 3-D chart?

15. Is there any difference between

   1. A column chart and

   2. A bar chart?

   Substantiate your answer

16. Explain the function of doughnut chart?

Short Answer Type - II   [3 Marks]

17. What does percentage in chart represent and how it being calculated by the software?

18. What are the difference between 2D charts and 3D charts

19. What are the different types of charts?

Long Answer Type   [5 Marks]

Q20. Differentiate between pie charts, line charts and column charts respectively?

Q21. The net profits of a firm for the last six years are given below. Draw a line chart.

Year	Net Profit
2009	1,25,800
2010	2,38,400
2011	1,86,500
2012	1,54,900
2013	2,51,000
2014	3,00,000

Data Base Management System for Accounting

Summary

Meaning of Database

Data is the most important component in any work that we do. We either use existing data or generate more data. When this data is gathered and analysed it yields information. The word "data" is the plural of the word "datum" which means facts. Thus, data means facts. These may be numeric, textual, pictorial or even vocal. And therefore, many different types of data are handled by information technology, e.g., text, voice and picture.

A data type in a programming language is a set of data with values having predefined characteristics. Examples of data types are integer, floating point number, character, string and pointer, usually a limited number of such data types come built into a language. The language usually signifies the range of values for a given data type, how the values are processed by the computer and how they are stored. With object oriented programming a programmer can create new data types to meet application needs.

Database is a general term for any collection of related information stored in a logical way on a computer. A number of general purpose database programmes are available for PCs of which the best known is probably Microsoft's Access. Using such software one can define new databases enter information and process the information in various ways. One of the most important processing operations is to search for data that matches certain criteria. In the transactional database model, the database is divided into a number of tables. Each table consists of a number of record.

There Are Majorly Four Types of Database

- Network Database: When the details of multiple members can be linked to the files of multiple owners and vice versa, it is called a network database.
- Hierarchical Database: When the data stored in the form of records and is connected to each other through links is called hierarchical database. Each record comprises fields and each field comprises only one value.
- Relational Database: When the data is organised as a set of tables comprising rows and columns with a pre-defined relationship with one another, it is called a relational database.
- Object-oriented Database – the information is represented as objects, with different types of relationships possible between two or more objects. Such databases use an object-oriented programming language for development.

Advantage of database/data source

1. All of the information is together
2. The information is portable

3. Information can be accessed at any time

4. Many users can access the same database at the same time.

5. Reduced data entry, storage and retrieval cost.

Disadvantages of database/Data source

1. Designing of database is a complex and time consuming process

2. Initial training is required for all the users

3. Installation cost is high

Components/Elements of Database System

1. **Fields**: Individual pieces of data in a database are called fields.

2. **Table**: rows and columns to present fields in a database is called table. When creating a table, the characteristics of each field to be defined.

3. **Forms**: Forms are used to enter or modify data (fields) in to tables. Forms allow the user to display the data in a Table or Query.

4. **Query**: Query is a question. Queries are used to view, change and analyse data in different ways. It creates a new table from the existing tables based upon the question/ request asked to the data base.

5. **Reports**: It is used to create and present information based on queries in a easily readable format

Planning (or Designing) A Database/Data Source

The first step in creating a database is to list down the various fields which are necessary for creating a database. The listed fields are used to create tables of the database. While entering fields into Tables, a primary key or an identifier is to be set for each table.

The primary key field cannot be left blank. The relationships of entities or tables can be created with the support of primary key. The relationships may be

- One -to-One

- One -to-Many

- Many-to-Many

The database created on the basis of relationships between different data tables is called relational database. The database design can be used to describe the structure of different parts of the overall data base. Avoiding the duplication of attributes/ fields is key criteria of database design.

Relations: In relational data model, the data is organised into tables(in the form of rows and columns) called relations

Attribute: A column in a relation.

Primary Key: A column or set of columns that uniquely identifies a row within a table is called primary key.

Candidate Key: Candidate keys are set of fields (columns with unique values) in the relation that are eligible to act as a primary key.

Alternate Key: A candidate key that is not the primary key is called alternate key.

Identification of Data to Be Stored in Tables

Tables allow us to create the framework for storing information in the database. Each column (also called 'field') of the table corresponds to a specific characteristic (or 'attribute' in database terms) of the stored information. Each row (also called 'record') corresponds to a particular instance of the information.

A set of tables often with well established relationships between them constitutes the database covering total spectrum of stored information. The term 'database design' can be used to describe the structure of different parts of the overall database.

Creating of Table in Access shows three columns i.e. Field Name, Data Type and description, which define the schema of a table is created. Field name refers to the column name of the table being created. Access supports different data types like Text, remove, Number, Date/ Time, Auto Number, Yes/No, OLE object and Hyperlink.

Creating Database Tables

1. click on the Start button on the Windows Taskbar

2. All Programs; then point to Microsoft Office; and then click Microsoft Office Access 2007.

3. Start > All Programs > Microsoft Office > Microsoft Access 2007)

4. You will be taken to the 'Getting Started with Microsoft Access' Screen . This screen is divided into three sections. The 'Template Categories' section on the left is for previewing and downloading standard database templates. In the centre you will see the 'New Blank Database' section for starting straightaway with a new database. On the right side is the 'Open Recent Database' section for opening the existing database files.

5. Click on Blank Database under central section. This will open up a dialogue box on the right section asking for database file name. This dialogue box could have also been opened by Clicking on the Office button located at the upper left corner of the screen and then Clicking New at the drop down menu

6. Enter the file name 'Pay Roll Application' and then click on the Create button .

    Avoiding duplication of information is key criteria of database design, which is achieved by breaking up of information into separate but related tables; and this process is called normalisation. We will also have to establish links between different tables so as to reconstruct the original information; and these links in database terms are called relationships. The database created on the basis of such relationships between different data tables is called relational database.

The process of matching rows in two tables based on their primary and foreign keys is called a Join. Joins along with Structured Query Language (SQL) serve as valuable tools for manipulating tables. But, these topics are beyond the scope of this book, and hence not elaborated further.

Creation of Query in Microsoft Access

The Queries provide the real power to a database in terms of its capabilities to answer more complex requests (or queries). In case of Access, Queries provide the capability of combining data from multiple tables and placing specific conditions for the retrieval of data. In its simplest form, you may consider a Query to be another tabular view of your data showing information from one or more tables.

Steps "=

1. Click on Create > Query Design. A Show Table dialogue box will appear with a Query Table in the background

2. In case you do not see this dialogue box click on Design > Show Table

3. In the Show Table dialogue box, select a table and click Add button to add it in the relationship window. Add all the five tables in this manner. Close the Show Table dialogue box by clicking on Close button

4. In working area above the Query Table, you will see all five table objects (with complete list of their fields) along with the one-to one relationship that has been established between tables earlier

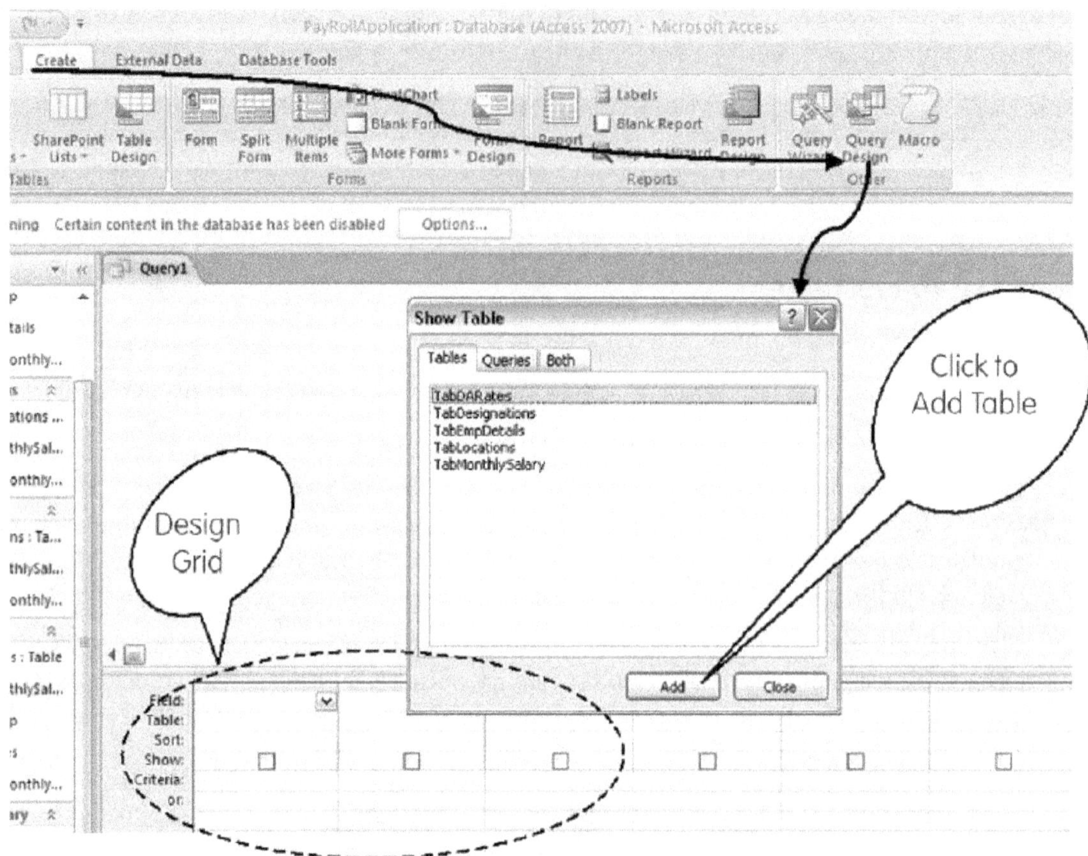

Creation of Forms in Microsoft Access

The Access 2007 provides facility for creation of a Simple Form wherein you can enter information for one record at a time. Access also provides tools for creation of a Split Form which shows the underlying datasheet in one half of the section and a Form in other half for entering information in the record selected in the datasheet. The two views in this form are synchronised so that scrolling in one view causes the scrolling of other view to same location of the record.

Create a form from an existing table or query in Access

To create a form from a table or query in your database, in the Navigation Pane, click the table or query that contains the data for your form, and on the Create tab, click Form.

Access creates a form and displays it in Layout view. You can make design changes like adjusting the size of the text boxes to fit the data, if necessary. For more information, see the article on using the form tool.

Create a blank form in Access

1. To create a form with no controls or preformatted elements: On the Create tab, click Blank Form. Access opens a blank form in Layout view, and displays the Field List pane.

2. In the Field List pane, click the plus sign (+) next to the table or tables that contain the fields that you want to see on the form.

3. To add a field to the form, double-click it or drag it onto the form. To add several fields at once, hold down CTRL and click several fields, and then drag them onto the form at the same time.

4. Use the tools in the Controls group on the Form Layout Tools tab to add a logo, title, page numbers, or the date and time to the form.

5. If you want to add a wider variety of controls to the form, click Design and use the tools in the Controls group

   To create a new split form by using the Split Form tool, in the Navigation Pane, click the table or query that contains the data, and then on the Create tab, click More Forms, and then click Split Form.

   Access creates the form and you can make design changes to the form. For example, you can adjust the size of the text boxes to fit the data, if necessary. For more information on working with a split form, see the article on creating a split form.

   Create a form that displays multiple records in Access

   A multiple item form, also known as a continuous form, and is useful if you want a form that displays multiple records but is more customizable than a datasheet, you can use the Multiple Items tool.

   1. In the Navigation Pane, click the table or query that contains the data you want to see on your form.

   2. On the Create tab and click More Forms > Multiple Items.

Creation of Reports in Microsoft Access

Accounting report display information that is acquired from data processing and transformation in an organised manner. Reports sent to reduce the level of uncertainly associated with decision-makers and also influence their positive actions. The output of the computerised is accounting reports. Financial accounting Reports such a Cash Books, Bank Book, Ledger and Trial Balance may be generated in Access by adhering to the report generation process.

The Report Wizard walks you through a series of decisions in order to build a report. To create a report using the Report Wizard, follow the steps below.

1. On the Create tab in the Reports group, click Report Wizard. The wizard starts

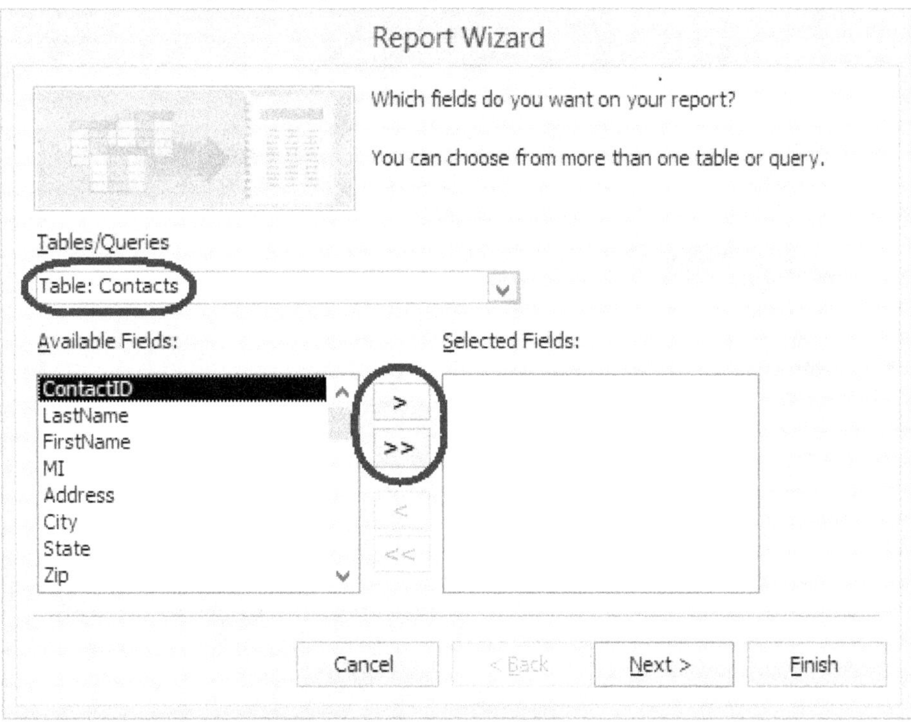

2. From the Tables/Queries drop-down list, select the table (or query) to base the report on. The fields for the selected table load in the Available Fields list box.

3. Move the fields to include on the report from the Available Fields list box to the Selected Fields list box. To do so, double-click a field name to move it or highlight the field name and click >. To move all fields at once, click >>.

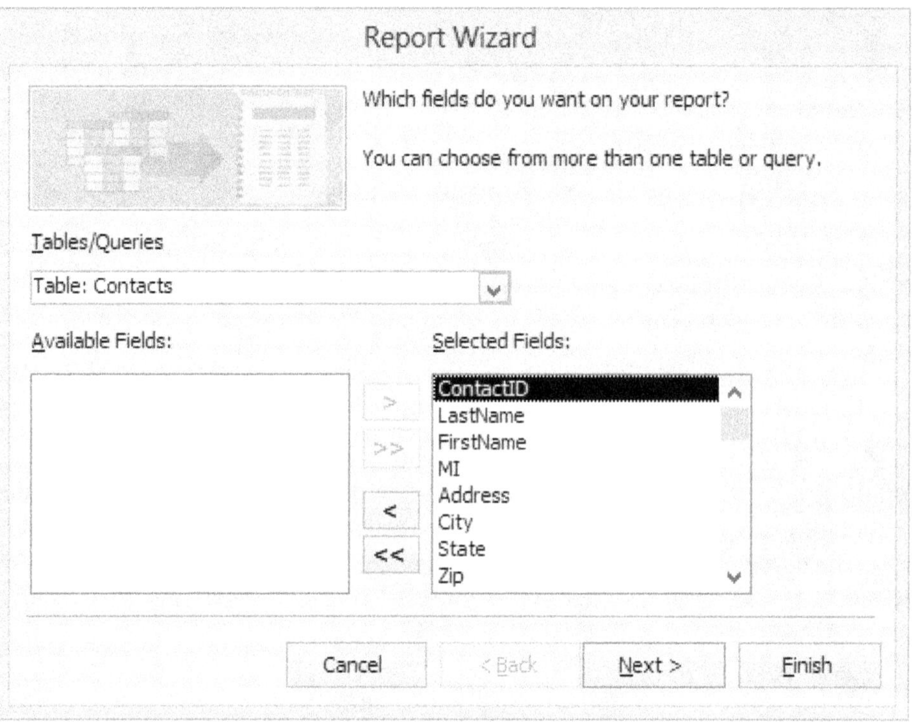

4. Click Next >.

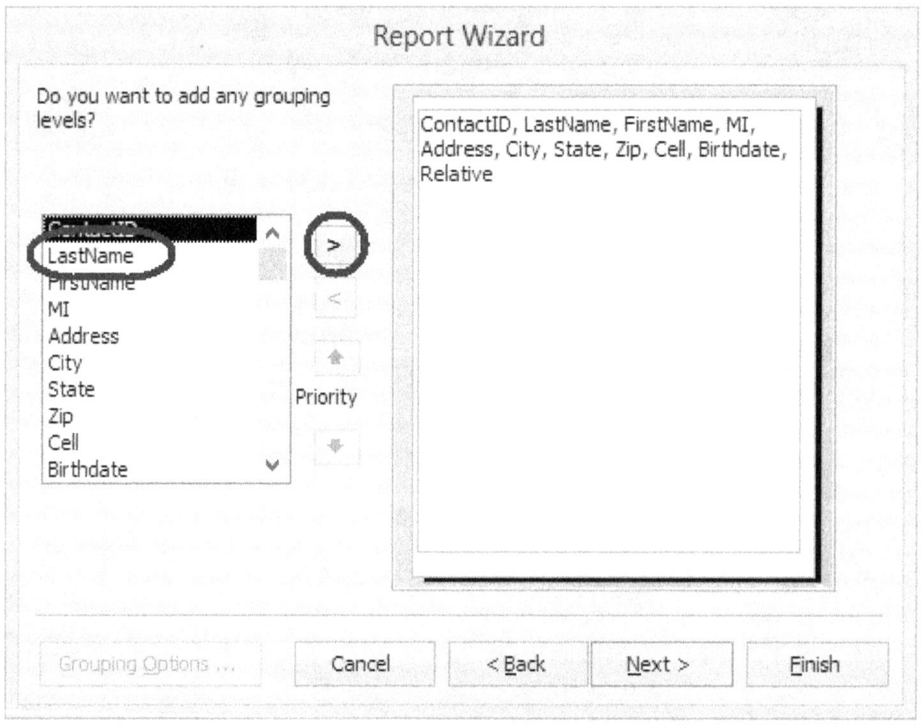

5. To group records on the report by a particular field, highlight the field in the list box and click >.

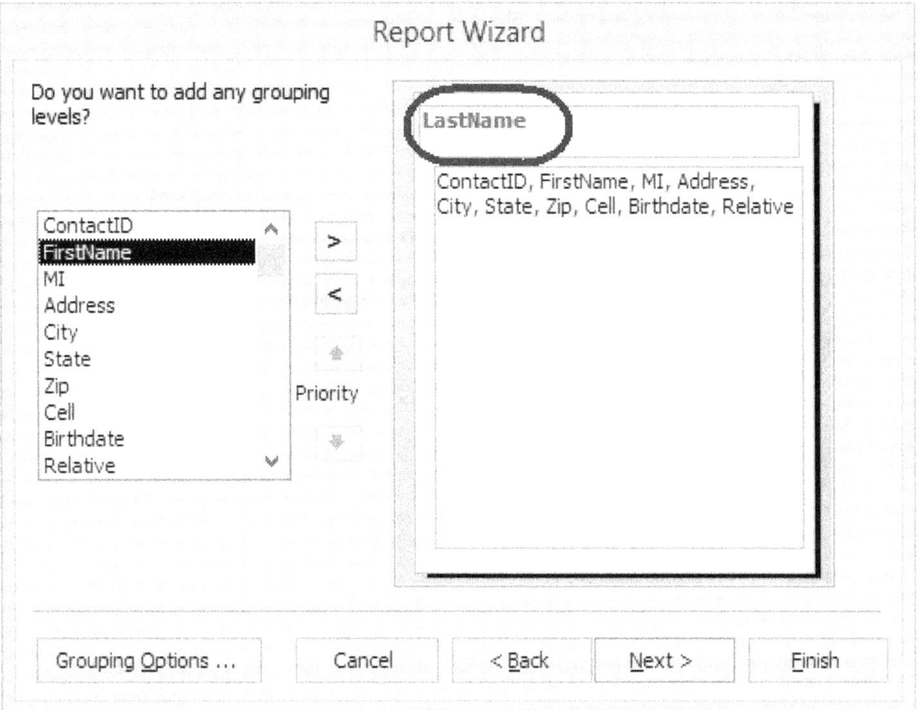

6. Add more grouping levels if desired. You can use the arrows to change the order of the grouping levels if needed.

7. When you finish defining how you want records grouped, click Next >.

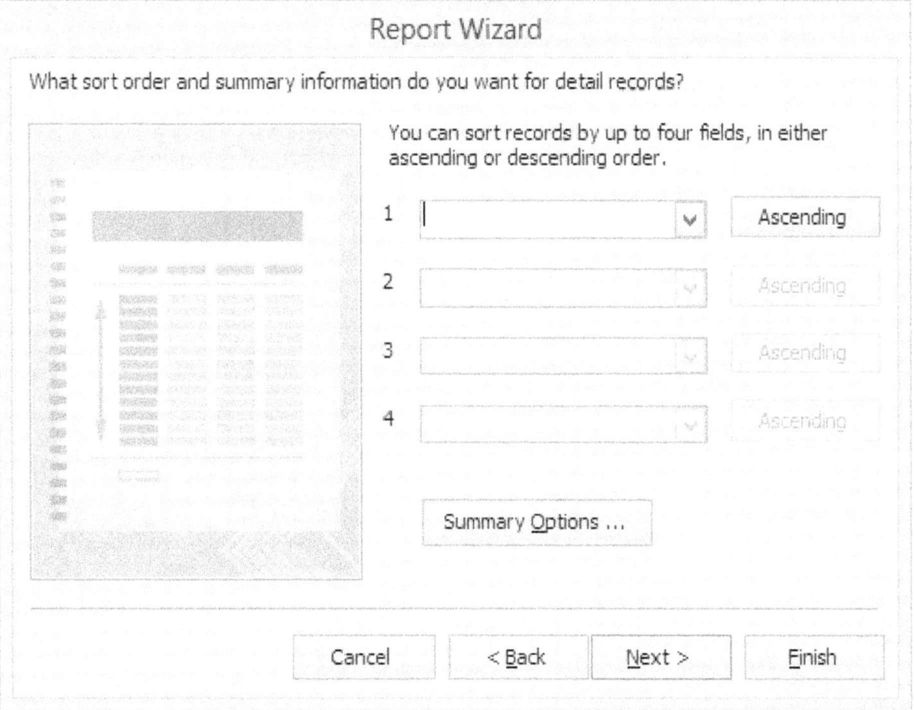

8. In the first drop-down list, select the field to sort records by. By default, records will be sorted in ascending order by the field you select. If you want to sort in descending order, click the Ascending button to change its label to "Descending".

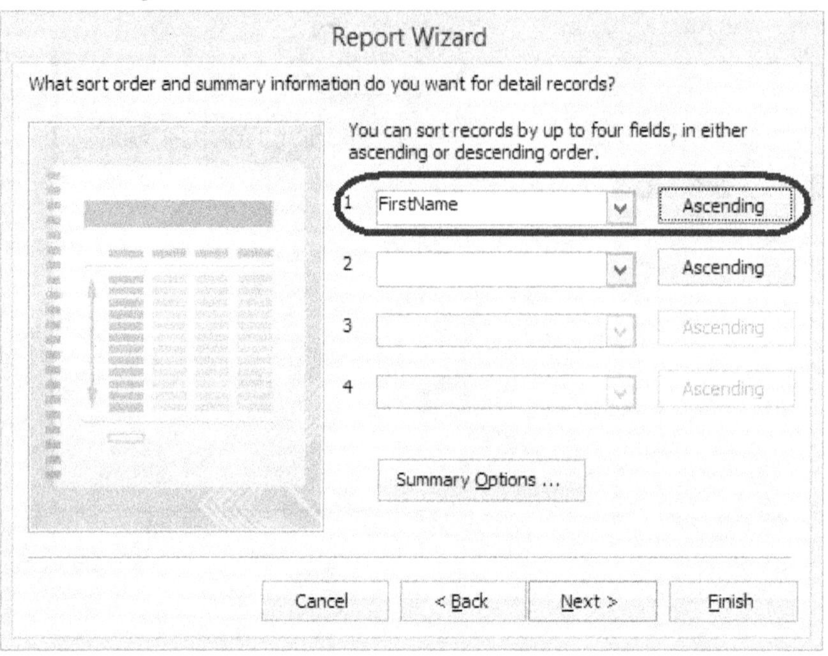

9. You can specify up to four levels of sorting. When you finish specifying sorting options, click Next >.

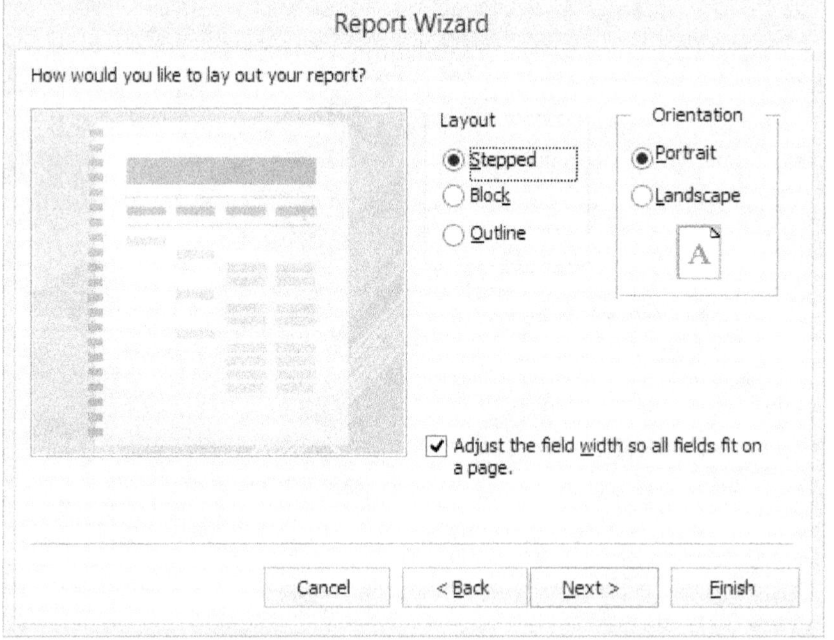

10. In the Layout field, select the format of the report. Your options are "Stepped", "Block", and "Outline". (Try the options to see a preview of the report layouts.)

11. In the Orientation field, select whether to lay out the report in portrait or landscape mode.

12. If you want all fields to fit on a single page, ensure the Adjust the field width so all fields fit on a page check box is marked.

13. Click Next >.

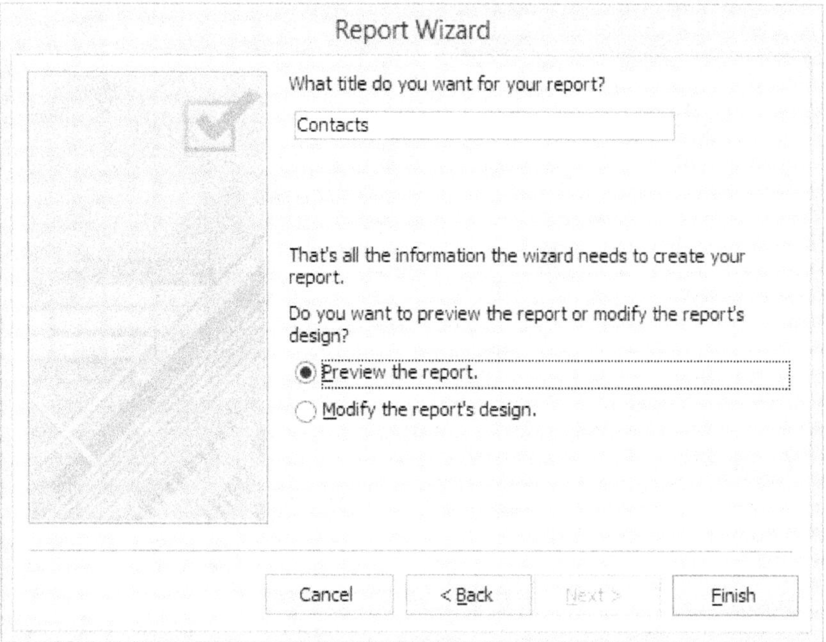

14. Enter a title for the report.

15. **Select an option for the view you want to open the report in. Your options are:**

    (a) Preview the report (opens in Print Preview mode).

    (b) Modify the report's design (opens in Design view).

16. Click Finish. The report loads in the view you selected.

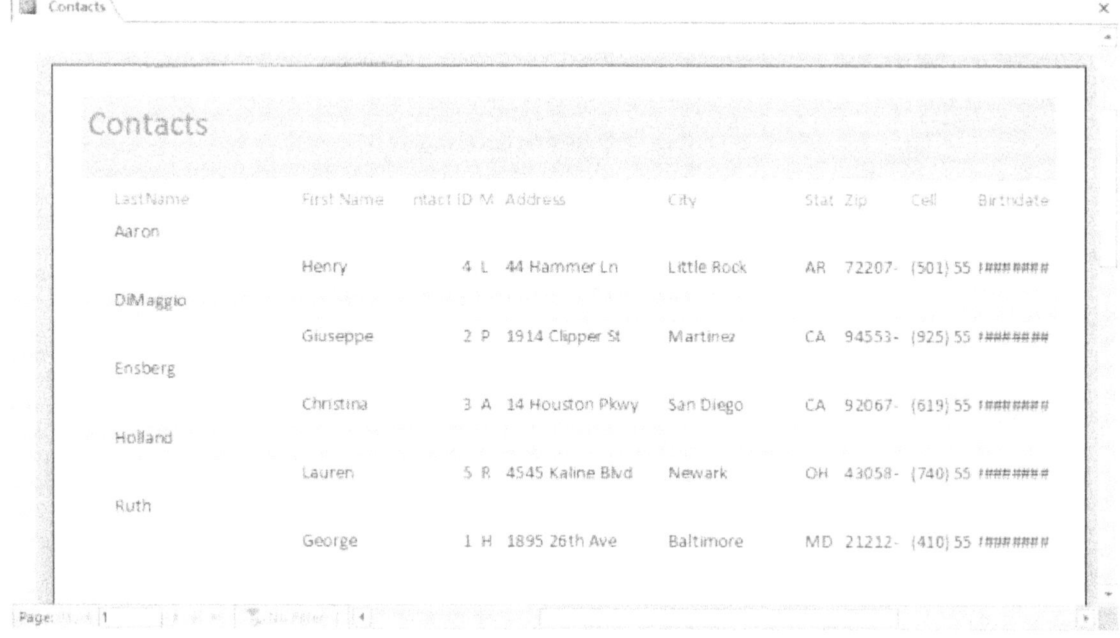

Print Preview

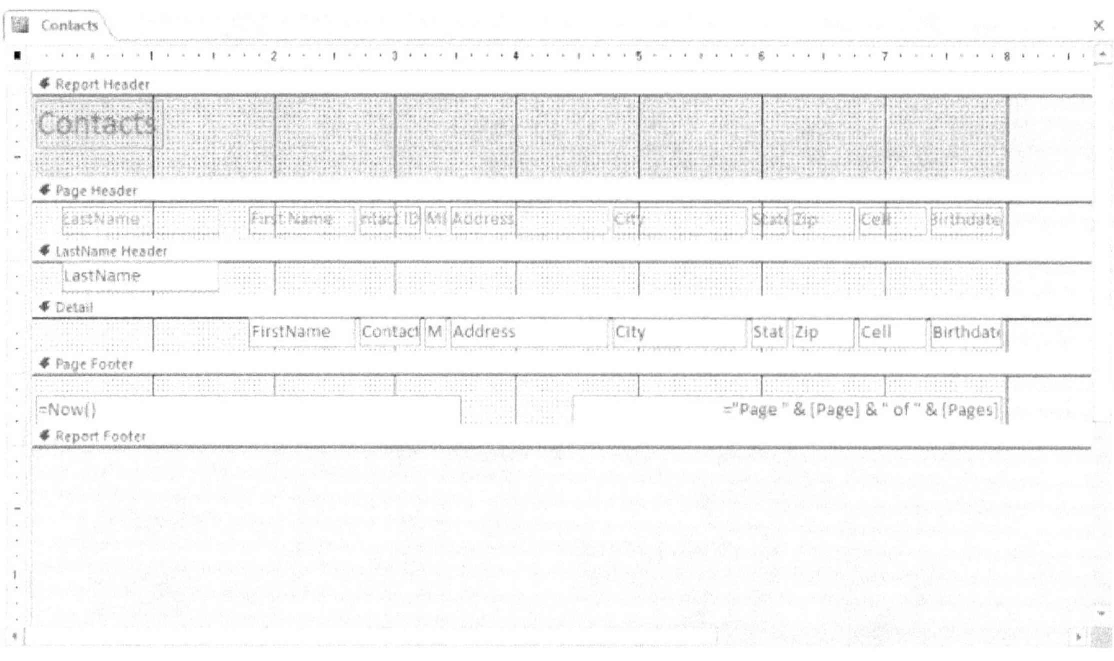

Design view

Multiple Choice Questions   [1 Mark]

1) What is fullform of DBMS?
   (a) Data Base Management Substance   (b) Data Base Management System
   (c) Data Base Managing System   (d) Data Base Maintaining System

2) Which is not DBMS software?
   (a) Oracle   (b) Access
   (c) Excel   (d) SQL Server

3) Where can you find data types and key of table entries?
   (a) Table view   (b) Design view
   (c) Report view   (d) None

4) From where can you make new table?
   (a) Create   (b) Home
   (c) Insert   (d) Design

5) What is not present in database tools option?
   (a) Relationships   (b) Create table
   (c) Analyze pane   (d) Macros

6) The query is completed when we see data in _____
   (a) Design view   (b) Edit view
   (c) Datasheet view   (d) Relationship table

7) Primary key in a table cannot have __________

  (a) Unique values   (b) Repeated values

  (c) Auto number as data type   (d) None

8) Horizontal row of the table is called ______

  (a) Data entry   (b) Record

  (c) Row   (d) Field

9) The term 'field' as applied to database table means ____

  (a) Vertical column of table   (b) Horizontal row of table

  (c) Name of table   (d) None

10) Which is not one of the advantage of database management system?

  (a) Reduce data redundancy   (b) Increase data consistency

  (c) Enhance efficiency   (d) Save space

Very Short Answer Type   **[1 Mark]**

1) What is normalization?

Ans. Normalisation is the process for removing data redundancy.

2) Where can we use desktop databases? Give one example of desktop database

Ans. the desktop databases – residing on standard personal computers – are oriented toward single-user applications

3) What is relational database?

Ans. Since the data stored in different tables may be related, such relationship is implemented by establishing links between tables. The database created on the basis of such relationships between different tables is called relational database.

4) What is primary key?

Ans. Primary key consists of minimum possible one or more than one attributes of a table, which uniquely identifies each row of that table

5) What is foreign key?

Ans. Foreign key consists of set of attributes, which from primary key in another (related) table

6) What is SQL?

Ans. SQL stands for Structured Query Language and it helps in data manipulation and calculation

7) What is wizard?

Ans. Wizards that will guide you through several steps for automatic creation of a database of your choice as well as linked queries and forms.

8) What functions are available in MS Access to take input, store and display data?

Ans. Tables, query, form, report

9) Why do we use form to insert data?

Ans. To make it less tedious and more convenient and avoid mistakes

10) Which are the two types of form in Access?

Ans. The Access 2007 provides facility for creation of a Simple Form wherein you can enter information for one record at a time. Access also provides tools for creation of a Split Form which shows the underlying datasheet in one half of the section and a Form in other half for entering information in the record selected in the datasheet.

Short Answer Type - I   [2 Marks]

1) Difference between desktop database and server database

Ans. Most of Computerised Accounting Systems are multi-user systems. These systems use 'server database' unlike single-user (or desktop) systems using 'desktop database'. In a multi user system, a user interacts with the software though the user interface, which is also termed as 'front-end'. Database, which is kept on a server, is termed as a 'back-end. MS-Access is an example of 'desktop database'. Oracle, SQL Server, IBMDB2 is examples of 'server databases', Desktop databases may be satisfactory for SOHO (Small Office Home Office) organisations as they offer inexpensive and simple solutions to many of business data storage and processing requirements

2) Why do we form relationships by storing data in different tables?

Ans. Avoiding duplication of information is key criteria of database design, which is achieved by breaking up of information into separate but related tables; and this process is called normalisation. We will also have to establish links between different tables so as to reconstruct the original information; and these links in database terms are called relationships.

3) What is required for a relationship between tables? Explain types of key fields

Ans. In order to establish relationship between any two tables, we will have to insert columns with matching values in the two related tables. The two common fields used in a relationship between tables are called the key fields. Primary key consists of minimum possible one or more than one attributes of a table, which uniquely identifies each row of that table. Foreign key consists of set of attributes, which from primary key in another (related) table

4) What are the uses of query in database?

Ans. The Queries provide the real power to a database in terms of its capabilities to answer more complex requests (or queries). In case of Access, Queries provide the capability of combining data from multiple tables and placing specific conditions for the retrieval of data. In its simplest form, you may consider a Query to be another tabular view of your data showing information from one or more tables

5) What are uses of report?

Ans. A Report is also used for the print purpose, though it allows for more flexibility in selecting the fields to print, and to have more control on the overall layout and format of the print output. The Report in Access is thus another object which is designed to print information from the database on to the screen, or to a file or directly to the printer.

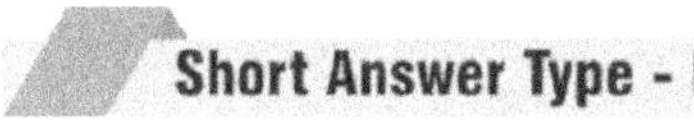
Short Answer Type - II   [3 Marks]

1. Define Candidate Key and Alternate Key with suitable examples from a table containing some meaningful data.

Ans. A table may have more than one such attribute/group of attributes that identifies a tuple uniquely, all such attribute(s) are known as Candidate Keys. All the candidate key except primary key are called Alternate key.

Table: Employee (empno, aadhar_no, voter_id, ename, deptno, sal, city)

In the above table Employee, empno,aadhar_no, voter_id all are candidate key If we define empno as primary key then remaining candidate keys will be alternate key.

2. Explain database management system?

Ans. Database Management System (DBMS) : Database is an important programme or software. It records all the useful and relevant information relating to a business at one centralized place. Data may relate to number of files, salaries appointments, retirements, sales, purchases, accounts receivables and accounts payable, incomes and expenditures etc. These data are generally stored on a floppy discs. The Database Management (DBM) converts the data into useful information. The data fed into the computer may be rearranged in a desired order and different calculations can be performed according to the need of the business. So, If the data of sales have been fed into the computer, we may very well know total sales of the month, average sale, the amount of collection, percentage of profit on sales, etc,

3. What do you understand by DBMS. Give names of two commarly available DBMS softwares?

Ans. DBMS stands Database Management System, which is kind of software used to design the store, manage, defined, and retrieve the data in the database.

- It is the system software used for managing as well as establishing the database. It makes it possible for the end-user to delete, create, update, and read the data within the database.

- It serves as the interface among the end-users and the databases, which ensures the data is organized consistently and accessible easily.

- It involve the performance tuning and monitoring, backup, change management, recovery and security of the data.

- The two commonly DBMS software easily available named are Oracle and Microsoft Access.

4. With suitable example illustrate the meaning of 'attributes' as applied to database?   **(NCERT)**

Ans. Entities are presented by means of their properties, called attributes. All attributes have values. For example, a student entity may have name, class, and age as attributes. Types **of Attributes**:-

- Simple Attribute: - Simple attributes are atomic values, which cannot be divided further. For example, a student's phone number is an atomic value of 10 digits.

- Composite Attribute:- Composite attributes are made of more than one simple attribute.

- Derived attribute:- Derived attributes are the attributes that do not exist in the physical database, but their values are derived from other attributes present in the database. For example Age can be derived from date of Birth.

- Multi-value attribute:- Multi-value attributes may contain more than one value. For example, a person can have more than one phone number, email address etc.

5. What do you understand by terms 'key field' , 'primary key' and 'secondary key' in a database?

Ans. (1) Primary Key-

- Primary key in the database is the constraint that uniquely defines or identifies every record in the table.

- It must contain unique values and could not contain the null values.

- Table could have only one primary key and it comprises multiple or single fields.

(2) Secondary Key-

- Secondary key is the key, which has not been chosen to be the primary key. In short, a candidate key that is not selected as the primary key will be called as the secondary key.

- In short, it is defined as the field, which is the basis for retrieval is referred to as the secondary key.

- Candidate key is the attributes set or the attribute, which the user could consider as the Primary key.

(3) Key Field-

- Key field is the field that holds the unique data that identifies the record from all the other databases.

- Customer name, account number, and product code are the key fields. And as an identifier, every key value needs to be unique in each and every record. **The key field** is the one which is very vital as it has unique data, **the primary key** is the one that attributes identify the record and **the secondary key** is the one which is made on the field that the user would like to index for the faster searches.

6. Distinguish between database and database management system

Ans. Database is a collection of data. It consists of inter-related data tables.

Database management system is a collection of programs that enables users to work on database. DBMS enables the user to create and maintain a database.

7. List down the advantages of using Database.

Ans. Advantage of database/ data source:

- All of the information is together

- The information is portable

- Information can be accessed at any time

- Many users can access the same database at the same time.

- Reduced data entry, storage and retrieval cost.

8. What is data?

Ans. Data is the most important component in any work that we do. We either use existing data or generate more data. When this data is gathered and analysed it yields information. The word "data" is the plural of the word "datum" which means facts. Thus, data means facts. These may be numeric, textual, pictorial or even vocal. And therefore, many different types of data are handled by information technology, e.g., text, voice and picture.

Long Answer Type   [5 Marks]

1. What do you understand by 'Form' object in Access and how are they useful?   **(NCERT)**

Ans. Form is a database object used for the process of data entry and data editing.

- Form can be used to customize your presentation of data allowing you to keep the data fields you want.

- Forms can also be used to control the application execution.

Thus, the form is an object that displays the data stored in your Access desktop database. It has the following uses-

1. Forms are used to enter, edit or to display data from the tables or queries i.e. primarily for data input and display.

2. Forms make it easier to view or get to the items of the database you want.

3. Forms are also used to create a user interface for a database application.

4. Forms are also used to control access to data in terms of which fields of data should display.

2. What do you understand by database? What are the ways in which data is stored and queried in an Access database?

Ans. A data set is a coordinated assortment of organized data, or information, normally put away electronically in a PC framework. The information would then be able to be handily gotten to, oversaw, adjusted, refreshed, controlled, and coordinated. Most information bases utilize organized question language (SQL) for composing and questioning information.

- Tables. An information base table is comparable in appearance to a bookkeeping page, in that information is put away in lines and sections.

- Structures. Structures permit you to make a UI in which you can enter and alter your information.

- Reports. Reports are what you use to arrange, sum up and present information.

- Questions.

- Macros.

- Modules.

3. Describe in brief the function of 'Table', 'Query', 'Form' and 'Report' object of Access program?

Ans. At the point when you make an information base in Microsoft Access, you have various sorts of item: tables, structures, reports, inquiries, macros and modules. You may likewise have – relying upon which rendition of Microsoft Access you're utilizing – information access pages. Yet, for the occasion, we'll adhere to the fundamental six sorts of item and go through every one of these thusly.

- Tables store information. Nothing else, no arranging, no arranging, no sifting, no figuring, simply putting away. The most essential, key assignment of an information base is to store information for simple recovery and the board, and it's tables that accomplish this jackass work. In the event that you've at any point worked in Excel, a table will be recognizable to **you in appearance – they look rather like Excel accounting pages**:

- Structures make that information accessible on the screen. With a structure, you can see and alter the information, show it pleasantly, sort it, add to it, erase it, etc. Structures let you work with your information

- Reports additionally show your information, however on paper. Not at all like Forms, Reports don't permit you to alter the information – they are intended to be static. All things considered, whenever you've printed your information on paper (or as a PDF) it will be quite static, so Reports mirror that.

- Regardless of whether it's an item list (as in the screen capture beneath) or a staff index, a receipt or an assembling agenda, if it's information on paper, it's a reports

4. Write the steps to create blank forms in Microsoft access?

Ans. To create a form with no controls or preformatted elements: On the Create tab, click Blank Form. Access opens a blank form in Layout view, and displays the Field List pane.

- In the Field List pane, click the plus sign (+) next to the table or tables that contain the fields that you want to see on the form.

- To add a field to the form, double-click it or drag it onto the form. To add several fields at once, hold down CTRL and click several fields, and then drag them onto the form at the same time.

- Use the tools in the Controls group on the Form Layout Tools tab to add a logo, title, page numbers, or the date and time to the form.

- If you want to add a wider variety of controls to the form, click Design and use the tools in the Controls group

5. Open the company information table ?

Ans. This is the company salary information of the electrical department.

SI.NO	MONTH/year	NAME	Rank	Salary
1	January 2020	Riaz Leo	Cheif electrician	100000
2	January 2020	Usman Emath	Assistant electrician	70000
3	January 2020	Beno Elzi	HR	90000
4	January 2020	Amanda Mary	EEE n-charge	50000
5	January 2020	Natasha Abi	Board controller	30000
6	January 2020	Jesika Jeno	Trainee	20000

ANSWERS & SOLUTIONS

PART-I

CHAPTER-1

Accounting for Partnership Firms – Fundamentals

1. (d)   **2.** (d)   **3.** (d)   **4.** (b)

5. (b)   **6.** (a)   **7.** (a)

8. Partners called individually - Partner Partners called collevtively - Firm

9. Misunderstanding and dispute can be easily resolved a partnership deed.

10. Fixed capital of partners may change :
   (i)   With further addition of capital.
   (ii) With the withdrawal of part of capital.

11. Interest on capital is allowed to compute a partner for contributing capital to be firm in excess of the profit sharing ratio.

12. In the case of partnership, profit and loss appropriation. Account is prepared after ascertaining net profit from profit & loss to show how profit is distributed among the partners VB, interest on capital, salary commission the partners, interest on drawings, profit share of partners etc.

13. (i) Minimum two partners.
   (ii) Maximum limit of partners is 50 (As per Sec. 464 of companies Act 2013)

14. Both oral and written terms and conditions of partnership and enforceable by law, however written partnership deed is better to resolve the misunderstanding and dispute at a later stage.

15. Journal

Date	Particulars	LF	DR ₹	CR ₹
2022 March 31	Ran's Current A/c To interest on drawings A/c (Being interest on drawings charged)		500	 500

16. Interest on drawings = (18000×4)

$$= 72000 \times \frac{6}{100} \times \frac{4.5}{12} = ₹1620$$

17. Loss after guarantee is ₹ 1,16,000 in the ratio 3 : 1.

i.e., ₹ 87000 to A and ₹ 29000 to C.

18. Profit and Loss Appropriation A/c for the year ending 31st March 2022

Particulars	Amount	Particulars	Amount
To interest on capital Jay　　　　5000 Vijay　　　4000	 9000	By profit & loss A/c (profit)	9000
	9000		**9000**

Note: Since total interest on capital is more than the profit so interest on capital can be paid only upto ₹ 9000 to Jay and Vijay in the ratio of 6000 : 4800 or 5 : 4.

Jay : $9000 \times \dfrac{5}{9} = ₹ 5000$

Vijay : $9000 \times \dfrac{4}{9} = ₹ 4000$

19. Statement Showing Adjustment

Particlars	Veena	Vasudha	Vandana	Total
(A) Interest on capital already credited @12 P.A.	9600	4800	6000	20400
Less : Interest should be credited @10% excess interest credited @2%	8000	4000	5000	17000
(B) Due to error profit will be increase ₹ 3400 so it should be credited in the ratio 7 : 6 : 4	1600	800	1000	3400
(C) Difference (A – B)	1400	1200	800	3400
	DR 200	CR 400	DR 200	–

Date	Particular	If	DR ₹	CR ₹
	Veena's Current A/c Dr Vandana's Current A/c Dr To Vasudha's Capital A/c (Beeing excess interest on capital credited now corrected).		200 200	 400

20. Profit and Loss Appropriation A/c for the year ending 31st March 2022.

Dr. **Cr.**

Particulars	Amount	Particulars	Amount
To profit transferred to Anita's Capital A/c 41000 Babita's Capital A/c 41000	 82,000	By profit & loss A/c 82000 Loss's interest & loss 3202 $\left(100000 \times \dfrac{8}{100} \times \dfrac{6}{16}\right)$	 82,000
	82,000		**82,000**

Note :

(i)   Interest on Loan allowed @ 6.2 P.A. in the   (not clear matter) of partnership dead.

(ii)   No. internal on capital .... on .... (not clear matter)

(iii) Profit sharing ratio will be .... (not clear matter) of partnership dead.

21. Calculation of Interest on Capital @8%P.A.

Veena	
On ₹ 200000 from 1 April to 30 June (3 Months)	4000
On ₹ 250000 from 1 July to 30 Sept. (3 Months)	5000
On ₹ 220000 from 1 Oct to 31 March (6 Months)	8800
Total ₹	17,800
Vasudha	
On ₹ 3,00,000 from 1 April to 30 June (3 Months)	6000
On ₹ 360000 from 1 July to 31 Dec. (6 Months)	14400
On ₹ 34500 from 1 Jan to 31 March (3 Months)	6900
Total ₹	27,300

22. Calculation of Interest on Drawings as at 31st March 2022 @ 9% P.A.

Date	Amount	Period/Months	Product
01.04.2021	16000	12	1,92,000
30.06.2021	15000	09	1,35,000
15.10.2021	10000	5.5	55000
31.12.2021	14000	03	42000
01.03.2022	11000	01	11000
	66,000	**Total of Product**	**4,35,000**

$$\textbf{Interest as Drawings} = \frac{\text{Total of Product} \times \text{Rate of Interest}}{100 \times 12}$$

$$\textbf{Interest on Drawings} = \frac{43500 \times 9}{100 \times 12} = ₹3262.50 \text{ or say } 3263$$

23. $\quad \text{Interest on Drawings} = \dfrac{\text{Total Amount} \times \text{Average Period} \times \text{Rate of Interest}}{100 \times 12}$

    (i)   Abhiyank's Interest on Drawings

$$(20000 \times 12) = \frac{240000 \times 5.5 \times 9}{100 \times 12} = ₹\,9900$$

    (ii)   Dipika's Interest on Drawings

$$(40000 \times 4) = \frac{160000 \times 7.5 \times 9}{100 \times 12} = ₹9000$$

24. Profit and Loss Appropriation A/c for the year ending 31st March 2022

DR   CR

Particulars	Amount	Particulars	Amount
To profit & loss A/c (loss) (200000 + 9000) To Kamal's Capital A/c	2,09,000 70,000	By loss transperred Anil's Capital A/c 186000 Sunil's Capital A/c 93000	 2,79000
	2,79000		**2,79000**

25. Adjustment Journal Entry

Date	Particlars		L$_F$	DR ₹	CR ₹
2022 March 31	Ashoka's Current A/c	Dr		6000	
	To Ravi's Current A/c				1000
	To Manoj's Current A/c				5000
	(Being interest on capital, salary and commission to parmers missed while distributing profit now adjusted)				

Statement Showing Adjustment

Particulars		Ravi	Ashok	Manoj	Total
(A)	Items Omitted				
	Interest on Capital	10000	4000	3000	17000
	Salary to Ravi	18000	–	–	18000
	Commission to Manoj	–	–	12000	12000
	Total	28000	4000	15000	47000
	Commission on Profit to Ravi				
	(100000 – 47000 = 53000 × 6/106)	3000			
		31000	4000	15000	50000
	Add : Profit share 3 : 1 : 1	30000	10000	10000	150000
	Amount should be credited	61000	14000	25000	100000

(B)	Due to commission profit was divided in ratio 3 : 1 : 1 so debited	60000	20000	20000	100000
(C)	Difference (A – B)	1000	6000	5000	
		CR	DR	DR	

26. Profit and Loss Appropriation A/c for the year ending 31st March 2022

Dr   **Cr**

Particulars	Amount	Particulars	Amount
To Interest on Capital		By Profit and Loss A/c 1,11,000	
Shailesh 5500		Less Rent 12000	99000
Shoubhik 5500	11000	By Interest on Drawings	
To Commission to Shailesh	9900	Shailesh 137	
(99000 × 10/100)		Shobhik 181	318
To Commission to Shoubhik	8910		
(99000 – 9900 = 89100)			
(89100 × 10/100)			
To Profit transferred			
Shailesh's Capital A/c 52131			
Shobhika's Capital A/c 17377	69508		
	99318		**99318**

Note : Calculation of Interest on Drawings :

Shailes : $350 \times 12 = \dfrac{4200 \times 6 \times 6.5}{100 \times 12} = 136.50$ or 137

Shobhik : $550 \times 12 = \dfrac{6600 \times 6 \times 5.5}{100 \times 12} = 181.50$ or 181

27. Ratio of effective capital of partners

Particulars	Product
Dharma = ₹ 60000 for 12 months	7,20,000
Sharma = ₹ 50000 for 6 months	
	3,00,000
= ₹ 70000 for 6 months	
	4,20,000
	7,20,000
Verma = ₹ 80000 for 8 months	6,40,000
	2,40,000
= ₹ 60000 for 4 months	8,80,000

Profit & Loss Approximation A/c for the year ending ....

Dr   **Cr**

Particular	Amount	Particular	Amount
To profit transfered to		By Net Profit	29000
Dharma (9/29) 9000			
Sharma (9/29) 9000			
Verma (11/29) 11000	29000		
	29000		**29000**

CHAPTER-2

Change In Profit Sharing Ratio

1. (d)   **2.** (b)   **3.** (a)   **4.** (c)

5. (b)   **6.** (a)   **7.** (b)   **8.** (b)

9. (d)   **10.** (d)

11. Revaluation Account-Debit side

12. (i) Retirement of a partner (ii) Death of a partner (iii) change in PSR.

13. Gaining ratio is the ratio in which remaining/continuing partners acquire the share of the outgoing partner(s).

14. Distributed among the partners in old profit sharing ratio

15. Gaining Partner, Sacrificing Partner

16. Bala's Capital A/c Dr. (Rs.50,000 × 1/10) 5,000, Anu's Capital A/c Cr.5,000

    W.NOTE.

    Sacrificed Share/ Gaining Share = Old Share – New Share

    Anu = 3/5 – 1/2 = 6 – 5/10 = 1/10 i.e. sacrifice made

    Bala = 2/5 – /2 = 4 – 5/10 = –1/10 (being negative, it is a gain)

17. C's capital a/c Dr., A's capital a/c Cr. By 13,500

    W.NOTE.net effect = 15000 + 60000 – 30000 = 45000 × 3/10 = 13500

    Sac of A = 3/10, B neither sac nor gain, C gain 3/10

18. A firm reconstituted in the event of.

- Change in the profit- sharing ratio among the existing partners
- Admission of a partner or partners
- The retirement of a partner

- Death of a partner
- The amalgamation of two or more partnership firms.

19. Investments are recorded in the book of a company at cost. However, in the market, it might change. It may be higher or lower than the book value. Investment fluctuation reserve is a reserve set aside out of profit to meet fall in the market value of the investment.

    The three types of the accounting treatment of Investment Fluctuation Reserve are.

    1. When the book value and market value of the investment are the same- The amount of investment fluctuation reserve is transferred to partners' capital account in their old profit-sharing ratio.

        - When the market value of investments is less than the book value- In this case, the treatment on investment fluctuation reserve depends on the amount of decrease.

        - When there is an increase in the market value of investment- The amount of investment fluctuation reserve is distributed among partners and an increase in the value of the investment is credited to revaluation account.

20. H's capital a/c Dr. = 16000,S's capital a/c Dr. = 4000, Advertisement suspense a/c Cr. = 20000

21. Calculation of Net Effect of Accumulated Profits/Losses

	Rs
General Reserves	1,60,000
Add: Profit and Losses a/c	80,000
	2,40,000
Less: Advertisement Suspense a/c	60,000
Net Effect	1,80,000

A's gain = 2/9, B = neither sac nor gain, C's sac = 2/9

A's Capital a/c Dr.	40000
To C's Capital a/c	40000

(For Adjustment of G R. P&L a/c balance and advertisement suspense a/c on change in Profit sharing ratio)

22. (b)	23. (c)	24. (a)	25. (a)	26. (d)

27. Dr   REVALUATION ACCOUNT   Cr.

Particulars	Rs.	Particulars	Rs.
To Stock A/c	20,000	By Land & Building A/c	1,00,000
To B's Capital A/c	10,000	By Provision for Doubtful	
To Gain on Revaluation		Debts A/c	25,000
transferred to:		By Salaries Payable A/c	15,000
A's Capital A/c 65,000		By Outstanding Expenses A/c	20,000
B's Capital A/c 39,000			
C's Capital A/c 26,000	1,30,000		
	1,60,000		**1,60,000**

28. Dr.   REVALUATION ACCOUNT   Cr.

Particulars	Rs.	Particulars	Rs.
To Stock A/c	10,000	By Building A/c	40,000
To Machinery A/c	15,900	By Sundry Creditors A/c	2,500
To Provision for Doubtful			
Debts A/c	2,200		
To Profit on Revaluation			
transferred to:			
A's Capital A/c (3/8)	5,400		
B's Capital A/c (3/8)	5,400		
C's Capital A/c (2/8)	3,600		
	42,500		**42,500**

CHAPTER-3

Reconstitution of a Partnership Firm - Admission of a Partner

1. (a)   **2.** (c)   **3.** (c)   **4.** (d)

5. (b)

6. Hidden goodwill will be difference between total capital on the bills of new partners capital for a given share and school capital of all partners.

7. Journal Entry

Revaluation A/c   Dr.

   To Liability A/c

8. According to only purchased goodwill cars be to the books.

9. Two rights acquired by new partner:

(i) Right to share the assets of the firm.

(ii) Right to share in the future profit of the firm.

10. To compensate the old partners for their

15.

Journal Entries

Date	Particulars		L.F.	Dr. (Rs.)	Cr. (Rs.)
(i)	Cash/Bank A/c	Dr.		120,000	
	To Ankit Capital A/c				120,000
	(Amount brought by Ankit for Capital)				

(ii)	Ankit Current A/c	Dr.		30,000	
	To Ajay's Capital A/c				15,000
	To Lakshya's Capital A/c				15,000
	(distributed in SR)				

Calculation of Hidden Goodwill

Total capital of firm 1,95,000 + 1,35,000 + 1,20,000 = 4,50,000

Capital of firm $= 1,20,000 \times \dfrac{5}{1} = $ Rs.6,00,000

Goodwill = 6,00,000 – 4,50,000 = 1,50,000

Share of Ankit $= 1,50,000 \times \dfrac{1}{5} = $ Rs.30,000

16.

Journal Entry

Date	Particulars		L.F.	Dr. (Rs.)	Cr. (Rs.)
2021 April 1	No entry is that to be passed when premium paid is privately)				
2022 April 1	Cash A/c To Primium for Goodwill A/c (Being cash brought by Hanu for his share of goodwill)	Dr.		40,000	40,000
	Premium for Goodwill To Kanu Capital A/c To Manu Capital A/c To Tanu Capital A/c (Goodwill distributed in SR)	Dr.		40,000	20,000 10,000 10,000
	To Kanu's Capital A/c To Manu's Capital A/c To Tanu's Capital A/c To Bank/Cash A/c (Being half of the goodwill withdrawn by old partners)	Dr. Dr. Dr.		10,000 5,000 5,000	20,000

Calculation of New Profit Sharing Ratio.

(i) On Tanu's Admission

$1 - \dfrac{1}{4} = \dfrac{3}{4}$ Remaining

Kanu $= \dfrac{3}{4} \times \dfrac{2}{3} = \dfrac{6}{12}$,　Manu $\dfrac{3}{4} \times \dfrac{1}{3} = \dfrac{3}{12}$,　Tanu $\dfrac{1}{4}$ or $\dfrac{3}{12}$

Or 6 : 3 : 3 or 2 : 1 : 1

(ii) On Hanu's Admission:

$$1 - \frac{1}{5} = \frac{4}{5}$$

$$\text{Kanu} = \frac{4}{5} \times \frac{6}{12} = \frac{2}{5}$$

$$\text{Manu} = \frac{4}{5} \times \frac{3}{12} = \frac{1}{5}$$

$$\text{Tanu} = \frac{4}{5} \times \frac{3}{12} = \frac{1}{5}$$

$$\text{Hanu} = \frac{1}{5}$$

New Ratio 2 : 1 : 1 : 1

17.

Journal

Date	Particulars		L.F.	Dr. (Rs.)	Cr. (Rs.)
(1)	Workmen's Compensation Reserve A/c	Dr.		80,000	
	Revaluation A/c			20,000	
	To claim for workmen				100,000
	(Workmen compensation claim adjusted)				
(2)	Investment Fluctation Reserve A/c	Dr.		30,000	
	To Investments				18,000
	To Aditya's Capital A/c				4,800
	To Gourav's Capital A/c				4,800
	To Madhur's Capital A/c				2,400
	(Being Loss on investment adjusted and excess amount of reserve transferred)				
(3)	Aditya's Capital A/c	Dr.		8,000	
	To Gourav's Capital A/c	Dr.		8,000	
	To Madhur's Capital A/c	Dr.		4,000	
	To Revaluation A/c				20,000
	(Being loss on revaluation debited in old profit sharing ration)				

18. (I) Share of Mukul & Nakul $= \frac{3}{5}, \frac{2}{5}$

(II) Share of Bakul $= \frac{1}{5}$

(III) Remaining share $= 1 - \frac{1}{5} = \frac{4}{5}$

(IV) Mukul $\dfrac{4}{5} \times \dfrac{3}{5} = \dfrac{12}{25}$ Nakul $\dfrac{2}{5} \times \dfrac{4}{5} = \dfrac{8}{25}$

Step I: Total Capital of firm $= 800 \times \dfrac{5}{1} = 400,000$

Step II: Mukul $40,000 \times \dfrac{12}{25} = \text{Rs.} 1,92,000$

Nakul $40,000 \times \dfrac{8}{25} = \text{Rs.} 1,28,000$

Bakul $40,000 \times \dfrac{1}{25} = \text{Rs.} 80,000$

Step III: Adjustment

Investment	Mukul	Nakul
Opening Capital	1,60,000	80,000
Add Revaluation Profit (3 : 2)	18,000	12,000
Add Reserve (3 : 2)	24,000	16,000
	2,02,000	1,08,000

Step: IV

Particular	Required Capital	Actual Capital	Difference	
Mukul	192,000	202,000	10,000	Excess
Nakul	128,000	108,000	20,000	Deficiency

Journal Entry

Date	Particulars		L.F.	Dr. (Rs.)	Cr. (Rs.)
(I)	Mukul's Capital A/c	Dr.		10,000	
	To Mukul's Current A/c				10,000
	(Being the excess of capital transferred)				
(II)	Nakul's Current A/c	Dr.		20,000	
	To Nakul's Capital A/c				20,000
	(Being the deficiancy brought in)				

CHAPTER-4

Retirement /Death of a Partner

1. (c) 1 : 2

2. (b) New Ratio - old ratio

3. (a) Retiring Partner's capital A/c

4. (b) 6% P.A.

5. Retirement of a partner is one of the modes of reconstituting the firm under which the existing partnership deed comes to an end and in its place a new one among the remaining partners comes into existence.

6. Journal Entry : All Partners Capital A/c   Dr.

To Goodwill A/c

(Being existing goodwill written off)

7. Profit & Loss Suspense A/c

8. Gaining ratio is required because the continuing partners will pay the amount of goodwill to the retiring partner in their gaining ratio.

9. Journal Entry:

Workmen Compensation Reserve At Dr.	60000
To Kmal's Capital A/c	20000
To Pankaj's Capital A/c	20000
To Saras's Capital A/c	20000
(Being balance of WCR transferred)	

10. Assets and Liabilities are revalued because the the profit or los due to their revaluation is divided between all partners (including the retiring partner) in their old profit sharing ratio.

11. (i) On Time Basis

(ii) On Sales Basis

12. Journal Entries

Date	Particulars		L.F.	Dr. (₹)	Cr. (₹)
(i)	Hanny's Capital A/c	Dr.		30,000	
	Pammy's Capital A/c	Dr.		20,000	
	Sunny's Capital A/c	Dr.		10,000	
	To Goodwill A/c				60000
	(Being goodwill written off in old profit ratio)				
(ii)	Hanny's Capital A/c	Dr.		14000	
	Sunny's Capital A/c	Dr.			
	To Pammy's Capital A/c	Dr.			28000
	(Being share of goodwill to Pammy adjusted in gain ratio)				

13. Calculation of share of profit to A

Total profit = 14000 + 18000 + 16000 (10000) + 16000 = 54000

$$\text{Average profit} = \frac{54000}{5} = 10800$$

Date	Particulars		L.F.	Dr (₹)	Cr (₹)
	B's Capital A/C (900 × 4/5)	Dr.		720	
	C's Capital A/C (900 × 1/5	Dr.		180	
	To A's Capital A/C			10,000	900
	(Being B's share of profit debited to remaining partners in gaining ratio)				

14. Calculation of profit to B

(i) Numbers of days from March 31 to June 12,2022 = 73 days

(ii) B's share in profit $= 15000 \times \dfrac{73}{365} \times \dfrac{2}{6} = ₹10000$

Journal

Date	Particulars		L.F.	Dr. (₹)	Cr. (₹)
	Profit and Loss suspense A/c	Dr.		10000	
	To B's Capital A/c				10000
	(Being B's share of profit credited)				

15.

Journal

Date	Particulars		L.F.	Dr (₹)	Cr. (₹)
(1)	Arpit's Capital A/c (2)	Dr.		16000	
	Gopal's Capital A/c (3)	Dr.		24000	
	Tushar's Capital A/c (4)	Dr.		32000	
	To Profit & Loss A/c				72000
	(Being accumulated loss debited in old profit ratio)				
(2)	Workmen compensation reserve at	Dr.		45000	
	To claim for compensation A/c				18000
	To Arpit's Capital A/c				6000
	To Gopal's Capital A/c				9000
	To Tushar's Capital A/c				12,000
	(Being WCR transferred to claim and excess transferred to capital A/c)				
(3)	General Reserve A/c	Dr.		120,000	
	To provision for Bad debts				30000
	To Arpit's Capital A/c				20000
	To Gopal's Capital A/c				30000
	To Tushar's Capital A/c				40000
	(Being 25% of General Reserve transferred to PBD and remaining to partners capital A/c)				

16.

JOURNAL

Date	Particulars		L.F.	Dr. (₹)	Cr. (₹)
	Kamal's Capital A/c	Dr.		60000	
	To Anil's Capital A/c (150000 × 1/10)				15000
	To Sunil's Capital A/c (150000 × 3/10)				45000
	(Being adjustment made for accumulated profits, losses on Sunil's retirement)				

Working Note:

Calculation of Net effect of accumulated profits/losses particulars

Particulars	Amount
General Reserve	1,20,000
Contingency Reserve	70,000
Less: Profit & Los A/c (Debit Balance)	(30000)
Loss: Advertisement suspense A/c	(10000)
Net Effect	1,50,000

(ii) Calculation of Sacrificing or Gaining ratio

$$\text{Anil} = \frac{5}{10} - \frac{2}{5} = \frac{5-4}{10} = \frac{1}{10} \ \text{Sacrifice}$$

$$\text{Komal} = \frac{2}{10} - \frac{3}{5} = \frac{2-6}{10} = \frac{4}{10} \ \text{Gain}$$

17. Total capital of firm = 140000 + 1,00,000

$$= \text{Rs. } 2,40,000$$

This capital should be in their profit ratio i.e:2 : 1

Particular	Required	Actual Capital		
Aditya 240000 × 2/3 =	1,60,000	140000	20000	Short
Ankit 240000 × 1/3 =	80000	1,00,000	20000	Excess

JOURNAL

Date	Particulars		L.F.	Dr. (₹)	Cr. (₹)
(i)	Bank A/c	Dr.		20000	
	To Aditya's Capital A/c				20000
	(Being capital brought by Aditya to maintain the balance)				
(ii)	Ankit's Capital A/c	Dr.		20000	
	(Being excess of capital withdraw)				20000

18.

Amitabh's Loan A/c

Date	Particulars	Amount	Date	Particulars	Amount
2019 March 31	To Bank A/c	2,80,000	2018 April 1	By Amitabh's Capital A/c	8,00,000
2019 March 31	To Balance c/d	6,00,000	2018 M. 31	By Interest	80,000
		8,80,000			8,80,000
2020 March 1	To Bank A/c	2,60,000	2019 April 1	By Balance b/d	60,0000
	To Balance c/d	4,00,000	March 1	By Interest	60,000
		6,60,000			6,60,000

2021 April 1	To Bank A/c	2,40,000	2020 April 21	By Balance c/d	4,00,000
	To Balance c/d	2,00,000	March 31	By Interest	40,000
		4,40,000			4,40,000
2020 March 31	To Bank A/c	2,20,000	2021 April 1	By Balance c/d	2,00,000
			March 31	By Interest	20,000
		2,20,000			2,20,000
2021 April 1	To Balance b/d	5,000	2022 March 3	By statement of P & L	5,000
		5,000			5,000

19.   Partners Capital A/c

Dr.   **Cr.**

Particular	Mukesh	Mahesh	Manish	Particular	Mukesh	Mahesh	Manish
To P. & L A/c	12500	7500	5000	By Balance b/d	150000	125000	75000
To P/Loss	25825	15495	10330	By G/Reserve	15000	9000	6000
To Mukesh	-	30000	120000	By Mahesh (1)	30000		
To Loan A/c	276675			By Manish (4)	12000		
To Balance c/d		81005		By Balance b/d			54330
	315000	134000	135330		315000	134000	135330

NEW BLANCE SHEET

Liabilities	Amount	Assets		Amount
Creditors	65000	Cash	45000	40000
Mukesh's Loan A/c	276675	Debtors	45000	
Capital A/c		Less: Bad depts	2000	
			43000	
Mahesh	81005	Less: PBD	2150	40850
		Stock		50000
		Machinery		142500
		Building		95000
		Manish's Capital A/C		54330
	422680			422680

20. Neena's Capital A/c

   (i) Calculation of profit and share to Neena

     Average profit = 150000 + 50000

$$= \frac{200000}{2} = 1,00,000$$

Share of Neena $= 100000 \times \dfrac{3}{12} \times \dfrac{5}{10} = ₹12500$

(ii) Calculation of Goodwill and share to Neena

Goodwill = Average profit × No of years of purchase

$= 100000 \times 2 = 2,00,000$

$= 200000 \times \dfrac{5}{10} = 1,00,000$

CHAPTER-5

Dissolution of the Partner

1. (c) **2.** (b) **3.** (d) **4.** (b)

5. (d)

6. If court finds that dissolution of firm is justified.

7. In case of dissolution of partnerhsip, the firm continues to do business but with a changed agreement. In case of dissolution of partnership firm, the firm creases to exist, the assets of the firm are realised and its liabilities are discharged.

8. Realisation account is prepared to know the amount of profit or loss arising from disposing off the assets of the firm and payment of all liabilities.

9. Partner's loan is not an outside liabilities. So it is not transferred to Realisation A/c.

10. When an assets is taken by a partner, his capital A/c id debited because the claim of his capital A/c is reduced to the extent of value of assets taken over by him.

11. Realisation A/c   Dr.

To Cash / Bank A/c

(Being payment of unrecorded liability)

12. No entry passed

13. Employees Provident Fund is a liability to the employees. Hence, it will be transferred to the credit side of Realisations A/c and will be paid.

14. Loss ₹30,000

15. Realisation A/c   Dr 56,000

To Cash/Bank A/c   56,000

(Being creditors paid off)

(80,000 – 10,000 = 70,000 – 14,000 = 56,000)

16. A firm can be dissolved in following circumstances:

(i) All the partners give their consent.

(ii) Business of firm becomes unlawful.

(iii) All partners of firm save one become insolvent.

(iv) Dissolution of firm under order of court.

(v) If any partner gives notice in case partnership is at will.

17. (i) Realisation Account

(ii) Partner's Loan A/C

(iii) Partner's Capital A/C

(iv) Bank / Cash A/C

18. The court may order a partnership firm to be dissolution on the following grounds :

(i) When a partner becomes insane.

(ii) When a partner becomes permanently incapable of performing his duties as a partner.

(iii) When a partner is guilty of misconduct which is likely to adversely affect the business of the firm.

(iv) When a partner persistently commits breach of partnership agreement.

(v) When a partner has transferred the whole of his interest in the firm to a third party.

19.

Memorandum Balance Sheet as on 31st march 2022

Liabilities	Amount	Assets	Amount
Creditors	24000	Cash in Hand	4000
Combined Capital of Partners		Sundry Assets	1,80,000
(100000 + 80000 + 60000) 2,40,000		(Balancing figure)	
Less : Drawings (10000 × 3) (30000)			
Less : loss in the year (5000)	160000		
	184000		**184000**

REALISATION ACCOUNT

Dr.   **Cr.**

Particulars	Amount	Particular	Amout
To Sunday Asset	180000	By Creditors	24,000
To Cash (Creditors)	23500	By Cash (Assets)	299500
to Partners Capital A/c			
Deep 48000			
Danish 36000			
Deny 36000	120000		
	323500		**323500**

20.

REALISATION ACCOUNT

Dr.   **Cr.**

Particulars	Amount	Particular	Amout
To Debtors	55000	By P.B.S (PROVISION)	2,000
To Stock	78000	By Creditors	80000
To Investment	89000	By Bank Overdraft	50000
To Building	250000	By Rajesh's Wife's Loan	77000
To Cash		By Invest. Flu. Fund	15000
Creditor 3000		By Yogesh (show) by Cash	4000
Bank Overdraft 50000	53000	Debtors 49000	
To Rajesh (Loan)	77000	Building 172000	
To Yogesh (Expenses)	17000	Investment 80000	301000
		By Partners Capital A/c	
		Rajesh 36000	
		Yogesh 54000	90000
	619000		**619000**

Yogesh's Loan A/c

Dr.   **Cr.**

Particular	Amount	Particular	Amount
To Cash A/c	28000	By Balance B/d	28000
	28000		**28000**

Yogesh's Loan A/c

Dr.   **Cr.**

Particular	Rajesh	Yogesh	Particular	Rajesh	Yogesh
To P & L A/c	4000	6000	By Balance b/d	150000	100000
To Realisation	-	4000	By Realisation	77000	17000
To Realisation (loss)	36000	54000			
To Cash A/c	187000	53000			
	227000	**117000**		**227000**	**117000**

Cash A/c

Dr.   **Cr.**

Particulars	Amount	Particulars	Amount
To Balance b/d	20000	By Realisation	53000
To Realisation	301000	By Yogesh's Loans	28000
		By Rajesh's Capital A/c	187000
		By Yogehs's Capital A/c	53000
	321000		**321000**

Dr.   **REALISATION A/C**   **Cr.**

Particulars	Amount	Particulars	Amount
To Lank & Building	47000	By Sundry Creditors	14000
To office equipment	8000	By Bills Payble	1000
To stock	56000	By Bank Overdraft	12000
To Sunday Debtors	18000	By Workmen Co. Reserve	5000
To Investment	15000	By Cash	
To Cash		Investment 9000	
Creditors 7000		Land & Building 120000	
Bills Payble 1000		Stock 40000	169000
Bank Overdraft 12000		By Vikas's Loan	15000
W. Compensation 5000	25000	By Vikas's Loan (Proit)	3000
To Cash (Expenses)	3000		
To Partners Capital A/c			
Vijay 9400			
Vikas 18800			
Vishwas 18800	47000		
	219000		**219000**

Dr.   **VIKAS'S LOAN A/C**   **Cr.**

Particular	Amount	Particular	Amount
To Realisation	15000	By Balance b/d	18000
To Realisation	3000		
	18000		
	18000		**18000**

Dr.   **PARTNERS CAPITAL A/C**   **Cr.**

Particulars	Vijay	Vikas	Vishwas	Particulars	VIjay	Vikas	Vishwas
To Bank A/c	31400	62800	62800	By Balance b/d	19000	38000	38000
Cash				By WCR	3000	6000	6000
				By R/Profit	9400	18800	18800
	31400	**62800**	**62800**		**31400**	**62800**	**62800**

CASH A/C

Particulars	Amount	Particulars	Amount
To Balance b/d	16000	By Realisation	25000
To Realisation	169000	By Realisation	3000
		By Vijay	31400
		By Vikas	62800
		By Vishwas	62800
	185000		**185000**

CHAPTER-6

Accounting for Share Capital

1. (b)	**2.** (d)	**3.** (a)	**4.** (a)
5. (b)	**6.** (d)	**7.** (b)	**8.** (a)
9. (b)	**10.** (c)		

11. Authorised or registered capital is the maximum amount of share capital which a company can issue during its life span. It is also called nominal capital of the company.

12. Expenses incurred by the company during the process of its formation are called preliminary expenses.

13. One Month

14. Calls in advance is shown in the Balance Sheet on Equity and Liabilities side under the head "Current Liabilities" under sub head 'other current Liabilities'.

15. No. Securities Premium Reserve can be used only for purposes specified under section 52(2) of companies Act 2013. Thus dividend can not be declared out of Securities Premium Reserve.

16. Maximum amount of discount at which the forfieted shares can be reissued is the amount forfeited on such shares.

17. As per to section 42 of the companies Act 2013, private placement to shares refers to issue and allotment of shares by the company to a selected group of persons in place of public issue no fresh offer under private placement of shares shall be made unless the allotments made earlier under this scheme have been completed.

18. As per section 62(1-6) a company can allot shares to its employees under a scheme of employee's stock option by passing a special resolution. The scheme is intended to retain high caliber employees to give them a sense of belonging in the company so a company may offer them equality share at a pre-determined price which is lower than the market price of the shares. The option is given to whole time directors, officers or employees which them right to purchase or subscribe share at a future date.

The basic objective of ESOP is:

(i) To inspire the employed of the company

(ii) To attract, retain and motivate the efficient employees of the company.

(iii) To creat long term weath for the employees

19. As per section 52(2) of the companies Act 2013, securities premium reserve account may be utilized for the following purpose: (Any three)

(A) for issuing fully paid bonus shares to equity shareholders.

(B) for writing off preliminary expenses.

(C) for writing off expenses or discount allowed on issue of shares or debentures or commission paid on issue of shares or debentures.

(D) for providing for payment of premium payable on redemption of preference share or securities.

(E) for purchase of its own shares or other securities under section 68(2).

20. Calculation of Purchase Consideration

Nominal Value of shares issued (10000 × 100)	10,00,000
Securities Premium Reserve	1,00.000
Bank draft	11,00,000
	22,00,000

PUCHASE CONSIDERATION JOURNAL

Date	Particulars		L.F.	Dr. (₹)	Cr. (₹)
(i)	Sunday Assets A/c	Dr.		25,00,000	
	Goodwell A/c (Balancing figure)			3,00,000	
	To Sunday Liabilities				6,00,000
	To Ravi Ltd.				22,00.00
	(Being Purchase of assets and Liabilities of Ravi Ltd.)				
(ii)	Ravi Ltd.	Dr.		22,00,000	
	To Equity share capital A/c				10,00,000
	To Securities Premium Rserve A/c				1,00,000
	To Bank A/C				11,00,000
	(Being equity shares issued at premium and Bank draft paid)				

21.
JOURNAL

Date	Particulars		LF.	Dr. (₹)	Cr. (₹)
(i)	Plant & Machinery A/c	Dr.		4,00,000	
	Building A/c	Dr.		6,00,000	
	Stock A/c	Dr.		5,00,000	
	Sunday Debtars	Dr.		3,00,000	
	To Sunday Creditors				2,00,000
	To Ashok Traders				15,00,000
	To Capital Reserve (Balancing figure)				1,00,000
	(Being the purchase of Assets and Liabilities of Ashok Traders)				
(ii)	Ashok Traders A/c	Dr.		15,00,000	
	To Bank A/c				3,00,000
	To Equity share capital A/c				10,00,000
	To Securities Premium Reesrve A/c				2,00,000
	(Being equity shares issued at premium and balance by draft)				

22.

JOURNAL

Date	Particulars		L.F.	Dr. (₹)	Cr. (₹)
Jan 1	Bank A/c	Dr.		20,000	
	To calls in Advance A/c				20,000
	(Being first call on 10000 shares @ ₹ 2 each reaceived in advance)				
Feb 15	Equity shares first call A/c	Dr.		20000	
	To equity share capital All				
	(Being first call due)				
	Calls in Advance A/c	Dr.		20000	
	To equity share first call A/c				20,000
	(Being calls in advance transferred)				

23.

JOURNAL

Date	Particulars		L.F.	Dr. (₹)	Cr. (₹)
(i)	Equity Share capital A/c (500 × 90)	Dr.		45000	
	To equity share first call all				15000
	To share forfeited A/c				30,000
	(Being 500 shares forfeited due to non payment)				
(ii)	Bank A/c	Dr.		65000	
	To equity shre capital A/c				50000
	To secirities premium reserve A/c				15000
	(Being 500 forfeited shares reissued at premium)				
(iii)	Share forfeited A/c			30000	
	To capital reseve A/c				30000
	(Being profit on reissue of shares transferred)				

24.

JOURNAL

Date	Particulars		L.F.	Dr. (₹)	Cr. (₹)
(i)	Equity share capital A/c (800 × 80)	Dr.		64000	
	To equity share first call A/c (800 × 30)				24000
	To share forfeited A/c (800 × 50)				40000
	(Being 800 shares forfeited due to non payment of 80 called up)				
(ii)	Bank A/c	Dr.		42000	
	To equity share capital A/c				40000
	To securities premium reserve A/c				
	(Being 400 shares reissued at premium)				
(iii)	Share forfeited A/c	Dr.		20000	20000
	To capital reserve A/c				
	(Being profit on reissue of 400 shares transferred)				

25.

JOURNAL

Date	Particulars		L.F.	Dr. (₹)	Cr. (₹)
(i)	Bank A/c (60000 × 2)	Dr.		120,000	
	To equity share application A/c				120,000
	(Being application money received				
(ii)	Equity share application A/c	Dr.		120,000	
	To equity share capital A/c				80000
	To equity share allotment A.c				40000
	(Being application money transferred)				
(iii)	Equity share allotment A/c	Dr.		200,000	
	To equity share capital A/c				120,000
	To securities Premium Reserve				80,000
	(Being allotment money due)				
(iv)	Bank A/c (160000 – 4000)	Dr.		156000	
	To equity share allotment A/c				156000
	(Being allotment money recd.)				
	(200000 – 40000 = 160000 × 1000/40000 ₹ 4000)				
(v)	Equity share first & final call A/c	Dr.		200,000	
	To equity share capital A/c				200,000
	(Being first & final call due)				
(vi)	Bank A/c	D.		185000	
	To equity share first & final call A/c				185000
	(Being first & final call money received (200000 – 5000 – 10000)				
(vii)	Equity share capital A/c (3000 × 10)	Dr.		30000	
	Securities premium A/c (1000 × 2)	Dr.		2000	
	To equity share allotment A/c				4000
	To equity share first & final call A/c				12000
	To share forfeited A/c			13000	
	(Being 3000 shares forfeited due to non payment)				
(viii)	Bank A/C (2000 × 8)	Dr.		16000	
	Share forfeited A/C (2000 × 2)	Dr.		4000	
	To equity share capital A/c				20000
	(Being 2000 shares reissued at descent)				
(ix)	Share forfeited A/c	Dr.		4000	
	To capital reserve A/c				4000
	(Being profit or reissue of shares transferred)				

(i)   Vineet alloated for 3000 × 4/6 = 2000 shares

(ii) Profit on reissue of shares

Profit on 1000 shares of Sandeep (forfeited   3000
Amount)

Share forfeited on 1000 shares of Vineet

10000 × 1000/2000   5000

Total   8000

Discount allowed   4000

Profit   4000

26.   **JOURNAL**

Particulars	Amount	Particulars	Amount
To Share application A/c	6000	By share application A/c	1200
To Share Allotment A/c	9016	By Balance c/d	23956
(10000 – 800 = 19200 – 174)			
To share first call A/c	5700		
(10000 – 4000 – 300)			
To share final call A/c	3800		
(3920 – 120)			
To share capital A/c	640		
	25156		**25156**

Date	Particulars		L.F.	Dr. (₹)	Cr. (₹)
(i)	Share Application A/c	Dr.		5200	
	To share capital A/c				4000
	To share allotment A/c				800
	(Being application money transferred and excess money adjusted)				
(ii)	Share allotment A/c	Dr.		10000	
	To share capital A/c				6000
	To securities premium reserve A/c				4000
	(Being allotment money due)				
(iii)	Share first call A/c			6000	
	To share capital A/c				6000
	(Being first call money due)				
(iv)	Shae capital A/c (40× 8)	Dr.		320	
	Securities premium reserve	Dr.		80	
	To share allotment A/c				184
	To share first call A/c				120
	To share forfeited A/c				96
	(Being 40 sares forfeited due to non payment Rs. 8 called up)				

(v)	Share final call A/c	Dr.		3920	
	To share capital A/c				3920
	(Being final call due on 1960 share)				
(vi)	Share capital A/c	Dr.		600	
	To share first call A/c				180
	To share final call A/c				120
	To share forfieted A/c				300
	(Being 60 shares forfeited)				
(vii)	Share forfeiture A/c	Dr.		160	
	To share capital A/c				160
	(Being 80 shares reissued)				
(viii)	Share forfeiture A/c	Dr.		136	
	To capital reserve A/c				136
	(Being profit on reissue of shares transferred)				

CHAPTER-7

Issue and Redemption of Debentures

1. (c) Bearer Debentures

2. (c) Loss on issue of debentures

3. (b) Rs. 6500 $\left(\dfrac{585000}{90}\right)$

4. (a) Rs. 48000 $(4000 \times 100 = 1,00,000 \times \dfrac{12}{100})$

5. (a) Any of the above

6. A debenture is an instrument issued by a company under its common seal as acknowledgement of a debt. It contains face value of debentures, rate of interest, mode of interest payment, tenure and terms of redemption.

7. Bond is similar to that of debentures. The term board was initially used for government debt instruments but not the term used by semi-government and non government institutions as well. Rate of interest of debentures is prefixed while bonds can be issued without a pre-determined rate of interest e.g. zero coupon bonds.

8. (i) Secured Debentures (ii) Unsecured or Naked Debentures.

9. There is no limit of discount on issue of debentures.

10. Personal account.

11. (i) Ownership : A share represents owned capital of the company

   A debenture represents debt taken by company

   (ii) Return : Dividend is paid on shares.

   Interest is paid on debentures

12.
JOURNAL

Date	Particulars		LF	DR Rs.	CR Rs.
(i)	Fixed Assets A/c	Dr.		17,30,000	
	To trade payables A/C				3,20,000
	To Vasudha oils				12,00,000
	To capital reserve A/C				2,10,000
	(Being purchases of assets and liabilities from Vasudha oils)				
(ii)	Vasudha oils	Dr		12,00,000	
	Discontinue issue of debentures	Dr		50000	
	To Bank A/C				190000
	To Bills Payables A/C				60000
	To 8% Debentures A/C				10,00,000
	(Amount paid by draft, B/P debentures issued on discount)				

13.
JOURNAL

Date	Particulars		LF	DR Rs.	CR Rs.
(i)	Bank A/c	Dr		15,00,000	
	To Bank Loan A/C				15,00,000
	(Being Loan taken from bank)				
(ii)	Debentures Suspense A/C	Dr		10,00,000	
	To 11% Debentures A/C				10,00,000
	(Being debentures issued as collect oral securities)				

An Extract of Balance Sheet

Particular	Note No.	Rs.
EQUITY AND LIABILITIES		
Non-Current Liabilities		
Long-Term Borrowings	1	15,00,000

Notes to Accounts:

Note	Particular		Rs.
1	Long Term Borrowings		
	Loan From Bank		15,00,000
	Long-Term Borrowings		15,00,000
	10,000 11% Debenture issued as		
	Collateral Securities	10,00000	
		10,00000	**15,00,000**

14. (a) No. of shares to be issued

$$= \frac{52,50,000}{105} = 50000$$

(b) Journal of Priyank Computer Ltd.

Date	Particulars	LF	DR Rs.	CR Rs.
April 1 2022	Debenture Application & Allotment A/C Dr.		52,20,000	
	Loss on issue of debentures A/C　　　　Dr.		5,00,000	
	To 6% Debentures A/C			50,00,000
	To securities premium reserve A/C			2,50,000
	(Being allotment of 50000, 6% debentures of Rs. 100 each made)			

(c) Journal

Date	Particulars	LF	DR Rs.	CR Rs.
March 31 2022	Securities Premium Reserve A/C　　　　Dr.		25,0000	
	Statement of Profit & Loss　　　　Dr.		25,0000	
	To Loss on issue of debentures A/C			5,00,000
	(Being loss on issue of debentures written off at the end of the year)			

(d) Interest on 6% Debentures

$$= 50,00,000 \times \frac{6}{100} = Rs.3,00,000 \text{ per annum}$$

(e) Loss on issue of debentures A/C

Date	Particulars	Amount	Date	Particulars	Amount
2022 April 1	To Premium on		2022 M 31	By Securities Pr. Res.	25,0000
	Redemption of Deb. A/C	5,00,000		By Statement of P & L	25,0000
					500,000
		50,0000			**500,000**

15. (a) Debentures issued at discount and redeemable at premium Journal of Rashi Ltd.

Date	Particulars	LF	DR Rs.	CR Rs.
(i)	Bank A/C (750×90)　　　　Dr.		67500	
	To 12% Debenture App. & Allotment A/C			67500
	(Being application money received)			
(ii)	12% Debenture Application & Allotment A/C Dr.		67500	
	Loss on issue of debentures A/C　　　　Dr.		11250	
	To 12% debentures A/C			75000

(iv)	To premium on red of debenture A/C				3750
	(Being allotment made of 750 debentures of ` 100 each made)				

(b) Debenture issued at 20% premium and Redeemable at premium Journal of Bhavik Ltd.

Date	Particulars	LF	DR Rs.	CR Rs.
(i)	Bank A/C (800 × 120) Dr.		96000	
	To 9% debenture application & allotment A/C			96000
	(Being application money received)			
(ii)	9% Debentures application & allotment A/C Dr.		96000	
	Loss on issue of debenture A/C Dr.		8000	
	To 9% debentures A/C			80000
(iv)	To securities premium reserve A/C			16000
	To Premium on red of debenture A/C			8000
	(Being allotment made for 800 debentures)			

16.   **JOURNAL OF SONIYA LTD.**

Date	Particulars	LF	DR Rs.	CR Rs.
2021 April 1	Bank A/C (500 × 48) Dr.		24000	
	To 9% debenture app. & allotment A/C			24000
	(Being application money received)			
2021 April 1	9% debenture application & allotment Dr.		24000	
	Discount on issue of debenture A/C Dr.		1000	
	To 9% debenture A/C			25000
	(Being 500 debentures allotted on 4% discount)			
2021 Sep 30	Debenture Interest A/C Dr.		1125	
	To debenture holders A/C			1012
	To T.D. S A/C			113
	(Being interest on debentures payable and T.D.S @ 10% deducted)			
2021 Sep 30	Debenture holders A/C Dr.		1012	
	T.D.S. A/C Dr.		113	
	To Bank A/C			1125
	(Being interest paid to debenture holders and TDS deposited)			

2022 M. 31	Debenture interest A/C Dr.	1125	
	To debenture holders A/C		1012
	ToTDS A/C		113
	(Being debenture interest payable and 10% T.D.S deducted)		

2022 M. 31	Debenture holders A/C Dr.	1012	
	T. D. S. A/C Dr.	113	
	To Bank A/C		1125
	(Being interest paid and T.D.S deposited)		
2022 M. 31	Statement of profit & loss Dr.	226	
	To debenture interest A/C		226
	(Being debenture interest transferred)		

17. (i) Amount of Discount on issue of debentures $= \dfrac{100000 \times 6}{100} = $ Rs.6000

(ii) Calculation of discount to be written off each year

Analytical Table

Beginning of the year	Debenture outstanding	Ratio	Discount to be written off
2016-17	100,000	5	6000 × 5/15 = 2000
2017-18	80000	4	6000 × 4/15 = 1500
2018-19	60000	3	6000 × 3/15 = 1200
2019-20	40000	2	6000 × 2/15 = 800
2020-21	20000	1	6000 × 1/15 = 400
		15	6000

Discount on issue of debentures A/C

Date	Particulars	Amount	Date	Particulars	Amount
2016 April 1	To 9% Debenture A/C	6000	2013 M. 31	By statement of P. & L	2000
				By balance	4000
		6000			6000
2015 April 1	To Balance b/d	4000	2018 M 31	By statement of P & L	1600
			2018 M 31	By Balance C/D	2400
		4000			**4000**

2018 April 1	To Balance b/d	2400	2019 M 31	By statement of P & L	1200
				By Balance c/d	1200
		2400			2400
					800
2019 April 1	To Balance b/d	1200	2020 M 31	By statement of P & L	400
				By Balance c/d	
		1200			1200
2020 April 1	To Balance b/d	400	2021 M. 3	By statement of P & L	400
		400			**400**

18. (a) Total amount of discount $= \dfrac{10,00,000 \times 10}{100}$ ⟶ 1,00,000

      Less: Balance in securities premium reserve   30000

      Balance will be written off   70,000

(b) Analytical Table

Beginning of the year	Debenture outstanding	Ratio	Discount to be written off
2016-17	10,00,000	4	70000 × 4/14 = 20000
2018-19	10,00,000	4	70000 × 4/14 = 20000
2019-20	750,000	3	70000 × 3/14 = 10000
2020-21	5,00,000	2	70000 × 2/14 = 10000
2021-22	2500000	1	70000 × 1/14 = 5000
		14	70000

Discount on issue of debentures A/C

Date	Particulars	Amount	Date	Particulars	Amount
2019 April 1	To 8% Debenture A/C	100000	2018 M. 31	By sec. Pre Reserve	30000
			2018 M. 31	By statement of P & L	20000
			2018 M. 31	By Balance C/D	50000
		1,00,000			1,00,000
2018 April 1	To Balance b/d	50000	2019 M 31	By statement of P & L	20000
			2018 M 31	By Balance C/D	30000
		50000			50000
2019 April 1	To Balance b/d	30000	2020 M 31	By statement of P & L	15000
				By Balance c/d	15000
		30000			30000
					800
2020 April 1	To Balance b/d	15000	2021 M 31	By statement of P & L	10000
				By Balance c/d	5000
		15000			15000
2021 April 1	To Balance b/d	5000	2022 M. 3	By statement of P & L	5000
		5000			**5000**

CHAPTER-8

Financial Statements of A Company

1. (a)	**2.** (b)	**3.** (c)	**4.** (b)

5. (b)

6. 'Operating cycle' is the time between the acquisition of assets for processing and their realisation in cash and cash equivalents.

7. The assets and liabilities of a company usually marshalded in Permanence.

8. Trade payables refers to the amount payable against goods purchased or services received in the normal course of business.

9. (i) Shareholders's Fund

(ii) Share application money pending allotment.

(iii) Non current liabilities

(iv) Current liabilities

10. (i) Capital Reserve

(ii) Securities Premium Reserve

(iii) Debenture Redemption Reserve

11. (i) Fixed Assets

(ii) Non current investment

12. As per AS-26, Prelimanery Expenses is written off from Securities Premium Reserve A/C or from statement of profit and loss A/C in the year in which it arises.

13. It is the principal revenue producing activity of the business. It includes

(i) Sale of product

(ii) Sale of service

(iii) Other operating revenue i.e., sale of scrap.

14. It refers to interest expenses on long term and short term borrowings of the company. It also includes other borrowing costs.

15. (i) Fuel & Power

(ii) Postage & Telephone expenses

(iii) Advertisement

(iv) Bad debts

16. Financial statement are the end products of accounting process. They provide information about the profitability and financial position of a business.

As per section 2(40) of the Companies Act 2013, financial statement in relation to a company, include the following :

(i) A balance sheet

(ii) A statement of profit and loss

(iii) Cash flow statement

(iv) A statement of change in equity

(v) Explanatory notes

17. Characteristics of financial statements are as below :

(i) Financial statements are related to past period and hence are historical documents

(ii) They are expressed in the terms of money

(iii) Financial statements show profitability through statements of profit and loss and financial position through balance sheet

18.

S. No.	Items	Headings	Sub-headings
1	Net loss as shown by statements of profit & loss	Share holders fund	Reserve and surplus as negative item
2	Capital redemption reserve	Share holders fund	Reserve & Surplus
3	Bond/Debontines	Non current liabilities	Long term borrowings
4	Unpaid dividend	Current-liabilites	Short term borrowings
5	Building	Non current assests	Fixed ansets – Tangible
6	Raw materials	Current assests	Inventory

19.

S.No.	Items	Headings	Sub-headings
1	Balance with bank	Current assets	Cash & cash equivalent
2	Investment in debeptures	Non current assels	Not current investments
3	Outstanding salaries	Current-liabilites	Other current liabilities
4	Authoirised capital	Share holders fund	Share capital
5	Acceptance/Bills Payable	Current Liabilites	Trade Paybles
6	Provision for Tqx	Current Liabilites	Short term provisions

20.

LAXMI AGRO LTD.

Balance Sheet as at 31st March, 2022

	Particulars	Note No.	Rs.
I.	**EQUITY AND LIABILITIES**		
	(1) Share Capital Fund		
	(a) Share Capital		
	(b) Reserve & Surplus	1	(2,00,000)
	(2) Long Term Borrowings (Debentum)		10,00,000
	Total		8,00,000
II.	**ASSETS**		
	(1) Non Current Assets		
	(2) Current Assests		
	(a) Cash and cash equivalents		8,00,000
	Total		8,00,000

Notes to Accounts :

	Particulars		Rs.
(1)	Reserve & Surplus		
	Statement of profit & loss		....
	Lens : Discount on issue of debprinters		(200000)
	Total		**(200000)**

CHAPTER-9

Analysis of Financial Statements

1. (d)   **2.** (a)   **3.** (b)

4. (c)   **5.** (d)

6. Financial analysis is the process of identifying the financial strengths and weakness of the firm by properly establishing relationship between the various items of balance sheet and statement of profit & loss.

7. The basic objectives of financial statement analysis is to know about the

(i) Operating performance and

(ii) Financial soundness of the business.

8. When an analyst the financial statements of an enterprises over a number of years, the analysis is called horizontal or dynamic analysis.

9. If different financial variables of a firm are analysed and compared over a period of time, it is called intra firm analysis.

10. (i) Comparative statements

(ii) Common size statements

(iii) Ratio analysis

(iv) Cash flow statements

11. By making financial analysis, public try to find out the financial efficiency of the business entity.

12. Comparison of analysis of financial statements of two or more business firms is called inter-firm analysis.

13. (i) Management

(ii) Shareholders

(iii) Financial institutions

(iv) Creditors

(v) Public

(vi) Government

14. Top management can judge the solvency, profitability and capital structure with the help of financial analysis.

15. Financial analysis is useful for the following purpose :

1. **To know the earning capicity or profitability:** The profitability and earining capicity of the business may be computed on the basis of financial statement which is an indicator of efficiency and success of a business enterprises.

2. **To know the solvency position :** It can be ascertained from financial analysis whether the business is in a position to pay its short- term and long term liabilities. It can be measure with the help of ratio analysis.

3. **To measure the financial strength :** The purpose of financial analysis is to help the management to make a comparative study and assess the financial potential of business. Analysis helps in providing answer related to fund and current repulation of the business.

16. The main features of financial analysis as below:

1. To present the complex data contained in financial statements in simple and understable form.

2. To classify the items contained in financial statements in convenient and rational group.

3. To make comparisons between various group to draw various condusions.

17. Financial statements analysis helps the interested parties to make an assessment of the earning capicity and financial soundness of a financial enterprises. But such analysis has its limitations. Some limitations are as follow :

1. **Affected by window dressing :** Some firm resort to window dressing their financial statements to cover up bad financial position on the eve of accounting date. For example, they may not record to purchase made at the end of the year or they may overvalued their closing stock. In such cases, the result obtained by analysis of financial statement will be misleading.

2. **Do not reflect changes in price level :** Figures given in financial statements do not show the effect of changes in price level. As such, the comparison of past years figure with current year figures may lead to misleading conclusions.

3. **Different Accounting Policies :** If two firms adopt different accounting policies, the comparison between the two will be unreliable. For example, one firm may provide depreciation on original cost method, whereas the other firm may adopt the written down value method for providing depreciation. The result obtained from comparison of financial statements of such firm may give misleading picture.

4. **Difficulty in fore casting :** Financial statements are a record of past events and historical facts. In the fast changing and developing modern business, the analysis of past information may not be much use in future forecasting. Continuous changes take place in the demand of the product, policies adopted by the firm, the position of competition etc. As such, no estimate based on analysis of historical facts can be made for future.

5. **Lack of qualitative analysis :** Financial statements record only monetary transactions and does not record qualitative factors which are non-monetary in nature like reputation of business, management etc. This these qualitative elements ignores in financial statement analysis.

CHAPTER-10

Accounting Ratios

1. (c)   **2.** (d)   **3.** (b)

4. (d)   **5.** (a)

6. According to Myres, Ratio analysis is a study of relationship among various items or group of items in financial statements.

7. Short-term Solvency Ratio indicate the ability of the firm to meet its current obligations maturing within a period of one year as within the period of operating cycle out of its current resources.

8. The standard ratio for current ratio is 2 : 1 and for liquid ratio is 1 : 1.

9. Shareholders fund as proprietor's fund or not worth.

10. Average holding period represents the period of retention of stock with entity before it generates sales on an average. It is computed as

    Average holding period = 365 days/Imentary Turnorer Ratio

11. The earing capicity of the business is assessed by computing gross profit ratio, operating ratio and net profit ratio.

12. Operating Cost = Cost of Revenue from operations + Operating exp.

13. Activity ratio shows the rapidity with which assets of the business are being utilised.

14. It establishe the relationship between profit earned and capital employed to earn it. This ratio computed as under :

$$\text{Return on Investment} = \frac{\text{P.B.I.T.} \times 100}{\text{capital employed}}$$

15. Sale of inventory at cost price.

16. Current Ratio will improve because both current Assets and current liabilities are decreased by the same amount.

17. Decrease, Reason: Current liabilities (creditors) will increase with no change in quick assets.

18. Debt-Equity ratio will decrease because conversion of debentures into prefrence share will reduce the long term debts but increase the shareholder's fund.

19. While calculating inventory turmover ratio it is not included in inventories.

20.   Operating Profit Ratio = 100 – Operating Ratio

        = 100 – 83.6% = 16.36%

21. Ratio analysis is a quantitative measurement of the performance of the futress. It ignores qualitations which are also usesful for telespretation. For example, credit may be generated to a customer on the basic of certain ratio of his but the and management abilityof the customer also is takes lets consideration.

    There may be different accuting painless adopted by different firms with regard to depretation, valuation method of stock etc. Such differences make the accounting ratio incomparable.

22. $\quad$ Current Ratio $= \dfrac{\text{Current Assets}}{\text{Current Liabilities}}$

$= 2.5 = \dfrac{17,00,000}{\text{Current Liabilities}}$

$\therefore$ Current liabilities $= 17,00,000 \div 2.5 = 680000$

$\because$ Quich Ratio $= \dfrac{\text{Quich Assets}}{\text{Current Liabilities}}$

$= 0.95 = \dfrac{\text{Quich Assets}}{\text{Rs.6,80,000}}$

Quich Assets $= 680000 \times 0.95 = 6,46,000$

Inventory $=$ Current Assets $-$ Quich Assets

$= 17,00,000 - 6,46,000 = 10,54,000$

Thus : $\qquad$ Current Liabilities $= 68,0000$

Inventory Liabilties $= 10,54,000$

OR

Let Current Liabilities $= x$

$\because$ Current Ratio is 4.5 : 1

So, Current Assets $= 4.5\,x$

$\therefore$ Liquid Ratio is 3 : 1

So, Liquid Assets $= 3x$

Liquid Assets $=$ Current Assets $-$ Inventories or

$= 3x = 4.5 - 3,00,000$

$1.5 = 3,00,000$

$\therefore \quad x = \dfrac{3,00,000}{1.5} = 2,00,000$

$\therefore$ Current Liabilities $= $ Rs.2,00,000

23. We know thatTotal Assets $=$ Total of equity and liabilities

$\therefore$ Shaeholder Fund $=$ Total Assets $-$ Total debts

$= 10,00,000 - 5,50,000 = 4,50,000$

Long Termn Debt $=$ Total Debt $-$ Current Liabilities

$= 5,50,000 - 2,00,000 = 3,50,000$

(i) Deb Equity Ratio $= \dfrac{\text{Long Term Debts}}{\text{Equity}}$

$= \dfrac{3,50,000}{4,50,000} = 0.78 : 1$

(ii) Total Assets to Debt Ratio $= \dfrac{\text{Total Assets}}{\text{Long Term Debts}}$

$= \dfrac{10,00,000}{3,50,000} = 2.86 : 1$

24.   Let net profit before tax = 100

Less tax provision = 50

Net profit after tax = 50

If net profit after tax = Rs. 20,5000.

Net profit after tax = 2,05,000

Net profit before tax $2,05,000 \times \dfrac{100}{50}$ = Rs. 4,10,000

Net profit before tax = 4,10,000

Add : 10% on Debentures $4,00,000 \times 10\%$ 40,000

Add : 8% on Loan $3,00,000 \times 8\%$ 24,000   } 82,000

Add : 9% on Public deposit $20,00,00 \times 9\%$ 18,000

Net profit before Interest 8C tax **4,92,000**

$$\text{Interest Coverage Ratio} = \dfrac{\text{Profit before Interest \& Tax}}{\text{Interest on Long Term Debts}}$$

25. $\text{Inventory Turnover Ratio} = \dfrac{\text{Cost of Revenue From Operation}}{\text{Average Inventory}}$

$$= \dfrac{6}{1} = \dfrac{3,00,000}{\text{Average Inventory}}$$

$\therefore$ $\text{Average Inventory} = \dfrac{3,00,000}{6}$ = Rs. 50,000

Calculation of Inventory

(i)   Operating Inventory = Average Inventory

$$= -\dfrac{1}{2} \text{ of } 10,000$$

$$= 50,000 - 5,000 = 45,000$$

(ii) Closing Inventory = Average Inventory + $\dfrac{1}{2}$ of 10,000

$$= 50,000 + 5,000 = 55,000$$

26. Let cost of Revenue from Operation = 100

Gross Profit   <u>25</u>

Revenue from Operation (Sales)   <u>125</u>

$\therefore$ Revenue from operation = Cost of Revenue from Operation $\times$ 125/100

$= 4,00,000 \times 125/100$ 5,00,000

Less: Cash sales $5,00,000 \times 20/100$ <u>1,00,000</u>

Net Credit Sales   <u>4,00,000</u>

$$\text{Average Trade Recelable} = \dfrac{(\text{Operaint} + \text{Closing Trade Receivables})}{2}$$

$$= \dfrac{70,000 + 90,000}{2} = 80,000$$

$$\text{Debtors Turnover Ratio} = \frac{\text{Net Credit Sales}}{\text{Average Trade Receivables}}$$

$$= \frac{4,00,000}{80,000} = 5 \text{ Times}$$

27. (A) Calculation of Returns on Investment

Capital employed = Fixed Assets + Current

Assets – Current liabilities = 7500,000 + 40,00,000 – 2700 = 88,00,000

$$\text{Return on Investment} = \frac{\text{Net Profit before Interest \&Tax}}{\text{Capital Employed}}$$

$$= \frac{14,50,000}{88,00,000} \times 100 = 16.47$$

(B) Calculation of total Assets to Debts Ratio Total Assets = Fixed Assets + Current Assets

$$= 75,00,000 + 40,00,000 = 1,15,00,000$$

$$\text{Total Assets to Debts Ratio} = \frac{\text{Total Assets}}{\text{Debentures}} = \frac{1,15,00,000}{80,00,000} = 1.44 : 1$$

28. (A) <u>Calculation of Gross Profit Ratio</u>

Gross Profit = Sales – Cost of Revenue from operation

$$= 1,500,00 - 120000 = 30000$$

$$\text{Gross Profit Ratio} = \frac{\text{Gross Profit}}{\text{Revenue from operation}} \times 100$$

$$= \frac{30,000 \times 100}{1,50,000} = 20\%$$

(B) <u>Stock Turnover Ratio</u>

$$\text{Stock Turnover Ratio} = \frac{\text{Cost of Revenue from operation}}{\text{Average Inventory}}$$

$$\text{Average Inventory} = \frac{\text{Opening} + \text{Closing Inventory}}{2}$$

Cost of Revenue from Operation = 1,20,000

$$\text{Average Inventory} = \frac{29,000 + 31,000}{2} = 30,000$$

$$\text{Stock Turnover Ratio} = \frac{1,20,000}{3,000} = 4 \text{ Times}$$

(C) <u>Calculating of Operating Ratio</u>

$$\text{Operating Ratio} = \frac{\text{Operating Cost}}{\text{Net Revenue from Operation}} \times 100$$

Operating Cost = Cost of Revenue from Operation + Operating Expenses

= 1,20,000 + 16,000 = 1,36,000

Operating Ratio = $\dfrac{1,36,000}{15,000} \times 100 = 90.67$

CHAPTER-11

Cash Flow Statement

1. (c)   **2.** (c)   **3.** (c)   **4.** (b)

5. (d)

6. Under Accounting standard-3 (Revised)

7. Cash Flow mean the inflow and outflows of cash and cash equivalents.

8. Because Cash Flow statement shows only the inflows and outflow of each whereas income statement shows both cash and non-cash items of revenue nature and also shows the net income during the year.

9. It will be (i) Cash inflow from operating activities in case of a finance co and (ii) Cash inflow from inresting activities in case of non finance co.

10. It will result in no flow of cash because it is a non cash transation.

11. Cash Flow Statement for the year ended 31st March 2022

Particulars	Amount
(C) Cash Flow from Financing Activities :	
Redemption of 12% Debentures	(3,00,000)
Proceeds from issue of 10% Debentures (500000 – 25000)	4,75,000
Interest paid on debentures	(46500)
Decrease in Bank overdraft	(20000)
Proposed dividend paid on Equity Share Capital (20,00,000 × 8%)	(16,0000)
Interest paid on Bank overdraft	(10000)
Net Cash used in financing Activities	(61500)

Note :

(i) Bonus Shares issued to existing equity shareholders without charging any amount from them. Hence, bonus shares are not shown in Cash Flow statement because there is no flow of cash.

(ii) Interest on Debentures :

12% on 3,00,000 for 3 months	Rs. 9000
10% on 5,00,000 for 9 months	Rs. 37500
Total	**Rs. 46500**

12. Cash Flow Statements for the year ending 31st March 2022

Particulars	Amount (Rs.)
(B) Cash Flow From Investing Activities	
Sale of Plant & Machinery Sale of Land	40000
	160000
Purchases of Plant & Machinery Purchase of non current investment	(260000)
	(60000)
Net Cash outflow from investing activities	(120000)

Dr.   **Land A/C**   Cr

To Balance b/d	200,000	By Bank (Balancing Fingues)	160000
		By Balance c/d	
To Gain on Sale of Land	60000		100000
	260000		**2,60,000**

Dr.   **Plant & Machinery A/C**   Cr

To Balance b/d	850,000	By Depreciation	50,000
To Bank	2,60,000	By Bank	40000
(Balancing figure)		By Loss on Sale of Machinery	20000
		By Balance c/d	10,00,000
	11,10,000		**11,10,000**

OR

Cash Flow Statement for the year ending 31st March 2022

Particulars	Rs.
(B) Cash Flow from Investing Activities :	
Purchases of Goodwill	(2,00,000)
Proceeds from Sale of Patent	100000
Proceeds from Sale of Machinery	50,000
Purchase of machinery	(4,40,000)
Purchase of 10% investment	(180000)
Proceeds from sale of investment	1,00,000
Interest Received (10% on 60000)	6000
Dividend Received (10% on 1,00,000)	10000
Rent Received	30000
Net Cash used in outflow investing activities	(524000)

Dr.   Patent A/c   Cr

Particulars	Amount	Particulars	Amount
To Balance b/d	2,80,000	By Statement of P & L (w/o)	40000
To Gain on Sale	20000	By Bank (Balancing figure) By Balance c/d	100000
			160000
	300000		**3,00,000**

Dr.   Machinery A/c   Cr

To Balance b/d	10,20,000	By Bank	50000
To Bank	4,40,000	By D. & L Loss	30000
(Balancing figures)		By Depreciation	1,40,000
		By Balancing c/d	12,40,000
	14,60,000		**14,60,000**

Dr.   10% Investment A/c   Cr

Cash flow statement for the year ending 31st March 2022

Particulars		Amount (Rs.)
(A) Cash Flow from Operating Activities		
Net Profit before Tax (80000 – 30000) = 50000 + 20000 + 15000		85000
Adjustment for non cash and non operating items.		
Add : Depreciation		10000
Operating profit before working capital changes		95000
Add : Increase in Trade payable	54000	
Less : Increase in Inventories	(30000)	
Less : Increase in Trade Receivables	(38000)	(8000)
Cash generated from operations		87000
Less : Income Tax Paid		(12000)
Net Cash inflow from Operating Activities		75000
(B) Cash Flow from Investing Activities		
Purchases of Plant & Machinery		(50000)
Net Cash used (outflow) in investing activities		(50000)

Particulars	Amount (Rs.)
(C) Cash Flow from Financing Activities	
Issue of Share Capital	1,00,000
Repayment of Loan	(75000)
Repayment of Short Term Borrowing (overdraft)	(12000)
Payment of Proposed dividend	(20000)
Net Cash used (outflow) in financing Activities	(7000)
Net Cash increase (75000 – 50000 – 7000)	18000
Add : Opening Cash & cash equivalents	25000
Closing cash and cash equivalents	43,000

Dr.   **PLANT & MACHINERY A/C**   **Cr**

Particulars	Amount	Paritation	Amount
To Balance b/d	3,50,000	By Balance c/d	4,00,000
To Bank A/c (Purchase) (Balancing Figures)	50000		
	400000		**4,00,000**

Dr.   **ACCUMULATED DEPRECIATION**   **Cr**

To Balance c/d	60000	By balance b/d	50000
		By Depreciation (Balancing figure)	10000
	60,000		**60,000**

Calculations of Cash and Cash Equivalents

Particulars	31.03.2022	31.02.2022
Cash and bank balance Current investments	13000	5000
	30000	20000
	43000	**25000**

PART-II

CHAPTER-1

Overview of Computerised Accounting System

1. (b) Assets, Capital, Liabilities, Revenues & Expenses

2. (c) Data Bank

3. (d) Management Information System

4. (a) Hierarchical relationship between groups and components

5. (a) The Encryption of data

6. (a) safeguard assets and optimise the use of resource

7. Procedure, Data , People , Hardware , Software.

8. Computerised Accounting System refers to the processing of accounting transaction through the use of hardware and software in order to produce accounting records and reports.

9. Encryption essentially scrambles the information so as to make its interpretation extremely difficult (almost impossible). Thus, Encryption ensures security of data even if it lands in wrong hands, because the receiver of data will not be able to decode and interpret it.

10. Revenue means inflow of resources, which results from the sale of goods or services in the normal course of business and increase in capital. Expenses imply consumption of resources in generating revenues.

11 This sub-system records expenses under broad groups such as manufacturing administrative, financial, selling and distributions and others.

12. Data is raw, unorganised facts that need to be processed. Data can be something simple and useless until it is organised.

When data is processed, organised, structured or presented in a given context so as to make it useful, it is called information. A computer is an information processing machine. Computers process data to produce information

13. • Collect data

• Organise data

• Communicate Accounting Information

14. This system generates information about changes in the cost that takes place during the period under review. It deals with the ascertainment of cost of goods produced. It has linkages with other accounting sub-systems for obtaining the necessary information about cost of material, labour, and other expenses.

15. Codification of accounts is needed where there are numerous accounts heads in an organisation. There is a hierarchical relationship between the groups and its components. In order to maintain the hierarchical relationships between a group and its sub-groups, proper codification is required. The coding scheme of account heads should be such that it leads to grouping of accounts at various levels so as to generate various reports.

16. The transaction is an exchange of monetary items or nonmonetary item or also exchange of any item which effect business statements for example buying or selling something, paid or receive something. Normally transactions are also recorded on accrual basis for example outstanding employees' salary is a transaction is businesses have to record in their financial statements.

17. 1. **SIMPLE AND INTEGRATED** : CAS is designed to automate and integrate all the business operations, such as sales, finance, purchase, inventory and manufacturing. CAS is integrated to provide accurate, up-to-date business information rapidly. The CAS may be integrated with enhanced MIS (Management Information System), Multi-lingual and Data Organisation capabilities to simplify all the business processes of the organisation easily and cost-effectively.

2. **ACCURACY AND SPEED**: CAS provides user-definable templates (data entry screens or forms) for fast, accurate data entry of the transactions. It also helps in generalising desired documents and reports.

3. **RELIABILITY** : CAS makes sure that the generalised critical financial information is accurate, controlled and secured.

18. Management Information System (MIS) deals with generation and processing of reports that are vital for management decision-making. The Information system should be so flexible as to provide customised reports to support various managerial functions such as planning, organising, staffing, oversight, control and decision-making including operational, functional and strategic nature. Management Information System, more commonly known as MIS is a computer-based system. MIS actually helps the organization, especially the managers, to organize and evaluate information and data, and provide information in a timely and efficient manner. This also helps the managers make decisions based on the information and analysis the MIS provides. Since it is a computer system, it includes elements of the computer system as well. It has software (that help make the decisions), users (managers), databases, all hardware necessary and applications (people and project management applications) as well. MIS generally focuses on accounting and economic aspects of a firm, analysing problems and providing solutions.

19. Following are the limitation of CAS software:

1. Faster obsolescence of technology necessitates investment in shorter period of time.

2. Data may be lost or corrupted due to power interruptions.

3. Data are prone to hacking.

4. Un-programmed and un-specified reports cannot be generated.

Ans.

Data	Information
1. It is used as input	1. It is the output of processed data
2. Data is the raw material	2. Information is the product
3. It doesn't carry a meaning	3. It must carry a logical meaning
4. It is an independent value	4. Information depends on data

21. (a) CASH AND BANK SUB-SYSTEM: It deals with the receipt and payment of cash both physical cash and electronic fund transfer. Electronic fund transfer takes place without having the physical entry or exit of cash by using the credit cards or electronic banking

(b) INVENTORY SUB-SYSTEM: It deals with the recording of different items purchased and issued specifying the price, quantity and date. It generates the inventory position and valuation report.

(c) PAYROLL ACCOUNTING SUB-SYSTEM: It deals with payment of wages and salary to employees. A typical wage report details information about basic pay, dearness allowance, and other allowances and deductions from salary and wages on account of provident fund, taxes, loans, advances and other charges. The system generates reports about wage bill, overtime payment and payment on account of leave encashment, etc.

(d) FIXED ASSETS ACCOUNTING SUB-SYSTEM: It deals with the recording of purchases, additions, deletions, usage of fixed assets such as land and buildings, machinery and equipment's, etc. it also generates reports about the cost, depreciation, and book value of different assets.

(e) TAX ACCOUNTING SUB-SYSTEM: This sub-system deals with compliance requirement value-added tax (VAT), excise, customs and income tax. This sub-system used in large size organisation.

CHAPTER-2

Spreadsheet

1. (b)

2. (c)

3. (d)

4. (c)

5. (d)

6. (c) SUM

7. The one variable Data Table allows us to identify a single decision variable in our model and see how changing the values for that variable affect the values calculated by one or more formulas in our model.

The two variable Data table allows us to Specify two decision variables and a variety of inputs and only a single formula.

8. There are 5 ways to enter data excel.

- Type directly into a cell
- Using the formula bar.
- autocomplete
- Copy paste
- Autofill

9. Arithmetic expression or a function.

10. A Pivot Table is utilized to sum up, sort, rearrange, bunch, check, aggregate or normal information put away in a table. It permits us to change segments into lines and lines into sections. It permits gathering by any field (segment), and utilizing progressed figurings on them.

11. These excel features are already given in the home tab of excel sheets and users can easily use these features. But use of these features is depending upon the requirements. It makes better display and appearance. Wrap text makes it easier to read the large text in a cell and take a printout. Merging the cells makes the work more presentable and completed it in a proper format.

12. A spreadsheet is a sheet of paper that shows accounting or other data in rows and columns. A spreadsheet also a computer application program that simulates a physical spreadsheet by capturing, displaying and manipulating data arranged in rows and column.

13. The syntax of PPMT function :

= PPMT (rate/payment in a year, 1, year * payment in a year, amount

14. A cell is the intersection between a row and a column on a spreadsheet that starts with alt.

A row is a series of data banks laid out in a horizontal fashion in a table or spreadsheet.

15.

A	B
1. Rows	1. Numerical numbers from top to bottom
2. Columns	2. Alpha characters from left to right
3. Cell	3. Intersection of a row & a column
4. Cell address	4. Unique identification code of a cell

16. 1. Workbook:

A file in spread sheet is known as a workbook. A work book is a collection of a number of work sheets.

2. Work sheets:

The work area which consists of rows and columns in a spreadsheet is called a worksheet. By default three work sheets-sheet 1, sheet -2, sheet -3 are available in work book.

17. The basic elements of M.S. Excel are as follows :

1. **Work Book**: Each file of excel is known as Work Book. There can be many work sheet in any work book. We can store information in an organised way in a single work book. A work book opens with their worksheet by default and maximum 255 worksheets can be there.

2. **Worksheet** : Worksheet can be called a window made of rows and columns. It is used for financial document or project planning of an organisation. Worksheet is used with mouse so it is easy to format.

3. **Row**: Row is a horizontal block made by cell. Which runs from left to right in a worksheet.

4. **Column**: It is a vertical block of cells which runs in entire worksheet there are 16,384 columns in a worksheet.

5. **Cell**: The smallest unit of Excel is called cell.

6. **Formula**: It is a sequence of standard, name, cell references functions and operators entered in a cell which give a new value together.

7. **Function**: Function's are predefined formulas which makes sometimes complex calculations and for this it uses a particular value in a particular sequence to get a result.

18. The following are the key features of spreadsheet:

1. Many types of data can be managed and used in a large quantity.

2. Data can be shown with the help of graph on chart.

3. Data can be brought and sent in spreadsheet through software.

4. Data's calculation can be done speed.

5. All calculation's done by using the formula once.

6. Spreadsheet can be used for different uses.

19. Importance and Uses of MS Excel Spreadsheet:

Microsoft Excel spreadsheet software has become an integral part of most business organisations across the world. MS Excel is used for various purposes by business establishments. Some organisations use this spreadsheet software for generating memos, track sales trends and other business data. Microsoft Excel spreadsheets software come with million rows of data and automate number crunching, but this popular spreadsheet software is capable of doing more than just figures. MS Excel has a simple interface that allows users to easily understand this software and also perform basic activities.

Ms Excel offers a grid interface that allows the users to organise any type of information that require. One of the major advantages of MS Excel spreadsheet software is its flexibility feature.

20. 1. Cell:

The intersection of a row and a column is called a cell. A cell is identified by a combination of alpha – numeric character eg: A1, B6, C10, etc. This alphanumeric character is called cell address. Hence each cell has a unique address.

2. Ranges:

Range is a group of adjacent cells that forms a rectangular area. A range is specified by giving the address for first cell in range and the last cell in the rage, eg: range starting from A10 to A20 is written as A10: A20 where colon (:) is the range operator.

3. Worksheets:

The work area which consists of rows and columns in a spreadsheet is called worksheet. By default three worksheets-sheet 1, sheet -2, sheet -3 are available in the workbook.

4. Workbook:

A file in a spreadsheet is known as a workbook. A workbook is a collection of a number of worksheets.

21. Spreadsheet Reference Functions:

The important spreadsheet reference functions are

1. **LOOKUP () functions**:

The LOOKUP function returns a value either from a one-row or one-column **range or from an array. The lookup function has two syntax forms**: Vector form and Array form.

The vector form of LOOUP looks in a one-row or one-column range (known as a vector) for a value and then returns a value from the same position in a second one-row or one-column range.

The array form of LOOKUP looks in the first row or column of an array for the specified value and then returns a value from the same position in the last row or column of the array.

LOOKUP (Vector from)

Syntax: = LOOKUP (search criterion, Search vector, Result vector)

LOOKUP (Array form)

Syntax: =(LOOKUP (lookup_value, array)

2. **VLOOK UP ()**:

VLOOK UP is the vertical LOOKUP function. Use VLOOK UP to search the first column (columns are vertical) of a block of data and return the value from another column in the same row.

Syntax: = VLOOKUP (Search criterion; Array; Index; Sort Order)

3. **HLOOKUP ( )**:

It is the Horizontal LOOKUP function, searches for a value in the first row of a table array and returns the corresponding value in the same column from another row of the same table array.

Syntax: HLOOKUP (search criteria; index; sorted)

CHAPTER-3

Use of Spreadsheet in Business Applications

1. (b) PV

2. (b) payroll

3. (a) Loan Repayment schedule

4. (a) Fixed Instalment Method

5. (b) Scrap value

6. (d) Provident Fund (It is a deduction)

7. Tax Deducted at Source (TDS)

8. Net Salary

9. Depreciation

10. Depreciation = 10000–2000/ 10

i.e., 1600

11. Amount of Depreciation (Yearly Depreciation) / Total Depreciable Amount (Cost) ×100

12. Methods of calculation of depreciation

1. Straight Line Method (SLM)

2. Written Down Value Method (WDV)

13. At the end of the loan period, the balance amount payable will be zero assuming that the repayments are made on regular basis. Therefore the future value FV is taken as zero.

14. IF (B3 < 10000, 250, 500)

15. Provident Fund (PF) : It is a statutory deduction, as part of social security.

16. Number of Effective Days Present (NOEDP) – is the Number of Days in a Month Minus Leave without Pay minus Unauthorised Absence, i.e. NOEDP = (Number of Days in a Month) NOEDP = (Number of Days in a Month) – (Leave without Pay) – (Unauthorised Absence) ; where (Number of Days in a Month) may be denoted by NODM.

17. 1. Basic Pay

2. Dearness Allowance

3. House Rent Allowance

4. Provident Fund

5. Professional Tax

6. ESI

18. • Net Salary Calculation:

Step 1 – Calculate Gross salary by using the given formula.

Gross salary /Gross Pay = Basic Pay + Grade Pay + Dearness Pay+ Dearness Allowance + House Rent Allowance + Any other Earnings.

• Step 2 – Calculate Total Deduction by using the following formula.

Total Deduction = Professional Tax+ Provident Fund + Tax deducted at source + Loan Recovery + Any other deductions

• Step 3- Calculate net salary by the given formula.

Net Salary = Gross salary – Total Deduction

19. LOAN REPAYMENT SCHEDULE:

Loan is a sum of borrowed money for a specified period at a pre-specified rate of interest. The loan is repaid through a number of periodic repayment instalments over the loan repayment period. LibreOffice Calc function PMT is used to calculate the loan repayment schedule. The parameters of the function PMT are as follows.

Parameter – Explanation

- Rate –   Interest rate
- Nper – Total Number of payments for the loan
- PV – Present value(Loan amount)
- FV – Future value, which is taken a zero, is the balance at the end of the loan period
- Type – Whether payment is made at the beginning (value = 1) or at the end (value = 0) of the period.

20. 1.   DA $\rightarrow$ C2 =B2 $\times$ 20%

HRA $\rightarrow$ D2 = B2 $\times$ 5%

GP $\rightarrow$ E2 = B2 + C2+ D2

TDS $\rightarrow$ F2 = E2 $\times$ 10%

NP $\rightarrow$ G2 = E2 – F2

21. PMT function can be used to prepare Loan Repayment Schedule in LibreOffice Calc.

The parameters of PMT function are:

Parameter – Explanation

- Rate – Interest on Loan
- Nper – Number of payments for the loan
- PV – Present value; (ie the loan amount)
- FV – Future value, which is taken a zero
- Type – If the payment is made at the beginning of the month, the value = 1 or at the end of the month, the value = 0

CHAPTER-4

Graphs and Charts for Business Data

1. (c) Bar chart

2. (a) Two

3. (d) All the above

4. (c) Move here

5. (c) Pie Chart

6. (b) DATA LABELS

7. Bar chart, Column Chart, Pie chart, Line chart, Area chart, Doughnut chart, etc.

8. • Chart and graphs covey lots of business information in a visual format

   • Different business Data variables plotted in charts and graphs show the trend of the business in an easy way

9. Area chart

10. Resizing of the chart means changing size of the chart as desired. This option can be used independently for the fonts, title, legends easily.

11. 2-D types of graphs/charts are line graphs, bar, area, surface column (horizontal or vertical), multiple line charts, radar chart, XY (scatter) or bubble chart.

12. 1. Chart area:

This is the total space that is enclosed by a chart. It is the background of the chart.

2. Chart wall:

In 2D chart, the wall or area is bounded by the X and Y-axis. In the 3D chart, the wall is bounded by three axes X, Y and Z

13. (a) 2D Chart

(b) 3D Chart

14. Charts can be prepared with three dimensional (3-D) effects. 3- D charts have a third axis. The third axis is called as Z-axis. So a 3-D chart has the following dimensions.

1.   Horizontal axis – Indicate the category – known as X-axis

2.   Vertical axis – Indicate the derived values – known as Y-axis

3.   Depth axis – Indicate the series – known as Z-axis

15. 1. Column Chart:

It is the most commonly used chart type. It shows a bar chart or bar graph with vertical bars. The X-axis shows the categories and Y-axis shows the value for each category. Column chart are used to compare values across categories.

2. Bar Chart:

This type of chart shows a bar graph or column chart with horizontal bars. The Y-axis shows categories and the X-axis shows the value for each category. It is suitable for comparing multiple values.

16. Doughnut charts display data in rings, where each ring represents a data series. doughnut chart can contain more than one data series. Each data series that you plot in a doughnut chart adds a ring to the chart. The first data series is displayed in the center of the chart.

17. The percentage in the chart represents whole information as a percentage format for ease of understanding.

The steps for calculating Percentage in excel are shown below:

1.   Select the date range you need and click Insert > Column > Stacked Column.

2.   Click at the column and then click Design > Switch Row/Column.

3.   In Excel 2007, click Layout > Data Labels > Centre. In Excel 2013 or the new version, click Design > Add Chart Element > Data Labels > Centre.

4. Then go to a blank range and type cell contents.

5. Then in the cell next to the column you type this =XX/Y$Y (XX is the cell value you want to show as a percentage, Y$Y is the total value), and drag the fill handle to the range needed.

6. Then go to the stacked column, and select the label you want to show as a percentage, then type = in the formula bar and select percentage cell and press Enter key.

18.

2D Chart	3D Chart
(a) The chart represents business data with just two dimensions	(a) The chart represents business data with three dimensions
(b) The two dimensions are length and height (No width)	(b) The Three dimensions are Length and Height and width (or depth)
(c) There are X-axis and Y-axis	(c) There is X-axis, Y-axis is and Z-axis
(d) The shape of the chart may be in the form of Rectangle, Square, Triangle, Polygon, etc	(d) The shape of the chart may be Cylinder, Cube, Pyramid, etc

19. 1. Column chart: column chart are used to compare values across categories

2. Line chart: Line charts are used to display trends over time

3. Pie chart: Pie charts display the contribution of each value to a total

4. Bar chart: Bar charts are best suited for comparing multiple values

5. Area chart: Area chart emphasis differences between several sets of data over a period of time.

6. Scatter chart: (XY chart) This chart compares pairs of values.

7. Radar chart: Display values relative to a centre point.

8. Doughnut chart: It shows the relationship of parts to a whole. This chart display data in rings, where each ring represents a data series.

20.

Basis	Column Chart	Pie Chart	Line Chart
Meaning	Column chart is the chart that uses vertical (rectangle shaped) bars to represent each category.	Pie chart is a circular chart which represents data in slices.	Line chart is a chart which is formed by connecting the data points together.
Use/Purpose	Column chart is well suited for depicting change in data over a time period.	Pie charts are will suitable where parts are to be compared to whole. It is used for proportional data.	Line charts are used to depict relationship between two sets of data in which oneset is always dependent on another.

| Negative values | Negative values can be shown here using downward vertical bars. | Pie chart cannot be used to depict negative values. | Negative values can be shown in Line charts by first clicking on vertical bar and pressing Ctrl+1 to bring up the format axis box. Then choose custom category from number section and add a (-) negative sign in format code box. Click add to incorporate negative values in the line chart. |
| How it looks? | Chart Title | ENGLISH | Chart Title |

21. **Procedure**:

Step 1 – Open a new blank worksheet

Step 2 – Enter the following data in the respective cells

	A	B
1	Year	Net Profit
2	2009	1,25,800
3	2010	2,38,400
4	2011	1,86,500
5	2012	1,54,900
6	2013	2,51,000
7	2014	3,00,000

Step 3 – Select the range A1: B7, which is to be shown in the chart

Step4- Click on Insert menu → Click on Chart → Chart Wizard → Click on Line Chart → Finish

Output:

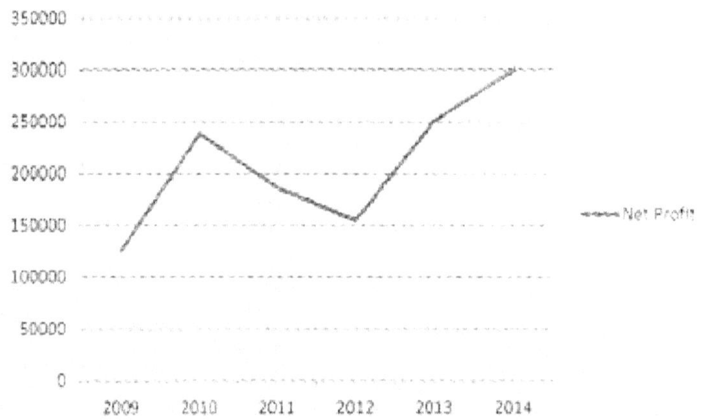

CUET UG

ACCOUNTANCY/BOOK KEEPING

Class XII

1. Match List I with List II

List I	**List II**
A. Excess of purchase consideration over value of net assets	I. Issue Debentures as collateral security.
B. Excess of net assets over purchase consideration	II. Goodwill
C. Debenture Suspense Account	III. Issue of Debentures for consideration other than cash
D. Assets received against Debentures	IV. Capital Reserve

   Choose the correct answer from the options given below :

   (a) A-IV, B-II, C-I, D-III   (b) A-II, B-IV, C-I, D-III

   (c) A-II, B-IV, C-III, D-I   (d) A-IV, B-II, C-III, D-I

2. Which among the following are the non-cash items?

   A. Deferred Tax   B. Goodwill write-off

   C. Depreciation   D. Increase in Stock

   Choose the correct answer from the options given below :

   (a) B and C only   (b) A, B and D only

   (c) B, C and D only   (d) A, B and C only

3. Operating Profit Ratio of XYZ Ltd. is 60%. The operating ratio of XYZ Ltd. is :

   (a) 30%   (b) 60%

   (c) 100%   (d) 40%

4. Which among the following are the modes of dissolution?

   A. Dissolution by Nature   B. Compulsory Dissolution

   C. Dissolution by Agreement   D. Dissolution by Notice

   Choose the correct answer from the options given below :

   (a) B, C and D only   (b) A, C and D only

   (c) A, B and C only   (d) A, D and B only

5. In the absence of any information regarding the acquisition of share in the profit of retiring/deceased partner by the remaining partners, it is assumed that they will acquire his/her share in the :

(*a*) Capital Ratio   (*b*) Equal Ratio

(*c*) New Profit Sharing Ratio   (*d*) Old Profit Sharing Ratio

6. Extract of Receipt and Payment Account for the year ended on March 31, 2021 is given.

Calculate the amout of Stationery to be shown in Income and Expenditure A/c.

Payments of Stationery : Rs. 23,000

Additional Information :

	1 April, 2020	31 Mar 2021
Stock of Stationary	4,000	3,000
Creditors for stationery	9,000	2,500

(*a*) Rs. 17,500   (*b*) Rs. 20,500

(*c*) Rs. 11,500   (*d*) Rs. 23,000

7. _________ is the amount received as per the will of a deceased person.

(*a*) Honorarium   (*b*) Entrance Fees

(*c*) Donation   (*d*) Legacy

8. From the following information of I Ltd., calculate Net Increase/Decrease in cash and cash equivalents during the year 2021-22.

(i)   Cash flow from Operation Activities : Rs. 2,35,000

(ii) Cash used in investing Activities : Rs. 4,35,000

(iii) Cash flow from financing activities : Rs. 2,35,000

(*a*) Rs. 35,000 Decrease   (*b*) Rs. 4,35,000 Decrease

(*c*) Rs. 4,70,000 Increase   (*d*) Rs. 35,000 Increase

9. Blue Prints Ltd. purchased a building worth Rs. 1,50,000, Machinery work Rs. 1,40,000 and Furniture worth Rs. 10,000 from XYZ Co. and took over its liabilities of Rs. 20,000 for a purchase consideration of Rs. 3,15,000.

Calculate the Goodwill/Capital Reserve to be recorded by Blue Print Ltd.

(*a*) Rs. 35,000 Capital Reserve   (*b*) Rs. 35,000 Goodwill

(*c*) Rs. 3,15,000 Goodwill   (*d*) Rs. 55,000 Goodwill

10. The Directors of Tivoli Plastics Ltd. resolved that 200 equity shares of Rs. 100 each be Forfeited for non-payment of the second and final call of Rs. 30 per share. Out of these, 150 shares were reissued at Rs. 60 per share as fully paid-up. How much amount will be transferred to Capital Reserve Account?

(*a*) Rs. 10,500   (*b*) Rs. 4,500

(*c*) Rs. 6,000   (*d*) Rs. 8,000

11. On 1/4/22, X and Y decided to dissolve their firm. On that date of dissolution, Goodwill appeared at Rs. 5,00,000 in the Balance Sheet. Goodwill will be :

(a) Transferred to the debit side of realisation A/C

(b) Transferred to the credit side of partner's Capital A/c in their profit sharing ratio

(c) Transferred to the credit side of realisation A/c

(d) Transferred to cash account

12. From the following information, calculate interest on Capital of C, a partner for the year ended 31st March, 2022.

C's Capital on 31/3/2022 : Rs. 12,00,000

Profit credited to C for the year ended 31/3/2022 : Rs. 3,00,000

Drawings made during the year : Rs. 1,00,000

Additional Capital introduced on 1/10/21 : Rs. 5,00,000

Rate of Interest = 12% p.a.

(a) Rs. 60,000   (b) Rs. 1,44,000

(c) Rs. 90,000   (d) Rs. 1,20,000

13. If the total income earned by Saket Club, a Not-for-Profit organisation is Rs. 2,60,000 and surplus earned is Rs. 85,000, then total expenditure incurred will be :

(a) Rs. 1,85,000   (b) Rs. 1,75,000

(c) Rs. 3,45,000   (d) Rs. 85,000

14. If X share of profit was to be calculated on the basis of Average Profit of the last three years, which were Rs. 1,36,000 for 2018 – 19, Rs. 1,54,000 for 2019-20 and Rs. 1,00,000 for 2020-21. X share of profit for the period from April 01, 2020 to June 30, 2020 shall be calculated on the basis of Average Profit. The profit sharing ration is 4 : 5 : 1 between X, Y and Z.

His share of profit will be :

(a) Rs. 26,000   (b) Rs. 13,000

(c) Rs. 10,000   (d) Rs. 12,000

15. Correct sequence of issue of shares is –

A. Receipt of Application   B. Issue of Prospectus

C. Letter of Allotment of Shares   D. Letter of Regret

Choose the correct answer from the options given below :

(a) A, B, C, D   (b) A, B, D, C

(c) B, A, C, D   (d) C, B, A, D

16. For computing Goodwill by capitalisation of Average Profit method, the following sequence would be followed :

A. Capitalise the average profit on the basis of Normal Rate of Return

B. Ascertain the firm's Capital - Total Assets - Outside Liabilities

C. Ascertain the average profits based on past year's performance

D. Compute the volume of Goodwill

Choose the correct answer from the options given below :

(a) B, C, A, D   (b) C, A, B, D

(c) A, B, C, D   (d) A, C, B, D

17. Earning Capacity of a Company is measured by :

(a) Working Capital Ratio   (b) Profitability Ratio

(c) Solvency Ratio   (d) Liquidity Ratio

18. Separate disclosure of cash flows from __________ activities is important because they represent the extent to which expenditure have been made for resources intended to generate future income and cash flows :

(a) Operating   (b) Investing

(c) Financing   (d) Extraordinary

19. In common size statement, if revenue from operations are Rs. 23,00,000 and other incomes are Rs. 3,00,000, then the percentage of "Total Revenue from Operations" to "Revenue from operations" will be :

(a) 110%   (b) 113.04%

(c) 12.04%   (d) 110.04%

20. Which A/c is credited for transfer of interest on Debenture Redemption Fund Investment?

(a) Debenture Redemption Fund A/c

(b) Debenture Redemption Fund Investment A/c

(c) Bank A/c

(d) Statement of P & L

21. The directors of a company forfeited 400 equity shares of Rs. 10 each fully called up on which Rs. 1,600 had been paid. All the forfeited shares were reissued upon payment of Rs. 3,000. Calculate the amout transferred to Capital Reserve

(a) Rs. 1,600   (b) Rs. 600

(c) Rs. 1,400   (d) 2,400

22. Raman and Naman were in partnership sharing profit and losses as 3 : 2. Their partnership firm was dissolved on 31st March 2022. On the date of dissolution, Naman's loan was Rs. 20,000. Naman agreed to take stock (already transferred to Realisation A/c) of Rs. 15,000 at Rs. 18,000 and balance in cash for the settlement of loan. Journal Entry for above transaction is :

(a) Naman's Loan A/c   Dr.   20,000
       To Realisation A/c   18,000
       To cash A/c   2,000

(b) Naman's Loan A/c   Dr.   20,000
       To Realisation A/c   15,000
       To cash A/c   5,000

(c) Naman's Loan A/c   Dr.   20,000
       To Realisation A/c   20,000

(d) Naman's Loan A/c   Dr.   20,000
       To Realisation A/c   12,000
       To cash A/c   8,000

23. Calculate the amount of adjusted profit for the year ended 31 March 2021 for the purposes of valuation of Goodwill from the following information :

Profit for the year ended 31 March 2021 : Rs. 80,000

On 1 July, 2020, a major plant repair was undertaken for Rs. 10,000 which was charged to Revenue. The said sum is to be capitalised for Goodwill valuation subject to adustment of depreciation @ 10% p.a. on reducing balance method.

(*a*) Rs. 90,000

(*b*) Rs. 89,000

(*c*) Rs. 89,750

(*d*) Rs. 89,250

24. Match List I with List II

List I	**List II**
A. Partner's Salary	I. P & L A/c Dr.
B. Manager's Salary	II. P & L Appropriation A/c Dr.
C. Distribution of Loss	III. P & L A/c Cr.
D. Commission Received	IV. P & L Appropriation A/c Cr.

Choose the correct answer from the options given below :

(*a*) A-I, B-II, C-III, D-IV

(*b*) A-II, B-I, C-IV, D-III

(*c*) A-III, B-II, C-IV, D-I

(*d*) A-IV, B-III, C-II, D-I

25. How will you deal with the following items while preparing for the Bombay Women Cricket Club, its Income and Expenditure Account for the year ending 31ˢᵗ March 2021, and its Balance Sheet, on the same date : Donation for the Pavilion construction Rs. 12,25,000, Expenditure incurred Rs. 10,80,000. Total estimate Rs. 25,00,000.

(*a*) Rs. 1,45,000 to be shown in Liability side of Balance Sheet

(*b*) Rs. 1,45,000 to be shown on Asset side of the Balance sheet and Rs. 25,00,000 to be shown on Liability side

(*c*) Rs. 12,75,000 to be shown on expenditure side of Income and Expenditure Account

(*d*) Rs. 12,75,000 to be shown on Income side of Income and Expenditure Account

26. X Ltd. has a Current Ration of 3.5 : 1 and Quick Ratio of 2 : 1. If excess of current assets over quick assets represented by inventories is Rs. 24,000. Calculate current liabilities.

(*a*) Rs. 16,000

(*b*) Rs. 56,000

(*c*) Rs. 36,000

(*d*) Rs. 32,000

27. Comparative Statements are also known as :

(*a*) Dynamic Analysis

(*b*) Horizontal Analysis

(*c*) Vertical Analysis

(*d*) External Analysis

28. The company purchased plant with a book value of Rs. 1,90,000 from National Victory Company and agreed to pay via issuing 2000, 10% Debentures of Rs. 100 each at a discount of 5%.

Amount that will be credited to 10% Debenture A/c will be :

(*a*) Rs. 1,90,000

(*b*) Rs. 2,00,000

(*c*) Rs. 2,40,000

(*d*) Rs. 10,000

29. Valuation of Goodwill takes place on which of the following occasions :

    A. Incorporation of a new business   B. Change in profit sharing ratio

    C. Amalgamation of partnership firm   D. Admission of a partner

    E. Dissolution of firm or closure of business

Choose the correct answer from the options given below :

    (*a*) A, B and D only   (*b*) B, C and D only

    (*c*) A, C, D only   (*d*) A, B, E only

30. Following items are categorised under Operating Activities :

    A. Purchase of Goodwill   B. Transfer to General Reserve

    C. Issue of fresh shares   D. Gain on sale of machinery

Choose the correct answer from the options given below :

    (*a*) B and D only   (*b*) A and B only

    (*c*) A and D only   (*d*) B and C only

31. Match List I with List II

List I	**List II**
A. Liquidity Ratio	I. Proprietary Ratio
B. Solvency Ratio	II. Current Ratio
C. Activity Ratio	III. Earning per Share
D. Profitability Ratio	IV. Current assets turnover ratio

Choose the correct answer from the options given below :

    (*a*) A-II, B-I, C-IV, D-III   (*b*) A-III, B-IV, C-I, D-II

    (*c*) A-I, B-II, C-III, D-IV   (*d*) A-III, B-II, C-I, D-IV

32. The money received from applicants to whom no debentures have been allotted will be __________ .

    (*a*) Refunded   (*b*) Adjusted

    (*c*) Used later on   (*d*) not refunded

33. What will be the share of decreased partner, whose ratio was $\frac{1}{4}$, if the turnover in year of death till the date of death was Rs. 8,00,000 and in previous year was Rs. 20,00,000? Profit in previous year was Rs. 4,00,000

    (*a*) Rs. 40,000   (*b*) Rs. 13,333

    (*c*) Rs. 1,60,000   (*d*) Rs. 1,00,000

34. If Amit, a partner, withdrew Rs. 10,000 per month in the end, what will be the amount of interest on drawing if it is calculated @8% p.a.?

    (*a*) Rs. 9,600   (*b*) Rs. 4,800

    (*c*) Rs. 5,200   (*d*) Rs. 4,400

35. Match List I with List II

List I	**List II**
A. Share forfeiture	I. Reserve Capital
B. Uncalled Capital	II. Pro-rata allotment
C. Over-subscription	III. Capital Reserve
D. Discount on issue of shares	IV. Reissue of shares

Choose the correct answer from the options given below :

(*a*) A-III, B-I, C-II, D-IV (*b*) A-IV, B-I, C-III, D-II

(*c*) A-II, B-III, C-IV, D-I (*d*) A-I, B-II, C-IV, D-III

36. X, Y, Z are partners who decided to dissolve their firm. Realisation expenses were to be borne by Y for which he was to be given remuneration of Rs. 10,000. Actual expenses were Rs. 12,000. How much amount will be transferred to Y's Capital A/c for it?

(*a*) Rs. 22,000 (*b*) Rs. 12,000

(*c*) Rs. 2,000 (*d*) Rs. 10,000

37. The default extension of MS Access (2007) file is :

(*a*) .accbd (*b*) .end

(*c*) .doc (*d*) .exe

38. Which of the following statement is not correct?

(*a*) A spreadsheet is a configuration of rows and columns

(*b*) A spreadsheet is different from worksheet

(*c*) Spreadsheet application is a computer programme

(*d*) Spreadsheet can be used for making Graphs also

39. The data that is entered in a cell may be either :

A. Numeric B. Alpha-Numeric

C. Date D. Label

Choose the correct answer from the options given below :

(*a*) C, D only (*b*) A, B and D only

(*c*) A, C and D only (*d*) A, B and C only

40. The computerised accounting System refers to :

(*a*) Processing of Balance Sheet only

(*b*) Processing of Accounting related transactions and produce Records and Reports

(*c*) Processing of accounting related data only

(*d*) Printing of Balance Sheet and Profit and Loss Account

Passage

Read the following information to answer.

On the basis of case study given below, answer the question which follows :

"Mikku on alumni of IIT Delhi, initiated his start-up" "Gajanan Ltd.," in the year 2016. His profit in the year 2020-21 after all appropriation was Rs. 6,25,000. This profit was arrived after taking following items into consideration :

Loss on sale of fixed Assets	Rs. 5,00,000
Goodwill written off	Rs. 3,80,000
Transfer to reserve	Rs. 3,55,000
Provision for tax	Rs. 2,70,000
Interest on Debentures paid	Rs. 1,65,000

Other Details are :

Particulars	2020 (in Rs.)	2021 (in Rs.)
Prepaid Expenses	25,000	10,000
Accrued interest	40,000	68,000
Trade payables	7,00,000	4,00,000
Inventories	6,50,000	5,50,000

41. Net profit before tax will be Rs. _________.

    (*a*) Rs. 9,80,000   (*b*) Rs. 8,95,000

    (*c*) Rs. 12,50,000   (*d*) Rs. 16,30,000

42. Operating Profit before working capital changes will be Rs. _________.

    (*a*) 22,95,000   (*b*) 20,95,000

    (*c*) 23,95,000   (*d*) 12,95,000

43. From among the following, choose the item which would be mentioned in financing activity also :

    (*a*) Provision for tax   (*b*) Interest on Debenture

    (*c*) Goodwill written off   (*d*) Loss on sale of fixed assets

44. Cash from operating activities before tax will be Rs. _________.

    (*a*) 20,82,000   (*b*) 26,82,000

    (*c*) 23,78,000   (*d*) 28,62,000

45. Cash flow from Operating Activities will be Rs. _________.

    (*a*) 30,72,000   (*b*) 1,81,2000

    (*c*) 26,82,000   (*d*) 24,12,000

Passage

Case Study

Read the following information to answer.

Arun and Ram are partners in a restaurant business sharing profits and losses in capital ratio. Their fixed capital from the beginning of the firm was Rs. 2,00,000 and Rs. 1,50,000 respectively.

The profit for the year ended 31 March 2022 before the appropriation of Salary and Interest on Capital was Rs. 2,20,000. Ram is allowed a salary of Rs. 2,000 per quarter and interest on capital @10% p.a.

Due to the further expansion of the business, they decided to enter Sanjeev as a new partner for $\frac{1}{5}$ share in profits. It was agreed that Sanjeev will bring Rs. 1,00,000 as capital and Rs. 50,000 as his share of Goodwill. It was decided that he will give Rs. 1,00,000 as loan to the firm for 3 years.

46. The amount of salary to be shown in the Dr. side of P & L Appropriation A/C will be :

   (a) Rs. 2,000   (b) Rs. 8,000

   (c) Rs. 12,000   (d) Rs. 24,000

47. Interest on capital will be shown on the Dr. side of Profit and Loss Appropriation A/c and _____ side of Partner's _____ A/c.

   (a) Cr, Capital   (b) Dr, Current

   (c) Cr, Current   (d) Dr, Capital

48. Rate of Interest on loan given by Sanjeev will be :

   (a) 8% P.A.   (b) 10% P.A.

   (c) NIL   (d) 6% P.A.

49. The amount of distributed profits of both the partner's will be :

   (a) Rs. 1,77,000   (b) Rs. 2,20,000

   (c) Rs. 1,71,000   (d) Rs. 2,00,000

50. The new profit sharing ratio of Arun, Ram and Sanjeev will be :

   (a) 1 : 1 : 1   (b) 14 : 10 : 6

   (c) 16 : 12 : 7   (d) 3 : 2 : 1

Answers

1. (b)	**2.** (a)	**3.** (d)	**4.** (a)	**5.** (d)	**6.** (a)	**7.** (d)	**8.** (d)	**9.** (a)	**10.** (b)
11. (a)	**12.** (c)	**13.** (b)	**14.** (b)	**15.** (c)	**16.** (b)	**17.** (b)	**18.** (d)	**19.** (b)	**20.** (d)
21. (b)	**22.** (a)	**23.** (d)	**24.** (b)	**25.** (a)	**26.** (a)	**27.** (b)	**28.** (b)	**29.** (b)	**30.** (c)
31. (a)	**32.** (a)	**33.** (a)	**34.** (d)	**35.** (a)	**36.** (d)	**37.** (a)	**38.** (b)	**39.** (c)	**40.** (b)
41. (c)	**42.** (a)	**43.** (b)	**44.** (a)	**45.** (b)	**46.** (b)	**47.** (c)	**48.** (d)	**49.** (a)	**50.** (c)

Solutions

1. (b) Match

2. (a) Goodwill & Depveciation are non case items.

3. (d) 100 – 60% = 40%

4. (a) Dissolution by nature is not a mode.

5. (d) Absence of information means old profit sharing ratio.

6. (a) 23000 + 4000 + 2500 – 3000 – 9000 = 17500

7. (d) Legacy is the amount of will of a decreased person.

8. (d) 235000 + 235000 – 435000 = 35000 Increase

9. (a) 150000 + 140000 + 10000

$$= \overset{\text{Dr}}{300000}, \overset{\text{Cr}}{335000} = \overset{\text{Goodwill}}{35000}$$

10. (b) $\overset{\text{Cr}}{\text{F/F } 1400}, \overset{\text{Dr}}{\text{F/F } 6000}, \overset{\text{Transfer}}{10500 - 6000} = 4500$

11. (a) At dissolution goodwill be transfer to realisation.

12. (c) OP Cap = 12L + 1L – (3L + 5L) = 5L

$$\text{IOC on OP Cap } 500000 \times \frac{12}{100} = 60000$$

$$\text{IOC on Addi Cap } 500000 \times \frac{12}{100} \times \frac{6}{12} = \frac{30000}{90000}$$

13. (b) 260000 – 85000 = 175000

14. (b) Total = 136000 + 154000 + 100000 = 390000

    AV = 390000 ÷ 3 = 130000

    Share of profit of period

$$= 130000 \times \frac{3}{12} \times \frac{4}{10} = 13000$$

15. (c)

16. (b) Match the col.

17. (b) Earning capacity is measured by profitability ratio.

18. (d)

19. (b) $\dfrac{2600000}{2300000} \times 100 = 113.04\%$

20. (d) Statement of P & L.

21. (b) F/F Cr = 1600, F/F Dr = 1000, Bal = 600

22. (A) 20000 – 18000 = 2000 Rs. in cash

23. (d) $\overset{\text{Plant}}{80000} + 10000 - \overset{\text{Dep of 9 month}}{750} = 89250$ Rs.

24. (b) Match

25. (a) $\overset{\text{Donation}}{1225000} - \overset{\text{Exp}}{1080000} = 145000$

26. (a) Inventories = CA – LA

    24000 = 3.5x – 2x

    24000 = 1.5x

$$\frac{24000}{1.5} = x$$

    16000 = C.L.

27. (b) Horizontal Analysis

28. (b) No. × Rs.

    2000 × 100 = 200000 Rs.

29. (b)

30. (c) Purchase of goodwill & Gain in sale of machinery are under operating activity.

31. (a) Liquidity ratio = Current ratio

    Solvency ratio = Proprietry ratio

32. (a) If debentures not allotted, full application money refunded.

33. (a) $\dfrac{400000}{2000000} \times 800000 = 160000$

$$160000 \times \frac{1}{4} = 40000$$

34. (d) Per month = 10000

Total Drawings = 10000 × 12 = 120000

$$\text{IOD} = 120000 \times \frac{8}{100} \times \frac{11}{2} \times \frac{1}{12} = 4400 \text{ Rs.}$$

35. (a) Share for feiture = Cap. Res.

Over subscription = Pro. rata allotment.

36. (d) Remuneration of Rs. 10000

37. (a)   **38.** (b)   **39.** (c)   **40.** (b)

41. (c) 625000 + 355000 + 270000 = 12,50,000

42. (a) 1250000 + 500000 + 380000 + 165000
= 2295000

43. (b)

44. (2082000) Rs.

2295000 + (15000 + 100000) – (28000 + 300000)

2295000 + 115000 – 328000

45. (1812000)   2082000 – 270000

46. (b) 2000 × 4 = 8000

47. (c) Cr side of current a/c

48. (d) 6% p.a. Int on Loan

49. (a)

P & L Appropriation A/c			
To salary	8000	By P & C	220000
To IOCA	20000		
R	13000		
To profit D is	177000		
	220000		220000

50. (c) 5's share = $\dfrac{1}{5}$

Remaining share = $1 - \dfrac{1}{5} = \dfrac{4}{5}$

A's share = $\dfrac{4}{5} \times \dfrac{4}{7} = \dfrac{16}{35}$

R's share = $\dfrac{4}{5} \times \dfrac{3}{7} = \dfrac{12}{35}$

A : R : S

$\dfrac{16}{35} : \dfrac{12}{35} : \dfrac{1}{5}$ or $\dfrac{16 : 12 : 7}{35}$

CBSE

ACCOUNTANCY (THEORY)

Class XII

Time Allowed: 90 minutes   Maximum Marks: 40

General Instructions

1. *This question paper contains 60 questions out of which 40 questions are to be attempted. All questions carry equal marks.*
2. *This question paper consists of three parts- Part I, II and III.*
3. *Part I is compulsory for all candidates. Attempt either Part II or Part III.*
4. *Part I comprises of three sections - Section A, B and C.*
5. *From Part I (Q. No. 1 to 36) – attempt any 14 questions each from Section A and B. Attempt any three questions from Section C.*
6. *From Part II OR III – (Q. No. 37 to 60) – attempt any four questions from Section A and any five questions from Section B.*
7. *Attempted first, desired number of questions only, in each Part/Section will be evaluated.*
8. *There is only one correct option for every multiple choice questions (MCQs). Marks will not be awarded for answering more than one option.*
9. *There is no negative marking.*

PART – I

Section A

Attempt any 14 questions from question number 1 to 16.

1. The document that contains the terms of partnership is called:

   (A) Partnership Agreement   (B) Partnership Contract

   (C) Partnership Deed   (D) Partnership Rules

2. A, B, C and D are partners in a firm. They want to expand their business for which additional capital and more managerial experts are required. For this they want to admit more members in their firm. What is the maximum number of additional members that can be admitted by them in the firm:

   (A) 02   (B) 50

   (C) 20   (D) 46

3. Vijay and Rattan are partners in a firm. The partnership agreement provides for interest on drawings @ 12% per annum. Which of the following accounts will be debited to transfer interest on drawings to Profit and Loss Appropriation Account :

(A) Interest of Drawings account   (B) Bank account

(C) Partner's Current accounts   (D) Partner's Capital accounts

4. A and B were partners in a firm. Their capitals at the end of the year ending on 31.3.2021 were ₹ 3,00,000 and ₹ 1,50,000 respectively. During the year B withdrew ₹ 10,000 which was debited to his capital account. Profit for the year ended 31st March, 2021 was ₹ 32,000 which was credited to their capital accounts. During the year B introduced additional capital ₹ 32,000. What was B's capital on 1.4.2020?

(A) ₹ 1,50,000   (B) ₹ 1,60,000

(C) ₹ 1,12,000   (D) ₹ 1,52,000

5. P, Q and R were partners in a firm sharing profits and losses in the ratio 2:2:1. They admitted L as a new partner for $\frac{1}{5}th$ share in the profits. L was given a guarantee that his share of profit shall be ₹ 1,00,000. Any deficiency arising on account of guarantee to L will be borne by Q. The profit of the firm during the year ended 31.3.3021 was ₹ 4,00,000. The amount of deficiency borne by Q was :

(A) ₹ 80,000   (B) ₹ 20,000

(C) ₹ 1,00,000   (D) ₹ 6,667

6. X and Y were partners in a firm sharing profits and losses equally. Their capitals were ₹ 2,00,000 and ₹ 3,00,000 respectively. Z was admitted as a new partner for $\frac{1}{4}th$ share in the profits of the firm. Z brought ₹ 2,00,000 as his capital. The goodwill of the firm was :

(A) ₹ 1,00,000   (B) ₹ 25,000

(C) ₹ 2,00,000   (D) ₹ 7,00,000

7. R and M were partners in a firm, sharing profits and losses in the ratio of 5 : 3. L was admitted as a new partner for 1/5th share in the profits of the firm. The new profit ratio was 2 : 2 : 1. L brought ₹ 1,54,000 for his capital and did not bring his share of goodwill premium. Goodwill of the firm of L's admission was estimated at ₹ 4,50,000. It was decided not to raise goodwill account of L's admission.

Out of the following what will be the correct treatment of good will on L's admission?

(A) Debit L's current A/c by ₹ 90,000 and credit R's and M's capital A/cs by ₹ 45,000 each.

(B) Debit L's current A/c by ₹ 90,000 Debit M's capital A/c by ₹ 11,250 credit R's capital A/c by ₹ 1,01,250.

(C) Debit L's current A/c by ₹ 90,000 and credit R's capital A/c by ₹ 56,250 and credit M's capital A/c ₹ 33,750.

(D) Debit L's current A/c by ₹ 4,50,000 and credit R's and M's capital A/c by ₹ 2,25,000 each.

8. Sharma and Verma were partners in a firm. The partnership deed provided that interest on partner's drawings will be charged @ 12% per annum. During the year Sharma withdrew ₹ 6,000. Interest on his drawings will be :

(A) ₹ 600   (B) ₹ 330

(C) ₹ 360   (D) ₹ 720

9. When a combined 'Share Application and Allotment Account' is opened in the books of the company, which of the following accounts will be debited for money refunded on rejected application :

(A) Share Application Account

(B) Share Application and Allotment Account

(C) Share Allotment Account

(D) Bank Account

10. Shubham Ltd. purchased a machinery of ₹ 3,80,000 from Ganpati Ltd. The payment was made by issue of ₹ 3,000 equity shares of ₹ 100 each at a premium of 10% and the balance by issuing a cheque. The amount of cheque issued in favour of Ganpati Ltd. was :

(A) ₹ 80,000   (B) ₹ 3,80,000

(C) ₹ 30,000   (D) ₹ 50,000

11. Pooja Ltd. issued ₹ 50,00,000 equity share of ₹ 100 each at a premium of ₹ 30 per share. Half of the premium amount was payable on allotment and the remaining half was payable on first call. Raja to whom 500 shares were allotted failed to pay the first call and second and final call. His shares were forfeited. On forfeiture of shares the amount debited to 'securities premium reserve account' was :

(A) ₹ 7,500   (B) ₹ 15,000

(C) Nil   (D) ₹ 50,000

12. Y Ltd. invited applications for issuing 1,00,000 equity shares of ₹ 10 each at a premium of ₹ 8 per share. The amount per share was payable as follows :

On Application - ₹ 8 per share (including ₹ 5 premium)

On Allotment - ₹ 8 per share (including ₹ 3 premium)

On first and final call - Balance.

Applications for 1,50,000 shares were received. Mohan who had applied for 4,000 shares paid the entire share money, on shares applied, with application. The application money received was :

(A) ₹ 12,00,000   (B) ₹ 8,00,000

(C) ₹ 12,40,000   (D) ₹ 10,00,000

13. Which of the following accounts will be debited for transferring loss on revaluation of assets and reassessment of liabilities at the time of admission of a new partner into the partnership firm :

(A) Old partner's capital accounts in old profit sharing ratio

(B) Old partners capital accounts in sacrificing ratio

(C) All partners capital accounts (including incoming partner) in new profit sharing ratio.

(D) Revaluation account

14. A business earned average profits of ₹ 60,000 during the last three years. The normal rate of return on similar business is 12%. The value of net assets of the business is ₹ 4,00,000. Its goodwill by capitalisation of Average Profits Method will be :

(A) ₹ 1,00,000

(B) ₹ 2,00,000

(C) ₹ 4,00,000

(D) ₹ 50,000

15. Due to change in the profit sharing ratio, Anisha's gain is 1/5th while Harit's sacrifice is 1/5th. They decided to adjust the following without affecting their book values, by passing a single adjustment entry :

General Reserve	₹ 20,000
Profit & Loss Account (Dr.)	₹ 30,000

The necessary adjustment entry will be :

(A) Debit Anisha's capital account by ₹ 2,000 and credit Harit's capital account by ₹ 2,000.

(B) Debit Anisha's capital account by ₹ 10,000 and credit Harit's capital account by ₹ 10,000.

(C) Debit Harit's capital account by ₹ 2,000 and credit Anisha's capital account by ₹ 2,000.

(D) Debit Harit's capital account by ₹ 10,000 and credit Anisha's capital account by ₹ 10,000.

16. Leela and Meeta were partners in a firm sharing profits and losses in the ratio of 7 : 3. Geeta was admitted as a new partner for a 3/13 share in the profits of the firm. The new profit sharing ratio will be :

(A) 7 : 3 : 7   (B) 7 : 3 : 3

(C) 3 : 7 : 7   (D) 1 : 1 : 1

Section B

Attempt any 14 questions from question number 17 to 32.

17. Given below are two statements one labelled as **Assertion (A)** and the other labelled as **Reason (R)** :

Assertion (A) : Co-ownership of property amounts to partnership.

Reason (R) : The element of business is present in co-ownership.

In the context of the above two statements which of the following is correct.

(A) Both (A) and (R) are correct and (R) is correct reason for (A).

(B) Both (A) and (R) are incorrect.

(C) (A) is correct but (R) is incorrect.

(D) Both (A) and (R) are correct but (R) is not the correct reason for (A).

18. Z Ltd. forfeited 800 shares of ₹ 10 each on which ₹ 8 per share was called and ₹ 6 per share was paid. The amount with which share capital account debited on the forfeiture of these shares was :

(A) ₹ 8,000

(B) ₹ 6,400

(C) ₹ 4,800

(D) ₹ 3,200

19. A situation where number of shares offered to the public for subscription are less than the number of shares for which applications have been received is called :

(A) Under subscription

(B) Fully subscribed

(C) Over subscription

(D) Both (B) and (C)

20. Which of the following statements are correct :

(i) The liability of a partner for acts of the firm is unlimited.

(ii) Private assets of a partner can also be used for paying the debts of the firm.

(iii)Each partner is liable jointly with all other partners and also severally to the third parties for all the act of the firm done, while he is a partner.

(iv)The liability of a partner is limited to the extent of his capital contribution.

(A) Only (iii)

(B) (i) and (ii)

(C) (i), (ii) and (iii)

(D) (i), (ii), (iii) and (iv)

21. Which of the following statement is not true for fixed capital account ?

(A) The capital account balance remains unchanged unless there is addition to or withdrawal of capital.

(B) The capital accounts always show a credit balance.

(C) Each partner has only one account, i.e., capital account, under this method.

(D) All adjustments for drawings, salary, interest on capital etc. are made in the current account.

22. Amar and Samar were partners in a firm sharing profits and losses in the ratio of 1 : 5. On 1.4.2021 Ganesh was admitted for 1/5th share in the profits. On the date of Ganesh's admission the balance sheet of Amar and Samar showed a debit balance of ₹ 60,000 in the profit and loss account. The accounting treatment for the same in the books of accounts of the firm on Ganesh's admission will be :

(A) Amar's and Samar's Capital Accounts will be debited by ₹ 10,000 and ₹ 50,000 respectively and Profit and Loss Account will be credited by ₹ 60,000.

(B) Profit and Loss Account will be debited by ₹ 60,000 and Amar's and Samar's Capital Accounts will be credited by ₹ 10,000 and ₹ 50,000 respectively.

(C) Revaluation Account will be debited by ₹ 60,000 and Profit and Loss Account will be credited by ₹ 60,000.

(D) Profit and Loss Appropriation Account will be debited by ₹ 60,000 and Profit and Loss Account will be credited by ₹ 60,000.

23. On the reconstitution of a firm, the value of land was to be appreciated ₹ 2,00,000 and plant and machinery was to be reduced to ₹ 7,00,000 from ₹ 10,00,000. Gain or Loss on revaluation will be :

(A) Gain ₹ 1,00,000

(B) Loss ₹ 1,00,000

(C) Loss ₹ 5,00,000

(D) Gain ₹ 5,00,000

24. Given below are two statements, one labelled as **Assertion (A)** and the other labelled as **Reason (R)**.

Assertion (A) : Goodwill is an intangible asset.

Reason (R) : It is the value of the reputation of a firm in respect of the profits expected in future over and above the normal profits.

In the context of the above statements which of the following is correct ?

(A) Both (A) and (R) are correct.

(B) (A) is wrong but (R) is correct.

(C) (A) is correct but (R) is wrong.

(D) Both (A) and (R) are wrong.

25. When a new partner is admitted, the balance of 'General Reserve' appearing in the Balance Sheet is credited to :

(A) Profit and Loss Appropriation Account

(B) Capital Accounts of all partners

(C) Revaluation Account

(D) Capital Accounts of old partners

26. Kavita and Karan are partners in a firm sharing profits and losses in the ratio 4 : 1. On 1st April, 2021, they admitted Mohit for 1/4th share in the profits of the firm. The balance sheet of Kavita and Karan showed stock at ₹ 45,000. On admission of new partner, the stock was found undervalued by 10%. The journal entry to give effect to the above adjustment on Mohit's admission wil be :

			Debit Amount (₹)	Credit Amount (₹)
(A)	Revaluation A/c	Dr.	5,000	
	To Stock A/c			5,000
(B)	Stock A/c	Dr.	4,500	
	To Revaluation A/c			4,500
(C)	Stock A/c	Dr.	5,000	
	To Revaluation A/c			5,000
(D)	Revaluation A/c	Dr.	4,500	
	To Stock A/c			4,500

27. Sangeet and Suman were partners in a firm sharing profits and losses in the ratio of 7 : 3. During the year ended 31.3.2021 the firm earned a proit of ₹ 1,00,000. After preparation of the financial statements it was discovered that salary to Suman @ ₹ 3,000 per month had been omitted. The necessary adjustment entry for the same will be :

			Dr. (₹)	Cr. (₹)
(A)	Profit and Loss Appropriation A/c Dr.		36,000	
	To Suman's Capital A/c			36,000
(B)	Sangeet's Capital A/c	Dr.	36,000	
	To Suman's Capital A/c			36,000
(C)	Profit and Loss Adjustment A/c	Dr.	36,000	
	To Suman's Capital A/c			36,000
(D)	Sangeet's Capital A/c	Dr.	25,200	
	To Suman's Capital A/c			25,200

28. Roopa and Daya were partners in a firm. They admitted Navin as a new partner for 1/3rd share in the profits. On Navin's admission it was found that there was a claim against the firm for damages for which a liability for damages should be created. Which of the following accounts will be debited for creating the liability.

(A) Profit and Loss Appropriation Account

(B) Profit and Loss Account

(C) Revaluation Account

(D) Profit and Loss Adjustment Account

29. Given below are two statements, one labelled as **Assertion (A)** and the other as **Reason (R)**.

Assertion (A) : In case the company fails to receive minimum subscription it cannot proceed for the allotment of shares.

Reason (R) : When the company fails to receive minimum subscription it has to return the application money within 120 days from the date of issue of prospectus. In the context of the above two statements which of the following is correct :

(A) Both (A) and (R) are correct.

(B) (A) is correct but (R) is incorrect

(C) Both (A) and (R) are incorrect

(D) (A) is incorrect but (R) is correct.

30. X Ltd. invited applications for issuing 10,00,000 equity shares of ₹ 10 each at a premium of ₹ 9 per share. The amount was payable as follows :

On Application – ₹ 6 per share (including premium ₹ 3)

On Allotment – ₹ 8 per share (including premium ₹ 4)

On first and final call – Balance

Applications for 15,00,000 shares were received. Shares were allotted on pro-rata basis to all applicants. Excess application money received with applications was adjusted towards sums due on allotment. Dharam to whom 600 shares were allotted failed to pay the allotment money. Allotment amount that was not paid by Dharam was :

(A) ₹ 4,800   (B) ₹ 600

(C) ₹ 3,000   (D) ₹ 2,400

31. PP Ltd. invited applications for issuing 10,000 equity shares of ₹ 10 each. Applications for 9, 500 shares were received and allotment was made to all the applicants. Ravi a shareholder holding 200 shares failed to pay allotment money and his shares were forfeited. Mohan to whom 100 shares were allotted failed to pay the first call and his shares were forfeited immediately after the first call was made. Afterwards the second and final call was made. The second and final call will be due on how many shares ?

(A) 9,500   (B) 9,300

(C) 9,200   (D) 10,000

32. Raman Ltd. was registered with an authorised capital of ₹ 5,00,00,000 divided into shares of ₹ 10 each. The company offered for subscription 4,00,000 shares. Applications were received for 4,50,000 shares. Applications for 50,000 shares were rejected. A shareholder holding 10,000 shares failed to pay the first and final call of ₹ 2 per share. The subscribed capital of the company is :

(A) ₹ 5,00,00,000   (B) ₹ 40,00,000

(C) ₹ 45,00,000   (D) ₹ 39,80,000

Section C

From question numbers 33 to 36 attempt any 3 questions.

Question numbers 33 and 34 are based on the hypothetical situation given below :

Sun India Ltd. invited applications for issuing equity shares fo ₹ 10 each at a premium of 10%. The premium was payable on allotment. Because of over-subscription all the applicants were divided into three categories for the purpose of allotment.

Category I – Applications for 1,00,000 shares were allotted shares in full.

Category II – 3,00,000 shares were allotted to the applicants of this category. For every 5 shares applied, 3 shares were allotted.

Category III – 8,00,000 shares were allotted to the applicants of 12,00,000 shares.

Amount payable per share was as follows :

On Application – ₹ 2 per share

On Allotment – ₹ 5 per share (including premium)

On First and Final call – Balance

Excess money received with applications was adjusted towards sums due on allotment.

33. How many shares were offered to the public for subscription ?

(A) 12,00,000   (B) 24,00,000

(C) 14,00,000   (d) 30,00,000

34. What was the amount of money received on allotment ?

(A) ₹ 60,00,000   (B) ₹ 12,00,000

(C) ₹ 6,00,00,000   (D) ₹ 48,00,000

Question number 35 and 36 are based on the hypothetical situation given below :

On 1.4.2018 A and B started business with capitals of ₹ 8,00,000 and ₹ 16,00,000 respectively. They decided to share the future profits in the ratio of their capitals. On 1.4.2019 they admitted C as a new partner. A surrendered 1/4th of his share in favour of C and B surrendered 1/9th from his share in favour of C. On 1.4.2020 D was admitted as a new partner for 1/6th share. On 1.4.2021, E was admitted for 1/5th share in the profits and it was decided that all the partners will share the future profits equally.

35. The profit sharing ratio of A, B and C was :

(A) 9 : 20 : 7   (B) 8 : 21 : 7

(C) 10 : 19 : 7   (D) 7 : 22 : 7

36. The profit sharing ratio of A, B, C and D was :

(A) 45 : 105 : 30 : 36   (B) 45 : 100 : 35 : 36

(C) 45 : 105 : 30 : 36   (D) 40 : 100 : 40 : 36

PART – II

Section A

Attempt any 4 questions from question, number 37 to 42.

37. The ratios that analyse profits in relation to revenue from operations or funds employed in the business are called :

(A) Profitability Ratios

(B) Turnover Ratios

(C) Solvency Ratios

(D) Liquidity Ratios

38. Because of exclusion of non-liquid current assets which of the following ratio is considered better than current ratio as a measure of liquidity position of the business?

(A) Debt - Equity Ratio

(B) Acid Test Ratio

(C) Proprietary Ratio

(D) Interest Coverage Ratio

39. Which of the following ratio establishes relationship of 'Shareholders funds' to 'Net assets'?

(A) Return on Investment

(B) Interest Coverage Ratio

(C) Proprietary Ratio

(D) Debt - Equity Ratio

40. Which of the following ratio establishes the relationship between 'Credit revenue from operations' and 'Trade receivables'?

(A) Inventory Turnover Ratio

(B) Interest Coverage Ratio

(C) Trade Payables Turnover Ratio

(D) Trade Receivables Turnover Ratio

41. Given below are two statements, one labelled as **Assertion (A)** and the other labelled as **Reason (R)** :

Assertion (A) : Profitability ratios are calculated to analyse the earning capacity of the business.

Reason (R) : Profitability ratios are calculated to determine the ability of the business to service its debt in the long run.

In the light of the above two statements which of the following is correct :

(A) Both (A) and (R) are correct.

(B) Both (A) and (R) are wrong.

(C) (A) is correct but (R) is wrong.

(D) (A) is wrong but (R) is correct.

42. Match the items given in Column I with the headings / sub-headings of Column II under which these are shown according to Schedule III Part I of the Companies Act, 2013 :

I	II
(i) Securities Premium Reserve	(a) Non current Liabilities
(ii) Patents	(b) Current Liabilities
(iii) Short Term Loans and Advances	(c) Current Assets
(iv) Trade Payables	(d) Intangible Assets
(v) Long Term Borrowings	(e) Reserves and Surplus

(A) (i) – (e), (ii) – (d), (iii) – (c), (iv) – (b), (v) – (a)

(B) (i) – (a), (ii) – (b), (iii) – (c), (iv) – (d), (v) – (e)

(C) (i) – (b), (ii) – (c), (iii) – (a), (iv) – (d), (v) – (e)

(D) (i) – (a), (ii) – (b), (iii) – (e), (iv) – (d), (v) – (e)

Section B

Attempt any 5 questions from question number 43 to 48.

43. Current ratio of a company is 3 : 1. The value of its current liabilities is ₹ 4,00,000.

Its current assets will be :

(A) ₹ 3,00,000   (B) ₹ 12,00,000

(C) ₹ 2,00,000   (D) ₹ 9,00,000

44. Gross Profit Ratio of a Company is 25%. Cost of revenue from operations are 3/4th of revenue from operations. If revenue from operations is ₹ 60,00,000, the Gross Profit of the Company will be :

(A) ₹ 25,00,000   (B) ₹ 45,00,000

(C) ₹ 15,00,000   (D) ₹ 11,25,000

45. Following information has been obtained from the statement of Profit and Loss of a Company :

Revenue from Operation – ₹ 20,00,000, cost of materials consumd – ₹ 8,00,000 Employees benefit expenses – ₹ 20,000, Finance cost – ₹ 5,000, Depreciation –₹ 25,000.

Its Profit before tax will be :

(A) ₹ 12,00,000

(B) ₹ 11,80,000

(C) ₹ 11,75,000

(D) ₹ 11,50,000

46. Given below are two statements, one labelled as **Assertion (A)** and the other labelled as **Reason (R)** :

Assertion (A) : 'Sale of goods for cash' does not effect Debt-Equity ratio.

Reason (R) : 'Sale of goods on cash basis' neither affect 'Debt' nor 'Equity'.

In the context of he above two statements which of the following is correct :

(A) Both (A) and (R) are correct and (R) is the correct reason of (A).

(B) Only (A) is correct.

(C) Only (R) is correct.

(D) Both (A) and (R) are incorrect.

47. Following are two statements, one labelled as **Assertion (A)** and the other labelled **Reason (R)** :

Assertion (A) : Operating ratio is = 100 – operating profit ratio.

Reason (R) : Operating ratio is computed to reveal the operating margin on products sold.

In the context of the above two statements which of the following is correct:

(A) Both statements are incorrect.

(B) (A) is correct but (R) is incorrect.

(C) (A) is incorrect but (R) is correct.

(D) Both (A) and (R) are correct and (R) is the correct reason of (A).

48. During the year ended 31.3.2021, Soma Ltd. earned net profit after tax ₹ 6,00,000.

The company has a long term 10% debt of ₹ 50,00,000. The tax rate is 40%. The interest coverage ratio of the company will be :

(A) 2 times   (B) 3 times

(C) 1.2 times   (D) 1.5 times

PART – III

Section A

From question number 49 to 54 attempt any 4 questions.

49. "Hardware, software and data are some of the components of computerised accounting system." Identify the missing component from the statement :

(A) Procedure and people   (B) Timely access

(C) Network   (D) Raw facts

50. Which of the following is not a feature of computerised accounting system :

(A) Transparency and control   (B) Data are prone to hacking

(C) Scalability   (D) Reliability

51. A sequential code is the one which :

(A) range of numbers is partitioned into desired number of sub-ranges.

(B) consists of alphabets or abbreviations as symbols to codify a piece of information.

(C) enables identification of missing documents.

(D) sub-ranges are allotted to specific groups.

52. Method of codification should be:

(A) An identification mark.

(B) Easy to understand, cryptic and leads to grouping of accounts.

(C) Explains a group of information.

(D) Such that it leads to grouping of accounts.

53. Which type of software package is suitable for an organisation where the volume of accounting transactions is very low and adaptability is very high :

(A) Specific   (B) Generic

(C) Tailored   (D) (A) and (C) both

54. Which of the following is not a limitation of computerised accounting system:

(A) Data may be lost or corrupted due to power interruptions.

(B) Faster obsolescence forces investment for shorter time.

(C) Data is not made available to everybody.

(D) Unprogrammed and un-specified reports cannot be generated.

Section B

From question number 55 to 60 attempt any 5 questions.

55. Which of the following is not contained on formula tab on Excel ribbon:

(A) Page layout   (B) Function library

(C) Defined names   (D) Calculations

56. Identify from the following what will be displayed on the screen when numeric value in the formula or function is invalid while working on excel:

(A) Correct a # REF! Error

(B) Correct a # NUM! Error

(C) Correct a # DIV/0! Error

(D) Correct a # N/A Error

57. As you type a number in a cell, what mode appears in the status bar:

(A) Ready mode   (B) Edit mode

(C) Enter mode   (D) Record mode

58. Which of the following is not included in calculation of 'Earning' while preparing payroll for current period?

(A) Basic pay

(B) Transport allowance

(C) Medical allowance

(D) Provident fund

59. What is the outcome of an arithmetic expression or function called?

(A) Basic Value

(B) Derived Value

(C) Vertical Vector

(D) Horizontal Vector

60. How is Navigation conducted from first to last filled cells of clusters when moving one cell at a time in a 'Row'?

(A) Home + Right arrow ($\rightarrow$)

(B) End + Right arrow ($\rightarrow$)

(C) CTRL + Right arrow ($\rightarrow$) successively

(D) CTRL + END

Answer Keys

1. (C)	**2.** (B)	**3.** (A)	**4.** (C)	**5.** (B)	**6.** (A)	**7.** (B)	**8.** (C)	**9.** (B)	**10.** (D)
11. (A)	**12.** (C)	**13.** (A)	**14.** (A)	**15.** (C)	**16.** (B)	**17.** (B)	**18.** (B)	**19.** (C)	**20.** (C)
21. (C)	**22.** (A)	**23.** (B)	**24.** (A)	**25.** (D)	**26.** (C)	**27.** (D)	**28.** (C)	**29.** (B)	**30.** (C)
31. (C)	**32.** (D)	**33.** (A)	**34.** (D)	**35.** (A)	**36.** (B)	**37.** (A)	**38.** (B)	**39.** (C)	**40.** (D)
41. (C)	**42.** (A)	**43.** (B)	**44.** (C)	**45.** (D)	**46.** (A)	**47.** (B)	**48.** (B)	**49.** (A)	**50.** (B)
51. (C)	**52.** (D)	**53.** (B)	**54.** (C)	**55.** (A)	**56.** (B)	**57.** (C)	**58.** (D)	**59.** (B)	**60.** (C)

Solution

1. (C) Partnership Deed

2. (B) 50 members.

3. (A) Interest on drawings A/c

4. (C) Opening capital = 1,12,000 Rs.

Dr.			On 1.4.2020		Cr.
			Partner's Capital A/c		
Particulars	A	B	Particulars	A	B
			By Bal b/d (OP Bal) B/F	-	112000
To Drawings	-	10000	By Cash (Add. Cap)	-	32000
To Bal c/d (C/0)	-	150000	By P&L APP.	-	16000
		160000			160000

5. (B) Deficiency bear by Q is 20,000 Rs.

Dr.				Cr.
	P & C Appropriation A/c			
	To Part. Cap A/c		By P & L (N.P.)	4,00,000
P	128000	128000		
Q	128000 - 20000	108000		
R	64000	64000		
L	80000 + 20000	100000		
		400000		400000

Guarnteed partner $\Rightarrow$ L

Guarnteed Amount = 1,00,000

Actual Amount = $\dfrac{1}{5} \times 400000 = 80,000$

Deficiency = 20000 bear by Q

6. (A) 100000 Rs. difference Amount is hidden goodwill.

Hidden goodwill

Capital should be $\dfrac{1}{4} \times 200000 = 800000$

Availble capital X 2,00,000

Y 3,00,000

Z $\underline{2,00,000}$ = $-\underline{7,00,000}$

H.G $\underline{1,00,000}$

7. (B) Goodwill not bring in cash so current A/c will be debited.

Dr   Dr   Cr

90000 + 11250 = 101250

8. (C) IOD = Drawings $\times \dfrac{R}{100} \times \dfrac{6}{12}$

$= 6000 \times \dfrac{12}{100} \times \dfrac{6}{12}$

= 360 Rs.

9. (B) Share application and allotment A/c will be debited.

10. (D) 50,000 Rs.

Total due   3,80,000

E.S. Capital $(-)\underline{3,30,000}$

Amount of cheque = $\underline{50,000}$

11. (A) 7500 Rs.

No. $\times$ Rs.

500 $\times$ 15

= 7500 Rs.

12. (C) 12,40,000 Rs.

150000 $\times$ 8 = 12,00,000 Due

4000 $\times$ 10   = $\underline{40,000}$ Adv.

$\underline{12,40,000}$ Total

13. (A) Always in old partners in old ratio.

14. (A) 1,00,000 (CV – CE)

Capitalised value = $\dfrac{\text{Net Asset}}{\text{Rate}} \times 100$

$= \dfrac{60000}{12} \times 100$ = 5,00,000

Cap. Employed = $-\underline{4,00,000}$

Diff g/w = $\underline{1,00,000}$

15. (C) 2000 Rs

Dr = 30,000

Cr = $-\underline{20000}$

Diff = $\overline{10000}$

Share 10000 $\times \dfrac{1}{5}$ = 2000 Rs.

16. (B) 7 : 3 : 3

L : M   G's share = $\dfrac{3}{13}$

Remaining share = $1 - \dfrac{3}{13} = \dfrac{10}{13}$

L's Share = $\dfrac{10}{13} \times \dfrac{7}{10} = \dfrac{7}{13}$

M's Share = $\dfrac{10}{13} \times \dfrac{3}{10} = \dfrac{3}{13}$

G's Share = $\dfrac{3}{13}$

17. (B) Assertion–Reason both are incorrect.

18. (B) 6400 Rs.

No. $\times$ Rs.

800 $\times$ 8 = Rs. 6400

19. (C) Over subscription (Applied > Offered)

20. (C) (iv) is incorrect as liabilities are unlimited

21. (C) In fixed capital account method two accounts are to be prepared. Capital A/c & Current A/c

22. (A) Amar's Cap. A/c Dr.   10,000

     Samar's Cap. A/c Dr.   50,000

     To Profit & Loss A/c   60,000

23. (B) Loss of Rs. 1,00,000

     Depreciate = 3,00,000

     Appreciate = 2,00,000

            Loss = 1,00,000

24. (A) Both are correct

25. (D) Capital A/c of old partners in old ratio

26. (C) Stock A/c   Dr.   5,000

     To Revaluation A/c   5000

$$\frac{45000}{90} \times 100 = 50000 \text{ New}$$

$$- \underline{45000} \text{ Old}$$

$$\underline{5000} \text{ Increase}$$

27. (D) Sangeet's Cap A/c. Dr.   25200

     To Suman's Cap. A/c   25200

     (Past Adj. made)

28. (C) Revaluation A/c debited by unrecorded Liability of claim.

29. (B) Assertion is correct but Reason is incorrect.

30. (C) 3000 Rs.   Due 600 × 8 = 4800

            Advance = −1800

               due = 3000

31. (C) 9200   [9500 − 200 − 100 = 9200]

32. (D) 45,00,000 Rs.

     [4,50,000 × 10 Rs.]

33. (A) 12,00,000

     [8,00,000 + 3,00,000 + 1,00,000]

34. (D) 48,00,000

     [60,00,000 − 12,00,000]

$$\begin{bmatrix} \text{II} & \text{I} \\ (4,00,000 + 2,00,000) \times 2 \end{bmatrix}$$

35. (A) 9 : 20 : 7

36. (B) 45 : 100 : 35 : 36

     A : B : C D is coming for $\dfrac{1}{6}$

     9 : 20 : 7

     Remaining Share $= 1 - \dfrac{1}{6} = \dfrac{5}{6}$

     A's Share $= \dfrac{5}{6} \times \dfrac{9}{36} = \dfrac{45}{216}$

     B's Share $= \dfrac{5}{6} \times \dfrac{20}{36} = \dfrac{100}{216}$

     C's = Share $= \dfrac{5}{6} \times \dfrac{7}{36} = \dfrac{35}{216}$

37. (A) Profitability ratios, related with profits to R.F.O.

38. (B) Acid test ratio/ Liquid ratio is better.

39. (C) Proprietory ratio shows relationship Shareholders funds to net assets.

40. (D) Trade receivable turn over ratio shows Relationship b/w credit RFO & Trade receivables.

41. (C) Assertion is correct but reason is wrong.

42. (A) i-e, ii-d, iii-c, iv-b, v-a

43. (B) 12,00,000 Rs.

$$CR = \frac{CA}{CL} = \frac{3}{1} \diagx \frac{CA}{400000}$$

     3 × 4,00,000 = CA

     12,00,000 = CA

44. (C) 15,00,000 Rs.

$$GPR = \frac{GP}{RFO} \times 100$$

GP = 25% of 60,00,000

     = 15,00,000 Rs.

45. (D) 11,50,000 Rs.

RFO	=	20,00,000
Cost	=	− 8,00,000
	=	12,00,000
Exp.	=	− 50,000
PBT =		11,50,000

46. (A) Both Assertion & Reason are correct & Reason is correct explanation.

47. (B) Assertion is correct Reason is wrong as operating profit ratio + OR = 100.

48. (B) 3 times

Interest coverage ratio

$$= \frac{NPBIT}{\text{Fixed Int. Charges}}$$

CBSE

ACCOUNTANCY

Class XII

Time Allowed : 2 Hours | Maximum Marks : 40

General Instructions

(i)   This question paper comprises of two Parts - A and B. There are 12 questions in the question paper. All questions are compulsory.

(ii) Part - A is compulsory for all candidates.

(iii) Part - B has two options i.e.

(i) Analysis of Financial Statements and

(ii) Computerised Accounting. Students must attempt only one of the given options.

(iv) Question Nos. 1 to 3 and 10 are short answer type -I questions carrying 2 marks each.

(v)   Question Nos. 4 to 6 and 11 are short answer type - II questions carrying 3 marks each.

(vi) Question Nos. 7 to 9 and 12 are long answer type questions carrying 5 marks each.

(vii) There is no overall choice. However, an internal choice has been provided in 3 questions of three marks and 1 question of five marks.

PART A

(Accounting for Not-for-Profit Organizations, Partnership Firms and Companies)

Q.1. Show the following information in the Balance Sheet of Ashoka Club as on 31.3.2021:   [2]

Particulars	Dr. (₹)	Cr. (₹)
Tournament Fund		2,50,000
Tournament Fund Investment	2,50,000	
Tournament Expenses	20,000	

Q.2. State any two situations when compulsory dissolution of a partnership firm takes place.   [2]

Q.3. Ajay, Vijay, Sanjay and Dhananjay are partners in a firm sharing profits and losses in the ratio of 2 : 2 : 1 : 1. Vijay decided to retire from the firm. The Goodwill of the firm was valued at ₹12,00,000.

Pass necessary journal entry for the treatment of Goodwill on Vijay's retirement without opening goodwill account.   [2]

Q.4. (a) From the following information, calculate the amount of sports material that will be debited to the Income and Expenditure Account of Arjun Sports Club for the year ended 31st March, 2021.

Particulars	1st April, 2020 (₹)	31st March, 2021 (₹)
Stock of Sports Material	1,50,000	2,20,000
Creditors for Sports Material	35,000	65,000

Additional Information:

During the year, ₹ 2,80,000 were paid to the creditors of sports material.   [3]

OR

(b) From the following extract of 'Receipts and Payments Account' and additional information, calculate the amount of subscriptions to be shown in 'Income and Expenditure Account' for the year ended 31st March, 2021 and 'Balance Sheet' as on that date.

RECEIPTS AND PAYMENTS ACCOUNT

for the year ended 31st March, 2021

Receipts		Amount (₹)	Payments	Amount (₹)
To Subscriptions:				
2019-20	9,000			
2020-21	40,000			
2021-22	6,000	55,000		

Additional Information :

The club has 500 members each paying an annual subscription of ₹100.

Subscriptions outstanding on 31st March, 2020 were ₹12,000.

Q.5. Vimal, Kamal and Nirmal were partners sharing profit & losses in the ratio of 3 : 2 : 1. Vimal died on 30th September, 2020 . The partnership deed provides that the share of profit of the deceased partner till the date of his death was to be calculated on the basis of the average profits of the last three years. The profit for the last three years were : 2017-18 ₹ 70,000; 2018-19 ₹ 80,000; 2019-20 ₹ 60,000.

Calculate Vimal's share of profit till the date of his death and pass necessary journal entry for the same.   [3]

Q.6. (a) Surya Ltd. purchased machinery from Mohan Equipment Ltd. The company paid the vendors by issue of 9% debentures and the balance through an acceptance in their favour payable after three months. The accountant of the company while Journalising the above mentioned transactions left some items blank. Fill in the blanks in the given below Journal of Surya Ltd. :   [3]

JOURNAL OF SURYA LTD.

Date	Particulars	LF	Debit Amount (₹)	Credit Amount (₹)	
2021 Jan.1	Machinery A/c. Dr. To __________ (Purchased Machinery for ₹ 12,50,000 from Mohan Equipment Ltd.)		________	________	1

" 1	Mohan Equipment Ltd. A/c. Dr.
	   To ________
	   To Securities Premium Reserve
	(Issued 8000, 9% Debentures of ₹ 100 each at a premium of 25%)
			________	________
				________
					1

" 1	__________ Dr. To __________ (__________)		________	________	1

(b) Sujata Ltd. invited applications for issuing 50,000, 9% debenture of ₹100 each at a discount of 10% redeemable at par after five years. The debentures were fully subscribed and all money was duly received. The company had a balance of ₹ 3,00,000 in 'Securities Premium Reserve' which it decided to use for writing off the discount/loss on issue of debentures. It also decided to write off the remaining discount/loss on issue of debentures in the first year.

Pass the Journal entries for issue of debentures and for writing off discount/loss on issue of debentures.

Q.7. (a) Chanda, Tara and Nisha were partners in a firm sharing profits and losses in the ratio of 3 : 2 : 1. They decided to dissolve the firm on 31st March, 2021. Pass necessary Journal Entries for the following transactions after all assets (other than cash and bank) and third party liabilities have been transferred to Realisation Account.   [3]

   (i)   A typewriter completely written off from the books was sold for ₹9,000 .

   (ii)   Chanda took over stock worth ₹ 96,000 at ₹ 84,000 .

   (iii) Nisha was to get remuneration of ₹ 42,000 for completing the dissolution process.

   (iv) Creditors of ₹ 23,500 took over all the investments at ₹10,000. Remaining amount was paid to them in Cash.

   (v)   Sundry Creditors amounting to ₹40,000 were settled at a discount of 10%.

OR

(b) Heena, Meena and Tina are partners in a firm sharing profits and losses equally. Their Balance Sheet on April 1st, 2020 was as follows :

Balance Sheet of Heena, Meena & Tina as on 1ˢᵗ April, 2020

Liabilities	Amount (₹)	Assets		Amount (₹)
Bills Payable	12,000	Building		40,000
Sundry Creditors	18,000	Machinery		30,000
General Reserve	12,000	Furniture		12,000
Capitals : Heena	30,000	Stock		22,000
Meena	30,000	Debtors	20,000	
Tina	28,000	Less : Provision for doubtful debts	1,000	19,000
		Bank		7,000
	1,30,000			**1,30,000**

Tina retired from the firm on the above date and the following was agreed upon :

(a) Building was to be appreciated by 20%.

(b) Machinery was to be depreciated by ₹1,500 .

(c) Provision for doubtful debts was to be increased to ₹1,500 .

(d) Goodwill was valued at ₹ 21,000 on Tina's retirement and the same was to be treated without opening goodwill account.

(e) The balance in Tina's Capital account will be transferred to her Loan account.

Prepare Revaluation Account and Partners' Capital Accounts.

Q.8. From the following 'Receipts and Payments Account' of Space Club, prepare an Income and Expenditure Account for the year ended 31ˢᵗ March, 2021.

Receipts and Payments Account of Space Club for the year ended 31ˢᵗ March, 2021

Receipts	Amount (₹)	Payments	Amount (₹)
To Balance b/d	5,000	By Salaries	31,000
To Subscriptions	73,000	By Machinery (1.7.2020)	40,000
To Sale of old furniture	800	By 8% Investments	30,000
(Book Value ₹ 2,000)		By Balance c/d	19,600
To Donations	41,800		
	1,20,600		**1,20,600**

Additional Information :

(i) Subscriptions in arrears on 31.03.2021were ₹ 2,000.

(ii) On 31ˢᵗ March, 2021, outstanding salaries were ₹ 4,000.

(iii) 8% Investments were purchased on 31ˢᵗ March, 2021.

(iv) The club owned Machinery of ₹ 1,00,000 on 1ˢᵗ April 2020. Depreciate Machinery@6% p.a.   **[5]**

Q.9. Pass journal entries for issue of debentures for the following transactions:

(i) Issued ₹ 3,000, 11% debentures of ₹ 100 each at par, redeemable at 5% premium.

(ii) Issued ₹ 4,000, 12% debentures of ₹ 100 each at 5% premium, redeemable at 10% premium.

(iii) Issued ₹ 3,00,000, 9% debentures of ₹ 100 each at par redeemable at par.

(iv) Issued ₹ 7,00,000, 9% debentures at a discount of 10% redeemable at par.

(v) Issued ₹ 10,00,000, 9% debentures of ₹ 100 each at 10% discount redeemable at 5% premium.　　[5]

PART B

Option-1

(Analysis of Financial Statements)

Q.10. State the objective of preparing 'Cash Flow Statement'.　　[2]

Q.11. (a) From the following information, prepare Comparative statement of Profit and Loss for the year ended 31st March 2021.　　[3]

Particulars	2020-21 (₹)	2019-20 (₹)
Revenue from Operations	4,00,000	2,00,000
Other Income	80,000	40,000
Expenses 50% of Revenue from operations		
Tax Rate @ 50%		

OR

(b) Prepare a 'Common Size statement of Profit and Loss' of Birla Ltd. for the year ended 31st March, 2021 from the following information :

Particulars	2020-21 (₹)	2019-20 (₹)
Revenue from Operations	20,00,000	10,00,000
Purchase of stock in trade	4,00,000	2,00,000
Other expenses	40,000	20,000
Tax Rate @ 50%		

Q.12. Following was the Balance Sheet of Bajaj Ltd. as on 31st March, 2021 :

BAJAJ LTD.

Balance Sheet as on 31st March, 2021

Particulars	Note No.	31.03.2021 (₹)	31.03.2020 (₹)
I. Equity and Liabilities :			
1. Shareholder's funds :			
(a) Share Capital		19,00,000	17,00,000
(b) Reserves and Surplus	1	6,00,000	3,00,000
2. Non-Current Liabilities:			
12% long term borrowings		5,00,000	4,00,000
3. Current Liabilities :			
(a) Short term Borrowings	2	1,70,0000	1,75,000
(b) Short term Provisions	3	2,00,0000	1,65,000
Total		**33,70,000**	**27,40,000**

II. Assets:			
1. Non Current Assets:			
Fixed Assets			
(i) Tangible Assets	4	25,00,000	21,00,000
(i) Intangible Assets	5	4,00,000	3,00,000
2. Current Assets:			
(a) Current Investments		1,40,0000	1,70,000
(b)Inventories		2,60,0000	1,30,000
(c)Cash & Cash Equivalents		70,000	40,0000
Total		**33,70,000**	**27,40,000**

Notes to Accounts

Note No.	Particulars	31.03.2021 (₹)	31.03.2021 (₹)
1	Reserves & Surplus :		
	Surplus i.e. Balance in Statement of Profit and Loss	6,00,000	3,00,000
2	Short term borrowings :Bank Overdraft	1,70,0000	1,75,000
3	Short term provisions :Provision for tax	2,00,000	1,65,000
4	Tangible Assets :Machinery	25,00,000	21,00,000
5	Intangible Assets :Goodwill	4,00,000	3,00,000

Additional Information :

(i) A machine of the book value of ₹ 40,000 was sold for ₹ 50,000.

(ii) Depreciation charged on machinery during the year was ₹ 2,00,000.

(iii) ₹ 1,00,000, 12% long term borrowings were obtained on 31-3-2021.

Calculate cash flows from investing and financing activities.　　　　[5]

PART B

Option - II

(Computerised Accounting)

Q.10. Give the meaning of the terms 'Report' and 'Report Wizard'.　　　[2]

Q.11. (a) Explain the terms 'Basic Pay', 'House Rent Allowance' and 'Tax Deducted at Source' as used in preparation of payroll.　　　[3]

OR

(b) Explain 'Accounts Group' and 'Loan' (Liabilities).

Q.12. State the steps in the installation of 'Computerised Accounting System'.　　　[5]

EXPLANATIONS

Part -A

1.

BALANCE SHEET OF ASHOKA CLUB
as at 31st March 2021

Liabilities		Amount	Asset	Amount
Tournament fund			Tournament fund Investment	2,50,000
Opening Balance	2,50,000			
(–) Tournament expenses	20,000			
		2,30,000		

$\left(\dfrac{1}{2}\times 4\right)=2$

2. Situations when compulsory dissolution of a partnership firm takes place　　$(1\times 2 = 2)$ marks

　a) When the business of the firm becomes illegal.

　b) When all the Partners or all but one partner becomes insolvent rendering them incompetent to sign a contract.

3.

JOURNAL

Date	Particulars	L.f	Debit (Dr.)	Credit (Cr.)
	Ajay's Capital A/c – Dr.		2,00,000	
	Sanjay's Capital A/c – Dr.		1,00,000	
	Dhanjay's Capital A/c – Dr.		1,00,000	
	To Vijay's Capital A/c			4,00,000
	(Being Vijay's Share of goodwill adjusted in the capital accounts of Ajay, Sanjay and Dhanjay in gaining ratio)			

$\left(\dfrac{1}{2}\text{ mark for share of Vijay's goodwill} + 1\dfrac{1}{2}\text{ for journal entry}\right) = 2$

4. (a) Dr.　　　　**STOCK OF SPORTS MATERIALS A/C**　　　　Cr.

Particulars	Amount (₹)	Particulars	Amount (₹)
To Balance b/d	1,50,000	By Income & Expenditure A/c	2,40,000
To Creditors	3,10,000	– Sports Material Consumers.	
(Credit Purchases)		By Balance c/d	2,20,000
	4,60,000		**4,60,000**

$\left(1\dfrac{1}{2}\right)$ Marks

Dr.　　　　**CREDITORS FOR SPORTS MATERIAL A/C**　　　　Cr.

Particulars	Amount (₹)	Particulars	Amount (₹)
To Cash/ Bank A/c	2,80,000	By Balance b/d	35,000
To Balance c/d	65,000	By Stock of Sports Material	3,10,000
		(Credit purchase)	
	3,45,000		3,45,000

$\left(1\dfrac{1}{2}\right)$ Marks

OR

(b)   **Income and Expenditure Account for the year ended 31ˢᵗ March, 2021.**

Expenditure	Amount (₹)	Income	Amount (₹)
		By subscriptions 40,000	
		(+) O/s for (2020-21) <u>10,000</u>	50,000

$\left(1\frac{1}{2}\right)$ Marks

Balance Sheet as on 31st March 2021

Liabilities	Amount (₹)	Assets	Amount (₹)
Subscriptions received in advance	6,000	Subscriptions Outstanding (3,000 + 10,000)	13,000

$\left(1\frac{1}{2}\right)$ Marks

5. Ratio $3 : 2 : 1$

$$\text{Average Profit} = \frac{(70,000 + 80,000 - 60,000)}{3} = \frac{90,000}{3} = 30,000.$$

Profit for 6 months $= 30,000 \div 2 = 15,000$

Vimal's share $= 15,000 \times \dfrac{3}{6} = 7500$ ₹

$\left(1\frac{1}{2}\right)$ Marks

JOURNAL

Date	Particulars	L.f	Debit(₹)	Credit (₹)
	P/L Suspense A/c Dr		7500	
	To Vimal's capital A/c			7500
	(Vimal's share of estimated profits till date of his death credited to his Capital Account)			

$\left(1\frac{1}{2}\right)$ Marks

6. (a)   **JOURNAL OF SURYA LTD.**

Date	Particulars	L.f	Debit (₹)	Credit (₹)
2021 1-Jan	Machinery A/c Dr. To Mohan Equipment Ltd. A/c		12,50,000	125,000
	(Purchased Machinery for ₹ 12,50,000 from Mohan Equipment Ltd.)			
1-Jan	Mohan Equipment ltd. Dr. To 9% Debentures A/c To Securities Premium Reserve.		1,000,000	8,00,000 2,00,000
	(Issued 8000, 9% debentures of ₹ 100 each at a premium of 25%)			
1-Jan	Mohan Equipment Ltd. Dr. To Bill Payable A/c		2,50,000	2,50,000
	(Acceptance given to Mohan Equipment Ltd.)			

$(1 \times 3 = 3)$ marks

OR

(b)

JOURNAL OF SURYA LTD.

Date	Particulars		L.f	Debit(₹)	Credit (₹)
	Bank A/c	Dr.		45,00,000	
	To 9% debenture appliction & allotment A/c.				45,00,000
	(Debenture Appliction money received)				
	9% debenture application & allotment A/c	Dr.		45,00,000	
	Discount/loss on issue of debenture A/c	Dr.		5,00,000	
	To 9% debentures A/c				50,00,000
	(Issue of 50,000, 9% debenture of ₹ 100 each @ 10% discount)				
	Securities Premium Reserve A/c	Dr.		3,00,000	
	Statement of Profit & Loss A/c	Dr.		2,00,000	
	To discount/ loss on issue of debenture A/c				5,00,000
	(Discount on issue of debenture written off)				

$(1 \times 3 = 3)$ marks

7. (a) Ratio = 3 : 2 : 1

JOURNAL

Date	Particulars		L.f	Debit (₹)	Credit (₹)
	Bank/Cash A/c	Dr.		9000	
	To Realisation A/c				9000
	(Old typewriter written off, now sold)				
	Chanda's Capital A/c	Dr.		84,000	
	To Realisation A/c				84,000
	(Stock taken over by Chanda)				
	Realisation A/c	Dr.		42,000	
	To Nisha's Capital A/c				42,000
	(Remuneration to Nisha)				
	Realisation A/c	Dr.		13,500	
	To Bank/Cash A/c				13,500
	(Balance creditors paid in cash)				
	Realisation A/c	Dr.		36,000	
	To Bank/Cash A/c				36,000
	(Creditors Paid at discount of 10%)				

$(1 \times 5 = 5)$ marks

OR

(b) H : M : T

1 : 1 : 1

(2 marks)

Dr.	REVALUATION A/C			Cr.
Particulars	**Amount**	**Particulars**	**Amounts**
To Machinery A/c	1500	By Building	8000
To Provision for Doubtful debts	500		
To gain on revaluation A/c			
Heena – 2000			
Meena – 2000			
Tina – 2000	6000		
	8000		**8000**

Dr.				Partner's Capital A/c			Cr.
Particulars	**Heena**	**Meena**	**Tina**	**Particulars**	**Heena**	**Meena**	**Tina**
To Tina's Capital	3500	3500		By Balance b/d	30,000	30,000	28,000
To Tina's loan			41,000	By General Reserve	4000	4000	4000
To Balance c/d	32,500	32,500		By Revaluation A/c	2000	2000	2000
				By Heena's Capital A/c			3500
				By Meena's Capital A/c			3500
	36,000	**36,000**	**41,000**		**36,000**	**36,000**	**41000**

(3 marks)

8.

Dr.	Income and Expenditure A/c of Space Club			Cr.
Expenditure		**Amount (₹)**	**Income**		**Amount (₹)**
To Loss on sale of old furniture		1200	By Subscription	73000	
To Salaries	31000		(+) o/s for (2020-21)	2000	75000
(+) o/s salaries (2020-21)	4000	35000	By Donations		41800
To depreciation on machinery (6000 + 1800)		7800			
To Surplus		72800			
		1,16,800			**1,16,800**

(5 marks)

9.

	JOURNAL			
Date	**Particulars**	**L.f.**	**Debit (₹)**	**Credit (₹)**
(i)	Bank A/c Dr.		3,00,000	
	To Debenture Application & Allotment A/c			3,00,000
	(Debenture application money received)			
	Debenture Application and Allotment A/c Dr.		3,00,000	
	Loss on issue of debenture A/c Dr.		15,000	
	To 11 % debenture A/c			3,00,000
	To Premium on redemption of debenture A/c.			15,000
	(Issue of 3000, 11% debenture of Rs.100 each at par, redeemable at 5% premium)			
(ii)	Bank A/c Dr.		4,20,000	
	To Debenture Application and allotment A/c			4,20,000
	(Debenture application money received)			
	Debenture Application and Allotment A/c Dr.		4,20,000	
	Loss on issue of debenture A/c Dr.		40,000	
	To 12% Debenture A/c			4,00,000
	To Securities Premium Reserve			20,000
	To Premium on Redemption of Debenture A/c			40,000
	(Issue of 4,000, 12% debenture of Rs. 100 each at 5% premium redeemable at 10% premium)			
(iii)	Bank A/c Dr.		3,00,000	
	To Debenture Application & Allotment A/c			3,00,000
	(Debenture application money received)			
	Debenture Application & Allotment A/c Dr.		3,00,000	
	To 9% debenture A/c			3,00,000
	(Debenture Redeemable at par)			
(iv)	Bank A/c Dr.		6,30,000	
	To Debenture Application & Allotment A/c			6,30,000
	(Debenture application money received)			
	Debenture Application & Allotment A/c Dr.		6,30,000	
	Discount / loss on issue Dr.		70,000	
	To 9% debenture A/c			7,00,000
	(Debenture at a discount of 10% redeemable at par)			

(v)	Bank A/c	Dr.	9,00,000	
	To Debenture Application & Allotment A/c			9,00,000
	(Debenture application money received)			
	Debenture Application & Allotment A/c	Dr.	9,00,000	
	Loss on issue of debenture A/c	Dr.	1,50,000	
	To 9% debenture A/c			10,00,000
	To Premium on redemption of debenture A/c			50,000
	(Debenture of 100 each at 10% discount redeemable at premium)			

$$\left(\frac{1}{2}\times 10 = 5\right)\text{marks}$$

Part -B (Option I)

10. The objective of preparing cash flow is to provide useful information about cash flows of an enterprise during a particular period under various heads i.e., operating activities, investing activities and financing activities.

(2 marks)

11. (a)   Comparative Statement of Profit & Loss for the year ended March 31, 2021

Particulars	2019-20 ₹	2020 – 21 ₹	Absolute Change	% change
I. Revenue from Operations	2,00,000	4,00,000	2,00,000	100
II. Other Income	40,000	80,000	40,000	100
III. Total Revenue (I + II)	2,40,000	4,80,000	2,40,000	100
IV. Expenses	1,00,000	2,00,000	1,00,000	100
V. Profit before Tax	1,40,000	2,80,000	1,40,000	100
VI. Less : Tax @ 50%	70,000	1,40,000	70,000	100
VII. Profit after Tax	70,000	1,40,000	70,000	100

$$\left(\frac{1}{2}\times 6 = 3\right)\text{marks}$$

OR

Common Size Statement of Profit & Loss of Birla Ltd. for the year ended on March 31st, 2020 & 2021

Particulars	Absolute Amount 31st March, 2020 (₹)	Absolute Amount 31st March, 2021 (₹)	% of Revenue from Operations 31st March, 2020	% of Revenue from Operations 31st March, 2021
Revenue from operation	10,00,000	20,00,000	100	100
(–) Expresses purchase of Stock – in- trade	2,00,000	4,00,000	20	20
Other expenses	20,000	40,000	2	2
Total Expenses	2,20,000	4,40,000	22	22
Profit before Tax	7,80,000	15,60,000	78	78
(–) Tax @ 50%	3,90,000	7,80,000	39	39
Profit after tax	**3,90,000**	**7,80,000**	**39**	**39**

$$\left(\frac{1}{2}\times 6 = 3\right)\text{marks}$$

12.   **Cash flow from investing & financing activities for the year ended on 31st March, 2021**

Particulars	Details (₹)	Amount (₹)
Cash flows from Investing activities		
Sale of Machinery	50,000	
Purchase of Machinery	(6,40,000)	
Purchase of Goodwill	(1,00,000)	
Cash used in investing activities		(6,90,000)
Cash flow from financing activities		
Proceeds from issue of shares	2,00,000	
Proceeds from long term Borrowings	1,00,000	
Repayment of Bank overdraft	(5000)	
Payment of interest on 12% long term borrowings	(48000)	
Cash flow from financing activities		2,47,000

$$\left(\frac{1}{2}\text{mark each} = 5 \text{ marks}\right)$$

Working Notes.

Dr.   **Machinery A/c**   Cr.

Expenditure	Amount	Income	Amount
To Balance b/d	21,00,000	By Bank A/c (Sale of machinery)	50,000
To Profit on sale	10,000	By Depreciation	2,00,000
To Bank A/c (Purchases)	6,40,000	By Balance c/d	25,00,000
(Balance figure)			
	27,50,000		27,50,000

Part B (Option II)

10. Report in Access is an object which is designed to print information from the database on to the screen or to a file or directly to the printer.

Report wizard is a tool that guides the designer through a series of dialogue boxes to create the most suitable report.

$$(1 \times 2 = 2 \text{ marks})$$

11. (a) **Basic Pay** : It is the pay in the pay scale plus grade pay, but does not include special pay.

House Rent Allowance : It is an amount paid to facilitate employee in acquiring on lease of residential accomodation.

Tax Deducted at Source : It is a statutory deduction, which is deducted monthly towards income tax liability of an employee. It is essentially an appointment of yearly income tax liability over 12 months.

$$(1 \times 3 = 3 \text{ marks})$$

OR

(b) Accounts group-loans consists of following sub-groups.

    (i) **Bank Overdraft :** In computerised accounting system, Current Bank Account, and Cash Credit is sub-group of Loan (liabilities) because Bank Overdraft and Cash Credit operation on day-to-day basis should be placed under this group.

    (ii) **Secured Loans :** Secured loans are fully secured against security like (Mortgage, pledge, etc) should be placed uder this group.

    (iii) **Unsecured Loans :** Such loans are without any security examples are : Loans from directors, friends, relatives, etc.   ($1 \times 3 = 3$ marks)

12. Steps in the installation of Computerised Accounting Systems ;

    a) Insert CD in the system.

    b) After inserting CD, select the option in the following steps ;

      i) Select any (C : or E : or D :) from My computer icon on the Desktop, Double click on install.exe.

OR

      ii) Select start > run > type the file name E : \ install. exe.

    c) After the above process the default directories of application, data and configuration opens in a window. In case, the user wants to change the default directories then it can be changed by providing the desired drive and file name/directory name.

    d) Click on install and installation process begins accounting software displays the message of successful installation, then the CD can be removed   (5 marks)

CPSIA information can be obtained
at www.ICGtesting.com
Printed in the USA
BVHW022316160623
666061BV00012B/158

9 789395 101417